T0176844

Design and Optimization for 5G Wireless Communications

Design and Optimization for 5G Wireless Communications

Haesik Kim
VTT Oulu, Finland

This edition first published 2020
© 2020 John Wiley & Sons Ltd

All rights reserved. No part of this publication may be reproduced, stored in a retrieval system, or transmitted, in any form or by any means, electronic, mechanical, photocopying, recording or otherwise, except as permitted by law. Advice on how to obtain permission to reuse material from this title is available at http //www.wiley.com/go/permissions.

The right of Haesik Kim to be identified as the author of this work has been asserted in accordance with law.

Registered Offices
John Wiley & Sons, Inc., 111 River Street, Hoboken, NJ 07030, USA
John Wiley & Sons Ltd, The Atrium, Southern Gate, Chichester, West Sussex, PO19 8SQ, UK

Editorial Office
The Atrium, Southern Gate, Chichester, West Sussex, PO19 8SQ, UK

For details of our global editorial offices, customer services, and more information about Wiley products visit us at www.wiley.com.

Wiley also publishes its books in a variety of electronic formats and by print-on-demand. Some content that appears in standard print versions of this book may not be available in other formats.

Limit of Liability/Disclaimer of Warranty
While the publisher and authors have used their best efforts in preparing this work, they make no representations or warranties with respect to the accuracy or completeness of the contents of this work and specifically disclaim all warranties, including without limitation any implied warranties of merchantability or fitness for a particular purpose. No warranty may be created or extended by sales representatives, written sales materials or promotional statements for this work. The fact that an organization, website, or product is referred to in this work as a citation and/or potential source of further information does not mean that the publisher and authors endorse the information or services the organization, website, or product may provide or recommendations it may make. This work is sold with the understanding that the publisher is not engaged in rendering professional services. The advice and strategies contained herein may not be suitable for your situation. You should consult with a specialist where appropriate. Further, readers should be aware that websites listed in this work may have changed or disappeared between when this work was written and when it is read. Neither the publisher nor authors shall be liable for any loss of profit or any other commercial damages, including but not limited to special, incidental, consequential, or other damages.

Library of Congress Cataloging-in-Publication Data applied for

ISBN HB: 9781119494553

Cover Design: Wiley
Cover Images: © sutadimage/Shutterstock

Set in 9.5/12.5pt STIXTwoText by SPi Global, Chennai, India

Printed and bound by CPI Group (UK) Ltd, Croydon, CR0 4YY

10 9 8 7 6 5 4 3 2 1

To my wife Hyeeun,
daughter Naul,
son Hanul
and
mother Hyungsuk

Contents

Preface

From 1G to 4G cellular networks, the main target of development was system capacity improvement. Thus, the current cellular systems have very efficient system architectures in terms of system capacity. However, it is not an optimal solution in terms of other system parameters (latency, energy efficiency, connection density, etc.). 5G systems have ambitious goals, and 5G applications cover various areas such as eHealth, factory automation, automated vehicles, critical communication, and so on. In recent mobile communications and networks events, leading mobile phone vendors and network equipment vendors have exhibited more than smartphones and networks. Connected and automated vehicles, smart cities, drones, and factory automations were highlighted, and they are highly related to latency, energy efficiency, mobility, and connection density. Thus, 5G systems no longer focus on system capacity only. Many other system parameters should be improved significantly. 5G applications can be classified into (i) enhanced mobile broadband communication (eMBB), (ii) ultra-reliable and low latency communication (URLLC), and (iii) massive machine type communication (mMTC). Their target system parameters are different in accordance with use cases. The key metrics of eMBB, URLL, and mMTC are system capacity, latency, and connection density, respectively. They also have different system requirements and architectures. In this book, we analyze and design 5G communication and network systems from a different perspective. We introduce mathematical tools and find an optimal, suboptimal or tradeoff point to meet the system requirements.

There is a big gap between theoretical design and practical implementation. Countless papers are published every year to optimize wireless communication systems in academia, but their practical use is very limited in industry. The reasons why they have a big gap can be summarized as simple system models, limited target parameters, and lack of a holistic design. First, optimization algorithms are applied under simple system models. The simple system models sometimes include unrealistic system parameters such as perfect channel state information, limited numbers of users, no interferences, and so on. They allow optimization algorithms to solve the problem nicely, but they are far from practical solutions. Secondly, each optimization algorithm targets only one system parameter (for example, energy efficiency) while other system parameters (for example, system throughput, latency, complexity, and so on.) are not close to an optimal solution, and are sometimes even worse. Thirdly, one optimization algorithm is applied to a small part or component of a communication architecture and it finds an optimal solution. From a holistic point of view, the solution is not optimal. For example, although we design an energy-efficient multicarrier modulation scheme and achieve significant energy savings, the other parameters might be worse and bring a higher energy consumption to another component. The architecture design is highly related to many other components of communications and networks. Sometimes there is a trade-off relationship and sometime there is no optimal point. One decision in one design step is highly related to another decision in the next design step. It is very difficult to optimize many metrics such as complexity, system capacity, latency, energy efficiency, connection density, and flexibility. Thus, a wireless communication system designer makes a decision subjectively and empirically. It is a big challenge to reduce the gap between theoretical design and practical implementation.

This book introduces mathematical methods and optimization algorithms for wireless communications and networks and helps audiences find an optimal, suboptimal or trade-off solution for each communication problem using the optimization algorithms. By this approach, audiences can understand how to obtain a solution under specific conditions and realize the limit of the solution.

This book is not a math book, and we skip the proofs of mathematical formulae and algorithms. This book focuses on design and optimization for 5G communication systems including eMBB, URLLC, and mMTC. The organization of the book is as follows: in Part I, mathematical methods and optimization algorithms for wireless communications are introduced. It will provide audiences with a mathematical background including approximation theory, LS estimation, MMSE estimation, ML and MAP estimation, matrix factorization, linear programming, convex optimization, gradient descent method, supervised and unsupervised learning, reinforcement learning, and so on. In Part II, 5G communication systems are designed and optimized using the mathematical methods and optimization algorithms. For example, the key metric of URLLC is latency. The latency is highly related to many PHY/MAC/network layer parameters such as frame size, transmit time interval, hybrid automatic repeat request (HARQ) processing time, round trip time, discontinuous reception, and so on. We look into them to minimize the latency. In addition, we design some key components using the optimization algorithms. It covers 5G NR, multiple input multiple output (MIMO), 5G waveforms (OFDMA, FBMC, GFDM, and UFMC), low-density parity-check (LDPC), short packet transmission theory, latency analysis of 4G and 5G networks, MEC optimizations, robust optimization, power control and management, wireless sensor networks, and so on. The main purpose of this book is to introduce mathematical methods and optimization algorithms and design 5G communication systems (eMBB, URLLC, mMTC) with a different perspective.

I am pleased to acknowledge the support of the VTT Technical Research Centre of Finland and John Wiley & Sons, and also the valuable discussion of my colleagues and experts in EU projects Flex5Gware, 5G-Enhance, and 5G-HEART. I am grateful for the support of my family and friends.

Haesik Kim
VTT Oulu, Finland

List of Abbreviations

1G	first generation
2G	second generation
3G	third generation
3GPP	Third Generation Partnership Project
4G	fourth generation
5G	fifth generation
5GC	5G core
ACK	acknowledge
ACLR	adjacent channel leakage ratio
ACM	adaptive coding and modulation
ADSL	asymmetric digital subscriber line
AI	artificial intelligence
AMF	access and mobility management function
AMPS	Advanced Mobile Phone Service
APP	a posteriori probability
AR	augmented reality
ARFCN	Absolute Radio Frequency Channel Number
ARO	adjustable robust optimization
ARQ	automatic repeat request
AS	access stratum
AWGN	additive white Gaussian noise
BBU	baseband unit
BCCH	broadcast control channel
BCH	broadcast channel
BER	bit error rate
BLER	block error ratio
BMSE	Bayesian mean squared error
BP	belief propagation
BPSK	binary phase shift keying
BWP	bandwidth part
CapEx	capital expenditure
CBG	code block group
CCCH	common control channel

CCE	control channel element
CCSDS	Consultative Committee for Space Data Systems
cdf	cumulative distribution function
CDMA	code-division multiple access
CINR	carrier-to-interference plus noise ratio
CN	core network
CORESET	configurable control resource set
CP	convex optimization problems
CP	cyclic prefix
CPU	central processing unit
C-plane	control-plane
CQI	channel quality indicator
CQP	convex quadratic programming
C-RAN	cloud radio access network
CRC	cyclic redundancy check
C-RNTI	cell radio network temporary identifier
CRSC	circular recursive systematic constituent
CSI	channel state information
CSI-RS	channel state information reference signal
CSIT	channel state information at transmitter
CSS	chirp spread spectrum
D2D	device-to-device
DARPA	Defense Advanced Research Projects Agency
D-BLAST	Diagonal Bell Laboratories Layered Space–Time
DCCH	dedicated control channel
DCI	downlink control information
DFT	discrete Fourier transform
DL	downlink
DL-SCH	downlink shared channel
DMC	discrete memoryless channel
DMRS	demodulation reference signal
DNS	domain name service
DRB	data radio bearer
DRX	discontinuous reception
DSN	distributed sensor network
DSSS	direct sequence spreading spectrum
DTCH	dedicated traffic channel
E2E	end-to-end
EC-GSM-IoT	extended coverage global system for mobile communications IoT
E-DCH	enhance dedicated channel
EDGE	Enhanced Data rates for GSM Evolution
eGPRS	enhanced general packet radio service
eMBB	enhanced mobile broadband communication
eMTC	enhanced machine-type communication
eNB	evolved Node B

EPC	enhanced packet core
ETSI	European Telecommunications Standard Institute
EV-DO	Evolution, Data Only
FA	false alarm
FBMC	filter bank multicarrier
FDD	frequency division duplexing
FDM	frequency division multiplexing
FDMA	frequency division multiple access
FD-MIMO	full-dimension MIMO
FER	frame error rate
FFT	fast Fourier transform
FM	frequency modulation
FONC	first-order necessary condition
GF	Galois Field
GFDM	generalized frequency division multiplexing
GMSK	Gaussian minimum shift keying
gNB	next-generation NodeB
GPO	generalized precoded OFDMA
GPRS	general packet radio services
GSM	global system for mobile communications
HARQ	hybrid automatic repeat request
HSCSD	high-speed circuit-switched data
HSDPA	high speed downlink packet access
HSPA	high-speed packet access
HSUPA	high-speed uplink packet access
ICI	inter-carrier interference
IDFT	inverse discrete Fourier transform
IFFT	inverse fast Fourier transform
IoT	Internet of Things
IPM	interior point method
ISI	inter-symbol interference
ITU	International Telecommunication Union
ITU-R	ITU's Radiocommunication Sector
KKT	Karush–Kuhn–Tucker
KPI	key performance indicator
LDC	linear dispersion code
LDPC	low-density parity-check
LIDAR	Light Detection and Ranging
LoRa	long range
LP	linear programming
LPWAN	lower power wide area network
LS	least squares
LTE	Long Term Evolution
LU	lower upper
M2M	machine-to-machine

MAC	medium access control
MAP	maximum a posteriori
MCG	master cell group
MD	missed detection
MDP	Markov decision problem/process
MEC	multi-access edge computing
MF	matched filter
MIB	master information block
MIMO	multiple input multiple output
ML	maximum likelihood
MME	mobility management entity
MMS	multimedia messaging services
MMSE	minimum mean-squared error
mMTC	massive machine type communication
mmWAVE	millimetre wave
MNO	mobile network operators
MRC	maximum ratio combining
MRT	maximum ratio transmission
MSE	mean square error
MVNO	mobile virtual network operators
MVU	minimum variance unbiased
NACK	negative acknowledge
NAS	non-access stratum
NAT	network address translation
NB-IoT	narrowband IoT
NB-PCID	narrowband physical cell identity
NEF	network exposure function
NFV	network functions virtualization
NGMN	Next Generation Mobile Network
NG-RAN	next generation RAN
NMT	Nordic Mobile Telephone
Node B	base station
NOMA	nonorthogonal multiple access
NP	nondeterministic polynomial
NPBCH	narrowband physical broadcast channel
NPDCCH	narrowband physical downlink control channel
NPDSCH	narrowband physical downlink shared channel
NPRACH	narrowband physical random access channel
NPSS	narrowband primary synchronization signal
NPUSCH	narrowband physical uplink shared channel
NR	new radio
NRS	narrowband reference signal
NSA	non-standalone
NSSI	network slice subnet instance
NSSS	narrowband secondary synchronization signal

NTT	Nippon Telegraph and Telephone
OFDM	orthogonal frequency division multiplexing
OFDMA	orthogonal frequency division multiple access
OMA	orthogonal multiple access
OOBE	out-of-band emission
OpEx	operational expenditure
OQAM	offset quadrature amplitude modulation
OSTBC	orthogonal space–time block code
OTT	over-the-top
PAPR	peak-to-average power ratio
PBCH	physical broadcast channel
PCCH	paging control channel
PCH	paging channel
PDCCH	physical downlink control channel
PDCP	packet data convergence protocol
pdf	probability density function
PDN-GW	packet data network gateway
PDSCH	physical downlink shared channel
PDU	protocol data unit
PEP	pairwise error probability
PHY	physical
pmf	probability mass function
PPN	polyphase network
PRACH	physical random access channel
PRB	physical resource block
PSM	power-saving mode
PSS	primary synchronization signal
PSTN	public switched telephone network
PTRS	phase tracking reference signal
PUCCH	physical uplink control channel
PUSCH	physical uplink shared channel
QAM	quadrature amplitude modulation
QCQP	quadratically constrained quadratic program
QFI	QoS flow ID
QoS	quality of service
QP	quadratic programming
QPSK	quadrature phase shift keying
RACH	random access channel
RAN	radio access network
RB	resource block
REG	resource element group
RF	radio frequency
RL	reinforcement learning
RLC	radio link control
RO	robust optimization

RRC	radio resource control
RRU	remote radio unit
RS	Reed-Solomon
RTT	round trip time
SA	standalone
SARSA	state-action-reward-state-action
SC-CPS	single carrier circularly pulse shaped
SC-FDM	single carrier frequency division multiplexing
SCG	secondary cell group
SDAP	service data adaption protocol
SDL	supplemental downlink
SDMA	space division multiple access
SDN	software defined networking
SDP	semidefinite programming
SDR	semidefinite relaxation
SDU	service data unit
SE	standard error
SGW	serving gateway
SIC	successive interference cancellation
SINR	signal-to-interference-plus-noise ratio
SIR	signal-to-interference ratio
SMDP	semi-Markov decision problem
SMF	session management function
SMS	short messaging service
SN	sequence number
SNR	signal-to-noise ratio
SOCP	second-order cone programming
SONC	second-order necessary condition
SOSC	second-order sufficient condition
SRS	sounding reference signal
SSB	synchronization signal block
SSE	sum of the squared errors
SSQ	sum of squares
SSS	secondary synchronization signal
STBC	space–time block code
STSK	space–time shift keying
STTC	space–time trellis code
SVD	singular value decomposition
SVM	support vector machine
SUMT	sequential unconstrained minimization technique
TCP	transmission control protocol
TCM	trellis-coded modulation
TD	temporal difference
TDD	time division duplexing
TDMA	time division multiple access

TM	transmission mode
TN	transport network
TRxP	transmission reception point
TTI	transmission time interval
UE	user equipment
UFMC	universal filtered multicarrier
UHD	ultra-high definition
UL	uplink
UL-SCH	uplink shared channel
UMTS	Universal Mobile Telecommunications Service
UPF	user plane function
U-plane	user-plane
URLLC	ultra-reliable and low latency communication
UTRAN	UMTS Terrestrial Radio Access Network
V-BLAST	Vertical Bell Laboratories Layered Space–Time
VLSI	very large-scale integration
VoIP	Voice over Internet Protocol
VR	virtual reality
WAP	wireless application protocol
WGN	white Gaussian noise
WSN	wireless sensor network
ZF	zero forcing
ZP	zero padding

Part I

Mathematical Methods and Optimization Theories for Wireless Communications

1

Historical Sketch of Cellular Communications and Networks

Cellular communication and network systems have changed rapidly over the past four decades and have adopted new technologies. The cellular communication and network industry has evolved from the first generation (1G) to the fifth generation (5G). The term "generation" is based on the 3GPP standard group's releases. In this chapter, we look into the evolution of cellular communications and networks in terms of technology enhancement, cost reduction, and use case expansion.

1.1 Evolution of Cellular Communications and Networks

Mobile phones have now become essential devices to people in their day-to-day lives. Their history began in the early 1900s. The predecessors of cellular systems were actually two-way radio systems for ships and trains. In 1906, a Canadian-born inventor Reginald Fessenden made the first two-way voice transmission using amplitude modulation. In 1926, the German National Railway (Deutsche Reichsbahn) provided first-class passengers with mobile telephony services on the train route between Berlin and Hamburg. After World War II, the developments for portable-size devices accelerated in many countries. At this stage, the mobile devices were not based on a cellular concept and did not need base stations. They supported only a few users and were very expensive. Thus, those mobile devices are regarded as the "zero generation" (0G).

In 1973, Martin Cooper and John F. Mitchell of Motorola demonstrated the first public mobile phone call using a device weighing 1.1 kg [1]. In 1979, Nippon Telegraph and Telephone (NTT) deployed the first commercial cellular network in Tokyo, Japan. In 1981, the Nordic Mobile Telephone (NMT) group launched the first mobile phone network supporting international roaming among Finland, Sweden, Norway, and Denmark. Two types of NMT are NMT-450 (450 MHz frequency bands) and NMT-900 (900 MHz frequency bands). NMT-900 had more channels than NMT-450. In 1983, Advanced Mobile Phone Service (AMPS) was launched in Chicago, USA, using the Motorola DynaTAC 8000x mobile phone. The DynaTAC was the pocket-sized phone supporting about 30 minutes talk time. It was a significant improvement and heralded a new era of cellular phones. This was the first generation (1G) cellular system supporting voice calls and using analogue technology. The technical specifications of 1G systems are summarized in Table 1.1.

Design and Optimization for 5G Wireless Communications, First Edition. Haesik Kim.
© 2020 John Wiley & Sons Ltd. Published 2020 by John Wiley & Sons Ltd.

Table 1.1 Technical specifications of 1G cellular systems.

	NMT (NMT-450 and NMT-900)	AMPS
Frequency band (MHz)	463 to 468 (Rx) and 453 to 458 (Tx) in NMT-450 standard, 935 to 960 (Rx) and 890 to 915 (Tx) in NMT-900 standard	824 to 849(Tx) and 869 to 894 (Rx)
Channel bandwidth	25 kHz in NMT-450 standard, 12.5 kHz in NMT-900 standard	30 kHz
Multiple access scheme	FDMA	FDMA
Duplex scheme	FDD	FDD
No. of channels	200 in NMT-450 and 1999 in NMT-900	832 in AMPS and 2496 in Narrow band AMPS
Modulation	Frequency modulation (FM)	Frequency modulation (FM)
Number of users per channel	One	One
Base station antenna	Omni-directional	Omni-directional
Switch type	Circuit switching	Circuit switching
Data rate	2.4 ~ 14.4 kbps	2.4 ~ 14.4 kbps

The 1G analogue system established the foundation of cellular networks and adopted key techniques such as frequency reuse, licensed spectrum and coordinated mobile network. The cellular concept [2] allows us to overcome many problems such as coverage, power consumption, user capacity, interference, and so on. The frequency reuse is a key idea of the cellular concept. Neighboring cells operate on different frequencies. Thus, the interference can be reduced and cell capacity can be increased. In addition, the mobile operator holds licensed spectrum for exclusive use and coordinates the call for seamless access. However, the 1G analogue system had the limitation of capacity because the frequency division multiple access (FDMA) system is inefficient. The FDMA of 1G systems supports only one user per channel. The 1G device was heavy, with a high energy consumption, and high cost.

In 1991, the second generation (2G) of cellular systems was commercially launched in Finland. The 2G systems can be divided into the global system for mobile communications (GSM) using time division multiple access (TDMA) technology, and IS-95 (or cdmaOne) using code-division multiple access (CDMA) technology. GSM is very widely deployed in all countries. About 80% of all 2G subscribers around the world used GSM [3]. IS-95 is deployed in the US and parts of Asia. About 17% of all 2G subscribers around the world used IS-95 [3]. In addition, TDMA-based IS-136 was developed as an AMPS evolution in the US but migrated to GSM. The 2G digital systems are voice-oriented systems supporting voice-mail and short messaging service (SMS). The GSM is based on a TDMA technique that support eight users per 200 kHz frequency band by assigning different time slots for

Table 1.2 Technical specifications of 2G cellular systems.

	GSM	IS-95
Frequency bands	850/900 MHz, 1.8/1.9 GHz	850 MHz/1.9 GHz
Channel bandwidth	200 kHz	1.25 MHz
Multiple access scheme	TDMA/FDMA	CDMA
Duplex scheme	FDD	FDD
Frame duration	20 ms	4.6 ms
Modulation	GMSK	BPSK
Modulation efficiency (bps/Hz)	1	1.35
Spectrum efficiency (conversation/cell/MHz)	12.1 ~ 45.1	5.0 ~ 6.6
Switch type	Circuit switching for voice and packet switching for data	Circuit switching for voice and packet switching for data

each user. As a modulation technique of the GSM system, Gaussian minimum shift keying (GMSK) is adopted. It allows the GSM system to have a constant envelope property, providing low power consumption. The technical specifications for 2G systems are summarized in Table 1.2.

The main disadvantages of the 1G systems were low capacity, high-energy consumption, and heavy and high-cost handsets. In 2G systems, the capacity problem was solved by voice compressing techniques and TDMA/CDMA techniques. The high energy consumption problem was solved by the lower radio power emission of the digital system. The heavy and high-cost handset problem was solved by low digital component cost and size. In addition, simple encryption was used in 2G systems. However, the 2G system still requires a large frequency spacing to reduce interference and does not support soft-handover. Most importantly, there were market requirements relating to data services such as real-time news, stock information, weather, location, and so on. The 2G system could not satisfy them and evolved to 2.5G systems. Thus, the general packet radio services (GPRS) appeared in the market and allowed limited web browsing and multimedia services such as wireless application protocol (WAP), multimedia messaging services (MMS), and email access. The main difference between 2G systems and 2.5G systems is the switching method. The 2G systems are designed for voice services in a circuit-switched network. However, the 2.5G systems are designed to support data services so it partially implements a packet-switched network. The reason why we call this system 2.5G is that it was not a major change but an upgrade over existing 2G infrastructure. It required some modification of base stations and mobile phones. Besides GPRS, there were Enhanced Data rates for GSM Evolution (EDGE) and high-speed circuit-switched data (HSCSD) as an evolution of TDMA systems, and IS-95B as an evolution of CDMA systems. However, the 2.5G systems were not deployed widely due to the following limitations:

(i) The actual data rate was much lower than advertised. The maximum data rate of 172.2 kbps could be achieved when a single user takes all radio resources (8 time-slots) without any error protection. However, a mobile operator should provide a subscriber with enough radio resources. Thus, the actual data rate was about 30–40 kbps.

(ii) Transit delays occurred. The GPRS data packets arrived at one destination from many different places. It caused packet loss or corruption over the radio links.

(iii) Applications were limited. It supported many applications such as email, internet access, location-based services, and so on. Traditional web browsers support access to full websites with high-resolution images, video, and lots of information. However, WAP scaled this down and supported a small-size image and text-based website. It did not meet the market requirement, and thus many mobile operators waited for the next generation (3G).

NTT Docomo launched the first pre-commercial 3G network in 1998, and then deployed the first commercial 3G network based on W-CDMA technology in Japan in October 2001. SK Telecom commercially launched the first 3G network based on CDMA200 technology in South Korea in January 2002. 3G systems provide us with much higher data rates, better voice quality and multimedia services. In order to achieve a global interoperability of mobile networks, the International Telecommunication Union (ITU) identified a global frequency band in the 2 GHz range and invited proposals for IMT-2000 to meet high data rate requirements: 2 Mbps for fixed users, 284 kbps for pedestrians, and 144 kbps for vehicular environments. The 3G services include global roaming, high-quality voice calls, location-based services, video conferencing, video on demand, online banking and so on. The ITU approved several proposals for IMT-2000. Two major proposals were the Universal Mobile Telecommunications Service (UMTS), also called W-CDMA, by the Third Generation Partnership Project (3GPP) standard (GSM camp), and the CDMA2000 by the 3GPP2 standard (IS-95 camp). They both selected CDMA as the multiple access technique because of multiple benefits: (i) more efficient spectrum use; (ii) increased system capacity; and (iii) better security. There are many similarities between the two systems: direct sequence spreading spectrum (DSSS) multiple access, orthogonal code channelization, random access, power control scheme, rake receivers, soft handover, voice decoder, and so on. The technical specifications of 3G systems are summarized in Table 1.3.

The UMTS was originally developed by the European Telecommunications Standard Institute (ETSI). However, the seven telecommunications standard development organizations (ETSI, ARIB, ATIS, CCSA, TSDSI, TTA, and TTC) built a partnership known as the 3GPP, and the 3GPP completed the UMTS standards as the evolution of GSM in 1999. The UMTS architecture supporting backward compatibility with GSM and GPRS architecture is composed of (i) a core network (CN) with functions of switching, routing, and subscriber management, (ii) UMTS Terrestrial Radio Access Network (UTRAN) connecting mobile phones to the public switched telephone network (PSTN) and packet networks, and (iii) user equipment (UE) such as mobile phones and any handheld devices. The CDMA2000 1× implies the same bandwidth (1.25 MHz) as the 2G (IS-95). The data rate of CDMA2000 1× has been increased but it could not meet the 3G requirements of the ITU. Thus, it was

Table 1.3 Technical specifications of 3G cellular systems.

	UMTS (3 GPP Release 99)	CDMA2000 (1x)
Frequency bands	850/900 MHz, 1.8/1.9/2.1 GHz	450/850 MHz 1.7/1.9/2.1 GHz
Channel bandwidth	5 MHz	1.25 MHz
Multiple access scheme	CDMA	CDMA
Duplex scheme	FDD/TDD	FDD
Data modulation	DSSS, QPSK	DSSS, BPSK/QPSK
Peak data rate	384~2048 kbps	307 kbps
Chip rate	3.84 Mcps	1.2288 Mcps
Frame length	5 ms (signaling), 20, 40, 80 ms physical layer frames	10 ms for physical layer, 10, 20, 40, and 80 ms for transport layer
Channel coding	Convolutional and turbo code	Convolutional and turbo code
Network synchronization	Synchronous/asynchronous	Synchronous
Core network	GSM-MAP	ANSI-41

evolved to CDMA200 EV-DO (Evolution, Data Only) in October 2000. As the name EV-DO implies, it supports data only. It provides up to 2.4 Mbps downlink data rate and up to 153 kbs uplink data rate, and includes new techniques such as adaptive coding and modulation, data optimized channel, and opportunistic scheduling. In the late 1990s, the data usage pattern was asymmetric. The higher data rates are required in downlink to access the internet, download a huge file and use video-on-demand services. In order to respond to market demands for much higher data rates, the next evolution is high-speed packet access (HSPA) as 3.5G systems by the 3GPP. In the HSPA family, high-speed downlink packet access (HSDPA) was introduced in 3GPP Release 5 in 2002. The HSDPA supported up to 14.4 Mbps peak data rate theoretically, but the typical user data rate was 500 kbps to 2 Mbps. The HSDPA adopted new advanced techniques (hybrid automatic repeat request [HARQ], link adaptation, fast dynamic scheduling) to deliver higher data rates and more capacity [4]. The HARQ improved the performance by reducing the retransmission rate. There are two types of HARQ: chase combining HARQ, and Incremental redundancy HARQ. The chase combining HARQ is regards as repetition coding. The retransmission includes the same information and redundancy. The receiver combines the received bits with the same bits from the previous transmission using maximum ratio combining (MRC). In contrast, the incremental redundancy HARQ uses multiple different sets of coded bits. They are transmitted in different channels and the receiver obtains additional information. Link adaptation techniques help to increase system throughput. The UE of HSDPA reports a channel quality indicator (CQI) to a base station (NodeB). Depending on this channel state information, the base station varies the modulation order and coding rate per user and frame. The fast dynamic scheduler provides us with better radio resource utilization by exploiting the diversity of channels and allocating more radio resource to a user whose channel condition is favorable. High-speed uplink packet access (HSUPA) was introduced in 3GPP Release 6 in 2004. The HSUPA supports up to 5.76 Mbps peak data rate theoretically, but a typical user data rate was 500 kbps to 1 Mbps. This high data rate allows us to use more applications such as Voice over Internet Protocol (VoIP). The HSUPA added the enhance dedicated channel (E-DCH) to UMTS and included new features such as a shorter transmission time interval (TTI). After that, evolved HSPA (HSPA+) was introduced in 3GPP Release 7. It provides us with high data rates (up to 42.2 Mbps in downlink and up to 22 Mbps in the uplink) and includes new techniques (high order modulation, 2×2 multiple input multiple output [MIMO]). The high order modulation such as 64QAM allows us to improve by about 50% more data transmission in the packets. The MIMO plays a key role in HSPA and beyond. About 25% average cell throughput gain is achieved by a HSPA+MIMO solution when compared with a single antenna system [5].

The driving force for 4G systems comes from market needs. Although 3G systems improved significantly over 2G systems, the main function was still voice communications on circuit switch systems. People preferred to use broadband data services offered by wired communication systems (ADSL, cable modem, and so on) and short-range wireless communication systems (WiFi) because the mobile data service by cellular systems was much more expensive than ADSL and WiFi. Thus, 4G systems were developed on a new network architecture. Voice services and data services are no longer separated. All IP core networks of 4G systems support both voice service and high-speed data services including multimedia services, mobile TV, video conferencing, and so on. Another driving force is popularization of the smartphone. Unlike a traditional cellular phone, smartphones have a full keyboard, large display, touch screen, cameras, video recorder, GPS navigation, microphones, and many sensors (accelerometer, gyroscope, magnetometer, light sensor, proximity sensor, barometer, thermometer, fingerprint sensor, etc.). Smartphones are powerful mobile devices as much as a laptop. Thus, data services became more important than voice services. In 2008, ITU defined requirements of IMT-Advanced (4G systems) including 100 Mbps for vehicular environments and 1 Gbps for fixed users or pedestrians. However, two major proposals, mobile WiMAX and LTE, known as 4G systems, do not fulfill the requirements of IMT-Advanced. Nevertheless, they were approved as 4G systems. After that, both systems gradually improved and met many parts of the requirements. In terms of technology, they both have many similarities such as all IP networks, orthogonal frequency division multiple access (OFDMA) based multiple access schemes, MIMOs, and so on. On the other hand, the differences are (i) compatibility: LTE is compatible with 3G, but WiMAX does not support coexistence of WiMAX and 3G; (ii) mobility support: LTE supports up to 450 km/h, but WiMAX supports up to 120 km/h; (iii) frame duration: LTE has 10 ms frame duration but WiMAX frame duration is 5 ms; (iv) channel bandwidth: LTE channel bandwidth is from 1.4 to 20 MHz but WiMAX uses from 5 to 10 MHz; and so on. The technical specifications of 4G systems are summarized in Table 1.4.

Table 1.4 Technical specifications of 4G cellular systems.

	LTE (3 GPP Release 8)	Mobile WiMAX (IEEE 802.16e-2005)
Frequency bands	700 MHz, 1.7/2.1 GHz, 2.6 GHz, 1.5 GHz	2.3 GHz, 2.6 GHz, and 3.5 GHz
Channel bandwidth	Scalable, 1.4, 3, 5, 10, 15, 20 MHz	Scalable, 5, 7, 8.75, 10 MHz
Data rate	150 Mbps (DL)/75 Mbps (UL)	46 Mbps(DL)/7 Mbps (UL)
Frame size	1 ms (sub-frame)	5 ms (frame)
Multiple access scheme	OFDMA (DL)/SC-FDMA (UL)	OFDMA
Duplex scheme	FDD/TDD	FDD/TDD
FFT size	128, 256, 512, 1024, 1536, 2048	128, 512, 1024, 2048
OFDMA symbol duration	71.8, 71.3, 83.2, and 166.6 μs	102.9 μs
Cyclic prefix	1/4, 1/8, 1/16 and 1/32	Normal, Extended
Modulation	QPSK, 16QAM, 64QAM	QPSK, 16QAM, 64QAM
Subcarrier spacing	7.5, 15 kHz	10.9375 kHz
Channel coding	Convolutional coding, Convolutional turbo coding	Convolutional coding, Convolutional turbo coding
MIMO	Multilayer precoded spatial multiplexing, space frequency block coding	Beamforming, space time coding and spatial multiplexing
Networks	All IP EUTRAN network, two-tier architecture (EUTRAN and EPC)	All IP network, two-tier architecture (ASN and CSN)

1.2 Evolution to 5G Networks

The 3GPP continuously evolves for more data capacity. Capacity of cellular systems has been improved by three different approaches: bandwidth increase, spectral efficiency increase, and frequency reuse. According to Shannon's capacity formula [6] and extended capacity for MIMO channels [7], channel capacity can be simply expressed as follows:

$$C = W \cdot n \cdot \log_2(1 + S/N) \tag{1.1}$$

where *C, W, n, S/N* are channel capacity, bandwidth, number of antennae and signal-to-noise ratio, respectively. The first approach (bandwidth increase) is to increase *W* by more bandwidth by regulation, carrier aggregation technique, and cognitive radio. The second approach (spectral efficiency increase) is to increase n by MIMO techniques and S/N by interference mitigation techniques, error correction coding, traffic adaptation, and so on. The third approach (frequency reuse) is to increase the number of cells or sections by cell sectorization and femto cells. The channel capacity in Equation (1.1) can be modified as follows:

$$C = W \cdot n \cdot \sum \log_2(1 + S/N) \tag{1.2}$$

Based on those approaches, cellular systems improved system capacity significantly. Now, we prepare for the 5G era and expect life enhancement, such as can be achieved by new features of 5G systems such as the Internet of Things (IoT), public safety, proximity service, vehicular communications, terrestrial TV, Gbps mobility, and so on. In order to achieve the goals for 5G, the standard bodies set high requirements, and industry and academia stay in line with them. From 1G to 4G, the main target metric was system capacity. However, 5G systems focus not only on system capacity but also latency, connection density and energy efficiency. The 5G applications can be classified into three main communication applications: (i) enhanced mobile broadband communication (eMBB); (ii) ultra-reliable and low latency communication (URLLC), and (iii) massive machine type communication (mMTC). The ITU defined 5G as IMT-2020 in 2015. The ITU's Radiocommunication Sector (ITU-R) Working Party 5D has the leading role and plans to deploy the 5G system in 2020 [8]. The 3GPP also plans to enhance the LTE system and meet the 5G requirements of ITU [9]. The 5G target of the 3GPP is to (i) improve LTE capacity and performance, and (ii) address a new business segment. The 3GPP standards keep expanding their platform to new 5G services while improving their system performance to meet ambitious 5G requirements. The initial features were completed in September 2016 and the broader framework was finalized in June 2017 (Release 14).

As we can observe in Figure 1.1, 3GPP 5G Phase 1/Release 15 is planned to complete in September 2018. Key features of Release 15 will be forward compatibility with previous versions, eMBB, roaming, charging, network sharing, QoS control, and so on. 3GPP 5G Phase 2/Release 16 is planned to complete in March 2020. Key features of Release 16 will be compatibility with non-3GPP access, IoT, satellite support, URLLC, 5G media for virtual reality, and so on. Cellular systems have evolved approximately every 20 years, as shown in Figure 1.2. We expect 5G to revolutionize our day-to-day life and various industries (telecommunications, transportation, public safety, healthcare, manufacturing, media, etc.) in the near future. In [10], ITU-R summarizes 5G use cases and applications: transportation,

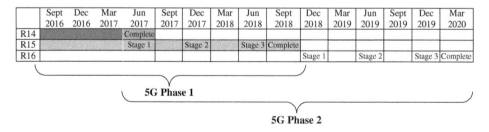

	Sept 2016	Dec 2016	Mar 2017	Jun 2017	Sept 2017	Dec 2017	Mar 2018	Jun 2018	Sept 2018	Dec 2018	Mar 2019	Jun 2019	Sept 2019	Dec 2019	Mar 2020
R14				Complete											
R15				Stage 1		Stage 2			Stage 3	Complete					
R16										Stage 1		Stage 2		Stage 3	Complete

5G Phase 1

5G Phase 2

Figure 1.1 Timeline of 3GPP 5G developments.

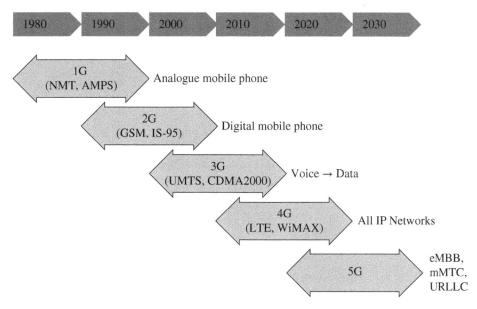

Figure 1.2 Evolution of cellular systems.

public safety, utilities, remote control, healthcare, education, Smart cities, wearables, Smart homes, agriculture, and enhanced multimedia. Among them, people pay attention to five key vertical sectors: automated driving, factory automation, smartgrids, eHealth, and augmented reality. In the next chapter, we look into their applications, system parameters and requirements. To sum up, 1G laid the foundation for mobile telephony, 2G popularized mobile telephony, 3G expanded mobile services from voice to data, 4G builds all IP core networks and achieves mobile broadband, and 5G includes new wireless features such as eMBB, URLL, and mMTC.

References

1 Edward C. Niehenke, "Wireless Communications: Present and Future: Introduction to Focused Issue Articles", IEEE Microwave Magazine 15, 2, 16–35 2014.

2 MacDonald, V.H. (1979). The cellular concept. *Bell System Technical Journal* 58 (1): 15–42.

3 GSM Association. (2010). GSM World Statistics. https://web.archive.org/web/20100521013451/http://www.gsmworld.com/newsroom/market-data/market_data_summary.htm

4 Holma, H., Toskala, A., Ranta-aho, K, Pirskanen, J. High-Speed Packet Access Evolution in 3GPP Release 7. IEEE Communications Magazine 45, 12, 29–35 2007.

5 GSM Association. (2010). MIMO in HSPA: the Real-World Impact. https://www.gsma.com/spectrum/wp-content/uploads/2012/03/umtsmimofinal.pdf

6 Shannon, C.E. (1948). A mathematical theory of communication. *Bell System Technical Journal* 27: 379, 623–423, 656.

7 Tse, D. and Viswanath, P. (2006). *Fundamentals of Wireless Communication.* Cambridge University Press.

8 International Telecommunication Union. (not dated). http://www.itu.int/en/ITU-R/study-groups/rsg5/rwp5d/imt-2020/Pages/default.aspx

9 3GPP (not dated). 3GPP standard systems heading into the 5G era. http://www.3gpp.org/news-events/3gpp-news/1614-sa_5g

10 International Telecommunication Union. (2015). Recommendation ITU-R M.2083-0, IMT Vision – Framework and overall objectives of the future development of IMT for 2020 and beyond. https://www.itu.int/rec/R-REC-M.2083-0-201509-I/en

2

5G Wireless Communication System Parameters and Requirements

From 1G to 4G, the cellular systems have been developed to meet high system capacity requirements and high data rates, and then provide us with high-quality voice services and high-throughput data services. In 5G wireless communication systems, a paradigm shift is required as target applications are diversified. In order to support various services and use cases, the various metrics (data rate, system capacity, mobility, latency, reliability, coverage, energy efficiency, connection density, CapEx and OpEx, accessibility, flexibility, security, quality of service, etc.) need to be improved significantly and new technological developments are required. In this chapter, we look into 5G key performance indicators (KPIs) and requirements and their relationships, and also introduce key enabling technologies and approaches.

2.1   5G Requirements

The 4G system provides a broadband service to people, and mobile broadband services are now popular in many countries. However, people want significant improvements in networks and mobile devices and expect better and various services. Basically, a user would require better battery life, higher user-experienced data rates, seamless user experience, better mobility, lower cost, and so on. 5G networks should improve scalability, capacity, flexibility, energy efficiency, coverage, security, compatibility, and cost efficiency. As we discussed in Chapter 1, the ITU-R Working Party 5D has a leading role in 5G system developments and defines the 5G minimum technical performance requirements [1]. Based on those criteria [1], ITU-R will accept the candidate standards for IMT-2020 as 5G. According to three usage scenarios (enhanced mobile broadband communication [eMBB], ultra-reliable and low latency communication [URLLC], and massive machine type communication [mMTC]), key requirements are defined.

The mMTC is a very important driver of 5G systems. In order to provide a subscriber with mMTC services in a dense area, device density is a key performance indicator. The estimated device density and traffic characteristics to support 10 000 households/km^2 in a city are summarized in Table 2.1 [2].

As we can see in Table 2.1, the message size is small but device density is high in the city scenario. Thus, the connection density of mMTC is a key requirement. ITU-R specifies a required connection density of 1 M devices/km^2, greater than 99% grade of service, and

Design and Optimization for 5G Wireless Communications, First Edition. Haesik Kim.
© 2020 John Wiley & Sons Ltd. Published 2020 by John Wiley & Sons Ltd.

Table 2.1 Traffic characteristics for mMTC city scenario [2].

	Typical message size (bytes)	Message interval	Device density (per km^2)
Water meters	100	12 h	10 000
Electricity meters	100	24 h	10 000
Gas meters	100	30 min	10 000
Vending machines	150	24 h	150
Bike fleet management	150	30 min	200
Pay-as-you-drive	150	10 min	2250

less than 10 seconds latency [1]. Another important requirement is battery life. The mMTC devices should send a short message (about 100 bytes) via an uplink (UL) channel to a gateway after receiving downlink (DL) acknowledgements from a gateway. According to a 3GPP LTE-M study [3, 4], the required power consumptions are 575 mW for uplink transmit power, 80 mW for downlink receive power, 3 mW for sleep mode, and 0.015 mW for deep sleep mode. However, those power consumptions are associated with transmit data packet structure, power amplifier efficiency, frequency bands, filter design, coverage, network deployments, and so on. The required battery life of mMTC devices is about 10 years without charging.

The URLLC is an important feature of 5G systems to support latency-sensitive services such as public safety, automated vehicles, factory automation, eHealth, smartgrid, and tactile internet. The mission-critical link of the URLLC should be anywhere and anytime. In order to meet these requirements, a high level of KPIs (latency, reliability, and availability) should be provided. It causes wireless communications system designers to face a new challenge and approach system design differently. The traditional communication model based on Shannon theory [5] assumes sufficiently long time and many channel uses. The channel capacity is defined to establish a deterministic and error-free transmission link. However, in the case of the URLLC scenario, limited channels are used and we cannot average out the variations of the trials. The metadata including channel estimation, synchronization, and so on becomes a big burden. Re-transmission techniques (automatic repeat request, ARQ) should be used in a limited way. In addition, due to a high reliability requirement (bit error rate [BER] less than 10^{-7}), very rare events in communication models (relationship of power, error, outage, and reliability) should be considered. ITU-R specifies 1 ms user plane latency, 20 ms control plane latency, 99.999% reliability with packet error rate less than 10^{-5} to 10^{-9}, and near-zero interruption time [1]. Depending on target applications, the latency requirements vary from 10 ms (smartgrid, vehicle parking, process automation, game, and so on) to less than 1 ms (safety related V2X communications, factory automation, tactile internet, and so on).

The eMBB as a successor of 4G is a service to meet market needs for an increasingly digital lifestyle including ultra-high definition (UHD) video, augmented reality (AR) and virtual reality (VR). The eMBB use cases can be classified as broadband access in

Table 2.2 5G eMBB requirements [1].

Metrics	eMBB requirements	Remarks
Peak data rate	DL:20 Gbps, UL:10 Gbps	
Peak spectral efficiency	DL: 30 bps/Hz (8×8 MIMO), UL:15 bps/Hz (4×4 MIMO)	
User experienced data rate	DL: 100 Mbps, UL:50 Mbps	5% point of the cumulative distribution function of the user throughput in urban
Area traffic capacity	DL: 10 Mbps/m^2	Indoor hotspot
Latency	User plane: 4 ms, Control plane: 20 ms	User plane: single user for small IP packet (e.g. 0 byte payload + IP header), for both downlink and uplink. Control plane: transition from idle to active
Mobility	10 km/h for indoor hotspot, 30 km/h for dense urban, 120–500 km/h for rural	
Normalized traffic channel link data rate	1.5 bps/Hz for indoor hotspot, 1.12 bps/Hz for dense urban, 0.8–0.45 bps/Hz for rural	

dense areas (urban centers, stadiums, shopping malls, and so on), broadband access everywhere (suburban and rural), and high-speed mobility (high-speed train, planes, and so on) [6]. Each eMBB use case has different requirements. For example, broadband access in dense areas requires higher connection density and traffic density. However, other use cases (broadband access everywhere and high-speed mobility) require relatively lower performance. In order to provide us with the eMBB services, the main requirement is high throughput. ITU-R specifies eMBB requirements as shown in Table 2.2 [1].

In order to deploy 5G systems, multiple architectures are studied in 3GPP standard. Phase 1 of 5G focuses on eMBB services. Phase 1 development is considered as non-standalone (NSA), which can connect both 4G LTE (Long Term Evolution) and 5G. In NSA, 5G devices maintain dual connectivity as user-plane (U-plane) connection for 5G and control-plane (C-plane) connection for 4G LTE. Thus, 5G devices monitor paging channels on 4G LTE and exchange control information including call set-up/termination, location registration, and so on. Phase 2 is considered as standalone (SA), which can connect only to 5G networks. In SA, 5G devices monitor paging channels on 5G networks and use both U-plane and C-plane. In addition, 3GPP standard defines service requirements and technical targets of 5G systems [7]. In [7], the 5G services are defined as: (i) fixed, mobile and satellite access technologies supports; (ii) scalable and customizable networks for vertical markets; (iii) resource efficient services from low data rate IoT services to high data

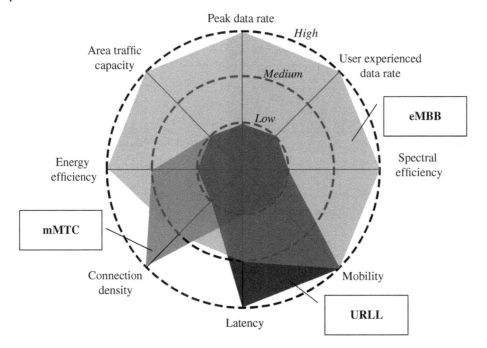

Figure 2.1 5G requirements [8].

rate multimedia services; (iv) energy efficient networks and battery power optimizations; (v) network capability exposure for the third-party service providers; and (vi) indirect connectivity supports. The technical requirements for different scenarios (urban, rural, and dense environments) are (i) user-experienced data rate from 25 Mbps (uplink)/50 Mbps (downlink) for rural, to 500 Mbps (uplink)/1 Gbps (downlink) for dense environments; (ii) 0.5 ms latency for mission-critical scenarios; (iii) 16 Tbps/km^2 with 250 K users/km^2 capacity for dense environments. These service and technical requirements are used as inputs for the 3GPP Working Group. Figure 2.1 summarizes the requirements of 5G eMBB, URLL, and mMTC [8].

2.2 Trade-off of 5G System Metrics

In the previous section, 5G key metrics and their requirements are discussed. Besides those metrics, we should consider many other parameters (complexity, signal quality, area, cost, and so on) to design 5G systems, and many of them have a trade-off relationship. For example, cell size is an important design parameter, which relates to both geographical coverage and the number of subscribers. In order to cover large area and reduce the cost, the cell size should be as large as possible. Thus, we can minimize the deployment cost. On the other hand, the cell size should be as small as possible because we maintain good signal quality and accommodate a large number of subscribers. In this section, we review the relationship between 5G key metrics. In [9, 10], the four fundamental metric relationships in an additive white Gaussian noise (AWGN) channel are expressed as follows:

$$\eta_{EE}(\eta_{SE}) = \frac{\eta_{SE}}{(2^{\eta_{SE}} - 1)N_0} \tag{2.1}$$

$$\eta_{EE}(\eta_{DE}) = \frac{\eta_{DE} \cdot C}{(2^{\eta_{DE} \cdot C/W} - 1)WN_0} \tag{2.2}$$

$$P(W) = WN_0(2^{R/W} - 1) \tag{2.3}$$

$$P(\tau) = WN_0(2^{1/W\tau} - 1) \tag{2.4}$$

where $\eta_{EE}, \eta_{SE}, \eta_{DE}, P, W, N_0, \tau, R$, and C represent energy efficiency, spectrum efficiency, deployment efficiency, the total transmit power, the total bandwidth, the additive noise power density, the transmission delay, the rate requirement and the deployment cost, respectively. The energy efficiency, spectrum efficiency, and deployment efficiency can be expressed as follows:

$$\eta_{EE} = \frac{W}{P} \log_2\left(1 + \frac{P}{WN_0}\right) \tag{2.5}$$

$$\eta_{SE} = \log_2\left(1 + \frac{P}{WN_0}\right) \tag{2.6}$$

$$\eta_{DE} = \frac{W}{C} \log_2\left(1 + \frac{P}{WN_0}\right) \tag{2.7}$$

Each metric is with regard to radio resources (spectrum, energy, cost, bandwidth, and so on). A dictionary definition of "efficiency" is an ability to avoid wasting resources (effort, energy, time, money, and so on) in producing a desired result, or a quality characterizing the correspondence between the consumed resources and the attained utility. Thus, energy efficiency formed by combining two words means how well a wireless communication and network system is designed without wasting energy. As we can observe for Equations (2.1)–(2.4), each relationship shows us a trade-off. However, the trade-off relationships will be different in practical systems. In terms of communication system conditions (such as size, type, environment, and so on), each metric and equation should be redefined. Nevertheless, those equations are meaningful for simple communication systems.

Equation (2.1) is derived from the Shannon formula for peer-to-peer communication links in AWGN channels. As we can observe for Equation (2.1), η_{EE} converges to a constant or zero when η_{SE} approaches zero or goes to infinity, respectively. The spectrum efficiency means the system throughput per bandwidth. The spectrum efficiency as a key metric from 1G systems is widely used for measuring how efficiently a spectrum is used and how cellular systems are optimized. The energy efficiency represents how efficiently power is consumed, and became an important aim in the implementation of 5G networks. About 3% of worldwide energy is consumed by information and communication infrastructures, and their power consumption is rising at 15–20% every year. In [11], base stations (BS) in the 3G mobile network use 57%, mobile switching systems use 20%, core transmission parts are responsible for 15% of usage and data centers use 6%. Thus, a base station is the most energy-consuming part of a mobile network. In addition, the energy efficiency of a base station is still very low. According to an ITU study [12], key factors impacting energy efficiency are higher data rate, lower latency, the IoT, carrier aggregation and multiple connectivity, massive MIMO, multilevel sleep modes, cloudification, virtualization, and network slicing. Among those factors, carrier aggregation can reduce fast fading losses and dual connectivity can reduce interferences at the cell border. However, in order to operate multiple radio equipment and wideband equipment on different frequencies, higher energy consumption (EC) is required. Massive MIMO antennae require many parallel transceivers and increase power consumption. Multilevel sleep modes of base stations are highly related to an impact on energy efficiency of 5G networks. Many of them are entangled with each other. The overall EC of a network can be formulated as follows [12]:

$$EC_{MN} = \sum_i \left(\sum_k EC_{BS_{i,k}} + EC_{SI_i} \right) + \sum_j EC_{BH_j} + \sum_l EC_{RC_l} \qquad (2.8)$$

where *EC* is energy consumption, BS is the base station in the mobile network (MN), BH is the backhauling, SI is the site infrastructure (including rectifier, battery losses, climate equipment, etc.), RC is the control node, i is an index over the number of sites, j is an index over the number of BH equipment connected to the i sites, k is the index over the number of BSs in the i-th site, and l is the index over the control nodes of the MN.

Equation (2.2) describes the trade-off of deployment efficiency and energy efficiency. The deployment efficiency means system throughput per deployment cost (including capital expenditure [CapEx] and operational expenditure [OpEx]). The CapEx is defined as equipment or materials required for the networks, for example, cost of spectrum, network equipment, permission to use the relevant infrastructure including fiber, and so on. The OpEx is defined as the regular operational expenses for the networks, for example, rental fees for base station installation, employee salaries, marketing costs, electricity costs, and so on. They are key design criteria for network planning. In order to minimize energy efficiency, a network planner prefers to design small cells while the deployment cost is increased. On the other hand, in order to minimize deployment cost, a network planner wants to design large cells where a high power is used.

Equation (2.3) represents the trade-off of transmit power and signal bandwidth. This is the fundamental communication metric relationship from Shannon's capacity formula. The channel capacity means how much information we can send through the given channel. The channel capacity can be increased by increasing power or bandwidth.

Equation (2.4) describes the trade-off of the latency and average consumed power. It was derived from Shannon's formula because of $\tau = 1/R$. If we consider information theory, the network architecture, and queueing theory, the latency equation will be more complicated. In order to operate 5G services including virtual reality, tactile internet, automated vehicles, and so on, ultra-low latency is required. The 5G latency goal of 1 ms is very challenging even if the processor performance is significantly increased, a new network component such as multi-access edge computing is introduced, and new radio techniques are adopted in 5G systems.

Summary 2.1 5G Requirements and Their Trade-off Relationships

1) The mMTC is a very important driver of 5G systems. ITU-R specifies a required connection density of 1 M devices km^{-2}, greater than 99% grade of service, and less than 10 seconds latency.
2) The URLL is an important feature of 5G systems to support the latency-sensitive services such as public safety, automated vehicles, factory automation, eHealth, smartgrid, and tactile internet. ITU-R specifies 1 ms user plane latency, 20 ms control plane latency, 99.999% reliability with a packet error rate less than 10^{-5} to 10^{-9}, and near-zero interruption time.
3) The eMBB as a successor to 4G is a service to meet market needs for an increasingly digital lifestyle including ultra-high definition (UHD) video, augmented reality (AR) and virtual reality (VR). ITU-R specifies 20 Gbps downlink peak data rate and 100 Mbps downlink user-experienced data rate.
4) We should consider many 5G system parameters (complexity, signal quality, area, cost, and so on) to design 5G systems, and many of them are involved in trade-off relationships.

Problems

2.1 Describe 5G requirements according to the mMTC use cases such as factory automation and production process.

2.2 Describe 5G requirements according to the URLL use cases such as remote medical surgery and automated vehicles.

2.3 Describe 5G requirements according to the eMBB use cases such as virtual reality and ultra-high definition (UHD) video.

2.4 Define technical challenges and key techniques to achieve the 1 ms 5G requirement.

2.5 Define technical challenges and key techniques to achieve the connection density of 1 M devices/km^2.

2.6 Define technical challenges and key techniques to achieve the 20 Gbps downlink peak data rate.

References

1 International Telecommunication Union – Radiocommunication Sector (ITU-R) (2017) . *Report M.2320 – Minimum Requirements Related to Technical Performance for IMT-2020 Radio Interface(s)*. ITU-R.

2 Ericsson. (2016). *Ericsson Mobility Report 2016*. www.ericsson.com/en/mobility-report/ reports

3 *TR 45.820 V13.1.0, Cellular System Support for Ultra-low Complexity and Low Throughput Internet of Things (CIoT)*. https://portal.3gpp.org/desktopmodules/Specifications/ SpecificationDetails.aspx?specificationId=2719

4 *TR 38.913 V14.3.0, Study on Scenarios and Requirements for Next Generation Access Technologies*. https://portal.3gpp.org/desktopmodules/Specifications/SpecificationDetails.aspx? specificationId=2996

5 Shannon, C.E. (1948). A mathematical theory of communication Part I and II. *Bell System Technical Journal* 27: 623–656.

6 Next Generation Mobile Networks. (2015). *5G White Paper*. http://www.ngmn.org/ uploads/media/NGMN$_$5G$_$White$_$Paper$_$V1$_$0.pdf

7 *Technical Specification TS22.261, Service Requirements for Next Generation New Services and Markets*. https://portal.3gpp.org/desktopmodules/Specifications/SpecificationDetails .aspx?specificationId=3107

8 International Telecommunication Union – Radiocommunication Sector (ITU-R). (2015). *Recommendation M.2083-0, IMT Vision – Framework and overall objectives of the future development of IMT for 2020 and beyond*. https://www.itu.int/rec/R-REC-M.2083

9 Zhang, S., Wu, Q., Xu, S., and Li, G.Y. (2017). Fundamental green tradeoffs: progresses, challenges, and impacts on 5G networks. *IEEE Communication Surveys and Tutorials* 19 (1): 33–56.

10 Y. Chen, S. Zhang, S. Xu, and G. Y. Li, Fundamental tradeoffs on green wireless networks. IEEE Communications Magazine 49, 6, 30–37 2011.

11 T. Edler (2008). *Green Base Stations – How to Minimize CO_2 Emissions in Operator Networks*. Ericsson seminar, Bath Base Station Conference 2008.

12 Mauro Boldi (ed.) (2017). *ITU-T Technical Paper LSTP-5GEE, Study on methods and metrics to evaluate energy efficiency for future 5G systems*. https://www.itu.int/dms_pub/ itu-t/opb/tut/T-TUT-ICT-2017-PDF-E.pdf

3

Mathematical Methods for Wireless Communications

Mathematics is the language of technology and science because it can provide us with precise expression of concepts, objects, or natural phenomena and we can share a meaning with others. It is important to understand the mathematical expression of wireless communication and network elements, formulate problems of wireless communications and networks, and find solutions to the problems. Thus, students, researchers, or developers who want to work in this field should be familiar with mathematical terms and theories. In addition, when designing communication devices and planning cellular networks, we should consider many design parameters including system capacity, radio resource allocations, traffic, base station location, signal propagation and regulation, and also examine many aspects of communication and network systems, which are security, quality of service, traffic engineering, switching, routing, mobility, wireless channels, and so on. Those communication and network topics are related to many mathematical theories such as statistics, stochastic analysis, queueing theory, game theory, coding theory, graph theory, linear/nonlinear programming, machine learning, and so on. For example, when we deal with traffic engineering in cellular networks, we solve some traffic problem using linear/nonlinear programming or statistics. When we solve some routing problem, we use graph theory or coding theory. Thus, we should investigate mathematical topics and pay attention to optimization problems in order to maximize radio resource efficiency and minimize the cost. As the first step, we simplify the practical cellular systems and define the related mathematical model. If we include most of the practical aspects, the mathematical model is too complex to solve the problem. Thus, the mathematical model unavoidably includes some assumptions and a gap exists between practical systems and mathematical models. In this chapter, a mathematical background will be provided to define a mathematical model of cellular systems, and design and optimize wireless communications.

3.1 Signal Spaces

Communications can be defined as the process of delivering information from a source to a destination via a channel. The channel is a physical transmission medium such as a copper wire, optical cable, or electromagnetic wave. The channel includes many types of noise which impairs the information. We can intuitively raise interesting questions: how should we deliver with no loss of information? How much information can we send via

Design and Optimization for 5G Wireless Communications, First Edition. Haesik Kim.
© 2020 John Wiley & Sons Ltd. Published 2020 by John Wiley & Sons Ltd.

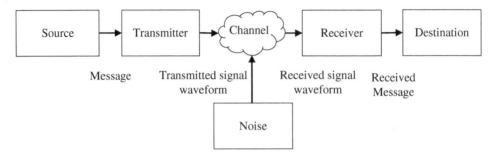

Figure 3.1 Shannon's communication architecture [1].

the channel? How long does it take to exchange the information between a mobile user and a server? How many mobile users can exchange information at the same time? How much energy is needed to operate cellular systems? How can we define the metrics about capacity, latency, and efficiency? How can we measure them? In this book, we find answers to these questions. In order to find answers, we should define a model of a communication system. In this section, we define the communication system model and an important concept of the model.

According to Shannon's communication architecture [1], the components of communications are source, transmitter, channel, receiver, destination, and noise, as shown in Figure 3.1. In this figure, the source produces the information (or message) to transmit, and the information can be voice, video, music, email, and so on. The transmitter has a role to transform the information into a suitable signal waveform for transmission over a channel. The channel is a physical medium. The receiver reconstructs the information from the received signal waveform. The destination is the location where the information arrives. The noise is a disruptive factor interfering with the transmission. This architecture developed by Shannon and Weaver in 1949 is very useful to understand and analyze communication systems because a communication system designer can treat each component of the communication system separately. Many communication systems are still based on Shannon's communication architecture. In this architecture, each component including signals and function blocks should be described mathematically. The signal space (or vector) representation of signals (or waveforms) is a very useful tool of modern communication theory, which is given in Wozencraft and Jacobs [2]. The basic idea is simple: waveforms as finite energy functions are vectors in a certain signal space (or vector space). Any set of waveforms is equivalent to a set of vectors. One important merit of the vector representation is that a signal space as a set of objects can be combined together using linear combinations. It is possible to describe how objects work precisely.

A finite-dimensional vector $\mathbf{x}$ can be written as

$$\mathbf{x} = \begin{bmatrix} x_1 \\ x_2 \\ \vdots \\ x_n \end{bmatrix} \tag{3.1}$$

where x_i, $i = 1, 2, \ldots, n$ is the element of the vector $\mathbf{x}$. The elements lie in the set of real numbers $x_i \in \mathbb{R}$ or the set of complex numbers $x_i \in \mathbb{C}$. These are called the sets of real vector space and complex vector space. If the vectors are represented as n-tuples of real numbers (or complex numbers), $\mathbb{R}^n$ (or $\mathbb{C}^n$) are the set of n-tuple real numbers (or complex numbers). $\mathbb{R}^2$ and $\mathbb{R}^3$ are geometrically represented by a plane and a three-dimensional space, respectively.

A linear vector space S over a set of scalar R is a collection of vectors. Addition and scalar multiplication satisfy the following properties:

Property 3.1 Addition in Vector Space S

For any $\mathbf{x}$ and $\mathbf{y} \in S$, $\mathbf{x} + \mathbf{y} \in S$. The addition is closed and the sum of $\mathbf{x}$ and $\mathbf{y}$ satisfies the following properties:

(i) There is a unique/identity element $\mathbf{0} \in S$ satisfying $\mathbf{x} + \mathbf{0} = \mathbf{0} + \mathbf{x} = \mathbf{x}$ for all $\mathbf{x} \in S$.

(ii) For every $\mathbf{x} \in S$, there is another $\mathbf{y} \in S$ such that $\mathbf{x} + \mathbf{y} = \mathbf{0}$ where $\mathbf{y}$ is the additive inverse of $\mathbf{x}$ and usually is $-\mathbf{x}$.

(iii) The addition is associative and commutative: for any $\mathbf{x}$, $\mathbf{y}$, and $\mathbf{z} \in S$,

$$(\mathbf{x} + \mathbf{y}) + \mathbf{z} = \mathbf{x} + (\mathbf{y} + \mathbf{z}),$$

$$\mathbf{x} + \mathbf{y} = \mathbf{y} + \mathbf{x}.$$

Property 3.2 Scalar Multiplication in Vector Space S

For any a, $b \in R$ and any $\mathbf{x}$ and $\mathbf{y} \in S$, the scalar multiplication of a and $\mathbf{x}$ satisfies the following properties:

(i) $a\mathbf{x} \in S$,

(ii) *Scalar associative property*: $a(b\mathbf{x}) = (ab)\mathbf{x}$,

(iii) *Distributive property*: $(a + b)\mathbf{x} = a\mathbf{x} + b\mathbf{x}$, $a(\mathbf{x} + \mathbf{y}) = a\mathbf{x} + a\mathbf{y}$,

(iv) *Unit multiplication*: For all $\mathbf{x} \in S$, there is a multiplicative identity element $1 \in R$ such that $1\mathbf{x} = \mathbf{x}$.

Example 3.1 *Addition and Scalar Multiplication in Vector Space*

For $\mathbb{R}^4$, a vector $\mathbf{x}$ is a 4-tuple of real number. When $\mathbf{x}, \mathbf{y} \in \mathbb{R}^4$ and

$$\mathbf{x} = \begin{bmatrix} 1 \\ 4 \\ 8 \\ 5 \end{bmatrix} \text{ and } \mathbf{y} = \begin{bmatrix} 4 \\ 0 \\ -2 \\ 2 \end{bmatrix}$$

find $\mathbf{x} + \mathbf{y}$ and $2\mathbf{x} + 4\mathbf{y}$.

Solution

$$\mathbf{x} + \mathbf{y} = \begin{bmatrix} 1 \\ 4 \\ 8 \\ 5 \end{bmatrix} + \begin{bmatrix} 4 \\ 0 \\ -2 \\ 2 \end{bmatrix} = \begin{bmatrix} 5 \\ 4 \\ 6 \\ 7 \end{bmatrix} \text{ and}$$

$$2\mathbf{x} + 4\mathbf{y} = 2\begin{bmatrix} 1 \\ 4 \\ 8 \\ 5 \end{bmatrix} + 4\begin{bmatrix} 4 \\ 0 \\ -2 \\ 2 \end{bmatrix} = \begin{bmatrix} 2 \\ 8 \\ 16 \\ 10 \end{bmatrix} + \begin{bmatrix} 16 \\ 0 \\ -8 \\ 8 \end{bmatrix} = \begin{bmatrix} 18 \\ 8 \\ 8 \\ 18 \end{bmatrix}$$

Example 3.2   *Geometrical Interpretation of $\mathbb{R}^2$*

For $\mathbb{R}^2$, a vector $\mathbf{x}$ and $\mathbf{y}$ is a 2-tuple of a real number. When $\mathbf{x}, \mathbf{y} \in \mathbb{R}^2$ and

$$\mathbf{x} = \begin{bmatrix} 2 \\ 4 \end{bmatrix} \text{ and } \mathbf{y} = \begin{bmatrix} 6 \\ 3 \end{bmatrix}$$

represent $\mathbf{x}, \mathbf{y}, \mathbf{x}{-}\mathbf{y}, \mathbf{x}/2, \mathbf{y}/2$, and $(\mathbf{x}{-}\mathbf{y})/2$ geometrically.

Solution

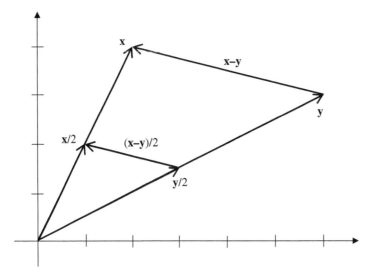

Figure p3.1   Geometric interpretation of **x, y, x − y, x/2, y/2**, and **(x − y)/2**.

As seen in Figure p3.1, vectors $\mathbf{x}$ and $\mathbf{y}$ are presented as directed lines from 0 in a plane, scalar multiplications $\mathbf{x}/2$ and $\mathbf{y}/2$ lie on the same line, and distributive property is recognized.

The term "vector" is used interchangeably with the terms "signal" or "waveform." In a discrete time domain, we can view the vector that is composed of the sample of the function in the set of n-tuple real numbers (or complex numbers). In a continuous time domain, the vector is the signal itself denoted by $x(t)$, which is the value corresponding to a specific argument t. In order to understand the concept of signal space, we should define several mathematical terms. The linear combination is defined as follows:

Definition 3.1 Linear Combination

Let S be a vector space over R. A set of vectors $\mathbf{p}_1, \mathbf{p}_2, \ldots, \mathbf{p}_m \in S$ spans S if every $\mathbf{x} \in S$ is a linear combination of $\mathbf{p}_1, \mathbf{p}_2, \ldots, \mathbf{p}_m$. For a set of scalars $c_1, c_2, \ldots, c_m, \in R$, we can represent the linear combination as follows:

$$\mathbf{x} = \sum_{i=1}^{m} c_i \mathbf{p}_i = c_1 \mathbf{p}_1 + c_2 \mathbf{p}_2 + \ldots + c_m \mathbf{p}_m$$

The linear combination synthesizes the vector $\mathbf{x}$ from a set of vectors $\{\mathbf{p}_i\} = \{\mathbf{p}_1 \, \mathbf{p}_2 \cdots \mathbf{p}_m\}$ as ingredients for other vectors. If the set of vectors is the m unit vectors of $\mathbb{R}^m$, $\mathbf{p}_1 = [1\, 0 \ldots 0]^T$, $\mathbf{p}_2 = [0\, 1 \ldots 0]^T, \ldots, \mathbf{p}_m = [0\ 0 \ldots 1]^T$ where $(\ )^T$ is the transpose. The vector $\mathbf{x}$ can be expressed as follows:

$$\mathbf{x} = \sum_{i=1}^{m} c_i \mathbf{p}_i = [c_1 \, c_2 \ldots c_m]^T \tag{3.2}$$

Now, we need to look into the uniqueness of the vector representation and the smallest set of vectors to synthesize any vector in S. Let V be a subset of S. A set of vectors V is linearly dependent if $\sum_{i=1}^{m} c_i \mathbf{p}_i = 0$ for a set of scalars not all equal to 0. If there is the only set of scalar satisfying the $\sum_{i=1}^{m} c_i \mathbf{p}_i = 0$ and $c_1 = c_2 = \ldots = c_m = 0$, it is linearly independent. If V is linearly independent and the span of V equals S, we call V a basis for S. As we can observe in Equation (3.2), the unit vectors of $\mathbb{R}^m$ are linearly independent and we call them the natural basis. A vector space V is finite-dimensional if V is spanned by a finite number of vectors. If a vector space is not finite-dimensional, it is said to be infinite dimensional. When designing mathematical models of wireless communications and networks, most vector spaces we deal with will be finite-dimensional vector spaces.

Example 3.3 *Linear Combination and Span*
Let $V = \{(1, 2), (2, 6)\}$ be in $\mathbb{R}^2$. Show the vector $(10,14) \in \text{span}(V)$.

Solution
By Definition 3.1, the vector $(10,14)$ should satisfy the following equation:

$$c_1(1,2) + c_2(2,6) = (10,14)$$

and should find scalars c_1 and c_2. If there are no such scalars, $(10,14) \notin \text{span}(V)$. The above equation can be rewritten as follows:

$$1c_1 + 2c_2 = 10,$$
$$2c_1 + 6c_2 = 14.$$

This is a linear equation with two variables. Thus, we can find a set of scalars $c_1 = 16$, $c_2 = -3$ by rewriting the equations and eliminating one of the variables. Therefore, $(10,14) \in \text{span}(V)$ due to $16(1,2) + -3(2,6) = (10,14)$.

If V is a subset of vector space S, span (V) is the smallest subspace of S containing set V. We can define span as follows:

Definition 3.2 Span

Let V be a set of vectors in a vector space S over a set of scalars R. If the set of vectors U can be generated by all linear combinations of the vectors in V, U is the span of the vectors in V. In other words,

$$U = \text{span}(V)$$

Generally speaking, a basis is a linearly independent spanning set. Let V be a basis for S: all elements of S can be expressed uniquely as a linear combination of the basis. Thus, we can conclude that a basis for the subspace is a smallest set of vectors whose linear combination can assemble every vector in the vector space S. The choice of basis vectors for a vector space is not unique. However, the number of basis vectors is unique. A vector space must include at least a zero vector, and a zero vector is unique. When we discuss the signal size in a vector space, there are several different ways of measuring the signal size. A norm is a way of defining the length of a vector. We can define it as follows:

Definition 3.3 Norm

Let S be a vector space over $\mathbb{R}$ (or $\mathbb{C}$) with elements $\mathbf{x}$ and $\mathbf{y}$. A norm on S is a real-valued function $\|\mathbf{x}\|$ with the following properties:

(i) $\|\mathbf{x}\| \geq 0$, for all $\mathbf{x} \in S$,
(ii) $\|\mathbf{x}\| = 0$ if and only if $\mathbf{x} = 0$,
(iii) $\|\alpha\mathbf{x}\| = |\alpha|\|\mathbf{x}\|$ for all $\mathbf{x} \in S$ and all $\alpha \in \mathbb{R}$ (or $\mathbb{C}$),
(iv) $\|\mathbf{x}+\mathbf{y}\| \leq \|\mathbf{x}\| + \|\mathbf{y}\|$, for all $\mathbf{x}, \mathbf{y} \in S$.

We call the property (iv) of Definition 3.3 the Cauchy-Schwarz inequality. This means that the sum of the two vectors has a length that is less than the sum of the lengths of each vector. It is a useful property for bounding values that are difficult to calculate.

When the vectors $\mathbf{x} = [x_1\ x_2 \ldots x_n]^T$ are represented as n-tuples of real numbers $\mathbb{R}^n$ (or complex numbers $\mathbb{C}^n$), Euclidean norm, maximum norm, and summation norm can be expressed as follows:

$$\text{Euclidean } norm: \|\mathbf{x}\| = \sqrt{x_1^2 + x_2^2 + \ldots + x_n^2} \tag{3.3}$$

$$\text{Maximum } norm: \|\mathbf{x}\| = \max\{|x_1|, |x_2|, \ldots, |x_n|\} \tag{3.4}$$

$$\text{Summation } norm: \|\mathbf{x}\| = |x_1| + |x_2| + \ldots + |x_n| \tag{3.5}$$

Among them, the Euclidean norm as the square root of the total energy is the most commonly used in wireless communication theory. If a vector space equips with a norm, we call it a normed vector space and express a pair $(S, \|\mathbf{x}\|)$ consisting of a vector space S and a norm $\|\mathbf{x}\|$.

Another important operation in a vector space is an inner product. Roughly speaking, the norm represents the length of a vector and the inner product provides us with the geometric interpretation about the direction of a vector. In addition, it is very useful for defining orthogonality between vectors or detecting similarity of them. We can define it as follows:

Definition 3.4 Inner Products

Let S be a vector space over $\mathbb{R}$ (or $\mathbb{C}$) with elements $\mathbf{x}$ and $\mathbf{y}$. The inner product of two vectors $\mathbf{x}$ and $\mathbf{y}$ is defined as

$$\langle \mathbf{x}, \mathbf{y} \rangle = \mathbf{x}^H \mathbf{y}$$

where $(\cdot)^H$ denotes the Hermitian transpose operator.

For two vectors $\mathbf{x}, \mathbf{y} \in \mathbb{R}^n$ in a finite-dimensional Euclidean space, the inner product between two vectors $\mathbf{x} = [x_1\, x_2 \ldots x_n]^T$, $\mathbf{y} = [y_1\, y_2 \ldots y_n]^T$ can be calculated as follows:

$$\langle \mathbf{x}, \mathbf{y} \rangle = \sum_{i=1}^{n} x_i y_i = x_1 y_1 + x_2 y_2 + \ldots + x_n y_n \tag{3.6}$$

This inner product is the dot product or Euclidean inner product and we can simply express

$$\langle \mathbf{x}, \mathbf{y} \rangle = \mathbf{x} \cdot \mathbf{y} = \mathbf{y}^T \mathbf{x} = \mathbf{x}^T \mathbf{y} \tag{3.7}$$

For two vectors $\mathbf{x}, \mathbf{y} \in \mathbb{C}^n$ in a finite-dimensional Euclidean space, the inner product is

$$\langle \mathbf{x}, \mathbf{y} \rangle = \sum_{i=1}^{n} x_i y_i^* = \mathbf{y}^H \mathbf{x} \tag{3.8}$$

Example 3.4 *Inner Product*
For finite-dimensional vectors $\mathbf{x}, \mathbf{y} \in \mathbb{R}^3$, $\mathbf{x} = [2\ 5\ 8]^T$, $\mathbf{y} = [7\ 3\ 4]^T$, find the inner product $\langle \mathbf{x}, \mathbf{y} \rangle$.

Solution
By Equation (3.6),

$$\langle \mathbf{x}, \mathbf{y} \rangle = 2 \cdot 7 + 5 \cdot 3 + 8 \cdot 4 = 14 + 15 + 32 = 61$$

The inner product satisfies the following properties:

Property 3.3 Inner Product Properties

(a) *Hermitian symmetry*: $\langle \mathbf{x}, \mathbf{y} \rangle = \langle \mathbf{y}, \mathbf{x} \rangle^*$ for all $\mathbf{x}, \mathbf{y} \in S$, where $(\cdot)^*$ denotes the complex conjugation.
(b) *Linearity*:

$$\langle \alpha \mathbf{x}, \mathbf{y} \rangle = \alpha \langle \mathbf{x}, \mathbf{y} \rangle \text{ for all } \mathbf{x}, \mathbf{y} \in S \text{ and all } \alpha \in \mathbb{R} \text{ (or } \mathbb{C}\text{)},$$

$$\langle \mathbf{x} + \mathbf{y}, \mathbf{z} \rangle = \langle \mathbf{x}, \mathbf{z} \rangle + \langle \mathbf{y}, \mathbf{z} \rangle \text{ for all } \mathbf{x}, \mathbf{y}, \mathbf{z} \in S.$$

(c) *Positivity*: $\langle \mathbf{x}, \mathbf{x} \rangle > 0$ if $\mathbf{x} \neq 0$ and $\langle \mathbf{x}, \mathbf{x} \rangle = 0$ if and only if $\mathbf{x} = 0$.

A vector space equipped with an inner product is an inner product space. In addition, the norm $\|\mathbf{x}\|$ can be expressed using an inner product as follows:

$$\|\mathbf{x}\| = \sqrt{\langle \mathbf{x}, \mathbf{x} \rangle} \tag{3.9}$$

and it means the distance from 0 to $\mathbf{x}$. If two vectors $\mathbf{x}$ and $\mathbf{y}$ satisfies $\langle \mathbf{x}, \mathbf{y} \rangle = 0$, they are orthogonal. For finite-dimensional vectors $\mathbf{x}, \mathbf{y} \in \mathbb{R}^2$ or $\mathbb{R}^3$, there is a geometric interpretation of the inner product as follows:

$$\mathbf{x} \cdot \mathbf{y} = \|\mathbf{x}\| \|\mathbf{y}\| \cos \theta \tag{3.10}$$

where θ is the angle between two vectors. From Equation (3.10), we can determine the angle between two vectors as follows:

$$\cos \theta = \frac{\mathbf{x} \cdot \mathbf{y}}{\|\mathbf{x}\| \|\mathbf{y}\|} \tag{3.11}$$

Since $-1 \leq \cos \theta \leq 1$, it can be shown that

$$-1 \leq \frac{\mathbf{x} \cdot \mathbf{y}}{\|\mathbf{x}\| \|\mathbf{y}\|} \leq 1 \tag{3.12}$$

and the angle θ is real number. It shows us direction in any inner product space. In addition, equality $\mathbf{x} \cdot \mathbf{y} = \|\mathbf{x}\| \|\mathbf{y}\|$ holds if and only if $\mathbf{y} = \alpha \mathbf{x}$ for some $\alpha \in \mathbb{R}$. It implies that $\mathbf{x}$ and $\mathbf{y}$ are linearly dependent.

Example 3.5 *Angle Between Two Vectors*
For finite-dimensional vectors $\mathbf{x}, \mathbf{y} \in \mathbb{R}^3$, $\mathbf{x} = [2 \ 5 \ 8]^T$, $\mathbf{y} = [7 \ 3 \ 4]^T$, find the angle between two vectors.

Solution
By Equation (3.11),

$$\cos \theta = \frac{61}{9.64 \cdot 8.6} = 0.74$$

Example 3.6 *Cauchy-Schwarz Inequality*
For finite-dimensional variables $x, y, z \in \mathbb{R}$, $x^2 + y^2 + z^2 = 1$, find the maximum of $3x + y + 2z$.

Solution
By the Cauchy-Schwarz inequality,

$$(3x + y + 2z)^2 \leq (3^2 + 1^2 + 2^2)(x^2 + y^2 + z^2)$$

$$(3x + y + 2z)^2 \leq 14$$

$$3x + y + 2z \leq \sqrt{14} = 3.74$$

Therefore, the maximum of $3x + y + 2z$ is 3.74.

If the vectors are orthogonal and each vector has a unit norm, they are said to be orthonormal. The term "orthogonal" is synonymous with "perpendicular" and we denote it by $\mathbf{x} \perp \mathbf{y}$. We define orthogonality as follows:

Definition 3.5 Orthogonality

Let S be an inner product space with elements **x** and **y**. Two vectors **x** and **y** are said to be orthogonal if

$$\langle \mathbf{x}, \mathbf{y} \rangle = 0.$$

The space of all vectors orthogonal to V is said to be the orthogonal complement of V. We denote it by $V^{\perp}$. We define it as follows:

Definition 3.6 Orthogonal Space

Let S be a vector space and V and U be subspaces of S. V and U are orthogonal if every vector $\mathbf{v} \in V$ is orthogonal to every vector $\mathbf{u} \in U$ as follows:

$$\langle \mathbf{v}, \mathbf{u} \rangle = 0$$

Example 3.7 *Orthogonality*

Let S be an inner product space with elements **x**, **y**, and $\mathbf{z} \in \mathbb{R}^3$. The elements are

$$\mathbf{x} = [2\,5\,2]^T, \mathbf{y} = [1\,2 - 6]^T, \mathbf{z} = [3\,6\,7]^T$$

Find which vectors are orthogonal.

Solution

By Equation (3.6),

$$\langle \mathbf{x}, \mathbf{y} \rangle = 2 \cdot 1 + 5 \cdot 2 - 2 \cdot 6 = 2 + 10 - 12 = 0$$

$$\langle \mathbf{x}, \mathbf{z} \rangle = 2 \cdot 3 + 5 \cdot 6 + 2 \cdot 7 = 6 + 12 + 14 \neq 0$$

$$\langle \mathbf{y}, \mathbf{z} \rangle = 1 \cdot 3 + 2 \cdot 6 - 6 \cdot 7 = 3 + 12 - 42 \neq 0$$

By Definition 3.5, **x** and **y** are orthogonal, while **x** and **z** as well as **y** and **z** are not orthogonal.

$T(V)$ is called the range of T. We can think of a linear transformation as an operator or a type of function. We define linear transformation as follows:

Definition 3.7 Linear Transformation

Let V and U be vector spaces over $\mathbb{R}$ (or $\mathbb{C}$). A function $T : V \to U$ is called a linear transformation if, for all vectors v, u in V and scalar α,

Multiplicativity: $T(\alpha v) = \alpha T(v)$ for all $v \in V$ and all $\alpha \in \mathbb{R}$(or $\mathbb{C}$)

Additivity: $T(v + u) = T(v) + T(u)$ for all v and $u \in V$

The nullspace of the linear transformation T is called the kernel of T. Figure 3.2 illustrates two properties (multiplicativity and additivity) of linear transformation.

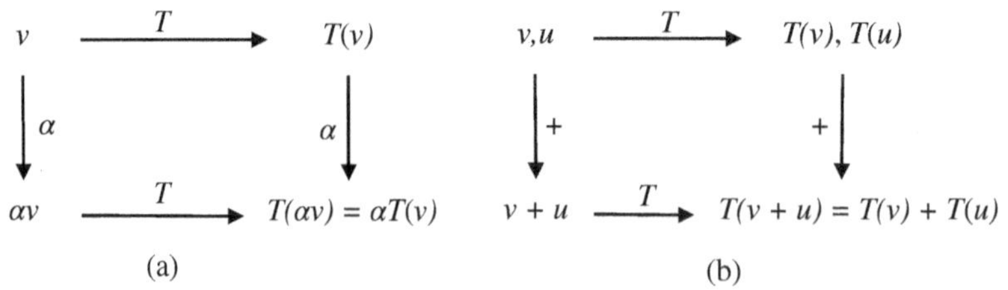

Figure 3.2 Properties of linear transformation: (a) multiplicativity and (b) additivity.

Example 3.8 *Linear Transformation*

Let $T : \mathbb{R}^3 \to \mathbb{R}^2$ be defined by

$$T\left(\begin{bmatrix} x_1 \\ x_2 \\ x_3 \end{bmatrix}\right) = \begin{bmatrix} 2x_1 + x_2 - 5x_3 \\ 3x_1 - 2x_2 + x_3 \end{bmatrix}$$

Verify that T is a linear transformation.

Solution

We can rewrite T in matrix notation as follows:

$$T\left(\begin{bmatrix} x_1 \\ x_2 \\ x_3 \end{bmatrix}\right) = \begin{bmatrix} 2 & 1 & -5 \\ 3 & -2 & 1 \end{bmatrix} \begin{bmatrix} x_1 \\ x_2 \\ x_3 \end{bmatrix}$$

Multiplicativity is satisfied as follows:

$$T\left(\alpha \begin{bmatrix} x_1 \\ x_2 \\ x_3 \end{bmatrix}\right) = \alpha \begin{bmatrix} 2 & 1 & -5 \\ 3 & -2 & 1 \end{bmatrix} \begin{bmatrix} x_1 \\ x_2 \\ x_3 \end{bmatrix} = \alpha T\left(\begin{bmatrix} x_1 \\ x_2 \\ x_3 \end{bmatrix}\right)$$

and additivity is satisfied as follows:

$$T\left(\begin{bmatrix} x_1 \\ x_2 \\ x_3 \end{bmatrix} + \begin{bmatrix} x_4 \\ x_5 \\ x_6 \end{bmatrix}\right) = T\left(\begin{bmatrix} x_1 + x_4 \\ x_2 + x_5 \\ x_3 + x_6 \end{bmatrix}\right) = \begin{bmatrix} 2 & 1 & -5 \\ 3 & -2 & 1 \end{bmatrix} \begin{bmatrix} x_1 + x_4 \\ x_2 + x_5 \\ x_3 + x_6 \end{bmatrix}$$

$$= \begin{bmatrix} 2x_1 + 2x_4 + x_2 + x_5 - 5x_3 - 5x_6 \\ 3x_1 + 3x_4 - 2x_2 - 2x_5 + x_3 + x_6 \end{bmatrix}$$

$$= \begin{bmatrix} 2x_1 + x_2 - 5x_3 \\ 3x_1 - 2x_2 + x_3 \end{bmatrix} + \begin{bmatrix} 2x_4 + x_5 - 5x_6 \\ 3x_4 - 2x_5 + x_6 \end{bmatrix} = T\left(\begin{bmatrix} x_1 \\ x_2 \\ x_3 \end{bmatrix}\right) + T\left(\begin{bmatrix} x_4 \\ x_5 \\ x_6 \end{bmatrix}\right)$$

Thus, T is a linear transformation.

Figure 3.3 Example of projection.

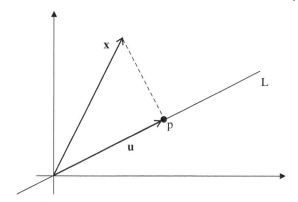

If we have a vector **x** and a line L as shown in Figure 3.3, what is the closest point to a vector **x** on the line L? As we can observe in Figure 3.3, the closet point p is located at the intersection by dropping a perpendicular onto the line L. The vector **u** is called the projection of **x** on to the line L. We write $\mathbf{u} = \text{proj}_L(\mathbf{x})$. This is the basic idea of a projection. We can generalize this idea in a vector space.

Let V be an inner product space with non-zero elements **x**, **y**, and **z**. We decompose a vector **y** as follows:

$$\mathbf{y} = \alpha\mathbf{x} + \mathbf{z}, \text{where } \mathbf{z} \in \mathbf{x}^{\perp} \tag{3.13}$$

Since **x** and **z** are orthogonal, we have

$$\langle \mathbf{x}, \mathbf{y} \rangle = \alpha \langle \mathbf{x}, \mathbf{x} \rangle \tag{3.14}$$

$$\alpha = \frac{\langle \mathbf{x}, \mathbf{y} \rangle}{\langle \mathbf{x}, \mathbf{x} \rangle} \tag{3.15}$$

Thus, we can define the orthogonal projection of **y** onto **x** as follows:

$$\text{proj}_{\mathbf{x}}(\mathbf{y}) = \frac{\langle \mathbf{x}, \mathbf{y} \rangle}{\langle \mathbf{x}, \mathbf{x} \rangle}\mathbf{x} \tag{3.16}$$

The linear transformation $\text{proj}_{\mathbf{x}}: V \to V$ is called the orthogonal projection of V onto **x**.

Example 3.9 *Orthogonal Projection*
Consider a vector $\mathbf{x} = [-3, 2]^T$ and a line L spanned by a vector $\mathbf{u} = [6, 4]^T$ over $\mathbb{R}^2$. Find the orthogonal projection onto the line L and the distance from **x** to L.

Solution
By Equation (3.16), the orthogonal projection onto the line L is

$$\text{proj}_{\mathbf{u}}(\mathbf{x}) = \frac{\langle \mathbf{u}, \mathbf{x} \rangle}{\langle \mathbf{u}, \mathbf{u} \rangle}\mathbf{u} = \frac{-18 + 8}{36 + 16}\begin{bmatrix} 6 \\ 4 \end{bmatrix} = -\frac{10}{52}\begin{bmatrix} 6 \\ 4 \end{bmatrix}$$

and we can find the distance from **x** to L as follows:

$$\mathbf{x}_{L^{\perp}} = \mathbf{x} - \text{proj}_{\mathbf{u}}(\mathbf{x}) = \begin{bmatrix} -3 \\ 2 \end{bmatrix} - \frac{10}{52}\begin{bmatrix} 6 \\ 4 \end{bmatrix} = \frac{1}{52}\begin{bmatrix} -216 \\ 64 \end{bmatrix}$$

$$\|\mathbf{x}_{L^{\perp}}\| = \frac{1}{52}\sqrt{216^2 + 64^2} \approx 4.33$$

> **Summary 3.1 Signal Spaces**
>
> 1) Communications can be defined as the process of delivering information from a source to a destination via a channel.
> 2) The components of Shannon's communication architecture are source, transmitter, channel, receiver, destination, and noise.
> 3) In the vector space representation of signal, waveforms as finite energy functions are vectors in a certain signal space (or vector space). Any set of waveforms is equivalent to a set of vectors.
> 4) The linear combination synthesizes the vector $\mathbf{x}$ from a set of vectors $\{\mathbf{p}_i\} = \{\mathbf{p}_1 \ \mathbf{p}_2 \ldots \mathbf{p}_m\}$ as ingredients for other vectors.
> 5) The inner product is very useful for defining orthogonality between vectors or detecting similarity of vectors.
> 6) We can define the orthogonal projection of $\mathbf{y}$ onto $\mathbf{x}$ as follows:
>
> $$\text{proj}_{\mathbf{x}}(\mathbf{y}) = \frac{\langle \mathbf{x}, \mathbf{y} \rangle}{\langle \mathbf{x}, \mathbf{x} \rangle} \mathbf{x}$$

3.2 Approximation and Estimation in Signal Spaces

3.2.1 Approximation Problems

Many research problems in areas of communications and networks can be expressed as approximation or optimization of performance metrics. In this section, we look into approximation problems and find a solution in vector spaces.

A complete inner product space (or a complete normed vector space with an inner product) is called a Hilbert space, and one example of a Hilbert space is the Euclidean space. It extends from two-dimensional or three-dimensional Euclidean space to a finite or infinite dimensional space. We analyze approximation problems in this vector space. Let a pair $(S, \|\cdot\|)$ be a normed linear vector space where S is a linear vector space and $\|\cdot\|$ is a norm on S. Let $U = \{\mathbf{p}_1, \mathbf{p}_2, \ldots, \mathbf{p}_m\}$ be a set of linearly independent vectors in S and $V = \text{span}(U)$. Given a vector $\mathbf{x} \in S$, we find the coefficients c_i of the approximation $\hat{\mathbf{x}}$ as follows:

$$\hat{\mathbf{x}} = c_1 \mathbf{p}_1 + c_2 \mathbf{p}_2 + \ldots + c_m \mathbf{p}_m = \sum_{i=1}^{m} c_i \mathbf{p}_i \tag{3.17}$$

The approximation error $\mathbf{e}$ can be defined as follows:

$$\|\mathbf{e}\| = \|\mathbf{x} - \hat{\mathbf{x}}\| \tag{3.18}$$

and the vector $\mathbf{x}$ can be expressed as follows:

$$\mathbf{x} = \hat{\mathbf{x}} + \mathbf{e} \tag{3.19}$$

We should find the coefficients where the approximation error is as small as possible. In order to simplify the problem and observe this geometrically, we assume that $U = \{\mathbf{p}_1, \mathbf{p}_2\}$

Figure 3.4 Approximation problem in $\mathbb{R}^3$.

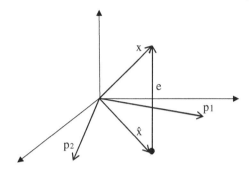

in $\mathbb{R}^3$ and a vector $\mathbf{x} \in \mathbb{R}^3$. The vector $\mathbf{x}$ can be expressed as follows:

$$\mathbf{x} = c_1\mathbf{p}_1 + c_2\mathbf{p}_2 + \mathbf{e} \tag{3.20}$$

and we can illustrate the approximation problem in Figure 3.4.

In this simple case, we can geometrically observe that the norm of the approximation error is minimized when the error vector is orthogonal to U. We can find the approximation vector $\hat{\mathbf{x}}$ when the vector $\mathbf{x}$ is projected onto the plane formed by two vectors $\mathbf{p}_1$ and $\mathbf{p}_2$. Since U contains two vectors $\mathbf{p}_1$ and $\mathbf{p}_2$, we have the following orthogonality conditions:

$$\mathbf{e} \perp \mathbf{p}_1 = \mathbf{0} \tag{3.21}$$

or

$$\langle \mathbf{x} - (c_1\mathbf{p}_1 + c_2\mathbf{p}_2), \mathbf{p}_1 \rangle = \mathbf{0} \tag{3.22}$$

and

$$\mathbf{e} \perp \mathbf{p}_2 = \mathbf{0} \tag{3.23}$$

or

$$\langle \mathbf{x} - (c_1\mathbf{p}_1 + c_2\mathbf{p}_2), \mathbf{p}_2 \rangle = \mathbf{0} \tag{3.24}$$

Using the inner product properties, Equations (3.22) and (3.24) can be changed as follows:

$$\langle \mathbf{x}, \mathbf{p}_1 \rangle = c_1 \langle \mathbf{p}_1, \mathbf{p}_1 \rangle + c_2 \langle \mathbf{p}_2, \mathbf{p}_1 \rangle \tag{3.25}$$

$$\langle \mathbf{x}, \mathbf{p}_2 \rangle = c_1 \langle \mathbf{p}_1, \mathbf{p}_2 \rangle + c_2 \langle \mathbf{p}_2, \mathbf{p}_2 \rangle \tag{3.26}$$

and Equations (3.25) and (3.26) can be represented in a matrix form as follows:

$$\begin{bmatrix} \langle \mathbf{x}, \mathbf{p}_1 \rangle \\ \langle \mathbf{x}, \mathbf{p}_2 \rangle \end{bmatrix} = \begin{bmatrix} \langle \mathbf{p}_1, \mathbf{p}_1 \rangle & \langle \mathbf{p}_2, \mathbf{p}_1 \rangle \\ \langle \mathbf{p}_1, \mathbf{p}_2 \rangle & \langle \mathbf{p}_2, \mathbf{p}_2 \rangle \end{bmatrix} \begin{bmatrix} c_1 \\ c_2 \end{bmatrix} \tag{3.27}$$

Now, we find the coefficients c_i of the approximation $\hat{\mathbf{x}}$ by solving the matrix Equation (3.27).

Example 3.10 *Approximation Problem in $\mathbb{R}^3$*

Consider $U = \{\mathbf{p}_1, \mathbf{p}_2\}$ where $\mathbf{p}_1 = [1 \ 1 \ 0]^T$ and $\mathbf{p}_2 = [1 \ 2 \ 0]^T$ in $\mathbb{R}^3$ and a vector $\mathbf{x} = [3 \ 1 \ 2]^T \in \mathbb{R}^3$. Find the approximation vector $\hat{\mathbf{x}}$.

Solution

By Equation (3.20), the vector $\mathbf{x}$ can be expressed as follows:

$$\mathbf{x} = c_1\mathbf{p}_1 + c_2\mathbf{p}_2 + \mathbf{e}$$

and the approximation vector $\hat{\mathbf{x}}$ can be represented as follows:

$$\hat{\mathbf{x}} = c_1 \mathbf{p_1} + c_2 \mathbf{p_2}$$

Using Equation (3.27), we have the following matrix:

$$\begin{bmatrix} \langle \mathbf{x}, \mathbf{p_1} \rangle \\ \langle \mathbf{x}, \mathbf{p_2} \rangle \end{bmatrix} = \begin{bmatrix} \langle \mathbf{p_1}, \mathbf{p_1} \rangle & \langle \mathbf{p_2}, \mathbf{p_1} \rangle \\ \langle \mathbf{p_1}, \mathbf{p_2} \rangle & \langle \mathbf{p_2}, \mathbf{p_2} \rangle \end{bmatrix} \begin{bmatrix} c_1 \\ c_2 \end{bmatrix}$$

$$\begin{bmatrix} 4 \\ 5 \end{bmatrix} = \begin{bmatrix} 2 & 3 \\ 3 & 5 \end{bmatrix} \begin{bmatrix} c_1 \\ c_2 \end{bmatrix}$$

By solving the above matrix, we obtain

$$\begin{bmatrix} c_1 \\ c_2 \end{bmatrix} \approx \begin{bmatrix} 5 \\ -2 \end{bmatrix}$$

Thus, the approximation vector $\hat{\mathbf{x}}$ is

$$\hat{\mathbf{x}} \approx 5 \begin{bmatrix} 1 \\ 1 \\ 0 \end{bmatrix} - 2 \begin{bmatrix} 1 \\ 2 \\ 0 \end{bmatrix} = \begin{bmatrix} 3 \\ 1 \\ 0 \end{bmatrix}$$

In Example 3.10, we have two equations and two unknown variables. Thus, we can find the solution. However, it often happens that the orthogonality matrix has no solution when there are more equations (or m rows) than unknown variables (or n columns). We call this an overdetermined system. In addition, we can find an exact solution when the approximation error $\mathbf{e}$ is zero, but the approximation vector $\hat{\mathbf{x}}$ is a least squares (LS) solution when the approximation error $\mathbf{e}$ is as small as possible. We generalize the orthogonality condition as follows:

$$\left\langle \mathbf{x} - \sum_{i=1}^{m} c_i \mathbf{p_i}, \mathbf{p_j} \right\rangle = 0, \quad j = 1, 2, \dots, n \tag{3.28}$$

and Equation (3.28) can be represented in a matrix form as follows:

$$\begin{bmatrix} \langle \mathbf{x}, \mathbf{p_1} \rangle \\ \langle \mathbf{x}, \mathbf{p_2} \rangle \\ \vdots \\ \langle \mathbf{x}, \mathbf{p_n} \rangle \end{bmatrix} = \begin{bmatrix} \langle \mathbf{p_1}, \mathbf{p_1} \rangle & \langle \mathbf{p_2}, \mathbf{p_1} \rangle & \cdots & \langle \mathbf{p_m}, \mathbf{p_1} \rangle \\ \langle \mathbf{p_1}, \mathbf{p_2} \rangle & \langle \mathbf{p_2}, \mathbf{p_2} \rangle & \cdots & \langle \mathbf{p_m}, \mathbf{p_2} \rangle \\ \vdots & \vdots & \ddots & \vdots \\ \langle \mathbf{p_1}, \mathbf{p_n} \rangle & \langle \mathbf{p_2}, \mathbf{p_n} \rangle & \cdots & \langle \mathbf{p_m}, \mathbf{p_n} \rangle \end{bmatrix} \begin{bmatrix} c_1 \\ c_2 \\ \vdots \\ c_n \end{bmatrix} \tag{3.29}$$

We can rewrite Equation (3.29) as follows:

$$\mathbf{x}^{\mathbf{xp}} = \mathbf{Rc} \tag{3.30}$$

where $\mathbf{x}^{\mathbf{xp}}$, $\mathbf{R}$, and $\mathbf{c}$ are cross-correlation vectors of $\mathbf{x}$ and $\mathbf{p_i}$, the inner product matrix and coefficient vector, respectively. We call this form ($\mathbf{Ax} = \mathbf{b}$) the normal equations, and the solution can be found by minimizing the square of the error.

Summary 3.2 Approximation Problems

1) Many research problems in areas of communications and networks can be expressed as approximation or optimization of performance metrics.
2) The norm of the approximation error is minimized when the error vector is orthogonal to a set of linearly independent vectors.
3) We can find an exact solution when the approximation error **e** is zero but the approximation vector $\hat{\mathbf{x}}$ is a least squares solution when the approximation error **e** is as small as possible.
4) Let $U = \{\mathbf{p}_1, \mathbf{p}_2, \ldots, \mathbf{p}_m\}$ be a set of linearly independent vectors in S and $V = \text{span}(U)$. Given a vector $\mathbf{x} \in S$, we find the coefficients c_i of the approximation $\hat{\mathbf{x}}$ as follows:

$$\hat{\mathbf{x}} = c_1\mathbf{p}_1 + c_2\mathbf{p}_2 + \ldots + c_m\mathbf{p}_m = \sum_{i=1}^{m} c_i\mathbf{p}_i$$

5) We generalize the orthogonality condition as follows:

$$\left\langle \mathbf{x} - \sum_{i=1}^{m} c_i\mathbf{p}_i, \mathbf{p}_j \right\rangle = 0, \quad j = 1, 2, \ldots, n$$

3.2.2 Least Squares Estimation

In wireless communication systems, we need to know how a microwave propagates via a wireless channel and how much noise is included by channel impairments such as fading, scattering, shadowing, and so on. If we can characterize wireless channels, we can build a reliable communication link and transmit a signal more efficiently. We call this technique or process "channel estimation". It has become an essential part of modern communication systems. This technique is based on data (or curve) fitting or regression analysis. Data fitting is a technique to construct data with the best fit to limited data points. Least squares (LS) is the simplest and most commonly used for many applications. The method of least squares was independently developed by Carl Friedrich Gauss in 1795, and Adrien Marie Legendre in 1805. Gauss developed this idea to calculate the orbits of celestial bodies, and Legendre published a method for determining the orbits of comets by fitting linear equations to data. This method immediately became famous.

Let $\mathbf{A} \in \mathbb{R}^{m \times n}$ and $\mathbf{b} \in \mathbb{R}^m$. The normal equation $\mathbf{A}\mathbf{x} = \mathbf{b}$ is overdetermined $(m > n)$ and there is no exact solution. We define least squares problem and error as follows:

Definition 3.8 Least Squares Problem and Error

The least squares problem consists of finding a vector $\mathbf{x} \in \mathbb{R}^n$ to minimize $\|\mathbf{A}\mathbf{x} - \mathbf{b}\|^2$. The vector $\mathbf{e} = \mathbf{A}\mathbf{x} - \mathbf{b}$ is called the least squares error (or residual) and $\|\mathbf{A}\mathbf{x} - \mathbf{b}\|^2$ is called the objective function.

We are interested in finding the vector $\mathbf{x}$ that minimizes the norm of squares of the residual. In wireless communication or signal processing, the energy of a vector $\mathbf{x}$ can be expressed as $\|\mathbf{x}\|^2$. The name "least square" comes from

$$\min_{\mathbf{x} \in \mathbb{R}^n} \|\mathbf{Ax} - \mathbf{b}^2\|$$

$\uparrow \quad \uparrow$

Least Square $\hfill (3.31)$

As we observed in Section 3.2.1, the minimum of $\|\mathbf{e}\|^2 = \|\mathbf{Ax} - \mathbf{b}\|^2$ can be found when $\mathbf{e}$ is orthogonal to each vector of the matrix $\mathbf{A}$. The objective function can be rewritten as follows:

$$\|\mathbf{e}\|^2 = \|\mathbf{Ax} - \mathbf{b}\|^2 = (\mathbf{Ax} - \mathbf{b})^T(\mathbf{Ax} - \mathbf{b}) \tag{3.32}$$

$$= \mathbf{b}^T\mathbf{b} - \mathbf{b}^T\mathbf{Ax} - \mathbf{x}^T\mathbf{A}^T\mathbf{b} + \mathbf{x}^T\mathbf{A}^T\mathbf{Ax} \tag{3.33}$$

Since $\mathbf{x}^T\mathbf{A}^T\mathbf{b}$ is the transpose of $\mathbf{b}^T\mathbf{Ax}$, the objective function is

$$\|\mathbf{e}\|^2 = \mathbf{b}^T\mathbf{b} - 2\mathbf{b}^T\mathbf{Ax} + \mathbf{x}^T\mathbf{A}^T\mathbf{Ax} \tag{3.34}$$

If we take the derivative of the objective function, we have

$$\frac{\partial}{\partial \mathbf{x}}\|\mathbf{e}\|^2 = -2\mathbf{A}^T\mathbf{b} + 2\mathbf{A}^T\mathbf{Ax} \tag{3.35}$$

The least squares estimation is obtained by minimizing it. Thus, we set the derivative equal to zero and we have

$$\frac{\partial}{\partial \mathbf{x}}\|\mathbf{e}\|^2 = -2\mathbf{A}^T\mathbf{b} + 2\mathbf{A}^T\mathbf{Ax} = 0 \tag{3.36}$$

$$\mathbf{A}^T\mathbf{b} = \mathbf{A}^T\mathbf{Ax} \tag{3.37}$$

If we assume that $\mathbf{A}^T\mathbf{A}$ is invertible, we can find the vector $\mathbf{x}$ as follows:

$$\mathbf{x} = (\mathbf{A}^T\mathbf{A})^{-1}\mathbf{A}^T\mathbf{b} \tag{3.38}$$

This is the least squares solution. The matrix $\mathbf{A}^\dagger = (\mathbf{A}^T\mathbf{A})^{-1}\mathbf{A}^T$ is called a pseudoinverse of $\mathbf{A}$. It is a left inverse of $\mathbf{A}$ as follows:

$$\mathbf{A}^\dagger\mathbf{A} = (\mathbf{A}^T\mathbf{A})^{-1}\mathbf{A}^T\mathbf{A} = \mathbf{I} \tag{3.39}$$

The approximation $\hat{\mathbf{x}}$ is

$$\hat{\mathbf{x}} = \mathbf{Ax} = \mathbf{A}(\mathbf{A}^T\mathbf{A})^{-1}\mathbf{A}^T\mathbf{b} = \mathbf{Pb} \tag{3.40}$$

where the matrix $\mathbf{P}$ is a projection matrix. It projects a vector $\mathbf{b}$ onto the space spanned by the column of $\mathbf{A}$. We could explain this approximation geometrically. When we want to solve the normal equation $\mathbf{Ax} = \mathbf{b}$ and it is overdetermined, there is no exact solution because the vector $\mathbf{x}$ is not in the space spanned by $\mathbf{A}$. Thus, we orthogonally project the vector $\mathbf{x}$ onto the space spanned by $\mathbf{A}$ and then find the best solution in the space.

When the confidence in data is reflected, a weight can be applied to the data point. In this case, we should minimize the weighted square error. Thus, the objective function is reformulated as follows:

$$\|\mathbf{e}\|_W^2 = \|\mathbf{Ax} - \mathbf{b}\|_W^2 \tag{3.41}$$

and we should minimize

$$\|\mathbf{W}^{1/2}(\mathbf{A}\mathbf{x} - \mathbf{b})\|^2 \tag{3.42}$$

where $\mathbf{W}$ is a diagonal matrix representing a weight. The weighted least square problem is

$$\min_{\mathbf{x} \in \mathbb{R}^n} \|\mathbf{W}^{1/2}(\mathbf{A}\mathbf{x} - \mathbf{b})\|^2 \tag{3.43}$$

and the weighted least square solution is

$$\mathbf{x} = (\mathbf{A}^T\mathbf{W}\mathbf{A})^{-1}\mathbf{A}^T\mathbf{W}\mathbf{b} \tag{3.44}$$

Example 3.11   *Least Square Problem*
Let $\mathbf{A} \in \mathbb{R}^{3 \times 2}$ and $\mathbf{b} \in \mathbb{R}^3$ and

$$\mathbf{A} = \begin{bmatrix} 2 & 0 \\ -3 & 5 \\ 1 & 7 \end{bmatrix} \quad \text{and} \quad \mathbf{b} = \begin{bmatrix} 2 \\ 1 \\ 3 \end{bmatrix}$$

Find the vector $\mathbf{x}$ of the normal equation $\mathbf{A}\mathbf{x} = \mathbf{b}$.

Solution
By Equation (3.38), the vector $\mathbf{x}$ is

$$\mathbf{x} = (\mathbf{A}^T\mathbf{A})^{-1}\mathbf{A}^T\mathbf{b}$$

We need a matrix calculation as follows:

$$\mathbf{A}^T\mathbf{A} = \begin{bmatrix} 2 & -3 & 1 \\ 0 & 5 & 7 \end{bmatrix} \begin{bmatrix} 2 & 0 \\ -3 & 5 \\ 1 & 7 \end{bmatrix} = \begin{bmatrix} 14 & -8 \\ -8 & 74 \end{bmatrix}$$

$$(\mathbf{A}^T\mathbf{A})^{-1} = \begin{bmatrix} 0.0761 & 0.0082 \\ 0.0082 & 0.0144 \end{bmatrix}$$

$$(\mathbf{A}^T\mathbf{A})^{-1}\mathbf{A}^T = \begin{bmatrix} 0.0761 & 0.0082 \\ 0.0082 & 0.0144 \end{bmatrix} \begin{bmatrix} 2 & -3 & 1 \\ 0 & 5 & 7 \end{bmatrix} = \begin{bmatrix} 0.1523 & -0.1872 & 0.1337 \\ 0.0165 & 0.0473 & 0.1091 \end{bmatrix}$$

Thus, the vector $\mathbf{x}$ is

$$\mathbf{x} = \begin{bmatrix} 0.1523 & -0.1872 & 0.1337 \\ 0.0165 & 0.0473 & 0.1091 \end{bmatrix} \begin{bmatrix} 2 \\ 1 \\ 3 \end{bmatrix} = \begin{bmatrix} 0.5185 \\ 0.4074 \end{bmatrix}$$

Now, we look into the least square algorithm in the context of a regression problem. When we acquire data with multiple variables, we need to know their relationship – for example, the relationship between people's weights and heights, the relationship between house price and location, the relationship between voting rates and ages, and so on. Regression analysis is a statistical technique to estimate the relationship between a target and a predictor. It is a useful tool for forecasting, error reduction or data analysis. Classification is also used for forecasting data. Simply, regression is used to predict continuous values but classification is used to predict discrete values. Linear regression is one of the most widely

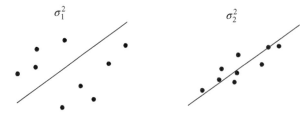

Figure 3.5 Comparison of the variance of the error term $(\sigma_1^2 > \sigma_2^2)$.

used methods for estimating the relationship between one dependent variable and one or more independent variables using a best-fit line.

In the regression model, the independent variable (or predictor variable, explanatory variable) is denoted as x along the horizontal axis and the dependent variable (or response variable, target variable) is denoted as y along the vertical axis. The purpose of the regression is to determine the best-fit line that connects x and y. If we believe the relationship between x and y is linear, we have a linear model as follows:

$$y = \beta_0 + \beta_1 x \tag{3.45}$$

where β_0 is an intercept term and β_1 is a slope coefficient. This is a linear regression problem. Finding β_0 and β_1 means determining the best-fit line. Assume there are n paired data points $(x_1, y_1), (x_2, y_2), \ldots, (x_n, y_n)$ and the paired observations satisfy a linear model. We can write that y_i as a function of x_i is generated as follows:

$$y_i = \beta_0 + \beta_1 x_i + \varepsilon_i \tag{3.46}$$

where ε_i is the error term. It means that the data do not fit the model. The error term can be expressed as Gaussian noise: $\varepsilon \sim \mathcal{N}(0, \sigma^2)$. We call this model a probabilistic model because the error term is a random variable. The variance σ^2 means how spread out the data are from the straight line as shown in Figure 3.5.

In this model, the least squares approach is to find a best-fit line to minimize the sum of the squared errors (SSE). We call this the least squared criterion. The least squares estimations of β_0 and β_1 are obtained by solving the following optimization problem:

$$\min_{\beta_0, \beta_1} \left(\sum_{i=1}^{n} \varepsilon_i^2 \right) = \min_{\beta_0, \beta_1} \left(\sum_{i=1}^{n} (y_i - (\beta_0 + \beta_1 x_i))^2 \right) \tag{3.47}$$

This problem is known as the least squares linear regression problem. The SSE term of Equation (3.47) is rewritten as follows:

$$\text{SSE} = \sum_{i=1}^{n} \varepsilon_i^2 = \sum_{i=1}^{n} (y_i^2 - 2y_i(\beta_0 + \beta_1 x_i) + \beta_0^2 + 2\beta_0 \beta_1 x_i + \beta_1^2 x_i^2) \tag{3.48}$$

The partial derivative of SSE with respect to β_0 is

$$\frac{\partial \text{SSE}}{\partial \beta_0} = \sum_{i=1}^{n} (-2y_i + 2\beta_0 + 2\beta_1 x_i) \tag{3.49}$$

and the partial derivative of SSE with respect to β_1 is

$$\frac{\partial \text{SSE}}{\partial \beta_1} = \sum_{i=1}^{n} (-2x_i y_i + 2\beta_0 x_i + 2\beta_1 x_i^2) \tag{3.50}$$

The values of β_0 and β_1 are obtained by setting

$$\frac{\partial SSE}{\partial \beta_0} = 0, \frac{\partial SSE}{\partial \beta_1} = 0 \tag{3.51}$$

Thus, Equation (3.49) is rewritten as follows:

$$\sum_{i=1}^{n} (-2y_i + 2\beta_0 + 2\beta_1 x_i) = 0 \tag{3.52}$$

$$\sum_{i=1}^{n} (-y_i + \widehat{\beta}_0 + \widehat{\beta}_1 x_i) = 0 \tag{3.53}$$

$$-n\bar{y} + n\widehat{\beta}_0 + \widehat{\beta}_1 n\bar{x} = 0 \tag{3.54}$$

$$\widehat{\beta}_0 = \bar{y} - \widehat{\beta}_1 \bar{x} \tag{3.55}$$

where $\widehat{\beta}_i$ is the predicted value of β_i and $\bar{y}$ and $\bar{x}$ are the sample means as follows:

$$\bar{y} = \frac{1}{n} \sum_{i=1}^{n} y_i \text{ and } \bar{x} = \frac{1}{n} \sum_{i=1}^{n} x_i \tag{3.56}$$

Likewise, Equation (3.50) is rewritten as follows:

$$\sum_{i=1}^{n} (-2x_i y_i + 2\beta_0 x_i + 2\beta_1 x_i^2) = 0 \tag{3.57}$$

$$\sum_{i=1}^{n} -x_i y_i + \widehat{\beta}_0 \sum_{i=1}^{n} x_i + \widehat{\beta}_1 \sum_{i=1}^{n} x_i^2 = 0 \tag{3.58}$$

$$-\sum_{i=1}^{n} x_i y_i + (\bar{y} - \widehat{\beta}_1 \bar{x}) \sum_{i=1}^{n} x_i + \widehat{\beta}_1 \sum_{i=1}^{n} x_i^2 = 0 \tag{3.59}$$

$$\widehat{\beta}_1 = \frac{\sum_{i=1}^{n} x_i (y_i - \bar{y})}{\sum_{i=1}^{n} x_i (x_i - \bar{x})} \tag{3.60}$$

$$\widehat{\beta}_1 = \frac{\sum_{i=1}^{n} (x_i - \bar{x})(y_i - \bar{y})}{\sum_{i=1}^{n} (x_i - \bar{x})^2} = \frac{S_{xy}}{S_{xx}} \tag{3.61}$$

where S_{xy} and S_{xx} are defined as follows:

$$S_{xx} = \sum_{i=1}^{n} (x_i - \bar{x})^2 = \sum_{i=1}^{n} (x_i)^2 + \frac{\left(\sum_{i=1}^{n} x_i \right)^2}{n} \tag{3.62}$$

$$S_{xy} = \sum_{i=1}^{n} (x_i - \bar{x})(y_i - \bar{y}) = \sum_{i=1}^{n} x_i y_i + \frac{\left(\sum_{i=1}^{n} x_i \right) \left(\sum_{i=1}^{n} y_i \right)}{n} \tag{3.63}$$

In addition, we can express Equation (3.61) as follows:

$$\widehat{\beta}_1 = \frac{\sum_{i=1}^{n} (x_i - \bar{x})(y_i - \bar{y})}{\sum_{i=1}^{n} (x_i - \bar{x})^2} = r \frac{s_y}{s_x} \tag{3.64}$$

where s_y and s_x are standard deviations of x and y, respectively. r is the correlation coefficient as follows:

$$r = \frac{1}{n-1} \sum_{i=1}^{n} \left(\frac{x_i - \bar{x}}{s_x} \right) \left(\frac{y_i - \bar{y}}{s_y} \right) \tag{3.65}$$

It means how much x is related to y, and r^2 is called the coefficient of determination. In order to assess accuracy of the estimated coefficients, the standard error (SE) is widely used, and we can define them as follows:

$$SE(\hat{\beta}_1) = \frac{\sigma}{\sqrt{\sum_{i=1}^{n}(x_i - \bar{x})^2}}, \tag{3.66}$$

$$SE(\hat{\beta}_0) = \sigma \sqrt{\frac{1}{n} + \frac{\bar{x}^2}{\sum_{i=1}^{n}(x_i - \bar{x})^2}}, \tag{3.67}$$

where the mean squared error σ^2 is

$$\sigma^2 = \frac{\sum_{i=1}^{n}(\hat{y}_i - y_i)^2}{n - 2} \tag{3.68}$$

where $\hat{y}_i$ is the predicted value of y_i. The standard error means how close x values are and how large the errors are. It reflects how much it varies under repeated sampling. If x values are very close, the standard error $SE(\hat{\beta}_1)$ is large and the slope is less confident. Thus, the standard error gets larger if the error gets bigger. The bigger error indicates a worse fit. In addition, the standard errors are used to calculate confidence intervals. The confidence interval tells us about how stable the estimation is. If we define 95% confidence interval, the 95% confidence interval β_1 will be $[\hat{\beta}_1 - 2 \cdot SE(\hat{\beta}_1), \hat{\beta}_1 + 2 \cdot SE(\hat{\beta}_1)]$.

Example 3.12 *Linear Least Square Regression*
Consider five paired data points (1, 1), (3, 5), (5, 7), (7, 11), (9, 15) where the paired data satisfy a linear model. Find β_0 and β_1 of the linear model and compare the paired data and the linear model.

Solution
In order to calculate Equations (3.55) and (3.61), the first step is to compute the following:

x	y	x^2	xy
1	1	1	1
3	5	9	15
5	7	25	35
7	11	49	77
9	15	81	135

and then we calculate sums of x, y, x^2 and xy as follows:

$$\sum_{i=1}^{5} x_i = 25, \quad \sum_{i=1}^{5} y_i = 39, \quad \sum_{i=1}^{5} x_i^2 = 165, \quad \sum_{i=1}^{5} x_i y_i = 265$$

By Equations (3.62) and (3.63),

$$S_{xx} = \sum_{i=1}^{5}(x_i)^2 + \frac{\left(\sum_{i=1}^{5} x_i\right)^2}{n} = 165 + \frac{25^2}{5} = 290$$

$$S_{xy} = \sum_{i=1}^{5} x_i y_i + \frac{\left(\sum_{i=1}^{5} x_i\right)\left(\sum_{i=1}^{5} y_i\right)}{n} = 265 + \frac{25 \cdot 39}{5} = 460$$

Now, we can obtain the slope and intercept as follows:

$$\hat{\beta}_1 = \frac{S_{xy}}{S_{xx}} = \frac{460}{290} = 1.5862$$

$$\hat{\beta}_0 = \bar{y} - \hat{\beta}_1 \bar{x} = \frac{39}{5} - 1.5862 \cdot \frac{25}{5} = -0.131$$

Thus, we obtain the following linear model:

$$\hat{y} = -0.131 + 1.5862x$$

We can compare the pair data and estimation as follows:

	x	*y*	**Estimation** *(ŷ)*	**Error** *(ε)*
1	1	1	1.4552	0.4552
2	3	5	4.6276	−0.3724
3	5	7	7.8	0.8
4	7	11	10.9724	−0.0276
5	9	15	14.1448	−0.8552

Figure p3.2 shows a comparison of the linear model and the paired data.

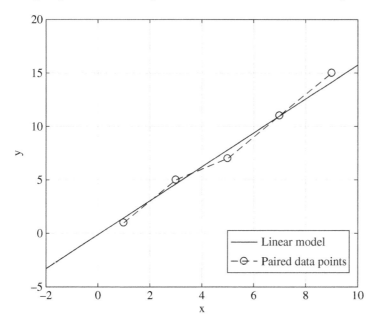

Figure p3.2 Comparison of the linear model and paired data points.

Many applications of regression analysis contain more than one independent variable. We call them multiple regression models, and predict the dependent variable *y* as a linear model of the different *x* independent variables as follows:

$$y = \beta_0 + \beta_1 x_1 + \beta_2 x_2 + \ldots + + \beta_n x_n \tag{3.69}$$

As we can observe from Equation (3.69), it is still linear in the coefficient β_j. However, this model is more versatile. For example, we can predict one dependent variable y (house price) as a function of multiple x independent variables (location, size, construction cost, and so on). In addition, we can easily transform to any nonlinear function by replacing one independent variable x_i with x_i^2. The coefficients can be estimated by least squares approaches. Assume there are n dependent variables y_i ($i = 1, 2, ..., n$) and k independent variables x_j ($j = 0, 1, 2, ..., k$ and $x_0 = 1$). We can write the linear regression model with multiple independent variables as follows:

$$y_i = \beta_0 + \beta_1 x_{i1} + \beta_2 x_{i2} + ... + \beta_k x_{ik} + \varepsilon_i \tag{3.70}$$

where ε_i is the error term. We can rewrite Equation (3.70) in the following matrix form:

$$\mathbf{y} = \mathbf{X}\boldsymbol{\beta} + \boldsymbol{\varepsilon} \tag{3.71}$$

where

$$\mathbf{y} = \begin{bmatrix} y_1 \\ y_2 \\ \vdots \\ y_n \end{bmatrix}, \mathbf{X} = \begin{bmatrix} 1 & x_{11} & \cdots & x_{1k} \\ 1 & x_{21} & \cdots & x_{2k} \\ \vdots & \vdots & \ddots & \vdots \\ 1 & x_{n1} & \cdots & x_{nk} \end{bmatrix}, \boldsymbol{\beta} = \begin{bmatrix} \beta_0 \\ \beta_1 \\ \vdots \\ \beta_k \end{bmatrix}, \boldsymbol{\varepsilon} = \begin{bmatrix} \varepsilon_1 \\ \varepsilon_2 \\ \vdots \\ \varepsilon_n \end{bmatrix} \tag{3.72}$$

In a similar way to Equation (3.47), the least squares approach is to minimize the SSE. The least squares estimation of $\boldsymbol{\beta}$ is obtained by solving the following optimization problem:

$$\min_{\boldsymbol{\beta}} \left(\sum_{i=1}^{n} \varepsilon_i^2 \right) = \min_{\boldsymbol{\beta}} \left(\sum_{i=1}^{n} (y_i - \mathbf{X}_i\boldsymbol{\beta})^2 \right) \tag{3.73}$$

where $\mathbf{X}_i$ is a row vector of the matrix $\mathbf{X}$. In a similar way to Equations (3.32) to (3.38), the least squares estimation of $\boldsymbol{\beta}$ is

$$\hat{\boldsymbol{\beta}} = (\mathbf{X}^T\mathbf{X})^{-1}\mathbf{X}^T\mathbf{y} \tag{3.74}$$

In order to solve this equation, it requires that k is smaller than or equal to n ($n > k$). If $(\mathbf{X}^T\mathbf{X})^{-1}$ does not exist, the solution may not be unique. If it exists, the columns of $\mathbf{X}$ are linearly independent. We can express the predicted value of $\hat{\mathbf{y}}$ as follows:

$$\hat{\mathbf{y}} = \mathbf{X}\hat{\boldsymbol{\beta}} = \mathbf{X}(\mathbf{X}^T\mathbf{X})^{-1}\mathbf{X}^T\mathbf{y} = \mathbf{H}\mathbf{y} \tag{3.75}$$

where $\mathbf{H}$ is a $n \times n$ projection matrix and it projects $\mathbf{y}$ onto the space spanned by the column of $\mathbf{X}$. The matrix $\mathbf{H}$ is often called the hat matrix. It plays an important role in diagnostics of a regression model.

Example 3.13   *Multiple Linear Least Square Regression*

Consider that we design a cellular network and measure a signal strength in terms of distance from base station, and mobility. We obtained the following dataset as shown in Table p3.1.

Find $\hat{\boldsymbol{\beta}}$ of a linear model and compare the paired data and the linear model.

Table p3.1 Measurement data of signal strength, distance from base station (BS), and mobility.

	Signal strength (y)	Distance from BS (x_1)	Mobility (x_2)		Signal strength (y)	Distance from BS (x_1)	Mobility (x_2)
1	9.76	10	10	14	3.89	77	71
2	9.64	15	13	15	1.10	98	99
3	7.26	36	37	16	2.01	89	89
4	6.57	55	45	17	5.98	61	51
5	7.55	34	36	18	6.67	54	43
6	9.89	5	8	19	3.95	78	71
7	8.45	27	25	20	8.65	23	23
8	2.53	85	85	21	7.87	31	31
9	8.56	23	26	22	6.98	49	41
10	6.56	45	46	23	2.89	81	82
11	5.87	67	52	24	1.87	92	92
12	7.78	32	33	25	8.67	22	27
13	3.98	79	71				

Solution

In order to calculate Equation (3.74), we have the matrix **X** and **y** as follows:

$$\mathbf{X} = \begin{bmatrix} 1 & 10 & 10 \\ 1 & 15 & 13 \\ 1 & 36 & 37 \\ \vdots & \vdots & \vdots \\ 1 & 92 & 92 \\ 1 & 22 & 27 \end{bmatrix}, \quad \mathbf{y} = \begin{bmatrix} 9.76 \\ 9.64 \\ 7.26 \\ \vdots \\ 1.87 \\ 8.67 \end{bmatrix}$$

The first step is to compute the following:

$$\mathbf{X}^T\mathbf{X} = \begin{bmatrix} 1 & 1 & 1 & \cdots & 1 & 1 \\ 10 & 15 & 36 & \cdots & 92 & 22 \\ 10 & 13 & 37 & \cdots & 92 & 27 \end{bmatrix} \begin{bmatrix} 1 & 10 & 10 \\ 1 & 15 & 13 \\ 1 & 36 & 37 \\ \vdots & \vdots & \vdots \\ 1 & 92 & 92 \\ 1 & 22 & 27 \end{bmatrix} = \begin{bmatrix} 25 & 1268 & 1207 \\ 1268 & 83664 & 79343 \\ 1207 & 79343 & 75841 \end{bmatrix}$$

$$(\mathbf{X}^T\mathbf{X})^{-1} = \begin{bmatrix} 25 & 1268 & 1207 \\ 1268 & 83664 & 79343 \\ 1207 & 79343 & 75841 \end{bmatrix}^{-1} = \begin{bmatrix} 0.17395 & -0.00139 & -0.00131 \\ -0.00139 & 0.00153 & -0.00158 \\ -0.00131 & -0.00158 & 0.00168 \end{bmatrix}$$

$$\mathbf{X}^T\mathbf{y} = \begin{bmatrix} 1 & 1 & 1 & \cdots & 1 & 1 \\ 10 & 15 & 36 & \cdots & 92 & 22 \\ 10 & 13 & 37 & \cdots & 92 & 27 \end{bmatrix} \begin{bmatrix} 9.76 \\ 9.64 \\ 7.26 \\ \vdots \\ 1.87 \\ 8.67 \end{bmatrix} = \begin{bmatrix} 154.93 \\ 6064.1 \\ 5741.72 \end{bmatrix}$$

The next step is to calculate $\hat{\boldsymbol{\beta}}$ as follows:

$$\hat{\boldsymbol{\beta}} = (\mathbf{X}^T\mathbf{X})^{-1}\mathbf{X}^T\mathbf{y}$$

$$\begin{bmatrix} \hat{\beta}_0 \\ \hat{\beta}_1 \\ \hat{\beta}_2 \end{bmatrix} = \begin{bmatrix} 0.17395 & -0.00139 & -0.00131 \\ -0.00139 & 0.00153 & -0.00158 \\ -0.00131 & -0.00158 & 0.00168 \end{bmatrix} \begin{bmatrix} 154.93 \\ 6064.1 \\ 5741.72 \end{bmatrix} = \begin{bmatrix} 10.97537 \\ -0.00082 \\ -0.09809 \end{bmatrix}$$

Thus, we obtain the following linear model:

$$\hat{y} = 10.97537 - 0.00082x_1 - 0.09809x_2$$

We can compare the pair data and estimation as follows:

	Signal strength (y)	Estimation (ŷ)	Error (ε)		Signal strength (y)	Estimation (ŷ)	Error (ε)
1	9.76	9.986	0.226	14	3.89	3.946	0.056
2	9.64	9.687	0.047	15	1.10	1.182	0.082
3	7.26	7.315	0.055	16	2.01	2.17	0.16
4	6.57	6.515	−0.054	17	5.98	5.921	−0.058
5	7.55	7.415	−0.134	18	6.67	6.712	0.042
6	9.89	10.186	0.296	19	3.95	3.945	−0.004
7	8.45	8.5	0.05	20	8.65	8.7	0.05
8	2.53	2.566	0.036	21	7.87	7.9	0.038
9	8.56	8.405	−0.154	22	6.98	6.912	−0.067
10	6.56	6.425	−0.134	23	2.89	2.864	−0.025
11	5.87	5.818	−0.051	24	1.87	1.874	0.004
12	7.78	7.711	−0.068	25	8.67	8.308	−0.361
13	3.98	3.944	−0.035				

Figure p3.3 illustrates the comparison between the linear model and the paired data. In this figure, the dot (•) and the surface represent the paired data and the linear model, respectively.

There are other algorithms (Cholesky factorization, QR factorization, and SVD [singular value decomposition]) to find least squares solutions. We discuss those below.

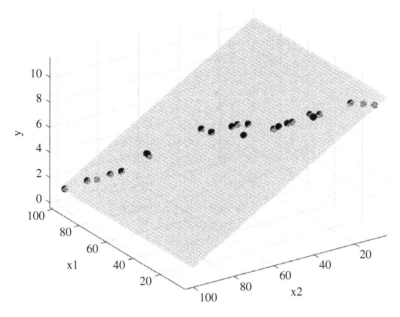

Figure p3.3 Comparison of the linear model and paired data points.

Summary 3.3 LS Estimation

1) Let $\mathbf{A} \in \mathbb{R}^{m \times n}$ and $\mathbf{b} \in \mathbb{R}^m$. The normal equation $\mathbf{Ax} = \mathbf{b}$ is overdetermined $(m > n)$ and there is no exact solution. The least squares problem consists of finding a vector $\mathbf{x} \in \mathbb{R}^n$ to minimize $\|\mathbf{Ax} - \mathbf{b}\|^2$.
2) The approximation $\hat{\mathbf{x}}$ is

$$\hat{\mathbf{x}} = \mathbf{Ax} = \mathbf{A}(\mathbf{A}^T\mathbf{A})^{-1}\mathbf{A}^T\mathbf{b} = \mathbf{Pb}$$

3) In the regression model, the independent variable (or predictor variable, explanatory variable) is denoted as x along the horizontal axis, and the dependent variable (or response variable, target variable) is denoted as y along the vertical axis. The purpose of the regression is to determine the best-fit line that connects x and y.
4) Many applications of regression analysis contain more than one independent variable. We call it multiple regression modeling and predict the dependent variable y as a linear model of the different x independent variables as follows:

$$y = \beta_0 + \beta_1 x_1 + \beta_2 x_2 + \ldots + + \beta_n x_n$$

3.2.3 Minimum Mean-Squared Error Estimation

In Section 3.2.2, no probabilistic model has been employed to find a solution. The optimization problem has been solved by minimizing the sum of squared error for the given data block itself. When dealing with a problem in wireless communications, the data block is a finite period of time and the solution of LS estimation can be optimal on the data block. However, it does not guarantee the optimal solution about other data blocks. Thus, we need to define and solve an approximation problem using a probabilistic model. In order to introduce minimum mean-squared error (MMSE) estimation based on a probabilistic model, we firstly review probability theory.

Wireless communication systems deal with uncertainty. If there is no noise in the communication architecture as shown in Figure 3.1, we can transmit messages without any distortion and do not need to investigate probability theory. However, received messages are impaired by thermal noise, interference, fading, and so on. Probability theory indicating how likely it is to happen is a very useful tool. We briefly discuss several important concepts and definitions of probability theory.

When modeling wireless communication systems, we assume that transmitted messages include a random signal and received messages cannot be predicted with certainty. A random variable is useful to express unpredictable signals. The random variable can be defined as a variable X whose possible values are numerical outcomes of a random phenomenon [3]. In addition, we can regard a random variable as a measurable function mapping outcomes to numerical quantities in the sample space of a random experiment. The random variables can be discrete when X has discrete values, or continuous when X has continuous values. We can extend the concept of a random variable to a random vector (or multivariate random variable). The random vector X can be defined as a function assigning a column (or row) vector to each outcome in sample space. We look into a collection (or ensemble) of random variables when analyzing a random variable. The probability distribution of a random variable comprises probabilities corresponding to each possible random value. It is difficult to express the probabilities of all possible events. Thus, probability density functions (pdf) and cumulative distribution functions (cdf) are widely used. The cdf $F_X(x)$ of a random variable X is defined as the probability of the event $(X \leq x)$:

$$F_X(x) = P(X \leq x), -\infty < x < \infty \tag{3.76}$$

and the pdf $f_X(x)$ of continuous random variable X is defined as the derivative of the cdf $F_X(x)$:

$$f_X(x) = \frac{dF_X(x)}{dx} \tag{3.77}$$

If a random variable X is discrete, the pdf $f_X(x)$ is

$$f_X(x) = \frac{\Delta F_X(x)}{\Delta x} \tag{3.78}$$

The probability that X lies between a and b is

$$P(a \leq X \leq b) = \int_a^b f_X(x)dx \tag{3.79}$$

The most important probability distribution in wireless communications is Gaussian (or normal) distribution [4]. It is defined as follows:

$$P(X) = \frac{1}{\sigma\sqrt{2\pi}}e^{-\frac{1}{2}\left(\frac{X-\mu}{\sigma}\right)^2} \tag{3.80}$$

where σ and μ are the standard deviation and mean of the distribution, respectively. The cdf of a Gaussian distribution is as follows:

$$F_X(x) = \frac{1}{2}\left[1 + erf\left(\frac{x-\mu}{\sqrt{2\sigma^2}}\right)\right] \tag{3.81}$$

where error function, erf( ), is defined as follows:

$$erf(x) = \frac{2}{\sqrt{\pi}}\int_0^x e^{-t^2}dt \tag{3.82}$$

The properties of the cdf and pdf are summarized as follows:

Property 3.4 Properties of the cdf

(i) $0 \leq F_X(x) \leq 1$
(ii) $\lim_{x\to\infty} F_X(x) = 1$, $\lim_{x\to-\infty} F_X(x) = 0$
(iii) $F_X(a) \leq F_X(b)$ if $a \leq b$
(iv) $F_X(b) - F_X(a) = P(a < X \leq b)$

Property 3.5 Properties of the pdf

(i) $f_X(x) > 0$
(ii) $\int_{-\infty}^{\infty} f_X(x)dx = 1$
(iii) $F_X(x) = \int_{-\infty}^{x} f_X(x)dx$

The expected value of the continuous random variable X is defined as follows:

$$E(X) = \mu = \int_{-\infty}^{\infty} x f_X(x)dx \tag{3.83}$$

and the expected value of the discrete random variable X is

$$E(X) = \sum_{i=1}^{n} x_i f_X(x_i). \tag{3.84}$$

The expected value represents the center of mass of the distribution of X. We also call it the mean or average. The properties of the expected value are summarized as follows:

Property 3.6 Properties of the Expected Value

Let $Y, X, X_1, X_2, \ldots, X_n$ be random variables in a sample space, and $a, b, c, c_1, c_2, c_n, c_{n+1}$ be constants.

(i) $E(X + Y) = E(X) + E(Y)$
(ii) $E(aX + b) = aE(X) + b$
(iii) $E(c_1X_1 + c_2X_2 + \ldots + c_nX_n + c_{n+1}) = c_1E(X_1) + c_2E(X_2) + \ldots + c_nE(X_n) + c_{n+1}$
(iv) If $X \leq Y$ and both $E(X)$ and $E(Y)$ exist, $E(X) \leq E(Y)$
(v) $|E(X)| \leq E(|X|)$
(vi) $E(XY) = E(X)E(Y)$ if X and Y are independent.

Example 3.14 *Expected Value*

Let a random variable X have pdf $f_X(x) = x^2/4$ and range $[0, 2]$. Find the expected value.

Solution

By Equation (3.83),

$$E(X) = \int_0^2 x \cdot x^2 dx = \int_0^2 x^3 dx = \left[\frac{x^4}{16}\right]_0^2 = 1$$

Let X be a random variable with the expected value μ. The variance of X is

$$\text{Var}(X) = E((X - \mu)^2) \tag{3.85}$$

Equation (3.85) can be expressed as follows:

$$\text{Var}(X) = E((X - \mu)^2) = E(X^2 - 2X\mu + \mu^2) \tag{3.86}$$

$$= E(X^2) - 2E(X)\mu + \mu^2 \tag{3.87}$$

$$= E(X^2) - 2\mu^2 + \mu^2 = E(X^2) - \mu^2 \tag{3.88}$$

Equation (3.88) is often easier to calculate the variance than Equation (3.85). The variance indicates how far apart data are spread out in relation to the expected value. The properties of the variance are summarized as follows:

Property 3.7 Properties of the Variance

(i) $\text{Var}(X + Y) = \text{Var}(X) + \text{Var}(Y)$ if X and Y are independent
(ii) $\text{Var}(aX + b) = a^2\text{Var}(X)$ if a and b are constants.

Example 3.15 *Variance*

Let a random variable X have pdf $f_X(x) = x^{-2}$ and range $[1, 2]$. Find the variance.

Solution

By Equation (3.83), the expected value is

$$E(X) = \mu = \int_1^2 x \cdot x^{-2} dx = \int_1^2 x^{-1} dx$$

$$= [\ln x]_1^2 = \ln 2 - \ln 1 = \ln 2$$

By Equation (3.88), the variance is

$$\text{Var}(X) = E(X^2) - \mu^2 = \int_1^2 x^2 \cdot x^{-2} dx - (\ln 2)^2$$

$$= \int_1^2 1 dx - (\ln 2)^2 = [x]_1^2 - (\ln 2)^2$$

$$= 1 - (\ln 2)^2 = 0.5195.$$

Sometimes, we need to investigate the relationship among two or more events, for example, the relationship between received signal power and location, the relationship between velocity and channel impairment, and so on. Thus, when two random variables

Table p3.2 Joint probability mass function of X and Y.

	$Y = 0$	$Y = 1$	$Y = 2$
$X = 0$	1/4	1/6	1/8
$X = 1$	1/6	1/8	1/6

are dependent and we need to investigate their relationship, we use different tools such as joint pdf, joint cdf, conditional pdf, Bayes' theorem, and so on. If X and Y are two random variables, the probability distribution defines their behaviors. If X and Y are discrete, the probability distribution can be expressed as a joint probability mass function (pmf). If X and Y are continuous, it can be described with a joint pdf. Firstly, the joint pmf of two discrete random variables for each pair of values (x, y) is defined as follows:

$$P_{XY}(x, y) = P(X = x, Y = y) \tag{3.89}$$

If we want to obtain the individual probability distribution for X or Y, the marginal probability distribution is used. The marginal distribution of X is defined as follows:

$$P_X(x) = \sum_y P_{XY}(x, y) \tag{3.90}$$

and the marginal distribution of Y is defined as follows:

$$P_Y(y) = \sum_x P_{XY}(x, y). \tag{3.91}$$

The properties of the joint pdf are summarized as follows:

Property 3.8 Properties of the Joint Probability Mass Function

(i) $P_{XY}(x, y) \geq 0$

(ii) $\sum_x \sum_y P_{XY}(x, y) = 1$

Example 3.16 *Joint Probability Mass Function*
Consider two discrete random variables X and Y as shown in Table p3.2. Find $P(X \leq 1, Y \leq 1)$ and the marginal distribution of X and Y.

Solution

$$P(X \leq 1, Y \leq 1) = P_{XY}(0, 0) + P_{XY}(1, 0) + P_{XY}(0, 1) + P_{XY}(1, 1)$$
$$= \frac{1}{4} + \frac{1}{6} + \frac{1}{6} + \frac{1}{8} = 0.7083$$

By Equation (3.90), the marginal distribution of X is

$$P_X(0) = \sum_y P_{XY}(x, y) = P_{XY}(0, 0) + P_{XY}(0, 1) + P_{XY}(0, 2)$$
$$= \frac{1}{4} + \frac{1}{6} + \frac{1}{8} = 0.5417$$

$$P_X(1) = \sum_y P_{XY}(x,y) = P_{XY}(1,0) + P_{XY}(1,1) + P_{XY}(1,2)$$

$$= \frac{1}{6} + \frac{1}{8} + \frac{1}{6} = 0.4583$$

$$P_X(x) = \begin{cases} 0.5417, & x = 0 \\ 0.4583, & x = 1 \end{cases}$$

By Equation (3.91), the marginal distribution of Y is

$$P_Y(0) = \sum_x P_{XY}(x,y) = P_{XY}(0,0) + P_{XY}(1,0)$$

$$= \frac{1}{4} + \frac{1}{6} = 0.4167$$

$$P_Y(1) = \sum_x P_{XY}(x,y) = P_{XY}(0,1) + P_{XY}(1,1)$$

$$= \frac{1}{6} + \frac{1}{8} = 0.2917$$

$$P_Y(2) = \sum_x P_{XY}(x,y) = P_{XY}(0,2) + P_{XY}(1,2)$$

$$= \frac{1}{8} + \frac{1}{6} = 0.2917$$

$$P_Y(y) = \begin{cases} 0.4167, & y = 0 \\ 0.2917, & y = 1 \\ 0.2917, & y = 2 \end{cases}$$

For two continuous random variables X and Y, we define the joint cdf as follows:

$$F_{XY}(x,y) = P(X \leq x, Y \leq y) \tag{3.92}$$

and the joint pdf as follows:

$$f_{XY}(x,y) = \frac{d}{dxdy} F_{XY}(x,y) \tag{3.93}$$

For any set $A \in \mathbb{R}^2$, we have

$$P((X,Y) \in A) = \iint_A f_{XY}(x,y)\, dxdy \tag{3.94}$$

The marginal pdf of a continuous random variable X is defined as follows:

$$f_X(x) = \int_y f_{XY}(x,y) dy \tag{3.95}$$

and the marginal pdf of a continuous random variable Y is defined as follows:

$$f_Y(y) = \int_x f_{XY}(x,y) dx \tag{3.96}$$

The properties of the joint pdf are summarized as follows:

> **Property 3.9 Properties of the Joint Probability Density Function**
>
> (i) $f_{XY}(x, y) \geq 0$ for all x and y
> (ii) $\int_{-\infty}^{\infty} \int_{-\infty}^{\infty} f_{XY}(x, y) dx dy = 1$

Example 3.17   *Joint Probability Density Function*

Consider two continuous random variables X and Y with the following joint pdf:

$$f_{XY}(x, y) = x + y^2, 0 \leq x \leq 1, 0 \leq y \leq 1$$

Find $P\left(0 \leq X \leq \frac{1}{2}, 0 \leq Y \leq \frac{1}{2}\right)$ and the marginal pdfs $f_X(x)$ and $f_Y(y)$.

Solution
By Equation (3.94), we have

$$P((X, Y) \in A) = \int_0^1 \int_0^1 f_{XY}(x, y) dx dy$$

$$P\left(0 \leq X \leq \frac{1}{2}, 0 \leq Y \leq \frac{1}{2}\right) = \int_0^{1/2} \int_0^{1/2} (x + y^2) dx dy$$

$$= \int_0^{1/2} \left[\frac{x^2}{2} + y^2 x\right]_0^{1/2} dy = \int_0^{1/2} \left(\frac{1}{8} + \frac{y^2}{2}\right) dy$$

$$= \left[\frac{y}{8} + \frac{y^3}{6}\right]_0^{1/2} = 0.0833$$

By Equations (3.95) and (3.96), the marginal pdfs of continuous random variables X and Y are

$$f_X(x) = \int_y f_{XY}(x, y) dy = \int_0^1 (x + y^2) dy$$

$$= \left[xy + \frac{y^3}{3}\right]_0^1 = x + \frac{1}{3}, \ 0 \leq x \leq 1$$

and

$$f_Y(y) = \int_x f_{XY}(x, y) dx = \int_0^1 (x + y^2) dx$$

$$= \left[\frac{x^2}{2} + y^2 x\right]_0^1 = \frac{1}{2} + y^2, \ 0 \leq x \leq 1$$

Sometimes, we already know that an event has happened, and we want to know what happens next. Conditional probability allows us to analyze this case. For discrete random variables X and Y, the conditional pmf of X given Y is

$$P_{X|Y}(x|y) = \frac{P_{XY}(x, y)}{P_Y(y)} \quad \text{for } P_Y(y) > 0 \tag{3.97}$$

and the conditional pmf of Y given X is

$$P_{Y|X}(y|x) = \frac{P_{XY}(x,y)}{P_X(x)} \quad \text{for } P_X(x) > 0 \tag{3.98}$$

For continuous random variables X and Y, the conditional pdf of X given Y is

$$f_{X|Y}(x|y) = \frac{f_{XY}(x,y)}{f_Y(y)} \quad \text{for } f_Y(y) > 0 \tag{3.99}$$

and the conditional pmf of Y given X is

$$f_{Y|X}(y|x) = \frac{f_{XY}(x,y)}{f_x(x)} \quad \text{for } f_X(x) > 0. \tag{3.100}$$

The properties of the conditional pmf and pdf are summarized as follows:

Property 3.10 Properties of the pmf and pdf

(i) $P_{X|Y}(x|y) \geq 0$ and $f_{X|Y}(x|y) \geq 0$

(ii) $\sum_X P_{X|Y}(x|y) = 1$ and $\int_{-\infty}^{\infty} f_{X|Y}(x|y)dx = 1$

Example 3.18 *Conditional Probability Density Function*
Consider two continuous random variables X and Y with the following joint pdf:

$$f_{XY}(x,y) = x + y^2, 0 \leq x \leq 1, 0 \leq y \leq 1$$

Find the conditional pdf of X given Y.

Solution
By Equation (3.99), the conditional pdf of X given Y is

$$f_{X|Y}(x|y) = \frac{f_{XY}(x,y)}{f_Y(y)}$$

From Example 3.17, the marginal pdf of a continuous random variable Y is

$$f_Y(y) = \frac{1}{2} + y^2, \ 0 \leq y \leq 1$$

Thus, we have

$$f_{X|Y}(x|y) = \frac{x + y^2}{\frac{1}{2} + y^2}, \ 0 \leq x \leq 1, 0 \leq y \leq 1$$

The Bayesian formula is an important tool for calculating conditional probabilities when the reserve conditional probability is known. In wireless communication theory, the Bayesian formula is used when we know a priori information and likelihood. We can conceptually describe the Bayesian formula as follows [4]:

$$(\text{Posteriori}) = \frac{(\text{Likelihood})(\text{Prior})}{(\text{Occurrence})} \tag{3.101}$$

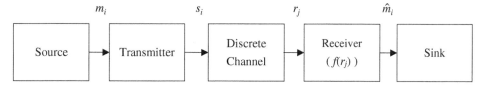

Figure 3.6 System model based on a discrete channel [4].

Let a discrete random variable x_i be one of n possible mutually exclusive events with $P_X(x_i) > 0$. The conditional probability for y given x_i is $P_{Y|X}(y|x_i)$. The total probability for y is

$$P_Y(y) = \sum_{i=1}^{n} P_{Y|X}(y|x_i)P_X(x_i) \tag{3.102}$$

and we define the Bayesian formula for discrete random variables as follows:

$$P_{X|Y}(x_i|y) = \frac{P_{Y|X}(y|x_i)P_X(x_i)}{P_Y(y)} = \frac{P_{Y|X}(y|x_i)P_X(x_i)}{\sum_{i=1}^{n} P_{Y|X}(y|x_i)P_X(x_i)} \tag{3.103}$$

Likewise, we can define the Bayesian formula for continuous random variables as follows:

$$f_{X|Y}(x|y) = \frac{f_{Y|X}(y|x)f_X(x)}{f_Y(y)} = \frac{f_{Y|X}(y|x)f_X(x)}{\int_{-\infty}^{\infty} f_{Y|X}(y|x)f_X(x)dx} \tag{3.104}$$

We consider a simple system model with a discrete channel [4] as shown in Figure 3.6. In this model, the message source produces a discrete message, m_i (where $i = 1, \ldots, M$) as a random variable. The probability the message, m_i, appears is a priori probability, $P(m_i)$. The transmitter produces a signal, s_i, which is the value corresponding to the message, m_i. The signal, s_i, becomes the input of the discrete channel. The output, r_j, can be expressed as a conditional probability, $P(r_j|s_i)$, which indicates the probability that the output, r_j, is received when the transmitter sends the signal, s_i. The receiver estimates the transmitted messages, $\hat{m}_i$, as the output of the receiver using the decision rule, $f(\ )$, namely $f(r_j) = \hat{m}_i$. The decision rule is a function mapping the received signal to the most probable value. The receiver is designed to minimize the probability of error, $P_\varepsilon = P(\hat{m}_i \neq m_i)$. The receiver minimizing the probability of error is called an optimum receiver. We can formulate the problem for the optimum receiver design using the Bayesian formula as follows:

$$P(s_i|r_j) = \frac{P(r_j|s_i)P(s_i)}{P(r_j)} \tag{3.105}$$

where $P(r_j) = \sum_i P(r_j|s_i)P(s_i)$. We can interpret this problem as shown in Figure 3.7.

As we can observe in Figure 3.7, multiple candidates are received including different levels of noise. Based on the data, we predict the most probable signal by minimizing the probability of error.

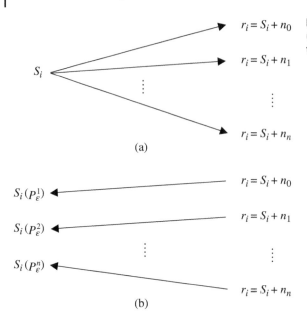

$r_i = S_i + n_0$

$r_i = S_i + n_1$

S_i

$r_i = S_i + n_n$

(a)

Figure 3.7 Optimum receiver model using Bayesian formula: (a) transmission and (b) prediction.

$S_i(P_\varepsilon^1)$ ← $r_i = S_i + n_0$

$S_i(P_\varepsilon^2)$ ← $r_i = S_i + n_1$

$S_i(P_\varepsilon^n)$ ← $r_i = S_i + n_n$

(b)

Example 3.19   *Bayesian Formula*

Consider a simple communication system with the system model shown in Figure p3.4, and a priori probability, $P(s_i)$, occurrence probability, $P(r_i)$, and conditional probability, $P(r_j|s_i)$. We have the following probabilities:

m_i $s_i = s_0$ or s_1 $r_j = r_0, r_1$ or r_2 $\hat{m}_i$

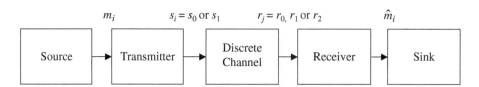

| Source | → | Transmitter | → | Discrete Channel | → | Receiver | → | Sink |

Figure p3.4 System model for Example 3.19.

i	$P(s_i)$	$P(r_0|s_i)$	$P(r_1|s_i)$	$P(r_2|s_i)$
0	0.7	0.7	0.2	0.1
1	0.3	0.2	0.3	0.5

Design the Bayesian rule with the minimum error probability.

Solution

The Bayesian decision rule, $f_{Bayesian}(\ )$, is designed by both a priori probability, $P(s_i)$, and a conditional probability, $P(r_j|s_i)$. By Equation (3.105), we have

$$P(s_0|r_0) = \frac{P(r_0|s_0)P(s_0)}{P(r_0)} = \frac{0.7 \cdot 0.7}{1} = 0.49$$

In the same way, we can calculate the following probabilities:

i	$P(s_i|r_0)$	$P(s_i|r_1)$	$P(s_i|r_2)$
0	**0.49**	**0.14**	0.07
1	0.06	0.09	**0.15**
$f_{Bayesian}(\ )$	0	0	1

If two discrete random variables X and Y are independent, one random variable does not affect the probability of the other. Thus, we can write

$$P_{X|Y}(x|y) = P_Y(y) \tag{3.106}$$

We can define independence of two discrete random variables as follows:

$$P_{XY}(x,y) = P(X = x, Y = y) = P(X = x)P(Y = y) \text{ for all } x, y \tag{3.107}$$

For independent continuous random variables X and Y, we have

$$f_{X|Y}(x|y) = f_X(x)f_Y(y) \text{ for all } x, y \tag{3.108}$$

When dealing with multiple random variables, a random vector is defined as a finite collection (or ensemble) of random variables. If it represents a random value of time, we call it a random process. It is a very useful model to describe wireless communication systems including an information source, transmission, and a random noise generator. A random vector is written as follows: $\mathbf{X} = [X_1, X_2, \ldots, X_n]^T$. The cdf and pdf of the random vector is the joint cdf and pdf of all random variables. The joint cdf of $\mathbf{X}$ is defined as follows:

$$F_{\mathbf{X}}(\mathbf{x}) = F_{X_1, X_2, \ldots X_n}(x_1, x_2, \ldots, x_n) = P(X_1 \le x_1, X_2 \le x_2, \ldots, X_n \le x_n) \tag{3.109}$$

and the joint pdf of $\mathbf{X}$ is defined as follows:

$$f_{\mathbf{X}}(\mathbf{x}) = \frac{\partial^n}{\partial x_1 \partial x_2 \ldots \partial x_n} F_{\mathbf{X}}(\mathbf{x}) = f_{X_1, X_2, \ldots, X_n}(x_1, x_2, \ldots, x_n) \tag{3.110}$$

In a similar way to scalar random variables, we can define the expected value vector, correlation matrix, and covariance matrix. The expected value vector of the random vector **X** is defined as follows:

$$E[\mathbf{X}] = \boldsymbol{\mu} = [E[X_1], E[X_2], \ldots, E[X_n]]^T = [\mu_1, \mu_2, \ldots, \mu_n]^T \tag{3.111}$$

The correlation matrix $\mathbf{R_X}$ is defined as follows:

$$\mathbf{R_X} = E[\mathbf{XX}^T] = \begin{bmatrix} E[X_1^2] & E[X_1X_2] & \cdots & E[X_1X_n] \\ E[X_2X_1] & E[X_2^2] & \cdots & E[X_2X_n] \\ \vdots & \vdots & \ddots & \vdots \\ E[X_nX_1] & E[X_nX_2] & \cdots & E[X_n^2] \end{bmatrix} \tag{3.112}$$

and the covariance matrix $\mathbf{C_X}$ is defined as follows:

$$\mathbf{C_X} = E[(\mathbf{X} - \boldsymbol{\mu})(\mathbf{X} - \boldsymbol{\mu})^T]$$

$$= \begin{bmatrix} E[(X_1 - \mu_1)^2] & \cdots & E[(X_1 - \mu_1)(X_n - \mu_n)] \\ E[(X_2 - \mu_2)(X_1 - \mu_1)] & \cdots & E[(X_2 - \mu_2)(X_n - \mu_n)] \\ \vdots & \ddots & \vdots \\ E[(X_n - \mu_n)(X_1 - \mu_1)] & \cdots & E[(X_n - \mu_n)^2] \end{bmatrix} \tag{3.113}$$

$$= \begin{bmatrix} \text{Var}(X_1) & \text{Cov}(X_1, X_2) & \cdots & \text{Cov}(X_1, X_n) \\ \text{Cov}(X_2, X_1) & \text{Var}(X_2) & \cdots & \text{Cov}(X_2, X_n) \\ \vdots & \vdots & \ddots & \vdots \\ \text{Cov}(X_n, X_1) & \text{Cov}(X_n, X_2) & \cdots & \text{Var}(X_n) \end{bmatrix} \tag{3.114}$$

where Var( ) and Cov( ) represent variance and covariance, respectively. The covariance matrix is a generalized form of the variance of a random variable. The covariance matrix indicates how one random variable is associated with other random variable. We can observe how they vary together. For example, If two random variables X and Y increase, $\text{Cov}(X,Y) > 0$. If X decreases and Y increases, $\text{Cov}(X,Y) < 0$. If they are not correlated, $\text{Cov}(X,Y) = 0$. The properties of the covariance are summarized as follows:

Property 3.11 Properties of the Covariance

(i) $\text{Cov}(X, Y) = E[XY] - E[X]E[Y]$
(ii) $\text{Var}(X) = \text{Cov}(X, X)$
(iii) $\text{Var}(X + Y) = \text{Var}(X) + \text{Var}(Y) + 2\text{Cov}(X, Y)$
(iv) $\text{Cov}(X, Y) = \text{Cov}(Y, X)$
(v) $\text{Cov}(aX, Y) = \text{Cov}(X, aY) = a\text{Cov}(X, Y)$ if a is constant
(vi) $\text{Cov}(X_1 + X_2, Y) = \text{Cov}(X_1, Y) + \text{Cov}(X_2, Y)$

Summary 3.4 Probability Theory

1) The random variable can be defined as a variable X whose possible values are numerical outcomes of a random phenomenon.
2) The random vector $\boldsymbol{X}$ can be defined as a function assigning a column (or row) vector to each outcome in sample space.
3) The cdf $F_X(x)$ of a random variable X is defined as the probability of the event $(X \leq x)$:

$$F_X(x) = P(X \leq x), -\infty < x < \infty$$

4) The pdf $f_X(x)$ of continuous random variable X is defined as the derivative of the cdf $F_X(x)$:

$$f_X(x) = \frac{dF_X(x)}{dx}$$

5) Gaussian (or normal) distribution is defined as follows:

$$P(X) = \frac{1}{\sigma\sqrt{2\pi}} e^{-\frac{1}{2}\left(\frac{X-\mu}{\sigma}\right)^2}$$

where σ and μ are standard deviation and mean of the distribution, respectively.
6) The expected value of continuous random variable X is defined as follows:

$$E(X) = \mu = \int_{-\infty}^{\infty} x f_X(x) dx$$

7) Let X be a random variable with the expected value μ. The variance of X is

$$\text{Var}(X) = E((X - \mu)^2)$$

8) We can conceptually describe the Bayesian formula as follows

$$(\text{Posteriori}) = \frac{(\text{Likelihood})(\text{Prior})}{(\text{Occurence})}$$

9) The receiver minimizing the probability of error is called an optimum receiver. We can formulate the problem for the optimum receiver design using the Bayesian formula as follows:

$$P(s_i|r_j) = \frac{P(r_j|s_i)P(s_i)}{P(r_j)}$$

where $P(r_j) = \sum_i P(r_j|s_i)P(s_i)$

Now, we discuss estimation theory. Estimation theory deals with estimating the values of some parameters based on observation, and the estimator approximates the unknown parameters. Estimation theory is widely used in many different areas such as equalization of wireless communications, motion detection in image processing, voice recognition in voice processing, range and angle estimation in radar techniques, and so on. There are two approaches to estimation: the Bayesian and Frequentist (or classical) approaches. In the Frequentist approach, the parameter we want to estimate is regarded as an unknown but deterministic parameter. However, the Bayesian approach exploits prior information and considers the parameter to be an outcome of a random process with knowledge of the distribution of the random variable. For example, we need to go from home to the workplace and decide which route we drive. We can say this is the shortest path-finding problem. In the Frequentist approach, we drive and find a path while observing the traffic. In the Bayesian approach, we find a path while observing the traffic and also have a mental model including our previous information such as a congested area. Simply speaking, the Frequentist approach depends on the likelihood for observed data, but the Bayesian approach depends on both the prior information and the likelihood for observed data. The prior information is very helpful in obtaining a better estimator. Thus, the Frequentist approach tends to be less computationally complex than the Bayesian approach. Since we now have powerful computers, big data, and VLSI technology, the Bayesian approach has been widely used in many different areas recently. In order to solve an estimation problem, we need to build models (linear model, Gaussian model, and so on) and have estimation techniques. If we want to estimate a parameter as a deterministic variable, we can use a least square estimator, maximum likelihood (ML) estimator, best linear unbiased estimator, minimum variance unbiased (MVU) estimator, and so on. If the parameter is regarded as a random variable, we can use a MMSE estimator.

Let a set of random variable $\mathbf{X} = [X_1 X_2 ... X_n]^T$ be independent and identically distributed according to pdf $p(x|\theta)$ where θ is unknown. The pdf $p(x|\theta)$ is a mathematical model of an n dataset parameterized by θ. We will determine a scalar parameter θ from an observed $\mathbf{X}$ by finding the highest probability of obtaining the observed data. We define an estimator as a function of n random variables as follows:

$$\hat{\theta} = g(X_1, X_2, \ldots, X_n) \tag{3.115}$$

where $\hat{\theta}$ is an estimate of the parameter θ and $g()$ is an estimator function. We statistically describe the performance of the estimator $\hat{\theta}$. An estimator is a function that assigns a value to the parameter θ from each realization of $\mathbf{X}$. An estimate for a particular realization $\mathbf{X}$ is $\hat{\theta} = g(\mathbf{X})$. We need to investigate how close an estimate is to a true value and define a natural criterion to know how good the estimator is. The estimation error $(\hat{\theta} - \theta)$ of an estimate $\hat{\theta}$ of a parameter θ measures the quality of the estimator. We can use $(\hat{\theta} - \theta)^2$ or $|\hat{\theta} - \theta|^2$ depending on ease of computation. We define the mean square error (MSE) as follows:

Definition 3.9 Mean Square Error

The MSE of an estimate $\hat{\theta}$ of a parameter θ is defined as follows:

$$\text{MSE}_{\hat{\theta}} = E((\hat{\theta} - \theta)^2) \tag{3.116}$$

We also call it a risk function of an estimator corresponding to the expected value of the squared error loss $(\hat{\theta} - \theta)^2$. Equation (3.116) can be rewritten as follows:

$$\text{MSE}_{\hat{\theta}} = E((\hat{\theta} - E(\hat{\theta}) + E(\hat{\theta}) - \theta)^2) \tag{3.117}$$

$$= E((\hat{\theta} - E(\hat{\theta}))^2 + 2(\hat{\theta} - E(\hat{\theta}))(E(\hat{\theta}) - \theta) + (E(\hat{\theta}) - \theta)^2) \tag{3.118}$$

$$= E((\hat{\theta} - E(\hat{\theta}))^2) + E(2(\hat{\theta} - E(\hat{\theta}))(E(\hat{\theta}) - \theta)) + E((E(\hat{\theta}) - \theta)^2) \tag{3.119}$$

We define the bias of an estimator $\hat{\theta}$ of a parameter θ as follows:

$$\text{Bias}(\hat{\theta}) = E(\hat{\theta}) - \theta \tag{3.120}$$

An estimator is called unbiased if bias $(\hat{\theta}) = 0$ for all θ. $E(\hat{\theta}) - \theta$ and $E(\hat{\theta})$ are constant. Equation (3.119) is rewritten as follows:

$$\text{MSE}_{\hat{\theta}} = E((\hat{\theta} - E(\hat{\theta}))^2) + 2(E(\hat{\theta}) - \theta)E(\hat{\theta} - E(\hat{\theta})) + (E(\hat{\theta}) - \theta)^2 \tag{3.121}$$

$$= E((\hat{\theta} - E(\hat{\theta}))^2) + 2(E(\hat{\theta}) - \theta)(E(\hat{\theta}) - E(\hat{\theta})) + (E(\hat{\theta}) - \theta)^2 \tag{3.122}$$

$$= E((\hat{\theta} - E(\hat{\theta}))^2) + (E(\hat{\theta}) - \theta)^2 \tag{3.123}$$

$$\text{MSE}_{\hat{\theta}} = \text{Var}(\hat{\theta}) + (\text{Bias}(\hat{\theta}))^2 \tag{3.124}$$

As we can observe by Equation (3.124), the MSE depends on both the variance and the bias. The MVU estimator is defined by constraining the bias to zero and minimizing the variance as follows:

Definition 3.10 MVU Estimator

$$\text{Minimum variance}: \hat{\theta}_{MVU} = \arg\min_{\hat{\theta}}(\text{Var}(\hat{\theta})) \tag{3.125}$$

$$\text{Unbiased}: E(\hat{\theta}) = \theta, \quad a < \theta < b \tag{3.126}$$

where $[a, b]$ is the range of possible values of θ.

An MVU estimator for linear models can be found by Cramer-Rao Lower Bound theorem. Generally, an MVU estimator does not always exist and it is difficult to find it because there is no simple and general procedure.

Example 3.20 *Two Estimators*
Consider a fixed signal A in white Gaussian noise (WGN) as follows:

$$X_i = A + w_i, \quad i = 0, 1, \ldots, N - 1$$

where A is the parameter θ to be estimated from observed data X_i and $w_i \sim \mathcal{N}(0, \sigma^2)$ is a noise with known pdf. Compare two estimators: $\hat{A}_a = X_0$ and $\hat{A}_b = \frac{1}{N}\sum_{i=0}^{N-1} X_i$.

Solution

The expected values of the two estimators are as follows:

$$E(\widehat{A}_a) = A$$

$$E(\widehat{A}_b) = E\left(\frac{1}{N}\sum_{i=0}^{N-1} X_i\right) = \frac{1}{N}\sum_{i=0}^{N-1} E(X_i) = \frac{1}{N}\sum_{i=0}^{N-1} A = \frac{1}{N}NA = A$$

Both estimators are unbiased. The variances of the two estimators are as follows:

$$\text{Var}(\widehat{A}_a) = \sigma^2$$

$$\text{Var}(\widehat{A}_b) = \text{Var}\left(\frac{1}{N}\sum_{i=0}^{N-1} X_i\right) = \frac{1}{N^2}\sum_{i=0}^{N-1} \text{Var}(X_i) = \frac{1}{N^2}\sum_{i=0}^{N-1} \sigma^2 = \frac{1}{N^2}N\sigma^2 = \frac{\sigma^2}{N}$$

The second estimator $\widehat{A}_b$ has smaller variance than the first estimator $\widehat{A}_a$. As we can observe, $\text{Var}(\widehat{A}_b) = \frac{\sigma^2}{N}$, $\text{Var}(\widehat{A}_b) \to 0$ when $N \to \infty$ and the estimator is consistent. We can say estimators are random variables. The fixed signal estimation is useful in wireless communications because a sinusoidal waveform is represented by a constant in the time and frequency domain.

The MMSE estimator is an estimation method to minimize the Bayesian mean squared error (BMSE), given statistical information such as a prior pdf $p_\theta(\theta)$. The MMSE estimator always exists, in contrast to the MVU estimator, and has a smaller BMSE than MVU estimator. Thus, it is widely used in wireless communications. However, the MMSE estimator is biased. Since both θ and $\mathbf{x}$ are random variables, there is a joint distribution $p_{\mathbf{x},\theta}(\mathbf{x}, \theta)$. The BMSE is defined as follows:

Definition 3.11 Bayesian Mean Squared Error

$$\text{BMSE}_{\widehat{\theta}} = E((\widehat{\theta} - \theta)^2) = \iint (\widehat{\theta} - \theta)^2 p_{\mathbf{x},\theta}(\mathbf{x}, \theta) d\mathbf{x} d\theta \qquad (3.127)$$

As we can observe for Equation (3.127), the dependence on θ in the BMSE is averaged out, whereas the classical MSE depends on the value of θ. We can rewrite Equation (3.127) as follows:

$$\text{BMSE}_{\widehat{\theta}} = \int \left(\int (\widehat{\theta} - \theta)^2 p_{\theta|\mathbf{x}}(\theta|\mathbf{x}) d\theta\right) p_{\mathbf{x}}(\mathbf{x}) d\mathbf{x} \qquad (3.128)$$

because we can write $p_{\mathbf{x},\theta}(\mathbf{x}, \theta) = p_{\theta|\mathbf{x}}(\theta|\mathbf{x}) p_{\mathbf{x}}(\mathbf{x})$. The MMSE estimator can be found by minimizing $\text{BMSE}_{\widehat{\theta}}$ as follows:

Definition 3.12 MMSE Estimator

$$\widehat{\theta}_{\text{MMSE}} = \arg\min_\theta \left(\int (\widehat{\theta} - \theta)^2 p_{\theta|\mathbf{x}}(\theta|\mathbf{x}) d\theta\right) \qquad (3.129)$$

because $p_{\mathbf{x}}(\mathbf{x}) \geq 0$ of all $\mathbf{x}$. By making the derivative with respect to $\hat{\theta}$ be zero, we obtain:

$$\frac{\partial}{\partial \hat{\theta}} \int (\hat{\theta} - \theta)^2 p_{\theta|\mathbf{x}}(\theta|\mathbf{x})d\theta = 2 \int (\hat{\theta} - \theta)p_{\theta|\mathbf{x}}(\theta|\mathbf{x})d\theta \tag{3.130}$$

$$= 2\hat{\theta} - 2 \int \theta p_{\theta|\mathbf{x}}(\theta|\mathbf{x})d\theta = 0 \tag{3.131}$$

Thus, the MMSE estimator is derived as

$$\hat{\theta}_{\text{MMSE}} = \int \theta p_{\theta|\mathbf{x}}(\theta|\mathbf{x})d\theta = E(\theta|\mathbf{x}) \tag{3.132}$$

This is the expectation of the posterior density $p_{\theta|\mathbf{x}}(\theta | \mathbf{x})$. The MMSE depends on both the prior information $(p_{\theta}(\theta).)$ and the data $(p_{\mathbf{x}|\theta}(\mathbf{x}|\theta))$.

Example 3.21   *MMSE Estimator*

Consider a similar signal to Example 3.20 as follows:

$$x_i = A + w_i, \quad i = 0, 1, \ldots, N - 1$$

where A is the parameter θ to be estimated and also a random variable with a prior pdf $p(A) \sim \mathcal{N}(\mu_A, \sigma_A^2)$, and $w_i \sim \mathcal{N}(0, \sigma^2)$ is a noise with known pdf. In addition, we assume that $p(\mathbf{x}|A) \sim \mathcal{N}(A, \sigma^2)$ and $\mathbf{x}$ and A are jointly Gaussian distributions. Find the MMSE estimator of A.

Solution

From Equation (3.132), we have

$$\hat{\theta}_{\text{MMSE}} = \int \theta p_{\theta|\mathbf{x}}(\theta|\mathbf{x})d\theta = E(\theta|\mathbf{x})$$

$$= E(A|\mathbf{x})$$

The posterior pdf $p_{A|\mathbf{x}}(A | \mathbf{x})$ is given by

$$p_{A|\mathbf{x}}(A|\mathbf{x}) = \frac{p_{\mathbf{x},A}(\mathbf{x}, A)}{p_{\mathbf{x}}(\mathbf{x})} = \frac{p_{\mathbf{x},A}(\mathbf{x}, A)}{\int p_{\mathbf{x},A}(\mathbf{x}, A)dA} = \frac{p_{\theta|\mathbf{x}}(\mathbf{x}|A)p_{\mathbf{x}}(A)}{\int p_{\theta|\mathbf{x}}(\mathbf{x}|A)p_{\mathbf{x}}(A)dA} = \mathcal{N}(\mu_{A|\mathbf{x}}, \sigma_{A|\mathbf{x}}^2)$$

After simplification, we have

$$\sigma_{A|\mathbf{x}}^2 = \frac{1}{\frac{N}{\sigma^2} + \frac{1}{\sigma_A^2}} \text{ and } \mu_{A|\mathbf{x}} = \left(\frac{N}{\sigma^2}\mathbf{x} + \frac{\mu_A}{\sigma_A^2}\right)\sigma_{A|\mathbf{x}}^2$$

Thus, the MMSE estimator of A is

$$\hat{A}_{\text{MMSE}} = \int A p_{A|\mathbf{x}}(A|\mathbf{x})dA = \mu_{A|\mathbf{x}} = \left(\frac{N}{\sigma^2}\bar{x} + \frac{\mu_A}{\sigma_A^2}\right)\left(\frac{1}{\frac{N}{\sigma^2} + \frac{1}{\sigma_A^2}}\right)$$

$$= \left(\frac{\sigma_A^2}{\sigma_A^2 + \frac{\sigma^2}{N}}\right)\bar{x} + \left(1 - \frac{\sigma_A^2}{\sigma_A^2 + \frac{\sigma^2}{N}}\right)\mu_A$$

where $\bar{x}$ is the sample mean. When N is small (we have small amounts of data), $\sigma_A^2 \ll \frac{\sigma^2}{N}$ and $\widehat{A}_{\mathrm{MMSE}}$ approaches to μ_A, which means that we can ignore the observed data. When N is large (we have large amounts of data), $\sigma_A^2 \gg \frac{\sigma^2}{N}$ and $\widehat{A}_{\mathrm{MMSE}}$ approaches to $\bar{x}$, which means that we can ignore the prior information.

Suppose that we estimate the value of a random variable θ based on a discrete random variable $\mathbf{x}=[x_0\, x_1\, \ldots x_{N-1}]^T$. We seek an estimator $\widehat{\theta}$ in the form of an affine function (affine functions are $f(x) = ax + b$, where a and b are arbitrary constants) of the observation $\mathbf{x}$ as follows:

$$\widehat{\theta} = \sum_{i=0}^{N-1} a_i x_i + a_N = \mathbf{a}^T \mathbf{x} + a_N \tag{3.133}$$

where $\mathbf{a}^T = [a_0\, a_1\, \ldots a_{N-1}]^T$ and a_N are scalars to be determined. We deal with the non-zero mean case. The estimation problem is to find the coefficient a_i to minimize the BMSE as follows:

$$\mathrm{BMSE}_{\widehat{\theta}} = E((\widehat{\theta} - \theta)^2) = E((\theta - \widehat{\theta})^2) \tag{3.134}$$

$$= E((\theta - \mathbf{a}^T\mathbf{x} - a_N)^2) = E\left(\left(\theta - \sum_{i=0}^{N-1} a_i x_i - a_N\right)^2\right) \tag{3.135}$$

We call the resultant estimator the linear MMSE estimator. If θ and $\mathbf{x}$ are jointly Gaussian, the MMSE estimator is linear and the linear MMSE is optimal. If θ and $\mathbf{x}$ are not jointly Gaussian, the linear MMSE is suboptimal. By making the derivative with respect to a_N to zero, we obtain:

$$\frac{\partial}{\partial a_N}\mathrm{BMSE}_{\widehat{\theta}} = \frac{\partial}{\partial a_N}E\left(\left(\theta - \sum_{i=0}^{N-1} a_i x_i - a_N\right)^2\right) \tag{3.136}$$

$$= -2E\left(\theta - \sum_{i=0}^{N-1} a_i x_i - a_N\right) = 0 \tag{3.137}$$

Thus, a_N is derived as

$$a_N = E(\theta) - E\left(\sum_{i=0}^{N-1} a_i x_i\right) = E(\theta) - \mathbf{a}^T E(\mathbf{x}) \tag{3.138}$$

By Equations (3.135) and (3.138), we obtain:

$$\mathrm{BMSE}_{\widehat{\theta}} = E\left(\left(\theta - \sum_{i=0}^{N-1} a_i x_i - E(\theta) - E\left(\sum_{i=0}^{N-1} a_i x_i\right)\right)^2\right) \tag{3.139}$$

$$= E((\mathbf{a}^T(\mathbf{x} - E(\mathbf{x})) - (\theta - E(\theta)))^2) \tag{3.140}$$

$$= E(\mathbf{a}^T(\mathbf{x} - E(\mathbf{x}))(\mathbf{x} - E(\mathbf{x}))^T\mathbf{a}) - E(\mathbf{a}^T(\mathbf{x} - E(\mathbf{x}))(\theta - E(\theta)))$$
$$- E((\theta - E(\theta))(\mathbf{x} - E(\mathbf{x}))^T\mathbf{a}) + E((\theta - E(\theta))^2) \tag{3.141}$$

a as a scalar can be moved outside of the expected value operator due to Property 3.6(c). We obtain

$$= \mathbf{a}^T \mathbf{C_{xx}} \mathbf{a} - \mathbf{a}^T \mathbf{C}_{x\theta} - \mathbf{C}_{\theta x}\mathbf{a} + C_{\theta\theta} \tag{3.142}$$

$$= \mathbf{a}^T \mathbf{C_{xx}} \mathbf{a} - 2\mathbf{a}^T \mathbf{C}_{x\theta} + C_{\theta\theta} \tag{3.143}$$

where $\mathbf{C_{xx}}$ is the $N \times N$ covariance matrix, $\mathbf{C}_{x\theta}$ is the $N \times 1$ cross-covariance vector, $C_{\theta\theta}$ is the covariance matrix, and $\mathbf{C}_{\theta x} = \mathbf{C}_{x\theta}{}^T$. By making the derivative with respect to **a** be zero, we obtain as follows:

$$\frac{\partial}{\partial \mathbf{a}} \mathrm{BMSE}_{\hat{\theta}} = \frac{\partial}{\partial \mathbf{a}}(\mathbf{a}^T \mathbf{C_{xx}} \mathbf{a} - 2\mathbf{a}^T \mathbf{C}_{x\theta} + C_{\theta\theta}) \tag{3.144}$$

$$= 2\mathbf{C_{xx}}\mathbf{a} - 2\mathbf{C}_{x\theta} = 0 \tag{3.145}$$

$$\mathbf{a} = \mathbf{C_{xx}}^{-1}\mathbf{C}_{x\theta} \text{ and } \mathbf{a}^T = \mathbf{C}_{\theta x}\mathbf{C_{xx}}^{-1} \tag{3.146}$$

By Equations (3.133), (3.138), and (3.146), we obtain the linear MMSE estimator $\hat{\theta}$ as follows:

$$\hat{\theta} = \mathbf{a}^T\mathbf{x} + a_N = \mathbf{C}_{x\theta}{}^T\mathbf{C_{xx}}^{-1}\mathbf{x} + E(\theta) - \mathbf{C}_{x\theta}{}^T\mathbf{C_{xx}}^{-1}E(\mathbf{x}) \tag{3.147}$$

$$= E(\theta) + \mathbf{C}_{\theta x}\mathbf{C_{xx}}^{-1}(\mathbf{x} - E(\mathbf{x})) \tag{3.148}$$

and the BMSE is obtain by Equations (3.143) and (3.146) as follows:

$$\mathrm{BMSE}_{\hat{\theta}} = \mathbf{a}^T\mathbf{C_{xx}}\mathbf{a} - 2\mathbf{a}^T\mathbf{C}_{x\theta} + C_{\theta\theta} \tag{3.149}$$

$$= \mathbf{C}_{\theta x}\mathbf{C_{xx}}^{-1}\mathbf{C_{xx}}\mathbf{C_{xx}}^{-1}\mathbf{C}_{x\theta} - 2\mathbf{C}_{\theta x}\mathbf{C_{xx}}^{-1}\mathbf{C}_{x\theta} + C_{\theta\theta} \tag{3.150}$$

$$= \mathbf{C}_{\theta x}\mathbf{C_{xx}}^{-1}\mathbf{C}_{x\theta} - 2\mathbf{C}_{\theta x}\mathbf{C_{xx}}^{-1}\mathbf{C}_{x\theta} + C_{\theta\theta} \tag{3.151}$$

$$= C_{\theta\theta} - \mathbf{C}_{\theta x}\mathbf{C_{xx}}^{-1}\mathbf{C}_{x\theta} \tag{3.152}$$

As we can observe from Equations (3.148) and (3.152), we need to calculate expected values, variances, and covariance to obtain the linear MMSE estimator. If we have zero mean, $\hat{\theta} = \mathbf{C}_{\theta x}\mathbf{C_{xx}}^{-1}\mathbf{x}$. If θ and $\mathbf{x}$ are statistically independent, we have $\mathbf{C}_{\theta x} = 0$. Thus, $\hat{\theta} = E(\theta)$ and $\mathrm{BMSE}_{\hat{\theta}} = C_{\theta\theta}$. This means that we do not need data and the estimator is based on prior information. Now, we can expand them in a matrix form. Equations (3.133) and (3.134) can be rewritten as follows:

$$\hat{\theta}_j = \sum_{i=0}^{N-1} a_{ji}x_i + a_{jN} \text{ and } \hat{\boldsymbol{\theta}} = \mathbf{A}\mathbf{x} + \mathbf{a} \tag{3.153}$$

$$\mathrm{BMSE}_{\hat{\theta}_j} = E((\theta_j - \hat{\theta}_j)^2) = E((\boldsymbol{\theta} - \hat{\boldsymbol{\theta}})(\boldsymbol{\theta} - \hat{\boldsymbol{\theta}})^T) \tag{3.154}$$

where $j = 1, 2, \ldots, p$. We estimate the realization of $\theta^T = [\theta_1\ \theta_2 \ldots \theta_p]^T$ by minimizing BMSE for each element. We already know the individual solutions and represent them in the matrix form. From Equations (3.148) and (3.152), the linear MMSE estimator and BMSE can be rewritten as follows:

$$\hat{\theta}_j = E(\theta_j) + \mathbf{C}_{\theta_j x}\mathbf{C_{xx}}^{-1}(\mathbf{x} - E(\mathbf{x})) \tag{3.155}$$

$$\hat{\theta} = \begin{bmatrix} E(\theta_1) \\ E(\theta_2) \\ \vdots \\ E(\theta_p) \end{bmatrix} + \begin{bmatrix} \mathbf{C}_{\theta_1\mathbf{x}}\mathbf{C}_{\mathbf{xx}}^{-1}(\mathbf{x} - E(\mathbf{x})) \\ \mathbf{C}_{\theta_2\mathbf{x}}\mathbf{C}_{\mathbf{xx}}^{-1}(\mathbf{x} - E(\mathbf{x})) \\ \vdots \\ \mathbf{C}_{\theta_p\mathbf{x}}\mathbf{C}_{\mathbf{xx}}^{-1}(\mathbf{x} - E(\mathbf{x})) \end{bmatrix} \tag{3.156}$$

$$\hat{\theta} = E(\boldsymbol{\theta}) + \mathbf{C}_{\cdot\mathbf{x}}\mathbf{C}_{\mathbf{xx}}^{-1}(\mathbf{x} - E(\mathbf{x})) \tag{3.157}$$

where $\mathbf{C}_{\theta\mathbf{x}}$ is $p \times N$ cross-covariance vector and

$$\text{BMSE}_{\hat{\theta}_j} = C_{\theta_j\theta_j} - \mathbf{C}_{\theta_j\mathbf{x}}\mathbf{C}_{\mathbf{xx}}^{-1}\mathbf{C}_{\mathbf{x}\theta_j} \tag{3.158}$$

$$\text{BMSE}_{\hat{\theta}_j} = [\mathbf{M}_{\hat{\theta}}]_{jj} \tag{3.159}$$

where $\mathbf{M}_{\hat{\theta}} = C_{\theta\theta} - \mathbf{C}_{\theta\mathbf{x}}\mathbf{C}_{\mathbf{xx}}^{-1}\mathbf{C}_{\mathbf{x}\theta}$ is the minimum MSE matrix whose diagonal elements are the minimum BMSE and $C_{\theta\theta}$ is a $p \times p$ prior covariance matrix. The properties of the linear MMSE estimator are summarized as follows:

Property 3.12 Properties of the Linear MMSE Estimator

(i) Invariance over affine transformations: $\boldsymbol{\alpha} = \mathbf{A}\boldsymbol{\theta} + \mathbf{b} \rightarrow \hat{\boldsymbol{\alpha}} = \mathbf{A}\hat{\boldsymbol{\theta}} + \mathbf{b}$
(ii) $\boldsymbol{\alpha} = \boldsymbol{\theta}_1 + \boldsymbol{\theta}_2 \rightarrow \hat{\boldsymbol{\alpha}} = \hat{\boldsymbol{\theta}}_1 + \hat{\boldsymbol{\theta}}_2$
(iii) Linear MMSE and MMSE are identical under the joint Gaussian assumption.

The MMSE estimator approaches the LSE estimators if the process is ergodic and the amount of data approaches infinity.

Summary 3.5 MMSE Estimation

1) Estimation theory deals with estimating the values of some parameters based on observation, and the estimator approximates the unknown parameters.
2) In the Frequentist approach, the parameter we want to estimate is regarded as an unknown but deterministic parameter. However, the Bayesian approach exploits a priori information and considers the parameter to be an outcome of random process with knowledge of the distribution of the random variable.
3) The mean square error (MSE) of an estimate $\hat{\theta}$ of a parameter θ is defined as follows

$$\text{MSE}_{\hat{\theta}} = E((\hat{\theta} - \theta)^2)$$

4) The minimum variance unbiased (MVU) estimator is defined by constraining the bias to zero and minimizing the variance as follows:

$$\text{Minimum variance}: \hat{\theta}_{MVU} = \arg\min_{\hat{\theta}}(\text{Var}(\hat{\theta}))$$

$$\text{Unbiased}: E(\hat{\theta}) = \theta, \ a < \theta < b$$

where $[a, b]$ is the range of possible values of θ.

---

5) The minimum mean square error (MMSE) estimator is an estimation method to minimize the Bayesian mean squared error (BMSE), given statistical information such as a priori pdf $p_\theta(\theta)$.

6) The MMSE estimator can be found by minimizing $\mathrm{BMSE}_{\hat{\theta}}$ as follows:

$$\hat{\theta}_{\mathrm{MMSE}} = \arg\min_\theta \left(\int (\hat{\theta} - \theta)^2 p_{\theta|\mathbf{x}}(\theta|\mathbf{x}) d\theta \right)$$

3.2.4 Maximum Likelihood and Maximum A Posteriori Estimation

We can write a Bayesian formula as follows:

$$p(\theta|x) \propto p(\theta)p(x|\theta) \tag{3.160}$$

where $p(\theta \,|\, x)$, $p(\theta)$, and $p(x \,|\, \theta)$ are the posterior density, the prior density and the likelihood, respectively. The omitted term $1/p(x)$ is called the constant of proportionality. As we can observe from Equation (3.160), the posterior is proportional to the prior and the likelihood. Since the a priori density is fixed by the a priori knowledge or assumption, we can regard it as an invariant term. Thus, we can define the likelihood $L(\theta \,|\, x)$ as follows:

Definition 3.13 Likelihood

$$L(\theta|x) \propto p(x|\theta) \tag{3.161}$$

As we can observe from Equation (3.161), the likelihood is proportional to the probability of the observed data. The MMSE depends on both the prior information and the observed data. We cannot calculate the MMSE if we do not have the prior information. However, the likelihood can be calculated without the prior information. Maximum likelihood estimation is a method of estimating the parameters by maximizing the likelihood. If the sample is large enough, the maximum likelihood (ML) estimation will give a good estimator of θ. It is one of the most widely used techniques in wireless communications. The ML estimator is defined as follows:

Definition 3.14 ML Estimator

$$\hat{\theta}_{ML} = \arg\max_\theta(L(\theta|x)) = \arg\max_\theta(p(x|\theta)) \tag{3.162}$$

Suppose that the random variables X_1, X_2, ..., X_n have a random sample $x_1, x_2, ..., x_n$ from a distribution $f(x \,|\, \theta)$ where θ could be a real unknown parameter or a vector unknown parameter. If the random variable is discrete, $f(x \,|\, \theta)$ is a pmf. If it is continuous, $f(x \,|\, \theta)$ is a pdf. If the random variables are independent and identically distributed, we can define the likelihood function of θ for the observed random samples as follows:

$$f(x_1, x_2, \ldots, x_n|\theta) = f(x_1|\theta)f(x_2|\theta) \ldots f(x_n|\theta) = \prod_{i=1}^{n} f(x_i|\theta) \tag{3.163}$$

where $f(x_1, x_2, \ldots, x_n \mid \theta)$ is the joint probability if it is discrete, and $f(x_1, x_2, \ldots, x_n \mid \theta)$ is the joint density function if it is continuous. The likelihood function depends on the unknown parameter θ. If we have actual data, the maximum likelihood estimate $\hat{\theta}$ will be a particular numerical value. If we do not have actual data, it will be a function of n random variables. We can rewrite Equation (3.163) as follows:

$$L(\theta) = \prod_{i=1}^{n} f(x_i \mid \theta) \tag{3.164}$$

The ML estimation maximizes the likelihood function $L(\theta)$ with respect to the parameter θ. The likelihood function $L(\theta)$ requires calculation of a product of n pmf or pdf. It is not simple computation. Thus, we define the log-likelihood function as follows:

$$\ln L(\theta) = \ln \prod_{i=1}^{n} f(x_i \mid \theta) = \sum_{i=1}^{n} \ln f(x_i \mid \theta) \tag{3.165}$$

It is usually simpler to work with the logarithm of the likelihood function because the log function is a monotonically increasing function. Maximizing the likelihood function is equivalent to maximizing the log-likelihood function. We can regard the problem of the ML estimation as a maximization problem. Sometimes, we use the negative logarithm and minimize the negative log-likelihood function. We can find the ML estimator by setting the derivative equal to zero. If θ is a vector with elements $(\theta_1, \theta_2, \ldots, \theta_k)$, the ML estimation of θ can be obtained by differentiating $\ln L(\theta)$ with respect to each element as follows:

$$\frac{\partial}{\partial \theta_1} \ln L(\theta) = 0$$

$$\frac{\partial}{\partial \theta_2} \ln L(\theta) = 0$$

$$\vdots \tag{3.166}$$

$$\frac{\partial}{\partial \theta_k} \ln L(\theta) = 0$$

We call Equation (3.166) Fisher's score function, and the solutions are the ML estimator $\hat{\theta}$.

Example 3.22 *ML Estimator for a Discrete Random Variable*
Consider a discrete random variable X with a pmf: $P(X = 0) = \theta/3$, $P(X = 1) = 2\theta/3$, $P(X = 2) = (1 - \theta)/3$, $P(X = 3) = 2(1 - \theta)/3$, where $0 \leq \theta \leq 1$. We have 10 samples as follows:

X_1	X_2	X_3	X_4	X_5	X_6	X_7	X_8	X_9	X_{10}
0	3	1	2	1	0	2	3	1	2

Find the maximum likelihood estimator.

Solution
From Equation (3.164), the likelihood of 10 samples is

$$L(\theta) = \prod_{i=1}^{10} P(X_i \mid \theta)$$

$$L(\theta) = P(X_1 = 0)P(X_2 = 3)P(X_3 = 1)P(X_4 = 2)P(X_5 = 1)P(X_6 = 0)$$
$$\times P(X_7 = 2)P(X_8 = 3)P(X_9 = 1)P(X_{10} = 2)$$
$$L(\theta) = (\theta/3)^2(2\theta/3)^3((1-\theta)/3)^3(2(1-\theta)/3)^2$$

From Equation (3.165), we have the log-likelihood function as follows:

$$\ln L(\theta) = \sum_{i=1}^{10} \ln P(X_i|\theta) = 2(\ln 1/3 + \ln \theta) + 3(\ln 2/3 + \ln \theta)$$
$$+ 3(\ln 1/3 + \ln(1-\theta)) + 2(\ln 2/3 + \ln(1-\theta))$$
$$= 5\ln \theta + 5\ln(1-\theta) + \alpha$$

where α is a constant. By making the derivative of $\ln L(\theta)$ with respect to θ be zero, we obtain as follows:

$$\frac{d}{d\theta}\ln L(\theta) = \frac{5}{\theta} - \frac{5}{1-\theta} = 0$$

$$1 - 2\theta = 0$$

Thus, the ML estimator is $\widehat{\theta}_{ML} = 0.5$.

Example 3.23   *ML Estimator for a Continuous Random Variable*

Consider continuous random variables $X_1, X_2, ..., X_n$ with a Poisson distribution are independent and identically distributed. Find the ML estimator.

Solution

For the Poisson distribution, we have the following likelihood function:

$$L(\theta) = \prod_{i=1}^{n} \frac{e^{-\theta}\theta^{X_i}}{X_i!} = \frac{e^{-n\theta}\theta^{\sum_{i=1}^{n} X_i}}{\prod_{i=1}^{n} X_i!}$$

From Equation (3.165), we have the log-likelihood function as follows:

$$\ln L(\theta) = \sum_{i=1}^{n} \ln\left(\frac{e^{-\theta}\theta^{X_i}}{X_i!}\right) = \sum_{i=1}^{n} \ln\left(\frac{e^{-n\theta}\theta^{\sum_{i=1}^{n} X_i}}{\prod_{i=1}^{n} X_i!}\right)$$

$$\ln L(\theta) = -n\theta + \sum_{i=1}^{n} X_i \ln \theta - \sum_{i=1}^{n} \ln X_i!$$

By making the derivative of $\ln L(\theta)$ with respect to θ be zero, we obtain as follows:

$$\frac{d}{d\theta}\ln L(\theta) = -n + \frac{\sum_{i=1}^{n} X_i}{\theta} = 0$$

Thus, the ML estimator is

$$\widehat{\theta}_{ML} = \frac{\sum_{i=1}^{n} X_i}{n}$$

As we can see in Examples 3.22 and 3.23, we found the ML estimator by making the derivative of the likelihood function with respect to the parameter equal to zero. However, this approach only works when the likelihood function is differentiable or there is an analytical solution. Another approach for obtaining the ML estimator is derivative-free grid search. It searches possible values producing the largest likelihood by approximation and iteration. However, this approach is not a practical solution in many cases and does not work if we do not know the range of possible values. The most common methods are numerical approaches such as Newton-Raphson and so on. We set an initial value for the ML estimator and make those numerical methods find the maximum by iteration. The iteration continues until it converges. However, this approach may converge to a local maximum (not the global maximum) if we do not set initial values and step sizes properly. This approach does not converge if the second derivative of the likelihood function is close to zero.

When we have large samples, the asymptotic properties of the ML estimator can be summarized as follows:

Property 3.13 Properties of the ML Estimator

(i) *Consistency*: The ML estimator $\widehat{\theta}_{ML}$ is asymptotically consistent ($n \to \infty$). Simply speaking, the more we have observed data, the greater accuracy we have.

(ii) *Asymptotic normality*: The ML estimator $\widehat{\theta}_{ML}$ is asymptotically normally distributed with minimal variance.

(iii) *Invariance*: If $\widehat{\theta}_{ML}$ is the ML estimator of θ, $\widehat{\gamma}_{ML} = g(\widehat{\theta}_{ML})$ is the ML estimator of $\gamma = g(\theta)$. The ML solution is invariant under the parameter change.

(iv) *Efficiency*: The asymptotic variance of the ML estimator is equal to the Cramer-Rao lower bound.

As the name suggests, maximum a posteriori (MAP) estimation uses posterior information and finds the unknown parameter θ by maximizing this. The posterior information contains all the knowledge about the unknown parameter θ that we can observe, as per Equation (3.160). The MAP estimator is defined as follows:

Definition 3.15 MAP Estimator

$$\widehat{\theta}_{MAP} = \arg\max_{\theta}(p(\theta|x)) \tag{3.167}$$

Definition 3.15 can be rewritten as follows:

$$\widehat{\theta}_{MAP} = \arg\max_{\theta}(p(x|\theta)p(\theta)) \tag{3.168}$$

by Bayes' theorem ($p(\theta \mid x) = p(x \mid \theta)p(\theta)/p(x)$ where $p(x)$ does not depend on the parameter θ). Similar to ML estimation for n random variables, we can rewrite Equation (3.168) as follows:

$$\widehat{\theta}_{MAP} = \arg\max_{\theta}\left(\prod_{i=1}^{n} p(x_i|\theta)p(\theta)\right) \tag{3.169}$$

and the logarithmic form of MAP estimation is

$$\hat{\theta}_{MAP} = \arg\max_{\theta} \left(\ln \prod_{i=1}^{n} p(x_i|\theta)p(\theta) \right) \tag{3.170}$$

$$= \arg\max_{\theta} \left(\sum_{i=1}^{n} \ln p(x_i|\theta)p(\theta) \right) \tag{3.171}$$

$$= \arg\max_{\theta} \left(\sum_{i=1}^{n} \ln p(x_i|\theta) + \ln p(\theta) \right) \tag{3.172}$$

When comparing MAP with ML, the only difference is the a priori term $p(\theta)$, by which the likelihood is weighted. The estimate can be shifted when the number of observations is low. Figure 3.8 illustrates the relationship among a posteriori, likelihood, and a priori. As we can observe in Figure 3.8, the a priori term gives a weight to the likelihood and the estimate of MAP is changed. If we consider a uniform a priori term with the same weight everywhere, we can ignore that term and MAP estimation is identical to ML estimation as follows:

$$\hat{\theta}_{MAP} = \arg\max_{\theta} \left(\sum_{i=1}^{n} \ln p(x_i|\theta) + \alpha \right) \tag{3.173}$$

$$= \arg\max_{\theta} \left(\sum_{i=1}^{n} \ln p(x_i|\theta) \right) = \hat{\theta}_{ML} \tag{3.174}$$

where α is constant. When comparing MAP and MMSE, both MAP and MMSE produce estimates as a function of the a posteriori density. However, the estimate of MAP is the peak of the posterior while the MMSE estimate is the mean. The MMSE estimator does not require the posteriori density itself but the conditional mean of the posterior density.

Similar to ML estimation, if the logarithm of the posteriori function is differentiable with respect to θ, the MAP estimate is obtained from

$$\frac{\partial}{\partial\theta} p(\theta|x) = 0 \tag{3.175}$$

We can also write the MAP solution by applying a logarithm as follows:

$$\frac{\partial}{\partial\theta} (\ln p(x|\theta) + \ln p(\theta)) = 0 \tag{3.176}$$

Example 3.24 *MAP Estimator*
Consider continuous random variables $X_1, X_2, \ldots, X_n$ with normal distributions $\mathcal{N}(0, \sigma^2)$ that are independent and identically distributed. A priori distribution of θ is given by the normal distribution $\mathcal{N}(0, \sigma_\theta^2)$. Find the MAP estimator.

Solution
For the normal distribution, we have the following joint density function:

$$p(X_1, X_2, \ldots, X_n|\theta) = \prod_{i=1}^{n} \frac{1}{\sqrt{2\pi}\sigma} \exp\left(-\frac{(X_i - \theta)^2}{2\sigma^2}\right)$$

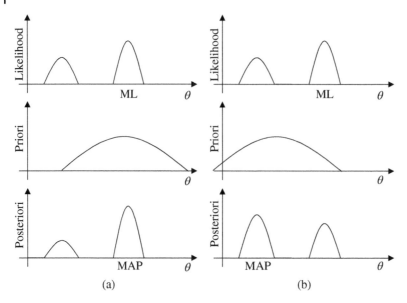

Figure 3.8 ML vs MAP: (a) MAP = ML; and (b) MAP ≠ ML.

and the priori distribution is

$$p(\theta) = \frac{1}{\sqrt{2\pi}\sigma_\theta} \exp\left(-\frac{\theta^2}{2\sigma_\theta^2}\right)$$

From Equation (3.176), we have

$$\frac{1}{\sigma^2}\sum_{i=1}^{n}(X_i - \theta) - \frac{\theta}{\sigma_\theta^2} = 0$$

Thus, the MAP estimator of the parameter θ is found as follows:

$$\widehat{\theta}_{MAP} = \frac{\sigma_\theta^2}{\sigma_\theta^2 + \sigma^2/n}\frac{1}{n}\sum_{i=1}^{n}X_i$$

As we can observe from the above equation, as $\sigma_\theta^2 \to \infty$, a priori distribution is close to a constant and $\widehat{\theta}_{MAP}$ approaches $\widehat{\theta}_{ML}$. Namely, MAP estimation would not be better performance than ML estimation if we have uninformative priori information. In addition, as $n \to \infty$ (when the number of observations is high enough), $\widehat{\theta}_{MAP}$ converges to $\widehat{\theta}_{ML}$. Namely, the priori term does not affect the likelihood when we have plenty of observations.

Summary 3.6 ML and MAP Estimation

1) The maximum likelihood (ML) estimator is defined as follows:

$$\widehat{\theta}_{ML} = \arg\max_{\theta}(L(\theta|x)) = \arg\max_{\theta}(p(x|\theta))$$

2) The MAP estimator is defined as follows:

$$\hat{\theta}_{MAP} = \arg\max_{\theta}(p(\theta|x)) = \arg\max_{\theta}(p(x|\theta)p(\theta))$$

3) The logarithmic form of MAP estimation is:

$$\hat{\theta}_{MAP} = \arg\max_{\theta}\left(\sum_{i=1}^{n}\ln p(x_i|\theta) + \ln p(\theta)\right)$$

4) When comparing MAP with ML, the only difference is the priori term $p(\theta)$ by which the likelihood is weighted. The estimate can be shifted when the number of observations is low.

3.3 Matrix Factorization

Matrix theory is very useful for both signal representation and information processing. It is very important tool to solve the problems of communication and network theory efficiently. In particular, multicarrier techniques, multiple input multiple output (MIMO) and detection and estimation techniques are adopted in many cellular communication systems because they improve the performance significantly. They require a matrix calculation. Matrix representation is very efficient for defining the problem and finding the solution for these techniques. In addition, matrix theory is very helpful for simplifying the problems, reducing computational complexity and optimizing the systems. There is an increasing demand to calculate large matrices and a requirement for faster and more efficient matrix computation algorithms. Most matrix computation from original data is not easy to calculate in an explicit way. Matrix factorization (or decomposition) allows us to rephrase some matrix forms in such a way that they can be solved more easily. Due to computational convenience and simplicity, matrix factorization is widely used in not only wireless communications but also signal processing. In particular, matrix computation is tricky and expensive in terms of hardware implementation. In this section, we review some important matrix decompositions.

3.3.1 LU Decomposition

When we need to solve a linear system of the form $\mathbf{Ax} = \mathbf{b}$ where $\mathbf{A} \in \mathbb{R}^{n\times n}$, $\mathbf{x} \in \mathbb{R}^n$ and $\mathbf{b} \in \mathbb{R}^n$, Lower Upper (LU) decomposition is a useful method. We can define it as follows:

Definition 3.16 LU Decomposition

A square matrix $\mathbf{A}$ can be factored into the product of a lower triangular matrix $\mathbf{L} \in \mathbb{R}^{n\times n}$ and an upper triangular matrix $\mathbf{U} \in \mathbb{R}^{n\times n}$ as follows:

$$\mathbf{A} = \mathbf{LU} \tag{3.177}$$

where $\mathbf{A}$, $\mathbf{L}$, and $\mathbf{U}$ are nonsingular.

For the case of a $n \times n$ matrix $\mathbf{A}$, Equation (3.177) can be represented as follows:

$$\begin{bmatrix} a_{11} & a_{12} & \cdots & a_{1n} \\ a_{21} & a_{22} & \cdots & a_{2n} \\ \vdots & \vdots & \ddots & \vdots \\ a_{n1} & a_{n2} & a_{n3} & a_{nn} \end{bmatrix} = \begin{bmatrix} l_{11} & 0 & \cdots & 0 \\ l_{21} & l_{22} & \cdots & 0 \\ \vdots & \vdots & \ddots & \vdots \\ l_{n1} & l_{n2} & l_{n3} & l_{nn} \end{bmatrix} \begin{bmatrix} u_{11} & u_{12} & \cdots & u_{1n} \\ 0 & u_{22} & \cdots & u_{2n} \\ \vdots & \vdots & \ddots & \vdots \\ 0 & 0 & 0 & u_{nn} \end{bmatrix} \tag{3.178}$$

Although we cannot represent all matrices in this form, this form can be transformed in many applications. The linear system of the form $\mathbf{Ax} = \mathbf{b}$ can be substituted by Equation (3.177) and associative properties of matrix multiplication as follows:

$$\mathbf{LUx} = \mathbf{b} \tag{3.179}$$

$$\mathbf{Ly} = \mathbf{b} \tag{3.180}$$

where $\mathbf{y} = \mathbf{Ux}$. We can solve for x using two steps. Firstly, we solve the lower triangular system Equation (3.180) for $\mathbf{y}$. Secondly, after obtaining y, we solve the upper triangular system $\mathbf{y} = \mathbf{Ux}$. The solution of a triangular set of these equations is trivial. Equation (3.180) can be solved by forward substitution as follows:

$$y_1 = \frac{b_1}{l_{11}}, \quad y_i = \frac{1}{l_{ii}} \left(b_i - \sum_{j=1}^{i-1} l_{ij} y_j \right) \text{ where } i = 2, 3, \dots, n \tag{3.181}$$

and then the equation $\mathbf{y} = \mathbf{Ux}$ can be solved by back-substitution as follows:

$$x_n = \frac{y_n}{u_{nn}}, \quad x_i = \frac{1}{u_{ii}} \left(y_i - \sum_{j=i+1}^{n} u_{ij} x_j \right) \text{ where } i = n-1, n-2, \dots, 1 \tag{3.182}$$

Example 3.25 *LU Decomposition*
Consider a square matrix $\mathbf{A} \in \mathbb{R}^{3 \times 3}$ as follows:

$$\mathbf{A} = \begin{bmatrix} 1 & 2 & 3 \\ 4 & 5 & 6 \\ 7 & 8 & 9 \end{bmatrix}$$

Find the LU decomposition of $\mathbf{A}$.

Solution
Using Gaussian elimination on $\mathbf{A}$, the upper triangular matrix $\mathbf{U}$ can be obtained as follows:

$$\text{Row\#2--4 Row\#1} \rightarrow \text{Row\#2:} \begin{bmatrix} 1 & 2 & 3 \\ 0 & -3 & -6 \\ 7 & 8 & 9 \end{bmatrix}$$

$$\text{Then, Row\#3--7 Row\#2} \rightarrow \text{Row\#3:} \begin{bmatrix} 1 & 2 & 3 \\ 0 & -3 & -6 \\ 0 & -6 & -12 \end{bmatrix}$$

$$\text{Then, Row\#3--2 Row\#2} \rightarrow \text{Row\#3:} \begin{bmatrix} 1 & 2 & 3 \\ 0 & -3 & -6 \\ 0 & 0 & 0 \end{bmatrix} = \mathbf{U}$$

The lower triangular matrix **L** can be obtained by the inverse operation as follows:

$$\mathbf{L} = \begin{bmatrix} 1 & 0 & 0 \\ l_{21} & 1 & 0 \\ l_{31} & l_{32} & 1 \end{bmatrix}$$

$$\begin{bmatrix} 1 & 2 & 3 \\ 4 & 5 & 6 \\ 7 & 8 & 9 \end{bmatrix} = \begin{bmatrix} 1 & 0 & 0 \\ l_{21} & 1 & 0 \\ l_{31} & l_{32} & 1 \end{bmatrix} \begin{bmatrix} 1 & 2 & 3 \\ 0 & -3 & -6 \\ 0 & 0 & 0 \end{bmatrix}$$

$$l_{21} = 4, l_{31} = 7, 2l_{31} - 3l_{32} = 8$$

$$l_{21} = 4, l_{31} = 7, l_{32} = 2$$

$$\mathbf{L} = \begin{bmatrix} 1 & 0 & 0 \\ 4 & 1 & 0 \\ 7 & 2 & 1 \end{bmatrix}$$

Thus, the LU decomposition of **A** is as follows:

$$\mathbf{A} = \begin{bmatrix} 1 & 2 & 3 \\ 4 & 5 & 6 \\ 7 & 8 & 9 \end{bmatrix} = \begin{bmatrix} 1 & 0 & 0 \\ 4 & 1 & 0 \\ 7 & 2 & 1 \end{bmatrix} \begin{bmatrix} 1 & 2 & 3 \\ 0 & -3 & -6 \\ 0 & 0 & 0 \end{bmatrix} = \mathbf{LU}$$

Example 3.26   *LU Decomposition for a Linear System*

Consider the following linear system:

$$10x_1 + 3x_2 + 4x_3 = 15$$
$$2x_1 - 10x_2 + 3x_3 = 37$$
$$3x_1 + 2x_2 - 10x_3 = -10$$

Find **x** using LU decomposition.

Solution

The linear system can be written in matrix form as follows:

$$\begin{bmatrix} 10 & 3 & 4 \\ 2 & -10 & 3 \\ 3 & 2 & -10 \end{bmatrix} \begin{bmatrix} x_1 \\ x_2 \\ x_3 \end{bmatrix} = \begin{bmatrix} 15 \\ 37 \\ -10 \end{bmatrix}$$

$$\mathbf{Ax} = \mathbf{b}$$

From Equation (3.177) we have

$$\mathbf{A} = \mathbf{LU}$$

$$\begin{bmatrix} 10 & 3 & 4 \\ 2 & -10 & 3 \\ 3 & 2 & -10 \end{bmatrix} = \begin{bmatrix} l_{11} & 0 & 0 \\ l_{21} & l_{22} & 0 \\ l_{31} & l_{32} & l_{33} \end{bmatrix} \begin{bmatrix} 1 & u_{12} & u_{13} \\ 0 & 1 & u_{23} \\ 0 & 0 & 1 \end{bmatrix}$$

$$\begin{bmatrix} 10 & 3 & 4 \\ 2 & -10 & 3 \\ 3 & 2 & -10 \end{bmatrix} = \begin{bmatrix} l_{11} & l_{11}u_{12} & l_{11}u_{13} \\ l_{21} & l_{21}u_{12} + l_{22} & l_{21}u_{13} + l_{22}u_{23} \\ l_{31} & l_{31}u_{12} + l_{32} & l_{31}u_{13} + l_{32}u_{23} + l_{33} \end{bmatrix}$$

Column 1: $l_{11} = 10, l_{21} = 2, l_{31} = 3$

Column 2: $l_{11}u_{12} = 3, l_{21}u_{12} + l_{22} = -10, l_{31}u_{12} + l_{32} = 2$

Column 3: $l_{11}u_{13} = 4, l_{21}u_{13} + l_{22}u_{23} = 3, l_{31}u_{13} + l_{32}u_{23} + l_{33} = -10$

From the above equations, we have

$$u_{12} = \frac{3}{10}, \quad l_{22} = -10 - 2\frac{3}{10} = -\frac{106}{10}, \quad l_{32} = 2 - 3\frac{3}{10} = \frac{11}{10}$$

$$u_{13} = \frac{4}{10}, u_{23} = \frac{\left(3 - 2\frac{4}{10}\right)}{\left(-\frac{106}{10}\right)} = -\frac{11}{53}, l_{33} = -10 - 3\frac{4}{10} - \left(\frac{11}{10}\right)\left(-\frac{11}{53}\right) = -\frac{1163}{106}$$

Thus, we have

$$\begin{bmatrix} 10 & 3 & 4 \\ 2 & -10 & 3 \\ 3 & 2 & -10 \end{bmatrix} = \begin{bmatrix} 10 & 0 & 0 \\ 2 & -10.6 & 0 \\ 3 & 1.1 & -10.97 \end{bmatrix} \begin{bmatrix} 1 & 0.3 & 0.4 \\ 0 & 1 & -0.2 \\ 0 & 0 & 1 \end{bmatrix}$$

From Equation (3.180) we have

$$\mathbf{Ly} = \mathbf{b}$$

$$\begin{bmatrix} 10 & 0 & 0 \\ 2 & -10.6 & 0 \\ 3 & 1.1 & -10.97 \end{bmatrix} \begin{bmatrix} y_1 \\ y_2 \\ y_3 \end{bmatrix} = \begin{bmatrix} 15 \\ 37 \\ -10 \end{bmatrix}$$

$$10y_1 = 15, 2y_1 - 10.6y_2 = 37, 3y_1 + 1.1y_2 - 10.97y_3 = -10$$

$$y_1 = 1.5, \quad y_2 = -3.2, \quad y_3 = 1$$

Now, we solve the upper triangular system $\mathbf{y} = \mathbf{Ux}$ as follows:

$$\begin{bmatrix} 1.5 \\ -3.2 \\ 1 \end{bmatrix} = \begin{bmatrix} 1 & 0.3 & 0.4 \\ 0 & 1 & -0.2 \\ 0 & 0 & 1 \end{bmatrix} \begin{bmatrix} x_1 \\ x_2 \\ x_3 \end{bmatrix}$$

$$x_1 + 0.3x_2 + 0.4x_3 = 1.5, \quad x_2 - 0.2x_3 = -3.2, \quad x_3 = 1$$

Therefore, we find $\mathbf{x}$ as follows:

$$x_1 = 2, \quad x_2 = -3, \quad x_3 = 1$$

In general, LU decomposition is not unique and there are many different LU decompositions. For example, $\mathbf{A} = \mathbf{LU} = \mathbf{LDD^{-1}U} = (\mathbf{LD})(\mathbf{D^{-1}U}) = \mathbf{L'U'}$ where $\mathbf{D}$ is a diagonal matrix. $\mathbf{L'U'}$ is another LU decomposition. However, there is a unique LU decomposition if L is a lower unit triangular matrix. Sometimes, LU decomposition does not exist. We can check it by the determinant of the leading principal submatrix. The $k \times k$ leading principal submatrix of a matrix A is found by looking at the upper left $k \times k$ corners. For example, we have the leading principal submatrices as follows:

$$\mathbf{A_1} = a_{11}, \mathbf{A_2} = \begin{bmatrix} a_{11} & a_{12} \\ a_{21} & a_{22} \end{bmatrix}, \dots, \mathbf{A_n} = \begin{bmatrix} a_{11} & a_{12} & \cdots & a_{1n} \\ a_{21} & a_{22} & \cdots & a_{2n} \\ \vdots & \vdots & \ddots & \vdots \\ a_{n1} & a_{n2} & a_{n3} & a_{nn} \end{bmatrix} \qquad (3.183)$$

The LU decompositions exists if and only if $|\mathbf{A_0}| \neq 0, i = 1, \dots, n$.

Example 3.27 *LU Decomposition Existence*
Consider the following two matrices:

$$\mathbf{A} = \begin{bmatrix} 1 & 2 & 4 \\ 2 & 6 & 10 \\ 1 & 4 & 9 \end{bmatrix}, \quad \mathbf{B} = \begin{bmatrix} 1 & -3 & 7 \\ -2 & 6 & 1 \\ 0 & 3 & -2 \end{bmatrix}$$

Find which of these matrices have an LU decomposition.

Solution
In order to check matrix **A**, the leading principal submatrices are

$$\mathbf{A_1} = 1, \mathbf{A_2} = \begin{bmatrix} 1 & 2 \\ 2 & 6 \end{bmatrix}, \mathbf{A_3} = \begin{bmatrix} 1 & 2 & 4 \\ 2 & 6 & 10 \\ 1 & 4 & 9 \end{bmatrix}$$

and the determinants of them are

$$|\mathbf{A_1}| = 1$$

$$|\mathbf{A_2}| = 1 \cdot 6 - 2 \cdot 2 = 2$$

$$|\mathbf{A_3}| = \begin{vmatrix} 6 & 10 \\ 4 & 9 \end{vmatrix} - 2 \begin{vmatrix} 2 & 10 \\ 1 & 9 \end{vmatrix} + 4 \begin{vmatrix} 2 & 6 \\ 1 & 4 \end{vmatrix} = 14 - 2 \cdot 8 + 4 \cdot 2 = 6$$

The LU decomposition of matrix **A** exists because none of these determinants is zero. In order to check matrix **B**, the leading principal submatrices are

$$\mathbf{B_1} = 1, \mathbf{B_2} = \begin{bmatrix} 1 & -3 \\ -2 & 6 \end{bmatrix}, \mathbf{B_3} = \begin{bmatrix} 1 & -3 & 7 \\ -2 & 6 & 1 \\ 0 & 3 & -2 \end{bmatrix}$$

and the determinants of them are

$$|\mathbf{B_1}| = 1$$

$$|\mathbf{B_2}| = 1 \cdot 6 - 3 \cdot 2 = 0$$

$$|\mathbf{B_3}| = \begin{vmatrix} 6 & 1 \\ 3 & -2 \end{vmatrix} + 3 \begin{vmatrix} -2 & 1 \\ 0 & -2 \end{vmatrix} + 7 \begin{vmatrix} -2 & 6 \\ 0 & 3 \end{vmatrix} = -15 + 3 \cdot 4 + 7 \cdot -6 = -45$$

The LU decomposition of the matrix **B** does not exist because $|\mathbf{B_2}| = 0$.

3.3.2 Cholesky Decomposition

In the linear system of the form $\mathbf{Ax} = \mathbf{b}$, Cholesky decomposition is useful if the matrix $\mathbf{A}$ is symmetric and positive definite. We can define Cholesky decomposition as follows:

> **Definition 3.17 Cholesky Decomposition**
>
> The matrix $\mathbf{A}$ is factored by Cholesky decomposition as follows:
>
> $$\mathbf{A} = \mathbf{LL}^T \tag{3.184}$$
>
> where $\mathbf{L}$ is a lower triangular matrix with real and positive diagonal elements.

In some case, Cholesky decomposition is rewritten in the form of $\mathbf{A} = \mathbf{U}^T\mathbf{U}$ where $\mathbf{U}$ is an upper triangular matrix. The advantages of Cholesky decomposition is that we need only a lower triangular to compute Cholesky decomposition. Thus, computation is faster than LU decomposition and less storage is required. However, it works only for symmetric positive definite matrices. As we can observe from Equation (3.184), Cholesky decomposition is composed of a lower triangular matrix $\mathbf{L}$ and its transpose $\mathbf{L}^T$ serving as an upper triangular part. The elements of $\mathbf{L}^T$ are related to the elements of the lower triangular matrix $\mathbf{L}$ as follows:

$$l_{ij}^T = l_{ji} \tag{3.185}$$

The diagonal elements (l_{kk}) of $\mathbf{L}$ are evaluated as follows:

$$l_{kk} = \sqrt{a_{kk} - \sum_{j=1}^{k-1} l_{kj}^2}, k = 1, 2, \ldots, n \tag{3.186}$$

and the other elements ($l_{ik}, i > k$) are

$$l_{ik} = \frac{1}{l_{kk}} \left(a_{ik} - \sum_{j=1}^{k-1} l_{ij} l_{kj} \right) \tag{3.187}$$

When we have a square matrix $\mathbf{A} \in \mathbb{R}^{3 \times 3}$, Equation (3.184) is rewritten as follows:

$$\begin{bmatrix} a_{11} & a_{12} & a_{13} \\ a_{21} & a_{22} & a_{23} \\ a_{31} & a_{32} & a_{33} \end{bmatrix} = \begin{bmatrix} l_{11} & 0 & 0 \\ l_{21} & l_{22} & 0 \\ l_{31} & l_{32} & l_{33} \end{bmatrix} \begin{bmatrix} l_{11} & l_{21} & l_{31} \\ 0 & l_{22} & l_{32} \\ 0 & 0 & l_{33} \end{bmatrix} \tag{3.188}$$

$$\begin{bmatrix} a_{11} & a_{12} & a_{13} \\ a_{21} & a_{22} & a_{23} \\ a_{31} & a_{32} & a_{33} \end{bmatrix} = \begin{bmatrix} l_{11}^2 & l_{21}l_{11} & l_{31}l_{11} \\ l_{21}l_{11} & l_{21}^2 + l_{22}^2 & l_{31}l_{21} + l_{32}l_{22} \\ l_{31}l_{11} & l_{31}l_{21} + l_{32}l_{22} & l_{31}^2 + l_{32}^2 + l_{33}^2 \end{bmatrix} \tag{3.189}$$

Equation (3.189) is symmetric. Thus, Equation (3.189) can be rewritten as follows:

$$\begin{bmatrix} a_{11} & a_{21} & a_{31} \\ a_{21} & a_{22} & a_{32} \\ a_{31} & a_{32} & a_{33} \end{bmatrix} = \begin{bmatrix} l_{11}^2 & l_{21}l_{11} & l_{31}l_{11} \\ l_{21}l_{11} & l_{21}^2 + l_{22}^2 & l_{31}l_{21} + l_{32}l_{22} \\ l_{31}l_{11} & l_{31}l_{21} + l_{32}l_{22} & l_{31}^2 + l_{32}^2 + l_{33}^2 \end{bmatrix} \tag{3.190}$$

From Equations (3.186) and (3.190), we can obtain the diagonal elements as follows:

$$l_{11} = \sqrt{a_{11}}, \ l_{22} = \sqrt{a_{22} - l_{21}^2}, l_{33} = \sqrt{a_{33} - (l_{31}^2 + l_{32}^2)} \tag{3.191}$$

From Equations (3.187) and (3.190), we can obtain the other elements as follows:

$$l_{21} = \frac{1}{l_{11}} a_{21}, \ l_{31} = \frac{1}{l_{11}} a_{31}, l_{32} = \frac{1}{l_{22}} (a_{32} - l_{31} l_{21}) \tag{3.192}$$

Example 3.28   Cholesky Decomposition

Consider the following matrix:

$$A = \begin{bmatrix} 25 & 15 & -5 \\ 15 & 18 & 0 \\ -5 & 0 & 11 \end{bmatrix}$$

Find the Cholesky decomposition of A.

Solution

From Equations (3.186) and (3.191), the diagonal element l_{11} is calculated as follows:

$$l_{11} = \sqrt{a_{11}} = \sqrt{25} = 5$$

From Equations (3.187) and (3.192), the element l_{21} below the diagonal is calculated as follows:

$$l_{21} = \frac{1}{l_{11}} a_{21} = \frac{1}{5} 15 = 3$$

Likewise, we can obtain the elements as follows:

$$l_{22} = \sqrt{a_{22} - l_{21}^2} = \sqrt{18 - 3^2} = 3$$

$$l_{31} = \frac{1}{l_{11}} a_{31} = \frac{1}{5}(-5) = -1$$

$$l_{32} = \frac{1}{l_{22}} (a_{32} - l_{31} l_{21}) = \frac{1}{3}(0 - (-1)(3)) = 1$$

$$l_{33} = \sqrt{a_{33} - (l_{31}^2 + l_{32}^2)} = \sqrt{11 - ((-1)^2 + (1)^2)} = 3$$

Therefore, we have

$$L = \begin{bmatrix} 5 & 0 & 0 \\ 3 & 3 & 0 \\ -1 & 1 & 3 \end{bmatrix}$$

and the Cholesky decomposition of A is

$$\begin{bmatrix} 25 & 15 & -5 \\ 15 & 18 & 0 \\ -5 & 0 & 11 \end{bmatrix} = \begin{bmatrix} 5 & 0 & 0 \\ 3 & 3 & 0 \\ -1 & 1 & 3 \end{bmatrix} \begin{bmatrix} 5 & 3 & -1 \\ 0 & 3 & 1 \\ 0 & 0 & 3 \end{bmatrix}$$

3.3.3   QR Decomposition

Both LU decomposition and Cholesky decomposition are valid for a square matrix. However, the QR decomposition can be used for both rectangular and square matrices.

QR decomposition is a very useful tool for solving linear systems, least squares problems, and so on. We can define QR decomposition as follows:

Definition 3.18 QR Decomposition

Let $\mathbf{A} \in \mathbb{R}^{m \times n}$ be an $m \times n$ matrix with linearly independent columns and $m > n > 1$. The matrix $\mathbf{A}$ can be factored as follows:

$$\mathbf{A} = \mathbf{QR} \tag{3.193}$$

where $\mathbf{Q} \in \mathbb{R}^{m \times n}$ (or $\mathbf{Q} \in \mathbb{R}^{m \times m}$) is an orthogonal matrix ($\mathbf{QQ}^\mathsf{T} = \mathbf{I}$) and $\mathbf{R} \in \mathbb{R}^{n \times n}$ (or $\mathbf{R} \in \mathbb{R}^{m \times n}$) is an upper triangular matrix with non-zero diagonal elements. (Reduced QR: $\mathbf{Q} \in \mathbb{R}^{m \times n}$ and $\mathbf{R} \in \mathbb{R}^{n \times n}$, Full QR: $\mathbf{Q} \in \mathbb{R}^{m \times m}$ and $\mathbf{R} \in \mathbb{R}^{m \times n}$.)

If $\mathbf{A}$ is nonsingular, the QR decomposition is unique. As we solve the linear system using LU decomposition and Cholesky decomposition, the QR decomposition can be used to solve the linear system with a square matrix $\mathbf{A} \in \mathbb{R}^{n \times n}$ as follows:

$$\mathbf{Ax} = \mathbf{b} \tag{3.194}$$

$$\mathbf{QRx} = \mathbf{b} \tag{3.195}$$

$$\mathbf{Rx} = \mathbf{Q}^T \mathbf{b} \tag{3.196}$$

As we can see from Equation (3.196), we firstly compute $\mathbf{y} = \mathbf{Q}^T \mathbf{b}$ and then we solve the equation $\mathbf{Rx} = \mathbf{y}$ by back-substitution. In addition, QR decomposition is useful for solving least squares problems. When the normal equation $\mathbf{Ax} = \mathbf{b}$ is overdetermined ($m > n$) and the columns of $\mathbf{A}$ are linearly independent, $\mathbf{AA}^T$ is nonsingular and the normal equation has a unique solution $\hat{\mathbf{x}} = (\mathbf{A}^T\mathbf{A})^{-1}\mathbf{A}^T\mathbf{b}$, as we reviewed in the least square problem in Section 3.2.2. We call this a full-rank least squares problem and can rewrite the solution of the least square problems using QR decomposition as follows:

$$\hat{\mathbf{x}} = (\mathbf{A}^T\mathbf{A})^{-1}\mathbf{A}^T\mathbf{b} \tag{3.197}$$

$$= ((\mathbf{QR})^T(\mathbf{QR}))^{-1}(\mathbf{QR})^T\mathbf{b} \tag{3.198}$$

$$= (\mathbf{R}^T\mathbf{Q}^T\mathbf{QR})^{-1}\mathbf{R}^T\mathbf{Q}^T\mathbf{b} \tag{3.199}$$

$$= (\mathbf{R}^T\mathbf{R})^{-1}\mathbf{R}^T\mathbf{Q}^T\mathbf{b} \tag{3.200}$$

$$= \mathbf{R}^{-1}\mathbf{R}^{-T}\mathbf{R}^T\mathbf{Q}^T\mathbf{b} \tag{3.201}$$

$$= \mathbf{R}^{-1}\mathbf{Q}^T\mathbf{b} \tag{3.202}$$

There are several algorithms for computing QR decomposition, such as the Gram-Schmidt method, the Modified Gram-Schmidt method, the Householder transformation, and Givens rotation. The Gram-Schmidt methods provide us with the least computational complexity, but it is not recommended in practice because it is sensitive to rounding errors. The Householder transformation uses a simple reflection operation and represents Q as a product of elementary orthogonal matrices. It is widely used in many applications. The Givens rotation (sometimes Jacobi rotation) is a simple two-dimensional rotation. Those algorithms are used to obtain an upper triangular matrix $\mathbf{R}$.

The Gram-Schmidt algorithm computes the matrix $\mathbf{Q}$ and $\mathbf{R}$ in column by column. Equation (3.193) is rewritten as follows:

$$[\mathbf{a_1}\ \mathbf{a_2} \ldots \mathbf{a_n}] = [\mathbf{q_1}\ \mathbf{q_2} \ldots \mathbf{q_n}] \begin{bmatrix} r_{11} & r_{12} & \cdots & r_{1n} \\ 0 & r_{22} & \cdots & r_{2n} \\ \vdots & \vdots & \ddots & \vdots \\ 0 & 0 & 0 & r_{nn} \end{bmatrix} \quad (3.203)$$

We can write down Equation (3.203) as

$$\mathbf{a}_1 = r_{11}\mathbf{q}_1,$$
$$\mathbf{a}_2 = r_{12}\mathbf{q}_1 + r_{22}\mathbf{q}_2,$$
$$\vdots \quad (3.204)$$
$$\mathbf{a}_n = r_{1n}\mathbf{q}_1 + r_{2n}\mathbf{q}_2 + \ldots + r_{nn}\mathbf{q}_n$$

and column vectors of $\mathbf{Q}$ can be obtained as follows:

$$\mathbf{q}_1 = \frac{\mathbf{a}_1}{r_{11}}$$
$$\mathbf{q}_2 = \frac{\mathbf{a}_2 - r_{12}\mathbf{q}_1}{r_{22}}$$
$$\vdots \quad (3.205)$$
$$\mathbf{q}_n = \frac{\mathbf{a_n} - \sum_{i=1}^{n} r_{in}\mathbf{q_i}}{r_{nn}}$$

The column vectors of $\mathbf{Q}$ are orthonormal and each $\mathbf{a}_i$ is a linear combination of previously generated column vectors. The orthonormality gives us the following condition:

$$\mathbf{q}_i^*\mathbf{q}_j = \begin{cases} 0 & \text{when } i \neq j \\ 1 & \text{when } i = j \end{cases} \quad (3.206)$$

Using those conditions, we can obtain r_{11} as follows:

$$\mathbf{q}_1^*\mathbf{q}_1 = \frac{\mathbf{a}_1^*\mathbf{a}_1}{r_{11}^2} = 1 \quad (3.207)$$
$$r_{11} = \sqrt{\mathbf{a}_1^*\mathbf{a}_1} = \|\mathbf{a}_1\| \quad (3.208)$$

r_{12} can be obtained as follows:

$$\mathbf{q}_1^*\mathbf{q}_2 = \frac{\mathbf{q}_1^*\mathbf{a}_2 - r_{12}\mathbf{q}_1^*\mathbf{q}_1}{r_{22}} = 0 \quad (3.209)$$

Since $\mathbf{q}_1^*\mathbf{q}_1 = 1$,

$$r_{12} = \mathbf{q}_1^*\mathbf{a}_2 \quad (3.210)$$

r_{22} can be determined by normalization as follows:

$$\mathbf{q}_2 = \frac{\mathbf{a}_2 - (\mathbf{q}_1^*\mathbf{a}_2)\mathbf{q}_1}{r_{22}} \quad (3.211)$$

Since $\mathbf{q}_2^*\mathbf{q}_2 = 1$ $(\|\mathbf{q}_2\| = 1)$

$$r_{22} = \|\mathbf{a}_2 - (\mathbf{q}_1^*\mathbf{a}_2)\mathbf{q}_1\| \tag{3.212}$$

In a similar way, we can obtain the remaining elements. The Gram-Schmidt algorithm is summarized as follows:

$$r_{ij} = \mathbf{q}_i^*\mathbf{a}_j, \quad i \neq j$$

$$r_{ij} = \left\| \mathbf{a}_j - \sum_{i=1}^{j-1} r_{ij}\mathbf{q}_i \right\|, \quad i = j$$

$$\mathbf{q}_j = \frac{\mathbf{a}_j - \sum_{i=1}^{j-1} r_{ij}\mathbf{q}_i}{r_{jj}} \tag{3.213}$$

Example 3.29 *Gram-Schmidt Algorithm for QR Decomposition*
Consider the following matrix:

$$\mathbf{A} = \begin{bmatrix} 2 & 4 & 0 \\ 0 & 3 & 3 \\ 1 & 0 & 1 \end{bmatrix}$$

Find the QR decomposition of $\mathbf{A}$ using the Gram-Schmidt algorithm.

Solution
From Equation (3.213), we firstly calculate r_{11} as follows:

$$r_{11} = \|\mathbf{a}_1\| = \sqrt{5}$$

and $\mathbf{q}_1$ is calculated as follows:

$$\mathbf{q}_1 = \frac{\mathbf{a}_1}{r_{11}} = \frac{1}{\sqrt{5}} \begin{bmatrix} 2 \\ 0 \\ 1 \end{bmatrix} = \begin{bmatrix} 0.89 \\ 0 \\ 0.45 \end{bmatrix}$$

In the second iteration, r_{12} is calculated as follows:

$$r_{12} = \mathbf{q}_1^*\mathbf{a}_2 = \frac{1}{\sqrt{5}} \begin{bmatrix} 2 & 0 & 1 \end{bmatrix} \begin{bmatrix} 4 \\ 3 \\ 0 \end{bmatrix} = \frac{8}{\sqrt{5}} = 3.58$$

and r_{22} is calculated as follows:

$$r_{22} = \|\mathbf{a}_2 - r_{12}\mathbf{q}_1\| = \left\| \begin{bmatrix} 4 \\ 3 \\ 0 \end{bmatrix} - \frac{8}{\sqrt{5}} \frac{1}{\sqrt{5}} \begin{bmatrix} 2 \\ 0 \\ 1 \end{bmatrix} \right\| = \left\| \begin{bmatrix} 4 \\ 3 \\ 0 \end{bmatrix} - \frac{8}{5} \begin{bmatrix} 2 \\ 0 \\ 1 \end{bmatrix} \right\| = \left\| \begin{bmatrix} 0.8 \\ 3 \\ -1.6 \end{bmatrix} \right\| = 3.5$$

$\mathbf{q}_2$ is calculated as follows:

$$\mathbf{q}_2 = \frac{\mathbf{a}_2 - r_{12}\mathbf{q}_1}{r_{22}} = \frac{1}{3.5}\begin{bmatrix} 0.8 \\ 3 \\ -1.6 \end{bmatrix} = \begin{bmatrix} 0.23 \\ 0.86 \\ -0.46 \end{bmatrix}$$

In the third iteration, we calculate r_{13}, r_{23}, and r_{33} as follows:

$$r_{13} = \mathbf{q}_1^*\mathbf{a}_3 = \frac{1}{\sqrt{5}}\begin{bmatrix} 2 & 0 & 1 \end{bmatrix}\begin{bmatrix} 0 \\ 3 \\ 1 \end{bmatrix} = \frac{1}{\sqrt{5}} = 0.45$$

$$r_{23} = \mathbf{q}_2^*\mathbf{a}_3 = \frac{1}{3.5}\begin{bmatrix} 0.8 & 3 & -1.6 \end{bmatrix}\begin{bmatrix} 0 \\ 3 \\ 1 \end{bmatrix} = 2.1$$

$$r_{33} = \|\mathbf{a}_3 - r_{13}\mathbf{q}_1 - r_{23}\mathbf{q}_2\| = \left\|\begin{bmatrix} 0 \\ 3 \\ 1 \end{bmatrix} - \frac{1}{\sqrt{5}}\frac{1}{\sqrt{5}}\begin{bmatrix} 2 \\ 0 \\ 1 \end{bmatrix} - 2.1\frac{1}{3.5}\begin{bmatrix} 0.8 \\ 3 \\ -1.6 \end{bmatrix}\right\|$$

$$= \left\|\begin{bmatrix} 0 \\ 3 \\ 1 \end{bmatrix} - \frac{1}{5}\begin{bmatrix} 2 \\ 0 \\ 1 \end{bmatrix} - 0.6\begin{bmatrix} 0.8 \\ 3 \\ -1.6 \end{bmatrix}\right\| = \left\|\begin{bmatrix} -0.88 \\ 1.2 \\ 1.76 \end{bmatrix}\right\| = 2.3$$

$\mathbf{q}_3$ is calculated as follows:

$$\mathbf{q}_3 = \frac{\mathbf{a}_3 - r_{13}\mathbf{q}_1 - r_{23}\mathbf{q}_2}{r_{33}} = \frac{1}{2.3}\begin{bmatrix} -0.88 \\ 1.2 \\ 1.76 \end{bmatrix} = \begin{bmatrix} -0.38 \\ 0.52 \\ 0.77 \end{bmatrix}$$

Thus, the QR decomposition of $\mathbf{A}$ is

$$\begin{bmatrix} 2 & 4 & 0 \\ 0 & 3 & 3 \\ 1 & 0 & 1 \end{bmatrix} = \begin{bmatrix} 0.89 & 0.23 & -0.38 \\ 0 & 0.86 & 0.52 \\ 0.45 & -0.46 & 0.77 \end{bmatrix}\begin{bmatrix} \sqrt{5} & 3.58 & 0.45 \\ 0 & 3.5 & 2.1 \\ 0 & 0 & 2.3 \end{bmatrix}$$

We can interpret the Gram-Schmidt algorithm as triangular orthogonalization using a series of transformations $(\mathbf{AR}_1\mathbf{R}_2\ldots\mathbf{R}_{n-1}\mathbf{R}_n = \mathbf{Q})$. An alternative approach to computing QR decomposition is to use orthogonal triangularization by a series of orthonormal transformations. This method is less susceptible to rounding errors as well as faster and more accurate than the Gram-Schmidt algorithm.

The Householder transformation uses orthogonal triangularization as follows:

$$\mathbf{Q}_n\mathbf{Q}_{n-1}\cdots\mathbf{Q}_2\mathbf{Q}_1\mathbf{A} = \mathbf{R} \tag{3.214}$$

$$
\begin{bmatrix} x & x & x & x \\ x & x & x & x \\ x & x & x & x \\ x & x & x & x \end{bmatrix} \xrightarrow{Q_1} \begin{bmatrix} x & x & x & x \\ 0 & x & x & x \\ 0 & x & x & x \\ 0 & x & x & x \end{bmatrix} \xrightarrow{Q_2} \begin{bmatrix} x & x & x & x \\ 0 & x & x & x \\ 0 & 0 & x & x \\ 0 & 0 & x & x \end{bmatrix} \xrightarrow{Q_3} \begin{bmatrix} x & x & x & x \\ 0 & x & x & x \\ 0 & 0 & x & x \\ 0 & 0 & 0 & x \end{bmatrix}
$$
$$
\quad \mathbf{A} \qquad\qquad \mathbf{Q_1 A} \qquad\qquad \mathbf{Q_2 Q_1 A} \qquad\quad \mathbf{Q_3 Q_2 Q_1 A}
$$

Figure 3.9 Concept of Householder transformation.

where $\mathbf{Q}_i$ is unitary. The idea is to reduce columns of $\mathbf{A} \in \mathbb{R}^{4\times4}$ to zero below the main diagonals, as shown in Figure 3.9. Here, x represents a non-zero entry. As we can observe in Figure 3.9, $\mathbf{Q_3 Q_2 Q_1 A} = \mathbf{R}$ and we need to multiply and transpose all the orthogonal matrices to obtain $\mathbf{Q}_i$. Thus, we can obtain $\mathbf{A} = \mathbf{Q_1^T Q_2^T Q_3^T R}$.

Let $\mathbf{Q_1} \in \mathbb{R}^{m\times m}$ be the Householder transformation with respect to the first column of the matrix $\mathbf{A} \in \mathbb{R}^{m\times n}$ as follows:

$$
\mathbf{A^1} = \mathbf{Q_1 A} = \begin{bmatrix} x & x & \cdots & x \\ 0 & x & \cdots & x \\ \vdots & \vdots & \ddots & \vdots \\ 0 & x & x & x \end{bmatrix} \tag{3.215}
$$

Let $\widetilde{\mathbf{Q}}_2 \in \mathbb{R}^{(m-1)\times(m-1)}$ be the Householder transformation with respect to the first column of $\mathbf{A}^1_{2:m\,2:n}$ and $\mathbf{Q_2}$ be of the form as follows:

$$
\mathbf{Q_2} = \begin{bmatrix} 1 & 0 \\ 0 & \widetilde{\mathbf{Q}}_2 \end{bmatrix} \tag{3.216}
$$

and

$$
\mathbf{A^2} = \mathbf{Q_2 Q_1 A} = \begin{bmatrix} x & x & \cdots & x \\ 0 & x & \cdots & x \\ 0 & 0 & \cdots & x \\ \vdots & \vdots & \ddots & \vdots \\ 0 & x & x & x \end{bmatrix} \tag{3.217}
$$

In a similar way, we can construct $\mathbf{Q}_k$ for $k = 1, 2, \ldots, n-1$ as the following form:

$$
\mathbf{Q}_k = \begin{bmatrix} I_{k-1} & 0 \\ 0 & \widetilde{\mathbf{Q}}_k \end{bmatrix} \tag{3.218}
$$

where I_{k-1} is a $(k-1)\times(k-1)$ identity matrix and $\widetilde{\mathbf{Q}}_k$ is a $(m-k+1)\times(n-k+1)$ matrix. We call $\widetilde{\mathbf{Q}}_k$ a Householder reflector. The Household reflector introduces zeros in the lower part of column k as follows:

$$
\mathbf{x} = \begin{bmatrix} x \\ x \\ \vdots \\ x \end{bmatrix}, \quad \widetilde{\mathbf{Q}}_k \mathbf{x} = \begin{bmatrix} \|x\| \\ 0 \\ \vdots \\ 0 \end{bmatrix} = \|x\| e_1 \tag{3.219}
$$

where $e_1 = [1\ 0...0]^T$. We have

$$
\mathbf{A}^k = \mathbf{Q}_k \mathbf{A}^{k-1} \tag{3.220}
$$

and the last iteration results in

$$
\mathbf{A}^{n-1} = \mathbf{Q}_{n-1}\mathbf{Q}_{n-2} \cdots \mathbf{Q}_2 \mathbf{Q}_1 \mathbf{A} \tag{3.221}
$$

which is the upper triangular $\mathbf{R}$. Therefore, the QR decomposition is obtained by $\mathbf{Q} = \mathbf{Q}_1^T \mathbf{Q}_2^T \cdots \mathbf{Q}_{n-1}^T$ and $\mathbf{R} = \mathbf{A}^{n-1}$ as follows:

$$
\mathbf{A} = \mathbf{QR} = \mathbf{Q}_1^T \mathbf{Q}_2^T \cdots \mathbf{Q}_{n-1}^T \mathbf{A}^{n-1} \tag{3.222}
$$

Now, we need to construct the Householder reflector $\widetilde{\mathbf{Q}}_k$. The Householder reflector is a linear transformation reflecting a vector $\mathbf{x}$ across the orthogonal complement $\mathbf{v}_\perp$ for any nonzero vector $\mathbf{v} \in \mathbb{R}^n$. The Householder reflector is

$$
\widetilde{\mathbf{Q}}_k = \mathbf{I} - 2\mathbf{P} = \mathbf{I} - 2\frac{\mathbf{v}\mathbf{v}^T}{\mathbf{v}^T\mathbf{v}} \tag{3.223}
$$

where a projector $\mathbf{P} = \mathbf{v}\mathbf{v}^T/\mathbf{v}^T\mathbf{v}$. $\widetilde{\mathbf{Q}}_k$ is orthogonal and symmetric, $\|\widetilde{\mathbf{Q}}_k\mathbf{x}\| = \|\mathbf{x}\|$ for any vector $\mathbf{x}$, and $\widetilde{\mathbf{Q}}_k\mathbf{x}$ is reflection of $\mathbf{x}$. The vector $\mathbf{v}$ can be expressed as follows:

$$
\mathbf{v} = \mathbf{x} + sign(x(1))\|\mathbf{x}\|e_1 \quad \text{where } sign(x) = \begin{cases} -1, & \text{if } x < 0 \\ 1, & \text{if } x \geq 0 \end{cases} \tag{3.224}
$$

where $x(1)$ is the first element of the vector $\mathbf{x}$.

Example 3.30 *Householder Transformation for QR Decomposition*
Consider the following matrix:

$$
\mathbf{A} = \begin{bmatrix} 1 & -1 & 9 \\ 2 & 1 & 0 \\ 2 & 2 & 0 \end{bmatrix}
$$

Find the upper triangular $\mathbf{R}$ using the Householder transformation.

Solution

Firstly, we compute the reflector $\mathbf{v}_1 = \mathbf{a}_1 + \text{sign}(a_{11})\|\mathbf{a}_1\|e_1$ as follows:

$$\mathbf{v}_1 = \begin{bmatrix} 1 \\ 2 \\ 2 \end{bmatrix} + 3 \begin{bmatrix} 1 \\ 0 \\ 0 \end{bmatrix} = \begin{bmatrix} 4 \\ 2 \\ 2 \end{bmatrix}$$

and the corresponding Householder matrix is calculated by Equation (3.223) as follows:

$$\mathbf{Q}_1 = \mathbf{I} - 2\frac{\mathbf{v}_1 \mathbf{v}_1^T}{\mathbf{v}_1^T \mathbf{v}_1} = \begin{bmatrix} 1 & 0 & 0 \\ 0 & 1 & 0 \\ 0 & 0 & 1 \end{bmatrix} - 2\frac{\begin{bmatrix} 4 \\ 2 \\ 2 \end{bmatrix}\begin{bmatrix} 4 & 2 & 2 \end{bmatrix}}{\begin{bmatrix} 4 & 2 & 2 \end{bmatrix}\begin{bmatrix} 4 \\ 2 \\ 2 \end{bmatrix}} = \begin{bmatrix} 1 & 0 & 0 \\ 0 & 1 & 0 \\ 0 & 0 & 1 \end{bmatrix} - \frac{1}{12}\begin{bmatrix} 16 & 8 & 8 \\ 8 & 4 & 4 \\ 8 & 4 & 4 \end{bmatrix}$$

$$= \begin{bmatrix} -0.5 & -0.67 & -0.67 \\ -0.67 & 0.67 & -0.33 \\ -0.67 & -0.33 & 0.67 \end{bmatrix}$$

We can find $\mathbf{Q}_1\mathbf{A}$ as follows:

$$\mathbf{Q}_1\mathbf{A} = \begin{bmatrix} -0.5 & -0.67 & -0.67 \\ -0.67 & 0.67 & -0.33 \\ -0.67 & -0.33 & 0.67 \end{bmatrix}\begin{bmatrix} 1 & -1 & 9 \\ 2 & 1 & 0 \\ 2 & 2 & 0 \end{bmatrix} = \begin{bmatrix} -3.17 & -1.5 & -4.5 \\ 0 & 0.67 & -6 \\ 0 & 1.67 & -6 \end{bmatrix}$$

In the next iteration, we have

$$\mathbf{A}^1 = \begin{bmatrix} 0.67 & -6 \\ 1.67 & -6 \end{bmatrix}$$

and we compute the reflector $\mathbf{v}_2$ as follows:

$$\mathbf{v}_2 = \begin{bmatrix} 0.67 \\ 1.67 \end{bmatrix} + 1.8 \begin{bmatrix} 1 \\ 0 \end{bmatrix} = \begin{bmatrix} 2.47 \\ 1.67 \end{bmatrix}$$

The corresponding Householder matrix is calculated as follows:

$$\tilde{\mathbf{Q}}_2 = \mathbf{I} - 2\frac{\mathbf{v}_2\mathbf{v}_2^T}{\mathbf{v}_2^T\mathbf{v}_2} = \begin{bmatrix} 1 & 0 \\ 0 & 1 \end{bmatrix} - 2\frac{\begin{bmatrix} 2.47 \\ 1.67 \end{bmatrix}\begin{bmatrix} 2.47 & 1.67 \end{bmatrix}}{\begin{bmatrix} 2.47 & 1.67 \end{bmatrix}\begin{bmatrix} 2.47 \\ 1.67 \end{bmatrix}} = \begin{bmatrix} 1 & 0 \\ 0 & 1 \end{bmatrix} - \frac{2}{8.89}\begin{bmatrix} 6.1 & 4.12 \\ 4.12 & 2.79 \end{bmatrix}$$

$$= \begin{bmatrix} -0.37 & -0.93 \\ -0.93 & 0.37 \end{bmatrix}$$

$$\mathbf{Q}_2 = \begin{bmatrix} 1 & 0 & 0 \\ 0 & -0.37 & -0.93 \\ 0 & -0.93 & 0.37 \end{bmatrix}$$

Thus, we find Q_2Q_1A as follows:

$$Q_2Q_1A = \begin{bmatrix} 1 & 0 & 0 \\ 0 & -0.37 & -0.93 \\ 0 & -0.93 & 0.37 \end{bmatrix} \begin{bmatrix} -3.17 & -1.5 & -4.5 \\ 0 & 0.67 & -6 \\ 0 & 1.67 & -6 \end{bmatrix} = \begin{bmatrix} -3.17 & -1.5 & -4.5 \\ 0 & -1.8 & 7.8 \\ 0 & 0 & 3.36 \end{bmatrix}$$

In the next iteration, we have

$$A^2 = [3.36]$$

and we compute the reflector v_3 as follows:

$$v_3 = [3.36] + 3.36[1] = [6.72]$$

The corresponding Householder matrix is calculated as follows:

$$\widetilde{Q}_3 = I - 2\frac{v_3 v_3^T}{v_3^T v_3} = [1] - 2\frac{[6.72][6.72]}{[6.72][6.72]} = [-1]$$

$$Q_3 = \begin{bmatrix} 1 & 0 & 0 \\ 0 & 1 & 0 \\ 0 & 0 & -1 \end{bmatrix}$$

Thus, we finally find $Q_3Q_2Q_1A$ as follows:

$$Q_3Q_2Q_1A = \begin{bmatrix} 1 & 0 & 0 \\ 0 & 1 & 0 \\ 0 & 0 & -1 \end{bmatrix} \begin{bmatrix} -3.17 & -1.5 & -4.5 \\ 0 & -1.8 & 7.8 \\ 0 & 0 & 3.36 \end{bmatrix} = \begin{bmatrix} -3.17 & -1.5 & -4.5 \\ 0 & -1.8 & 7.8 \\ 0 & 0 & -3.36 \end{bmatrix} = R$$

3.3.4 SVD Decomposition

SVD is a very useful tool in wireless communications. In particular, the MIMO channel can be decomposed into independent signal paths by SVD. We can calculate the capacity of MIMO systems by signal covariance matrix. The SVD is defined as follows:

Definition 3.19 SVD

The SVD is the factorization of a rectangular matrix $A \in \mathbb{R}^{m \times n}$ into the product of three matrices: an orthogonal matrix $U \in \mathbb{R}^{m \times m}$, a diagonal matrix $\Sigma \in \mathbb{R}^{m \times n}$, and the transpose of an orthogonal matrix $V \in \mathbb{R}^{n \times n}$. The SVD is expressed as follows:

$$A = U\Sigma V^T \tag{3.225}$$

where $UU^T = I$ and $V^TV = I$.

The columns of U and V are orthonormal eigenvectors of AA^T and A^TA, respectively. The matrix U is called a left singular vector matrix and the matrix V is called a right singular vector matrix. The matrices U and V are not uniquely determined by A. The matrix $\Sigma \in \mathbb{R}^{m \times n}$ is a diagonal matrix containing diagonal elements $\sigma_1, \sigma_2, \ldots, \sigma_p$. The scalars σ_i are uniquely determined by $\mathbf{A}$ and $\sigma_1 \geq \sigma_2 \geq \ldots \geq \sigma_p$ with $p = \min(m, n)$. We call them singular values of $\mathbf{A}$, and the diagonal matrix can be expressed as follows:

$$\Sigma = \begin{bmatrix} \sigma_1 & 0 & \cdots & 0 & 0 & \cdots & 0 \\ 0 & \sigma_2 & \cdots & 0 & 0 & \cdots & 0 \\ \vdots & \vdots & \ddots & \vdots & \vdots & \ddots & \vdots \\ 0 & 0 & 0 & \sigma_m & 0 & \cdots & 0 \end{bmatrix}, \quad \text{when } m \leq n \tag{3.226}$$

$$\Sigma = \begin{bmatrix} \sigma_1 & 0 & \cdots & 0 \\ 0 & \sigma_2 & \cdots & 0 \\ \vdots & \vdots & \ddots & \vdots \\ 0 & 0 & 0 & \sigma_n \\ 0 & 0 & \cdots & 0 \\ \vdots & \vdots & \ddots & \vdots \\ 0 & 0 & \cdots & 0 \end{bmatrix}, \quad \text{when } m \geq n \tag{3.227}$$

or

$$\Sigma = \begin{bmatrix} \sigma_1 & 0 & \cdots & 0 \\ 0 & \sigma_2 & \cdots & 0 \\ 0 & 0 & \ddots & 0 \\ \vdots & \vdots & \sigma_p & \vdots \\ 0 & 0 & \cdots & 0 \end{bmatrix}, \quad \text{where } p = \min(m, n) \tag{3.228}$$

Equation (3.225) has the following matrix structure:

$$\mathbf{A} = \mathbf{U}\Sigma\mathbf{V}^T = \begin{bmatrix} \mathbf{u_1} & \mathbf{u_2} & \cdots & \mathbf{u_m} \end{bmatrix} \begin{bmatrix} \sigma_1 & 0 & \cdots & 0 \\ 0 & \sigma_2 & \cdots & 0 \\ 0 & 0 & \ddots & 0 \\ \vdots & \vdots & \sigma_p & \vdots \\ 0 & 0 & \cdots & 0 \end{bmatrix} \begin{bmatrix} \mathbf{v}_1^T \\ \mathbf{v}_2^T \\ \vdots \\ \mathbf{v}_n^T \end{bmatrix} \tag{3.229}$$

If matrix A is symmetric positive definite, its eigenvectors are orthogonal and the SVD is identical to the eigenvalue decomposition. Equation (3.229) can be rewritten as follows:

$$\mathbf{A} = \mathbf{Q}\Sigma\mathbf{Q}^T \tag{3.230}$$

where $\mathbf{Q} = \mathbf{U} = \mathbf{V}$. Equation (3.230) is called the eigenvalue decomposition. It is only defined for square matrices and also does not use an orthonormal basis. This is a special case of the SVD.

The SVD is based on the properties of the eigenvalues of $\mathbf{A}^T\mathbf{A}$ and $\mathbf{A}\mathbf{A}^T$. If λ is an eigenvalue and $\mathbf{x}$ is the corresponding eigenvector of $\mathbf{A}^T\mathbf{A}$, we have

$$\mathbf{A}^T\mathbf{A}\mathbf{x} = \lambda\mathbf{x} \tag{3.231}$$

$$(\mathbf{A}^T\mathbf{A} - \lambda)\mathbf{x} = 0 \tag{3.232}$$

In a matrix form, we have

$$(\mathbf{A}^T\mathbf{A} - \lambda\mathbf{I})\mathbf{x} = 0 \tag{3.233}$$

and the SVD finds eigenvalues satisfying the following equation:

$$|\mathbf{A}^T\mathbf{A} - \lambda\mathbf{I}| = 0. \tag{3.234}$$

This determinant calculation produces an nth degree polynomial in the variable λ. This polynomial is called the characteristic polynomial. Let $\mathbf{v}_i$ be an orthonormal basis for $\mathbb{R}^n$ consisting of eigenvectors of $\mathbf{A}^T\mathbf{A}$ and also let λ_i be the corresponding eigenvalues of $\mathbf{A}^T\mathbf{A}$ where $1 \leq i \leq n$. We have

$$\begin{aligned} \mathbf{A}\mathbf{v}_i{}^2 &= (\mathbf{A}\mathbf{v}_i)^T\mathbf{A}\mathbf{v}_i \\ &= \mathbf{v}_i^T\mathbf{A}^T\mathbf{A}\mathbf{v}_i \end{aligned} \tag{3.235}$$

and we can rewrite Equation (3.235) as follows:

$$\|\mathbf{A}\mathbf{v}_i\|^2 = \mathbf{v}_i^T\lambda_i\mathbf{v}_i = \lambda_i \tag{3.236}$$

because $\mathbf{v}_i$ is an eigenvector of $\mathbf{A}^T\mathbf{A}$ and a unit vector. We call $\mathbf{v}_i$ a singular vector of the matrix $\mathbf{A}$. The eigenvalues are arranged as $\lambda_1 \geq \dots \geq \lambda_n \geq 0$. The singular values σ_i of the matrix $\mathbf{A}$ are the square roots of the eigenvalues λ_i of $\mathbf{A}^T\mathbf{A}$ as follows:

$$\sigma_i = \sqrt{\lambda_i}, \ 1 \leq i \leq n \tag{3.237}$$

In addition, we can interpret that the singular values of the matrix A are the lengths of the vectors $\mathbf{A}\mathbf{v}_i$. Now, we find an orthogonal basis for the row space which is transformed to an orthogonal basis for the column space. The Gram-Schmidt algorithm is a useful tool to find an orthogonal basis. Thus, we can formulate the problem as follows:

$$\mathbf{A}[\mathbf{v}_1\,\mathbf{v}_2\dots\mathbf{v}_p] = [\mathbf{u}_1\mathbf{u}_2\dots\mathbf{u}_p]\begin{bmatrix} \sigma_1 & 0 & \cdots & 0 \\ 0 & \sigma_2 & \cdots & 0 \\ \vdots & \vdots & \ddots & \vdots \\ 0 & 0 & 0 & \sigma_p \end{bmatrix} = [\sigma_1\mathbf{u}_1\,\sigma_2\mathbf{u}_2\dots\sigma_p\mathbf{u}_p] \tag{3.238}$$

where $\mathbf{v}_i$ and $\mathbf{u}_i$ are an orthonormal basis for the row space of the matrix $\mathbf{A}$ and an orthonormal basis for the column space of the matrix $\mathbf{A}$, respectively. If we add $\mathbf{v}_{p+1}, \dots, \mathbf{v}_n$ in the nullspace of the matrix A, the diagonal elements $\sigma_{p+1}, \dots, \sigma_n$ will be zero. We have the following equation:

$$\mathbf{AV} = \mathbf{U\Sigma} \tag{3.239}$$

The properties of the SVD can be summarized as follows:

Property 3.14 Properties of the SVD

(i) Non-zero eigenvalues of $\mathbf{A}^T\mathbf{A}$ are non-zero singular values and eigenvectors are $\mathbf{v}_i$.
(ii) Non-zero eigenvalues of $\mathbf{AA}^T$ are non-zero singular values and eigenvectors are $\mathbf{u}_i$.
(iii) The rank of the matrix $\mathbf{A}$ is given by the number of non-zero singular values p.
(iv) Range($\mathbf{A}$) = $\langle\mathbf{u}_1, \dots, \mathbf{u}_p\rangle$ and null($\mathbf{A}$) = $\langle\mathbf{v}_{p+1}, \dots, \mathbf{v}_n\rangle$.
(v) If $\mathbf{A} = \mathbf{A}^T$, singular values of $\mathbf{A}$ are the absolute values of the eigenvalues of $\mathbf{A}$.
(vi) If the matrix $\mathbf{A}$ is square, $|\det(\mathbf{A})| = \prod_{i=1}^m \sigma_i$.

Example 3.31 *SVD Decomposition*

Consider the following matrix:

$$\mathbf{A} = \begin{bmatrix} -1 & 3 & 1 \\ 3 & 1 & 1 \end{bmatrix}$$

Find the SVD of $\mathbf{A}$.

Solution

Firstly, we find the eigenvalues and corresponding eigenvectors of $\mathbf{A}^T\mathbf{A}$. The transpose of $\mathbf{A}$ is

$$\mathbf{A}^T = \begin{bmatrix} -1 & 3 \\ 3 & 1 \\ 1 & 1 \end{bmatrix}$$

and $\mathbf{A}^T\mathbf{A}$ is

$$\mathbf{A}^T\mathbf{A} = \begin{bmatrix} -1 & 3 \\ 3 & 1 \\ 1 & 1 \end{bmatrix} \begin{bmatrix} -1 & 3 & 1 \\ 3 & 1 & 1 \end{bmatrix} = \begin{bmatrix} 10 & 0 & 2 \\ 0 & 10 & 4 \\ 2 & 4 & 2 \end{bmatrix}$$

This matrix gives us the eigenvectors $\mathbf{v}_i$ and the singular values σ_i. The eigenvalues and corresponding eigenvectors of $\mathbf{A}^T\mathbf{A}$ are calculated as follows:

$$\begin{bmatrix} 10 & 0 & 2 \\ 0 & 10 & 4 \\ 2 & 4 & 2 \end{bmatrix} \begin{bmatrix} x_1 \\ x_2 \\ x_3 \end{bmatrix} = \lambda \begin{bmatrix} x_1 \\ x_2 \\ x_3 \end{bmatrix}$$

$$10x_1 + 2x_3 = \lambda x_1$$

$$10x_2 + 4x_3 = \lambda x_2$$

$$2x_1 + 4x_2 + 2x_3 = \lambda x_3$$

$$(10 - \lambda)x_1 + 2x_3 = 0$$

$$(10 - \lambda)x_2 + 4x_3 = 0$$

$$2x_1 + 4x_2 + (2 - \lambda)x_3 = 0$$

$$\begin{bmatrix} 10 - \lambda & 0 & 2 \\ 0 & 10 - \lambda & 4 \\ 2 & 4 & 2 - \lambda \end{bmatrix} \begin{bmatrix} x_1 \\ x_2 \\ x_3 \end{bmatrix} = 0$$

We can solve these equations by setting the determinant of the coefficient matrix to zero as follows:

$$\begin{vmatrix} 10 - \lambda & 0 & 2 \\ 0 & 10 - \lambda & 4 \\ 2 & 4 & 2 - \lambda \end{vmatrix} = 0$$

$$(10 - \lambda) \begin{vmatrix} 10 - \lambda & 4 \\ 4 & 2 - \lambda \end{vmatrix} + 2 \begin{vmatrix} 0 & 10 - \lambda \\ 2 & 4 \end{vmatrix} = 0$$

$$(10 - \lambda)((10 - \lambda)(2 - \lambda) - 4 \cdot 4) + 2(0 \cdot 4 - 2(10 - \lambda)) = 0$$

$$(10 - \lambda)(10 - \lambda)(2 - \lambda) - 16(10 - \lambda) - 4(10 - \lambda) = 0$$

$$(10 - \lambda)(10 - \lambda)(2 - \lambda) - 20(10 - \lambda) = 0$$

$$(10 - \lambda)((10 - \lambda)(2 - \lambda) - 20) = 0$$

$$(10 - \lambda)(12 - \lambda)\lambda = 0$$

Thus, the eigenvalues of $A^T A$ are

$$\lambda = 10, \quad \lambda = 12, \quad \lambda = 0$$

We have three eigenvalues for $A^T A$ because it is a third-degree polynomial. These values can be used to find the eigenvector. When $\lambda = 10$, we have

$$2x_3 = 0$$

$$4x_3 = 0$$

$$2x_1 + 4x_2 - 8x_3 = 0$$

$$x_1 = -2x_2$$

$$x_3 = 0$$

These equations are a ratio of x_1 and x_2, and we choose x_1 and x_2 such that the elements of the diagonal matrix are the square roots of the eigenvalues. Thus, we have the eigenvectors $v_1 = [2 - 1\ 0]$ corresponding to the eigenvalues $\lambda = 10$. When $\lambda = 12$, we have

$$-2x_1 + 2x_3 = 0$$

$$-2x_2 + 4x_3 = 0$$

$$2x_1 + 4x_2 - 10x_3 = 0$$

From the above equations, we have the eigenvectors $v_2 = [1\ 2\ 1]$ corresponding to the eigenvalues $\lambda = 12$. When $\lambda = 0$, we have

$$10x_1 + 2x_3 = 0$$

$$10x_2 + 4x_3 = 0$$

$$2x_1 + 4x_2 + 2x_3 = 0$$

From the above equations, we have the eigenvectors $v_3 = [1\ 2 - 5]$ corresponding to the eigenvalues $\lambda = 0$. The eigenvectors become column vectors of the matrix U in decreasing order. Namely, the eigenvector with the largest eigenvalue is placed in the first column and the eigenvector with the smallest eigenvalue is placed in the last column. Thus, we have the matrix

$$\begin{bmatrix} v_2 & v_1 & v_3 \end{bmatrix} = \begin{bmatrix} v_1' & v_2' & v_3' \end{bmatrix} = \begin{bmatrix} 1 & 2 & 1 \\ 2 & -1 & 2 \\ 1 & 0 & -5 \end{bmatrix}$$

In order to obtain an orthonormal basis, we use the Gram-Schmidt algorithm as follows:

$$\mathbf{e}_1 = \frac{\mathbf{v}_1'}{\|\mathbf{v}_1'\|} = \begin{bmatrix} 1/\sqrt{6} \\ 2/\sqrt{6} \\ 1/\sqrt{6} \end{bmatrix}$$

$$\mathbf{w}_2 = \mathbf{v}_2' - \frac{\langle \mathbf{v}_1', \mathbf{v}_2' \rangle}{\langle \mathbf{v}_1', \mathbf{v}_1' \rangle} \mathbf{v}_1' = \begin{bmatrix} 2 \\ -1 \\ 0 \end{bmatrix} - \frac{0}{6} \begin{bmatrix} 1 \\ 2 \\ 1 \end{bmatrix} = \begin{bmatrix} 2 \\ -1 \\ 0 \end{bmatrix}$$

$$\mathbf{e}_2 = \frac{\mathbf{w}_2}{\|\mathbf{w}_2\|} = \begin{bmatrix} 2/\sqrt{5} \\ -1/\sqrt{5} \\ 0 \end{bmatrix}$$

$$\mathbf{w}_3 = \mathbf{v}_3' - \frac{\langle \mathbf{v}_1', \mathbf{v}_3' \rangle}{\langle \mathbf{v}_1', \mathbf{v}_1' \rangle} \mathbf{v}_3' - \frac{\langle \mathbf{w}_2, \mathbf{v}_3' \rangle}{\langle \mathbf{w}_2, \mathbf{w}_2 \rangle} \mathbf{v}_3' = \begin{bmatrix} 1 \\ 2 \\ -5 \end{bmatrix} - \frac{0}{6} \begin{bmatrix} 1 \\ 2 \\ -5 \end{bmatrix} - \frac{0}{5} \begin{bmatrix} 1 \\ 2 \\ -5 \end{bmatrix} = \begin{bmatrix} 1 \\ 2 \\ -5 \end{bmatrix}$$

$$\mathbf{e}_3 = \frac{\mathbf{w}_3}{\|\mathbf{w}_3\|} = \begin{bmatrix} 1/\sqrt{30} \\ 2/\sqrt{30} \\ -5/\sqrt{30} \end{bmatrix}$$

Thus, we obtain

$$\mathbf{V} = \begin{bmatrix} 1/\sqrt{6} & 2/\sqrt{5} & 1/\sqrt{30} \\ 2/\sqrt{6} & -1/\sqrt{5} & 2/\sqrt{30} \\ 1/\sqrt{6} & 0 & -5/\sqrt{30} \end{bmatrix}$$

and its transpose is

$$\mathbf{V}^T = \begin{bmatrix} 1/\sqrt{6} & 2/\sqrt{6} & 1/\sqrt{6} \\ 2/\sqrt{5} & -1/\sqrt{5} & 0 \\ 1/\sqrt{30} & 2/\sqrt{30} & -5/\sqrt{30} \end{bmatrix}$$

We find singular values as follows:

$$\sigma_1 = \sqrt{12} = 2\sqrt{3}, \quad \sigma_2 = \sqrt{10}, \quad \sigma_3 = \sqrt{10} = 0$$

and the non-zero singular values are the diagonal elements of the matrix $\mathbf{D}$ as follows:

$$\mathbf{D} = \begin{bmatrix} 2\sqrt{3} & 0 \\ 0 & \sqrt{10} \end{bmatrix}$$

The diagonal matrix $\mathbf{\Sigma}$ is composed of the matrix $\mathbf{D}$ in the upper left corner and zeros in the other elements as follows:

$$\mathbf{\Sigma} = \begin{bmatrix} 2\sqrt{3} & 0 & 0 \\ 0 & \sqrt{10} & 0 \end{bmatrix}$$

The matrix $\mathbf{A}$ has two non-zero singular values and the rank of $\mathbf{A}$ is 2. The column vectors $\mathbf{u}_i$ of $\mathbf{U}$ are obtained from normalized $\mathbf{A}\mathbf{v}_i$ as follows:

$$\mathbf{u}_i = \frac{1}{\|\mathbf{A}\mathbf{v}_i\|}\mathbf{A}\mathbf{v}_i = \frac{1}{\sigma_i}\mathbf{A}\mathbf{v}_i$$

Thus, we have

$$\mathbf{u}_1 = \frac{1}{2\sqrt{3}}\begin{bmatrix} -1 & 3 & 1 \\ 3 & 1 & 1 \end{bmatrix}\begin{bmatrix} 1/\sqrt{6} \\ 2/\sqrt{6} \\ 1/\sqrt{6} \end{bmatrix} = \begin{bmatrix} 1/\sqrt{2} \\ 1/\sqrt{2} \end{bmatrix}$$

$$\mathbf{u}_2 = \frac{1}{\sqrt{10}}\begin{bmatrix} -1 & 3 & 1 \\ 3 & 1 & 1 \end{bmatrix}\begin{bmatrix} 2/\sqrt{5} \\ -1/\sqrt{5} \\ 0 \end{bmatrix} = \begin{bmatrix} -1/\sqrt{2} \\ 1/\sqrt{2} \end{bmatrix}$$

and obtain

$$\mathbf{U} = \begin{bmatrix} 1/\sqrt{2} & -1/\sqrt{2} \\ 1/\sqrt{2} & 1/\sqrt{2} \end{bmatrix}$$

Therefore, the SVD of the matrix $\mathbf{A}$ is

$$\mathbf{A} = \mathbf{U}\mathbf{\Sigma}\mathbf{V}^T$$

$$\begin{bmatrix} -1 & 3 & 1 \\ 3 & 1 & 1 \end{bmatrix} = \begin{bmatrix} 1/\sqrt{2} & -1/\sqrt{2} \\ 1/\sqrt{2} & 1/\sqrt{2} \end{bmatrix}\begin{bmatrix} 2\sqrt{3} & 0 & 0 \\ 0 & \sqrt{10} & 0 \end{bmatrix}\begin{bmatrix} 1/\sqrt{6} & 2/\sqrt{6} & 1/\sqrt{6} \\ 2/\sqrt{5} & -1/\sqrt{5} & 0 \\ 1/\sqrt{30} & 2/\sqrt{30} & -5/\sqrt{30} \end{bmatrix}$$

Summary 3.7 Matrix Factorization

1) Most matrix computation from original data is not easy to calculate in an explicit way. Matrix factorization (or decomposition) allows us to rephrase some matrix forms in such a way that they can be solved more easily.

2) A square matrix $\mathbf{A}$ can be factored into the product of a lower triangular matrix $\mathbf{L} \in \mathbb{R}^{n \times n}$ and an upper triangular matrix $\mathbf{U} \in \mathbb{R}^{n \times n}$ as follows:

$$\mathbf{A} = \mathbf{L}\mathbf{U}$$

where $\mathbf{A}$, $\mathbf{L}$ and $\mathbf{U}$ are nonsingular.

3) The matrix $\mathbf{A}$ is factored by Cholesky decomposition as follows:

$$\mathbf{A} = \mathbf{L}\mathbf{L}^T$$

where $\mathbf{L}$ is a lower triangular matrix with real and positive diagonal elements.

(Continued)

4) Let $A \in \mathbb{R}^{m \times n}$ be an $m \times n$ matrix with linearly independent columns and $m > n > 1$. The matrix A can be factored as follows:

$$A = QR$$

where $Q \in \mathbb{R}^{m \times n}$ (or $Q \in \mathbb{R}^{m \times m}$) is an orthogonal matrix ($QQ^T = I$) and $R \in \mathbb{R}^{n \times n}$ (or $R \in \mathbb{R}^{m \times n}$) is an upper triangular matrix with non-zero diagonal elements.

5) The SVD is the factorization of a rectangular matrix $A \in \mathbb{R}^{m \times n}$ into the product of three matrices: an orthogonal matrix $U \in \mathbb{R}^{m \times m}$, a diagonal matrix $\Sigma \in \mathbb{R}^{m \times n}$, and the transpose of an orthogonal matrix $V \in \mathbb{R}^{n \times n}$. The SVD is expressed as follows:

$$A = U\Sigma V^T$$

where $UU^T = I$ and $V^T V = I$.

Problems

3.1 Compare Shannon's communication architecture with 5G communication architecture.

3.2 For $\mathbb{R}^3$, a vector x is a 3-tuple of real number. When $x, y \in \mathbb{R}^3$ and

$$x = \begin{bmatrix} 1 \\ 3 \\ 7 \end{bmatrix} \text{ and } y = \begin{bmatrix} -3 \\ 5 \\ 11 \end{bmatrix},$$

find $x + 4y$ and $3x + 5y$ and represent $x, y, x - y$ geometrically.

3.3 Let $V = \{(1, 3), (2, 5)\}$ be in $\mathbb{R}^2$. Show whether or not the vector $(4, 10) \in \text{span}(V)$.

3.4 For finite-dimensional vectors $x, y \in \mathbb{R}^3$, $x = [1\ 2\ 5]^T$, $y = [2\ 7\ 9]^T$, find the inner product $\langle x, y \rangle$.

3.5 For finite-dimensional vectors $x, y \in \mathbb{R}^3$, $x = [2\ 5\ 7]^T$, $y = [1\ 6\ 9]^T$, find the angle between two vectors.

3.6 For finite-dimensional variables $y, z \in \mathbb{R}$, $x^2 + y^2 + z^2 = 1$, find the maximum of $x + 2y + 5z$.

3.7 Let S be an inner product space with elements x, y, and $z \in \mathbb{R}^3$. The elements are

$$x = [1\ 5\ 7]^T, y = [1\ 6\ -2]^T, z = [2\ 8\ 3]^T.$$

Show whether or not the vectors are orthogonal.

3.8 Prove that a set of vectors is linear dependent if and only if one of them can be expressed by a linear combination.

3.9 Let $\mathbf{x}$ and $\mathbf{y}$ be vector in an inner product space $\mathbb{R}$. Prove the Cauchy-Schwarz inequality $\|\mathbf{x} + \mathbf{y}\| \leq \|\mathbf{x}\| + \|\mathbf{y}\|$.

3.10 Let S be a normed vector space with elements $\mathbf{x}$ and $\mathbf{y}$. Prove that $\|\mathbf{x} - \mathbf{y}\| \geq |\|\mathbf{x}\| - \|\mathbf{y}\||$ for for all $\mathbf{x}, \mathbf{y} \in S$.

3.11 Let $T : \mathbb{R}^3 \to \mathbb{R}^2$ be defined by

$$T\left(\begin{bmatrix} x_1 \\ x_2 \\ x_3 \end{bmatrix}\right) = \begin{bmatrix} 8x_1 - 5x_3 \\ 3x_1 + 7x_2 \end{bmatrix}.$$

Verify that T is a linear transformation.

3.12 Consider $U = \{\mathbf{p}_1, \mathbf{p}_2\}$ where $\mathbf{p}_1 = [1\ 0\ 1]^T$ and $\mathbf{p}_2 = [2\ 1\ 0]^T$ in $\mathbb{R}^3$ and a vector $\mathbf{x} = [1\ 5\ 3]^T \in \mathbb{R}^3$. Find the approximation vector $\hat{\mathbf{x}}$.

3.13 Let $\mathbf{A} \in \mathbb{R}^{3 \times 2}$ and $\mathbf{b} \in \mathbb{R}^3$ and

$$\mathbf{A} = \begin{bmatrix} 1 & 3 \\ -2 & 0 \\ 4 & 9 \end{bmatrix} \text{ and } \mathbf{b} = \begin{bmatrix} 3 \\ 1 \\ 5 \end{bmatrix}.$$

Find the vector $\mathbf{x}$ of the normal equation $\mathbf{A}\mathbf{x} = \mathbf{b}$.

3.14 Consider 10 paired data points $(1, 0.5), (3, 5.5), (5, 7.4), (7, 11), (9, 14.5)\ (11, 16)\ (13, 19.5)\ (15, 22)\ (17, 25)\ (19, 27)$ and the paired data satisfy a linear model. Find β_0 and β_1 of a linear model and compare the paired data and the linear model.

3.15 In Problem 3.14, the first 5 data points are fairly accurate but the next 5 data points are known to be corrupted by noise. When giving 1.5 weight to the first 5 data points, find a linear model and compare them with the result of Problem 3.14.

3.16 Let a random variable X have pdf $f_X(x) = x^3/2$ and range $[0, 3]$. Find the expected value and variance.

3.17 Let a random variable X have pdf $f_X(x) = x^2/2$ and range $[1, 5]$. Find the expected value and variance.

3.18 Consider two continuous random variables X and Y with the following joint pdf:

$$f_{XY}(x, y) = x^2 + y/2, 0 \leq x \leq 1, 0 \leq y \leq 1.$$

Find $P\left(0 \leq X \leq \frac{1}{2}, 0 \leq Y \leq \frac{1}{2}\right)$, the marginal pdf $f_X(x)$ and $f_Y(y)$, and the conditional pdf of X given Y.

3.19 In Example 3.19, compare the Bayesian decision rule with other decision rules such as a posterior decision rule.

3.20 Consider a signal $x_i \sim \mathcal{N}(0, 1)$ in white Gaussian noise (WGN) as follows:

$$y_i = x_i + w_i, \quad i = 0, 1, \ldots, N-1$$

where $w_i \sim \mathcal{N}(0, \sigma^2)$ is a noise with known pdf. Find the MMSE estimator.

3.21 Consider continuous random variables $X_1, X_2, \ldots, X_n$ with a normal distribution with unknown mean μ and variance σ^2 are independent and identically distributed. Find the ML estimator.

3.22 Consider $X_1, X_2, \ldots, X_n$ are represented by a uniform distribution $U(a,b)$. Find the ML estimator for a and b.

3.23 Consider two independent measurements (x_1, x_2) of $\mathbf{x}$ and the errors are described as $p(x_1|\theta) \sim \mathcal{N}(\theta, \sigma_1^2)$ and $p(x_2|\theta) \sim \mathcal{N}(\theta, \sigma_2^2)$. Find the ML estimator of $\mathbf{x}$.

3.24 Compare MAP and ML. Under which condition is ML or MAP estimation better?

3.25 Consider a square matrix $\mathbf{A} \in \mathbb{R}^{3 \times 3}$ as follows:

$$\mathbf{A} = \begin{bmatrix} 4 & 3 & 9 \\ 2 & -2 & 10 \\ 8 & 1 & -1 \end{bmatrix}$$

Find the LU decomposition of $\mathbf{A}$.

3.26 Consider the following linear system:

$$x_1 + 5x_2 - 2x_3 = 10$$
$$3x_1 - 15x_2 + 2x_3 = 21$$
$$5x_1 - 7x_2 - 3x_3 = -9$$

Find $\mathbf{x}$ using LU decomposition.

3.27 Consider the following matrix:

$$\mathbf{A} = \begin{bmatrix} 21 & -10 & 7 \\ -10 & 6 & 1 \\ 7 & 1 & 12 \end{bmatrix}$$

Find the Cholesky decomposition of $\mathbf{A}$.

3.28 Consider the following matrix:

$$A = \begin{bmatrix} 6 & 7 & 0 \\ 0 & 2 & 2 \\ 8 & 1 & 8 \end{bmatrix}$$

Find the QR decomposition of **A** using the Gram-Schmidt algorithm.

3.29 Consider same matrix A as Problem 3.28. Find the QR decomposition of **A** using the Householder transformation.

3.30 Consider the following matrix:

$$A = \begin{bmatrix} -10 & 7 & 1 \\ 5 & 1 & 2 \end{bmatrix}$$

Find the SVD of **A**.

References

1 Shannon, C.E. (1948). A mathematical theory of communication Part I and II. *Bell System Technical Journal* 27: 623–656.

2 Wozencraft, J.M. and Jacobs, I.M. (1965). *Principles of Communication Engineering*. New York: Wiley.

3 Blitzstein, J.K. and Hwang, J. (2014). *Introduction to Probability*. CRC Press. ISBN 9781466575592.

4 Kim, H. (2015). *Wireless Communications Systems Design*. Wiley.

4

Mathematical Optimization Techniques for Wireless Communications

4.1 Introduction

When we design wireless communications and networks, we deal with empirical data from field tests as well as data from simulation models. Wireless communication systems are based on many algorithms and theories such as information theory, coding theory, decision/estimation theory, mathematical modeling, optimization theory, and so on. Among them, mathematical modeling and optimization is a study with a long history. The term "modeling" is derived from the Latin word "modellus" which means copying the reality. We can simply define modeling as "a simplified system description copying the reality." Mathematical modeling describes a system using mathematical concepts and terms, and is helpful for the explanation of physical phenomena. If we obtain a good mathematical model, it allows us to make good predictions or decisions.

Mathematical optimization (or mathematical programming, optimization) techniques play an important role in many practical systems and research areas such as science, engineering, economics, statistics, medicine, and so on. Optimization is a large subject and includes linear/nonlinear programming, integer programming, fractional programming, combinatorial optimization, dynamic optimization, convex optimization, network flow theory, and so on. Taking a look at a brief history of optimization, the great ancient mathematicians laid the foundations for mathematical optimization in order to solve geometric and arithmetic problems. In this era, geometry and arithmetic were the main topics of mathematics. Euclid of Alexandria (325–265 BCE), known as the founder of geometry, published the book *The Elements* and solved the earliest optimizations [1]. He studied geometry and proved that a square has the greatest area among all rectangles with given total length of the edges. Heron of Alexandria (10–75 CE) published the book *Catoptrica*, stating that vision occurs as a result of light emissions by the eyes with infinite velocity, and proved that light travels between two points through the path with shortest length when reflecting from a mirror [2]. Pappus of Alexandria (290–350 CE) proved that a honeycomb shape (a repeating hexagonal pattern) is the optimal way of storing honey and formulated the famous problem under the title "On the Sagacity of Bees" [2]. In the seventeenth and eighteenth centuries, mathematical tools were developed and partial optimization problems were investigated. A French mathematician and philosopher Rene Descartes (1596–1650) defined any geometric object like a line or circle in terms of algebraic equations and made significant contributions [3]. We can say that this was the first step towards all analytical optimization

Design and Optimization for 5G Wireless Communications, First Edition. Haesik Kim.
© 2020 John Wiley & Sons Ltd. Published 2020 by John Wiley & Sons Ltd.

solutions. He described any position on a plane using a pair of numbers with a horizontal and vertical axis [3]. This description becomes coordination, assigning the horizontal as x and the vertical as y. Pierre de Fermat (1601–1665) solved the tangent line problem with a different approach [2]. In addition, he found the derivative and calculated the optimal point when the slope is zero. He shows that light always travels the shortest possible path. Two famous pioneers of calculus, Isaac Newton (1643–1727) and Gottfried Wilhelm Leibniz (1646–1716), created mathematical analysis forming the basis of calculus of variations and differential equations. Calculus of variations deals with the optimization of functions mapping from a set of functions to real numbers. It is very common to use differential equations for finding a solution of optimization problems. They worked at the same time but their approaches were different. Newton approached functions changing in time, but Leibniz thought of variables x and y as ranging over sequences of infinitely close values, dx and dy [2]. They investigated some finite optimization problems. Leonhard Euler (1701–1783) created many mathematical tools that are used today. For example, he proposed $f(x)$ for a function, e for the base of natural logs, π for pi, Σ for summation, i for the square root of the negative number -1, and so on [2]. He developed the general theory of calculus of variations. Joseph-Louis Lagrange (1736–1813) made a significant contribution at the age of 19. He discovered that the tautochrone (or isochrone curve) is the curve on which a weighted particle will always arrive at a fixed point in a fixed amount of time independent of its initial position [2]. His discovery is used in many optimization solutions.

In the nineteenth century, the first optimization algorithms were presented. Many mathematicians developed calculus of variations significantly. The least square approximation is one of the crucial optimization problems. Carl Friedrich Gauss (1777–1855) developed a solution for this problem, which minimizes the sum of the squares of the errors. The first iterative optimization algorithm was invented by Isaac Newton, Joseph Raphson (1648–1715), Thomas Simpson (1710–1761), and Jean-Baptiste-Joseph Fourier (1768–1830) [2]. This algorithm is known as the Newton-Raphson method. J.B.J Fourier formulated a linear programming (LP) problem for solving mechanics problems [4]. Augustin-Louis Cauchy (1789–1857) published the method of the gradient descent that is a fundamental derivative-based iterative procedure.

In the twentieth century, calculus of variations was further developed and important optimization techniques were developed by many brilliant mathematicians. Leonid Vitaliyevich Kantorovich (1912–1986) developed linear programming in 1939, but this algorithm was kept secret until George Bernad Dantzig (1914–2005) published the simplex method in 1947 [2]. A Hungarian-American mathematician John von Neumann (1903–1957) made a significant contribution to a number of fields such as operations research, representation theory, ergodic theory, numerical analysis, quantum mechanics, game theory, computing, statistics, and so on. One of his contributions is the theory of duality as a solution of linear programming. In addition, he proved the minimax theorem in game theory, founded the field of continuous geometry, established a mathematical framework for quantum mechanics, and made significant contributions to many areas. He was the foremost mathematician in the twentieth century. William Karush (1917–1997), Harold William Kuhn (1925–), and Albert William Tucker (1905–1995) developed optimality conditions for nonlinear problems. We call this Karush–Kuhn–Tucker (KKT) theorem and it provides us with conditions for the existence of an optimal solution to nonlinear programming [5]. Richard Bellman (1920–1984) developed dynamic programming. This method is commonly used for solving complex problems by breaking them down into a sequence of decision steps over time. Herbert Ellis Robbins (1915–2001) and Sutton Monro (1919–1995) developed stochastic approximation [6]. This approach was different from the deterministic processes that many mathematicians studied so far. Stochastic approximation as a family of iterative stochastic optimization algorithms is to find the minimum or maximum of an unknown function with unknown derivatives. Nils Aall Barricelli (1912–1993) developed evolutionary algorithms that were inspired by biological evolution (including reproduction, mutation, recombination and selection). Ingo Rechenberg (1934–) invented an evolution strategy technique for functional optimization and machine learning [2]. John Holland (1929–) developed genetic algorithms based on an evolutionary algorithm. He presented the concept of adaptive digital systems using evolutionary operators: mutation, selection and crossover [7]. In 1950, Alan Turing published the paper "Computing Machinery and Intelligence" and mentioned the possibility of creating machines that think [8]. In 1959, machine learning as a subset of artificial intelligence (AI) was coined by Arthur Samuel [9]. As computers become more powerful in the 1980s, heuristic algorithms and large-scale problems were investigated. In the last two decades, optimization techniques have grown along with advances in computer and communication technologies. In the twenty-first century, optimization techniques have become one of the key technologies in modern science and engineering. In particular, interest in the application of artificial intelligence (AI) is growing rapidly because AIs have the capability to adapt to nonlinearity and discontinuity of systems.

Many optimization problems include multiple conflicting objectives that we consider simultaneously. We call it the vector optimization problem. Modeling becomes very complicated and it is very tricky to find a solution. We here raise several key questions about mathematical modeling and optimizations: how is the model close to reality? How is the optimization problem tractable? Is the problem solvable? We try to find an answer in this chapter. This book is not a math book, and we skip the proof of algorithms. We cannot cover all the techniques, as well as deal with several key techniques for wireless communications.

4.2 Mathematical Modeling and Optimization Process

It is not possible to find a general solution of real-world problems and solve them efficiently. What we can do is to find a trade-off between generality and efficiency. In order to solve real-world problems, mathematical modeling and optimization is a very useful tool. We can summarize the process of mathematical modeling and optimization as follows: (i) observing the real-world phenomena and defining parameters to optimize; (ii) constructing a mathematical model in terms of the parameters; (iii) formulating a mathematical problem (or optimization problem); (iv) finding a mathematical solution using optimization algorithms, computer simulations, or empirical study; (v) evaluating the solution; (vi) refining the mathematical model and adjusting the parameters. In this book, we will focus on step 2: constructing a mathematical model; step 3: formulating a mathematical problem; and step 4: finding a mathematical solution.

A good mathematical model definition is very important because an inadequate model causes wrong directions to be followed and false conclusions to be drawn. It is very effective to model a real-world system because it could reduce the cost of experimentation and reduce risk. Basically, a mathematical model reflects a real-world system as closely as possible. However, if too many conditions and too many parameters are included, the system model will be too complex. It would be extremely difficult to find a solution. On the other hand, it is too simple to reflect a real-world system if the model simplifies too much – the solution would not be accurate. Thus, a system designer always confronts a trade-off between validity and tractability of a mathematical model. Since a mathematical system model is a simplified version and a real world system is much more complex than that, we should admit the gap between them. Thus, it is an important step to formulate a mathematical problem while reducing the gap, representing the relationship among parameters, and expressing key conditions of real-world systems. The mathematical model must have an objective function to optimize.

The purpose of optimization is to find the best possible value of the objective function. Optimization problems are composed of three elements: objective function, constraints, and optimization variables. The objective function is the main goal we optimize and it should be minimized or maximized. The constraints are restrictions that variables take, and it allows us to exclude certain values. The optimization variables control the values of the objective function. The optimization problem is to find values of the optimization variables by minimizing or maximizing the objective function under the given constraints. We can express the standard form of a mathematical optimization problem as follows:

$$\min_{\mathbf{x}} f(\mathbf{x})$$

subject to

$$C_1 : g_j(\mathbf{x}) \leq a_j, \ \ j = 1, 2, \ldots, m$$
$$C_2 : h_k(\mathbf{x}) = b_k, \ \ k = 1, 2, \ldots, p \tag{4.1}$$

where $\mathbf{x} = [x_1 \ x_2 \ldots x_n]^T \in \mathbb{R}^n$ is the real column vector of optimization variables x_i, $f(\mathbf{x})$ is the objective function, $g_j(\mathbf{x})$ is the inequality constraint function, $h_k(\mathbf{x})$ is the equality constraint function, and a_i and b_j are the limits of the constraint functions. The functions $f(\mathbf{x})$, $g_j(\mathbf{x})$ and $h_k(\mathbf{x})$ are scalar functions of the optimization variables $\mathbf{x}$. The solution of Equation (4.1) is denoted as the optimum vector $\mathbf{x}^*$ and the corresponding optimum value of the objective function is $f(\mathbf{x}^*)$. This standard form is defined as a minimization problem. If we assume the negative objective function, the standard form is regards as a maximization problem.

Optimization problems can be classified in many ways. Firstly, the optimization problems can be classified as linear, nonlinear, quadratic, polynomial, geometric, or convex, according to the nature of the objective function. For example, it is a linear programming problem if both objective functions and constraints are linear. It is a nonlinear programming problem if both objective functions and constraints are nonlinear. This is the very general form of an optimization problem. It is a quadratic programming (QP) problem if an objective function is quadratic and constraints are linear. A general optimization problem is very difficult to solve and we cannot always find the solution. Based on this classification, we can check whether or not the problem is solvable and find computational methods.

Secondly, according to existence of constraints, optimization problems can be classified as a constrained or an unconstrained optimization problem. Constraints allow us to exclude certain values of variables. The space in which all constraints are satisfied is the feasible space. Constrained optimization searches optimum values in the feasible space.

Thirdly, according to types of variables, they can be classified as integer or real and deterministic or stochastic problems. If the optimization variables are integer values, the optimization problem is an integer programming problem. If they are real values, we call it a real valued programming problem. In addition, optimization problems can be stochastic if optimization variables are stochastic (namely, the variables are represented as probability). If the variables are deterministic, the problem is a deterministic optimization problem.

Fourthly, according to the number of objective functions, we can classify the problems: single-objective optimization problem, and multi-objective optimization problem. Many optimization theories deal with the single-objective optimization problem and it is relatively easy to find a solution. Multi-objective optimization problems have more than one objective function and we should minimize them simultaneously. Thus, it is difficult to find an optimum solution.

We consider a simple quadratic programming as an unconstrained one-dimensional minimization. The objective function with a single real variable x can be expressed as follows:

$$f(x) = ax^2 + bx + c \tag{4.2}$$

where a, b and c are constants. We can formulate the optimization problem as follows:

$$\min_x f(x), \ x \in \mathbb{R} \tag{4.3}$$

In order to find an optimum solution x^*, we intuitively know that the following condition should be satisfied

$$f(x) > f(x^*), \ \text{ for all } x \tag{4.4}$$

and the derivative of $f(x)$ should be zero (namely, the slope of the objective function is zero) as follows:

$$\frac{d}{dx} f(x) = 2ax + b = 0 \tag{4.5}$$

Thus, we can determine the optimum solution x^* and value $f(x^*)$ as follows:

$$x^* = -\frac{b}{2a} \text{ and } f(x^*) = f\left(-\frac{b}{2a}\right) \tag{4.6}$$

Figure 4.1 illustrates quadratic optimization and shows us a strong local minimum.

We can generalize the solution of the unconstrained optimization problem. The optimization problem with vector $\mathbf{x} = [x_1, x_2, \ldots, x_n]^T$ is formulated as follows:

$$\min_{x_i} f(x_1, x_2, \ldots, x_n), \ x_i \in \mathbb{R}, i = 1, 2, \ldots n \tag{4.7}$$

where the function $f(\mathbf{x})$ is continuous and the first-order derivative of the function $f(\mathbf{x})$ exists. In order to obtain the minimum of the function $f(\mathbf{x})$, the derivative of $f(x_1, x_2, \ldots, x_n)$ should be zero as follows:

$$\frac{\partial}{\partial x_1} f(x_1, x_2, \ldots, x_n) = 0, \ldots, \frac{\partial}{\partial x_n} f(x_1, x_2, \ldots, x_n) = 0 \tag{4.8}$$

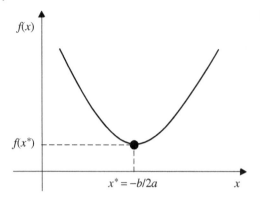

Figure 4.1 Quadratic optimization.

From Equation (4.8), we obtain n equations with n unknown variables and candidate solution points can be found. If the second-order derivative of the function $f(\mathbf{x})$ exists, we can have the Hessian matrix as follows:

$$\mathbf{H}_{i,j} = \frac{\partial^2}{\partial x_i \partial x_j} f(x_1, x_2, \dots, x_n) = \begin{bmatrix} \frac{\partial^2 f}{\partial x_1^2} & \frac{\partial^2 f}{\partial x_1 \partial x_2} & \cdots & \frac{\partial^2 f}{\partial x_1 \partial x_n} \\ \frac{\partial^2 f}{\partial x_2 \partial x_1} & \frac{\partial^2 f}{\partial x_2^2} & \cdots & \frac{\partial^2 f}{\partial x_2 \partial x_n} \\ \vdots & \vdots & \ddots & \vdots \\ \frac{\partial^2 f}{\partial x_n \partial x_1} & \frac{\partial^2 f}{\partial x_n \partial x_2} & \cdots & \frac{\partial^2 f}{\partial x_n^2} \end{bmatrix} \tag{4.9}$$

where $i = 1, 2, \dots, n$ and $j = 1, 2, \dots, n$. The function $f(\mathbf{x})$ is a minimum/maximum if the Hessian matrix is positive/negative definite.

We consider a function $f(\mathbf{x})$ of two variables $\mathbf{x} = [x_1, x_2]^T$ in a quadratic form. The algebraic expression of $f(\mathbf{x})$ is as follows:

$$f(x_1, x_2) = ax_1^2 + 2bx_1x_2 + cx_2^2 \tag{4.10}$$

and the matrix expression of $f(\mathbf{x})$ is as follows:

$$f(x_1, x_2) = [x_1 \ x_2] \begin{bmatrix} a & b \\ b & c \end{bmatrix} \begin{bmatrix} x_1 \\ x_2 \end{bmatrix} = \mathbf{x}^T \mathbf{A} \mathbf{x} \tag{4.11}$$

A quadratic form of three variables $\mathbf{x} = [x_1, x_2, x_3]^T$ is

$$\begin{aligned} f(x_1, x_2, x_3) = \ & a_{11}x_1^2 + a_{12}x_1x_2 + a_{13}x_1x_3 \\ & + a_{21}x_2x_1 + a_{22}x_2^2 + a_{23}x_2x_3 \\ & + a_{31}x_3x_1 + a_{32}x_3x_2 + a_{33}x_3^2 \end{aligned} \tag{4.12}$$

We have a generalized quadratic form with n variables as follows:

$$\begin{aligned} f(x_1, x_2, \dots, x_n) = \ & a_{11}x_1^2 + a_{12}x_1x_2 + \dots + a_{1n}x_1x_n + \\ & a_{21}x_2x_1 + a_{22}x_2^2 + \dots + a_{2n}x_2x_n + \\ & \vdots \qquad\qquad \ddots \qquad \vdots \\ & a_{n1}x_nx_1 + a_{n2}x_nx_2 + \dots + a_{nn}x_n^2 \end{aligned} \tag{4.13}$$

$$f(x_1, x_2, \ldots, x_n) = \sum_{i,j}^{n} a_{ij} x_i x_j \tag{4.14}$$

and the matrix expression of $f(\mathbf{x})$ is as follows:

$$f(\mathbf{x}) = [x_1 \ldots x_n] \begin{bmatrix} a_{11} & \cdots & a_{1n} \\ \vdots & \ddots & \vdots \\ a_{n1} & \cdots & a_{nn} \end{bmatrix} \begin{bmatrix} x_1 \\ \vdots \\ x_n \end{bmatrix} = \mathbf{x}^T \mathbf{A} \mathbf{x} \tag{4.15}$$

where $\mathbf{x}$ and $\mathbf{A}$ are an $n \times 1$ vector and an $n \times n$ matrix, respectively. The matrix $\mathbf{A}$ is a symmetric matrix and we call this positive definite if $f(\mathbf{x}) > 0$ for all $\mathbf{x} \neq 0$. A necessary and sufficient condition for positive definite is that all the determinants (det[A]) are positive. The determinant is called the discriminant of the function $f(\mathbf{x})$. Equation (4.10) can be rewritten as follows:

$$f(x_1, x_2) = ax_1^2 + 2bx_1x_2 + cx_2^2 = a\left(x_1 + \frac{b}{a}x_2\right)^2 + \frac{ac - b^2}{a}x_2^2$$

$$= D_1\left(x_1 + \frac{b}{a}x_2\right)^2 + \frac{D_2}{D_1}x_2^2 \tag{4.16}$$

where $D_1 = a$ and $D_2 = ac - b^2$. We call them leading principal minors of the matrix **A**. From this form, we observe definiteness of the quadratic form. Namely, it is positive definite if $D_1 > 0$ and $D_2 > 0$. It is negative definite if $D_1 < 0$ and $D_2 > 0$. It is indefinite if $D_2 < 0$. We can generalize n variable quadratic forms as follows:

$$f(x_1, x_2, \ldots, x_n) = |D_1| l_1^2 + \frac{|D_2|}{|D_1|} l_2^2 + \cdots + \frac{|D_n|}{|D_{n-1}|} l_n^2 \tag{4.17}$$

where D_i $(i = 1, 2, \ldots, n)$ are leading principal minors of the matrix **A** as follows:

$$|D_1| = |a_{11}|, |D_2| = \begin{vmatrix} a_{11} & a_{12} \\ a_{21} & a_{22} \end{vmatrix}, \ldots, |D_n| = \begin{vmatrix} a_{11} & \cdots & a_{1n} \\ \vdots & \ddots & \vdots \\ a_{n1} & \cdots & a_{nn} \end{vmatrix} \tag{4.18}$$

and l_i $(i = 1, 2, \ldots, n)$ are expressed as follows:

$$\begin{bmatrix} l_1 \\ \vdots \\ l_n \end{bmatrix} = \begin{bmatrix} p_{11} & \cdots & p_{1n} \\ \vdots & \ddots & \vdots \\ p_{n1} & \cdots & p_{nn} \end{bmatrix} \begin{bmatrix} x_1 \\ \vdots \\ x_n \end{bmatrix} \tag{4.19}$$

$$\mathbf{L} = \mathbf{P}\mathbf{x} \tag{4.20}$$

where the matrix P is a nonsingular matrix. Basically, determining the definiteness of the function $f(\mathbf{x})$ is related to optimality.

Example 4.1 *Definiteness of Two-Variable Quadratic Function*

Consider a function $f(\mathbf{x})$ of two variables $\mathbf{x} = [x_1, x_2]^T$ in a quadratic form as follows:

$$f(x_1, x_2) = x_1^2 + x_1x_2 + x_2^2, \quad x_1, x_2 \in \mathbb{R}$$

Confirm the definiteness of the function.

Solution

From Equation (4.16), we have

$$f(x_1, x_2) = x_1^2 + x_1 x_2 + x_2^2 = ax_1^2 + 2bx_1 x_2 + cx_2^2$$

From the above equation, $a = 1$, $b = 1/2$ and $c = 1$. Thus, we have

$$D_1 = a = 1 > 0 \text{ and } D_2 = ac - b^2 = 1 - \frac{1}{4} = \frac{3}{4} > 0$$

Thus, the function $f(x_1, x_2)$ is the form of $x_1^2 + x_2^2$ and it is positive definite. In addition, we can calculate the Hessian matrix as follows:

$$\mathbf{H}_{1,2} = \frac{\partial^2}{\partial x_1 \partial x_2} f(x_1, x_2) = \begin{bmatrix} \dfrac{\partial^2 f}{\partial x_1^2} & \dfrac{\partial^2 f}{\partial x_1 \partial x_2} \\ \dfrac{\partial^2 f}{\partial x_2 \partial x_1} & \dfrac{\partial^2 f}{\partial x_2^2} \end{bmatrix} = \begin{bmatrix} 2 & 1 \\ 1 & 2 \end{bmatrix}$$

$$\mathbf{x}^T \mathbf{H}_{1,2} \mathbf{x} = [x_1 \ x_2] \begin{bmatrix} 2 & 1 \\ 1 & 2 \end{bmatrix} \begin{bmatrix} x_1 \\ x_2 \end{bmatrix} = 2(x_1^2 + x_1 x_2 + x_2^2) = 2\left(\left(x_1 + \frac{1}{2} x_2 \right)^2 + \frac{3}{4} x_2^2 \right)$$

$$\mathbf{x}^T \mathbf{H}_{1,2} \mathbf{x} > 0 \text{ for all } \mathbf{x} \neq 0$$

Thus, $\mathbf{H}_{1,2}$ is positive definite and the function $f(\mathbf{x})$ is a minimum at the candidate points. In order to obtain the minimum of the function $f(\mathbf{x})$, the derivative of $f(x_1, x_2)$ should be zero as follows:

$$\frac{\partial}{\partial x_1} f(x_1, x_2) = 2x_1 + x_2 = 0$$

$$\frac{\partial}{\partial x_2} f(x_1, x_2) = x_1 + 2x_2 = 0$$

From the above equations, the candidate minimum solution points are

$$[x_1^*, x_2^*]^T = [0, 0]^T$$

As we observe in the above simple optimization problem, some functions may or may not have an optimal point. We intuitively raise some questions: does a function have a minimum or maximum point? Is the optimal point unique? What is the optimality condition? We need to define the conditions precisely and take a look at optimality conditions. The optimality conditions are useful in order to understand optimization problems and design optimization algorithms.

An optimum solution x^* is a point in the constraint set (or feasible set) S satisfying the following condition:

$$f(x) > f(x^*), \quad \forall x \in S \tag{4.21}$$

and an optimum solution may or may not be unique or exist. Figure 4.2 illustrates examples of possible optimum solutions when an optimization problem is bounded. The shaded area represents the constraint set S. As we can observe, the optimum solution of Figure 4.2a is unique, but we have two optimum solutions in Figure 4.2b.

Figure 4.3 illustrates examples of optimum solutions when an optimization problem is unbounded. As we can observe, the optimum solution of Figure 4.3a does not exist, but the optimum value converges to zero. The optimum solution of Figure 4.3b converges to zero

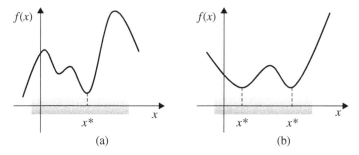

Figure 4.2 Examples of possible optimum values when the problem is bounded: (a) unique optimum value; and (b) optimum value exists, but not unique.

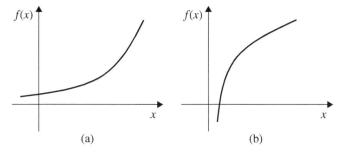

Figure 4.3 Examples of possible optimum values when the problem is unbounded: (a) the optimum value converges to zero; and (b) the optimum value diverges to negative infinity.

and the optimum value diverges to negative infinity. We can define the optimality conditions as follows:

Definition 4.1 Global Minimum and Strict Global Minimum

A point $x^* \in S$ is a global minimum of $f(x)$ over S if

$$f(x) > f(x^*), \quad \forall x \in S \tag{4.22}$$

and a strict global minimum if

$$f(x) > f(x^*), \quad \forall x \in S, \ x \neq x^* \tag{4.23}$$

Definition 4.2 Local Minimum and Strict Local Minimum

A point $x^* \in S$ is a local minimum of $f(x)$ over S if

$$\exists \varepsilon > 0 \text{ such that } f(x) > f(x^*), \quad \forall x \in S \cap B(x^*, \varepsilon) \tag{4.24}$$

and a strict local minimum if

$$\exists \varepsilon > 0 \text{ such that } f(x) > f(x^*), \quad \forall x \in S \cap B(x^*, \varepsilon), \ x \neq x^* \tag{4.25}$$

where $B(x^*, \varepsilon) := \{x \in \mathbb{R}^n \mid \|x - x^*\| < \varepsilon\}$ is the Euclidean ball with radius ε centred at x^*.

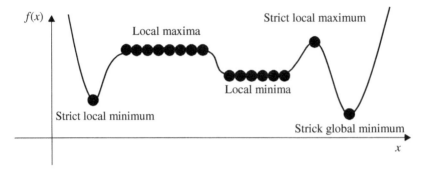

Figure 4.4 Examples of global and local minima and maxima when the problem is unbounded.

In addition, a point $\mathbf{x}^* \in S$ is a stationary point of $f(\mathbf{x})$ over S if

$$g(\mathbf{x}^*) = 0 \tag{4.26}$$

where $g(\mathbf{x})$ is the gradient of $f(\mathbf{x})$. The first derivative vector has the following components:

$$g(\mathbf{x}) = \frac{\partial}{\partial x_i} f(\mathbf{x}) \tag{4.27}$$

If the second-order derivative of the function $f(\mathbf{x})$ exists (the Hessian matrix exists), the point $\mathbf{x}^* \in S$ is a strict local minimum of $f(\mathbf{x})$. Likewise, we can define global and local maxima. Figure 4.4 illustrates examples of global and local minima and maxima.

Suppose that a differentiable function f of one variable is defined on an interval $[a\ b]$. If an interior point x^* is a local minimizer of f, $\nabla f(x^*) = 0$ where ∇ is a differential operator. If the left-end point $x^* = a$ and the right-end point $x^* = b$ are a local minimizer, we have $\nabla f(a) \geq 0$ and $\nabla f(b) \leq 0$, respectively. We call this condition the first-order necessary condition (FONC). The second-order necessary condition (SONC) for a minimum can be given in terms of the Hessian matrix. If f is twice differentiable and x^* is a local minimizer of f, we must have $\nabla f(x^*) = 0$ and $\nabla^2 f(x^*) \geq 0$ (the Hessian at x^* is positive semi-definite). These conditions cannot distinguish between local minimizers, local maximizers or saddle points. The necessary conditions are still not sufficient for optimality. If f is twice differentiable and we have $\nabla f(x^*) = 0$ and $\nabla^2 f(x^*) > 0$ (the Hessian at x^* is positive definite), x^* is a strict local minimizer of f. We call this the second-order sufficient condition (SOSC).

Example 4.2 *The First-Order Necessary Condition*
Consider a simple signal-to-interference model of two base stations as shown in Figure p4.1. We assume that the signal power is highly related to the distance between a sender and a receiver and we calculate the received power at a mobile station as follows: $P_r = 1/\text{distance}$ between a base station and a mobile station. Find a position of the mobile station maximizing the signal to interference ratio.

Solution
We simply calculate the received signal power and interference as follows:

$$P_r = 1/(1 + (2 - x)^2)$$
$$P_i = 1/(1 + x^2)$$

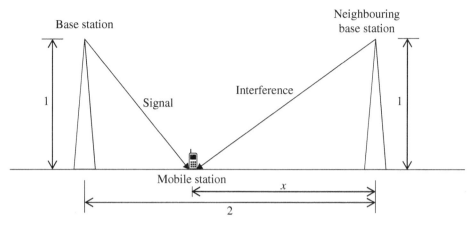

Figure p4.1 A simple model of signal-to-interference in two base stations.

and the signal-to-interference ratio is represented as follows:

$$f(x) = \frac{P_r}{P_i} = \frac{1/(1 + (2 - x)^2)}{1/(1 + x^2)} = \frac{1 + x^2}{1 + (2 - x)^2}$$

We can formulate the problem as follows:

$$\max_x f(x)$$

According to the FONC, we must have $\nabla f(x^*) = 0$ in order to find the optimal position x^*. The derivative of $f(x)$ is

$$\nabla f(x) = \frac{\partial}{\partial x}\left(\frac{1 + x^2}{1 + (2 - x)^2}\right) = \frac{-2x(1 + (2 - x)^2) - 2(2 - x)(1 + x^2)}{1 + (2 - x)^2} = \frac{4(x^2 - 2x - 1)}{1 + (2 - x)^2}$$

Thus, we have $x^* = 1 - \sqrt{2}$ or $1 + \sqrt{2}$. The position of the mobile station maximizing the signal to interference ratio is the position $1 - \sqrt{2}$ from the neighboring base station.

Summary 4.1 Mathematical Modeling and Optimization Process

1) The process of mathematical modeling and optimization is as follows: (i) observing the real-world phenomena and defining parameters to optimize; (ii) constructing a mathematical model in terms of the parameters; (iii) formulating a mathematical problem (or optimization problem); (iv) finding a mathematical solution using optimization algorithms, computer simulations, or empirical study; (v) evaluating the solution; and (vi) refining the mathematical model and adjusting the parameters.
2) The purpose of optimization is to find the best possible value of the objective function. Optimization problems are composed of three elements: objective function, constraints, and optimization variables.

(Continued)

---

3) The standard form of a mathematical optimization problem is as follows:

$$\min_{x} f(\mathbf{x})$$

subject to

$$C_1 : g_j(\mathbf{x}) \leq a_j, \; j = 1, 2, \ldots, m$$
$$C_2 : h_k(\mathbf{x}) = b_k, \; k = 1, 2, \ldots, p$$

where $\mathbf{x} = [x_1 \, x_2 \ldots x_n]^T \in \mathbb{R}^n$ is the real column vector of optimization variables x_j, $f(\mathbf{x})$ is the objective function, $g_j(\mathbf{x})$ is the inequality constraint function, $h_k(\mathbf{x})$ is the equality constraint function, and a_i and b_j are the limits of the constraint functions.

4.3 Linear Programming

Linear programming was the first widely used tool of optimization. In 1939, Kantorovich presented a number of solutions to problems of production and transportation planning. During World War II, Koopmans solved transportation problems using linear programming. Efficient methods were developed in World War II in order to maximize resource utilization. The term "programming" was a military term regarding planning schedules or deploying men efficiently. In 1975, Kantorovich and Koopmans were awarded a Nobel Prize in economics for their work on the theory of optimal allocation of resources [10]. In 1947, Dantzig developed the simplex method of optimization in order to solve linear programming problems. Since then, many mathematicians and economists have developed new methods and explored their applications [10].

As we briefly reviewed the optimization problem and solution in the previous section, two logical steps (problem formulation and solution finding) are needed. In the step of problem formulation, a system model is defined. The objective function and constraints are defined in terms of variables. In the step of solution finding, the solution is sought. Suitable algorithms are used to find an optimal solution and computer simulation comes up with solvers using heuristic or empirical methods. The linear programming problem can be formulated as follows: we firstly identify decision variables and represent them as algebraic symbols. The decision variables represent unknown variables to be made. Secondly, all constraints are defined and they are expressed as linear equations or inequalities of the decision variables. Thirdly, the objective function is defined and expressed as a linear function of the decision variables, which is to be minimized or maximized. We finally have a linear programming model composed of the decision variables, objective function and constraints. There are several assumptions on which the linear programming relies. One important assumption is that any variable in the constraint inequalities is proportional to the variable in the objective function, and also any variable to the constraints or objective functions is independent of the values of the other variables. Namely, the relationships between constraints and objective functions are linear. The decision variables are continuous (this means decision variables can be fractions). All coefficients in the objective function and constraints are known with certainty.

Linear programming is a highly useful tool of analysis and optimization. However, there are several limitations. Linear programming complies with the linear relationship but one assumption that all relationships are linear may not hold well in the real world. The objective functions and constraints should be clearly identified in quantitative terms, but this may not be possible in real life. A large number of variables or constraints may be involved in the model, so it requires a large amount of computation. In this case, it is a very complex method to solve the problem.

A linear programming problem can be defined as the problem of maximizing or minimizing a linear objective function subject to linear constraints. The goal of linear programming is to determine the values of decision variables. We consider an example of a simple linear programming problem as follows:

$$\max_{x,y}(x + y) \tag{4.28}$$

subject to

$$x \geq 0$$
$$y \geq 0$$
$$x + 2y \leq 4$$
$$2x + y \leq 4$$
$$-x + y \leq 1 \tag{4.29}$$

In this linear programming problem, we have one objective function for maximization, two decision variables, and five linear constraints. The first two constraints $x \geq 0$ and $y \geq 0$ are non-negativity constraints and the other constraints define a feasible set. Using the constraints, we can find a feasible region and the solution lies at a vertex of the feasible region. Figure 4.5 illustrates the feasible region as the shaded area.

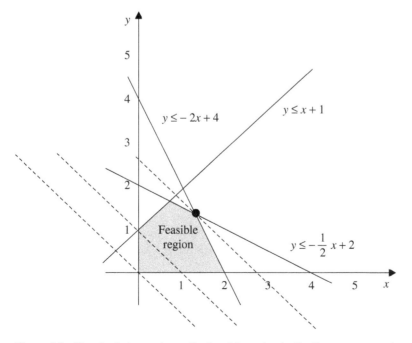

Figure 4.5 The shaded area shows the feasible region in the linear programming example.

In this problem, we should find two decision variables maximizing $x + y$ in the feasible region. The objective function $x + y$ is constant on lines with slope -1. We move this line in the feasible region and find a point achieving the maximum of the objective function. In Figure 4.5, the dashed line represents the search. The intersection of the lines $y = -2x + 4$ and $y = -\frac{1}{2}x + 2$ are the optimal point. Thus, we have $(x, y) = \left(\frac{4}{3}, \frac{4}{3}\right)$ and the value of the objective function is 8/3. To sum up, the constraints define the feasible region, the objective function takes on its maximum or minimum by search, and the optimal value is located at a vertex of the feasible region.

Now, we generalize the linear programming. A linear program is an optimization problem that can be expressed as the following standard form:

$$\text{Minimize } c_1 x_1 + c_2 x_2 + \cdots + c_n x_n \tag{4.30}$$

subject to

$$a_{11} x_1 + a_{12} x_2 + \cdots + a_{1n} x_n \leq b_1$$
$$a_{21} x_1 + a_{22} x_2 + \cdots + a_{2n} x_n \leq b_2$$
$$\vdots$$
$$a_{m1} x_1 + a_{m2} x_2 + \cdots + a_{mn} x_n \leq b_m$$

$$x_1 \geq 0, x_2 \geq 0, \cdots, x_n \geq 0 \tag{4.31}$$

where x_i is a decision variable to be determined, and c_i, a_i, b_i are constants.

Definition 4.3 Linear Programming

In compact form, the standard linear programming problem can be defined as follows:

$$\min_{\mathbf{x}} \mathbf{c}^{\mathsf{T}} \mathbf{x} \tag{4.32}$$

subject to

$$\mathbf{A}\mathbf{x} \leq \mathbf{b}, \mathbf{x} \geq 0 \tag{4.33}$$

where $\mathbf{x} \in \mathbb{R}^n$ is an n-dimensional vector of decision variables and each component of the vector $\mathbf{x}$ is non-negative, $\mathbf{c} \in \mathbb{R}^n$ and $\mathbf{b} \in \mathbb{R}^m$ are vectors of known coefficients, and $\mathbf{A} \in \mathbb{R}^{m \times n}$ are known matrices of coefficients.

Some variation of the canonical form is possible. For example, the objective function can be maximized. The constraints can be expressed as $\mathbf{A}\mathbf{x} \leq \mathbf{b}$. When a vector $\mathbf{x}$ satisfies all of the constraints, we call it a feasible solution. A feasible solution $\mathbf{x}^*$ minimizing or maximizing the objective function is called an optimal feasible solution. The value of $\mathbf{c}^{\mathsf{T}} \mathbf{x}^*$ is called the optimal objective value. Linear programming problems that have two decision variables ($\mathbf{x} \in \mathbb{R}^2$) can be solved graphically as in the previous simple example.

Example 4.3   *Linear Programming Problem with Two Decision Variables*
Consider the following linear programming problem:

$$\min_{\mathbf{x}} \mathbf{c}^T \mathbf{x}$$

subject to

$$\mathbf{A}\mathbf{x} \geq \mathbf{b}$$

$$\mathbf{x} \geq 0$$

where

$$\mathbf{c} = \begin{bmatrix} 1 \\ 4 \end{bmatrix}, \mathbf{x} = \begin{bmatrix} x_1 \\ x_2 \end{bmatrix}, \mathbf{A} = \begin{bmatrix} 1 & 3 \\ 1 & 1 \\ 0 & 1 \end{bmatrix} \text{ and } \mathbf{b} = \begin{bmatrix} 9 \\ 5 \\ 3 \end{bmatrix}.$$

Find the optimal value of the decision variable vector $\mathbf{x}$.

Solution
We can use a graphical method to solve this linear programming problem. In this problem, we find two decision variables x_1 and x_2 minimizing $x_1 + 4x_2$ in the feasible region. The objective function is constant on lines with slope $-1/4$ and the feasible region is defined by five constraints. Figure p4.2 illustrates the feasible region. The dashed line represents the search of the objective function. We move this line in the feasible region and find a point achieving the minimum of the objective function. The intersection of the lines $x_2 = 3$ and $x_2 = -x_1 + 5$ is the smallest point for the objective function. Thus, we have $(x_1, x_2) = (2, 3)$ and the value of the objective function is 14.

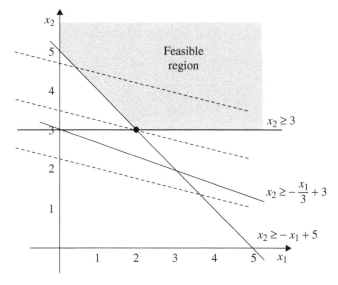

Figure p4.2   The shaded area shows the feasible region in Example 4.3.

Example 4.4 *Linear Programming Problem with Three Decision Variables*
Consider the following linear programming problem:

$$\max_{\mathbf{x}} \mathbf{c}^T\mathbf{x}$$

subject to

$$\mathbf{Ax} \le \mathbf{b}$$
$$\mathbf{x} \ge 0$$

where

$$\mathbf{c} = \begin{bmatrix} 1 \\ 1 \\ 1 \end{bmatrix}, \mathbf{x} = \begin{bmatrix} x_1 \\ x_2 \\ x_3 \end{bmatrix}, \mathbf{A} = \begin{bmatrix} 1 & 0 & 0 \\ 0 & 1 & 0 \\ 0 & 0 & 1 \end{bmatrix} \text{ and } \mathbf{b} = \begin{bmatrix} 1 \\ 1 \\ 1 \end{bmatrix}.$$

Find the optimal value of the decision variable vector **x**.

Solution
In this linear programming problem, we have three variables: think of the values of variables as a point (x_1, x_2, x_3) in three-dimensional space. Each constraint forms a boundary and the boundary can be described by $0 \le x_1 \le 1$, $0 \le x_2 \le 1$ and $0 \le x_3 \le 1$. Basically, it is not easy to draw the feasible region when there are more than two decision variables. For a linear programming problem with three decision variables, the feasible region can be visualized as a polyhedron. The shape is bounded by flat polygons. Like the two-variable case, the optimal point can be found at some corner point. In this problem, we can easily see that the feasible region is the unit cube as shown in Figure p4.3. The point $(1,1,1)$ is the biggest point for the objective function. Thus, we have $(x_1, x_2, x_3) = (1, 1, 1)$ and the value of the objective function is 3.

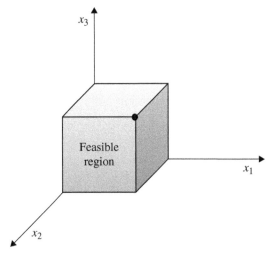

Figure p4.3 The shaded area shows the feasible region in Example 4.4.

In the above examples, we can find a single optimal point. However, there are three different possible cases: a single optimal solution, an infinite number of optimal solutions, or no optimal solution. Figure 4.6 illustrates the three different cases. As we can observe in Figure 4.6, the optimal solution is always located at corner points if an optimal solution exists. The constraints of the linear programming problems define a boundary, and

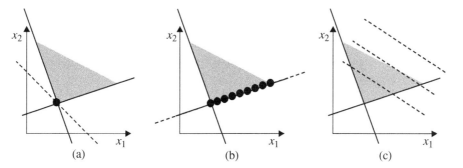

Figure 4.6 Three different cases: (a) a single optimal solution; (b) an infinite number of optimal solutions; and (c) no optimal solution.

geometrically it is a polyhedron. If we can determine all boundaries and have all corner points of the polyhedron, we can find an optimal solution by calculating the objective function at each corner point. The simplex algorithm is based on this idea, and it moves from one corner to another corner until the optimal solution is found.

Summary 4.2 Linear Programming

1) A linear programming problem can be defined as the problem of maximizing or minimizing a linear objective function subject to linear constraints. The goal of linear programming is to determine the values of decision variables.

2) The linear programming problem can be formulated as follows:
   - Firstly, we identify decision variables and represent them as algebraic symbols. The decision variables represent unknown variables to be made.
   - Secondly, all constraints are defined and they are expressed as linear equations or inequalities of the decision variables.
   - Thirdly, the objective function is defined and expressed as a linear function of the decision variables, which is to be minimized or maximized.
   - Lastly, we have a linear programming model composed of the decision variables, objective function and constraints.

3) One important assumption of linear programming is that any variable in the constraint inequalities is proportional to the variable in the objective function, and also any variable to the constraints or objective functions is independent of the values of the other variables.

Now, we consider the general case of a linear programming problem with n decision variables. There are several solutions for linear programming problems: the simplex algorithm, the ellipsoid algorithm and Karmarkar's algorithm. Among them, the simplex algorithm developed in the 1940s is the most commonly used solver. The basic idea is to search some corner of the feasible region repeatedly. We start at one corner of the feasible region, look at other neighboring corners of the current corner, and move to another corner if the value of the objective function is better. Finally, we stop the iteration when there are no neighboring corners with a higher value of the objective function. The key idea is based on (i) the optimal point is located at a corner, and (ii) there are no local maxima because the feasible region is convex. This approach works well. However, it might take an exponential number of iterations to converge if there are an exponential number of corners.

The ellipsoid algorithm was developed by Naum Z. Shor in 1972 for general convex optimization problems. In 1980 Khachiyan applied this method and proved the polynomial time solution for linear programming problems. This is a useful tool for a large class of convex optimization problems, but it is very slow and not competitive with the simplex algorithm. The basic idea is to localize the solution in an ellipsoid instead of a polyhedron. Firstly, a big ellipse containing the feasible region is defined and we check whether it violates any constraints. Then, we repeatedly find a new smaller ellipse while checking for constraint violations. One important property of the ellipsoid algorithm is that the volume of the ellipsoid shrinks in every iteration.

Another polynomial time algorithm for linear programming is Karmarkar's algorithm as the class of interior point algorithms. This algorithm uses feasible points like the simplex algorithm. However, it docs not search corners but looks into the interior of the feasible region. In this section, we focus on the simplex algorithm.

In order to solve linear programming problems, the geometric method is useful only for problems with two decision variables and few constraints. The simplex method is a matrix-based method to solve linear programming problems with any number of decision variables. It is an algebraic method but its concept is geometric because we can characterize corner points algebraically and geometrically. The steps of the simplex algorithm are as follows: The first step is to check whether the linear programming problem is a standard maximum type problem or converts to a standard maximum type problem. The standard maximum type problem should satisfy the following conditions: (i) the objective function is linear and should be maximized; (ii) all variables should be non-negative; and (iii) all constraints are in the form $a_{11}x_1 + a_{12}x_2 + \cdots + a_{1n}x_n \le b_1$ and $b_1 \ge 0$. The second step is to add slack variables and convert the inequality constraints to equivalent equality constraints in the form $a_{11}x_1 + a_{12}x_2 + s_1 = b_1$. The slack variables are always non-negative. The third step is to rewrite the objective function to match the form of the slack equations. It should be an equation in the form where the left-hand side $= 0$, for example, $z = a_{11}x_1 + a_{12}x_2 \rightarrow -a_{11}x_1 - a_{12}x_2 + z = 0$. The fourth step is to write the initial simplex tableau. We place the equality constraints into a matrix and put the objective function in the bottom row. The fifth step is to find the pivot element and perform the pivot operation. The pivot column is selected by finding the most negative indicator in the last row of the tableau. The pivot row is the row including the smallest non-negative ratio. It is selected by dividing the last column by the pivot column for each corresponding element except negative elements and the bottom element. In the simplex algorithm, we call decision variables nonbasic variables and we set them equal to zero. The slack variables are basic. Pivoting means that one nonbasic variable enters the basic and one basic variable leaves the basis. We perform the basis change by a pivot operation in this step. Once we find the pivot column and row, the pivot element is selected as the intersection of the pivot column and the row. We can perform the pivot operation on the pivot element. For example, when a_{rs} in the tableau is the pivot element, the update rules of the tableau are as follows: (i) in the pivot row, $a_{rj}/a_{rs} \rightarrow a_{rs}$ for $j = 1,\ldots, n+m$; (ii) in pivot column, $1 \rightarrow a_{rs}$ and $0 \rightarrow a_{is}$ for $i = 0,\ldots, m$,

$i \neq r$; (iii) in other elements, $a_{ij} - a_{rj}a_{is}/a_{rs} \rightarrow a_{ij}$. We could summarize the pivot operation as follows:

$$\begin{bmatrix} a_{ij} & a_{is} \\ a_{rj} & a_{rs} \end{bmatrix} \rightarrow \begin{bmatrix} a_{ij} - a_{rj}a_{is}/a_{rs} & 0 \\ a_{rj}/a_{rs} & 1 \end{bmatrix} \tag{4.34}$$

When all non-negative indicators are obtained, the pivot operation stops. We now set the nonbasic variables to zero and obtain a basic feasible solution to the linear programming problem.

Example 4.5 Simplex Algorithm for a Two Decision Variables Linear Programming Problem

Consider the following linear programming problem:

$$\max_{\mathbf{x}} \mathbf{c}^T \mathbf{x}$$

subject to

$$\mathbf{Ax} \leq \mathbf{b}$$

$$\mathbf{x} \geq 0$$

where

$$\mathbf{c} = \begin{bmatrix} 7 \\ 5 \end{bmatrix}, \mathbf{x} = \begin{bmatrix} x_1 \\ x_2 \end{bmatrix}, \mathbf{A} = \begin{bmatrix} 4 & 3 \\ 2 & 1 \end{bmatrix} \text{ and } \mathbf{b} = \begin{bmatrix} 24 \\ 10 \end{bmatrix}.$$

Find the optimal value of the decision variable vector $\mathbf{x}$ using the simplex method.

Solution

The first step is to check whether the problem is a standard maximum type problem. This is a standard maximization problem in standard form. The second step is to rewrite two constraints as equivalent equality constraints by using slack variables s_1 and s_2. Thus, we have the following constraints:

$$4x_1 + 3x_2 + s_1 = 24$$

$$2x_1 + x_2 + s_2 = 10$$

The third step is to rewrite the objective function and put it together with the constraints as follows:

$$4x_1 + 3x_2 + s_1 = 24$$

$$2x_1 + x_2 + s_2 = 10$$

$$-7x_1 - 5x_2 + z = 0$$

Now, this problem becomes three linear equations with five variables and we find z to maximize. The fourth step is to write the initial simplex tableau as shown in Table p4.1.

Table p4.1 Initial simplex tableau for Example 4.5.

	x_1	x_2	s_1	s_2	z	
s_1	4	3	1	0	0	24
s_2	2	1	0	1	0	10
z	-7	-5	0	0	1	0

From the initial simplex tableau, the initial solution is $x_1 = 0$, $x_2 = 0$, $s_1 = 24$, $s_2 = 10$, and $z = 0$. The fifth step is to find the pivot element and perform the pivot operation. We select the pivot column with the most negative indicator in the last row of the initial simplex tableau and the pivot row with the smallest non-negative ratio as shown in Table p4.2.

We perform the pivot operation: (i) Row#2/2 → Row#2, (ii) -4Row #2 + Row#1 → Row#1, and (iii) 7Row #2 + Row#3 → Row#3 and have the simplex tableau as shown in Table p4.3.

Now we have $x_1 = 5$, $x_2 = 0$, $s_1 = 4$, $s_2 = 0$, and $z = 35$. We keep pivoting until all non-negative indicators are obtained. We select the next pivot column and row as shown in Table p4.4.

Table p4.2 First selection of pivot column and row.

	x_1	x_2	s_1	s_2	z	
s_1	4	3	1	0	0	24 (24/4 = 6)
s_2	②	1	0	1	0	10 (10/2 = 5)
z	-7	-5	0	0	1	0

The most negative indicator   The smallest positive pivot row

Table p4.3 Second simplex tableau.

	x_1	x_2	s_1	s_2	z	
s_1	0	1	1	-2	0	4
x_1	1	1/2	0	1/2	0	5
z	0	-1.5	0	3.5	1	35

Table p4.4 Third simplex tableau.

	x_1	x_2	s_1	s_2	z	
s_1	0	①	1	-2	0	4 (4/1 = 4)
x_1	1	1/2	0	1/2	0	5 (5/(1/2) = 10)
z	0	-1.5	0	3.5	1	35

The most negative indicator   The smallest positive pivot row

Table p4.5 Final simplex tableau.

	x_1	x_2	s_1	s_2	z	
s_1	0	1	1	-2	0	4
x_1	1	1/2	-1/2	3/2	0	3
z	0	0	1.5	0.5	1	41

We perform the pivot operation: (i) -Row#1/2 + Row#2 → Row#2 and (ii) 1.5Row #1 + Row#3 → Row#3 and have the simplex tableau as shown in Table p4.5.

In this simplex tableau, there is no negative number in the last row, and this tableau provides us with the maximum value of z. Thus, we have $x_1 = 3$, $x_2 = 4$, $s_1 = 0$, $s_2 = 0$, and the optimal value of the objective function is $z = 41$.

Example 4.6 *Simplex Algorithm for Three Decision Variables Linear Programming Problem*

Consider the following linear programming problem:

$$\max_{\mathbf{x}} \mathbf{c}^T \mathbf{x}$$

subject to

$$\mathbf{Ax} \le \mathbf{b}$$

$$\mathbf{x} \ge 0$$

where

$$\mathbf{c} = \begin{bmatrix} 6 \\ 14 \\ 13 \end{bmatrix}, \mathbf{x} = \begin{bmatrix} x_1 \\ x_2 \\ x_3 \end{bmatrix}, \mathbf{A} = \begin{bmatrix} 1 & 4 & 2 \\ 1 & 2 & 4 \end{bmatrix} \text{ and } \mathbf{b} = \begin{bmatrix} 48 \\ 60 \end{bmatrix}.$$

Find the optimal value of the decision variable vector **x**.

Solution

The first step is to check whether the problem is a standard maximum type problem. This is a standard maximization problem in standard form. The second step is to rewrite two constraints as equivalent equality constraints by using slack variables s_1 and s_2. Thus, we have the following constraints:

$$x_1 + 4x_2 + 2x_3 + s_1 = 48$$

$$x_1 + 2x_2 + 4x_3 + s_2 = 60$$

The third step is to rewrite the objective function and put it together with the constraints as follows:

$$x_1 + 4x_2 + 2x_3 + s_1 = 48$$

$$x_1 + 2x_2 + 4x_3 + s_2 = 60$$

$$-6x_1 - 14x_2 - 13x_3 + z = 0$$

Table p4.6 Initial simplex tableau for Example 4.6.

	x_1	x_2	x_3	s_1	s_2	z	
s_1	1	4	2	1	0	0	48
s_2	1	2	4	0	1	0	60
z	−6	−14	−13	0	0	1	0

Table p4.7 First selection of pivot column and row.

	x_1	x_2	x_3	s_1	s_2	z	
s_1	1	④	2	1	0	0	48 (48/4=12)
s_2	1	2	4	0	1	0	60 (60/2=30)
z	−6	−14	−13	0	0	1	0

The most negative indicator   The smallest positive pivot row

Table p4.8 Simplex tableau 2.

	x_1	x_2	x_3	s_1	s_2	z	
x_2	0.25	1	0.5	0.25	0	0	12
s_2	0.5	0	3	−0.5	1	0	36
z	−2.5	0	−6	3.5	0	1	168

Now, this problem became three linear equations with six variables and we find z to maximize. The fourth step is to write the initial simplex tableau as shown in Table p4.6.

The fifth step is to find the pivot element and perform the pivot operation as shown in Table p4.7.

We perform the pivot operation: (i) Row#1/4 → Row#1, (ii) −2Row#1+ Row#2 → Row#2, (iii) 14Row#1+ Row#3 2 → Row#3 and generate Table p4.8.

We keep pivoting until all non-negative indicators are obtained. We select the next pivot column and row as shown in Table p4.9.

We perform the pivot operation: (i) Row#2/3 → Row#1, (ii) −Row#2/2+ Row#1 →Row#1, (iii) 6Row#1+ Row#3 → Row#3 and generate Table p4.10.

We keep pivoting until all non-negative indicators are obtained. We select the next pivot column and row as shown in Table p4.11.

We perform the pivot operation: (i) 6Row#1 → Row#1, (ii) −Row#1/6+ Row#2 → Row#2, (iii) 1.5Row#1+ Row#3 → Row#3 and generate Table p4.12.

Table p4.9 Second selection of pivot column and row.

	x_1	x_2	x_3	s_1	s_2	z	
x_2	0.25	1	0.5	0.25	0	0	12 $(12/0.5=24)$
s_2	0.5	0	③	−0.5	1	0	36 $(36/3=12)$
z	−2.5	0	−6	3.5	0	1	168

The most negative indicator   The smallest positive pivot row

Table p4.10 Simplex tableau 3.

	x_1	x_2	x_3	s_1	s_2	z	
x_2	1/6	1	0	1/3	−1/6	0	6
x_3	1/6	0	1	−1/6	1/3	0	12
z	−1.5	0	0	2.5	2	1	240

Table p4.11 Third selection of pivot column and row.

	x_1	x_2	x_3	s_1	s_2	z	
x_2	①/6	1	0	1/3	−1/6	0	6 $(6/(1/6)=36)$
x_3	1/6	0	1	−1/6	1/3	0	12 $(12/(1/6)=72)$
z	−1.5	0	0	2.5	2	1	240

The most negative indicator   The smallest positive pivot row

Table p4.12 Final simplex tableau.

	x_1	x_2	x_3	s_1	s_2	z	
x_1	1	6	0	2	−1	0	36
x_3	0	−1	1	−0.5	0.5	0	6
z	0	9	0	5.5	0.5	1	294

In this final simplex tableau, there is no negative number in the last row and this tableau provides us with the maximum value of z. Thus, we have $x_1 = 36$, $x_2 = 0$, $x_3 = 6$, $s_1 = 0$, $s_2 = 0$, and the optimal value of the objective function is $z = 294$.

Summary 4.3 Simplex Method

1) The simplex method is a matrix-based method to solve linear programming problems with any number of decision variables.
2) The steps of the simplex algorithm are as follows:
   - The first step is to check whether the linear programming problem is a standard maximum type problem or to convert it to standard maximum type problem.
   - The second step is to add slack variables and convert the inequality constraints to equivalent equality constraints in the form $a_{11}x_1 + a_{12}x_2 + s_1 = b_1$. The slack variables are always non-negative.
   - The third step is to rewrite the objective function to match the form of the slack equations. It should be an equation in the form where the left-hand side $= 0$.
   - The fourth step is to write the initial simplex tableau. We place the equality constraints into a matrix and put the objective function in the bottom row.
   - The fifth step is to find the pivot element and perform the pivot operation.
   - Lastly, the pivot operation stops when all non-negative indicators are obtained. We now set the nonbasic variables to zero and obtain a basic feasible solution to the linear programming problem.

4.4 Convex Optimization

The classical categorization view of optimization problems was linear or nonlinear. Linear programming is easy to solve and nonlinear programming is harder. However, after studying convex optimization and developing solutions such as interior point methods (IPMs) for them, optimization problems are categorized as convex optimization problems or non-convex optimization problems. Convex optimization problems are fundamentally tractable while other optimization problems cannot be efficiently solved. A convex optimization problem is more general than linear programming problems and is a subset of optimization problems that minimizes a convex function over a convex set. Convex optimization covers convexity analysis, modeling and problem formulation, optimization, and numerical analysis. It became an important tool for wireless communication systems design for multiple reasons: (i) convex optimization problems are computationally tractable; (ii) it can be solved by polynomial time complexity algorithms; (iii) it always achieves a global minimum; (iv) a first-order optimality condition is sufficient; (v) a real valued convex function has properties of differentiability; (vi) and efficient software tools exist. Among them, the most appealing to a system designer is that it finds a global optimum. Most optimization algorithms only guarantee a local optimum, and it is very difficult to find a global optimum for general nonlinear functions.

Definition 4.4 Convex Optimization

Convex optimization is a subset of optimization where functions are convex. Convex function simply means bowl-shaped function, and it makes optimization easier than general optimization because a local minimum becomes a global minimum.

A convex optimization problem is expressed as the following standard form [5]:

$$\min_{\mathbf{x}} f_0(\mathbf{x}) \tag{4.35}$$

subject to

$$f_i(\mathbf{x}) \leq 0, i = 1, 2, \ldots, m$$
$$h_j(\mathbf{x}) = 0, \quad j = 1, 2, \ldots, p \tag{4.36}$$

where the objective function f_0 and the constraint functions $f_1, \ldots, f_m$ are convex satisfying

$$f_i(\alpha \mathbf{x} + \beta \mathbf{y}) \leq \alpha f_i(\mathbf{x}) + \beta f_i(\mathbf{y}) \tag{4.37}$$

for all $\mathbf{x}, \mathbf{y} \in \mathbb{R}^n$ and all $\alpha, \beta \in [0, 1]$ with $\alpha + \beta = 1$. The equality constraint function ($h_j(\mathbf{x}) = \mathbf{a}_j^T \mathbf{x} - b_j$ where $\mathbf{a}_j$ is a column vector and b_j is a real number) must be affine and convex equality constraints are linear. Figure 4.7 illustrates examples of convex and non-convex functions. Roughly speaking, a function is convex when satisfying this condition: if $z = \alpha x + \beta y$ varies over the line $[x, y]$, the point $(z, f(z))$ is located below the line connecting two points $(x, f(x))$ and $(y, f(y))$.

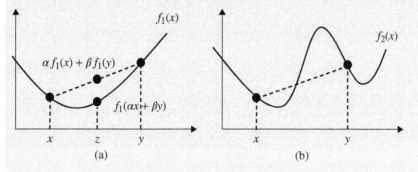

Figure 4.7 Examples of (a) a convex function $f_1(\mathbf{x})$; and (b) a non-convex function $f_2(\mathbf{x})$.

Least squares problems and linear programming problems are special cases of convex optimization problems. In addition, quadratic programming problems, second-order cone programming (SOCP) problems, and semidefinite programming (SDP) problems are part of the general convex optimization problem. Generally, a hierarchical structure of convex optimization problems is as follows [11]: convex optimization problems (CP) $\supset$ semidefinite programming (SDP) $\supset$ second-order cone programming (SOCP) $\supset$ convex quadratic programming (CQP) $\supset$ linear programming (LP). There are no generalized analytical solutions for convex optimization problems. Finding a generalized solution is still an active research area. In order to solve convex optimization problems, there are two approaches

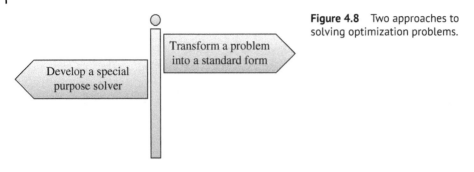

Figure 4.8 Two approaches to solving optimization problems.

as shown in Figure 4.8. The first approach is to transform a problem into a standard convex optimization problem form, put it into the form of LP, CQP, SOCP, SDP, or CP, and then use an existing solver for that specific class of optimization problems. There are reliable and effective methods such as Newton's method and the interior-point method. The interior-point method solves the problem in a number of iterations (typically 10–100). The other approach is a case-by-case and empirical approach. Special purpose solvers can be developed for specific optimization problems.

Now, we introduce a specific class of optimization problems. A quadratic programming (QP) problem is an optimization problem with a quadratic objective function of decision variables and constraints that are all linear functions of variables. A general quadratic programming problem can be formulated as follows:

$$\min_x f(\mathbf{x}) \tag{4.38}$$

subject to

$$\mathbf{A}\mathbf{x} \leq \mathbf{b}$$

$$\mathbf{x} \geq 0 \tag{4.39}$$

where $f(\mathbf{x}) = \frac{1}{2}\mathbf{x}^T\mathbf{Q}\mathbf{x} + \mathbf{q}^T\mathbf{x}$, $\mathbf{x} \in \mathbb{R}^n$, $\mathbf{Q} \in \mathbb{R}^{n \times n}$, $\mathbf{q} \in \mathbb{R}^n$, $\mathbf{A} \in \mathbb{R}^{m \times n}$, and $\mathbf{b} \in \mathbb{R}^m$. When the matrix $\mathbf{Q}$ is positive semidefinite or positive definite, we call this a convex quadratic programming (CQP) problem. As we can observe from Equations (4.38) and (4.39), a linear programming problem is a special case of a QP problem if the matrix $\mathbf{Q}$ is equal to 0. In order to solve the inequality constrained QP problem, there are two classes of algorithms: active-set method and interior-point method (IPM). Conjugated gradient methods are used to solve the unconstrained QP problem ($\min_x f(\mathbf{x})$) when the matrix $\mathbf{Q}$ is symmetric and positive definite. Iterative project algorithms are used to solve boxed constrained QP problems ($\min_x f(\mathbf{x})$ s.t. $\mathbf{a} \leq \mathbf{x} \leq \mathbf{b}$). In order to solve the equality constrained QP ($\min_x f(\mathbf{x})$ s.t. $\mathbf{A}\mathbf{x} = \mathbf{b}$), a gradient projection method can be used. A SOCP problem is a convex optimization problem in which a linear function is minimized over the intersection of an affine set and the product of second-order cones (also called the Lorentz cone). Feasible regions are intersections of conic regions. A SOCP problem can be formulated as follows:

$$\min_x f(\mathbf{x}) \tag{4.40}$$

subject to

$$\|\mathbf{A}_i\mathbf{x} + \mathbf{b}_i\| \leq \mathbf{c}_i^T\mathbf{x} + \mathbf{d}_i, \quad i = 1, \ldots, m \tag{4.41}$$

where $f(\mathbf{x}) = \mathbf{f}^T\mathbf{x}$, $\mathbf{x} \in \mathbb{R}^n$, $\mathbf{f} \in \mathbb{R}^n$, $\mathbf{A}_i \in \mathbb{R}^{n_i \times n}$, $\mathbf{b}_i \in \mathbb{R}^{n_i}$, $\mathbf{c}_i \in \mathbb{R}^n$, $\mathbf{d}_i \in \mathbb{R}$. The norm $\|\cdot\|$ is the standard Euclidean norm. We call the constraint a second-order cone constraint of dimension n_i. As we can observe from Equations (4.40) and (4.41), this linear programming problem is a special case of a SOCP problem if the matrix $\mathbf{A}_i$ is equal to 0. If the vector $\mathbf{c}_i$ is equal to 0, it becomes a convex, quadratically constrained, linear programming problem. The standard second-order cone of dimension k is defined as follows [11]:

$$C_k = \left\{ \begin{bmatrix} \mathbf{u} \\ t \end{bmatrix} \mid \mathbf{u} \in \mathbb{R}^{k-1}, t \in \mathbb{R}, \|\mathbf{u}\| \leq t \right\} \tag{4.42}$$

For $k = 1$, the standard second-order cone becomes

$$C_1 = \{ t \mid t \in \mathbb{R}, 0 \leq t \} \tag{4.43}$$

The set of points satisfying a second-order cone constraint is the inverse image of a second-order cone under an affine mapping as follows:

$$\|\mathbf{A}_i\mathbf{x} + \mathbf{b}_i\| \leq \mathbf{c}_i^T\mathbf{x} + \mathbf{d}_i \leftrightarrow \begin{bmatrix} \mathbf{A}_i \\ \mathbf{c}_i^T \end{bmatrix} \mathbf{x} + \begin{bmatrix} \mathbf{b}_i \\ \mathbf{d}_i \end{bmatrix} \in C_{n_i} \tag{4.44}$$

and it is convex [11]. Thus, the SOCP is a convex programming problem because both objective function and constraints are convex. The SOCP can be solved by IPMs. A SDP is a generalization of linear programming over the intersection of the cone of positive semidefinite matrices. The SDP minimizes a linear objective function subject to the constraints that an affine combination of symmetric matrices is positive semidefinite. The SDP problem is a convex optimization problem and can be efficiently solved by IPMs. The computational complexity is approximately the same as for linear programming. Thus, the SDP finds many applications in communication and network theory, control engineering, and combinatorial optimization. It deserves credit for the most exciting development of optimization theory in the 1990s. A SDP problem can be formulated as follows:

$$\min_{\mathbf{x}} f(\mathbf{X}) \tag{4.45}$$

subject to

$$\mathbf{A}_i \circ \mathbf{X} = b_i, \quad i = 1, \ldots, m$$
$$\mathbf{X} \geq 0 \tag{4.46}$$

where $f(\mathbf{X}) = \mathbf{C} \circ \mathbf{X} = \sum_{i=1}^{n} \sum_{j=1}^{n} C_{ij} X_{ij}$, $\mathbf{X} \in \mathbb{S}^n$, $\mathbb{S}^n$ is a linear space of $n \times n$ symmetric matrices, $\mathbf{A}_i \in \mathbb{S}^n$, and $b_i \in \mathbb{R}$. As we can observe from Equations (4.45) and (4.46), the objective function is linear and there are two types of constraints: affine constraints with m linear equations with regard to the decision variable matrix $\mathbf{X}$, and the decision variable matrix $\mathbf{X}$ must lie in the closed convex cone of positive semidefinite symmetric matrices. The standard form of the SDP is very similar to that of the LP. The different part between them is the semidefinite constraint. In the LP, the constraint $\mathbf{x} \geq 0$ addresses that the decision variables must be non-negative. In the SDP, the semidefinite constraint $\mathbf{X} \succ 0$ addresses that each of the n eigenvalues of the decision variable matrix must be non-negative.

Summary 4.4 Convex Optimization

1) Convex optimization is an important tool of wireless communication systems design for multiple reasons: (i) convex optimization problems are computationally tractable; (ii) they can be solved by polynomial time complexity algorithms; (iii) they always achieve a global minimum; (iv) a first-order optimality condition is sufficient; (v) a real valued convex function has properties of differentiability; and (vi) efficient software tools exist.

2) The standard form of convex optimization problems is as follows:

$$\min_{\mathbf{x}} f_0(\mathbf{x})$$

subject to

$$i = 1, 2, \ldots, m$$
$$j = 1, 2, \ldots, p$$

where the objective function f_0 and the constraint functions $f_1, \ldots, f_m$ are convex satisfying $f_i(\alpha \mathbf{x} + \beta \mathbf{y}) \le \alpha f_i(\mathbf{x}) + \beta f_i(\mathbf{y})$ for all $\mathbf{x}, \mathbf{y} \in \mathbb{R}^n$ and all $\alpha, \beta \in [0, 1]$ with $\alpha + \beta = 1$.

3) A hierarchical structure of convex optimization problems is as follows: convex optimization problems (CP) $\supset$ semidefinite programming (SDP) $\supset$ second-order cone programming (SOCP) $\supset$ convex quadratic programming (CQP) $\supset$ linear programming (LP).

4) There are two approaches to convex optimization. The first approach is to transform a problem into a standard convex optimization problem form, put it into the form of LP, CQP, SOCP, SDP, or CP, and then use an existing solver for a specific class of optimization problems. The other approach is a case-by-case and empirical approach. Special purpose solvers can be developed for specific optimization problems.

4.4.1 Barrier Method

The IPMs play an important role in convex optimization. As we briefly reviewed the hierarchical structure of convex optimization problems, the IPM impacts on LP, CQP, SOCP, and SDP. The IPM is a very useful tool for many convex optimization problems and is applied in practice. However, it requires differentiability of the objective function and constraints. If the size of the problem is very large, it is not efficient. Gradient descent methods are more suited for medium accuracy solutions in large convex optimization problems. The IPM starts searching for a solution from the interior of the feasible region and keep updating until converging to an optimal solution. Thus, the interior of the feasible region should not be empty, and also most of iterations should be in the interior of the

Figure 4.9 Approach of the interior point method.

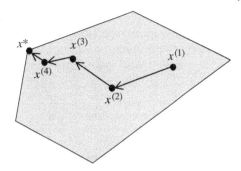

feasible region. The basic idea is to approximate the constraints of optimization problems using Newton's method. Firstly, the optimization problem is formulated in a standard form. Next, an optimal solution in the feasible region is iteratively searched by Newton's method. There are two algorithms of the IPMs: the barrier method and the primal-dual method. They are similar, but the primal-dual IPM is more efficient because it is more accurate with similar iterations and solves larger optimization problems. Figure 4.9 illustrates the IPM approach; we start with the initial solution $x^{(1)}$ inside the feasible region. If the current solution is good enough by optimality conditions, we stop iteration. If not, the solution moves in the interior of the feasible region by a feasible direction and step-length. In the next iteration, $x^{(2)}$ is found. After we keep updating, the optimal solution x^* is finally obtained.

Consider the following convex optimization problem:

$$\min_x f_0(\mathbf{x}) \tag{4.47}$$

subject to

$$f_i(\mathbf{x}) \leq 0, \quad i = 1, 2, \ldots, m$$
$$\mathbf{Ax} = \mathbf{b} \tag{4.48}$$

where f_i are convex and twice continuously differentiable and the matrix $\mathbf{A} \in \mathbb{R}^{p \times n}$ has rank $\mathbf{A} = p$. The IPM solves the problem by applying Newton's method. It puts the inequality constraints in the objective and the problem becomes a sequence of the equality-constrained problem. The convex optimization problem given in Equations (4.47) and (4.48) is transformed as follows:

$$\min_x f_0(\mathbf{x}) + (1/t)\phi(\mathbf{x}) \tag{4.49}$$

subject to

$$\mathbf{Ax} = \mathbf{b} \tag{4.50}$$

where ϕ is the logarithmic barrier function ($\phi(\mathbf{x}) = -\sum_{i=1}^{m} \ln -f_i(\mathbf{x})$) and $t > 0$ is a penalty parameter about the accuracy of the approximation. As t increases, the approximation becomes more accurate but the Hessian of the objective function varies rapidly near the boundary of the feasible set. Thus, we should consider a trade-off between accuracy and stability. Its domain (**dom** $\phi = \{\mathbf{x} \in \mathbb{R}^n \,|\, f_i(\mathbf{x}) < 0,\ i = 1,\ \ldots,\ m\}$) is the set of points satisfying all inequality constraints. We assume that the optimal value $f_0(\mathbf{x}^*) = p^*$ is finite and attained and also the problem is strictly feasible. Thus, strong duality holds and dual optimum is attained. Under the assumption, $\mathbf{x}^*$ is an optimal if and only if there exist dual optimal $\boldsymbol{\lambda}^* \in \mathbb{R}^m$ and $\boldsymbol{\nu}^* \in \mathbb{R}^p$ (λ and ν are called Lagrange multipliers or dual variables) satisfying the Karush–Kuhn–Tucker (KKT) conditions.

Definition 4.5 KKT Conditions

KKT conditions are defined as follows:

$$\text{Primal feasibility}: \mathbf{A}\mathbf{x}^* = \mathbf{b}, \quad f_i(\mathbf{x}^*) \leq 0, \quad i = 1, \ldots, m \tag{4.51}$$

$$\text{Dual feasibility}: \boldsymbol{\lambda}^* > 0 \tag{4.52}$$

$$\text{Lagrangian optimality in } \mathbf{x}: \nabla f_0(\mathbf{x}^*) + \sum_{i=1}^{m} \lambda^* \nabla f_i(\mathbf{x}^*) + \mathbf{A}^T \boldsymbol{\nu}^* = 0 \tag{4.53}$$

$$\text{Complementary slackness}: \lambda_i^* f_i(\mathbf{x}^*) = 0, \quad i = 1, \ldots, m \tag{4.54}$$

In general, when we have the following standard optimization problem (or primal problem):

$$\min_{\mathbf{x}} f_0(\mathbf{x}) \tag{4.55}$$

subject to

$$f_i(\mathbf{x}) \leq 0, \quad i = 1, 2, \ldots, m$$
$$h_j(\mathbf{x}) = 0, \quad j = 1, 2, \ldots, p \tag{4.56}$$

and its optimal value is p^* and $\mathbf{x} \in \mathbb{R}^n$ is in domain $\mathbb{D}$, the Lagrangian is defined as follows:

$$L(\mathbf{x}, \boldsymbol{\lambda}, \boldsymbol{\nu}) = f_0(\mathbf{x}) + \sum_{i=1}^{m} \lambda_i f_i(\mathbf{x}) + \sum_{j=1}^{p} \nu_j h_j(\mathbf{x}) \tag{4.57}$$

where λ_i and ν_j are the Lagrange multipliers associated with $f_i(\mathbf{x}) \leq 0$ and $h_j(\mathbf{x}) = 0$, respectively. In addition, we have a Lagrangian dual problem as follows:

$$\max_{\lambda, \nu} \theta(\lambda, \nu) \tag{4.58}$$

subject to

$$\lambda \geq 0 \tag{4.59}$$

where the Lagrangian dual function is defined as follows:

$$\theta(\lambda, \nu) = \inf_{\mathbf{x} \in \mathbb{D}} L(\mathbf{x}, \lambda, \nu) \tag{4.60}$$

where inf denotes the infimum of the domain $\mathbb{D}$. If $\mathbf{x}$ is primal feasible, $\theta(\lambda, \nu) \leq f_0(\mathbf{x})$ and $f_0(\mathbf{x}) - \theta(\lambda, \nu)$ is called the duality gap. This problem is convex optimization and finds the best lower bound on p^* obtained from the dual function. When the optimal value of the dual problem is d^*, $p^* - d^*$ is the optimal duality gap. We call weak duality and strong duality when $d^* \leq p^*$ and $d^* = p^*$, respectively. This dual approach is not always guaranteed to succeed, but it often allows us to have a simpler optimization problem. Thus, IPMs can solve the KKT conditions. The convex optimization problem in Equations (4.49) and (4.50) can be equivalently reformulated as follows:

$$\min_{\mathbf{x}} t f_0(\mathbf{x}) + \phi(\mathbf{x}) \tag{4.61}$$

subject to

$$\mathbf{Ax} = \mathbf{b} \tag{4.62}$$

We assume an optimal solution $\mathbf{x}^*(t)$ for the problem Equations (4.61) and (4.62) exists for $t > 0$. The central path for the problem Equations (4.61) and (4.62) is defined as the set $\{\mathbf{x}^*(t) \mid t > 0\}$. Every central point is a lower bound on the optimal value p^*. It is an important aspect of IPMs. The central path is a path of strictly feasible points and converges to the optimal solution as $t \to \infty$. The central points on the central path are characterized by the following necessary and sufficient conditions: strict feasibility

$$\mathbf{Ax}^*(t) = \mathbf{b} \text{ and } f_i(\mathbf{x}^*(t)) \leq 0, \quad i = 1, 2, \dots, m \tag{4.63}$$

and the centrality condition, there exists a $\hat{\boldsymbol{\nu}} \in \mathbb{R}^p$ such that

$$t \nabla f_0(\mathbf{x}^*(t)) + \sum_{i=1}^{m} \frac{1}{-f_i(\mathbf{x}^*(t))} \nabla f_i(\mathbf{x}^*(t)) + \mathbf{A}^T \hat{\boldsymbol{\nu}} = 0 \tag{4.64}$$

Therefore, $\mathbf{x}^*(t)$ minimizes the Lagrangian as follows:

$$L(\mathbf{x}, \boldsymbol{\lambda}^*(t), \boldsymbol{\nu}^*(t)) = f_0(\mathbf{x}) + \sum_{i=1}^{m} \lambda_i^*(t) f_i(\mathbf{x}) + \boldsymbol{\nu}^*(t)^T (\mathbf{Ax} - \mathbf{b}) = 0 \tag{4.65}$$

where

$$\lambda_i^*(t) = -\frac{1}{t f_i(\mathbf{x}^*(t))}, \quad i = 1, \dots, m \text{ and } \boldsymbol{\nu}^*(t) = \frac{\hat{\boldsymbol{\nu}}}{t} \tag{4.66}$$

The dual function $g(\boldsymbol{\lambda}^*(t), \boldsymbol{\nu}^*(t))$ is finite as follows:

$$g(\boldsymbol{\lambda}^*(t), \boldsymbol{\nu}^*(t)) = L(\mathbf{x}^*(t), \boldsymbol{\lambda}^*(t), \boldsymbol{\nu}^*(t)) = f_0(\mathbf{x}^*(t))$$

$$+ \sum_{i=1}^{m} \lambda_i^*(t) f_i(\mathbf{x}^*(t)) + \boldsymbol{\nu}^*(t)^T (\mathbf{Ax}^*(t) - \mathbf{b})$$

$$= f_0(\mathbf{x}^*(t)) - \frac{m}{t}. \tag{4.67}$$

This dual function implies a duality gap m/t. This confirms that $f_0(\mathbf{x}^*(t)) \to p^*$ if $t \to \infty$ as follows:

$$f_0(\mathbf{x}^*(t)) - \frac{m}{t} \leq p^* \tag{4.68}$$

Now, we can have a modified KKT condition. The vector $\mathbf{x}$ is equal to $\mathbf{x}^*(t)$ if and only if there exists λ and ν such that

$$\text{Primal feasibility}: \mathbf{Ax} = \mathbf{b}, \quad f_i(\mathbf{x}) \leq 0, \quad i = 1, \dots, m \tag{4.69}$$

Dual feasibility: $\lambda > 0$ (4.70)

Lagrangian optimality in $\mathbf{x}$: $\nabla f_0(\mathbf{x}) + \sum_{i=1}^{m} \lambda_i \nabla f_i(\mathbf{x}) + \mathbf{A}^T \boldsymbol{\nu} = 0$ (4.71)

Complementary slackness: $-\lambda_i f_i(\mathbf{x}) = 1/t, \quad i = 1, \ldots, m$ (4.72)

Comparing Equations (4.51)–(4.54) with Equations (4.69)–(4.72), only complementary slackness is relaxed from 0 to $1/t$. When t is large enough, approximate complementary slackness converges to the original complementary slackness and an optimal solution $\mathbf{x}^*(t)$ and a dual feasible pair $\lambda^*(t), \nu^*(t)$ satisfy the original KKT optimality conditions Equations (4.51)–(4.54).

The barrier method (also called path-following method or sequential unconstrained minimization technique [SUMT]) solves a sequence of linearly constrained (or unconstrained) minimization problems like Equations (4.61) and (4.62). We compute $\mathbf{x}^*(t)$ for increasing values of $t > 0$, until $m/t \leq \varepsilon$ where ε is tolerance (or desired accuracy). It guarantees to have a ε-suboptimal solution for the original problem Equations (4.47) and (4.48). We start at $t = t^{(0)} > 0$ and solve the problem using Newton's method at the centering step to produce $\mathbf{x}^{(0)} = \mathbf{x}^*(t)$. Then, we increase t for a barrier parameter $\mu > 1$. We can summarize the steps of the barrier method as follows:

Initial conditions: Strictly feasible $\mathbf{x}$, $t = t^{(0)} > 0$, $\mu > 1$ and $\varepsilon > 0$
Repeat
- ***Step 1***: Centering step. Compute $\mathbf{x}^*(t)$ solving $\min_{\mathbf{x}} t f_0(\mathbf{x}) + \phi(\mathbf{x})$ subject to $\mathbf{A}\mathbf{x} = \mathbf{b}$
- ***Step 2***: Update. Produce $\mathbf{x}^{(k)} = \mathbf{x}^*(t)$ at $t = t^{(k)}$ for $k = 1, 2, \ldots$
- ***Step 3***: Stop condition. Stop if $m/t \leq \varepsilon$
- ***Step 4***: Increase penalty. $t^{(k+1)} = \mu t$
Until it converges: $m/t \leq \varepsilon$

The Step 1 centering steps are regarded as outer iterations, and computing $\mathbf{x}^*(t)$ using Newton's method as inner iterations. It terminates with $f_0(\mathbf{x}^*(t)) - p^* \leq \varepsilon$. There are two important parameters we carefully choose: μ and $t^{(0)}$. The choice of μ involves a trade-off between number of inner iterations and number of outer iterations. If μ is small, many outer iterations are needed. If μ is big, Newton's method needs many iterations to converge. Typical values of μ are 10–20. Choice of $t^{(0)}$ involves a trade-off between number of inner iterations within the first outer iteration and number of outer iterations. If $t^{(0)}$ is small, many outer iterations are needed. If $t^{(0)}$ is big, the first outer iteration requires many iterations to compute $\mathbf{x}^{(0)}$. The number of centering steps is required as follows [5]:

$$\left\lceil \frac{\log(m/(\varepsilon t^{(0)}))}{\log \mu} \right\rceil$$ (4.73)

where m and ε are the number of inequality constraints and tolerance (or desired accuracy), respectively. In Step 1, Newton's method is used for linearly constrained minimization. We eliminate the variable λ_i from the modified KKT equations and apply Newton's method to solve the equations. The Newton step $\Delta\mathbf{x}_{NT}$ and associated dual variable $\mathbf{v}_{NT}$ are given by the linear equations as follows:

$$\begin{bmatrix} t\nabla^2 f_0(\mathbf{x}) + \nabla^2\phi(\mathbf{x}) & \mathbf{A}^T \\ \mathbf{A} & 0 \end{bmatrix} \begin{bmatrix} \Delta\mathbf{x}_{NT} \\ \mathbf{v}_{NT} \end{bmatrix} = \begin{bmatrix} -t\nabla f_0(\mathbf{x}) - \nabla\phi(\mathbf{x}) \\ 0 \end{bmatrix} \tag{4.74}$$

The Newton step directly solves the modified KKT Equations (4.69)–(4.72). The Lagrangian optimality condition and primal feasibility condition of the modified KKT conditions are rewritten by eliminating λ_i ($\lambda_i = -1/(tf_i(\mathbf{x}))$) as follows:

$$\nabla f_0(\mathbf{x}) + \sum_{i=1}^{m} \frac{1}{-tf_i(\mathbf{x})} \nabla f_i(\mathbf{x}) + \mathbf{A}^T \mathbf{v} = 0 \tag{4.75}$$

$$\mathbf{A}\mathbf{x} = \mathbf{b} \tag{4.76}$$

In order to find the Newton step, we use a Taylor approximation. For v is small, we have

$$\nabla f_0(\mathbf{x} + v) + \sum_{i=1}^{m} \frac{1}{(-tf_i(\mathbf{x}+v))} \nabla f_i(\mathbf{x}+v) \approx \nabla f_0(\mathbf{x}) + \sum_{i=1}^{m} \frac{1}{(-tf_i(\mathbf{x}))} \nabla f_i(\mathbf{x}) + \nabla^2 f_0(\mathbf{x})v$$

$$+ \sum_{i=1}^{m} \frac{1}{(-tf_i(\mathbf{x}))} \nabla^2 f_i(\mathbf{x})v + \sum_{i=1}^{m} \frac{1}{tf_i(\mathbf{x})^2} \nabla f_i(\mathbf{x})\nabla f_i(\mathbf{x})^T v \tag{4.77}$$

and Equations (4.75) and (4.76) are rewritten as follows:

$$\mathbf{H}v + \mathbf{A}^T \mathbf{v} = -\mathbf{g} \tag{4.78}$$

$$\mathbf{A}v = 0 \tag{4.79}$$

where

$$\mathbf{H} = \nabla^2 f_0(\mathbf{x}) + \sum_{i=1}^{m} \frac{1}{(-tf_i(\mathbf{x}))} \nabla^2 f_i(\mathbf{x}) + \sum_{i=1}^{m} \frac{1}{tf_i(\mathbf{x})^2} \nabla f_i(\mathbf{x})\nabla f_i(\mathbf{x})^T = \nabla^2 f_0(\mathbf{x}) + (1/t)\nabla^2\phi(\mathbf{x}) \tag{4.80}$$

$$\mathbf{g} = \nabla f_0(\mathbf{x}) + \sum_{i=1}^{m} \frac{1}{(-tf_i(\mathbf{x}))} \nabla f_i(\mathbf{x}) = \nabla f_0(\mathbf{x}) + (1/t)\nabla\phi(\mathbf{x}) \tag{4.81}$$

Thus, the Newton step $\Delta\mathbf{x}_{NT}$ and associated dual variable $\mathbf{v}_{NT}$ satisfy the following:

$$t\mathbf{H}\Delta\mathbf{x}_{NT} + \mathbf{A}^T \mathbf{v}_{NT} = -t\mathbf{g} \text{ and } \mathbf{A}\Delta\mathbf{x}_{NT} = 0 \tag{4.82}$$

due to $v = \Delta\mathbf{x}_{NT}$ and $\mathbf{v} = \mathbf{v}_{NT}/t$.

Summary 4.5 Barrier Method

1) The interior point methods play an important role in convex optimization. There are two algorithms of the interior point methods: the barrier method and the primal-dual method.
2) We can summarize the steps of the barrier method as follows:

(Continued)

Initial conditions: Strictly feasible $\mathbf{x}$, $t = t^{(0)} > 0$, $\mu > 1$ and $\varepsilon > 0$
Repeat
- **Step 1**: Centering step. Compute $\mathbf{x}^*(t)$ solving $\min_\mathbf{x} t f_0(\mathbf{x}) + \phi(\mathbf{x})$ subject to $\mathbf{Ax} = \mathbf{b}$
- **Step 2**: Update. Produce $\mathbf{x}^{(k)} = \mathbf{x}^*(t)$ at $t = t^{(k)}$ for $k = 1,2,\ldots$
- **Step 3**: Stop condition. Stop if $m/t \le \varepsilon$
- **Step 4**: Increase penalty. $t^{(k+1)} = \mu t$

Until it converges: $m/t \le \varepsilon$

4.4.2 Primal-Dual Interior Point Method

Primal-dual IPMs are also motivated by Newton's method and are similar to the barrier method. Some advantages over the barrier method are as follows: (i) it is more efficient because there is no distinction between inner iterations and outer iterations – both primal and dual variables are updated at each iteration; (ii) it can start at an infeasible point for equality constraints; and (iii) it empirically converges faster. In the primal-dual method, both the primal variable $\mathbf{x}$ and the associated dual variables λ, ν are updated. From the modified KKT condition, we define a residual $r_t(\mathbf{x}, \lambda, \nu) \in \mathbb{R}^n \times \mathbb{R}^m \times \mathbb{R}^p$ as follows:

$$r_t(\mathbf{x}, \lambda, \nu) = \begin{bmatrix} r_d \\ r_c \\ r_p \end{bmatrix} = \begin{bmatrix} \nabla f_0(\mathbf{x}) + Df(\mathbf{x})^T \lambda + \mathbf{A}^T \nu \\ -\mathrm{diag}(\lambda) f(\mathbf{x}) - (1/t)\mathbf{e} \\ \mathbf{Ax} - \mathbf{b} \end{bmatrix} \tag{4.83}$$

where $t > 0$, $\mathbf{e}$ is the vector of all 1s of m dimension, diag () is a diagonal matrix, and $f(\mathbf{x})$ and the derivative matrix $Df(\mathbf{x})$ are represented as follows:

$$f(\mathbf{x}) = \begin{bmatrix} f_1(\mathbf{x}) \\ \vdots \\ f_m(\mathbf{x}) \end{bmatrix} \quad \text{and} \quad Df(\mathbf{x}) = \begin{bmatrix} \nabla f_1(\mathbf{x})^T \\ \vdots \\ \nabla f_m(\mathbf{x})^T \end{bmatrix} \tag{4.84}$$

In Equation (4.83), r_d, r_c and r_p are called the dual residual, centrality residual and primal residual, respectively. $\mathbf{x}^*(t), \lambda^*(t)$ and $\nu^*(t)$ satisfy $r_t(\mathbf{x}, \lambda, \nu) = 0$ and $f_i(\mathbf{x}^*(t)) < 0, i = 1, \ldots, m$ with duality gap m/t. Thus, we solve $r_t(\mathbf{x}, \lambda, \nu) = 0$ through the first-order Taylor approximation. Given $\mathbf{y} = (\mathbf{x}, \lambda, \nu)$, we find Newton step $\Delta \mathbf{y} = (\Delta \mathbf{x}, \Delta \lambda, \Delta \nu)$ by the following linear equations:

$$r_t(\mathbf{y} + \Delta \mathbf{y}) \approx r_t(\mathbf{y}) + Dr_t(\mathbf{y})\Delta \mathbf{y} = 0 \tag{4.85}$$

$$\Delta \mathbf{y} = -Dr_t(\mathbf{y})^{-1} r_t(\mathbf{y}) \tag{4.86}$$

Specifically, in terms of $\mathbf{x}, \lambda,$ and ν, we have

$$-\begin{bmatrix} r_d \\ r_c \\ r_p \end{bmatrix} = \begin{bmatrix} \nabla^2 f_0(\mathbf{x}) + \sum_{i=1}^m \lambda_i \nabla^2 f_i(\mathbf{x}) & Df(\mathbf{x})^T & \mathbf{A}^T \\ -\mathrm{diag}(\lambda)Df(\mathbf{x}) & -\mathrm{diag}(f(\mathbf{x})) & 0 \\ \mathbf{A} & 0 & 0 \end{bmatrix} \begin{bmatrix} \Delta \mathbf{x} \\ \Delta \lambda \\ \Delta \nu \end{bmatrix} \tag{4.87}$$

The primal-dual search direction $\Delta \mathbf{y}_{pd}$ is the solution of Equation (4.87) and the main difference from the barrier method is $\Delta \lambda$. In the primal-dual IPM, it is not easy to evaluate a duality gap because both the primal variable $\mathbf{x}$ and the associated dual variables λ, $\mathbf{v}$ are not necessarily feasible. Thus, the surrogate duality gap is defined as follows:

$$\hat{\eta}(\mathbf{x}, \lambda) = -f(\mathbf{x})^{-1}\lambda \tag{4.88}$$

It is equal to the duality gap when the primal variable $\mathbf{x}$ and the associated dual variables λ, $\mathbf{v}$ are primal and dual feasible, respectively. Now, we can summarize the steps of the primal-dual interior point method as follows:

Initial conditions: Start with a feasible point $\mathbf{x}$ with $f(\mathbf{x}) < 0$, $\lambda > 0$, $\mu > 1$, tolerance $\varepsilon_f > 0$, $\varepsilon > 0$

Repeat
- ***Step 1***: Determine t. Set $t = \mu m / \hat{\eta}$
- ***Step 2***: Compute primal-dual search direction $\Delta \mathbf{y}_{pd}$
- ***Step 3***: Line search on λ, $f(\mathbf{x})$ and $\|r_t\|$
  - ***Step 3a***: Start with the step size $s = 0.99 s^{max}$ where $s^{max} = \min\{1, \min\{-\lambda_i/\Delta\lambda_i \mid \Delta\lambda_i < 0\}\}$, $s > 0$
  - ***Step 3b***: Continue $s = \beta s$ until $f(\mathbf{x} + s\Delta\mathbf{x}) < 0$, $\|r_t(\mathbf{y} + s\Delta\mathbf{y}_{pd})\| > (1 - \alpha s)\|r_t(\mathbf{y})\|$ where α and β are typically in the range $[0.01\ 0.1]$ and $[0.3\ 0.8]$, respectively
- ***Step 4***: Update. $\mathbf{y} = \mathbf{y} + s\Delta\mathbf{y}_{pd}$

Until $\|r_p\| \leq \varepsilon_f$, $\|r_d\| \leq \varepsilon_f$ and $\hat{\eta} \leq \varepsilon$

As we discussed in Section 4.3, we assume that a convex optimization problem is strictly feasible and have a dual optimal satisfying KKT conditions. The solutions of convex optimization problems can be found by solving the original problem with equality constraints or solving KKT conditions.

Now, we look into a simpler case: the primal-dual IPM for nonlinear programming problems with inequality constraints. Consider the following simplest nonlinear programming problem:

$$\min_{\mathbf{x}} f(\mathbf{x}) \tag{4.89}$$

subject to

$$g_i(\mathbf{x}) \geq 0, \quad i = 1, 2, \ldots, m. \tag{4.90}$$

We introduce slack variables to turn all inequality constraints $g_i(\mathbf{x}) \geq 0$ into non-negativities as follows:

$$\min_{\mathbf{x}} f(\mathbf{x}) \tag{4.91}$$

subject to

$$g_i(\mathbf{x}) - s_i = 0, \quad s_i \geq 0, \quad i = 1, 2, \ldots, m \tag{4.92}$$

where $s = [s_1, \ldots, s_m]$ is the vector of the slack variables. Next, the logarithmic barrier function is introduced and the non-negativity constraints of the slack variables $s_i \geq 0$ are removed as follows:

$$\min_{\mathbf{x}} f(\mathbf{x}) - \gamma \sum_{i=1}^{m} \ln s_i \tag{4.93}$$

subject to

$$g_i(\mathbf{x}) - s_i = 0, \quad i = 1, 2, \ldots, m \tag{4.94}$$

where γ is positive. We call this the barrier problem. The approximation of the barrier problem is highly related to the parameter γ. The parameter γ is similar to the penalty parameter t concerning the accuracy of the approximation in the previous section. As γ decreases, the approximation becomes more accurate. The primal-dual IPM iteratively solves the barrier problem for different values of γ. In order to solve the barrier problem, we define its Lagrangian function as follows:

$$L(\mathbf{x}, \mathbf{s}, \mathbf{z}) = f(\mathbf{x}) - \gamma \sum_{i=1}^{m} \ln s_i - \mathbf{z}^T (g(\mathbf{x}) - \mathbf{s}) \tag{4.95}$$

where $\mathbf{z}$ is the Lagrange multiplier and its first-order optimality conditions are as follows:

$$\nabla_{\mathbf{x}} L(\mathbf{x}, \mathbf{s}, \mathbf{z}) = \nabla_{\mathbf{x}} f(\mathbf{x}) - J(\mathbf{x})^T \mathbf{z} = 0 \tag{4.96}$$

$$\nabla_{\mathbf{s}} L(\mathbf{x}, \mathbf{s}, \mathbf{z}) = -\gamma \mathbf{S}^{-1} \mathbf{e} + \mathbf{z} = 0 \tag{4.97}$$

$$\nabla_{\mathbf{z}} L(\mathbf{x}, \mathbf{s}, \mathbf{z}) = g(\mathbf{x}) - \mathbf{s} = 0 \tag{4.98}$$

where $J(\mathbf{x})$ is a Jacobian matrix of the function $g(\mathbf{x})$, $\mathbf{S}$ is the diagonal matrix $\mathbf{S} = \text{diag}(s_1, \ldots, s_m)$, and $\mathbf{e}$ is a vector of all 1s. We rearrange Equations (4.96)–(4.97) by multiplying Equation (4.97) by $\mathbf{S}$ as follows:

$$\nabla_{\mathbf{x}} f(\mathbf{x}) - J(\mathbf{x})^T \mathbf{z} = 0 \tag{4.99}$$

$$-\gamma \mathbf{e} + \mathbf{S}\mathbf{z} = 0 \tag{4.100}$$

$$g(\mathbf{x}) - \mathbf{s} = 0 \tag{4.101}$$

As we can observe from Equations (4.99)–(4.101), these conditions are the optimality conditions of the original problem when $\gamma = 0$. We reduce γ to zero and make it converge to an optimal point. Now, we apply Newton's method to determine the search directions at an iteration k as follows:

$$\begin{bmatrix} H(\mathbf{x}^k, \mathbf{z}^k) & 0 & -J(\mathbf{x}^k)^T \\ 0 & \mathbf{Z}^k & \mathbf{S}^k \\ J(\mathbf{x}^k) & -\mathbf{I} & 0 \end{bmatrix} \begin{bmatrix} \Delta \mathbf{x}^k \\ \Delta \mathbf{s}^k \\ \Delta \mathbf{z}^k \end{bmatrix} = \begin{bmatrix} -\nabla_{\mathbf{x}} f(\mathbf{x}^k) + J(\mathbf{x}^k)^T \mathbf{z}^k \\ \gamma \mathbf{e} - \mathbf{S}^k \mathbf{Z}^k \mathbf{e} \\ -g(\mathbf{x}^k) + \mathbf{s}^k \end{bmatrix} \tag{4.102}$$

where the Hessian matrix of the Lagrange function $H(\mathbf{x}^k, \mathbf{z}^k) = \nabla^2 f(\mathbf{x}^k) - \sum_{i=1}^{m} z_i^k \nabla^2 g_i(\mathbf{x}^k)$, $\mathbf{Z}$ is the diagonal matrix $\mathbf{Z} = \text{diag}(z_1, \ldots, z_m)$ and $\mathbf{I}$ is the identity matrix. It can be symmetrized by negating the first equation and multiplying the second equation by $-\mathbf{S}^{k-1}$ as follows:

$$\begin{bmatrix} -H(\mathbf{x}^k, \mathbf{z}^k) & 0 & J(\mathbf{x}^k)^T \\ 0 & -\mathbf{S}^{k-1} \mathbf{Z}^k & -\mathbf{I} \\ J(\mathbf{x}^k) & -\mathbf{I} & 0 \end{bmatrix} \begin{bmatrix} \Delta \mathbf{x}^k \\ \Delta \mathbf{s}^k \\ \Delta \mathbf{z}^k \end{bmatrix} = \begin{bmatrix} \nabla_{\mathbf{x}} f(\mathbf{x}^k) - J(\mathbf{x}^k)^T \mathbf{z}^k \\ -\gamma \mathbf{S}^{k-1} \mathbf{e} + \mathbf{z}^k \\ -g(\mathbf{x}^k) + \mathbf{s}^k \end{bmatrix} \tag{4.103}$$

Using the second equation to solve for Δs^k, we have the reduced KKT as follows:

$$\begin{bmatrix} -H(\mathbf{x}^k, \mathbf{z}^k) & J(\mathbf{x}^k)^T \\ J(\mathbf{x}^k) & S^k Z^{k-1} \end{bmatrix} \begin{bmatrix} \Delta\mathbf{x}^k \\ \Delta\mathbf{z}^k \end{bmatrix} = \begin{bmatrix} \nabla_x f(\mathbf{x}^k) - J(\mathbf{x}^k)^T \mathbf{z}^k \\ -g(\mathbf{x}^k) + \gamma Z^{k-1}\mathbf{e} \end{bmatrix} \tag{4.104}$$

Equation (4.104) gives a linear symmetric matrix with a lower dimension than Equation (4.103). Next, we perform the following iterations:

$$\begin{aligned} \mathbf{x}^{k+1} &= \mathbf{x}^k + \alpha^k \Delta\mathbf{x}^k \\ \mathbf{s}^{k+1} &= \mathbf{s}^k + \alpha^k \Delta\mathbf{s}^k \\ \mathbf{z}^{k+1} &= \mathbf{z}^k + \alpha^k \Delta\mathbf{z}^k \end{aligned} \tag{4.105}$$

where the step length α^k is determined to ensure that the barrier function $(f(\mathbf{x}) - \gamma \sum_{i=1}^{m} \ln s_i)$ or the infeasibility $(\|-g(\mathbf{x}^k) + \mathbf{s}^k\|)$ is reduced and $\mathbf{s}^k > 0$, $\mathbf{z}^k > 0$. To choose the step length, we use either a merit function or filter methods. The merit function is defined by a linear combination of the barrier function and the infeasibility [12] as follows:

$$\Psi_{\beta,\gamma}(\mathbf{x}, \mathbf{s}) = f(\mathbf{x}) - \gamma \sum_{i=1}^{m} \ln s_i + \frac{\beta}{2}\|g(\mathbf{x}) - \mathbf{s}\|^2 \tag{4.106}$$

where β is a parameter such that the solution of Equation (4.103) is a descent direction for the merit function. The role of the merit function is to ensure that the objective and the infeasibility reduce at every iteration, and the solutions approach an optimal point for the original problem. Simply, we could set α^k to combine the objective function with constraints and cause the merit function to decrease.

Example 4.7   *The Barrier Problem*

Consider the following problem:

$$\min_x f(x)$$

subject to

$$x \geq 0$$

where $f(x) = (x-1)^2$. Find the barrier problem of the problem and discuss the effect of parameter γ.

Solution

From Equations (4.93) and (4.92), the problem can be transformed as follows:

$$\min_x (x-1)^2 + \gamma \ln x$$

and the objective function is

$$B(x) = (x-1)^2 + \gamma \ln x$$

When $\gamma = 1$, 5, and 20, Figure p4.4 illustrates $B(x)$.

As we can observe from Figure p4.4, it converges when γ decreases.

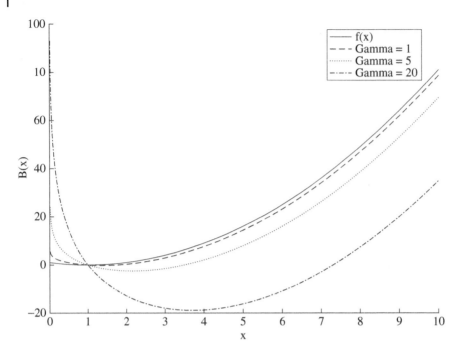

Figure p4.4 For Example 4.7, $B(x)$ when $\gamma = 1$, 5, and 20.

Example 4.8 *Primal-Dual Interior Point Method*

Consider the following problem:

$$\min_x f(x)$$

subject to

$$-x + 8 \geq 0, \quad x \geq 1$$

where $f(x) = x^2$. Find the optimal point using the primal-dual interior point method.

Solution

This optimization problem includes one decision variable and two constraints. Firstly, we introduce slack variables s_1, s_2 to turn all inequality constraints into non-negativities as follows:

$$\min_x x^2$$

subject to

$$-x + 8 - s_1 = 0, \quad x - 1 - s_2 = 0$$
$$s_1 \geq 0, s_2 \geq 0$$

Next, the logarithmic barrier function is introduced and the non-negativity constraints of the slack variables are removed as follows:

$$\min_x x^2 - \gamma \sum_{i=1}^{2} \ln s_i$$

subject to

$$-x + 8 - s_1 = 0, \quad x - 1 - s_2 = 0$$

where $g_1(x) = -x + 8$ and $g_2(x) = x - 1$. As initial conditions, we set $x^0 = 3$, $s_1^0 = 5$ and $s_2^0 = 2$ and also $\gamma^0 = 2$, $\alpha^0 = 0.5$, $z_1^0 = 1$ and $z_2^0 = 1$. We have $f(x^0) = 9$, $g_1(x^0) = 5$ and $g_2(x^0) = 2$. From Equation (4.102), we determine the search directions at an iteration k as follows:

$$
\begin{bmatrix} H(\mathbf{x}^k, \mathbf{z}^k) & 0 & -J(\mathbf{x}^k)^T \\ 0 & \mathbf{Z}^k & \mathbf{S}^k \\ J(\mathbf{x}^k) & -\mathbf{I} & 0 \end{bmatrix} \begin{bmatrix} \Delta \mathbf{x}^k \\ \Delta \mathbf{s}^k \\ \Delta \mathbf{z}^k \end{bmatrix} = \begin{bmatrix} -\nabla_x f(\mathbf{x}^k) + J(\mathbf{x}^k)^T \mathbf{z}^k \\ \gamma e - \mathbf{S}^k \mathbf{Z}^k e \\ -g(\mathbf{x}^k) + \mathbf{s}^k \end{bmatrix}
$$

where

$$
H(\mathbf{x}^k, \mathbf{z}^k) = \nabla^2 f(\mathbf{x}^k) - \sum_{i=1}^m z_i^k \nabla^2 g_i(\mathbf{x}^k) = \nabla^2 f(x^k) + z_1^k \nabla^2 g_1(x^k) + z_2^k \nabla^2 g_2(x^k)
$$

$$
= 2 + 1(0) + 1(0) = 2
$$

$$
J(\mathbf{x}^k) = \begin{bmatrix} \nabla g_1(x^k) \\ \nabla g_2(x^k) \end{bmatrix} = \begin{bmatrix} -1 \\ 1 \end{bmatrix}
$$

$$
\mathbf{Z}^k = \mathbf{Z}^0 = \begin{bmatrix} z_1^0 & 0 \\ 0 & z_2^0 \end{bmatrix} = \begin{bmatrix} 1 & 0 \\ 0 & 1 \end{bmatrix}
$$

$$
\mathbf{S}^k = \mathbf{S}^0 = \begin{bmatrix} s_1^0 & 0 \\ 0 & s_2^0 \end{bmatrix} = \begin{bmatrix} 5 & 0 \\ 0 & 2 \end{bmatrix}
$$

In the first iteration, we have the following coefficient matrix:

$$
\begin{bmatrix} H(\mathbf{x}^k, \mathbf{z}^k) & 0 & -J(\mathbf{x}^k)^T \\ 0 & \mathbf{Z}^k & \mathbf{S}^k \\ J(\mathbf{x}^k) & -\mathbf{I} & 0 \end{bmatrix} = \begin{bmatrix} 2 & 0 & 0 & 1 & -1 \\ 0 & 1 & 0 & 5 & 0 \\ 0 & 0 & 1 & 0 & 2 \\ -1 & -1 & 0 & 0 & 0 \\ 1 & 0 & -1 & 0 & 0 \end{bmatrix}
$$

and the residual matrix is calculated as follows:

$$
-\nabla_x f(\mathbf{x}^k) + J(\mathbf{x}^k)^T \mathbf{z} = -2x^0 + \begin{bmatrix} -1 & 1 \end{bmatrix} \begin{bmatrix} 1 \\ 1 \end{bmatrix} = -6
$$

$$
\gamma e - \mathbf{S}^k \mathbf{Z}^k e = 2 \begin{bmatrix} 1 \\ 1 \end{bmatrix} - \begin{bmatrix} 5 & 0 \\ 0 & 2 \end{bmatrix} \begin{bmatrix} 1 & 0 \\ 0 & 1 \end{bmatrix} \begin{bmatrix} 1 \\ 1 \end{bmatrix} = \begin{bmatrix} 2 \\ 2 \end{bmatrix} - \begin{bmatrix} 5 \\ 2 \end{bmatrix} = \begin{bmatrix} -3 \\ 0 \end{bmatrix}
$$

$$
-g(\mathbf{x}^k) + \mathbf{s}^k = -\begin{bmatrix} 5 \\ 2 \end{bmatrix} + \begin{bmatrix} 5 \\ 2 \end{bmatrix} = \begin{bmatrix} 0 \\ 0 \end{bmatrix}
$$

Thus, we can find search directions from the following matrix:

$$
\begin{bmatrix} 2 & 0 & 0 & 1 & -1 \\ 0 & 1 & 0 & 5 & 0 \\ 0 & 0 & 1 & 0 & 2 \\ -1 & -1 & 0 & 0 & 0 \\ 1 & 0 & -1 & 0 & 0 \end{bmatrix} \begin{bmatrix} \Delta x^0 \\ \Delta s_1^0 \\ \Delta s_2^0 \\ \Delta z_1^0 \\ \Delta z_2^0 \end{bmatrix} = \begin{bmatrix} -6 \\ -3 \\ 0 \\ 0 \\ 0 \end{bmatrix}
$$

and obtain

$$
\begin{bmatrix}
\Delta x^0 \\
\Delta s_1^0 \\
\Delta s_2^0 \\
\Delta z_1^0 \\
\Delta z_2^0
\end{bmatrix}
=
\begin{bmatrix}
-2 \\
2 \\
-2 \\
-1 \\
1
\end{bmatrix}
$$

From Equation (4.105), we perform the following iterations:

$$x^1 = x^0 + \alpha^0 \Delta x^0 = 3 + 0.5(-2) = 2$$

$$s_1^1 = s_1^0 + \alpha^0 \Delta s_1^0 = 5 + 0.5(2) = 6$$

$$s_2^1 = s_2^0 + \alpha^0 \Delta s_2^0 = 2 + 0.5(-2) = 1$$

$$z_1^1 = z_1^0 + \alpha^0 \Delta z_1^0 = 1 + 0.5(-1) = 0.5$$

$$z_2^1 = z_2^0 + \alpha^0 \Delta z_2^0 = 1 + 0.5(1) = 1.5$$

and have $f(x^1) = 4$. Now, we check convergence criteria: $\|r_p\| \le \epsilon_f$, $\|r_d\| \le \epsilon_f$ and $\hat{\eta} \le \epsilon$. If KKT conditions are satisfied with a tolerance, we stop the iteration. In addition, we reduce the step length to keep slack variables and Lagrange multipliers positive. In a similar way, we keep performing the iteration and find the optimal point $f(x^*) = 1$ at $x^* = 1$.

Example 4.9   *Primal-Dual Interior Point Method*

Consider the following problem:

$$\min_x f(\mathbf{x})$$

subject to

$$g(\mathbf{x}) \ge 0,$$

where $f(\mathbf{x}) = x_1^4 + 2x_1^2 x_2 + x_1 + 2x_2^2 + 1$ and $g(\mathbf{x}) = -x_1^2 - 2x_1 x_2 + x_2$. Find the optimal point using the primal-dual interior point method.

Solution

This optimization problem includes two decision variables and one constraint. Firstly, we introduce slack variable s_1 to turn the inequality constraint into non-negativity as follows:

$$\min_x x_1^4 + 2x_1^2 x_2 + x_1 + 2x_2^2 + 1$$

subject to

$$-x_1^2 - 2x_1 x_2 + x_2 - s = 0,$$
$$s \ge 0.$$

Next, the logarithmic barrier function is introduced and the non-negativity constraint of the slack variable are removed as follows:

$$\min_x x_1^4 + 2x_1^2 x_2 + x_1 + 2x_2^2 + 1 - \gamma \ln s$$

subject to

$$-x_1^2 - 2x_1 x_2 + x_2 - s = 0.$$

As initial conditions, we set $x_1^0 = -1, x_2^0 = 2$ and $s^0 = 5$ and also $\gamma^0 = 3$, $\alpha^0 = 0.5$, and $z^0 = 1$. We have $f(x^0) = 13$ and $g(x) = 5$. From Equation (4.102), we determine the search directions at an iteration k as follows:

$$
\begin{bmatrix} H(\mathbf{x}^k, \mathbf{z}^k) & 0 & -J(\mathbf{x}^k)^T \\ 0 & \mathbf{Z}^k & \mathbf{S}^k \\ J(\mathbf{x}^k) & -\mathbf{I} & 0 \end{bmatrix} \begin{bmatrix} \Delta \mathbf{x}^k \\ \Delta \mathbf{s}^k \\ \Delta \mathbf{z}^k \end{bmatrix} = \begin{bmatrix} -\nabla_x f(\mathbf{x}^k) + J(\mathbf{x}^k)^T \mathbf{z}^k \\ \gamma \mathbf{e} - \mathbf{S}^k \mathbf{Z}^k \mathbf{e} \\ -g(\mathbf{x}^k) + \mathbf{s}^k \end{bmatrix}
$$

where

$$
H(\mathbf{x}^k, \mathbf{z}^k) = \nabla^2 f(\mathbf{x}^k) - z^k \nabla^2 g(\mathbf{x}^k) = \nabla^2 f(\mathbf{x}^0) + z^0 \nabla^2 g(\mathbf{x}^0)
$$

$$
= \begin{bmatrix} 12x_1^{0^2} + 4x_2^0 & 4x_1^0 \\ 4x_1^0 & 4 \end{bmatrix} + z^0 \begin{bmatrix} -2 & -2 \\ -2 & 0 \end{bmatrix} = \begin{bmatrix} 16 & -4 \\ -4 & 4 \end{bmatrix} + \begin{bmatrix} -2 & -2 \\ -2 & 0 \end{bmatrix}
$$

$$
= \begin{bmatrix} 14 & -6 \\ -6 & 4 \end{bmatrix}
$$

$$
J(\mathbf{x}^k) = \nabla g(\mathbf{x}^k) = \begin{bmatrix} -2x_1^0 - 2x_2^0 & -2x_1^0 + 1 \end{bmatrix} = \begin{bmatrix} -2 & 3 \end{bmatrix}
$$

$$
\mathbf{Z}^k = \mathbf{Z}^0 = z^0 = 1
$$

$$
\mathbf{S}^k = \mathbf{S}^0 = s^0 = 5
$$

In the first iteration, we have the following coefficient matrix:

$$
\begin{bmatrix} H(\mathbf{x}^k, \mathbf{z}^k) & 0 & -J(\mathbf{x}^k)^T \\ 0 & \mathbf{Z}^k & \mathbf{S}^k \\ J(\mathbf{x}^k) & -\mathbf{I} & 0 \end{bmatrix} = \begin{bmatrix} 14 & -6 & 0 & 2 \\ -6 & 4 & 0 & -3 \\ 0 & 0 & 1 & 5 \\ -2 & 3 & -1 & 0 \end{bmatrix}
$$

and the residual matrix is calculated as follows:

$$
-\nabla_x f(\mathbf{x}^k) + J(\mathbf{x}^k)^T \mathbf{z} = -\begin{bmatrix} 4x_1^{0^3} + 4x_1^0 x_2^0 + 1 \\ 2x_1^{0^2} + 4x_2^0 \end{bmatrix} + \begin{bmatrix} -2x_1^0 - 2x_2^0 \\ -2x_1^0 + 1 \end{bmatrix} z^0 = \begin{bmatrix} 11 \\ 10 \end{bmatrix} + \begin{bmatrix} -2 \\ 3 \end{bmatrix} = \begin{bmatrix} 9 \\ 13 \end{bmatrix}
$$

$$
\gamma \mathbf{e} - \mathbf{S}^k \mathbf{Z}^k \mathbf{e} = 3 \cdot 1 - 5 \cdot 1 \cdot 1 = 3 - 5 = -2
$$

$$
-g(\mathbf{x}^k) + \mathbf{s}^k = -5 + 5 = 0
$$

Thus, we can find search directions from the following matrix:

$$
\begin{bmatrix} 14 & -6 & 0 & 2 \\ -6 & 4 & 0 & -3 \\ 0 & 0 & 1 & 5 \\ -2 & 3 & -1 & 0 \end{bmatrix} \begin{bmatrix} \Delta x_1^0 \\ \Delta x_2^0 \\ \Delta s^0 \\ \Delta z^0 \end{bmatrix} = \begin{bmatrix} 9 \\ 13 \\ -2 \\ 0 \end{bmatrix}
$$

and obtain

$$
\begin{bmatrix} \Delta x_1^0 \\ \Delta x_2^0 \\ \Delta s^0 \\ \Delta z^0 \end{bmatrix} = \begin{bmatrix} 4.1706 \\ 7.2118 \\ 13.2941 \\ -3.0588 \end{bmatrix}
$$

From Equation (4.105), we perform the following iterations:

$$x_1^1 = x_1^0 + \alpha^0 \Delta x_1^0 = -1 + 0.5(4.1706) = 1.0853$$

$$x_2^1 = x_2^0 + \alpha^0 \Delta x_2^0 = 2 + 0.5(7.2118) = 5.6059$$

$$s^1 = s^0 + \alpha^0 \Delta s^0 = 5 + 0.5(13.2941) = 11.6471$$

$$z^1 = z^0 + \alpha^0 \Delta z^0 = 1 + 0.5(-3.0588) = -0.5294$$

and have $f(\mathbf{x}^1) = 79.531$. In a similar way to Example 4.8, we check convergence criteria and decide to stop or perform the next iteration.

Summary 4.6 Primal-Dual Interior Point Method

1) Primal-dual interior point methods are also motivated by Newton's method and are similar to the barrier methods. Some advantages over the barrier method are as follows: (i) it is more efficient because there is no distinction between inner iterations and outer iterations – both primal and dual variables are updated at each iteration; (ii) it can start at an infeasible point for equality constraints; (iii) it empirically converges faster.

2) We can summarize the steps of the primal-dual interior point method as follows:

Initial conditions: Start with a feasible point $\mathbf{x}$ with $f(\mathbf{x}) < 0$, $\lambda > 0$, $\mu > 1$, tolerance $\varepsilon_f > 0$, $\varepsilon > 0$

Repeat
- *Step 1*: Determine t. Set $t = \mu m / \hat{\eta}$
- *Step 2*: Compute primal-dual search direction $\Delta \mathbf{y}_{pd}$
- *Step 3*: Line search on λ, $f(\mathbf{x})$ and $\|r_t\|$
  - *Step 3a*: Start with the step size $s = 0.99 s^{max}$ where $s^{max} = \min \{1, \min \{-\lambda_i / \Delta \lambda_i \mid \Delta \lambda_i < 0\}\}$, $s > 0$
  - *Step 3b*: Continue $s = \beta s$ until $f(\mathbf{x} + s\Delta \mathbf{x}) < 0$, $\|r_t(\mathbf{y} + s\Delta \mathbf{y}_{pd})\| > (1 - \alpha s)\|r_t(\mathbf{y})\|$ where α and β are typically in the range [0.01 0.1] and [0.3 0.8], respectively
- *Step 4*: Update. $\mathbf{y} = \mathbf{y} + s\Delta \mathbf{y}_{pd}$
Until $\|r_p\| \leq \varepsilon_f$, $\|r_d\| \leq \varepsilon_f$ and $\hat{\eta} \leq \varepsilon$

4.5 Gradient Descent Method

The gradient descent method is one of the most widely used optimization methods because it is simple and suitable for large-scale problems, and also works very well with few assumptions. The gradient descent method is an iterative optimization algorithm for finding the minimum of an objective function (or cost function) by moving in the direction of steepest descent. In machine learning, a gradient descent algorithm is used to update the parameters of a system model. Consider the unconstrained optimization problem

$$\min_x f(\mathbf{x}) \qquad (4.107)$$

where $\mathbf{x} \in \mathbb{R}^n$ and the objective function $f: \mathbb{R}^n \to \mathbb{R}$ is convex and differentiable. In this section, the gradient descent algorithm is mainly discussed for unconstrained optimization problems. However, it is possible to apply it to constrained optimization problems. The method is based on the observation that the minimum of the objective function $f(\mathbf{x})$ lies at a point $\mathbf{x}^*$ where $\nabla f(\mathbf{x}^*) = 0$ and a negative gradient step decreases the objective function. $\nabla f(\mathbf{x})$ denotes the gradient of $f(\mathbf{x})$ at the point $\mathbf{x}$. Thus, the gradient descent method finds the minimum of $f(\mathbf{x})$ by starting from an initial point and iteratively searching the next point in the steepest descent direction until it converges. We start at the initial point $\mathbf{x}^{(0)}$. When we have a point $\mathbf{x}^{(k)}$, we can find the next point $\mathbf{x}^{(k+1)}$ using the following equation:

$$\mathbf{x}^{(k+1)} = \mathbf{x}^{(k)} - \alpha^{(k)} \nabla f(\mathbf{x}^{(k)}) \qquad (4.108)$$

where $\alpha^{(k)} > 0$ is the step size (or the learning rate). Convergence of the gradient descent method depends on the step size and the number of iterations. The step size should be chosen carefully. Too large a step size causes overshooting or divergence and too small a step size results in very slow convergence. $\Delta \mathbf{x}^{(k)} = -\nabla f(\mathbf{x}^{(k)})$ is a search direction of gradient descent method at the point $\mathbf{x}^{(k)}$. We call this the steepest descent direction. The step size can be a small constant or be adapted as the iteration increases. Constant step size is usually not efficient. Adapting the step size is efficient and achieves a faster convergence. The step size $\alpha^{(k)}$ can be chosen to minimize the value of the next point and maximize the decrease in the objective function at each step. Thus, the step size $\alpha^{(k)}$ is defined as follows:

$$\alpha^{(k)} = \arg\min_{\alpha \geq 0} f(\mathbf{x}^{(k)} - \alpha \nabla f(\mathbf{x}^{(k)})) = \arg\min_{\alpha \geq 0} \phi(\alpha) \qquad (4.109)$$

We call this step-size computation a line search. The stop condition of the gradient descent method is ideally when the FONC $|\nabla f(\mathbf{x}^{(k)})| = 0$. However, this is not practical. Thus, we usually predefine precision (or tolerance) ε and use practical stop conditions as follows: $|\nabla f(\mathbf{x}^{(k)})| < \varepsilon$, $|f(\mathbf{x}^{(k+1)}) - f(\mathbf{x}^{(k)})| < \varepsilon$, or $|\mathbf{x}^{(k-1)} - \mathbf{x}^{(k)}| < \varepsilon$.

Definition 4.6 Gradient Descent Method

Gradient descent (or steepest descent) method is an iterative optimization method used to minimize an objective function. It is motivated by the observation that the minimum of the objective function $f(\mathbf{x})$ lies at a point $\mathbf{x}^*$ where $\nabla f(\mathbf{x}^*) = 0$ and a negative gradient step decreases the objective function.

Now, we can summarize the steps of the gradient descent method under the given precision $\varepsilon > 0$ as follows:

Initial conditions: Start with an initial point $\mathbf{x}^{(0)}$, step size $\alpha^{(k)}$, tolerance $\varepsilon > 0$
Repeat
- ***Step***: Determine the next point by $\mathbf{x}^{(k+1)} = \mathbf{x}^{(k)} - \alpha^{(k)} \nabla f(\mathbf{x}^{(k)})$
Until it converges: $|\nabla f(\mathbf{x}^{(k)})| < \varepsilon$

Example 4.10 *Gradient Descent Method*

Consider the following problem:

$$\min_x f(\mathbf{x})$$

where $f(\mathbf{x}) = x_1^2 - x_1 x_2 + 2x_2^2$ and the initial point $\mathbf{x}^{(0)} = (3, 3)$. Find the optimal point using the gradient descent method.

Solution

Firstly, we compute the search direction of gradient descent method as follows:

$$\nabla f(x_1, x_2) = (2x_1 - x_2, 4x_2 - x_1)$$

and obtain

$$\nabla f(x_1^{(0)}, x_2^{(0)}) = \nabla f(3, 3) = (3, 9)$$

From Equation (4.109), we find the step size. At the initial point, we have

$$\phi(\alpha) = f(\mathbf{x}^{(0)} - \alpha \nabla f(\mathbf{x}^{(0)})) = f((3, 3) - \alpha \nabla f(3, 3))$$
$$= f((3, 3) - \alpha(3, 9)) = f(3 - 3\alpha, 3 - 9\alpha)$$

The minimum of the function $\phi(\alpha)$ can be found by computing

$$\phi'(\alpha) = -\nabla f(3 - 3\alpha, 3 - 9\alpha)(3, 9)$$
$$= -(2(3 - 3\alpha) - (3 - 9\alpha), 4(3 - 9\alpha) - (3 - 3\alpha))(3, 9)$$
$$= -(3 + 3\alpha, 9 - 33\alpha)(3, 9)$$
$$= 306\alpha - 90$$

and $\alpha = \frac{90}{306} = 0.2941$

From Equation (4.108), we find the next point as follows:

$$\mathbf{x}^{(1)} = \mathbf{x}^{(0)} - \alpha^{(0)} \nabla f(\mathbf{x}^{(0)})$$
$$= (3, 3) - 0.2941(3, 9)$$
$$= (2.1177, 0.3531)$$

We repeat this process and find the optimal point $\mathbf{x}^* = (0, 0)$. Figure p4.5 illustrates iteration of the gradient descent method.

There are three types of gradient descent method depending on the amount of data: batch gradient descent, stochastic gradient descent, and mini-batch gradient descent. The batch gradient descent method is a straightforward method that updates parameters after all training sets have been evaluated. The stochastic gradient descent method updates the parameters for each training set. It can achieve faster convergence for large datasets due to fewer iterations. The mini-batch gradient descent method splits the training data into small batches. Thus, it performs parameter updates for each mini-batch. They are a trade-off between accuracy and convergence time. In addition, there are extensions of gradient descent methods [13, 14]: subgradient methods, projected gradient methods, proximal gradient methods, coordinated descent methods, and so on.

Subgradient methods [13] are iterative algorithms for minimizing a nondifferentiable convex function. When the objective function is convex but nondifferentiable, we cannot

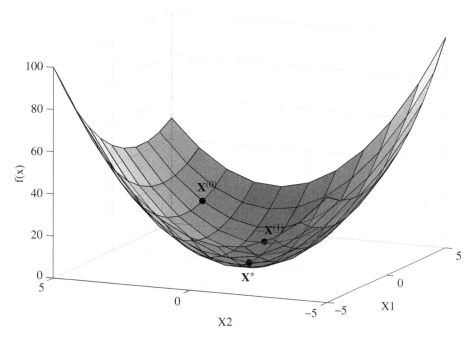

Figure p4.5 Iteration of the gradient descent method.

use the gradient descent method. However, we can generalize the ordinary gradient method. The subgradient method starts at the initial point $\mathbf{x}^{(0)}$ and uses the following iteration:

$$\mathbf{x}^{(k+1)} = \mathbf{x}^{(k)} - \alpha^{(k)}\mathbf{q}^{(k)} \tag{4.110}$$

where $\mathbf{q}^{(k)}$ is a subgradient of f at $\mathbf{x}^{(k)}$ and satisfies the following inequality:

$$f(\mathbf{y}) \geq f(\mathbf{x}) + \mathbf{q}^{T}(\mathbf{y} - \mathbf{x}) \quad \text{for all } \mathbf{y} \tag{4.111}$$

This method is not a descent method and the value of the objective function may increase as the iterations progress. Like the gradient descent method, we perform in the direction of a negative subgradient step.

The basic idea of the projected gradient method is to project points onto the feasibility set and take a gradient step at each iteration. Figure 4.10 illustrates the basic idea of the projected gradient method.

The projected gradient method solves the constrained convex optimization problem:

$$\min_{\mathbf{x}} f(\mathbf{x}) \tag{4.112}$$

subject to

$$\mathbf{x} \in S \tag{4.113}$$

where S is a convex set. The projected gradient method starts at the initial point $\mathbf{x}^{(0)}$ and computes

$$\mathbf{y}^{(k+1)} = \mathbf{x}^{(k)} - \alpha^{(k)}\nabla f(\mathbf{x}^{(k)}) \tag{4.114}$$

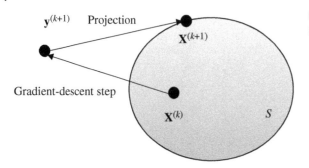

Figure 4.10 Approach of the projected gradient method.

$$\mathbf{x}^{(k+1)} = P_S(\mathbf{y}^{(k+1)}) \tag{4.115}$$

where the projection operator P_S onto S is defined as follows:

$$P_S(l) = \min_{m \in S}|l - m| \tag{4.116}$$

This computation is performed iteratively until a convergence criterion is satisfied.

The proximal gradient method is useful when the objective function is decomposed into two functions as follows:

$$f(\mathbf{x}) = g(\mathbf{x}) + h(\mathbf{x}) \tag{4.117}$$

where $g(\mathbf{x})$ is convex and differentiable and $h(\mathbf{x})$ is convex but not necessarily differentiable. The proximal gradient method starts at the initial point $\mathbf{x}^{(0)}$ and computes

$$\mathbf{x}^{(k+1)} = \text{prox}_{\alpha^{(k)}h}(\mathbf{x}^{(k)} - \alpha^{(k)}\nabla g(\mathbf{x}^{(k)})) \tag{4.118}$$

where the proximal operator of a function h is defined as follows:

$$\text{prox}_h(l) = \arg\min_m h(m) + \frac{1}{2}|m - l|^2 \tag{4.119}$$

and the step size $\alpha^{(k)}$ is a positive constant or can be determined by a line search. The computation is iteratively performed until a convergence criterion is satisfied.

The coordinate gradient method solves optimization problems by decoupling n-dimensional problems and successively performing approximate minimizations of a multivariable function along one direction at a time. Consider the following unconstrained convex optimization problem:

$$\min_{\mathbf{x}} f(\mathbf{x}) \tag{4.120}$$

where $f(\mathbf{x}) = f(x_1, x_2, \ldots, x_n)$, $\mathbf{x} \in \mathbb{R}^n$ and $f : \mathbb{R}^n \to \mathbb{R}$ is continuous and convex. We restructure the problem as follows:

$$\min_{\mathbf{x}} g(\mathbf{x}) + \sum_{i=1}^{n} h_i(x_i) \tag{4.121}$$

where $g(\mathbf{x})$ is convex and differentiable and $h_i(x_i)$ is convex but not necessarily differentiable. The coordinate gradient method starts at the initial point $\mathbf{x}^{(0)}$. At each iteration, we choose one component and adjust it while maintaining all other components as follows:

$$x_i^{(k+1)} = \arg\min_{x_i \in \mathbb{R}} f(x_1^{(k)}, \ldots, x_i, \ldots, x_n^{(k)}) \qquad (4.122)$$

The iteration performs until a convergence criterion is satisfied.

Example 4.11   *Gradient Descent Method for Linear Regression*
Consider the following dataset:

	x	y		x	y		x	y
1	3.8166	5.0546	11	5.3893	7.0708	21	24.147	22.203
2	3.2522	5.7107	12	3.1386	6.1891	22	12.592	6.1101
3	15.505	14.164	13	21.767	20.27	23	9.1302	5.5277
4	3.1551	5.734	14	4.263	5.4901	24	13.662	8.5186
5	7.2258	8.4084	15	5.1875	6.3261	25	4.854	7.0032
6	0.71618	5.6407	16	3.0825	5.5649	26	6.8233	5.8598
7	3.5129	5.3794	17	22.638	18.945	27	11.886	8.3829
8	5.3048	6.3654	18	13.501	12.828	28	4.3483	7.4764
9	0.56077	5.1301	19	7.0467	10.957	29	12	8.5781
10	3.6518	6.4296	20	14.692	13.176	30	6.5987	6.4862

Fit the linear regression parameters to the dataset using the gradient descent method.

Solution
As discussed in the previous chapter, linear regression is a statistical method to find the relationships of variables. Figure p4.6 illustrates the scatter plot of the dataset. As we can observe, the dataset shows a linear relationship and we find a linear regression line as the form $y = a + bx$. In order to fit the best line, we use the metric of the sum of squared errors (SSE). This metric represents the sum difference between actual data and predicted data. The SSE is defined as follows:

$$\text{SSE} = \sum_{i=1}^{n} (y_i - \bar{y})^2$$

where y_i and $\bar{y}$ are dependent variables and average of dependent variables, respectively. We find a linear regression model to make the SSE as small as possible. In the previous chapter, we used the least squares method and found the best line. In this problem, we use the gradient descent method to find a minimum value of the objective function (or cost function). We find minimum errors as differences of predicted values and actual values. Firstly, we represent the hypothesis h_θ as a linear function x

$$h_\theta(x) = \theta_0 + \theta_1 x$$

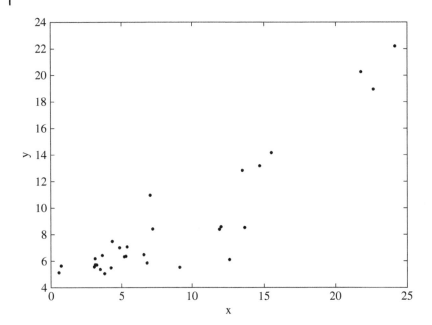

Figure p4.6 Scatterplot of the dataset for Example 4.11.

where θ_i is the parameter we adjust to minimize the errors. Secondly, we define the objective function (or cost function) as follows:

$$J(\theta_0, \theta_1) = \frac{1}{2n} \sum_{i=1}^{n} (h_\theta(x^{(i)}) - y^{(i)})^2$$

where $n = 1, \ldots, 30$. We can measure the accuracy of the hypothesis by this objective function. From Equation (4.108), we repeatedly perform the following:

$$\theta_j = \theta_j - \alpha \frac{\partial}{\partial \theta_j} J(\theta_0, \theta_1)$$

where α is the step size (or learning rate). The above equation can be rewritten as follows:

$$\theta_0 = \theta_0 - \alpha \frac{1}{n} \sum_{i=1}^{n} (h_\theta(x^{(i)}) - y^{(i)})$$

and

$$\theta_1 = \theta_1 - \alpha \frac{1}{n} \sum_{i=1}^{n} (h_\theta(x^{(i)}) - y^{(i)}) x^{(i)}$$

As an initial condition, we have $\alpha = 0.01$ and start $\theta_0 = 0$ and $\theta_1 = 0$. Figure p4.7 illustrates the objective function.

After performing the gradient descent repeatedly, we obtain $\theta_0 = 3.0342$ and $\theta_1 = 0.6669$ and $h_\theta(x) = 3.0342 + 0.6669x$. Figure p4.8 illustrates the best-fit line for the data.

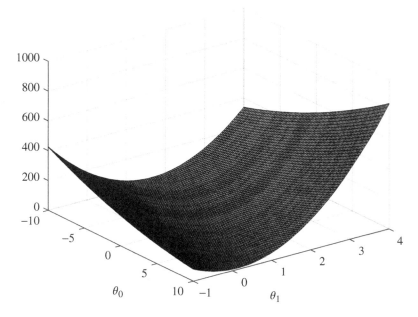

Figure p4.7 Objective function for Example 4.11.

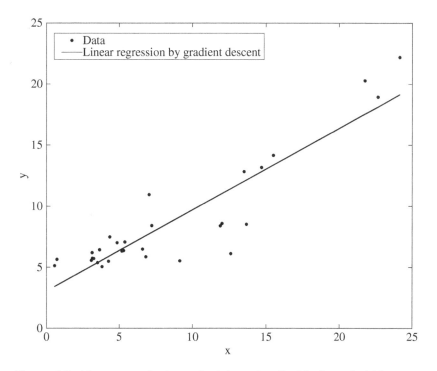

Figure p4.8 Linear regression by gradient descent method for Example 4.11.

Summary 4.7 Gradient Descent Method

1) The gradient descent method is an iterative optimization algorithm for finding the minimum of an objective function (or cost function) by moving in the direction of steepest descent.
2) The gradient descent method is based on the observation that the minimum of the objective function $f(\mathbf{x})$ lies at a point $\mathbf{x}^*$ where $\nabla f(\mathbf{x}^*) = 0$ and a negative gradient step decreases the objective function.
3) We can summarize the steps of the gradient descent method under the given precision $\varepsilon > 0$ as follows:

Initial conditions: Start with an initial point $\mathbf{x}^{(0)}$, a step size $\alpha^{(k)}$, tolerance $\varepsilon > 0$
Repeat
   Step: Determine the next point by $\mathbf{x}^{(k+1)} = \mathbf{x}^{(k)} - \alpha^{(k)} \nabla f(\mathbf{x}^{(k)})$
Until it converges: $|\nabla f(\mathbf{x}^{(k)})| < \varepsilon$

Problems

4.1   Describe the process of system modeling and optimization.

4.2   A system designer always confronts a trade-off in terms of performance. Describe key performance indicators of wireless communications and explain their trade-off.

4.3   Describe the classification of optimization problems and explain their solvers.

4.4   Consider a function $f(\mathbf{x})$ of two variables $\mathbf{x} = [x_1, x_2]^T$ in a quadratic form as follows:

$$f(x_1, x_2) = 4x_1^2 - 2x_1x_2 + x_2^2, \quad x_1, x_2 \in \mathbb{R}.$$

Observe definiteness of the function.

4.5   Describe the optimality conditions FONC, SONC, and SOSC, and then explain their limits.

4.6   Find a real-life optimization problem and formulate it in the standard form.

4.7   Describe the advantages and disadvantages of linear programming.

4.8   Find a real-life linear programming problem and formulate it in the compact form of the standard linear programming problem.

4.9 Consider the following linear programming problem:

$$\min_x \mathbf{c}^T \mathbf{x}$$

subject to

$$\mathbf{Ax} \geq \mathbf{b}$$

$$\mathbf{x} \geq \mathbf{0}$$

where

$$\mathbf{c} = \begin{bmatrix} 3 \\ 9 \end{bmatrix}, \mathbf{x} = \begin{bmatrix} x_1 \\ x_2 \end{bmatrix}, \mathbf{A} = \begin{bmatrix} 2 & 5 \\ 2 & 2 \\ 5 & 0 \end{bmatrix} \text{ and } \mathbf{b} = \begin{bmatrix} 8 \\ 2 \\ 1 \end{bmatrix}$$

Find the optimal value of the decision variable vector **x**.

4.10 Compare the geometric method with the simplex method of linear programming problems, and then explain their limits.

4.11 Consider the following linear programming problem:

$$\max_x \mathbf{c}^T \mathbf{x}$$

subject to

$$\mathbf{Ax} \leq \mathbf{b}$$

$$\mathbf{x} \geq \mathbf{0}$$

where

$$\mathbf{c} = \begin{bmatrix} 2 \\ 8 \end{bmatrix}, \mathbf{x} = \begin{bmatrix} x_1 \\ x_2 \end{bmatrix}, \mathbf{A} = \begin{bmatrix} 3 & 7 \\ 5 & 1 \end{bmatrix} \text{ and } \mathbf{b} = \begin{bmatrix} 16 \\ 5 \end{bmatrix}$$

Find the optimal value of the decision variable vector **x** using the simplex method.

4.12 Consider the following linear programming problem:

$$\max_x \mathbf{c}^T \mathbf{x}$$

subject to

$$\mathbf{Ax} \leq \mathbf{b}$$

$$\mathbf{x} \geq \mathbf{0}$$

where

$$\mathbf{c} = \begin{bmatrix} 8 \\ 21 \\ 15 \end{bmatrix}, \mathbf{x} = \begin{bmatrix} x_1 \\ x_2 \\ x_3 \end{bmatrix}, \mathbf{A} = \begin{bmatrix} 2 & 1 & 6 \\ 1 & 6 & 3 \end{bmatrix} \text{ and } \mathbf{b} = \begin{bmatrix} 45 \\ 36 \end{bmatrix}$$

Find the optimal value of the decision variable vector **x**.

4.13 Describe standard form of the convex optimization problem and explain the merits and limits.

4.14 Define convex sets and operations.

4.15 Describe the convex function and non-convex function.

4.16 Find a convex optimization problem in cellular networks and formulate it in the standard form.

4.17 In the hierarchical structure of convex optimization problems, select one problem and formulate it for cellular networks.

4.18 Describe the meaning of KKT conditions.

4.19 Explain why Lagrangian is useful.

4.20 Describe Newton's method for linearly constrained minimization.

4.21 After formulating the convex optimization problem for 4.17, solve the problem using the barrier method.

4.22 Compare the barrier method with primal-dual interior point method, and then describe their advantages and disadvantages.

4.23 Consider the following problem:

$$\min_x f(x)$$

subject to

$$-2x + 12 \geq 0, \quad x \geq 1$$

where $f(x) = x^2 + 2x + 1$. Find the optimal point using the primal-dual interior point method.

4.24 Consider the following problem:

$$\min_x f(\mathbf{x})$$

subject to

$$g(\mathbf{x}) \geq 0,$$

where $f(\mathbf{x}) = 4x_1^4 + 6x_1^2 x_2 + 2x_2^2 + 8$ and $g(\mathbf{x}) = -4x_1^2 - x_1 x_2 + 2x_2$. Find the optimal point using the primal-dual interior point method.

4.25 Compare the gradient descent method with the interior point method and then describe their advantages and disadvantages.

4.26 Describe how to select the step size for the gradient descent method and how it affects the performance.

4.27 Consider the following problem:
$\min_{\mathbf{x}} f(\mathbf{x})$ where $f(\mathbf{x}) = 6x_1^2 - 3x_1x_2 + x_2^2$ and the initial point $\mathbf{x}^{(0)} = (9, 6)$. Find the optimal point using the gradient descent method.

4.28 Describe the advantages and disadvantages of the subgradient method, projected gradient method, proximal gradient method, and coordinated descent method.

4.29 Find a convex optimization problem in cellular networks, formulate it in the standard form, and solve it using an extension of the gradient descent method.

4.30 Find a dataset of two variables showing us a linear relationship and fit the linear regression parameters to the dataset using the gradient descent method.

References

1 Artmann, B. (1999). *Euclid – The Creation of Mathematics*. New York, NY, ISBN 0-387-98423-2: Springer.

2 Kiranyaz, S., Ince, T., and Gabbouj, M. (2014). *Multidimensional Particle Swarm Optimization for Machine Learning and Pattern Recognition*. Springer, ISBN 978-3-642-37846-1.

3 Scoot, J.F. (1987). *The Scientific Work of Rene Descartes*. Facsimiles-Garl, ISBN-10:0824046722.

4 Williams, H.P. (1986). Fourier's method of linear programming and its dual. *The American Mathematical Monthly* 93 (9): 681–695.

5 Boyd, S. and Vandenberghe, L. (2004). *Convex Optimization*. Cambridge University Press, ISBN 978-0-521-83378-3.

6 Robbins, H.E. and Monro, S. (1951). A stochastic approximation method. *Annals of Mathematical Statistics* 22: 400–407.

7 Holland, J.H. (1992). *Adaptive in Natural and Artificial Systems: An Introductory Analysis with Applications to Biology, Control and Artificial Intelligence*. MIT Press Cambridge, ISBN:0262082136.

8 Turing, A.M. (1950). Computing machinery and intelligence. *Mind* LIX (236): 433–460. https://academic.oup.com/mind/article/LIX/236/433/986238.

9 Samuel, A.L. (1959). Some studies in machine learning using the game of checkers. *IBM Journal of Research and Development* 3, 3.

10 Chong, E.K.P. and Zak, S.H. (2001). *An Introduction to Optimization*. Wiley, ISBN:0-471-39126-3.

11 Lobo, M., Vandenberghe, L., Boyd, S., and Lebret, H. (1998). Applications of second order cone programming. *Linear Algebra and Its Applications*, Special Issue on Linear Algebra in Control, Signals and Image Processing 284: 193–228.

12 Fiacco, A.V. and McCormick, G.P. (1968). *Nonlinear Programming: Sequential Unconstrained Minimization Techniques*. Wiley.

13 Shor, N.Z. (1985). *Minimization Methods for Non-differentiable Functions*, Springer Series in Computational Mathematics. Springer.

14 Bubeck, S. (2015). *Convex optimization: algorithms and complexity. Foundations and Trends in Machine Learning* 8 (3–4): 231–357.

5

Machine Learning

In recent years, many research groups have paid attention to machine learning algorithms and they are now used in numerous areas including spam email filtering, web searching, advertising, fraud detection, automated vehicles, factory automation, and others. In modern communications and networks systems, we generate a huge amount of data every day due to high capacity network systems. We need to analyze the data to find useful information and make the system more efficient. Machine learning algorithms have become an essential part of 5G communications and networks because they help us with resource allocation and scheduling, system monitoring, traffic management, fault prediction, network security, optimization, and others.

What is machine learning? There are many research papers, lectures, and books defining machine learning and explaining it from a different angles (mathematics, computer science, statistics, business, and so on.). For example, "machine learning algorithms can figure out how to perform important tasks by generalizing from examples" University of Washington [1]. "The field of machine learning seeks to answer the question 'How can we build computer systems that automatically improve with experience, and what are the fundamental laws that govern all learning processes?'" Carnegie Mellon University [2]. "Machine learning is the science of getting computers to act without being explicitly programmed" Stanford University [3]. This book is about wireless communications and networks. From this point of view, machine learning can be defined as follows: "machine learning is the research area of getting wireless communications and networks systems to learn and act like humans do and improve the performance autonomously by observing and interacting with the real world." Machine learning algorithms are composed of representation, evaluation, and optimization [1]. Representation is a hypothesis space or a set of classifiers that could be expressed in some formal language that a computer or machine understands. Evaluation (which means evaluation function, objective function, utility function, loss function, or scoring function) is about how we judge one model. Optimization is about how we find the space of the model in order to evaluate it. This component is similar to the optimization methods discussed in Chapter 4. In machine learning, we carry out optimization on the training data and then check its performance on a new dataset. Thus, we could not know what a new dataset might look like. On the other hand, in conventional optimizations, we could know what a dataset looks like. Due to generalization of the current and future data, machine learning allows us to interpret a new dataset that we have never seen before.

Design and Optimization for 5G Wireless Communications, First Edition. Haesik Kim.
© 2020 John Wiley & Sons Ltd. Published 2020 by John Wiley & Sons Ltd.

5.1 Artificial Intelligence, Machine Learning, and Deep Learning

In 5G systems, artificial intelligence (AI), machine learning, and deep learning are hot topics and provide us with new opportunities. Simply speaking, machine learning and deep learning are subsets of artificial intelligence (AI). Figure 5.1 illustrates the relationships of AI, machine learning and deep learning.

Artificial intelligence is a general term meaning an intelligence demonstrated by a machine. It mimics human abilities and can be in the form of human mental processes such as perception, comprehension, learning, decision-making, problem-solving, and so on. AI as an academic discipline was coined in 1956 [4] and produced various subfields including neural networks, evolutionary computation, robotics, speech and image processing, machine learning, deep learning, and so on. They cover both scientific and engineering areas. In its scientific aspects, it studies thought processes including natural language processing, knowledge representation, reasoning, learning, and so on. In its engineering aspect, it solves real-world problems including finding mathematical solutions, playing chess or Go, driving a car, network planning, diagnosing diseases, and so on. Psychologists, linguists, and philosophers are more interested in the scientific aspects. They study how humans behave, how a human brain processes data, how humans recognize images and voices, how a human mind operates, and so on. They build models of how the human brain system operates. Artificial intelligent systems imitate human behavior by using the models. Obviously, computer scientists and communication and network engineers are more interested in the engineering aspects.

Machine learning as one aspect of AI is a data analysis method for extracting knowledge from data. One key aspect of machine learning is an iterative method to learn from previous computations and adapt independently. Machine learning was coined by Arthur Samuel from IBM in 1959 [4]. He defined it as the ability to learn without being explicitly programmed [4]. According to [5], machine learning will be the driver of the next big

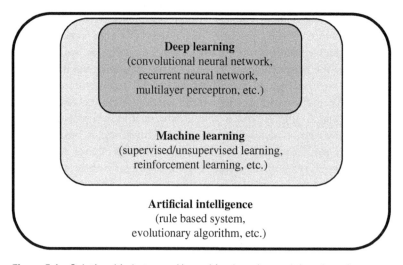

Figure 5.1 Relationship between AI, machine learning and deep learning.

wave of innovation. Machine learning is classified into supervised learning, unsupervised learning, and reinforcement learning (RL). Unsupervised learning finds hidden patterns based on input data. Supervised learning predict future outputs from both input and output data. Reinforcement learning solves Markov decision problems (MDPs). What we can do using machine learning is classification (e.g. spam or email), regression (e.g. interpolation), clustering (e.g. recognition of car, human, and others in video) and decision-making (e.g. automated car, chess machine, etc.). Classification is to predict the target class by looking at experience and choosing one among many candidates. Regression is to predict a value by looking at experience and making a decision in a context. Clustering is to find hidden patterns or similarities in observed data. Supervised learning is used for classification and regression. Unsupervised learning is used for clustering. Reinforcement learning is a learning algorithm that enables an agent to learn, interact with an environment and maximize the total rewards. It is used to solve MDPs or semi-Markov decision problems (SMDPs). Both supervised learning and reinforcement learning use mapping between input and output. Supervised learning predicts the output from the input if the training process converges. However, reinforcement learning uses a reward and policy function. The reward represents how much we optimize and the policy function tell us how much we maximize the expected sum of rewards.

Deep learning as a subset of machine learning is inspired by the human brain structure, including interconnection of many neurons. Neural networks mimic the human brain structure. Deep learning shows us a better performance than machine learning when we have a large amount of data (approximately 1 million sample). In big data era, this is acceptable. However, it does not work well with small amounts of data. High computational power and resources are required. Deep learning is getting more attention in the 5G era for two reasons: (i) 5G produces large amounts of labeled data, and (ii) cloud computing can reduce the training time for deep learning. The main difference between machine learning and deep learning is the decision process itself. Machine learning starts with pre-processing or manual feature extraction and then creates a model for classification. However, deep learning performs end-to-end learning through its own data processing. This is closer to how a human identifies, thinks, and makes a decision.

5.2 Supervised and Unsupervised Learning

Depending on system models and data types of the communication and network problems, there are different approaches to machine learning. In this section, we discuss two categories of machine learning: supervised and unsupervised learning. The main difference between them is the type of data they use. Supervised learning uses known and labeled input data, but the data used by unsupervised learning is neither known nor labeled. This means that their approach is completely different and their applications are distinguished. As the name suggests, supervised learning has the process learning from the training data and it looks like a supervisor of the learning process. Supervised learning algorithms iteratively predict the training dataset and is corrected by a supervisor until we reach an acceptable level of results. On the other hands, unsupervised learning does not have a feedback for predicting the results (there is no supervisor to correct data), and does not know what the results should look like. What it can do is to derive inherent structure from the input data. Another difference is computational complexity. Supervised learning is more complex than unsupervised learning because it should understand the labeled data. Another difference is accuracy and reliability. Supervised learning is more accurate and reliable than unsupervised learning because supervised learning already knows the labeled data and it finds the hidden pattern or predicts the future output. Computation time is also a point of difference. Unsupervised learning can perform real-time data analysis but supervised learning cannot. Due to those differences, supervised learning is useful for solving classification and regression problems and unsupervised learning is used to derive the structure by clustering the data. Table 5.1 summarizes the differences and Figure 5.2 illustrates the classification for supervised learning and clustering for unsupervised learning.

In mathematics, there are two "no free lunch" theorems: one for supervised machine learning [6] and one for optimization [7]. Briefly speaking, there is no one algorithm for every machine learning problem or optimization problem. In other words, one algorithm

Table 5.1 Comparison of supervised learning and unsupervised learning.

	Supervised learning	**Unsupervised learning**
Input data	Known and labeled input data	Unknown input data
Output data	Continuous output data in a regression problem, discrete output data in a classification problem	No corresponding output data, continuous output data in dimensionality reduction, discrete output data in clustering
Real time	Off-line analysis	Real-time analysis
Computational complexity	High	Medium
Accuracy and reliability of results	High	Medium
Algorithms	K nearest-neighbor algorithm, linear regression algorithm, SVMs, logistic regression, random forests, etc.	K means for clustering, a priori algorithm for association, etc.
Tasks	Classification and regression	Clustering and dimensionality reduction

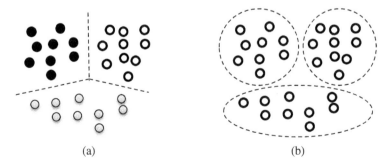

(a) (b)

Figure 5.2 (a) Classification for supervised learning, and (b) clustering for unsupervised learning.

cannot always be better than another algorithm due to many different factors (e.g. data type, initial background knowledge, feedback type, system model, etc.). Thus, we should try to find a proper machine learning algorithm for each system model and environment. In this section, we discuss support vector machines (SVMs) as one key supervised machine learning algorithm, and K means clustering as an unsupervised machine learning algorithm.

Based on statistical learning theory, SVMs were introduced in 1995 [8] and became important algorithms in machine learning [9]. They have been used for a wide variety of applications for classification and regression. In classification, applications of SVMs are face recognition, speaker identification, biological data processing, handwriting recognition, and so on. In regression, applications are control systems and communications. The main idea of SVMs is to determine an optimal separating hyperplane maximizing the margin (minimum gap between classes and decision boundary) and minimizing the number of misclassified training samples. There is a trade-off relationship. The basic approach is to formulate a constraint optimization problem and then find the best classifier boundary hyperplane using quadratic programming. In order to understand the concept of SVMs, let us consider linearly separable training samples and find a linear classifier as shown in Figure 5.3. Figure 5.4 illustrates examples of linearly separable samples.

In Figures 5.3 and 5.4, we can find a linear separating line. However, if data are not linearly separable and there is no decision line separating classes, a separating hyperplane

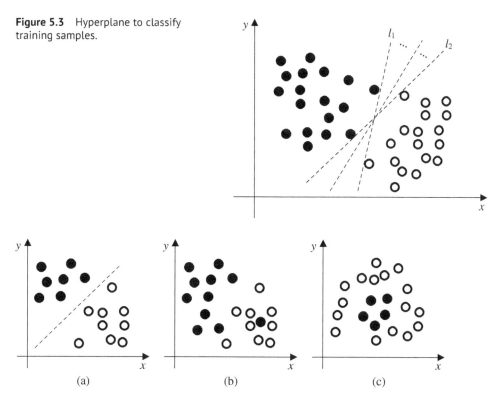

Figure 5.3 Hyperplane to classify training samples.

Figure 5.4 Examples of (a) a linearly separable sample, and (b) and (c) not linearly separable samples.

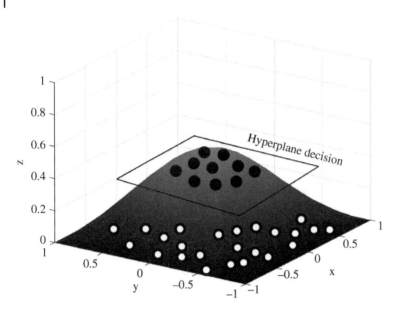

Figure 5.5 Example of hyperplane decision in multidimensional space.

surface in higher dimensional space can be found and the data can be separated as shown in Figure 5.5.

As we can observe in Figure 5.3, many lines $(l_1, \ldots, l_2)$ (or hyperplanes in multidimensional space) are possible for classification. However, which one is the best? A SVM defines the margin of the lines as the width between the lines and the closest samples on each side. A good margin gives larger separation for both classes and a bad margin is one that is very close to one class. In Figure 5.3, not all training samples are important when finding a line (or hyperplane). Some points, which are the closest points to the optimal line (or hyperplane), are important. We call them support vectors. Support vectors are the critical elements of the training samples. The problem of finding the best line (or optimal separating hyperplane) is an optimization problem. It is a quadratic programming problem and we can solve it using Lagrange multipliers in a standard form. It would be the optimal choice when maximizing the margin. Figure 5.6 illustrates the support vectors and maximum margin.

This concept is intuitionally acceptable and it provides us with empirically good performance in various applications. Generally speaking, there is a trade-off relationship between the margin and generalization error (or misclassified points). In Figure 5.7a, all samples are linearly separated but the margin is small. In Figure 5.7b, the margin is big, but one sample violates the constraint.

We consider n training samples of the form: $\{\mathbf{x}_i, y_i\}$ where the input vector $\mathbf{x}_i \in \mathbb{R}^d$ with $i = 1, \ldots, n$ is of dimensionality d and belongs to the response variables $y_i \in \{-1, +1\}$. We assume that the data is linearly separable and find a linear classifier for a binary classification problem. The line $f(\mathbf{x}) = \mathbf{w}^T\mathbf{x} - b$ classifies samples with $y_i = -1$ on one side $(f(\mathbf{x}_i) < 0)$ and samples with $y_i = +1$ on the other side $(f(\mathbf{x}_i) > 0)$. The separating line (or hyperplane) can be described as follows:

$$\mathbf{w}^T\mathbf{x} = b \tag{5.1}$$

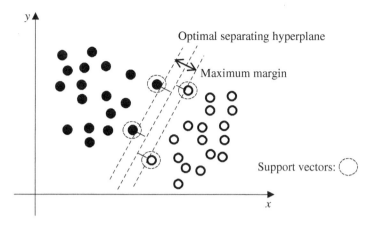

Figure 5.6 Maximum margin and support vectors.

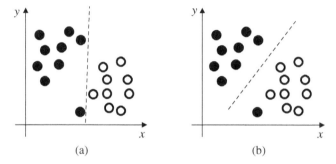

Figure 5.7 Trade-off between margin and misclassified points.

where the vector $\mathbf{w}$ is perpendicular to the line $\mathbf{w}^T\mathbf{x} = b$ and $b/\|\mathbf{w}\|$ is the perpendicular distance between the origin and the separating line. The separating line acts as a linear classifier. Support vectors are the closest to the separating line. Using the support vectors, we define two lines parallel to the separating line. The two lines cut through the closest training samples on each side. We call those support lines. The distances between them are d_1 and d_2. The margin γ is defined as addition of d_1 and d_2. Two support lines are described as follows:

$$\mathbf{w}^T\mathbf{x} = b + \delta \text{ and } \mathbf{w}^T\mathbf{x} = b - \delta \tag{5.2}$$

where δ is the offset on both sides. The SVM finds the optimal $\mathbf{w}$ for any δ. Thus, any non-zero offset establishes a margin optimization. The margin γ is twice distance d ($=d_1$ or d_2) of the closest samples to the separating line because of being equidistant from both support lines. Thus, the margin γ is $2/\|\mathbf{w}\|$. Given a vector $\mathbf{x}_i$, the following equations should be satisfied:

$$\mathbf{w}^T\mathbf{x}_i - b \leq -1 \text{ for } y_i = -1 \tag{5.3}$$

$$\mathbf{w}^T\mathbf{x}_i - b \geq +1 \text{ for } y_i = +1 \tag{5.4}$$

and Equations (5.3) and (5.4) can be written as follows:

$$y_i(\mathbf{w}^T\mathbf{x}_i - b) - 1 \geq 0, 1 \leq i \leq n \tag{5.5}$$

Equation (5.5) becomes the constraint of the optimization problem. Now, we formulate the primal problem of linear SVMs as follows:

$$\min\frac{1}{2}\|\mathbf{w}\|^2 \tag{5.6}$$

subject to

$$y_i(\mathbf{w}^T\mathbf{x}_i - b) - 1 \geq 0, \ 1 \leq i \leq n \tag{5.7}$$

This is a constrained quadratic programming problem. We maximize the margin subject to the constraint that all data fall on one side or the other. It cannot be solved by quadratic optimization when the number of training samples is large. Thus, we transform to the dual formulation and use the method of Lagrange multipliers α as follows:

$$L(\mathbf{w}, b, \boldsymbol{\alpha}) = \frac{1}{2}\|\mathbf{w}\|^2 - \boldsymbol{\alpha}(y_i(\mathbf{w}^T\mathbf{x}_i - b) - 1), \ 1 \leq i \leq n \tag{5.8}$$

$$= \frac{1}{2}\|\mathbf{w}\|^2 - \sum_{i=1}^{n}\alpha_i(y_i(\mathbf{w}^T\mathbf{x}_i - b) - 1) \tag{5.9}$$

$$= \frac{1}{2}\|\mathbf{w}\|^2 - \sum_{i=1}^{n}\alpha_i y_i(\mathbf{w}^T\mathbf{x}_i - b) + \sum_{i=1}^{n}\alpha_i \tag{5.10}$$

Finding the minimum of $L(\mathbf{w}, b, \boldsymbol{\alpha})$ means that we differentiate it with respect to $\mathbf{w}$ and b and set the derivatives to zero as follows:

$$\frac{\partial L}{\partial \mathbf{w}} = 0 \rightarrow \mathbf{w} = \sum_{i=1}^{n}\alpha_i y_i \mathbf{x}_i \tag{5.11}$$

$$\frac{\partial L}{\partial b} = 0 \rightarrow 0 = \sum_{i=1}^{n}\alpha_i y_i \tag{5.12}$$

In addition, inequality constraint and complementary slackness should be satisfied as follows: $y_i(\mathbf{w}^T\mathbf{x}_i - b) - 1 \geq 0$ and $\boldsymbol{\alpha}(y_i(\mathbf{w}^T\mathbf{x}_i - b) - 1) = 0$. This condition means that the inequality constraint is satisfied when $\alpha_i \geq 0$ and the inequality is saturated when $\alpha_i = 0$. By substituting Equations (5.11) and (5.12) into Equation (5.10), we have its dual form as follows:

$$\max_{\boldsymbol{\alpha}} L = \sum_{i=1}^{n}\alpha_i - \frac{1}{2}\sum_{i=1}^{n}\sum_{j=1}^{n}\alpha_i\alpha_j y_i y_j \mathbf{x}_i^T \mathbf{x}_j \tag{5.13}$$

subject to

$$\sum_{i=1}^{n}\alpha_i y_i = 0, \alpha_i \geq 0, \ 1 \leq i \leq n \tag{5.14}$$

This dual form is a constrained quadratic programming problem as well, but the number of new variables $\boldsymbol{\alpha}$ is same as the number of training samples. The term L of Equation (5.13) can be rewritten as follows:

$$L = \sum_{i=1}^{n}\alpha_i - \frac{1}{2}\sum_{i=1}^{n}\sum_{j=1}^{n}\alpha_i\alpha_j y_i y_j \mathbf{x}_i^T \mathbf{x}_j = \sum_{i=1}^{n}\alpha_i - \frac{1}{2}\sum_{i=1}^{n}\sum_{j=1}^{n}\alpha_i H_{ij}\alpha_j \tag{5.15}$$

$$L = \sum_{i=1}^{n} \alpha_i - \frac{1}{2}\boldsymbol{\alpha}^T \mathbf{H}\boldsymbol{\alpha} \tag{5.16}$$

where $H_{ij} = y_i y_j \mathbf{x}_i^T \mathbf{x}_j$. The dual form is rewritten as follows:

$$\max_{\boldsymbol{\alpha}} \sum_{i=1}^{n} \alpha_i - \frac{1}{2}\boldsymbol{\alpha}^T \mathbf{H}\boldsymbol{\alpha} \tag{5.17}$$

subject to

$$\sum_{i=1}^{n} \alpha_i y_i = 0, \alpha_i \geq 0, 1 \leq i \leq n \tag{5.18}$$

In some cases, the training samples may not be separable, some samples may lie within the margin, and they cannot be classified correctly. Thus, a cost penalty C is used. If $C \to 0$, it maximizes the margin and misclassified points are allowed. If $C \to \infty$, it minimizes the number of misclassified points and no errors are allowed. The cost penalty C acts like a regularizing parameter. We can generalize linear SVM. The classifier in Equation (5.5) can be rewritten by n non-negative slack variables s_i as follows:

$$y_i(\mathbf{w}^T\mathbf{x}_i - b) \geq 1 - s_i, 1 \leq i \leq n \tag{5.19}$$

and the cost function becomes

$$\|\mathbf{w}\|^2 + C \sum_{i=1}^{n} s_i^m \tag{5.20}$$

where m is an integer. The cost penalty C represents the effect of the slack variables, and the slack variables s_i affect misclassified points, generalization, or computational efficiency. Thus, the generalized optimal separating hyperplane is formulated as follows:

$$\min \frac{1}{2}\|\mathbf{w}\|^2 + C \sum_{i=1}^{n} s_i^m \tag{5.21}$$

subject to

$$y_i(\mathbf{w}^T\mathbf{x}_i - b) \geq 1 - s_i, s_i \geq 0, \ 1 \leq i \leq n \tag{5.22}$$

After including the slack variables, the associated dual form is

$$\max_{\boldsymbol{\alpha}} \sum_{i=1}^{n} \alpha_i - \frac{1}{2}\boldsymbol{\alpha}^T \mathbf{H}\boldsymbol{\alpha} \tag{5.23}$$

subject to

$$\sum_{i=1}^{n} \alpha_i y_i = 0, 0 \leq \alpha_i \leq C, \ 1 \leq i \leq n \tag{5.24}$$

As we can observe from Equations (5.17), (5.18), (5.23), and (5.24), the only difference is the constraint of the Lagrange multipliers. It includes an upper bound C. If $C \to 0$, misclassified points are not allowed. If $C \to \infty$, it is same as the original problem and implies smaller errors on the training samples. There is a trade-off relationship. A support vector $\mathbf{x}_s$ satisfies Equation (5.12) and we have the following equation:

$$y_s(\mathbf{w}^T\mathbf{x}_s - b) = 1 \tag{5.25}$$

By substituting Equation (5.25) into Equation (5.11), we have

$$y_s \left(\sum_{l \in S} \alpha_l y_l \mathbf{x}_l \cdot \mathbf{x}_s - b \right) = 1 \tag{5.26}$$

where S is the set of support vectors. If a sample is not a support vector, $\alpha_i = 0$. If a sample is a support vector, $\alpha_i > 0$ and it satisfies Equation (5.26). From Equations (5.3) and (5.4), $y_s^2 = 1$. Thus, Equation (5.26) can be rewritten as follows:

$$y_s^2 \left(\sum_{l \in S} \alpha_l y_l \mathbf{x}_l \cdot \mathbf{x}_s - b \right) = y_s \tag{5.27}$$

$$\left(\sum_{l \in S} \alpha_l y_l \mathbf{x}_l \cdot \mathbf{x}_s - b \right) = y_s \tag{5.28}$$

$$b = \sum_{l \in S} \alpha_l y_l \mathbf{x}_l \cdot \mathbf{x}_s - y_s \tag{5.29}$$

Using Equation (5.29) and support vectors, we can determine b. In order to achieve numerical stability, we can take an average over all of the support vectors. Alternatively, we can find it from the complementary slackness condition as follows:

$$0 = y_i(\mathbf{w}^T \mathbf{x}_i - b) - 1 \text{ when } \alpha_i > 0 \tag{5.30}$$

$$b = -\frac{1}{y_i} + \mathbf{w}^T \mathbf{x}_i \tag{5.31}$$

In addition, we can find $\mathbf{w}$ using Equation (5.11). Thus, we have both variables b and $\mathbf{w}$ to define the separating line. The important thing is that samples appear only through the inner products of $\mathbf{x}_i^T \mathbf{x}_j$. When dealing with samples in a higher dimensional space, we can replace them with kernel matrices.

The dataset we will face in practice will most likely not be linearly separable. Thus, we need to change to nonlinear SVMs and apply them to non-separable cases. We relax the constraints for Equations (5.3) and (5.4) by introducing slack variables s_i as follows:

$$\mathbf{w}^T \mathbf{x}_i - b \leq -1 + s_i \text{ for } y_i = -1 \tag{5.32}$$

$$\mathbf{w}^T \mathbf{x}_i - b \geq +1 - s_i \text{ for } y_i = +1 \tag{5.33}$$

$$s_i \geq 0, 1 \leq i \leq n \tag{5.34}$$

where the slack variables allow for misclassified points. The primal problem has been reformulated to Equations (5.21) and (5.22) using the penalty function $C \sum_{i=1}^{n} s_i^m$ of Equation (5.20). The penalty function becomes a part of the objective function. When m is a small integer (e.g. 1 and 2), it is still a quadratic programming problem. The penalty function represents how many samples are misclassified. Now, we reformulate Equations (5.21) and (5.22) using a Lagrangian as follows:

$$L(\mathbf{w}, b, s, \boldsymbol{\alpha}, \boldsymbol{\mu}) = \frac{1}{2} \|\mathbf{w}\|^2 + C \sum_{i=1}^{n} s_i - \sum_{i=1}^{n} \alpha_i(y_i(\mathbf{w}^T \mathbf{x}_i - b) - 1 + s_i) - \sum_{i=1}^{n} \mu_i s_i \tag{5.35}$$

We derive the KKT conditions as follows:

$$\frac{\partial L(\mathbf{w}, b, s, \boldsymbol{\alpha}, \boldsymbol{\mu})}{\partial \mathbf{w}} = 0 \rightarrow \mathbf{w} - \sum_{i=1}^{n} \alpha_i y_i \mathbf{x}_i = 0 \tag{5.36}$$

Figure 5.8 Example of a non-linear classification in (a) one dimension and (b) two dimensions.

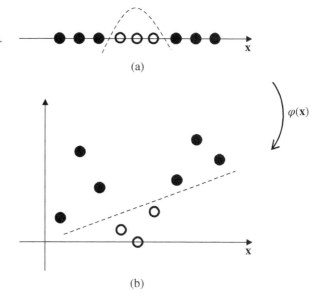

(a)

(b)

$$\frac{\partial L(\mathbf{w}, b, s, \boldsymbol{\alpha}, \boldsymbol{\mu})}{\partial b} = 0 \rightarrow \sum_{i=1}^{n} \alpha_i y_i = 0 \tag{5.37}$$

$$\frac{\partial L(\mathbf{w}, b, s, \boldsymbol{\alpha}, \boldsymbol{\mu})}{\partial s} = 0 \rightarrow C - \alpha_i - \mu_i = 0 \tag{5.38}$$

$$y_i(\mathbf{w}^T \mathbf{x}_i - b) - 1 + s_i \geq 0 \tag{5.39}$$

$$s_i \geq 0, \alpha_i \geq 0, \mu_i \geq 0 \tag{5.40}$$

$$\alpha_i(y_i(\mathbf{w}^T \mathbf{x}_i - b) - 1 + s_i) = 0 \tag{5.41}$$

$$\mu_i s_i = 0 \tag{5.42}$$

In the non-separable case, we can use a linear classifier by projecting the dataset into a higher dimension using a function $\varphi(\mathbf{x})$ as shown in Figure 5.8. However, we should deal carefully with this projection due to the curse of dimensionality. As the number of dimensions increases, the amount of data we need to generalize correctly increases exponentially and there is a risk of overfitting the data. In addition, computational complexity increases with the dimension of the space. We call this the curse of dimensionality. In order to avoid this problem, we define an implicit mapping to a higher-dimensional feature space, and computation in a high dimension is performed implicitly using kernel functions. We also control a measure of complexity by maximizing the margin of the hyperplane.

Example 5.1 *Support Vector Machine for Six Samples*
Consider the following dataset:

> Class A: $(1,6), (2,9), (4,9)$

> Class B: $(5,2), (7,7), (10,3)$

Find a classifier using SVM.

Solution

Firstly, we create two matrices from the given dataset as follows:

$$\mathbf{X} = \begin{bmatrix} 1 & 6 \\ 2 & 9 \\ 4 & 9 \\ 5 & 2 \\ 7 & 7 \\ 10 & 3 \end{bmatrix}, \quad \mathbf{y} = \begin{bmatrix} 1 \\ 1 \\ 1 \\ -1 \\ -1 \\ -1 \end{bmatrix}$$

Figure p5.1 illustrates the dataset.

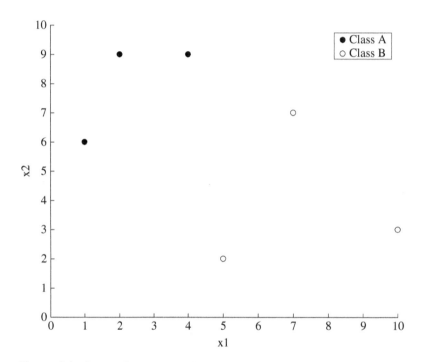

Figure p5.1 Dataset for Example 5.1.

Secondly, we find the matrix $\mathbf{H}$ using $H_{ij} = y_i y_j \mathbf{x}_i^T \mathbf{x}_j$ as follows:

$$\mathbf{H} = \begin{bmatrix} 37 & 56 & 58 & -17 & -49 & -28 \\ 56 & 85 & 89 & -28 & -77 & -47 \\ 58 & 89 & 97 & -38 & -91 & -67 \\ -17 & -28 & -38 & 29 & 49 & 56 \\ -49 & -77 & -91 & 49 & 98 & 91 \\ -28 & -47 & -67 & 56 & 91 & 109 \end{bmatrix}$$

Thirdly, we solve a constrained quadratic programming problem:

$$\max_{\alpha} \sum_{i=1}^{n} \alpha_i - \frac{1}{2} \alpha^T H \alpha$$

subject to

$$\sum_{i=1}^{n} \alpha_i y_i = 0, \ \alpha_i \geq 0, \ 1 \leq i \leq n$$

We need to transform the minimization optimization problem to standard form as follows:

$$\min_{\alpha} - \sum_{i=1}^{6} \alpha_i + \frac{1}{2} \begin{bmatrix} \alpha_1 \\ \vdots \\ \alpha_6 \end{bmatrix}^T H \begin{bmatrix} \alpha_1 \\ \vdots \\ \alpha_6 \end{bmatrix}$$

subject to

$$\sum_{i=1}^{6} \alpha_i y_i = 0, \alpha_i \geq 0, \ 1 \leq i \leq 6$$

We rewrite the above problem as follows:

$$\min_{\alpha} f^T \alpha + \frac{1}{2} \begin{bmatrix} \alpha_1 \\ \vdots \\ \alpha_6 \end{bmatrix}^T H \begin{bmatrix} \alpha_1 \\ \vdots \\ \alpha_6 \end{bmatrix}$$

subject to

$$B\alpha = b, \ A\alpha \leq a, \ 1 \leq i \leq 6$$

where α, B, b, A and a are

$$f = \begin{bmatrix} -1 \\ \vdots \\ -1 \end{bmatrix}, B = \begin{bmatrix} y_1 & \cdots & y_6 \\ 0 & \cdots & 0 \\ \vdots & \ddots & \vdots \\ 0 & \cdots & 0 \end{bmatrix}, b = \begin{bmatrix} 0 \\ \vdots \\ 0 \end{bmatrix}, A = \begin{bmatrix} -1 & \cdots & 0 \\ \vdots & \ddots & \vdots \\ 0 & \cdots & -1 \end{bmatrix}, a = \begin{bmatrix} 0 \\ \vdots \\ 0 \end{bmatrix}$$

Using a quadratic programming solver, we find α as follows:

$$\alpha = \begin{bmatrix} 0 \\ 0 \\ 0.15 \\ 0 \\ 0.15 \\ 0 \end{bmatrix}$$

This means the support vectors are (4, 9) and (7, 7).

Fourthly, we find **w** as follows:

$$\mathbf{w} = \sum_{i=1}^{6} \alpha_i y_i x_i = \begin{bmatrix} -0.46 \\ 0.30 \end{bmatrix}$$

Fifthly, since $\alpha_3 > 0$, we find b as follows:

$$b = -\frac{1}{y_3} + \mathbf{w}^T x_3 = -0.077$$

Figure p5.2 illustrates the classifier using SVM.

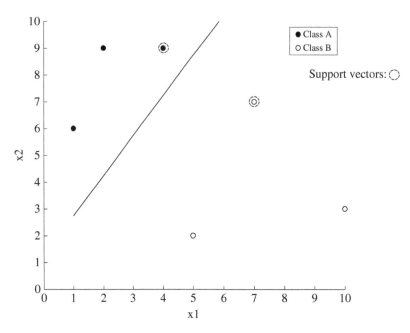

Figure p5.2 Classifier for the Example 5.1 dataset.

Example 5.2 *Support Vector Machine for 40 Samples*
Consider the following dataset:

Class A: (8,10), (6,2), (2,1), (5,4), (6,6), (10,6), (9,10), (10,6), (7,5), (5,6), (10,8), (5,1), (3,9), (4,2), (8,5), (6,3), (8,4), (10,7), (10,2), (6,3)

Class B: (12,19), (12,17), (13,14), (19,18), (15,20), (14,15), (11,15), (20,13), (14,10), (19,12), (16,11), (14,15), (19,10), (18,20), (15,17), (18,10), (19,10), (14,12), (13,15), (16,11)

Find a classifier using SVM.

Solution

In the same manner as Example 5.1, we find a classifier. Figure p5.3 illustrates the dataset.

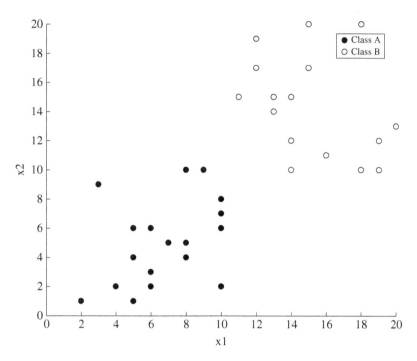

Figure p5.3 Dataset for Example 5.2.

After finding the matrix **H** using $H_{ij} = y_i y_j \mathbf{x}_i^T \mathbf{x}_j$ and solving a constrained quadratic programming problem, we find α as follows:

$$\alpha = [0\,0\,0\,0\,0\,0\,0.10\,0\,0\,0\,0\,0\,0\,0\,0\,0\,0\,0\,0\,0\,0\,0\,0\,0\,0\,0\,0.04\,0\,0\,0.06\,0\,0\,0\,0\,0\,0\,0\,0\,0\,0]^T$$

Thus, the support vectors are $(9,10)$, $(11,15)$, and $(14,10)$. Then, we find **w** as follows:

$$\mathbf{w} = \sum_{i=1}^{40} \alpha_i y_i \mathbf{x}_i = \begin{bmatrix} -0.4 \\ -0.24 \end{bmatrix}$$

Since $\alpha_7 > 0$, we find b as follows:

$$b = -\frac{1}{y_7} + \mathbf{w}^T \mathbf{x}_7 = 6.99$$

Figure p5.4 illustrates the classifier using SVM.

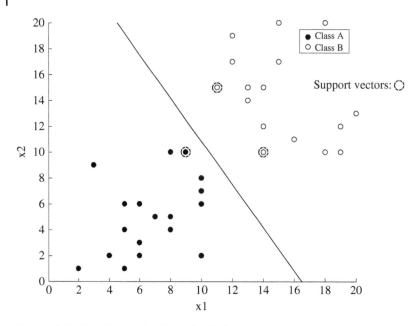

Figure p5.4 Classifier for the Example 5.2 dataset.

Summary 5.1 Support Vector Machine

1) Finding the matrix **H** using $H_{ij} = y_i y_j \mathbf{x}_i^T \mathbf{x}_j$.
2) Solving a constrained quadratic programming problem:

$$\max_{\alpha} \sum_{i=1}^{n} \alpha_i - \frac{1}{2} \alpha^T \mathbf{H} \alpha$$

subject to

$$\sum_{i=1}^{n} \alpha_i y_i = 0, \alpha_i \geq 0, 1 \leq i \leq n.$$

3) Finding **w** using $\mathbf{w} = \sum_{i=1}^{n} \alpha_i y_i \mathbf{x}_i$.
4) Determining the set of support vectors.
5) Finding b using $b = \sum_{l \in S} \alpha_l y_l \mathbf{x}_l \cdot \mathbf{x}_s - y_s$.
6) Each sample is classified by $y_c = \text{sgn}(\mathbf{w}^T \mathbf{x} - b)$.

The purpose of clustering is to show that elements or objects in a cluster are similar to one another or different from those in other clusters. Clustering algorithms are techniques for finding similarity groups in data. Definition of the similarity measure is important for clustering algorithms. Similarity is highly related to distance. There are different distance definitions (Euclidean distance d_e, Manhattan distance d_m, Chebyshev distance d_c, and non-linear distance d_n) as follows:

$$d_e(x_i, x_j) = \sqrt{\sum_{k=1}^{d} (x_i^k - x_j^k)^2} \tag{5.43}$$

$$d_m(x_i, x_j) = \sum_{k=1}^{d} |x_i^k - x_j^k| \tag{5.44}$$

$$d_c(x_i, x_j) = \max_{1 \le k \le d} |x_i^k - x_j^k| \tag{5.45}$$

$$d_n(x_i, x_j) = \|\varphi(x_i) - \varphi(x_j)\| \tag{5.46}$$

The Euclidean distance is the straight-line distance between two points in Euclidean space. The Manhattan distance (or rectilinear distance, city block distance) is the sum of the lengths of the projections of the line segment. The computational cost is cheaper than for the Euclidean distance. The Chebyshev distance (or chessboard distance) is defined as the distance between two points with standard coordinates. The computational cost is the lowest among the three metrics. These distance metrics are useful in various cases depending on their important aspects. The nonlinear distance can be defined according to specific clustering or functions.

When we have data as in Figure 5.9a, the Euclidean distance will be a useful metric. For data as in Figure 5.9b, nonlinear distance may be useful. Good clustering means that the inter-class similarity (between clusters) is low and the intra-class similarity (intra-cluster) is high. This technique is useful when we do not know what we are searching for, because it is helpful for finding a pattern in data. In the 1850s, an English physician John Snow plotted the locations of cholera deaths and found that the locations were clustered around polluted wells. Thus, he traced the source of a cholera outbreak in London and solved the problem. This is one application of the clustering approach. There are two types of clustering: partitioning clustering (K-means clustering, Gaussian mixture models and so on) and hierarchical clustering (agglomerative clustering (bottom-up), divisive clustering (top-down) and so on). Partitioning clustering means a division of the set of data objects into

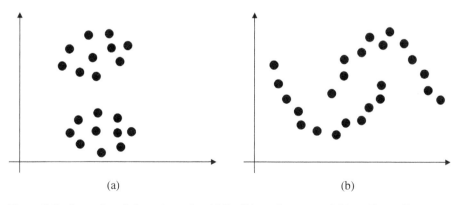

(a)   (b)

Figure 5.9 Examples of clustering using (a) Euclidean distance and (b) nonlinear distance.

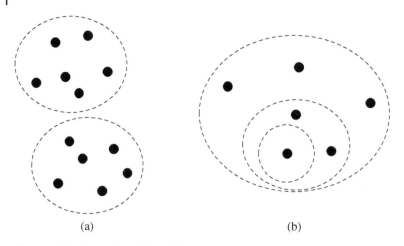

(a)   (b)

Figure 5.10 Examples of (a) partitioning clustering and (b) hierarchical clustering.

non-overlapping clusters. Hierarchical clustering means a set of nested clusters organized as a tree. Figure 5.10 illustrates the types of clustering.

One of the major clustering algorithms is based on the sum of squares (SSQ) criterion [10]. This is also known as "K-means" where K represents the number of clusters. K-means clustering algorithm as a partitioning clustering is one of the simplest unsupervised machine learning algorithms. The purpose of this algorithm is to find a cluster in data by iteratively minimizing the measure between the cluster center of the group and the given observation. The K-means clustering algorithm is easy to implement and provides us with rapid computation if K is small. However, it is not easy to predict the number of clusters, and the initial conditions strongly affect the results. Thus, the initialization is highly related to convergence speed and overall clustering performance. One safe choice is to try multiple initializations and find a better result.

Given n samples $x_1, \dots, x_n \in \mathbb{R}^d$ and the cluster number k, we find k cluster centers $\mu_1, \dots, \mu_k \in \mathbb{R}^d$ minimizing the following

$$f_k = \sum_i \min_j \|x_i - \mu_j\|^2, i = 1, \dots, n \text{ and } j = 1, \dots, k \tag{5.47}$$

As we can observe from Equation (5.47), the partition is achieved by minimizing the sum of the squared distance between all points to their closest cluster center. Lloyd's algorithm [11] as a modified version of the K-means clustering algorithm works well in practice. It is a simple iterative algorithm to find a local minimum. Equation (5.47) is modified as follows:

$$\arg_{C_j} \min_i \text{SSE} \tag{5.48}$$

where SSE is the sum of squared error:

$$\text{SSE} = \sum_j \sum_i \|x_i - \mu_j\|^2, i \in C_j \text{ and } j = 1, \dots, k \tag{5.49}$$

and C_j is the set of points closest to the cluster center. The K-means clustering algorithm is performed as the following steps:

Initial conditions: Set k cluster centers $\mu_1, \dots, \mu_k \in \mathbb{R}^d$ randomly (or choose any k samples)
Repeat
- ***Step 1***: Assign each x_i to its closest cluster center as follows:

$$\arg_{C_j} \min_i \text{SSE}$$

- ***Step 2***: Compute new cluster centers μ_j as follows:

$$\mu_j = \frac{1}{|C_j|} \sum_{i \in C_j} x_i$$

Until: It converges (when cluster centers do not change or objects in each cluster do not change)

As we can observe from the K-means clustering algorithm, finding the optimum of the objective is NP-hard (see Chapter 7) and K-means clustering is a heuristic approach. The algorithm terminates at a local optimum but it is difficult to find a global optimum due to complexity.

Example 5.3   *K-means Clustering Algorithm for One-Dimensional Data*
Consider the following one-dimensional dataset:

Data A : 14,15,16,17,22,23,24,27,33,35,40,41,46,50,62

Find two clusters using the K-means clustering algorithm.

Solution
As initial conditions, we choose two cluster centers as follows:

$$\mu_1 = 16, \quad \mu_2 = 24$$

We compute the Euclidean distance between the objects and cluster centers as follows:

$$d_1(x_i, \mu_1) = |x_i - \mu_1|, d_2(x_i, \mu_2) = |x_i - \mu_2|$$

and obtain the distance matrix shown in Table p5.1.
Based on the assigned group, we compute the new cluster centers as follows:

$$\mu_1 = \frac{1}{4}(14 + 15 + 16 + 17) = 15.5$$

$$\mu_2 = \frac{1}{11}(22 + 23 + 24 + 27 + 33 + 35 + 40 + 41 + 46 + 50 + 62) = 36.64$$

We re-compute the Euclidean distance and obtain the distance matrix shown in Table p5.2.

Table p5.1 The first iteration for Example 5.3.

x_i	μ_1	μ_2	d_1	d_2	Closest cluster center
14	16	24	2	10	μ_1
15	16	24	1	9	μ_1
16	16	24	0	8	μ_1
17	16	24	1	7	μ_1
22	16	24	6	2	μ_2
23	16	24	7	1	μ_2
24	16	24	8	0	μ_2
27	16	24	11	3	μ_2
33	16	24	17	9	μ_2
35	16	24	19	11	μ_2
40	16	24	24	16	μ_2
41	16	24	25	17	μ_2
46	16	24	30	22	μ_2
50	16	24	34	26	μ_2
62	16	24	46	38	μ_2

Table p5.2 The second iteration for Example 5.3.

x_i	μ_1	μ_2	d_1	d_2	Closest cluster center
14	15.5	36.64	1.5	22.64	μ_1
15	15.5	36.64	0.5	21.64	μ_1
16	15.5	36.64	0.5	20.64	μ_1
17	15.5	36.64	1.5	19.64	μ_1
22	15.5	36.64	6.5	14.64	μ_1
23	15.5	36.64	7.5	13.64	μ_1
24	15.5	36.64	8.5	12.64	μ_1
27	15.5	36.64	11.5	9.64	μ_2
33	15.5	36.64	17.5	3.64	μ_2
35	15.5	36.64	19.5	1.64	μ_2
40	15.5	36.64	24.5	3.36	μ_2
41	15.5	36.64	25.5	4.36	μ_2
46	15.5	36.64	30.5	9.36	μ_2
50	15.5	36.64	34.5	13.36	μ_2
62	15.5	36.64	46.5	25.36	μ_2

Table p5.3 The third iteration for Example 5.3.

x_i	μ_1	μ_2	d_1	d_2	Closest cluster center
14	18.71	41.75	4.71	27.75	μ_1
15	18.71	41.75	3.71	26.75	μ_1
16	18.71	41.75	2.71	25.75	μ_1
17	18.71	41.75	1.71	24.75	μ_1
22	18.71	41.75	3.29	19.75	μ_1
23	18.71	41.75	4.29	18.75	μ_1
24	18.71	41.75	5.29	17.75	μ_1
27	18.71	41.75	8.29	14.75	μ_1
33	18.71	41.75	14.29	8.75	μ_2
35	18.71	41.75	16.29	6.75	μ_2
40	18.71	41.75	21.29	1.75	μ_2
41	18.71	41.75	22.29	0.75	μ_2
46	18.71	41.75	27.29	4.25	μ_2
50	18.71	41.75	31.29	8.25	μ_2
62	18.71	41.75	43.29	20.25	μ_2

In the same way, we compute the new cluster centers as follows:

$$\mu_1 = \frac{1}{7}(14 + 15 + 16 + 17 + 22 + 23 + 24) = 18.71$$

$$\mu_2 = \frac{1}{8}(27 + 33 + 35 + 40 + 41 + 46 + 50 + 62) = 41.75$$

We re-compute the Euclidean distance and obtain the following distance matrix (Table p5.3):

In the same way, we compute the new cluster centers as follows:

$$\mu_1 = \frac{1}{8}(14 + 15 + 16 + 17 + 22 + 23 + 24 + 27) = 19.75$$

$$\mu_2 = \frac{1}{7}(33 + 35 + 40 + 41 + 46 + 50 + 62) = 43.86$$

We re-compute the Euclidean distance and obtain the distance matrix shown in Table p5.4).

In the fourth iteration, the grouping is not changed and K-means clustering algorithm terminates. We have two clusters as follows:

Cluster A: 14,15,16,17,22,23,24,27

Cluster B: 33,35,40,41,46,50,62

Table p5.4 The fourth iteration for Example 5.3.

x_i	μ_1	μ_2	d_1	d_2	Closest cluster center
14	19.75	43.86	5.75	29.86	μ_1
15	19.75	43.86	4.75	28.86	μ_1
16	19.75	43.86	3.75	27.86	μ_1
17	19.75	43.86	2.75	26.86	μ_1
22	19.75	43.86	2.25	21.86	μ_1
23	19.75	43.86	3.25	20.86	μ_1
24	19.75	43.86	4.25	19.86	μ_1
27	19.75	43.86	7.25	16.86	μ_1
33	19.75	43.86	13.25	10.86	μ_2
35	19.75	43.86	15.25	8.86	μ_2
40	19.75	43.86	20.25	3.86	μ_2
41	19.75	43.86	21.25	2.86	μ_2
46	19.75	43.86	26.25	2.14	μ_2
50	19.75	43.86	30.25	6.14	μ_2
62	19.75	43.86	42.25	18.14	μ_2

Example 5.4 *K-means Clustering Algorithm for Two-Dimensional Data*
Consider the following two-dimensional dataset:

$$\text{Data A}: (1,1), (1,2), (2,3), (4,4.5), (6,7), (7,8)$$

Find two clusters using the K-means clustering algorithm.

Solution
As an initial condition, we choose two cluster centers as follows:

$$\mu_1 = (1,1), \quad \mu_2 = (4,4.5)$$

We compute the Euclidean distance between the objects and cluster centers as follows:

$$d_1(x_i, \mu_1) = \sqrt{(x_{i,1} - \mu_{1,1})^2 + (x_{i,2} - \mu_{1,2})^2}$$

$$d_2(x_i, \mu_2) = \sqrt{(x_{i,1} - \mu_{2,1})^2 + (x_{i,2} - \mu_{2,2})^2}$$

and obtain the distance matrix as shown in Table p5.5.
Based on the assigned group, we compute the new cluster centers as follows:

$$\mu_1 = \left(\frac{1+1+2}{3}, \frac{1+2+3}{3} \right) = (1.33, 2)$$

$$\mu_2 = \left(\frac{4+6+7}{3}, \frac{4.5+7+8}{3} \right) = (5.67, 6.5)$$

We re-compute the Euclidean distance and obtain the distance matrix shown in Table p5.6.

Table p5.5 The first iteration for 5.4.

x_i	μ_1	μ_2	d_1	d_2	Closest cluster center
(1,1)	(1,1)	(4,4.5)	0	4.61	μ_1
(1,2)	(1,1)	(4,4.5)	1	3.91	μ_1
(2,3)	(1,1)	(4,4.5)	2.24	2.5	μ_1
(4,4.5)	(1,1)	(4,4.5)	4.61	0	μ_2
(6,7)	(1,1)	(4,4.5)	7.81	3.2	μ_2
(7,8)	(1,1)	(4,4.5)	9.22	4.61	μ_2

Table p5.6 The second iteration for 5.4.

x_i	μ_1	μ_2	d_1	d_2	Closest cluster center
(1,1)	(1.33,2)	(5.67,6.5)	1.05	7.22	μ_1
(1,2)	(1.33,2)	(5.67,6.5)	0.33	6.49	μ_1
(2,3)	(1.33,2)	(5.67,6.5)	1.20	5.07	μ_1
(4,4.5)	(1.33,2)	(5.67,6.5)	3.66	2.61	μ_2
(6,7)	(1.33,2)	(5.67,6.5)	6.84	0.6	μ_2
(7,8)	(1.33,2)	(5.67,6.5)	8.26	2	μ_2

In the second iteration, the grouping does not change and the K-means clustering algorithm terminates. We have two clusters as follows:

Cluster A: (1,1), (1,2), (2,3)

Cluster B: (4,4.5), (6,7), (7,8)

Example 5.5   *K-means Clustering Algorithm Using Computer Simulation*
Consider 120 two-dimensional data points as shown in Figure p5.5. Find four clusters using the K-means clustering algorithm.

Solution
As an initial condition, we choose four cluster centers as follows:

$$\mu_1 = (-0.37,0.65), \mu_2 = (0.2,2),\quad \mu_3 = (0.89,0.46),\quad \mu_4 = (1.05,2.27)$$

We compute the Euclidean distance between the objects and cluster centers as follows:

$$d_1(x_i, \mu_1) = \sqrt{(x_{i,1} - \mu_{1,1})^2 + (x_{i,2} - \mu_{1,2})^2}$$

$$d_2(x_i, \mu_2) = \sqrt{(x_{i,1} - \mu_{2,1})^2 + (x_{i,2} - \mu_{2,2})^2}$$

and obtain the clusters ($\bigcirc$, $+$, $\Diamond$, $\square$) as shown in Figure p5.6. In this figure, * represents the cluster centers.

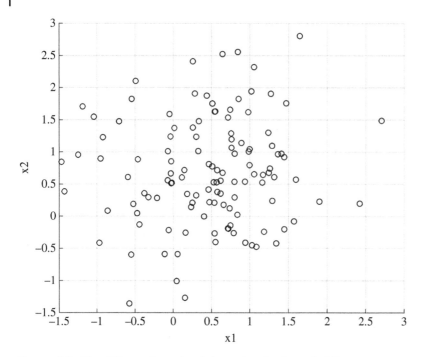

Figure p5.5 The 120 two-dimensional data points for Example 5.5.

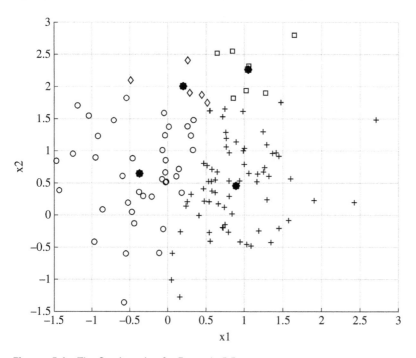

Figure p5.6 The first iteration for Example 5.5.

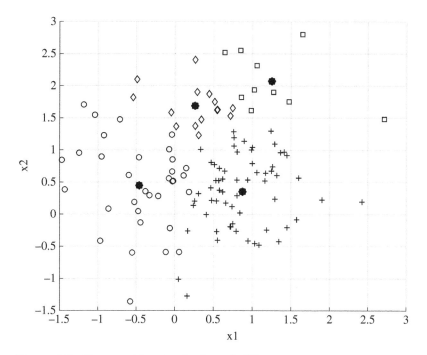

Figure p5.7 The second iteration for Example 5.5.

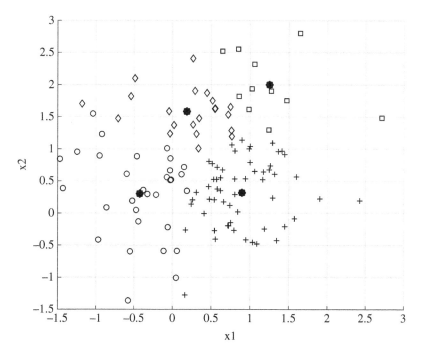

Figure p5.8 The third iteration for Example 5.5.

Based on the assigned group, we compute the new cluster centers as follows:

$$\mu_1 = (-0.46, 0.45), \quad \mu_2 = (0.26, 1.69), \mu_3 = (0.87, 0.35), \quad \mu_4 = (1.25, 2.07)$$

and perform the second iteration to obtain the clusters shown in Figure p5.7. In the third iteration, we have the following new cluster centers:

$$\mu_1 = (-0.43, 0.3), \quad \mu_2 = (0.18, 1.58), \quad \mu_3 = (0.9, 0.32), \quad \mu_4 = (1.25, 2)$$

and obtain the next clusters as shown in Figure p5.8. In the fourth iteration, we have the following new cluster centers:

$$\mu_1 = (-0.38, 0.17), \quad \mu_2 = (0.12, 1.56), \quad \mu_3 = (0.92, 0.36), \quad \mu_4 = (1.25, 2)$$

and obtain the next clusters as shown in Figure p5.9. The algorithm terminates because the cluster center μ_4 does not change.

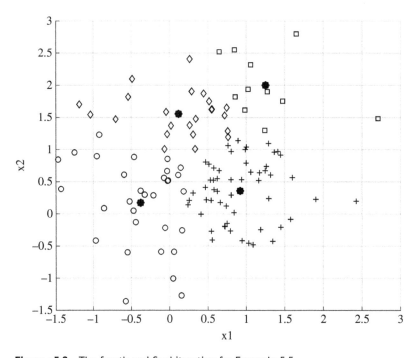

Figure p5.9   The fourth and final iteration for Example 5.5.

Summary 5.2 K-means Clustering Algorithm

Input: n samples $x_1, \ldots, x_n \in \mathbb{R}^d$ and the cluster number k
Initial conditions: Set k cluster centers $\mu_1, \ldots, \mu_k \in \mathbb{R}^d$ randomly (or choose any k samples)

Repeat
- *Step 1*: Assign each x_i to its closest cluster center as follows:

$$\arg\min_{C_j} \text{SSE}_i$$

- *Step 2*: Compute new cluster centers μ_j as follows:

$$\mu_j = \frac{1}{|C_j|} \sum_{i \in C_j} x_i$$

Until: It converges (when cluster centers do not change or objects in each cluster do not change)

5.3 Reinforcement Learning

In the previous section, we solved classification and clustering problems using supervised and unsupervised learning. However, a major component of artificial intelligence is decision-making. Reinforcement learning (RL) deals with sequential decision-making problems under uncertainty. Training data (or sample data) for supervised learning and unsupervised learning are labeled or unlabeled datasets, respectively. RL uses training data including state, action, transition probability, reward, and discount, and develops an optimal policy to maximize cumulative rewards. The goal of a sequential decision-making problem is to select actions to maximize long-term rewards. RL is also called adaptive (or approximate) dynamic programming or neurodynamic programming. RL has emerged as a powerful method for many different areas. The typical data-streaming process for RL is illustrated in Figure 5.11. Most RL algorithms are based on this process. As we can observe from Figure 5.11, the typical data streaming model is an agent–environment interacting data stream which provides us with numeric rewards. An agent interacts with a dynamic environment and receives a feedback in the form of rewards. Actions affect the state of the stochastic and uncertain environment. RL finds the optimal policy to maximize the long-term rewards. If we have a static environment, it is possible to have

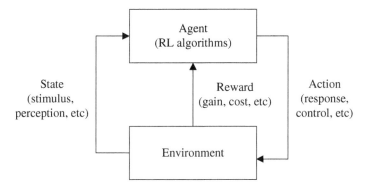

Figure 5.11 The interaction process of reinforcement learning.

deterministic actions and fully observable perception. This process keeps performing until the environment sends the agent a final state.

This interaction process is a finite Markov decision process (MDP). The RL problem can be formulated mathematically in a MDP. One important property of the MDP is the Markov property: the system is memoryless. It implies that a set of possible actions and transition does not rely on the sequence of events. The MDP is defined as (S,A,T,R) with the following elements:

- A finite set of states S, where $s_t \in S$ is the state at t.
- A finite set of actions A, where $a_t \in A$ is the action selected at t.
- A transition function $T(s, a, s')$, which can be denoted as a transition probability $p(s'|s, a)$. It represents how the environment evolves under the actions.
- A reward function $R(s, a)$. It is a feedback to the agent.
- A discount factor γ, where $0 \leq \gamma < 1$. It discounts for future rewards.
- A policy π, which is a strategy by which the agent determines the next action. A deterministic policy $a = \pi(s)$ means that the agent always executes the same action from a state. A stochastic policy $a \sim p_\pi(a|s)$ means that the agent selects an action from probability by the policy.
- A state value function $V^\pi(s)$ at the state s. It is the expected cumulative reward from a policy.
- A state action value function $Q^\pi(s, a)$. It denotes the expected sum of discounted rewards of the current state s when taking action a under the policy π.

The objective in a MDP is to find an optimal policy π^* maximizing the long-term reward. There are two types of RL: model-based methods and model-free methods. The model-based RL is to learn an approximate model of a transition function and a reward function based on experiences, and use them to get an optimal policy as if the model is correct. It can use dynamic programming algorithms on the model and the computational cost is high. On the other hand, the model-free RL uses a trial-and-error method to update its knowledge and to derive an optimal policy without learning the model. Computational cost and memory usage are low, but it may be slower than the model-based RL. In addition, there are two types of model-free RL: policy-based methods and value-based methods. The policy-based methods directly update policy evaluation and improvement until a policy converges, where policy evaluation is to find the corresponding value function for a given policy and policy improvement is to find a policy with a higher value. It defines the RL problem as an optimization problem. The policy estimation is performed by simulation. It is efficient when the simulation is fast and some prior information is available. However, value-based methods find an optimal value function under one policy using temporal difference (TD) learning (temporal difference learning, state-action-reward-state-action (SARSA) and Q learning). There is another important category: on-policy learning and off-policy learning. The on-policy learning methods (temporal difference learning and SARSA) learn the value based on its current action and policy, whereas the off-policy learning methods (Q learning and so on) learn the value of a different policy. On-policy learning may get stuck in local maxima, but off-policy learning will not if enough experiences are given. In the real world, the convergence of the optimal policy rarely happens. Thus, we face a trade-off between exploitation and exploration. If we focus on exploitation, it provides us with the

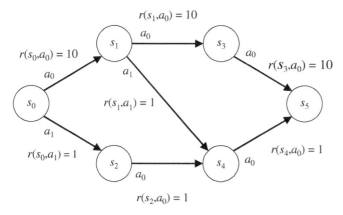

Figure 5.12 Example of a Markov decision process (MDP).

best decision under the current information. If we choose the exploration approach, it maximizes long-term rewards. For example, when finding a good restaurant, the exploitation approach is to go to a favorite restaurant, whereas exploration is to try a new restaurant. The exploration approach may include short-term sacrifices and the exploitation approach may get stuck in a bad policy. Thus, we can say they have a trade-off relationship. In this section, we focus on the value-based methods.

We consider a simple MDP example as shown in Figure 5.12. As we can observe from the figure, each decision affects the next decision and each action receives a reward. We should learn a policy by selecting actions to maximize the total rewards and can easily find three possible paths (policies) for this example: $\pi_1 = s_0 \to s_1 \to s_3 \to s_5$, $\pi_2 = s_0 \to s_1 \to s_4 \to s_5$, and $\pi_3 = s_0 \to s_2 \to s_4 \to s_5$. Each policy receives the following rewards: $\sum_{\pi_1} r(s,a) = 30$, $\sum_{\pi_2} r(s,a) = 12$, and $\sum_{\pi_3} r(s,a) = 3$. In this example, the value function $V^\pi(s)$ can be found for a fixed policy as follows: $V^{\pi_1}(\mathbf{s}) = [V^{\pi_1}(s_0), V^{\pi_1}(s_1), V^{\pi_1}(s_3)] = [30,20,10]$, $V^{\pi_2}(\mathbf{s}) = [V^{\pi_2}(s_0), V^{\pi_2}(s_1), V^{\pi_2}(s_4)] = [12,2,1]$, and $V^{\pi_3}(\mathbf{s}) = [V^{\pi_3}(s_0), V^{\pi_3}(s_2), V^{\pi_3}(s_4)] = [3,2,1]$. The state action value function $Q^\pi(s, a)$ can be found without a specific policy as follows: $Q^\pi(s_4, a_0) = 1$, $Q^\pi(s_3, a_0) = 10$, $Q^\pi(s_1, a_0) = 20$, $Q^\pi(s_1, a_1) = 2$, $Q^\pi(s_2, a_0) = 2$, $Q^\pi(s_0, a_0) = 30$, and $Q^\pi(s_0, a_1) = 3$. As we can observe both value functions, both have similar form and we can find the optimal policy by maximizing the value functions. In this MDP example, the optimal policy is π_1^*.

Now, we generalize the RL algorithms. In the value-based method, one way to find an optimal policy is to find all possible behaviors and then select one policy with the highest value as described in the above example. However, if there are too many possible behaviors, this approach is not possible. Thus, we define value functions and determine one policy using them. The basic idea of the value-based RL methods is to observe each experience in the form $(s_t, a_t, r(s, a), s_{t+1})$, generate a new experience, and improve a policy or value function. The state value function $V^\pi(s_t)$ with a policy π at a state s_t is defined as follows:

$$V^\pi(s_t) = \sum_{i=0}^{\infty} \gamma^i r_i^{\pi(s_t)} \tag{5.50}$$

where $r_i^{\pi(s_t)}$ and γ^i represent a reward and a discount factor, respectively. The sequence of the reward $r_i^{\pi(s_t)}$ is found on the ith time by repeatedly executing the policy π starting in the state s_t. A discount factor γ^i is a constant determining the relationship between the future rewards and the immediate rewards. This term implies that the future rewards are not as valuable as the immediate rewards because the future rewards are exponentially discounted. If we set $\gamma \sim 1$, the future rewards have as much of an impact as the immediate rewards. If we set $\gamma = 0$, there is no impact from the future rewards. We can find an optimal policy by maximizing $V^\pi(s_t)$ for all states as follows:

$$\pi^* = \arg\max_\pi V^\pi(s_t) \tag{5.51}$$

When we find a deterministic policy, a policy can be expressed by mapping states to actions. However, this is a special class of behaviors. More generally, a stochastic policy maps states to distributions over an action. Thus, we consider that the rewards are random variables and the effects of actions are random. A transition probability $p(s'|s, a)$ is the probability that an action a in state s will move to the next state s'. The state value function $V^\pi(s_t)$ can be defined as follows:

$$V^\pi(s_t) = E\left[\sum_{i=0}^{\infty} \gamma^i r_i^{\pi(s_t)}\right] \tag{5.52}$$

and we can rewrite this using Bellman optimality equations [12] as follows:

$$V^\pi(s) = r(s, \pi(s)) + \gamma \sum_{s'} p(s'|s, \pi(s))V^\pi(s') \tag{5.53}$$

where $r(s, \pi(s))$ is the expected immediate reward and $p(s'|s, \pi(s))$ is the probability of transiting the state s' when executing the action at the state s with a policy π. The summation means all possible next states. We define the optimal value function as the best possible expected sum of the discounted reward with any policy as follows:

$$V^*(s) = \max_\pi V^\pi(s) \tag{5.54}$$

By the Bellman optimality equation [12], the optimal value function is

$$V^*(s) = \max_a \left(r(s, a) + \gamma \sum_{s'} p(s'|s, a)V^*(s') \right) \tag{5.55}$$

where the max operation means taking the best possible actions in a MDP. According to [12], dynamic programming provides us with computation methods for the optimal value function and we can find at least one optimal policy π^*. The optimal policy corresponds with taking the best action in any state. From Equation (5.55), we can easily find the optimal policy as follows:

$$\pi^*(s) = \arg\max_a \left(r(s, a) + \gamma \sum_{s'} p(s'|s, a)V^*(s') \right) \tag{5.56}$$

and the optimal policy π^* satisfies

$$V^*(s) = V^{\pi^*}(s) \geq V^\pi(s) \tag{5.57}$$

for all states.

Temporal difference (TD) learning methods use the state value function and update an estimate of the state value function by learning from every experience. TD learning is similar to dynamic programming and Monte Carlo methods. The TD learning methods learn from the environment directly, like Monte Carlo methods, and update state value functions from the current estimates like dynamic programming. Thus, we can say that it combines the sampling of the Monte Carlo method and the bootstrapping of dynamic programming. When these updated estimates are based on other estimates, we call this bootstrapping. In addition, Monte Carlo methods wait for a final outcome to update the state value function, but TD learning only waits until the next time step. Thus, TD learning needs less memory and peak computation, and learns from incomplete sequences. The Monte Carlo method works well in a nonstationary environment. The simple Monte Carlo method can be described as follows:

$$V(s) \leftarrow V(s) + \alpha(R - V(s)) \tag{5.58}$$

where R is the actual return following the state s and $\alpha > 0$ is a step-size parameter. The simple dynamic programming can be described as follows:

$$V(s) \leftarrow E[r + \gamma V(s)] \tag{5.59}$$

where $r + \gamma V(s)$ is an estimate of the return. In Equation (5.53), we cannot update all states because we do not know $p(s'|s, \pi(s))$ for all states. However, s' is a sample of the transition probability $p(s'|s, \pi(s))$ and we can update as follows:

$$V^\pi(s) = r + \gamma V^\pi(s') \tag{5.60}$$

We assume that s' is the only possible next state. From Equations (5.58), (5.59), and (5.60), we can express the simplest TD methods as follows:

$$V(s) \leftarrow V(s) + \alpha[r + \gamma V(s') - V(s)] \tag{5.61}$$

Now, we can describe a tabular TD(0) algorithm as the following steps:

Initial conditions: $V(s)$ for all s
Repeat for each episode
  – Initialize s
    Repeat for each step in episode
  – **Step 1**: Sample action in the current state by a policy π: $a \leftarrow p_\pi(a\,|\,s)$
  – **Step 2**: Transition to the next state: take action a and observe r and next state s
  – **Step 3**: Update $V(s) \leftarrow V(s) + \alpha[r + \gamma V(s') - V(s)]$
  – **Step 4**: Reset current state $s \leftarrow s'$
Until: s is terminal

In the learning algorithms, the episode means one sequence of the agent–environment interactions from initial states to terminal states. This is one or more periods that a learner is engaged in the learning process. The state value function $V^\pi(s)$ is to converge to the optimal value function $V^*(s)$ after an infinite number of experiences. However, policy convergence is more important than value convergence. In practice, policy convergence happens sooner than value convergence. Thus, in order to update more efficiently, we need to trace where the agent has been. We call the term "$r + \gamma V(s') - V(s) = V^{new} - V^{old}$" of Equation (5.61) temporal difference (TD) error. The TD error is a temporal difference estimate error. The TD(0) algorithm uses one-step returns to update the state value function, but the update rule of the TD(λ) algorithm [13] is given as multistep returns. The parameter λ is the trace decay parameter with $0 \leq \lambda \leq 1$ and it is used to combine estimates obtained from various distances. The TD(λ) algorithm can be sensitive with respect to the parameter λ. When it has a higher value, it requires longer lasting traces. The TD(λ) algorithm tunes the decay rate.

In order to find an optimal policy using the state value function, we need all rewards and transition probabilities at all states and actions. In many practical cases, this is not possible. Thus, we explore how the environments react to actions and learn good state–action pairs. Incremental dynamic programming [14] takes this approach. A state–action value function $Q^{\pi}(s, a)$ is expressed as follows:

$$Q^{\pi}(s, a) = E[r(s, a)] + \gamma E[V^{\pi}(s')] \tag{5.62}$$

where the Q function is the value of starting at state s, executing action a, and then following policy π. $E[r(s, a)]$ is the average value of the immediate reward when executing action a at state s. The optimal value function can be expressed using the Q function as follows:

$$V^*(s) = \max_a Q^{\pi^*}(s, a) \tag{5.63}$$

and the corresponding optimal policy is given by

$$\pi^*(s) = \arg\max_a Q^{\pi^*}(s, a) \tag{5.64}$$

In Equation (5.64), the optimal policy is expressed as the Q function, which means we can choose optimal actions even if we have no knowledge of the rewards or transition probabilities. In small-size MDPs, we can store the values of the Q function in a look-up table and use them for calculation. When a MDP is known, we can compute the Q function with dynamic programming. In [12], the Q function is expressed in terms of Q values:

$$Q^{\pi^*}(s, a) = \max_a(E[r(s, a)] + \gamma E[Q^{\pi^*}(s', a)]) \tag{5.65}$$

$$Q^{\pi^*}(s, a) = E[r(s, a)] + \gamma \sum_{s'} p(s'|s, a) \max_{a'} Q(s', a') \tag{5.66}$$

and the optimal policy is

$$\pi^*(s) = \arg\max_a Q^{\pi^*}(s, a) \tag{5.67}$$

Equation (5.65) is described as the Q function and it is a recursive form. Thus, we can start with an arbitrary policy and an arbitrary value function and then repeat the equation. One of the recursive algorithms using the Q function was proposed in [14]. We could rewrite the Q function as follows:

$$\hat{Q}(s, a) \leftarrow r + \gamma \max_{a'} \hat{Q}(s', a') \tag{5.68}$$

where the $\hat{Q}$ function is a hypothesis (or an estimate) of the actual Q function. Equation (5.68) executes the action in the environment and then observes the new state and rewards repeatedly. It does not need to know general functions about rewards or transitions. If we perform a policy iteration, we need to carry out both policy improvement and policy evaluation at each step. Even policy evaluation is an iterative process. It makes the policy-based methods slow. On the other hand, policy evaluation is not performed at each step in value iteration. It makes the value-based methods fast. However, each iteration is slow when considering all actions. The update rule Equation (5.68) may work well in deterministic environments. However, if a reward function generates different values at each iteration, it may not converge. Thus, we rewrite the update rule by adjusting weights of active features as follows:

$$\hat{Q}_n(s,a) \leftarrow \hat{Q}_{n-1}(s,a) + \alpha_n(r + \gamma \max_{a'} \hat{Q}_{n-1}(s',a') - \hat{Q}_{n-1}(s,a)) \tag{5.69}$$

where $0 \le \alpha_n \le 1$ is a learning rate and implies how much new information affects the old information. It is related to how much Q values update and how rapidly the algorithm converges. If we set $\alpha_n \sim 0$, Q values are not updated. If we set $\alpha_n \sim 1$, the algorithm learns very quickly and considers only the most recent information. In a nonstationary environment, α_n is a constant (typically, $0.3 \le \alpha_n \le 0.5$). Equation (5.69) is the update rule of Q learning. In Equation (5.69), the term "$r + \gamma \max_{a'} \hat{Q}_{n-1}(s',a')$" is the learned value, the term "$\hat{Q}_{n-1}(s,a)$" is the old value, and the term "$\hat{Q}_n(s,a)$" is the new value. The term "$\max_{a'} \hat{Q}_{n-1}(s',a')$" represents that we take the best next action. Q learning is an off-policy algorithm and updates the Q function independent of the policy. The SARSA is similar to Q learning. The update rule of SARSA is expressed as follows:

$$\hat{Q}_n(s,a) \leftarrow \hat{Q}_{n-1}(s,a) + \alpha_n(r + \gamma \hat{Q}_{n-1}(s',a') - \hat{Q}_{n-1}(s,a)) \tag{5.70}$$

This is similar to Equation (5.69) except it takes the actual next state into account. In Equation (5.70), the term "$\hat{Q}_{n-1}(s',a')$" is the estimate of the future value and the term "$r + \gamma \hat{Q}_{n-1}(s',a')$" is the learned value. Q learning learns from the optimal Q value based on the maximum rewards, whereas the SARSA learns from the Q values consistent with the policy. One good example in [15] provides us with a comparison of Q learning and SARSA. Consider the cliff walking task shown in Figure 5.13, where we compare Q learning and SARSA.

The task is to begin a cliff walk at a start point and finish at an end point. Each action (up, down, left, and right) on the ground causes a reward −1, but an action on the cliff brings a penalty reward of −100. When stepping into the cliff region, we send it back to the start point. The goal is to find the shortest path. Q learning finds the optimal path but SARSA chooses a slightly longer safe path. However, Q learning falls into the cliff region more often.

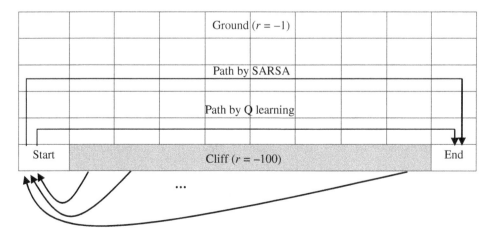

Figure 5.13 Comparison of Q learning and SARSA [15].

Table 5.2 Comparison of TD learning, Q learning, and SARSA.

	Update rule	Features
TD learning	$V(s) \leftarrow V(s) + \alpha[r + \gamma V(s') - V(s)]$	TD learning = Monte Carlo + dynamic programming
Q learning	$Q(s, a) \leftarrow Q(s, a) + \alpha(r + \gamma \max_{a'} Q(s', a') - Q(s, a))$	Off-policy, value iteration-based methods, relatively easier to implement but convergence may be slower than others
SARSA	$Q(s, a) \leftarrow Q(s, a) + \alpha(r + \gamma Q(s', a') - Q(s, a))$	On-policy, generalized policy iteration method, balances between exploration and exploitation, similar to Q learning but active policy controls the action a'

The Q learning algorithm is performed as the following steps:

Initial conditions: $Q(s, a)$ for all s and a
Repeat for each episode
    Initialize s
    Repeat for each step in episode
        – ***Step 1***: Choose a from s from Q
        – ***Step 2***: Take a, observe r and s'
        – ***Step 3***: Update $Q(s, a) \leftarrow Q(s, a) + \alpha(r + \gamma \max_{a'} Q(s', a') - Q(s, a))$
        – ***Step 4***: Reset current state $s \leftarrow s'$
    Until: s is terminal

The SARSA algorithm is performed as the following steps:

Initial conditions: $Q(s, a)$ for all s and a
Repeat for each episode
    Initialize s
    Choose a in s using a policy derived from Q
    Repeat for each step in episode
        – ***Step 1***: Take a, observe r and s'
        – ***Step 2***: Choose a' in s' from Q
        – ***Step 3***: Update $Q(s, a) \leftarrow Q(s, a) + \alpha(r + \gamma Q(s', a') - Q(s, a))$
        – ***Step 4***: Reset current state $s \leftarrow s'$, $a \leftarrow a'$
    Until: s is terminal

Table 5.2 summarizes the comparison of TD learning, Q learning and SARSA.

Example 5.6 *TD Learning*
Consider a gridworld as a simple MDP as shown in Figure p5.10. In the gridworld, we have

– States $S = \{(i, j) \mid i \text{ and } j = 1, 2, 3, 4, 5\}$
– Actions $A = \{$up, down, left, and right$\}$, the agent cannot move off the grid or into the shaded area
– Reward $r(s, a) = \begin{cases} -1 & \text{for nonterminal states} \\ 10 & \text{for terminal state} \end{cases}$

- Deterministic transitions
- $\alpha = 1$ and $\gamma = 1$

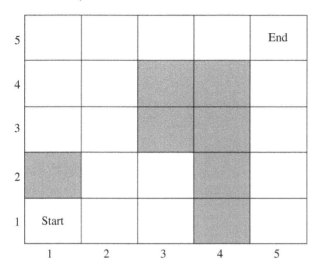

Figure p5.10 Gridworld for Example 5.6.

Find an optimal path using TD learning.

Solution

From $\alpha = 1$, $\gamma = 1$ and TD learning update rule Equation (5.61), we have

$$V(s) \leftarrow r + V(s')$$

and the state value function can simply be calculated using Equation (5.50). Thus, we have the state values as shown in Figure p5.11.

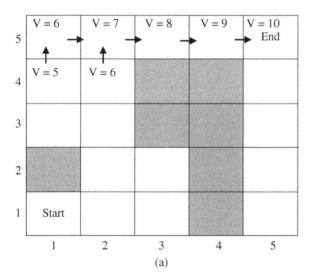

Figure p5.11 For Example 5.6, state values (a) at (2,4) and (b) after the first iteration.

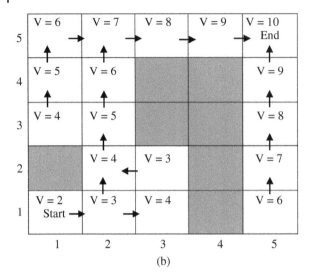

(b)

Figure p5.11 *(Continued)*

In the first iteration, we can find the optimal path: $(1,1) \to (2,1) \to (2,2) \to (2,3) \to (2,4) \to (2,5) \to (3,5) \to (4,5) \to (5,5)$

Example 5.7 *Q Learning*

Consider a gridworld as a simple MDP as shown in Figure p5.12. In the gridworld, we have

- States $S = \{(i, j) \mid i \text{ and } j = 1, 2, 3, 4, 5\}$
- Actions $A = \{$up, down, left, and right$\}$, the agent cannot move off the grid. If the agent moves into the shaded area, it should move back to the start.
- Reward $r(s, a) = \begin{cases} 0 & \text{for nonterminal states} \\ 10 & \text{for terminal state} \\ -100 & \text{for shaded area states} \end{cases}$
- Deterministic transitions
- $\alpha = 0.5$ and $\gamma = 1$

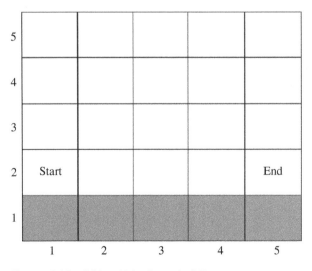

Figure p5.12   Gridworld for Example 5.7.

Find an optimal path using Q learning.

Solution

From $\alpha = 0.5$, $\gamma = 1$ and the Q learning update rule Equation (5.69), we have

$$Q(s, a) \leftarrow Q(s, a) + 0.5(r + \max_{a'} Q(s', a') - Q(s, a))$$

As the initial condition, $Q(s, a)$ for all s and a is set as zero as shown in Figure p5.13.

	1	2	3	4	5
5	$Q(s, u) = 0$ $Q(s, d) = 0$ $Q(s, l) = 0$ $Q(s, r) = 0$	$Q(s, u) = 0$ $Q(s, d) = 0$ $Q(s, l) = 0$ $Q(s, r) = 0$	$Q(s, u) = 0$ $Q(s, d) = 0$ $Q(s, l) = 0$ $Q(s, r) = 0$	$Q(s, u) = 0$ $Q(s, d) = 0$ $Q(s, l) = 0$ $Q(s, r) = 0$	$Q(s, u) = 0$ $Q(s, d) = 0$ $Q(s, l) = 0$ $Q(s, r) = 0$
4	$Q(s, u) = 0$ $Q(s, d) = 0$ $Q(s, l) = 0$ $Q(s, r) = 0$	$Q(s, u) = 0$ $Q(s, d) = 0$ $Q(s, l) = 0$ $Q(s, r) = 0$	$Q(s, u) = 0$ $Q(s, d) = 0$ $Q(s, l) = 0$ $Q(s, r) = 0$	$Q(s, u) = 0$ $Q(s, d) = 0$ $Q(s, l) = 0$ $Q(s, r) = 0$	$Q(s, u) = 0$ $Q(s, d) = 0$ $Q(s, l) = 0$ $Q(s, r) = 0$
3	$Q(s, u) = 0$ $Q(s, d) = 0$ $Q(s, l) = 0$ $Q(s, r) = 0$	$Q(s, u) = 0$ $Q(s, d) = 0$ $Q(s, l) = 0$ $Q(s, r) = 0$	$Q(s, u) = 0$ $Q(s, d) = 0$ $Q(s, l) = 0$ $Q(s, r) = 0$	$Q(s, u) = 0$ $Q(s, d) = 0$ $Q(s, l) = 0$ $Q(s, r) = 0$	$Q(s, u) = 0$ $Q(s, d) = 0$ $Q(s, l) = 0$ $Q(s, r) = 0$
2	$Q(s, u) = 0$ $Q(s, d) = 0$ $Q(s, l) = 0$ $Q(s, r) = 0$	$Q(s, u) = 0$ $Q(s, d) = 0$ $Q(s, l) = 0$ $Q(s, r) = 0$	$Q(s, u) = 0$ $Q(s, d) = 0$ $Q(s, l) = 0$ $Q(s, r) = 0$	$Q(s, u) = 0$ $Q(s, d) = 0$ $Q(s, l) = 0$ $Q(s, r) = 0$	$Q(s, a) = 0$
1	$Q(s, a) = 0$	$Q(s, a) = 0$	$Q(s, a) = 0$	$Q(s, a) = 0$	$Q(s, a) = 0$

Figure p5.13 Initial condition of $Q(s, a)$ for Example 5.7.

When the agent moves right until the end point, we have the following state action values:
For the first iteration,

$$Q((5,2), a) \leftarrow 0 + 0.5(10 + 0 - 0) = 5$$

For the second iteration,

$$Q((4,2), r) \leftarrow 0 + 0.5(0 + 5 - 0) = 2.5$$

$$Q((5,2), r) \leftarrow 5 + 0.5(10 + 0 - 5) = 7.5$$

For the third iteration,

$$Q((3,2), r) \leftarrow 0 + 0.5(0 + 2.5 - 0) = 1.25$$

$$Q((4,2), r) \leftarrow 2.5 + 0.5(0 + 7.5 - 2.5) = 5$$

$$Q((5,2), r) \leftarrow 7.5 + 0.5(10 + 0 - 7.5) = 8.75$$

For the fourth iteration,

$$Q((2,2), r) \leftarrow 0 + 0.5(0 + 1.25 - 0) = 0.625$$

$$Q((3,2), r) \leftarrow 1.25 + 0.5(0 + 5 - 1.25) = 3.125$$

$$Q((4,2), r) \leftarrow 5 + 0.5(0 + 8.75 - 5) = 6.875$$

$$Q((5,2), r) \leftarrow 8.75 + 0.5(10 + 0 - 8.75) = 9.375$$

For the fifth iteration,

$$Q((1,2), r) \leftarrow 0 + 0.5(0 + 0.625 - 0) = 0.3125$$

$$Q((2,2), r) \leftarrow 0.625 + 0.5(0 + 3.125 - 0.625) = 1.875$$

$$Q((3,2), r) \leftarrow 3.125 + 0.5(0 + 6.875 - 3.125) = 5$$

$$Q((4,2), r) \leftarrow 6.875 + 0.5(0 + 9.375 - 6.875) = 8.125$$

$$Q((5,2), r) \leftarrow 9.375 + 0.5(10 + 0 - 9.375) = 9.6875$$

Figure p5.14 illustrates the action state values when moving right to the end point.

	1	2	3	4	5
5	$Q(s, u) = 0$ $Q(s, d) = 0$ $Q(s, l) = 0$ $Q(s, r) = 0$	$Q(s, u) = 0$ $Q(s, d) = 0$ $Q(s, l) = 0$ $Q(s, r) = 0$	$Q(s, u) = 0$ $Q(s, d) = 0$ $Q(s, l) = 0$ $Q(s, r) = 0$	$Q(s, u) = 0$ $Q(s, d) = 0$ $Q(s, l) = 0$ $Q(s, r) = 0$	$Q(s, u) = 0$ $Q(s, d) = 0$ $Q(s, l) = 0$ $Q(s, r) = 0$
4	$Q(s, u) = 0$ $Q(s, d) = 0$ $Q(s, l) = 0$ $Q(s, r) = 0$	$Q(s, u) = 0$ $Q(s, d) = 0$ $Q(s, l) = 0$ $Q(s, r) = 0$	$Q(s, u) = 0$ $Q(s, d) = 0$ $Q(s, l) = 0$ $Q(s, r) = 0$	$Q(s, u) = 0$ $Q(s, d) = 0$ $Q(s, l) = 0$ $Q(s, r) = 0$	$Q(s, u) = 0$ $Q(s, d) = 0$ $Q(s, l) = 0$ $Q(s, r) = 0$
3	$Q(s, u) = 0$ $Q(s, d) = 0$ $Q(s, l) = 0$ $Q(s, r) = 0$	$Q(s, u) = 0$ $Q(s, d) = 0$ $Q(s, l) = 0$ $Q(s, r) = 0$	$Q(s, u) = 0$ $Q(s, d) = 0$ $Q(s, l) = 0$ $Q(s, r) = 0$	$Q(s, u) = 0$ $Q(s, d) = 0$ $Q(s, l) = 0$ $Q(s, r) = 0$	$Q(s, u) = 0$ $Q(s, d) = 0$ $Q(s, l) = 0$ $Q(s, r) = 0$
2	$Q(s, u) = 0$ $Q(s, d) = 0$ $Q(s, l) = 0$ $Q(s, r) = 0.3125$	$Q(s, u) = 0$ $Q(s, d) = 0$ $Q(s, l) = 0$ $Q(s, r) = 1.875$	$Q(s, u) = 0$ $Q(s, d) = 0$ $Q(s, l) = 0$ $Q(s, r) = 5$	$Q(s, u) = 0$ $Q(s, d) = 0$ $Q(s, l) = 0$ $Q(s, r) = 8.125$	$Q(s, a) = 9.6875$
1	$Q(s, a) = 0$	$Q(s, a) = 0$	$Q(s, a) = 0$	$Q(s, a) = 0$	$Q(s, a) = 0$

Figure p5.14 Q value updates when moving right for Example 5.7.

Likewise, we keep updating the state action values. When they converge to specific values, we can find the optimal policy. As we discussed for Figure 5.13, Q learning finds the shortest path as an optimal path.

Example 5.8 *Q Learning Using Computer Simulation*

Consider a gridworld as a simple MDP as shown in Figure p5.15. In the gridworld, we have

- States $S = \{(i, j) \mid i \text{ and } j = 1, 2, \ldots, 16\}$
- Actions $A = \{$up, down, left, right, diagonally down-right, diagonally down-left, diagonally up-right and diagonally up-left$\}$. The agent cannot move off the grid.
- Reward $r(s, a) = \begin{cases} 0 & \text{for nonterminal states} \\ 10 & \text{for terminal state} \\ -100 & \text{for shaded area states} \end{cases}$
- Deterministic transitions
- Maximum iteration $= 30$
- $\alpha = 0.2$ and $\gamma = 0.9$

Find an optimal path using Q learning.

START

Figure p5.15 Gridworld for 5.8.

Solution

Like Example 5.7, we initialize the state and update the state action values using the following update rule:

$$Q(s, a) \leftarrow Q(s, a) + 0.2(r + 0.9 \max_{a'} Q(s', a') - Q(s, a))$$

The matrix size is 16×16 and it is not easy to calculate without a computer. Using computer simulation, we obtain the optimal path: $(1,16) \rightarrow (2,15) \rightarrow (3,14) \rightarrow (4,14) \rightarrow (5,13) \rightarrow (6,12) \rightarrow (7,11) \rightarrow (8,10) \rightarrow (7,9) \rightarrow (7,8) \rightarrow (8,7) \rightarrow (7,6) \rightarrow (6,5) \rightarrow (7,4) \rightarrow (8,3) \rightarrow (9,3) \rightarrow (10,4) \rightarrow (11,4) \rightarrow (12,4) \rightarrow (13,3) \rightarrow (14,2) \rightarrow (15,2) \rightarrow (16,1)$. Figure p5.16 illustrates the optimal path in the gridworld.

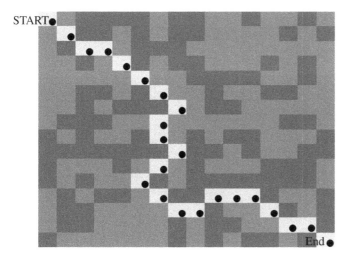

Figure p5.16 Optimal path for 5.8.

Summary 5.3 TD(0) Learning Algorithm

Input: A policy π to be evaluated, a sequence of step size α, mapping state to feature vectors.
Initial conditions: $V(s)$ for all s
Repeat for each episode
   Initialize s
   Repeat for each step in episode
      – *Step 1*: Sample action in the current state by a policy π: $a \leftarrow p_\pi(a\,|\,s)$
      – *Step 2*: Transition to the next state: take action a and observe r and next state s
      – *Step 3*: Update $V(s) \leftarrow V(s) + \alpha[r + \gamma V(s') - V(s)]$
      – *Step 4*: Reset current state $s \leftarrow s'$
      – *Until*: s is terminal

Summary 5.4 Q Learning Algorithm

Initial conditions: $Q(s, a)$ for all s and a
Repeat for each episode
   Initialize s
   Repeat for each step in episode
      – *Step 1*: Choose a from s from Q
      – *Step 2*: Take a, observe r and s'
      – *Step 3*: Update $Q(s, a) \leftarrow Q(s, a) + \alpha(r + \gamma \max_{a'} Q(s', a') - Q(s, a))$
      – *Step 4*: Reset current state $s \leftarrow s'$
      – *Until*: **s** is terminal

Summary 5.5 SARSA Learning Algorithm

Initial conditions: $Q(s, a)$ for all s and a
Repeat for each episode
   Initialize s
   Choose a in s using a policy derived from Q
   Repeat for each step in episode
      – *Step 1*: Take a, observe r and s'
      – *Step 2*: Choose a' in s' from Q
      – *Step 3*: Update $Q(s, a) \leftarrow Q(s, a) + \alpha(r + \gamma Q(s', a') - Q(s, a))$
      – *Step 4*: Reset current state $s \leftarrow s'$, $a \leftarrow a'$
      – *Until*: **s** is terminal

Problems

5.1 Compare artificial intelligence, machine learning, and deep learning.

5.2 From a communication and network engineering point of view, describe some applications of artificial intelligent systems.

5.3 Compare classification, regression, clustering, and decision-making. Then, find examples in communications and networks.

5.4 Compare supervised learning and unsupervised learning.

5.5 Define support vectors of SVM and describe how to find them.

5.6 Explain why margin and generalization error of SVM are a trade-off relationship.

5.7 Explain the curse of dimensionality.

5.8 Consider the following dataset:

Class A: (1,5), (2,4), (3,7), (4,8), (5,11)

Class B: (4,2), (6,8), (11,2), (12,4), (13,3)

Find a classifier using SVM.

5.9 Compare Euclidean distance d_e, Manhattan distance d_m, Chebyshev distance d_c, and non-linear distance d_n. Then, describe their pros and cons.

5.10 Consider the following one-dimensional dataset:

Data A: 10,12,15,16,17,21,23,25,31,35,41,45,46,55,69

Find two clusters using the K-means clustering algorithm.

5.11 Consider the following two-dimensional dataset:

Data A : (1,2), (2,5), (4,7), (5,8), (6,12), (7,18), (8,21), (9,24)

Find two clusters using the K-means clustering algorithm.

5.12 Describe the properties of the Markov decision process.

5.13 Describe the elements of the Markov decision process.

5.14 Compare the RL interaction processes with deterministic and stochastic environments.

5.15 Compare model-based RL methods and model-free RL methods.

5.16 Compare policy-based RL methods and value-based RL methods.

5.17 Compare off-policy learning methods and on-policy learning methods. Then, describe their pros and cons.

5.18 Explain the exploitation and exploration approaches of RL methods.

5.19 Compare TD learning, Q learning, and SARSA.

5.20 Consider a gridworld as a simple MDP as shown in Figure p5.17. In the gridworld, we have
- States $S = \{(i, j) \mid i \text{ and } j = 1, \ldots, 10\}$
- Actions $A = \{$up, down, left, and right$\}$, the agent cannot move off the grid or into the shaded area.
- Reward $r(s, a) = \begin{cases} 0 & \text{for nonterminal states} \\ 10 & \text{for terminal state} \\ -100 & \text{for shaded area states} \end{cases}$
- Deterministic transitions
- $\alpha = 0.2$ and $\gamma = 0.9$

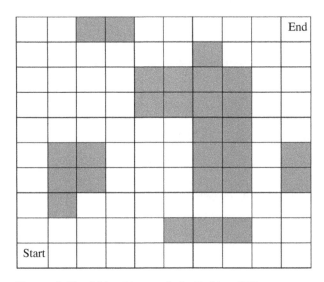

Figure p5.17   Gridworld example for Problem 5.20.

Find optimal paths using TD learning, Q learning, and SARSA. Then, compare the results.

References

1 Domingos, P. (2012). A few useful things to know about machine learning. *Magazine Communications of the ACM* 55 (10): 78–87.

2 Tom M. Mitchell (2006). The Discipline of Machine Learning, *CMU-ML-06-108*. Machine Learning Department, Carnegie Mellon University. http://reports-archive .adm.cs.cmu.edu/anon/anon/home/ftp/ml/CMU-ML-06-108.pdf.

3 Ng, A. (2018). *Machine Learning Lecture Note*. Stanford University https://www.coursera .org/learn/machine-learning.

4 Russel, S. and Norvig, P. (2009). *Artificial Intelligence: A Mordern Approach*, 3e. Pearson ISBN-10: 0136042597.

5 J. Manyika, M. Chui, B. Brown, et al. (2011). Big Data: The Next Frontier for Innovation, Competition, and Productivity. Technical report, McKinsey Global Institute. https://www.mckinsey.com/business-functions/digital-mckinsey/our-insights/big-data-the-next-frontier-for-innovation.

6 Wolpert, D.H. (1996). The lack of a priori distinctions between learning algorithms. *Neural Computation* 8 (7): 1341–1390.

7 Wolpert, D.H. and Macready, W.G. (1997). No free lunch theorems for optimization. *IEEE Transactions on Evolutionary Computation* 1 (1): 67–82.

8 Cortes, C. and Vapnik, V. (1995). Support vector networks. *Journal of Machine Learning* 20 (3): 273–297.

9 Vapnik, V.N. (1995). *The Nature of Statistical Learning Theory*. Springer-Verlag. ISBN: 0-387-98780-0.

10 Cox, D.R. (1955). Note on grouping. *Journal of the American Statistical Association* 52: 543–547.

11 Lloyd, S.P. (1982). Least squares quantization in PCM. *IEEE Transactions on Information Theory* 28: 129–137.

12 Bellman, R.E. (1957). *Dynamic Programming*. Princeton: Princeton University Press.

13 Sutton, R.S. (August 1988). Learning to predict by the methods of temporal differences. *Machine Learning* 3 (1): 9–44.

14 C. J. C. H. Watkins (1989). Learning from delayed rewards. PhD thesis. University of Cambridge.

15 Sutton, R.S. and Barto, A.G. (1998). *Introduction to Reinforcement Learning*. MIT Press.

Part II

**Design and Optimization for 5G Wireless Communications
and Networks**

6

Design Principles for 5G Communications and Networks

The cellular communication and network systems have been incrementally evolving and the old and new network equipment coexists for certain periods. Likewise, the 4G equipment will continuously roll out, adopt new features, and evolve to 5G systems, which will be deployed progressively. The transition to 5G may take longer than for 4G because many different features should be included, and also we need a game-changing approach. The 5G rollout will redefine the networks depending on the required services. In order to support them all, 5G requires significant network investment. According to [1], a high volume of investment is needed. The estimated costs to deploy a small cell for a small city or a large dense city are USD 6.8 million and 55.5 million, respectively. A large dense city is more commercially attractive from a mobile operator's point of view. Major mobile operators are more interested in investments in urban areas than rural areas. Thus, the digital divide between them may increase in the 5G era. A policymaker should try to find a balance between a rural service and an urban service. A policymaker's role is getting more important. The report [1] identified 16 key issues to stimulate investment in 5G networks as follows: the investment case, 4G network strategy, harmonizing the spectrum, the spectrum roadmap, spectrum sharing, spectrum pricing, the 700 MHz spectrum, fiber investment incentives, fiber tax, copper migration to fiber, wireless backhaul, access/sharing of passive infrastructure, access costs, asset databases, wayleave agreements, and 5G test beds. These issues are mixed as technical, political, and commercial issues. A 5G system designer considers them all and develops 5G devices and networks. In Chapter 2, we reviewed 5G wireless communication and networks system parameters and requirements. The demand for a wider broadband service will increase continuously and the device connection with humans, cars, appliances, apparel, and factory machines are required. 5G systems created demand for higher throughputs, lower latency and massive connectivity, and the need to develop attractive services and use cases for customers. In order to support richer content and new services, 5G systems should be developed in a cost-effective, energy-efficient, and high-performance manner. The 5G roles can be summarized as follows: (i) support richer contents like 8K, virtual reality (VR) and augmented reality (AR) videos and improve ultra-low latency and higher efficiency; (ii) support connection everywhere; (iii) support tailoring services and networks for B2B and B2C; (iv) enhance security and safety; and (v) digitalize business models of telecoms and vertical industries. New design principles for 5G communications and networks are required to satisfy these requirements and to provide policymakers with solutions of the key issues. In this chapter, we introduce design principles for 5G systems in order to meet

Design and Optimization for 5G Wireless Communications, First Edition. Haesik Kim.
© 2020 John Wiley & Sons Ltd. Published 2020 by John Wiley & Sons Ltd.

5G requirements and roles. The purpose of this chapter is to provide the reader with the big picture of the whole 5G system.

6.1 New Design Approaches and Key Challenges of 5G Communications and Networks

In order to meet 5G requirements and overcome the current limitations of 4G systems, a new design approach is required to develop 5G communications and networks. The approaches could be both evolutions of 4G to meet future demands, and revolutions in cellular communication devices and network architectures to support new features of 5G systems. In this section, we address new design approaches and key challenges for 5G system design.

6.1.1 5G Frequency Bands

Greater bandwidth allows us to support higher data rates and larger amounts of traffic. The bandwidths are strongly related to coverage and throughput of cellular systems. Thus, 5G spectrum allocation will play an important role in 5G system design. 5G bandwidth is much greater than 4G. Although the 5G bandwidths will vary between countries, they can be categorized as (i) sub 1 GHz for wide range coverage, (ii) prime 5G mid bands around 3.5 GHz for dense urban high data rates, (iii) 26, 28, and 39 GHz for hotspots, and (iv) WRC-19 (ITU World Radiocommunication Conference in 2019, above 24 GHz) bands for future mmWAVE options. Table 6.1 summarizes 5G spectrum usages.

5G needs to harmonize these spectrums globally in order to support 5G deployments and services including roaming, cross-border interferences and interoperability. In addition, the harmonized 5G spectrum will be able to deploy 5G systems more efficiently in terms of cost and performance. From the radio frequency (RF) design point of view, the unprecedented wide and different frequencies of 5G systems are big research challenges. This means that RF devices should support multiple frequencies and have multiple independent RF

Table 6.1 5G spectrum usages.

	Low frequencies (sub 1 GHz)	Medium frequencies (around 3.5 GHz)	High frequencies (above 24 GHz)
Frequencies	694~700 MHz in Europe, around 600 MHz in USA	3.4~3.8 GHz in Europe, 3.1~3.55, 3.7~4.2 GHz in USA	24~27 GHz in Europe, 27.5~28.35, 37~40, 64~71 GHz in USA
5G use cases	mMTC, URLLC	URLLC, eMBB, mMTC	eMBB
Capacity	Low	Medium	High
Coverage	Wide (rural and urban areas)	Medium (urban areas)	Narrow (Hot spots)
Remarks	Supplemental downlink (SDL) in combination with 5G prime band	5G prime bands, 100 MHz contiguous spectrum	800 MHz contiguous spectrum

pathways, and so this requires substantial change (antenna bandwidth increase, high complexity of signal routing, and so on). In addition, the major drawback of 5G multi-carrier techniques is a high peak-to-average power ratio (PAPR). This drawback causes signal distortion and high energy consumption. It is essential that a transmitter includes a power amplifier providing suitable power for transmission. The power amplifier is very sensitive to operational areas requiring a linear characteristic. The high PAPR causes a nonlinear operation problem and this problem causes a signal distortion. Thus, the PAPR is highly related to power amplifier efficiency. 5G new waveform, wide bandwidth and scalable numerology results in high PAPR and lower energy efficiency. Massive multiple input multiple output (MIMO) and beamforming techniques increase complexity and difficulty of 5G RF design. The performance of massive MIMO systems depends on channel correlation. There are two types of channel correlation: spatial correlation and antenna mutual coupling. In a practical MIMO system, each MIMO channel is related to another channel by different degrees, depending on the multipath channel environment. This is spatial correlation. Antenna mutual coupling is caused by the interaction among transmit antennas. This effect becomes a very serious problem if antenna spacing is very small, like a massive MIMO system. In addition, thermal dissipation caused by the large number of antenna elements is another RF design challenge. If we consider dual connectivity as 5G non-standalone (NSA) supporting both 4G LTE and 5G, it will add significantly more complexity because the 5G NSA should support multiple 4G bands while receiving a signal in 5G bands.

6.1.2 Low Latency

The key metrics of 5G URLLC (ultra-reliable and low latency communication) are latency, reliability, and availability. In particular, low latency is a key feature of 5G URLLC systems. 5G URLLC plays an important role in supporting connectivity solutions for automated vehicles, tactile internet, factory automation, remote surgery, and so on. Latency can be defined in many different ways. In 3GPP standard documentation [2], 5G URLLC requires (i) 1 ms user plane radio latency (the radio latency is defined as the duration from the reception of a packet by layer-2 radio protocol at the transmitting end to the delivery of the packet to the layer-3 protocol at the receiving end) with an outage probability of less than 10^{-5} for small data packets (e.g. 32 bytes) and (ii) 0.5 ms user plane average latency for both uplink (UL) and downlink (DL). The Next Generation Mobile Network (NGMN) alliance report [3] proposes 1 ms end-to-end (E2E) latency (E2E latency means the duration between the transmission from the application layer of the source node and the reception at the application layer of the destination node) for URLLC extreme-use cases, and 10 ms E2E in general cases. However, these requirements could not cover all 5G use cases. Depending on use cases, the latency requirement will be more stringent. This is one of the most difficult goals in 5G system design. The ITU defines the user plane latency T_t as follows [4]:

$$T_t = 2T_{L1/L2} + T_a + \sum T_p + \sum T_{tx} \tag{6.1}$$

where $T_{L1/L2}$, T_a, T_p, and T_{tx} are layer 1 and 2 processing delays, alignment delay, UE/gNB processing time, and transmission time, respectively. In Equation (6.1), the propagation delay is neglected because it is lower than the transmission time interval (TTI). In order

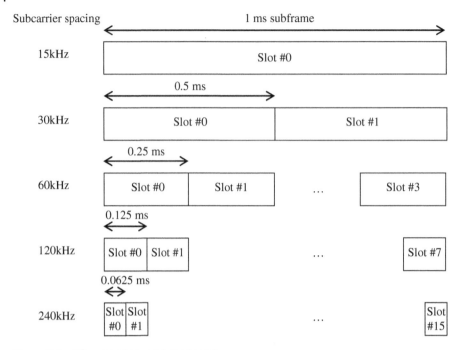

Figure 6.1   5G numerology and slot length.

to reduce the latency, the 3GPP release 15 and 16 standards proposed a new direction. The 5G NR (new radio) frame structure is designed to support the low latency connectivity. In 4G LTE, the subcarrier spacing is fixed as 15 kHz and the symbol period is accordingly $1/15\,\text{kHz} = 66.7\,\mu s$. However, 5G NR subcarrier spacing is scalable by $2^{\mu}\cdot15\,\text{kHz}$ where μ is 0, 1, 2, 3, 4, 5. Due to this configurable subcarrier spacing, it is possible to accommodate more symbols in one subframe. Shorter TTI and mini-slot can reduce the transmission time. The frame length is 10 ms and each subframe is 1 ms. The normal subframe is composed of 14 orthogonal frequency division multiplexing (OFDM) symbols. As numerology increases, the number of slots in a subframe increases. Figure 6.1 illustrates the slot length.

The slot is a unit for transmission by resource allocation and scheduling mechanism. A 5G NR mini-slot occupies only 2, 4, 7 OFDM symbols and they are not tied to a strict frame structure. It allows the 5G system to support non-slot-based scheduling, which can be positioned asynchronously. It helps to achieve short transmission and minimize inter-ferences to other 5G transmissions. Another important feature of 5G frame structure is that transmissions are not restricted to slot boundaries. In addition, when we have a mixed traffic of URLLC and enhanced mobile broadband communication (eMBB), pre-emptive schedul-ing [5] will be helpful for reducing latency. Using this scheduling mechanism, URLLC data can be immediately transmitted from next-generation NodeB (gNB) to user equipment (UE) without waiting for ongoing scheduling processes by overwriting of an eMBB transmission. Another approach is to reduce the processing time by a fast decoding process and fast hybrid automatic repeat request (HARQ). Fast decoding can be achieved by the mini-slot targeted parallelized channel coding. A 4G HARQ scheme needs a feedback (ACK/NACK signal) at every iteration but 5G allows the HARQ scheme to perform without waiting for a feedback at every transmission. Thus, the processing time can be reduced and also unnecessary transmissions can be prevented. 5G supports code block group (CBG) based transmission with single or multi-bit ACK feedback. CBGs divide the transport blocks into smaller groups and they can be decoded by the UE quickly. In addition, uplink grant free transmission reduces the latency significantly. An uplink grant free transmission scheme does not need a resource request and can avoid a regular handshake delay (request resource allocation and scheduling and then wait for the grant).

6.1.3 More Efficient Radio Resource Utilization

One important approach to 5G systems seeks more efficient radio resource utilization. The 100 MHz 4G LTE bandwidth is divided into five channels (5×20 MHz) and carrier aggregation techniques can be used. However, 5G NR uses a single contiguous wide bandwidth carrier with 100 MHz bandwidth. Thus, the 5G carrier is more efficient than the 4G carrier because overhead (10% guard bands) can be reduced. In addition, it helps us to support faster load balancing in heterogeneous cells. Dynamic (or flexible) time division duplexing (TDD) and full duplexing techniques will be able to increase the spectral efficiency of 5G systems. In 4G systems, TDD or frequency division duplexing (FDD) are used. FDD uses separate uplink (UL) and downlink (DL) frequency bands. However, TDD uses the same frequency bands for them and uplink and downlink are separated in the time domain. Both TDD and FDD have benefits for specific applications. The advantages of FDD over TDD are lower interferences and wider coverage. The advantages of TDD over FDD are channel reciprocity and asymmetric link supports. TDD is adopted in specific cases but FDD is more widely implemented in cellular systems. However, TDD may be widely adopted in 5G systems in order to use the spectrum more efficiently. Thus, one possible combination of 5G network deployment is to implement FDD at macro cells and TDD at small cells. The TDD operation allows us to adjust the amount of time domain radio resources according to channel and traffic conditions. In 4G systems, static TDD configurations are available with seven different uplink and downlink configuration subframes in 10 ms TDD frame [6]. 4G static TDD operation could not satisfy the fast adaptation required for 5G traffic demands. In order to meet the 5G requirements, dynamic TDD provides us with tailored TDD configurations in each cell or cluster as well as more flexible switching. It improves not only spectral efficiency but also energy efficiency and latency. However, a major challenge for this technique is interference mitigation because UL/DL transmission may interfere with DL/UL of a neighboring cell. Full duplexing technique allows us to transmit and receive a packet at the same time and frequency band. It provides us with roughly doubled channel capacity for single link transmission. Thus, the spectral efficiency increases significantly but self-interference cancellation is an essential part of this technique. A strong self-interference signal prevents proper detection of a signal. Typically, the self-interference signal is 100 dB stronger than the intended receiving signal [7]. Due to improvements in signal processing techniques, such as passive suppression (directional diversity antenna separation), analogue cancellation (antenna cancellation, pre-coding, minimum mean-squared error (MMSE) filtering, etc.), and digital cancellation, self-interference cancellation capability is up to 110 dB [8] and the interference can be mostly removed. In addition, 5G unlicensed spectrum or spectrum sharing provides us with other benefits such as higher spectral efficiency and new business models. In 3GPP standard, unlicensed spectrum uses in 5G NR are studied as (i) NR carrier aggregation in unlicensed spectrum and licensed anchor, and (ii) NR standalone operations in unlicensed spectrum. Lean carrier [9] allows us to minimize control channels and reduce redundancy. In 4G, continuous transmission of cell-specific reference signals is required. Synchronization and broadcasting is carried out every 5 and 10 ms, respectively. However, due to lean carrier, 5G NR does not need cell-specific reference signals. Synchronization and broadcasting is carried out every 20 and 20 ms, respectively. Thus, it increases resource utilization and decreases base station power.

6.1.4 Small Cells and Ultra-Dense Networks

Small cells are literally smaller than macro-cells and encompass pico-cells, micro-cells, and femto-cells. The base stations (or access nodes) are deployed as close as possible to the mobile users. Short range and low power transmission covers a geographically small area. In 5G, it will play an important role in providing high-speed transmission, increasing coverage, and improving overall network efficiency. The small cell concept was motivated by the traffic trends of cellular networks in recent decades and was included in 3GPP Release 8 for use in dense urban areas. It is especially useful when macro-cells cannot cover some area due to obstacles or poor propagation. In addition, the biggest costs in deploying mobile network equipment is site-leasing fees, fiber, and maintenance costs. Self-organizing small cells will be helpful for overall installation and maintenance costs by eliminating expensive rooftop base stations. The benefits of 5G small cells can be summarized as follows: Coverage improvement, efficient traffic management, high throughputs, faster deployment, relatively lower location requirements, low power consumption, and so on. Due to these benefits, 5G could drive densification, and ultra-dense network deployment of small cells is considered in 5G networks. As we reviewed in Chapter 2, area traffic capacity in 5G should be 10 Mbps/m^2 in eMBB downlink. Dense deployment of small cells improves area traffic capacity significantly. Main differences from macro-cells and design challenges can be summarized as follows:

(i) Severe inter-cell interferences caused by close proximity of small cells.
(ii) Inactive and active small cell management (idle mode).
(iii) Novel frequency reuse requirements.
(iv) Backhaul capacity management.
(v) Horizontal (small cell – small cell) and vertical (small cell – macro cell) handover.
(vi) Energy-efficient small cell operation.

To satisfy these, system optimization or trade-offs among different performance metrics is required.

6.1.5 Higher Flexibility

5G networks will be more complex, flexible, and scalable than 4G networks. Flexibility is highly related to network design cost, deployment time, equipment configuration, and maintenance cost. According to 3GPP release 15, the first wave of 5G networks will be deployed as a NSA scenario, which coexists together with 4G infrastructure, and then the next wave will be deployed as a standalone scenario. This approach provides us with many different deployment options and also requires interworking between existing 4G equipment and new 5G equipment. Flexibility is an essential requirement of 5G to enable this network deployment scenario. In addition, new technologies and new use cases should be gradually included in 5G systems. The network configuration will be different depending on what use cases are supported, where gNB is deployed, where self-organizing small cells are installed, and so on. The scalable and flexible network platform to encompass them all will be an important part of 5G system design. Most importantly, 3GPP keeps releasing new specifications and 5G networks will be continuously evolving. In order to satisfy new requirements and include new functionality, greater flexibility of 5G systems is required. Thus, network virtualization, software defined networking (SDN), and clouding computing are key elements of 5G networks.

6.1.6 Virtualization

Service providers deploy various network functions such as network address translation (NAT), domain name service (DNS), caching, firewalls, encryption, and so on. In 5G, network functions virtualization (NFV) offers a new design approach by decoupling software from hardware. The NFV implements them on virtual machines and delivers the network components when a user requests a network function. Leveraging the NFV, mobile operators obtain many benefits including capital expenditure (CapEx) and operating expenditure (OpEx) reduction, time reduction to deploy a network service, and network scalability improvements. In addition, the NFV enables us to optimize network resource provision and support network slicing, allowing virtual networks to operate on a single physical network. SDN is also one important approach to virtualizing 5G networks. SDN is similar to NFV because both techniques enable network architectures to be abstracted in software. However, SDN facilitates programmable network management and configuration, abstracts physical network resources (e.g. routing, switching, and so on), separates network control functions from network forwarding functions, and improves network performance. SDN detaches data plane from control plane and centralizes control plane. Thus, SDN orchestrates the network functions by making a decision of traffic control in software and handling the traffic in hardware. The advantages of SDN are summarized as follows: programmable network control and configuration, dynamic and agile traffic control, centralized network intelligence, and standardized protocols and interfaces. Based on both techniques, 5G networks can be more scalable and faster to adapt to a new service, while 4G static network architectures are limited to expanding services to meet future requirements. Network slicing is virtual networking as one family of NFV and SDN. 5G network slicing is helpful for building virtual E2E networks tailored to different 5G applications such as eMBB, URLLC, and mMTC. In order to serve one business customer, 4G should implement tailor-made functions for a specific customer and build a dedicated network. This is not an efficient or cost-effective solution. The concept of network slicing is a radical change of network implementation. It allows us to build virtually independent networks and operate multiple logical

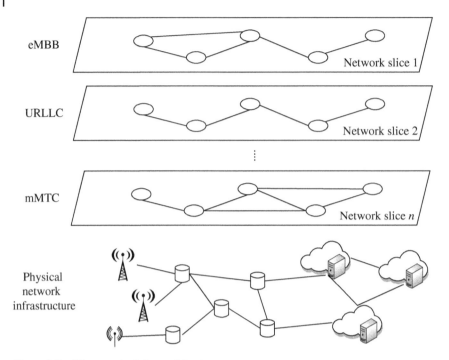

eMBB

URLLC

mMTC

Physical
network
infrastructure

Figure 6.2 5G network slicing architecture.

networks on the top of a single network infrastructure. Figure 6.2 illustrates the concept of network slicing.

Customized services by network slicing can be composed of network connection services and network resource services. Network connection services represent a level of connectivity that a mobile operator identifies network performance by network metrics (latency, throughput, mobility, reliability, scalability, energy efficiency, connection density, etc.). Network resource services means data management services, including big data analysis, charging, positioning, cloud storage, different levels of security, and so on. In addition, the concept of cloud radio access network (C-RAN) moves processing functions from base stations to virtualized edge data centers. Thus, it allows service providers to scale radio access resource dynamically and offer a better end-user performance. C-RAN architecture is composed of centralized baseband units (BBUs), remote radio units (RRUs), and front-hauls (or transport network [TN]). Sometimes, C-RAN is called centralized RAN because baseband processing functions are centralized. In this architecture, BBUs are centralized but RRUs are distributed. Front-hauls interconnect them. The advantages of C-RAN include a low maintenance cost, more efficient radio resource, infrastructure reuse, easy support for new technology, faster network deployment, and better network scalability.

6.1.7 Distributed Network Architecture

Centralized computing systems have been mainstream network architectures in previous cellular systems and have managed huge volumes of data traffic. However, they are ineffective and costly in computing high volumes of data traffic and supporting a large number of customers at the same time. Distributed computing systems can be defined as the systems whose components are distributed in different places and components are connected in networks and communicate with each other. Distributed computing systems will be more efficient in 5G networks due to their scalability, resilience, fault tolerance, and lower network congestion. Multi-access edge computing (MEC) is a distributed network architecture concept integrating multiple technologies: network virtualization, cloud computing, SDN, small cells, and network slicing. The benefits of MEC are to reduce latency and network congestion and also to improve reliability and scalability. The basic idea is that the computing is performed at the edge of a network and more content is cached at the edge. Thus, it offloads the traffic from the core network (CN), manages traffic flows efficiently and dynamically, adjusts network resources for each application, and reduces E2E latency. It allows us to open up a new class of cloud-based networks. Its use cases are automated vehicles, augmented reality, and virtual reality requiring ultra-low latency and high throughput. The concept of fog computing [10] extends both the edge computing concept and the cloud computing concepts. Fog computing distributes resources, computing powers, and controls and provides us with many benefits such as better privacy and security and operation cost reduction.

6.1.8 Device-Centric Communications

Device-to-device (D2D) communication allows devices to communicate directly with each other, with or without network infrastructure. This device-centric communication technique has been included in 3GPP standard Release 12. This technique keeps evolving the 5G network architecture and allows us to find better traffic flows with different priorities and transfer a large amount of data in short range. This technique will improve network performance such as capacity improvement by reducing overhead data, coverage extension without additional network infrastructure, user experience data rate improvements due to the proximity connectivity, and latency improvement due to the direct link. The small cell concept can enhance system capacity in a dense area, but the densification of small cells may make deployment and maintenance costs increase. Thus, D2D communication could be another approach for high-quality link support in a dense area. Many application scenarios for D2D communications are considered as follows: public safety when infrastructures collapse, proximity-based social and commercial services, advertisements for pedestrians, cooperative D2D communications, vehicular communications, and so on. In order to include D2D communication functions in 5G systems, several research challenges must be addressed:

(i) How to select a D2D communication mode or cellular communication mode? We could select a better quality link based on channel state information. In addition, it is possible that a mobile user requests D2D communication link directly.

(ii) How to discover neighboring devices and synchronize them? Like discovery and synchronization of Bluetooth communications, the device could search geographically close devices, send them a request for a D2D link, and synchronize them. However, this approach is based on one condition: both transmitter and receiver know each other. If the receiver does not recognize the transmitter, the monitoring function is required not to miss the request signal. The constant monitoring results in battery drain and power consumption will increase. Another approach is to establish the D2D link by cellular network support. Cellular networks manage control flow only and the D2D link is used for data flow.

(iii) How to manage interferences? The D2D link may reuse the cellular spectrum and the frequency reuse causes intra-cell interferences. If the intra-cell interferences are high, the system capacity will decease significantly and the benefit of the D2D link will decrease.

(iv) How to achieve optimal resource allocation? Multiple heterogeneous networks and D2D links coexist in 5G cellular networks. One key design topic is to find an optimal resource allocation policy to reduce signal overhead and complexity and increase network performance.

6.1.9 New Air Interfaces

In the initial stages, 5G air interfaces will be made available through the evolution of 4G air interfaces. However, they will be replaced by new 5G air interfaces. 3GPP Release 14 started studying 5G new radio in 2016 and 3GPP Release 15 included the first 5G new radio. 5G NR air interfaces support a huge number of services, allow deployment of different types of network, and improve network performance. The key components of 5G new air interfaces can be summarized as follows: (i) OFDM-based waveform with cyclic prefix is a baseline, and windowing, pre-coding and filtering can be added; (ii) flexible frame structure including different numerologies and wide carrier bandwidth; (iii) high order modulation; (iv) new channel coding schemes including low-density parity-check (LDPC) codes for the user plane and polar codes for the control plane; and (v) massive MIMO and beamforming.

6.1.10 Big Data Management

5G networks will support rich applications and services and manage a huge volume of data due to proliferation of network traffic. Since 5G networks act as a bridge between data sources and end users and also handles the traffic, 5G systems should continuously monitor system and service performance and manage configurations. Huge volume data monitors and analysis are new challenges in 5G systems. In addition, mobile operators provides storage and data analysis and the process is performed in cloud networks. Big data management is one of the essential parts in 5G networks, and includes data acquisition, storage, processing, analysis, and visualization. In 5G applications, many different types of data will flow in the networks. One edge component collects big data, a cloud computing processor analyzes them, and automatic action is carried out directly.

Summary 6.1 5G System Design Principles

1) 5G frequency bands can be categorized as (i) sub 1 GHz for wide range coverage; (ii) prime 5G mid bands around 3.5 GHz for dense urban high data rates; (iii) 26, 28, and 39 GHz for hotspots; and (iv) WRC-19 (ITU World Radiocommunication Conference in 2019, above 24 GHz) bands for future mmWAVE options.

2) 5G URLLC plays an important role in supporting connectivity solutions for auto-mated vehicles, tactile internet, factory automation, remote surgery, and so on. Depending on use cases, the latency requirement will be more stringent.

3) 5G carrier is more efficient than 4G carrier because overhead (10% guard bands) can be reduced.

4) Small cells will play an important role in providing high-speed transmission, increased coverage, and improved overall network efficiency.

5) 5G networks will be more complex and scalable than 4G networks.

6) Network virtualization offers a new design approach by decoupling software from hardware.

7) Distributed computing systems will be more efficient in 5G networks due to their scalability, resilience, fault tolerance, and lower network congestion.

8) The D2D technique will improve network performance such as capacity improve-ment by reducing overhead data, coverage extension without additional network infrastructure, user experience data rate improvement, and latency improvement.

9) 5G NR air interfaces support a huge number of services, allowing us to deploy different types of network, and improve network performance.

10) 5G networks will support rich applications and services and manage a huge volume of data due to proliferation of network traffic. Big data management includes data acquisition, storage, processing, analysis, and visualization.

6.2 5G New Radio

5G new radio (NR) has been designed to meet an extreme variation of 5G connectivity requirements and deployment types. One single technology improvement is not enough to meet them all. 5G NR includes multiple technologies and innovations to support wider frequency bands, various deployment scenarios and diverse use cases. In this section, we briefly review 5G new radio, which has been defined in the 3GPP standard.

6.2.1 5G Radio Access Network Architecture

In the 5G network architecture, a logical split between radio access network (RAN), core network (CN), and service layer functions is allowed to evolve them independently and also to provide us with more flexibility. Thus, RAN-based network operation is possible. For example, RAN-based paging for dense area operation, sleep mode operation for small cells, and multi-access edge computing operations can be instigated. Figure 6.3 illustrates the functional split between next generation RAN (NG-RAN) and 5G core (5GC) [11].

In Figure 6.3, the 5G new RAN nodes (new base stations) are called gNB (or gNodeB) and the 4G RAN nodes are called eNB (or eNodeB, evolved Node B). In 5G networks, eNB coex-ists with gNB and will be gradually replaced by gNB. The RAN nodes connect to the 5GC network including access and mobility management function (AMF), user plane function (UPF), and session management function (SMF). Figure 6.4 illustrates the 5G NR network architecture.

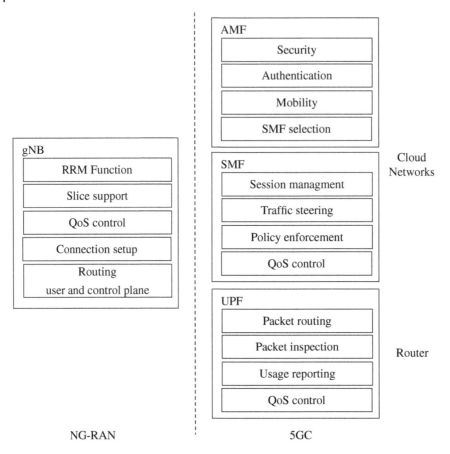

Figure 6.3 Functional split between NG-RAN and 5GC.

In 3GPP standard, the 5G RAN is generally referred to as the NG-RAN. As we can observe in Figure 6.4, NG-RAN consists of a set of gNBs and ng-eNB. 5G core (5GC) offers NFV, SDN, cloud services, network slicing, and so on. Thus, it is flexible and scalable. gNB and ng-eNB provide NR and E-UTRA user/control plane protocol termination toward the UE, respectively. They are interconnected with each other via Xn interface and connect to AMF and UPF via a NG interface. The user plane protocol carries user data in protocol data unit (PDU) session service. The control plane protocol manages the PDU session and controls traffic flows such as service requests, resource management, handover, and so on.

6.2.2 5G NR Deployment Scenarios

Different phases, configurations, and scenarios can be deployed by 5G NR. The cellular networks will gradually evolve and the old and new network equipment will coexist for a certain period. Thus, the 5G mobile devices should support both 4G and 5G networks. In order to support them, the 3GPP standard defined two main modes: NSA and standalone (SA). Figure 6.5 illustrates 5G NSA and SA. As we can observe from Figure 6.5a, NSA operation supports existing 4G networks (eNB, enhanced packet core [EPC], and so on). The 5G

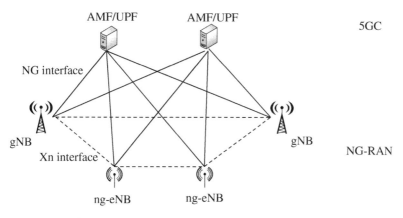

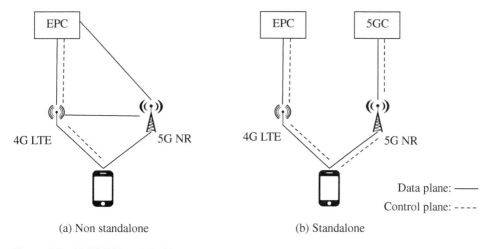

Figure 6.4 5G NR network architecture.

(a) Non standalone   (b) Standalone

Figure 6.5 (a) 5G NSA and (b) SA.

devices connect to gNB for data transmission, but still rely on 4G infrastructure for non-data features (call connection and termination, paging, location registration and so on). On the other hand, SA operation allows the 5G devices to connect to gNB for both data transmission and control. The first 5G NR deployment will be based on NSA and then the next deployment is considered as SA.

6.2.3 Frame Structure

The 5G NR frame structures have been defined in the 3GPP 38 series [12] and designed to satisfy the 5G requirements, with support forward and backward compatibility, and will reduce strict timing control across slots and transmissions. It supports FDD and TDD transmission and operates in licensed and unlicensed spectrums. The 5G NR supports OFDM transmission numerologies, and the subcarrier spacing scales from 15 to 240 kHz, as summarized in Table 6.2.

Table 6.2 5G NR numerology.

Subcarrier spacing (kHz)	Slot configuration				
	15	**30**	**60**	**120**	**240**
Symbol duration (μs)	66.7	33.3	16.6	8.33	4.17
CP duration (μs)	4.7	2.41	1.205 (normal CP), 4.13 (extended CP)	0.6	0.3
Nominal max. bandwidth (MHz)	50	100	100 (sub-6 GHz), 200 (mmWAVE)	400	400
Max. FFT size	4096	4096	4096	4096	4096
Symbols per slot	14	14	14 (normal CP), 12 (extended CP)	14	14
Slots per subframe	1	2	4	8	16
Usage	Outdoor large cell (<3 GHz)	Outdoor small cell (>3 GHz)	Indoor wideband cell (5 GHz) Small cell (>6 GHz)	Very small cell (28 GHz)	Indoor very small cell

As we can observe from Table 6.2, 5G NR is scalable and adopts flexible subcarrier spacing of $2^\mu \cdot 15$ kHz. The 5G NR frame has 10 ms duration and consists of 10 subframes. Subframe duration is 1 ms. Each subframe is divided into OFDM symbols and the number of OFDM symbols relies on the numerology as μ. Subcarrier spacing 15 kHz occupies one slot per subframe. Each slot occupies 14 OFDM symbols for normal cyclic prefix (CP) or 12 OFDM symbols for extended CP. The scalability allows us to support a wide range of deployment scenarios and frequency bands. The 5G NR numerologies are selected in terms of cell size, frequency band and applications. At low frequency, a large cell size is suitable because they have a large time dispersion at the receiver and large CP is needed. Thus, short subcarrier spacing (15 or 30 kHz) is enough. At high frequency, delay spread is typically small and phase noise will be severe. Thus, wide subcarrier spacing (60 or 120 kHz) is needed because it is less susceptible to phase noise. The physical layer timing unit (sampling time) of 5G NR can be calculated as follows:

$$T_c = 1/\Delta f_m N_f \tag{6.2}$$

where T_c, Δf_m, and N_f are sampling time, subcarrier spacing, and fast Fourier transform (FFT) size, respectively. The 5G NR frame duration (T_f) and subframe duration (T_{sf}) can be calculated as follow:

$$T_f = (\Delta f_m N_f/100)T_c = 10 \text{ ms} \tag{6.3}$$

and

$$T_{sf} = (\Delta f_m N_f/1000)T_c = 1 \text{ ms} \tag{6.4}$$

For example, when we have 240 kHz subcarrier spacing and 4096 FFT size, the sampling time is $T_c = \frac{1}{\Delta f_m N_f} = \frac{1}{(240000)(4096)} = 1.017$ ns. In 5G NR frame structure, OFDM symbols in

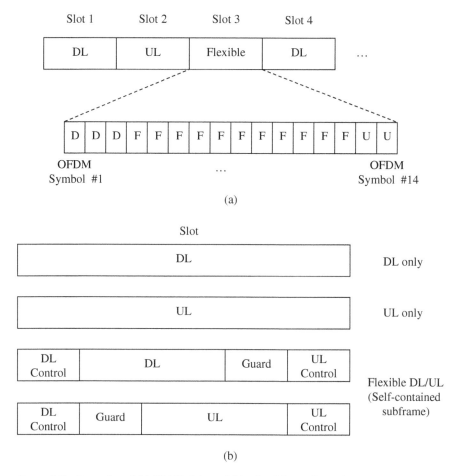

Figure 6.6 Examples of (a) 5G NR slots and (b) a flexible configuration.

a slot can be used for uplink, downlink, or flexible. The 5G NR slot format indicates which symbols are used for uplink, downlink, or flexible. In addition, slot aggregation is possible in 5G NR. Thus, transmission can be scheduled in multiple ways. In order to support agile and efficient use of radio resource, the flexible slot is useful. We can allocate all downlink, all uplink or a mixed downlink and uplink to the resource blocks (RBs). Figure 6.6 illustrates an example of 5G NR slots and flexible configuration. As we can observe from Figure 6.6 that downlink and uplink controls are allocated at the beginning and end of the slot, respectively. We can configure the mixed downlink and uplink slot dynamically depending on user requirements and applications. It will be helpful for more efficient resource management and scheduling as well as lower latency, because the self-contained transmission is decodable on its own data in a slot without any dependency on other slots.

One 5G NR resource grid is created for one numerology and antenna port. One resource element is the smallest unit of the resource grid as one subcarrier in one OFDM symbol. A 5G NR resource block (RB) (or physical resource block [PRB]) is defined as N_{sc}^{RB}

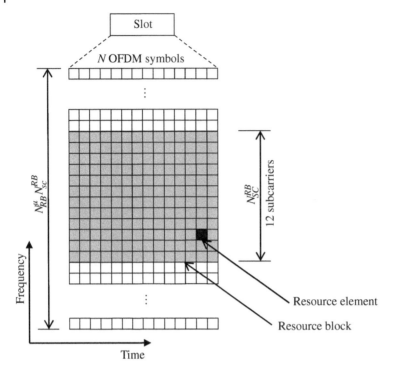

Figure 6.7 5G NR resource grid and resource blocks.

consecutive 12 subcarriers in frequency domain. 4G LTE RB bandwidth is fixed as 180 kHz, but 5G NR RB bandwidth relies on numerology. Figure 6.7 illustrates 5G NR resource blocks and resource elements. Table 6.3 summarizes the 5G NR RB configuration.

The 5G NR supports different subcarrier spacings within the same channel. We need to specify the starting RB location in the frequency domain and have a reference coordinate system. A common reference point called Point A is defined in 3GPP standard. Point A can be obtained from [13] (i) offsetToPointA for a PCell downlink where offsetToPointA represents the frequency offset between point A and the lowest subcarrier of the lowest resource block, and (ii) absoluteFrequencyPointA for all other cases where absoluteFrequencyPointA represents the frequency–location of point A expressed as an Absolute Radio Frequency Channel Number (ARFCN). In 4G frame structure, all mobile devices (UEs) must support the full carrier bandwidth. However, 5G NR frame structure allows them to support less than the carrier bandwidth. In order to support bandwidth adaptation and save power consumption on mobile devices, the bandwidth part (BWP) is defined as a subset of the carrier bandwidth. Each BWP consists of a set of contiguous PRBs that are configured by a gNB. The PRBs have a certain number of PRBs (e.g. PRB 0–N) that varies across BWPs, and a maximum of 4 BWPs can be specified in downlink and uplink. Mobile devices should transmit and receive only within the configured BWPs. Many different parameters can be configured in each BWP. Figure 6.8 illustrates an example of 5G NR frame structure in the frequency domain. As we can observe from the figure, different BWP numerologies on the same carrier frequency for mobile devices can be multiplexed.

Table 6.3 5G NR RB configuration.

μ	0	1	2	3	4
Subcarrier spacing (kHz)	15	30	60 (normal CP)	120	240
RB bandwidth (kHz)	180 (15×12)	360 (30×12)	720 (60×12)	1440 (120×12)	2880 (240×12)
RB duration (ms)	1	0.5	0.25	0.125	0.0625
Min. RBs	24	24	24	24	24
Max. RBs	275	275	275	275	138
Min. channel BW (MHz)	4.32	8.64	17.28	34.56	69.12
Max. channel BW (MHz)	49.5	99	198	396	397.44

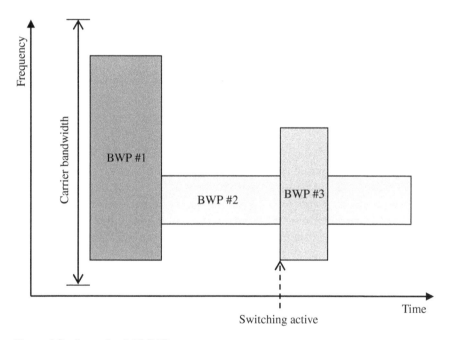

Figure 6.8 Example of 5G BWPs.

An initial BWP is signaled by physical broadcast channel (PBCH) and BWP configuration for one carrier can be signaled to a mobile device (UE).

6.2.4 5G Logical, Transport, and Physical Channels

There are three channel types: logical channels, transport channels, and physical channels. Figure 6.9 illustrates the types of 5G channels and protocol layers. Logical channels define

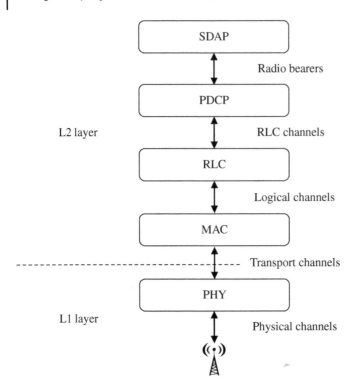

Figure 6.9 5G channel types.

the data type to be transferred. They are classified into traffic channels transferring user plane (user data traffic) and control channels transferring control plane (control and configuration information). It provides us with a service between the radio link control (RLC) layer and the medium access control (MAC) layer. Transport channels define how the information is carried and what characteristics of the information is transmitted to the physical layer. It serves between the MAC layer and the physical (PHY) layer. Physical channels define resource elements carrying information from higher layers.

Table 6.4 summarizes 5G logical, transport, and physical channels. In logical channels, broadcast control channel (BCCH) is used in standalone mode to transmit system information from a base station to a mobile device and obtain the network information. Paging control channel (PCCH) is used to transfer paging information in standalone mode. Common control channel (CCCH) is used to transmit control information in terms of random access. Dedicated control channel (DCCH) is used for transmission of control information for individual mobile device configuration. Dedicated traffic channel (DTCH) is used for user data transmission. In transport channels, broadcast channel (BCH) is used for broadcast transmission from BCCH. Paging channel (PCH) is used for paging signal transmission from PCCH. It supports discontinuous reception to save mobile device battery consumption. Downlink shared channel (DL-SCH) and uplink shared channel (UL-SCH) as the main transport channels are used for downlink and uplink data transmission, respectively. Random access channel (RACH) is in the uplink direction to establish the initial connection between a mobile device and a base station. In physical channels, physical downlink

Table 6.4 5G NR logical, transport, and physical channels.

	Channels	Channel full name
Logical channels	BCCH	Broadcast control channel
	PCCH	Paging control channel
	CCCH	Common control channel
	DCCH	Dedicated control channel
	DTCH	Dedicated traffic channel
Transport channels	BCH	Broadcast channel
	PCH	Paging channel
	DL-SCH	Downlink shared channel
	UL-SCH	Uplink shared channel
	RACH	Random access channel
Physical channels	PUSCH	Physical uplink shared channel
	PUCCH	Physical uplink control channel
	PRACH	Physical random access channel
	PDSCH	Physical downlink shared channel
	PDCCH	Physical downlink control channel
	PBCH	Physical broadcast channel

shared channel (PDSCH) and physical uplink shared channel (PUSCH) are used for actual user data transmission. Physical downlink control channel (PDCCH) informs a mobile device about resource allocation and scheduling of PCH and DL-SCH. Physical uplink control channel (PUCCH) is used for channel report, HARQ ACK, scheduling requests, and so on. Physical random access channel (PRACH) is used for the initial connection from RACH. PBCH is a broadcast channel carrying system control information from BCH.

In addition, the 5G NR physical layer includes physical signals: synchronization signals (PSS and SSS) and reference signals (DM-RS, PT-RS, CSI-RS, and SRS). Table 6.5 summarizes the 5G NR physical signals. The primary synchronization signal (PSS) is used for a mobile device to get the radio frame boundary. Compared with 4G PSS, the main difference is the type of sequence. 5G PSS uses an m-sequence made up of 127 values, but 4G PSS is based on the Zadoff-Chu sequence. The secondary synchronization signal (SSS) is used for a mobile device to get the subframe boundary. Both 5G SSS and 4G SSS are based on m-sequence. However, 5G SSS is allocated to 127 active subcarriers while 4G SSS is mapped to 72 subcarriers. A demodulation reference signal (DMRS) is used for channel estimation in downlink and uplink and acquisition of PBCH, PDCCH, PDSCH, PUCCH, and PUSCH. A phase tracking reference signal (PTRS) is used for phase tracking of the local oscillator and noise compensation in downlink and uplink. PTRS is allocated to a few subcarriers per symbol. It is designed to have low density in the frequency domain and high density in the time domain. The phase noise of a transmitter increases as the frequency increases. PTRS plays an important role at high frequency to minimize the phase noise. A channel

Table 6.5 5G NR physical signals.

Signals	Full name	Remarks
PSS	Primary synchronization signal	Downlink
SSS	Secondary synchronization signal	Downlink
DMRS	Demodulation reference signals (for PDSCH/PDCCH, PUSCH/PUCCH, and PBCH)	Downlink/uplink
PTRS	Phase tracking reference signal (for PDSCH and PUSCH)	Downlink/uplink
CSI-RS	Channel-state information reference signal	Downlink
SRS	Sounding reference signal	Uplink

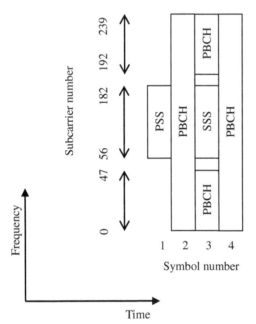

Figure 6.10 5G SS/PBCH block configuration.

state information reference signal (CSI-RS) is used for channel estimation in downlink, and a mobile device reports channel quality information to a base station using this signal. A sounding reference signal (SRS) is transmitted to obtain the channel quality information in uplink. A base station uses this information and allocates radio resource to a mobile station and configures link adaptation and MIMO management.

Figure 6.10 illustrates one example of a SS/PBCH block configuration.

Figure 6.11 illustrates 5G channel mappings among logical, transport, and physical channels in downlink and uplink. As we can observe from Tables 6.4 and 6.5 and Figure 6.10, 5G NR logical and transport channels and their mapping are similar to 4G. However, physical channels have some differences to meet 5G requirements. For example, 5G NR PDSCH requires DMRS instead of a cell-specific reference signal (4G physical signal). DMRS is required for scheduling in downlink and uplink.

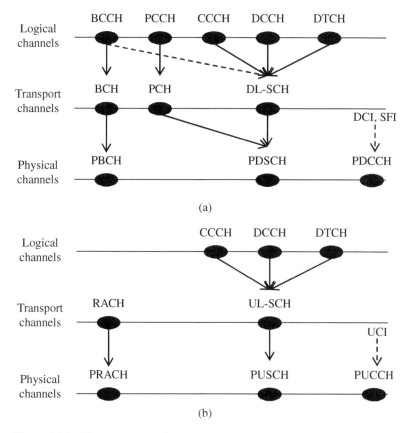

Figure 6.11 5G channel mapping for (a) downlink and (b) uplink.

6.2.5 5G Protocol Layers

The protocol layers of 5G systems inherit the advantages of 4G systems and support to meet 5G requirements. One difference between them is connectivity of a mobile device. In 4G systems, a signaling and context of a mobile device is managed as one key label connecting to one cell. This approach is efficient for managing radio resource, but it can cause a long delay and increase complexity in the connectivity and mobility of a mobile device. In 5G systems, signaling is simplified to support a low latency connectivity, and a user-centric protocol is required to meet various 5G applications. In addition, service data adaption protocol (SDAP) is included as a new layer of 5G protocols. Each QoS (quality of service) flow is identified by a QoS flow ID (QFI) and defined by a QoS profile. The 5G NR packets are marked with the QFI. It provides us with QoS control for each data stream by making QoS flow ID in both downlink and uplink, and mapping QoS flows to data radio bearers (DRBs). 5G protocol layers are composed of user plane and control plane. Layer 1 is the physical layer. Layer 2 includes MAC, RLC, PDCP, and SDAP. Layer 3 is the radio resource control (RRC) layer. Figure 6.12 illustrates the 5G protocol layers.

The user plane takes care of data traffic, and the control plane deals with user authentication, connection management, QoS policies, and so on. The control and user plane

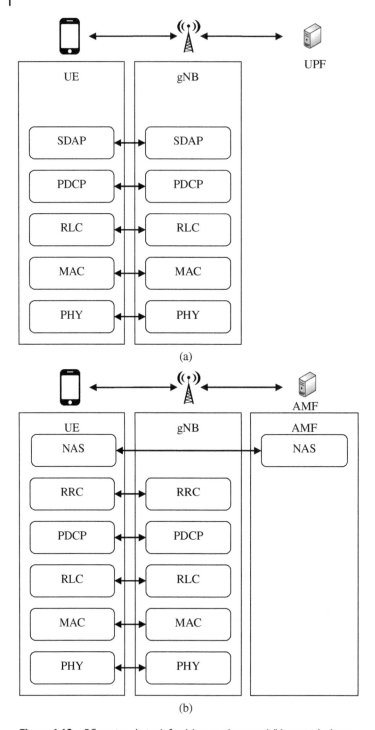

Figure 6.12 5G protocol stack for (a) user plane and (b) control plane.

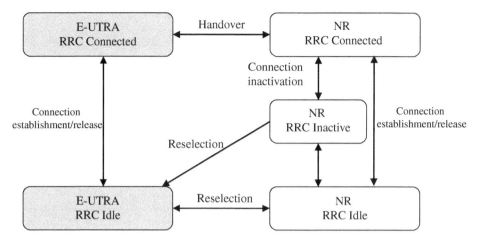

Figure 6.13 UE state machine and transitions in NR and between NR and E-UTRAN.

separation allows their functions to scale independently, as well as operators to deploy networks flexibly. For example, when data traffic increases, we can add more data plane nodes without additional control plane function. The main role of the RRC layer is to configure radio resources to establish a connectivity between mobile devices and base stations. The functions of the RRC layer can be summarized as follows: broadcasting of access stratum (AS) and non-access stratum (NAS) system information; paging by NG-RAN or 5GC; establishment, maintenance and release of RRC connection between UE and NG-RAN; security and mobility functions (key management, handover and context transfer, cell addition and release, etc.); UE measurement and control reporting; QoS management functions; and so on. The RRC layer is operated by a state machine including three states (NR RRC connected, NR RRC inactive, and NR RRC idle). Figure 6.13 illustrates the UE state machine and transitions.

As we can observe in Figure 6.13, 5G RRC state transitions allow us to access 4G radio access technology. The shaded left blocks (E-UTRA RRC connected and E-UTRA RRC Idle) are 4G RRC states and transition. Comparing with 4G RRC states, 5G RRC includes a new state (NR RRC inactive). The main purpose of this new state is to maintain the RRC connection and conserve radio and network resources in order to minimize power consumption and signaling. When UE is power up in NR RRC idle, the state is moved to NR RRC connected as the initial connection. If there is no UE activity for a short time, the state is moved to NR RRC inactive and its session is suspended. This mechanism is helpful for minimizing always-on transmissions. In layer 2, 5G packet data convergence protocol (PDCP) is almost the same as 4G PDCP. The main functions of PDCP are transfer of data in user plane and control plane, header compression and decompression, ciphering and deciphering of data, integrity protection and verification of control plane data, PDCP service data unit (SDU) discard and retransmission, PDCP PDU routing and duplicating, and so on. 5G RLC is almost the same as 4G RLC. There is a transparent mode (no RLC header, Tx buffering, no segmentation and reassembly, no ACK and NACK), an unacknowledged mode (RLC header, Tx/Rx buffering, segmentation and reassembly, no ACK and NACK), and an acknowledge mode (RLC header, Tx/Rx buffering, segmentation and reassembly, ACK and NACK). Each logical

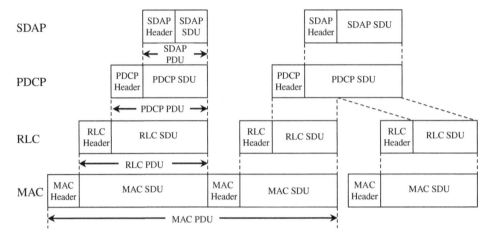

Figure 6.14 Example of 5G packet segmentation and reassembly.

channel uses one of the RLC modes. The main functions of RLC are transfer of upper layer PDU, error correction using ARQ, segmentation and reassembly, reordering of RLC data, RLC reestablishment, and so on. Figure 6.14 illustrates one example of 5G packet segmentation and reassembly.

The main roles of 5G MAC can be summarized as follows: data transfer by mapping between logical channels and transport channels, multiplexing and demultiplexing of MAC SDUs, logical channel prioritization, beam management, random access procedure, HARQ signaling, scheduling information report and channel quality indication (CQI). The main difference between 5G MAC and 4G MAC is the location of subheaders. In 4G MAC, all MAC subheaders are located in the beginning of a MAC PDU and the subheaders and corresponding data might be located in different areas. However, 5G MAC subheaders are closely placed in front of the corresponding data.

6.2.6 5G NR Physical Layer Processing

The 5G NR physical layer receives data in the form of a certain size transport block and transmits them through each antenna. The 5G NR physical layer processing scheme consists of many complicated steps according to different physical layer channels and transmission modes (TMs). In 4G physical layer processing, many parameters of the transport block are fixed and the RRC parameters affect the physical layer processing. However, in 5G NR physical layer processing, we should consider many transport parameters and configuration changes as well as the influence of RRC parameters. Figure 6.15 illustrates 5G NR physical layer processing for PDSCH.

As we can observe from Figure 6.15, the baseband signals representing a downlink physical channel PDSCH are processed in terms of the following steps:

(i) Transport block size calculation is based on modulation order, target code rate, modulation and coding scheme index, and so on.
(ii) A cyclic redundancy check (CRC) is attached to each transport block.
(iii) LDPC base graph per transport block size is selected.

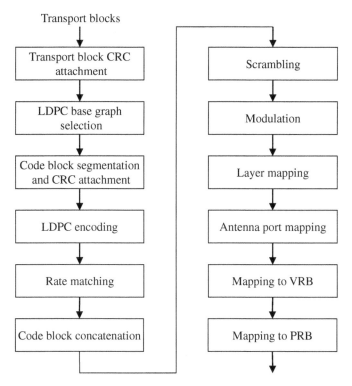

Figure 6.15 5G NR physical channel processing for PDSCH.

(iv) The transport block is segmented to code blocks and CRC is attached to each code block.

(v) Each code block is encoded.

(vi) The code rate is matched.

(vii) The code block is concatenated to form transmission codewords. About two codewords are transmitted over one PDSCH channel.

(viii) Scrambling is applied to all codewords.

(ix) Modulation (QPSK, 16QAM, 64QAM, or 256QAM) is performed and generates complex-valued modulation symbols.

(x) Layer mapping is performed to transmit on MIMO antenna.

(xi) Antenna mapping is configured to support different MIMO schemes.

(xii) Resource element mapping allocates complex-valued modulation symbols to the resource elements of the resource blocks. A virtual resource block (VRB) is created for each antenna.

(xiii) Mapping from virtual resource to PRBs is performed.

A PDCCH channel is used to carry downlink control information (DCI) and the physical layer processing is different from PDSCH channel processing. Figure 6.16 illustrates 5G NR physical layer processing for PDCCH.

4G control channels are allocated across a whole system bandwidth. However, 5G PDCCH channels take certain subcarriers and are transmitted in a configurable control

Transport blocks

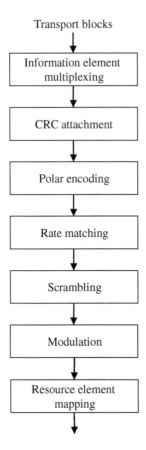

Figure 6.16 5G NR physical channel processing for PDCCH.

resource set (CORESET). The CORESET is defined as a set of resource element groups (REGs) under a given numerology. REG is composed of 12 resource elements of one OFDM symbol in one resource block. In the time domain, CORESET occupies up to three consecutive OFDM symbols. Figure 6.17 illustrates one example of PDCCH CORESET.

As we can observe Figure 6.16, the baseband signals representing a downlink physical channel PDCCH are processed in a similar way to PDSCH channel processing. The different parts are information element multiplexing and polar coding. In order to accommodate various DCI, a PDCCH channel is transmitted by control channel elements (CCEs). A CCE is composed of six REGs. The polar codes are simpler than LDPC codes and have good performance in short length packets. Figure 6.18 illustrates 5G NR physical layer processing for PUSCH. As we can observe in Figure 6.18, the PUSCH physical layer processing is similar to the PDSCH processing. The different parts are data and control multiplexing and precoding. Table 6.6 summarizes the characteristics of 5G NR downlink and uplink.

6.2.7 5G Initial Access Procedure and Beam Management

When a mobile device turns on or enters in the coverage of new cells, a cell search process is performed. Due to mobility and handover of devices, cell search and selection is performed frequently. The initial access procedure includes a RACH process to acquire

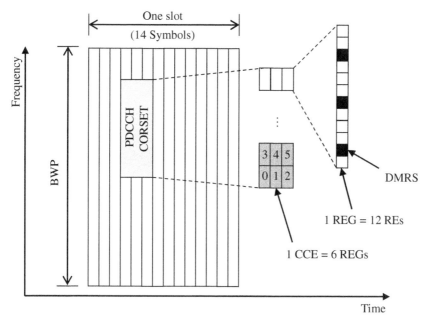

Figure 6.17 Example of PDCCH CORESET.

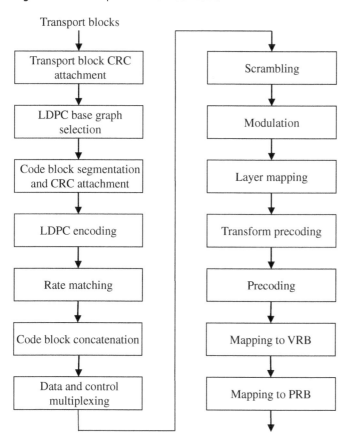

Figure 6.18 5G NR physical channel processing for PUSCH.

Table 6.6 5G NR physical layer.

Downlink/ uplink	PHY channels	Waveform	Bandwidth	Reference signals	Modulation	Channel coding
Downlink	PDSCH	CP-OFDM (precoding, filtering, and windowing)	Numerology	DM-RS	Up to 256QAM	LDPC
	PDCCH	CP-OFDM (precoding, filtering, and windowing)	Localized in BWP	DM-RS	QPSK	Polar
Uplink	PUSCH	CP-OFDM (precoding, filtering, and windowing) or DFT-s-OFDM	Numerology	DM-RS	Up to 256QAM	LDPC
	PUCCH	CP-OFDM (precoding, filtering, and windowing) or DFT-s-OFDM	Numerology	DM-RS	QPSK, $\pi/2$-BPSK	RM/ polar

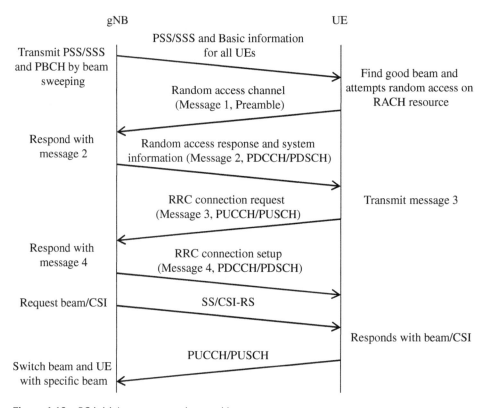

Figure 6.19 5G initial access procedure and beam management.

synchronization and obtain cell ID. The 5G RACH process is similar to the 4G RACH process. The 4G cell search and selection process can be summarized as three steps. In the first step, we perform symbol timing acquisition and frequency synchronization and obtain a physical layer ID using PSS. The second step is to perform frame boundary detection, CP length detection and FDD/TDD detection, and obtain the cell ID using SSS. The third step is to detect a cell-specific reference signal and PBCH. The 5G initial access procedure and beam management are summarized as shown in Figure 6.19.

As we can observe from Figure 6.19, the base station (or gNB) periodically transmits the SS/PBCH block (as shown in Figure 6.10) using beam sweeping and finds the best beam during the process. Message 1 indicates RACH configuration. The mobile device (or UE) selects a beam and uses the same beam during RACH transmission. Message 2 is the random access response. Message 3 is the RRC connection request. Message 4 is the RRC connection setup. Once the initial access procedure is complete, the dedicated connection with specific beam is established between them. Beam management is used to acquire and maintain a set of transmission reception points (TRxP) using the following operations: beam sweeping (operation of covering a spatial area with a set of beams), beam measurement (quality of the received sign such as RSRQ, SINR, and so on), beam determination (selection of the most suitable based on beam measurement) and beam reporting (UE reports beam quality and decision information to gNB). Simply speaking, the base station sweeps beams using different downlink beams of the synchronization signal block (SSB) and the mobile station determines the best beam and informs the base station using reference signals (PSS, SSS, and PBCH DMRS in idle mode, and CSI-RS and SRS in connected mode).

Summary 6.2 5G New Radio

1) A logical split between 5G radio access network (RAN), core network (CN) and service layer functions allows them to evolve independently and also provides us with more flexibility.

2) The cellular networks will gradually evolve and the old and new network equipment will coexist for a certain period. Different phases, configurations, and scenarios are possible to deploy 5G NR.

3) The 5G NR frame structure has been designed to satisfy the 5G requirements, support forward and backward compatibility, and reduce strict timing control across slots and transmissions.

4) Logical channels define the data type to be transferred. They are classified into traffic channels transferring user plane (user data traffic) and control channels transferring control plane (control and configuration information). Transport channels define how the information is carried and what characteristics of the information are transmitted to the physical layer. Physical channels define resource elements carrying information from higher layers.

5) In 5G systems, signaling is simplified to support a low latency connectivity and a user-centric protocol is required to meet various 5G applications. Layer 1 is the physical layer. Layer 2 includes MAC, RLC, PDCP, and SDAP. Layer 3 is the RRC layer.

(Continued)

---

6) The 5G NR physical layer receives data in the form of a certain size transport blocks and transmit them through each antenna.
7) When a mobile device turns on or enters in the coverage of new cells, a cell search process is performed. The 5G RACH process is similar to the 4G RACH process but includes beam management to acquire and maintain a set of transmission reception points.

6.3 5G Key Enabling Techniques

In this section, 5G key enabling techniques are reviewed. These techniques improve 5G KPIs and allow the 5G system to meet a high level of requirements.

6.3.1 5G Waveforms

Waveform is a key component of physical layer design in any wireless communication system. As we reviewed under the 5G design approaches and principles in the previous section, the 5G waveform should satisfy the following requirements: high spectrum efficiency, numerology, scalable bandwidth extension, high-order modulation support, efficient structure for MIMO, and so on. There are many changes from 4G radio systems. However, 5G NR still selected the OFDM-based waveform because it satisfies the requirements and also has several more attractive properties: for example, simple channel estimation, and low complexity equalization. In [14], the baseline of 5G waveform below 52.6 GHz is cyclic prefix (CP)-OFDM, and additional signal processing such as precoding, windowing, and filtering is possible to overcome two disadvantages: poor PAPR, and out-of-band emission (OOBE). The OFDM-based technique suffers from a high PAPR. This drawback causes signal distortion and high energy consumption. The OOBE increases the guard band overhead and causes poor spectrum utilization. The additional signal processing allows us to suppress the OOBE, PAPR, and adjacent channel leakage ratio (ACLR), and improve spectral efficiency. Figure 6.20 illustrates the OFDM-based 5G transmitter. The candidate 5G waveform can be summarized as CP-OFDM, filter bank multicarrier (FBMC), universal filtered multicarrier (UFMC), and generalized frequency division multiplexing (GFDM). 5G waveforms are further discussed in Chapter 7.

As we can observe in Figure 6.20, precoding is performed before the inverse fast Fourier transform (IFFT) block and helpful for reducing OOBE and PAPR. Discrete Fourier transform (DFT) spread OFDM (DFT-s-OFDM) waveform (known as single carrier frequency division multiple access [FDMA]) is one of the representative precoding methods. 4G LTE adopted this method for uplink transmission because it reduces PAPR significantly and it is more suitable for power-limited environments. There are many precoding methods for 5G waveforms, such as guard interval DFT-s-OFDM, unique word DFT-s-OFDM, zero tail DFT-s-OFDM, single carrier circularly pulse shaped (SC-CPS), generalized precoded OFDMA (GPO), and so on. The precoding method is relatively easier to improve OOBE with less deterioration than filtering. An OFDM symbol is composed of unfiltered subcarriers

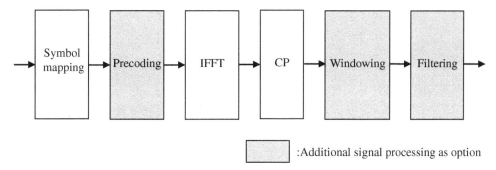

:Additional signal processing as option

Figure 6.20 OFDM-based 5G waveform.

so that the out-of-band spectrum decreases slowly, depending on the number of subcarriers. A larger number of subcarriers decrease more rapidly. The FFT size of 5G is up to 4096. Thus, windowing is useful for making the spectrum go down faster. Windowing is of relatively lower complexity and smaller PAPR overhead than filtering. However, the detection performance in the receiver side would be degraded due to inter-symbol interference by symbol extension. Filtering uses a digital filter with pre-specified frequency response and reduces the OOBE straightforwardly. It is simple, but causes guard period reduction by delay spread. In addition, filter design is not simple at high carrier frequency and should incorporate power amplifier nonlinearity.

6.3.2 5G Multiple Access Schemes

Multiple access schemes are techniques to share radio resources by multiple users in a cell, and can be categorized as orthogonal multiple access (OMA) or nonorthogonal multiple access (NOMA). There are various multiple access schemes such as frequency division multiple access FDMA, time division multiple access (TDMA), code-division multiple access (CDMA), and orthogonal frequency division multiple access (OFDMA), which are used in cellular systems from 1G to 4G. They are based on OMA schemes. The resource block in time, frequency, code, and space domains is exclusively allocated to users in order to avoid inter-user interferences. On the other hand, NOMA techniques allow multiple users to use nonorthogonal radio resources concurrently. Each user signal in NOMA schemes is multiplexed by different power allocation coefficients or signatures such as codeword, sequence, interleaver, and preamble. NOMA techniques can be categorized as power domain multiple access or code domain multiple access. The power domain multiple access scheme allocates multiple users to different power coefficients in terms of channel condition. Each user signal in transmitter is superimposed and successive interference cancellation (SIC) in the receiver is used for decoding each user signal. Multiple users in the code domain multiple access scheme are assigned in different codes but the same time frequency. In 5G, the OMA scheme still plays an important role for uplink and downlink transmission. In 3GPP standard, the NOMA study item was approved in March 2017. The study of NOMA continues to enhance system capacity, reduce latency and signal overhead and power consumption, and accommodate massive connectivity. Figure 6.21 illustrates a comparison of OMA and NOMA.

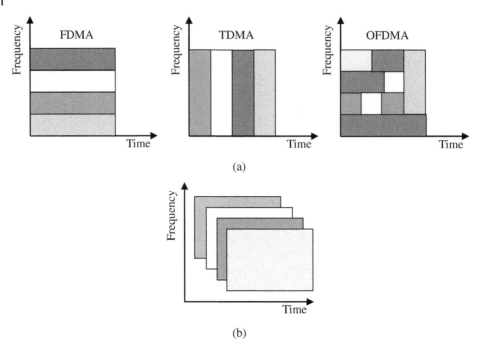

Figure 6.21 Comparison of (a) OMA and (b) NOMA.

6.3.3 Channel Coding Schemes

In modern wireless communication systems, channel coding techniques are an essential part of protecting and recovering messages. In 5G systems, two types of channel coding scheme (polar codes and LDPC codes) have been introduced for data and control channels [15]. Polar codes and LDPC codes of 5G NR replace convolutional codes and turbo codes of 4G LTE, respectively. Polar codes are used for control channels (PDCCH, PUCCH) and the broadcast channel (PBCH). LDPC codes are used for data channels (PDSCH and PUSCH). Polar codes are a class of capacity-achieving codes introduced in [16]. The main motivation for the introduction of polar codes was theoretical, to show the existence of a family of codes that are provably capacity-achieving and have a well-defined rule for code construction. The basic idea is to transform a pair of identical binary input channels into a better channel and worse channel than the original channel. When the codeword length is large enough, some bits in the better channel are error-free and the others in the worse channel are very noisy. The input bits to the better channel and worse channel are known as frozen bits and nonfrozen bits, respectively. The nonfrozen bits are used to transmit the information. Its characteristics can be summarized as follows: (i) the block length of a polar code is normally a power of two but the code length can be adjusted by usual code shortening methods; (ii) the rate of a polar code can be adjusted to any number between 0 and 1 in increments of $1/N$; (iii) polar codes are available in systematic form; (iv) polar codes have a recursive structure which makes them suitable for low-complexity implementations; and (v) polar codes have no error floor. Figure 6.22 illustrates the polar encoding structure for 5G NR.

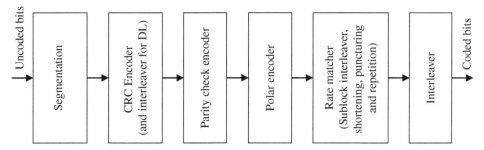

Figure 6.22 Polar encoding for 5G NR.

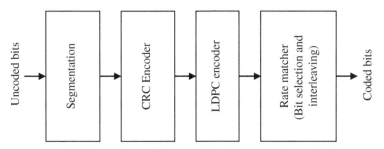

Figure 6.23 LDPC encoding for 5G NR.

LDPC codes were originally invented by R. Gallager in 1962 [17]. However, the LDPC codes did not get much attention until D.J.C. Mackay and R.M. Neal [18] rediscovered them. As the name implies, LDPC codes are linear block codes with a sparse parity check matrix. Basically, LDPC code structures are the same as conventional linear block code structures except for the sparseness of the parity check matrix **H**. The sparseness means that **H** contains relatively few 1s among many 0s. The main difference between LDPC codes and conventional linear block codes is the decoding algorithm. The decoding of LDPC codes is performed iteratively between bit nodes and check nodes in a Tanner graph. The decoding scheme of LDPC codes is known as the message passing algorithm, which passes messages forward and backward between the bit nodes and check nodes. Two types of message passing algorithm are widely used: the bit flipping algorithm based on a hard decision decoding algorithm, and the belief propagation algorithm based on a soft decision decoding algorithm. Further details of LDPC code encoding and decoding are discussed in Chapter 7. Figure 6.23 illustrates the LDPC encoding structure for 5G NR.

Two base matrices (matrix 1 and matrix 2) for LDPC code construction are used in 5G NR [15]. Matrix 1 is designed for large block sizes and high code rates. The parameters of matrix 1 are as follows: matrix size = 46×68, block size K = $22 \times 384 = 8448$, min. code rate = 1/3, and the number of non-zero elements = 316. On the other hand, matrix 2 is designed for small block sizes and low code rates. The parameters of matrix 2 are as follows: matrix size = 42×52, block size K = $10 \times 384 = 3840$, min. code rate = 1/5, and the number of non-zero elements = 197.

6.3.4 MIMO

MIMO techniques are widely employed in wireless communication systems because they provide us with significant performance improvement including diversity gain, array gain, and multiplexing gain. Each different gain is related to different types of system performance. Diversity gain improves link reliability and transmission coverage by mitigating multipath fading. The array gain improves transmission coverage and QoS. The multiplexing gain increases spectral efficiency by transmitting independent signals via different antennas. 5G systems takes advantage of various types of MIMO such as massive MIMO, multi-user MIMO, and beamforming. Standard MIMO systems equip only two or four antennas as transmitters or receivers, but a massive MIMO (or a large-scale MIMO) uses a large number of antennas (e.g. more than 100 antennas). The greater the number of antennas the base stations or mobile devices are equipped with, the better performance (e.g. data rate and link reliability) they can achieve. In particular, massive MIMO systems as multi-user MIMO and beamforming improve the performance significantly. However, a large number of antennas requires estimation of a bigger MIMO channel matrix. This is one big problem with a massive MIMO system. Multi-user MIMO assigns each data sequence to each user. It is especially useful for uplink systems due to the limited number of antennas at mobile stations. Sometime, this is called collaborative MIMO or collaborative spatial multiplexing.

The beamforming technique was first investigated in radar technology in the 1960s. However, this technique was given more attention in the 1990s when cellular systems gave rise to a new wireless communication. Beamforming has become a key technique in recent years and provides us with significant advantages for 5G systems. Due to the beam direction toward mobile devices, signal power is not wasted and interference to other mobile devices is significantly reduced. Particularly, antenna size is getting smaller in higher frequency, and also programmable high directivity is possible. The 3GPP standard defined different MIMO TMs for different usages of MIMO antennas (transmit diversity, spatial multiplexing and beamforming). The 3GPP release 8 included MIMO techniques such as 1D antenna array and 4 antenna ports, and defined 7 TMs: TM1 single antenna transmission, TM2 open loop transmit diversity, TM3 open loop spatial multiplexing, TM4 closed loop spatial multiplexing, TM5 multi-user MIMO, TM6 closed loop transmit diversity, and TM7 beamforming. In 3GPP release 9, TM 8 dual layer beamforming with reciprocity-based precoding was included. 3GPP release 10 supports TM9 eight-layer spatial multiplexing. 3GPP release 11 supports TM10 coordinated multipoint. 3GPP release 12 supports 8 antenna ports. In 3GPP release 13, massive MIMO including 16 antenna ports and 2D antenna arrays are supported. Discussion of full-dimension MIMO (FD-MIMO) has started. FD-MIMO allows the antenna system to form beams horizontally and vertically, and also to scale up the number of antennas. Thus, it can cover anywhere in the cell. 3GPP release 14 supports massive MIMO with 32 antenna ports. In 5G NR, MIMO techniques become even more important because 5G NR is a beam-based air interface. In order to improve capacity and coverage, 5G NR MIMO supports both sub- and above 6 GHz frequencies, as well as both TDD and FDD. The deployment scenarios of massive MIMO systems in sub- and above 6 GHz frequencies are different. In sub-6 GHz, the coverage is urban areas with high mobility users. The dominant characteristic of MIMO channels is multipath fading channel.

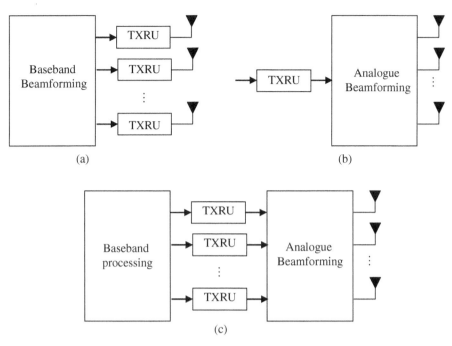

Figure 6.24 Antenna array architecture for (a) digital beamforming, (b) analogue beamforming, and (c) hybrid beamforming.

The main benefit is high spatial multiplexing gain and spectral efficiency. On the other hand, for above 6 GHz, the coverage is hotspot type, with low mobility users. The dominant characteristic of MIMO channels is few propagation paths. The main benefit is link budget improvement by beamforming. Hybrid beamforming (combining analogue and digital beamforming) will be used because it allows us to reduce the number of RF chain, hardware complexity, and cost. Analogue beamforming requires one RF chain for all antennas, but high power is consumed. Digital beamforming includes baseband precoding and multiple RF chains. When high numbers of antennas are required, hardware complexity and cost is high. Hybrid beamforming is good trade-off. Figure 6.24 illustrates antenna array architecture for a MIMO system. Further details of 5G MIMO system design are given in Chapter 7.

6.3.5 mmWAVE

The spectrum is tightly regulated all the time because spectrum scarcity is a primary problem faced by the telecommunication industry. Most mobile services from 1G to 4G are deployed in sub-3 GHz and the frequency bands are heavily crowded. The spectrum shortage motivates the use of millimeter wave (mmWAVE) bands in 5G systems. The range of mmWAVE band is from 30 to 300 GHz and the wavelength is between 1 and 10 mm. It provides us with huge bandwidths and also allows us to have large numbers of antennas and narrow beams. Thus, the mmWAVE enables 5G systems to provide high speed services. The mmWAVE is one of the key 5G enabling technologies. It will be used for hotspot or indoor environments because of high propagation loss, diffraction loss, absorption from rain and humidity, and reflection by cement and brick buildings. Thus, the key research challenges come from the propagation characteristics of mmWAVE. At high frequency, path loss, diffraction, atmospheric loss, reflection, scattering, and penetration loss all increase. They can be summarized as follows: (i) vulnerability to blockage; (ii) channel impairments (e.g. severe Doppler effect, beam misalignment, etc.) for mobile users; (iii) different propagation characteristics; (iv) RF impairments (e.g. phase noise, in-phase and quadrature imbalance, nonlinearity of PA, etc.); (v) high computational complexity and power consumption caused by ultra-wide bandwidth; (vi) channel model development above 6 GHz bands. In particular, it would be difficult to acquire mobile devices using a narrow beam antenna by high dimension antenna arrays.

6.3.6 Network Slicing

5G networks need to support multiple and different needs from multiple vertical industries such as healthcare, automotive, agriculture, factory automation, energy, and so on. Traditional networks could not support these diverse requirements and isolated use cases. Thus, 5G introduced the concept of "service based architecture" based on network virtualization. The network slicing technique of 5G supports customized services of applications (eMBB, mMTC, and URLLC) over a common network infrastructure. It provides us with low cost and logically isolated network capabilities to meet 5G requirements. We can summarize the characteristics of network slicing as customization, dedicated service, quality guarantee, and common infrastructure. This approach allows us to create new business models and network management services. It is possible to provide a customer with a cost-effective, tailor-made network service. For example, if a customer in a vertical industry requests a network service with specific requirements (e.g. slice type: eMBB, data rate: 1 Gbps, reliability: 99.99%, latency: 50 ms, connection density: 10^5 km^{-2}, etc.), a mobile operator creates one network slice to meet these requirements by installing and managing network components (e.g. RAN, TN, and core network). The customer receives the network service and obtains management information for the network slice. In addition, new players could join in the business. In the business model of current mobile networks, main players are mobile network operators (MNOs), mobile virtual network operators (MVNOs), and over-the-top (OTT) players. The 5G business model including network slicing techniques could invite new players: an infrastructure slice provider who is an owner of the infrastructure from one network slice, and the infrastructure slice tenant who is the user of a specific network slice, for which customized services are hosted. In 3GPP standard, the network slicing architecture is defined as a subnet group of network functions based on service-oriented network architecture. A network slice subnet instance (NSSI) may or may not be shared across different slices. Figure 6.25 illustrates 3GPP network slicing architecture. As we can observe from the figure, the E2E slice management system controls resource orchestration, identifies network slices, and provisions network slicing by RAN, TN, and CN management.

6.3.7 Multi-access Edge Computing

The European Telecommunications Standard Institute (ETSI) introduced mobile edge computing in 2014 based on a cloud computing platform to serve delay-sensitive applications, where the "edge" means both base stations and data centers. Since 2017, the ETSI has

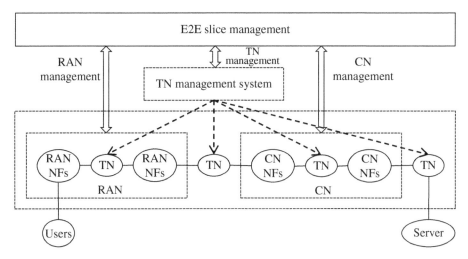

Figure 6.25 3GPP network slicing architecture.

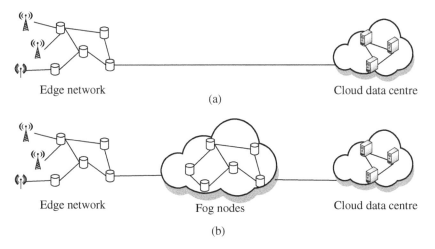

Figure 6.26 Comparison of (a) MEC and (b) fog computing.

renamed mobile edge computing to multi-access edge computing (MEC) to reflect aspects of noncellular system models. The concept of multi-access edge computing comes from cloud computing and edge computing. The basic idea is to put processing and storage tasks near to mobile users because the capability of network equipment and mobile devices as well as connectivity become more powerful. Thus, we reduce backhaul and core network congestion and in-network data processing, and also improve network performance such as low latency. Cloud computing and fog computing are similar concepts to MEC. Figure 6.26 illustrates the network architectures of MEC and fog computing.

As we can observe from Figure 6.26, fog nodes as physical and logical network elements sit between the edge and the cloud. Fog computing has a deeper hierarchy and extends cloud functions to the fog computing domain at the edge. On the other hand, the MEC nodes are located in the base station or radio network controller, which assumes that a

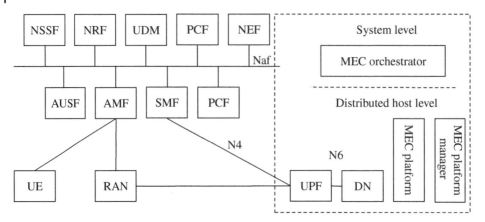

Figure 6.27 MEC deployment in a 5G network.

service provider is aware of a mobile user's location. The MEC nodes provide a user with real-time information on the edge network itself. The key function of the MEC node is the application server providing us with processing tasks, storage capacity and connectivity to RAN. Figure 6.27 illustrates the MEC deployment in a 5G network.

As we can observe from Figure 6.27, at a system level, the MEC orchestrator interacts with the network exposure function (NEF), and at a host level, the MEC platform manager interacts with 5G network functions. The MEC management system orchestrates the operation of MEC hosts and deploys the application. The distributed MEC accommodates a MEC platform service and the UPF steers user plane traffics. The major challenges of MEC deployment can be summarized as follows:

(i) Remote management: the edge node equips servers and a mobile user may require frequent handoffs. Thus, remote management and monitoring may increase operational costs.

(ii) Location acquisition: in order to deploy the MEC nodes, fiber networks are required and enough power should be supported. This will be more tricky a condition than location acquisition for a conventional base station.

MEC design and optimization are described in Chapter 8.

Summary 6.3 5G Key Enabling Techniques

1) 5G NR selected the OFDM-based waveform because it satisfies the requirements, as well as several more attractive properties: simple channel estimation, low complexity equalization, and so on.

2) 5G multiple access schemes can be categorized as orthogonal multiple access (OMA) and nonorthogonal multiple access (NOMA). In OMA, the resource block in time, frequency, code, and space domains is exclusively allocated to users in order to avoid inter-user interferences. On the other hand, NOMA techniques allow multiple users to use nonorthogonal radio resources concurrently. Each user signal in NOMA

schemes is multiplexed by different power allocation coefficients or signatures such as codeword, sequence, interleaver, and preamble.

3) In 5G NR, polar codes are used for control channels (PDCCH, PUCCH) and the broadcast channel (PBCH). LDPC codes are used for data channels (PDSCH and PUSCH).

4) 5G NR MIMO supports both sub- and above 6 GHz frequencies as well as both TDD and FDD. In sub-6 GHz, the coverage is urban areas with high mobility users. The dominant characteristic of MIMO channels is multipath fading channel. The main benefit is high spatial multiplexing gain and spectral efficiency. On the other hands, for above 6 GHz, the coverage is hotspots with low mobility users. The dominant characteristic of MIMO channels is few propagation paths. The main benefit is link budget improvement by beamforming.

5) The spectrum shortage motivates the use of millimeter wave (mmWAVE) bands in 5G systems. The mmWAVE provides us with huge bandwidths and also allows us to have large numbers of antennas and narrow beams.

6) 5G introduced the concept of "service based architecture" based on network virtualization. The network slicing technique of 5G supports customized services of applications (eMBB, mMTC, and URLLC) over a common network infrastructure.

7) The MEC reduces backhaul and core network congestion and in-network data processing, and also improves network performance such as low latency.

Problems

6.1 Compare key research challenges of 4G and 5G communications and networks.

6.2 Describe the pros and cons of 5G spectrum usages (low frequencies, medium frequencies, and high frequencies).

6.3 Describe the pros and cons of multicarrier techniques.

6.4 Describe the benefits and research challenges of massive MIMO in terms of spectral efficiency, diversity, and energy efficiency.

6.5 Define latency in device level and network level.

6.6 Define the smallest time unit in 5G numerology.

6.7 Compare the processing time between 4G and 5G HARQ.

6.8 Compare TDD and FDD in terms of RF and baseband design.

6.9 Describe the pros and cons of small cell concepts when used for eMBB, URLLC, and mMTC.

6.10 Describe possible non-standalone and standalone deployment scenarios for 5G systems.

6.11 Define key research challenges of NFV and SDN when designing eMBB, URLLC, and mMTC.

6.12 Compare centralized network architecture and distributed network architecture in terms of OpEx and CapEx.

6.13 Describe signaling of D2D communications with and without infrastructure.

6.14 Describe the roles of gNB, AMF, SMF, and UPF.

6.15 Describe one coexistence scenario for 4G and 5G networks.

6.16 Describe the difference between when OFDM symbol has normal CP or extended CP.

6.17 Describe channel differences in terms of indoor/outdoor, small/macro cell, and low/high frequency.

6.18 Describe the pros and cons of self-contained subframe.

6.19 Compare resource blocks of 4G and 5G.

6.20 Describe the role of each logical, transport, and physical channel.

6.21 Describe the relationship among logical, transport, and physical channels.

6.22 Compare physical signals of 4G and 5G.

6.23 Describe step-by-step physical channel processing of PDSCH, PDCCH, PUSCH, and PUCCH.

6.24 Describe the 5G initial access procedure in standalone and non-standalone scenarios.

6.25 Compare CP-OFDM, FBMC, UFMC, and GFDM.

6.26 Describe the pros and cons of CP-OFDM in terms of eMBB, URLLC, and mMTC applications.

6.27 Compare OMA and NOMA.

6.28 Describe why polar codes are used for control channels and LDPC codes are used for data channels.

6.29 Describe the pros and cons of digital, analogue, and hybrid beamforming architecture.

6.30 Describe the key research challenges of mmWAVE in terms of RF design.

6.31 Develop one scenario of network slicing for mMTC.

6.32 Describe the pros and cons of MEC in terms of eMBB, URLLC, and mMTC.

References

1 Brahim Sanou. (2018). Setting the Scene for 5G: Opportunities and Challenges. *ITU Discussion Paper*. https://www.itu.int/en/ITU-D/Documents/ITU_5G_REPORT-2018.pdf.

2 3GPP (2018). 3GPP TR 38.915 v15, Study on Scenarios and Requirements for Next Generation Access Technologies (Release 15). https://www.3gpp.org/release-15.

3 NGMN Alliance (2015). NGMN 5G White Paper, Feb. 2015. https://www.ngmn.org/wp-content/uploads/NGMN_5G_White_Paper_V1_0.pdf.

4 ITU-R (2017). Minimum requirements related to technical performance for IMT-2020 radio interface(s). International Telecommunication Union, Tech. Rep. https://www.itu.int/pub/R-REP-M.2410-2017.

5 3GPP (2017). 3GPP TR 38.802 v14, Study on New Radio (NR) Access Technology; Physical Layer Aspects. https://portal.3gpp.org/desktopmodules/Specifications/SpecificationDetails.aspx?specificationId=3066.

6 3GPP (2012). 3GPP TR 36.828, Further enhancements to LTE Time Division Duplex for Downlink-Uplink Interference Management and Traffic Adaptation. https://portal.3gpp.org/desktopmodules/Specifications/SpecificationDetails.aspx?specificationId=2507.

7 Hong, S., Brand, J., Choi, J. et al. (2014). Applications of self-interference cancellation in 5G and beyond. *IEEE Communications Magazine* 52 (2): 114–121.

8 D. Bharadia, E. McMilin, and S. Katti. "Full duplex radios," *Proceedings of ACM SIGCOMM*, Hong Kong, 375–386, 2013.

9 Hoymann, C., Larsson, D., Koorapaty, H., and Cheng, J. (2013). A lean carrier for LTE. *IEEE Communications Magazine* 51 (2): 74–80.

10 Bonomi, F., Milito, R., Zhu, J., and Addepalli, S. (2012). Fog computing and its role in the internet of things. In: *Proceedings of the First Edition of the MCC Workshop on Mobile Cloud Computing*, Helsinki, 13–15. https://conferences.sigcomm.org/sigcomm/2012/paper/mcc/p13.pdf.

11 3GPP (2017). 3GPP TS 38.300, NR Overall Description, Stage-2 (Release 15). https://portal.3gpp.org/desktopmodules/Specifications/SpecificationDetails.aspx?specificationId=3191.

12 3GPP (2018). 3GPP TS 38.214, v15.2.0, NR; Physical layer procedures for data. https://portal.3gpp.org/desktopmodules/Specifications/SpecificationDetails.aspx? specificationId=3216.

13 3GPP (2018). 3GPP TS 38.211 v15.4.0, NR; Physical channels and modulation. https://portal.3gpp.org/desktopmodules/Specifications/SpecificationDetails.aspx? specificationId=3213.

14 3GPP (2017). 3GPP TR 38.802 v. 14.2.0, Study on New Radio Access Technology; Physical Layer Aspects. https://portal.3gpp.org/desktopmodules/Specifications/ SpecificationDetails.aspx?specificationId=3066.

15 3GPP (2018). 3GPP TS 38.212, v15.0.0, NR; Multiplexing and channel coding. https://portal.3gpp.org/desktopmodules/Specifications/SpecificationDetails.aspx? specificationId=3214.

16 Arikan, E. (2009). Channel polarization: a method for constructing capacity-achieving codes for symmetric binary-input memoryless channels. *IEEE Transactions on Information Theory* 55 (7): 3051–3073.

17 Gallager, R.G. (1963). *Low Density Parity Check Codes*, Monograph. MIT Press.

18 MacKay, D.J.C. and Neal, R.M. (1996). Near Shannon limit performance of low density parity check codes. *Electronics Letters* 32 (18): 1645.

7

Enhanced Mobile Broadband Communication Systems*

7.1 Introduction

In Part I, we discussed how to develop a mathematical model, analyze the model in terms of the target metrics, quantify the impact of the model, and optimize the systems under a mathematical model. Many optimization problems in 5G communications and networks are hard to solve. In some cases, the optimization problems are converted to decision problems by searching for an optimum value such as key metrics or cost. After formulating optimization problems, it is important to know whether or not the problems are solvable and if an efficient algorithm can be found. We can find an answer by the theory of NP completeness in computer science. This is about the relationship between complexity class P (polynomial time) or NP (nondeterministic polynomial time). Simply speaking, if a problem can be solved in polynomial time by a non-deterministic Turing machine, the problem is classified within the NP problems. Class P holds the problems whose solutions can be found efficiently. NP complete problems within NP problems are the problems whose solutions can be verified but are unknown in polynomial time. NP hard problems are formally defined as at least as hard as the hardest problem in NP. The solutions of NP hard problems can or cannot be verified and unknown in polynomial time. Thus, the difficulty of finding a solution increases in the order of P, NP, NP complete, and NP hard problems. Figure 7.1 illustrates the complexity relationship for P, NP, NP complete, and NP hard problems.

Unfortunately, many network optimization problems are NP hard problems. Thus, approximation, heuristic methods, and others are used to solve the problems. In many cases, network optimization problems are converted to conventional mathematical problems such as clustering problems, path-finding problems, small world problems, salesman traveling problems, and so on. These problems are solved by relaxing the parameters, simplifying the mathematical models, and applying the conventional algorithms. As we discussed in the previous chapters, the mathematical model of the optimization or decision problems is composed of variables, constraints, and objective functions. The objective function of the network optimization problems can be a cost function or a utility function. We optimize in terms of performance metrics under the given constraints. In Chapter 6, we reviewed 5G NR systems. The enhanced mobile broadband (eMBB) is one of three 5G

---

* This chapter is based on the book by Haesik Kim (2015), *Wireless Communications Systems Design* (Wiley), and includes 5G features and design issues.

Design and Optimization for 5G Wireless Communications, First Edition. Haesik Kim.
© 2020 John Wiley & Sons Ltd. Published 2020 by John Wiley & Sons Ltd.

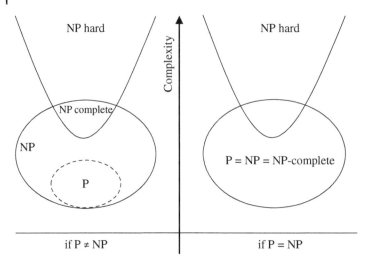

Figure 7.1 Euler diagram for P, NP, NP complete, and NP hard problems [1].

use cases and an extension of 4G broadband services. It provides us with higher data rates, better connectivity, and higher mobility. In this chapter, we consider a system model of 5G eMBB communications and discuss techniques for improving throughput and system capacity.

7.2 Design Approaches of eMBB Systems

The key metric of eMBB systems is throughput. In general terms, throughput is defined as the successful information delivery rate over a channel. However, throughput is affected by a lot of factors such as bandwidth, packet loss, power, latency, user density, channel type, network protocol, network topology, and so on. Thus, the definition of throughput depends on system models and assumptions. For example, in queuing theory, the throughput can be defined as $\lambda(1 - P_B)$ where λ and P_B are arrival rate and blocking probability, respectively. In the physical layer, the definition is more straightforward as how much data is successfully transmitted in a second (throughput [bps] = data [bit]/time [s]). The bandwidth represents the capacity of a medium for data delivery. However, it is a theoretical rate for data transmission over a medium. The throughput is a more practical rate because it considers noise, error, interference, and so on. Figure 7.2 illustrates the comparison of bandwidth and throughput.

One simplified definition of the network throughput (or area throughput) can be expressed as follows:

$$\text{Network throughput [bit/s/km}^2] = \text{Bandwidth [Hz]} \cdot \text{Cell density [cell/km}^2]$$
$$\cdot \text{Spectral efficiency [bit/s/Hz/cell]} \qquad (7.1)$$

As we can observe from Equation (7.1), a high network throughput can be obtained by allocating more available bandwidth, increasing cell density, or improving spectral efficiency. Among them, spectral efficiency represents how efficiently a radio frequency

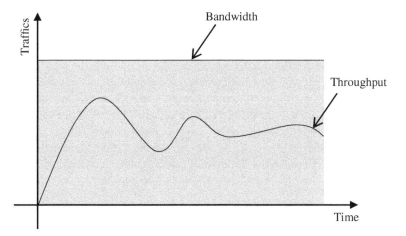

Figure 7.2 Bandwidth vs throughput.

Table 7.1 Approaches for increasing network throughput.

	Approaches			
5G techniques	**Bandwidth increase**	**Cell density increase**	**Spectral efficiency increase**	**Remarks**
Small cell		v		Network planning
Heterogeneous networks		v		Network planning
mmWAVE	v			Physical layer
Massive MIMO			v	Physical layer
Flexible TDD			v	Physical layer
Full duplex	v			Physical layer
OFDM based waveforms			v	Physical layer
LDPC and polar codes			v	Physical layer
D2D link		v		Physical layer and Layer 2
Resource allocation and scheduling			v	Layer 2: MAC, RLC, PDCP
Carrier aggregation	v			Physical layer and Layer 2

is used. The spectral efficiency is defined as the number of information bits that can be reliably transmitted over the channel under consideration. In 5G systems, three approaches are adopted to improve the network throughput. In order to increase available bandwidth, 5G spectrum uses high frequency bands and it is much wider than 4G. Flexible time division duplexing (TDD) and full duplex techniques are considered. In order to increase cell density, cell size is getting smaller, heterogeneous networks are adopted, and higher cell density is considered. In order to improve spectral efficiency, new techniques such as massive multiple input multiple output (MIMO) and low-density parity-check

(LDPC) codes are adopted. Table 7.1 summarizes three approaches for increasing network throughput. As we can observe from the table, each technique improves the throughput in different ways and 5G protocol layers. The throughput in each 5G protocol layer can be calculated a little differently. The throughput in the physical layer represents the maximum achievable throughput for the channel and bandwidth. This throughput is not close to user experience. In higher layers, we take into account overheads such as medium access control (MAC) or transmission control protocol (TCP) headers. They are close to user experience throughput. Those techniques in Table 7.1 are key components of 5G eMBB systems. In this chapter, we discuss some of the key techniques (MIMO, multicarrier techniques, and LDPC codes) to improve the throughput.

Summary 7.1 Design Approaches of eMBB

1) The bandwidth represents the capacity of a medium for data delivery. However, it is a theoretical rate for data transmission over a medium. The throughput is a more practical rate because it considers noise, error, interference, and so on.
2) The network throughput (or area throughput) can be expressed as follows:

$$\text{Network throughput [bit/s/km}^2] = \text{Bandwidth [Hz]} \cdot \text{Cell density [cell/km}^2]$$
$$\cdot \text{Spectral efficiency [bit/s/Hz/cell]}$$

3) A high network throughput can be obtained by allocating more available bandwidth, increasing cell density, or improving spectral efficiency.
4) 5G techniques for improving throughput are summarized as small cell, heterogeneous networks, mmWAVE, MIMO, flexible TDD, full duplex, multicarrier techniques, LDPC codes, D2D link, carrier aggregation, and so on.

7.3 MIMO

The MIMO techniques are key components of 5G systems because they significantly improve performances such as diversity gain, array gain, and multiplexing gain. The multiple antennas of a transmitter and a receiver allow us to have a new spatial dimension and improve system performances. Each gain is related to different uses (e.g. space–time coding, beamforming, and spatial multiplexing) of MIMO systems. The diversity gain, array gain, and multiplexing gain can improve link reliability, transmission coverage, and spectral efficiency, respectively. There is a trade-off between these usages. The goal of spatial diversity is to improve the reliability using one data stream. Space–time coding is designed for this purpose. On the other hand, the goal of spatial multiplexing is to improve the transmission rate while maintaining a certain level of reliability using multiple data streams. Vertical Bell Laboratories Layered Space–Time (V-BLAST) and precoding is used for this purpose. Space–time coding provides us with good performance at a low signal-to-noise ratio (SNR) and spatial multiplexing shows us good performance at a high SNR. Figure 7.3 illustrates the spectral efficiency comparison of space–time coding and spatial multiplexing.

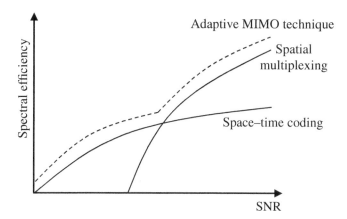

Figure 7.3 Spectral efficiency comparison of different MIMO techniques.

Multipath fading is one of the fundamental characteristics of wireless communication channels. Diversity is defined as the number of available independent wireless channels for which signal replicas can be transmitted. The diversity techniques are classified into time diversity, frequency diversity, space (or antenna) diversity, polarization diversity, and multi-user diversity. The basic idea of MIMO techniques uses space correlation properties of the wireless channels and obtains multiple uncorrelated signal replicas. Space diversity of MIMO systems can be achieved by multiple transmit antennas and multiple receive antennas. The multiple transmit antennas allow us to achieve transmitter space diversity and obtain uncorrelated fading signals. The transmit diversity (or degrees of freedom) can be defined as the number of independent channels exploited by the transmitter. The multiple receive antennas allow us to achieve receiver space diversity and obtain independent fading signals at the receiver. The receiver diversity can be defined as the number of independent channels exploited by the receiver. Thus, the MIMO performance depends on channel correlation. Channel correlation is defined as follows: a MIMO channel $\mathbf{H}_t \in \mathbb{C}^N$ is spatially uncorrelated if the MIMO channel gain $\|\mathbf{H}_t\|^2$ and the MIMO channel direction $\mathbf{H}_t / \|\mathbf{H}_t\|$ are independent random variables, and the MIMO channel direction is uniformly distributed over the unit-sphere in $\mathbb{C}^N$. The uncorrelated Rayleigh fading is denoted as $\mathbf{H}_t \sim CN(0, \beta\mathbf{I}_N)$ where β is the variance and $\mathbf{I}_N$ is the identity matrix. The correlated Rayleigh fading is expressed as $\mathbf{H}_t \sim CN(0, \mathbf{R})$ where the covariance matrix $\mathbf{R}$ is also the correlation matrix. In order to achieve the best performance, the MIMO channel should be full rank.

7.3.1 Capacity of MIMO Channel

We assume a time-invariant MIMO channel and compute the capacity of the channel [2]. Figure 7.4 illustrates the point-to-point MIMO channel (or single-user MIMO) with N_t transmit antennas and N_r receive antennas.

In the figure, $h_{ji}{}^t$, $s^i{}_t$, and $r^j{}_t$ denote channel gain from transmit antenna i to receive antenna j, a transmitted symbol, and a received symbol, respectively. The index t represents

N_t antennas N_r antennas

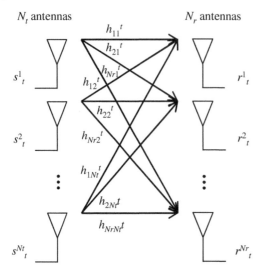

Figure 7.4 Point-to-point MIMO channel.

frame length in the time domain. The received signal at each antenna can be expressed as follows:

$$r_t^j = \sum_{i=1}^{N_t} h_{ji}^t s_t^i + n_t^j \tag{7.2}$$

where n_t^j represents an independent complex Gaussian noise and $1 \leq j \leq N_r$. The MIMO channel is represented by the $\mathbf{H}_t \in \mathbb{C}^{N_r \times N_t}$ matrix as follows:

$$\mathbf{H}_t = \begin{bmatrix} h_{11}^t & h_{12}^t & \cdots & h_{1N_t}^t \\ h_{21}^t & h_{22}^t & & h_{2N_t}^t \\ \vdots & & \ddots & \vdots \\ h_{N_r 1}^t & h_{N_r 2}^t & \cdots & h_{N_r N_t}^t \end{bmatrix} \tag{7.3}$$

and the received signals are expressed in the matrix form as follows:

$$\begin{bmatrix} r_t^1 \\ r_t^2 \\ \vdots \\ r_t^{N_r} \end{bmatrix} = \begin{bmatrix} h_{11}^t & h_{12}^t & \cdots & h_{1N_t}^t \\ h_{21}^t & h_{22}^t & & h_{2N_t}^t \\ \vdots & & \ddots & \vdots \\ h_{N_r 1}^t & h_{N_r 2}^t & \cdots & h_{N_r N_t}^t \end{bmatrix} \begin{bmatrix} s_t^1 \\ s_t^2 \\ \vdots \\ s_t^{N_t} \end{bmatrix} + \begin{bmatrix} n_t^1 \\ n_t^2 \\ \vdots \\ n_t^{N_r} \end{bmatrix} \tag{7.4}$$

The received signal vector is expressed as follows:

$$\mathbf{r}_t = \mathbf{H}_t \mathbf{s}_t + \mathbf{n}_t \tag{7.5}$$

where $\mathbf{r}_t \in \mathbb{C}^{N_r}$, $\mathbf{s}_t \in \mathbb{C}^{N_t}$, and $\mathbf{n}_t \in CN(0, N_0 \mathbf{I}_{N_r})$ representing the received signal, the transmitted signal, and Gaussian noise, respectively. The MIMO channel $\mathbf{H}_t$ is deterministic and assumes a constant channel matrix at all times. Both the transmitter and the receiver know the channel state information (CSI) of the MIMO channel. As we reviewed in Chapter 3, matrix theory is helpful for simplifying problems and reducing the computational complexity of the system. Matrix computation of the MIMO channel matrix $\mathbf{H}_t$ is not easy to calculate in an explicit way. Matrix decomposition allows us to rephrase some matrix forms in such a way that it can be solved more easily. Thus, the MIMO channel is transformed to parallel and independent scalar subchannels by matrix decomposition. Singular value decomposition (SVD) [3] is commonly used to decompose the MIMO channel as follows:

$$\mathbf{H}_t = \mathbf{U}_t \mathbf{\Lambda}_t \mathbf{V}_t^H \tag{7.6}$$

where $\mathbf{U}_t \in \mathbb{C}^{N_r \times N_r}$ and $\mathbf{V}_t \in \mathbb{C}^{N_t \times N_t}$ represent the left and right unitary matrices, respectively. $(\ )^H$ denotes Hermitian operation. They have the following property: $\mathbf{U}_t^H \mathbf{U}_t = \mathbf{I}$ and $\mathbf{V}_t \mathbf{V}_t^H = \mathbf{I}$. In Equation (7.6), $\mathbf{\Lambda}_t \in \mathbb{R}^{N_r \times N_r}$ is a rectangular matrix with non-negative real numbers as diagonal elements and zero as off-diagonal elements. The diagonal elements of $\mathbf{\Lambda}_t$ are the singular values ($\lambda_1 \geq \lambda_2 \geq \dots \geq \lambda_{n_{min}}$ where $n_{min} = \min(N_t, N_r)$) of the MIMO channel matrix $\mathbf{H}_t$. If $\lambda_i = 0$, the ith MIMO channel could not contribute to the capacity. This means that n_{min} parallel channels are created. The received signal vector Equation (7.5) can be rewritten using Equation (7.6) as follows:

$$\mathbf{r}_t = \mathbf{U}_t \mathbf{\Lambda}_t \mathbf{V}_t^H \mathbf{s}_t + \mathbf{n}_t \tag{7.7}$$

$$\mathbf{U}_t^H \mathbf{r}_t = \mathbf{U}_t^H \mathbf{U}_t \mathbf{\Lambda}_t \mathbf{V}_t^H \mathbf{s}_t + \mathbf{U}_t^H \mathbf{n}_t \tag{7.8}$$

$$\mathbf{U}_t^H \mathbf{r}_t = \mathbf{\Lambda}_t \mathbf{V}_t^H \mathbf{s}_t + \mathbf{U}_t^H \mathbf{n}_t \tag{7.9}$$

where $\mathbf{U}_t^H \mathbf{r}_t$ is the projection of $\mathbf{r}_t$ on the left eigenvector space $\mathbf{U}$ ($\tilde{\mathbf{r}}_t = \mathbf{U}_t^H \mathbf{r}_t$) and $\mathbf{V}_t^H \mathbf{s}_t$ is the projection of $\mathbf{s}_t$ on the right eigenvector space $\mathbf{V}$ ($\tilde{\mathbf{s}}_t = \mathbf{V}_t^H \mathbf{s}_t$). We define $\tilde{\mathbf{n}}_t = \mathbf{U}_t^H \mathbf{n}_t$ and rewrite Equation (7.9) as follows:

$$\tilde{\mathbf{r}}_t = \mathbf{\Lambda}_t \tilde{\mathbf{s}}_t + \tilde{\mathbf{n}}_t \tag{7.10}$$

where $\tilde{\mathbf{n}}_t$ is a complex Gaussian vector. Power levels of $\mathbf{s}_t$ and $\mathbf{n}_t$ are maintained because $\mathbf{U}$ and $\mathbf{V}$ are unitary. Equation (7.10) is re-written as n_{min} parallel Gaussian channels as follows:

$$\tilde{r}_t^k = \lambda_k \tilde{s}_t^k + \tilde{n}_t^k, k = 1, 2, \dots, n_{min} \tag{7.11}$$

Figure 7.5 illustrates the equivalent representation of the MIMO channel conversion through SVD.

We need metrics to know how many effective spatial links exist in the MIMO system. With high SNR, large capacity can be obtained if the eigenvalues are less spread out. However, with low SNR, the optimal policy is to assign power only to the strongest eigenmode [3]. The condition (or condition number) is used for the indicator of spatial selectivity. The condition of the MIMO channel matrix $\mathbf{H}_t$ is calculated as a ratio of the maximum and minimum eigenvalues as follows:

$$K(\mathbf{H}_t) = \lambda_{max} / \lambda_{min} \geq 1 \tag{7.12}$$

where λ_{max} and λ_{min} are the maximum singular value and the minimum singular value of the matrix $\mathbf{H}_t$, respectively. If the condition is close to 1, the MIMO channel matrix is well-conditioned, meaning higher capacity. The high number implies an ill-conditioned channel matrix. Another important metric is the rank of the MIMO channel matrix $\mathbf{H}_t$.

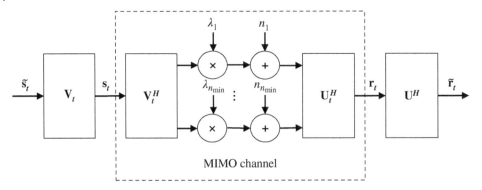

Figure 7.5 Point-to-point MIMO channel conversion through SVD.

The rank is used for the indicator of the number of multiplexing channels. The rank is defined as the number of singular values not equal to zero. The capacity of the MIMO channel can be found via waterfilling power allocations as follows [3]:

$$C_{\text{MIMO}} = \sum_{i=1}^{n_{\min}} \log\left(1 + \frac{P_i^* \lambda_i^2}{N_0}\right) \tag{7.13}$$

where P_i^* denotes the optimal powers by the waterfilling power allocations as follows:

$$P_i^* = \left(\mu - \frac{N_0}{\lambda_i^2}\right)^+ \tag{7.14}$$

where $(x)^+ = \max(x, 0)$ and μ is the water level satisfying the total power constraint $\sum_i P_i^* = P$. With high SNR, degree of freedom is more significant and uniform power allocation is asymptotically optimal. Thus, Equation (7.13) can be rewritten as follows:

$$C_{\text{MIMO}} \approx \sum_{i=1}^{k} \log\left(1 + \frac{P \lambda_i^2}{k N_0}\right) \approx k \log \text{SNR} + \sum_{i=1}^{k} \log\left(\frac{\lambda_i^2}{k}\right) \tag{7.15}$$

where k is the rank of $\mathbf{H}_t$ and $\text{SNR} = \frac{P}{N_0}$. As we can observe from Equation (7.15), k determines how many data streams can be spatially multiplexed in the MIMO channel. We call full rank if all rows and columns of the matrix are linearly independent. If it does not have full rank, the matrix is rank deficient. Thus, full rank of the matrix is important to the capacity of the MIMO channel. However, this is not enough. If a singular value of the MIMO channel matrix is less than 1, the second term of Equation (7.15) is negative and the capacity of the MIMO channel is limited. Thus, in order to maximize the second term, we use Jensen's inequality:

$$\frac{1}{k} \sum_{i=1}^{k} \log\left(1 + \frac{P \lambda_i^2}{k N_0}\right) \leq \log\left(1 + \frac{P}{k N_0}\left(\frac{1}{k} \sum_{i=1}^{k} \log \lambda_i^2\right)\right) \tag{7.16}$$

and

$$\sum_{ij} |h_{ji}^t|^2 = \text{Tr}\left(\mathbf{H}_t \mathbf{H}_t^H\right) = \sum_{i=1}^{k} \lambda_i^2 \tag{7.17}$$

where Tr $(\mathbf{X})$ is a trace of the matrix $\mathbf{X}$. Thus, maximum capacity can be obtained when all λ_i are equal. We can interpret that a well-conditioned channel matrix attains high capacity. With low SNR, capacity can be rewritten as follows [3]:

$$C_{\text{MIMO}} \approx \frac{P}{N_0}(\max \lambda_i^2)\log_2 e \qquad (7.18)$$

As we can observe from Equation (7.18), the rank or condition is not significant and the power becomes important to the capacity of a MIMO channel.

Example 7.1 SVD, Rank and Condition of MIMO Channel

Consider the following MIMO channel matrix:

$$\begin{bmatrix} 0.8 + 0.2i & 0.1 - 0.4i \\ -0.4 + 0.4i & -0.6 - 0.2i \end{bmatrix}$$

Decompose the MIMO channel using SVD and find the rank and condition of the matrix.

Solution

From Equation (7.6), we have

$$\mathbf{H}_t = \mathbf{U}_t\mathbf{\Lambda}_t\mathbf{V}_t^H$$

$$\begin{bmatrix} 0.8 + 0.2i & 0.1 - 0.4i \\ -0.4 + 0.4i & -0.6 - 0.2i \end{bmatrix} = \begin{bmatrix} -0.785 - 0.066i & -0.156 - 0.596i \\ 0.545 - 0.286i & -0.577 - 0.536i \end{bmatrix}\begin{bmatrix} 1.027 & 0 \\ 0 & 0.719 \end{bmatrix}$$

$$\times \begin{bmatrix} -0.949 & -0.316 \\ -0.314 - 0.039i & 0.941 + 0.118i \end{bmatrix}^H$$

The rank of the matrix is 2 because the number of non-zero diagonal elements is 2. From Equation (7.12), the condition number is calculated as follows:

$$K(\mathbf{H}_t) = \frac{\lambda_{\max}}{\lambda_{\min}} = \frac{1.027}{0.719} = 1.428$$

Thus, the MIMO channel is not the best but has good condition for spatial multiplexing.

Example 7.2 Capacity of MIMO Channel

Consider the same MIMO channel matrix as for Example 7.1 and find the capacity of the MIMO channel.

Solution

From Example 7.1, we obtained the singular values (λ_1, λ_2) of $\mathbf{\Lambda}_t$ as follows:

$$\lambda_1 = 1.027, \quad \lambda_2 = 0.719$$

From Equation (7.13), we can calculate the capacity of the MIMO channel as follows:

$$C_{\text{MIMO}} = \sum_{i=1}^{n_{\min}} \log\left(1 + \frac{P_i^*\lambda_i^2}{N_0}\right) = \log\left(1 + (1.027)^2\frac{P_i^*}{N_0}\right) + \log\left(1 + (0.719)^2\frac{P_i^*}{N_0}\right)$$

Assuming uniform power allocation, we obtain the Figure p7.1 as follows:

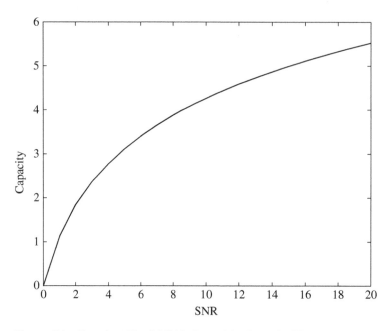

Figure p7.1 Capacity of 2×2 MIMO channel for Example 7.2.

When calculating the capacity of the MIMO channel, we assumed that the channel is time invariant and both the transmitter and the receiver have the CSI. We need to investigate the characteristics of the MIMO channel, such as channel reciprocity, channel parameterization, channel hardening, favorable propagation, and pilot contamination. Acquisition of accurate CSI influences the capacity of the MIMO techniques. If the MIMO channel is not constant over a bandwidth and also varying rapidly, it would be difficult to establish a reliable radio link and use MIMO techniques. Thus, in order to maintain the assumption, the MIMO techniques should be operated in the coherence bandwidth (B_c) and coherence time (T_c). They are defined [2] as follows. The coherence bandwidth is a statistical measurement of the bandwidth where the channel is regarded as a flat channel, which means two signals passing through the channel experience similar gain and phase rotation. The coherence time is the time interval over which a channel impulse response is regarded as invariant. In addition, the coherence block ($\tau_p = B_c T_c$) is defined as an approximately constant and flat fading channel block [4]. In TDD mode, pilot signals are used to obtain the CSI. If the channel reciprocity holds, both downlink and uplink match exactly. However, in frequency division duplexing (FDD) mode, uplink and downlink channels are different. Pilot signals in both uplink and downlink should be sent and feedback signals are needed. Thus, the packet overhead becomes a big problem when increasing the number of antennas. The TDD mode is suitable for massive MIMO due to channel reciprocity.

When designing MIMO systems, another channel characteristic we should consider is channel parameterization. In some propagation environments such as line of sight propagation, N-dimensional channel response can be parameterized using much fewer than N parameters. The channel model relies on the array geometry and angle between the base station and the mobile station. Channel hardening means that a fading channel acts as a deterministic channel. When the channel gain is close to its mean value ($\|\mathbf{H}_t\|^2 \to E[\|\mathbf{H}_t\|^2]$), the fading channel has little impact on performance and we call it channel hardening. Simply speaking, channel hardening happens when the channel fluctuation is small. Favorable propagation is defined as mutual orthogonality among the vector valued channels to the mobile stations [4]. When the channel directions maintain the orthogonality, this mitigates interference among the mobile stations and improves spectral efficiency by linear combination and precoding. Both channel hardening and favorable propagation have been validated as an experiment in [5]. Pilot contamination occurs when multiple mobile stations transmit pilot signals simultaneously or pilot signals are corrupted by other interferences or noises. The base station receives the mixed signals and the pilot signals are contaminated. The interference affects the channel estimation quality. The pilot contamination prevents us from estimating the MIMO channel accurately. In massive MIMO systems, pilot contamination might be a key aspect of the MIMO channel due to more frequent use of pilots.

In fading channel, the ergodic capacity and outage capacity of the MIMO fading channel are used. The ergodic capacity is an ensemble average of instantaneous capacity over all possible MIMO channel matrices. The ergodic capacity C_{Erg} of the MIMO fading channel is defined as follows:

$$C_{\text{Erg}} = E(I(\mathbf{s}_t; \mathbf{r}_t \mid \mathbf{H}_t)) \tag{7.19}$$

where the mutual information between channel input and output as a random variable is

$$I(\mathbf{s}_t; \mathbf{r}_t \mid \mathbf{H}_t) = \log \det \left(\mathbf{I}_{N_r} + \frac{1}{N_0} \mathbf{H}_t \mathbf{K}_s \mathbf{H}_t^H \right) \tag{7.20}$$

where the random variable $\mathbf{s}_t$ is independent of the noise and $\mathbf{K}_s = E(\mathbf{s}\mathbf{s}^H)$ is a transmit covariance matrix. If CSI is available, $\mathbf{K}_s$ can be optimized by maximizing Equation (7.20). However, if CSI is not available, $\mathbf{K}_s$ is a constant for all transmissions. In general, the computation of the ergodic capacity is not easy. In MIMO fading channel, the capacity is a random variable. The outage capacity is more useful than ergodic capacity because there is delay limitation. The outage capacity represents the maximum data rate without errors. The $q\%$ outage capacity of the MIMO fading channel is defined as follows:

$$P(I(\mathbf{s}_t; \mathbf{r}_t \mid \mathbf{H}_t) < C_{\text{outage},q\%}) = q\% \tag{7.21}$$

where q is the error probability and only $1 - q$ transmissions are correctly received. If we have the minimum outage probability for a constant transmission rate C_0 as follows: $P(I(\mathbf{s}_t; \mathbf{r}_t \mid \mathbf{H}_t) < C_0) \leq q\%$, C_0 is the $q\%$ outage capacity. We can say that minimizing the outage probability for a given constant rate is same as maximizing the outage capacity for the given outage probability. In general, outage capacity is much lower than additive white Gaussian noise (AWGN) channel capacity.

The key issues of MIMO design can be summarized as follows: (i) trade-off between multiplexing gain and diversity gain; and (ii) trade-off between performance and complexity. The MIMO techniques have been improved to find an optimal solution for them. The concept of space division multiple access (SDMA) using smart antennas on the same frequency in different locations was proposed in the early 1990s. The key idea of employing multiple antennas to a single user and obtaining the multiplexing gain was proposed by Foschini in 1996 [6]. In 1998, Wolniansky proposed the V-BLAST scheme as a simplified implementation [7]. Alamouti proposed a 2×2 MIMO scheme and obtained the full transmit diversity [8]. In 1999, Tarokh generalized the Alamouti scheme and discovered half-rate space–time block codes (STBCs) for 2, 4, and 8 transmit antennas [9]. In 2002, Hassibi proposed a new class of linear dispersion code (LDC) which drops the orthogonality requirements of STBC and improves the STBC capacity [10]. Heath proposed capacity achieving LDC for both full multiplexing gain and diversity gain [11]. In 2004, spatial modulation was proposed in [12]. In 2010, in order to add diversity gain to spatial modulation, space–time shift keying (STSK), combining LDC and spatial modulation, was proposed in [13]. Massive MIMO was proposed by the Nokia Bell Lab [14]. Massive MIMO operates in TDD mode and multi-cell scenarios, and relies on spatial multiplexing.

Summary 7.2 Capacity of MIMO Channel

1) The multiple antennas of a transmitter and a receiver allow us to have a new spatial dimension and improve system performances: diversity gain, array gain, and multiplexing gain.

2) We need metrics to know how many effective spatial links exist in the MIMO system. The condition (or condition number) is used for the indicator of spatial selectivity. If the condition is close to 1, the MIMO channel matrix is well-conditioned. Well-conditioned represents higher capacity. Another important metric is the rank of the MIMO channel matrix. The rank is used for the indicator of the number of multiplexing channels. The rank is defined as the number of singular values not equal to zero.

3) The capacity of a MIMO channel can be found via waterfilling power allocations as follows

$$C_{\text{MIMO}} = \sum_{i=1}^{n_{\min}} \log\left(1 + \frac{P_i^* \lambda_i^2}{N_0}\right)$$

where P_i^* denotes the optimal powers by the waterfilling power allocations.

4) The ergodic capacity C_{Erg} of the MIMO fading channel is defined as follows:

$$C_{\text{Erg}} = E(I(\mathbf{s}_t; \mathbf{r}_t \mid \mathbf{H}_t))$$

5) The outage capacity is more useful than ergodic capacity because there is delay limitation. The outage capacity represents the maximum data rate without errors. The q % outage capacity of the MIMO fading channel is defined as follows:

$$P(I(\mathbf{s}_t; \mathbf{r}_t \mid \mathbf{H}_t) < C_{\text{outage},q\%}) = q\%$$

where q is the error probability and only $1 - q$ transmissions are correctly received.

7.3.2 Space–Time Coding Design

Space–time coding is a joint design of channel coding, modulation, and diversity scheme. There are two types of space–time coding: STBCs and space–time trellis codes (STTCs). The STBCs are constructed from an orthogonal matrix over antennas and time and simply decoded by maximum likelihood (ML) decoding. They can achieve full diversity but show a lack of coding gain. On the other hand, STTCs transmit multiple and diverse data sequences over antennas and time and reconstruct the actual data sequence at the receiver. They can achieve both diversity gain and coding gain. However, the decoding complexity is higher because the decoding process is based on a joint maximum likelihood sequence estimation.

In order to design STBCs, we consider the point-to-point MIMO channel with N_t transmit antennas and N_r receive antennas as shown in Figure 7.6 [2]. The information source block generates m symbols as follows:

$$\mathbf{c}_t = (c_t^1, c_t^2, \ldots, c_t^m) \tag{7.22}$$

In the space–time encoder, m symbols $\mathbf{c}_t$ are mapped into N_t modulation symbols from a signal set of $M = 2^m$ and the transmit vector is represented as follows:

$$\mathbf{s}_t = (s_t^1, s_t^2, \ldots, s_t^{N_t})^T \tag{7.23}$$

We assume the MIMO channel is memoryless and the MIMO system operates over a slowly varying flat fading MIMO channel. The transmit vector has L frame length at each

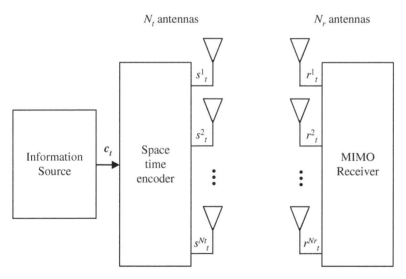

Figure 7.6 $N_r \times N_t$ MIMO channel for space–time block coding.

antenna. The $N_t \times L$ space–time codeword matrix is defined as follows:

$$\mathbf{S} = [\mathbf{s_1}, \mathbf{s_2}, \dots, \mathbf{s_L}] = \overset{\text{Time}}{\underset{\text{Space}}{\begin{bmatrix} s_1^1 & s_2^1 & \cdots & s_L^1 \\ s_1^2 & s_2^2 & & s_L^2 \\ \vdots & & \ddots & \vdots \\ s_1^{N_t} & s_2^{N_t} & \cdots & s_L^{N_t} \end{bmatrix}}}$$

(7.24)

and the MIMO channel matrix is given as Equation (7.3). Each column of $\mathbf{S}$ is transmitted at a given channel. Since m symbols in L channels are transmitted, the STBC rate is $R = m/L$ symbols/s. If we have a constellation of order M, the bit rate is $R_b = \frac{m}{L} \log M$. Linear STBCs are considered and the mapping between symbols and transmitted matrices is linear as follows:

$$\mathbf{S} = \sum_{k=1}^{m} (\mathbf{A_k} c_k + \mathbf{B_k} c_k^*)$$

(7.25)

where c_k^* is the complex conjugate of c_k and the $N_t \times L$ matrices $\mathbf{A_k}$ and $\mathbf{B_k}$ are fixed. The mapping rule is designed to optimize diversity gain and multiplexing gain and determine the performance of space–time coding. For example, if Alamouti code ($L = 2$, $m = 2$) is defined, both matrices are as follows:

$$\mathbf{A_1} = \begin{bmatrix} 1 & 0 \\ 0 & 0 \end{bmatrix}, \ \mathbf{A_2} = \begin{bmatrix} 0 & 0 \\ 1 & 0 \end{bmatrix}, \ \mathbf{B_1} = \begin{bmatrix} 0 & 0 \\ 0 & 1 \end{bmatrix}, \ \mathbf{B_2} = \begin{bmatrix} 0 & -1 \\ 0 & 0 \end{bmatrix}$$

(7.26)

Another representation is possible. We divide m complex symbols into their real and imaginary parts as follows:

$$r_k = \begin{cases} Re(c_k), k = 1, \dots, m \\ Im(c_k), k = m+1, \dots, 2m \end{cases}$$

(7.27)

where space–time codewords can be represented as follows:

$$\mathbf{S} = \sum_{k=1}^{m} (\mathbf{A_k} c_k + \mathbf{B_k} c_k^*) = \sum_{k=1}^{2m} \mathbf{C_k} r_k$$

(7.28)

where $\mathbf{C_k}$ is expressed as follows:

$$\mathbf{C_k} = \begin{cases} \mathbf{A_k} + \mathbf{B_k}, k = 1, \dots, m \\ j(\mathbf{A_{k-m}} - \mathbf{B_{k-m}}), k = m+1, \dots, 2m \end{cases}$$

(7.29)

For example, if Alamouti code ($L = 2$, $m = 2$) is defined, the matrix $\mathbf{C_k}$ is as follows:

$$\mathbf{C_1} = \begin{bmatrix} 1 & 0 \\ 0 & 1 \end{bmatrix}, \ \mathbf{C_2} = \begin{bmatrix} 0 & -1 \\ 1 & 0 \end{bmatrix}, \ \mathbf{C_3} = \begin{bmatrix} j & 0 \\ 0 & -j \end{bmatrix}, \ \mathbf{C_4} = \begin{bmatrix} 0 & j \\ j & 0 \end{bmatrix}$$

(7.30)

Orthogonal space–time block codes (OSTBCs) are one special class of linear STBCs. Attractive features of OSTBCs are summarized as: (i) full diversity gain; (ii) simple receiver structure by maximum likelihood decoding; (iii) maximum SNR or minimum MSE; and (iv) easy-to-cancel inter-symbol interference (ISI) due to orthogonality. The OSTBCs are optimal in terms of diversity gain and receiver complexity but suboptimal in terms of rate. The space–time codeword matrix of OSTBCs has the following property:

$$\mathbf{S}^H\mathbf{S} = \|\mathbf{c}_t\|^2\mathbf{I} \tag{7.31}$$

where

$$\|\mathbf{c}_t\|^2 = \sum_{k=1}^{m} |c_t^k|^2 \tag{7.32}$$

and the rows of the codewords are orthogonal with norm $\|\mathbf{c}_t\|^2$. In addition, the matrix $\mathbf{C}_k$ of the complex OSTBCs must satisfy

$$\mathbf{C}_k^H\mathbf{C}_l = \begin{cases} \mathbf{I}, k = l \\ -\mathbf{C}_l^H\mathbf{C}_k, k \neq l \end{cases} , k, l = 1, \ldots, 2m \tag{7.33}$$

In LDCs [11], the matrices $\mathbf{A}_k$ and $\mathbf{B}_k$ are selected to maximize the mutual information between a transmitter and a receiver. However, it is not easy to find an optimal solution because this is a nonconvex problem. Numerical solution is one approach. The maximum likelihood (ML) decoding scheme and perfect CSI are assumed at the receiver. Thus, the receiver has the following decision metric:

$$\sum_{t=1}^{L} \sum_{j=1}^{N_r} \left| r_t^j - \sum_{i=1}^{N_t} h_{ji}^t s_t^i \right|^2 \tag{7.34}$$

The ML decoder finds the codewords to minimize Equation (7.34). We can calculate the pairwise error probability (PEP) that the receiver decides erroneously as follows:

$$P(\mathbf{S}, \hat{\mathbf{S}} \mid \mathbf{H}) = Q\left(\frac{d(\mathbf{S}, \hat{\mathbf{S}})}{2\sigma}\right) \leq \exp\left(-\frac{d^2(\mathbf{S}, \hat{\mathbf{S}})E_s}{4N_0}\right) \tag{7.35}$$

where $\hat{\mathbf{S}}$ is the estimated erroneous sequence as follows:

$$\hat{\mathbf{S}} = [\hat{\mathbf{s}}_1, \hat{\mathbf{s}}_2, \ldots, \hat{\mathbf{s}}_L] = \begin{bmatrix} \hat{s}_1^1 & \hat{s}_2^1 & \cdots & \hat{s}_L^1 \\ \hat{s}_1^2 & \hat{s}_2^2 & & \hat{s}_L^2 \\ \vdots & & \ddots & \vdots \\ \hat{s}_1^{N_t} & \hat{s}_2^{N_t} & \cdots & \hat{s}_L^{N_t} \end{bmatrix} \tag{7.36}$$

and $d^2(\mathbf{S}, \hat{\mathbf{S}})$ is the modified Euclidean distance as follows:

$$d^2(\mathbf{S}, \hat{\mathbf{S}}) = \sum_{t=1}^{L} \sum_{j=1}^{N_r} \left| \sum_{i=1}^{N_t} h_{ji}^t(\hat{s}_t^i - s_t^i) \right|^2 = \|\mathbf{H}(\hat{\mathbf{S}} - \mathbf{S})\|^2 \tag{7.37}$$

where $\mathbf{H}$ is the channel response sequence at each time as follows:

$$\mathbf{H} = [\mathbf{H}_1, \mathbf{H}_2, \ldots, \mathbf{H}_L] \tag{7.38}$$

We define the codeword difference matrix $\mathbf{B(S,\hat{S})}$ and codeword distance matrix $\mathbf{A(S,\hat{S})}$ as follows:

$$\mathbf{B(S,\hat{S})} = \mathbf{S} - \hat{\mathbf{S}} = \begin{bmatrix} s_1^1 - \hat{s}_1^1 & s_2^1 - \hat{s}_2^1 & \cdots & s_L^1 - \hat{s}_L^1 \\ s_1^2 - \hat{s}_1^2 & s_2^2 - \hat{s}_2^2 & & s_L^2 - \hat{s}_L^2 \\ \vdots & & \ddots & \vdots \\ s_1^{N_t} - \hat{s}_1^{N_t} & s_2^{N_t} - \hat{s}_2^{N_t} & \cdots & s_L^{N_t} - \hat{s}_L^{N_t} \end{bmatrix} \tag{7.39}$$

and

$$\mathbf{A(S,\hat{S})} = \mathbf{B(S,\hat{S})}\mathbf{B}^H(\mathbf{S,\hat{S}}) \tag{7.40}$$

$$= \begin{bmatrix} (s_1^1 - \hat{s}_1^1)\overline{(s_1^1 - \hat{s}_1^1)} & (s_2^1 - \hat{s}_2^1)\overline{(s_2^1 - \hat{s}_2^1)} & \cdots & (s_L^1 - \hat{s}_L^1)\overline{(s_L^1 - \hat{s}_L^1)} \\ (s_1^2 - \hat{s}_1^2)\overline{(s_1^2 - \hat{s}_1^2)} & (s_2^2 - \hat{s}_2^2)\overline{(s_2^2 - \hat{s}_2^2)} & & (s_L^2 - \hat{s}_L^2)\overline{(s_L^2 - \hat{s}_L^2)} \\ \vdots & & \ddots & \vdots \\ (s_1^{N_t} - \hat{s}_1^{N_t})\overline{(s_1^{N_t} - \hat{s}_1^{N_t})} & (s_2^{N_t} - \hat{s}_2^{N_t})\overline{(s_2^{N_t} - \hat{s}_2^{N_t})} & \cdots & (s_L^{N_t} - \hat{s}_L^{N_t})\overline{(s_L^{N_t} - \hat{s}_L^{N_t})} \end{bmatrix}$$

$$\tag{7.41}$$

where $\overline{(\,)}$ is a complex conjugate. After simple manipulations [2], the modified Euclidean distance in Equation (7.37) is rewritten as follows:

$$d^2(\mathbf{S,\hat{S}}) = \sum_{j=1}^{N_r} \mathbf{h}_j \mathbf{A(S,\hat{S})} \mathbf{h}_j^H \tag{7.42}$$

where $\mathbf{h}_j = [h_{j1}, h_{j2}, \dots, h_{jN_t}]$ because a slow fading channel is assumed and channel gains at each frame are constant as follows:

$$h_{ji}^1 = h_{ji}^2 = \dots = h_{ji}^L \tag{7.43}$$

The matrix $\mathbf{A(S,\hat{S})}$ is written as follows:

$$\mathbf{V} \cdot \mathbf{A(S,\hat{S})} \cdot \mathbf{V}^H = \mathbf{\Lambda} \tag{7.44}$$

where $\mathbf{\Lambda}$ is a diagonal matrix as follows:

$$\mathbf{\Lambda} = \begin{bmatrix} \lambda_1 & 0 & \cdots & 0 \\ 0 & \lambda_2 & & 0 \\ \vdots & & \ddots & \vdots \\ 0 & 0 & \cdots & \lambda_{N_t} \end{bmatrix}, \quad \lambda_i \geq 0 \text{ for the eigenvalues of } \mathbf{A(S,\hat{S})} \tag{7.45}$$

and $\mathbf{V}$ is an orthonormal matrix ($\mathbf{V}^H\mathbf{V} = \mathbf{I}$). The row vectors $[\mathbf{v}_1, \mathbf{v}_2, \dots, \mathbf{v}_{N_t}]$ of $\mathbf{V}$ are the eigenvectors of $\mathbf{A(S,\hat{S})}$. Let $[\beta_{j1}, \beta_{j2}, \dots, \beta_{jN_t}] = \mathbf{h}_j\mathbf{V}^H$, and we express the term $\mathbf{h}_j\mathbf{A(S,\hat{S})}\mathbf{h}_j^H$ as follows:

$$\mathbf{h}_j\mathbf{A(S,\hat{S})}\mathbf{h}_j^H = \mathbf{h}_j\mathbf{V}^H \mathbf{\Lambda} \mathbf{V}\mathbf{h}_j^H = \sum_{i=1}^{N_t} \lambda_i|\beta_{ji}|^2 \tag{7.46}$$

Thus, Equation (7.42) is rewritten as follows:

$$d^2(\mathbf{S,\hat{S}}) = \sum_{j=1}^{N_r}\sum_{i=1}^{N_t} \lambda_i|\beta_{ji}|^2 \tag{7.47}$$

and Equation (7.35) is rewritten using Equation (7.46) as follows:

$$P(\mathbf{S}, \hat{\mathbf{S}} \mid \mathbf{H}) \le \prod_{j=1}^{N_r} \exp\left(-\frac{E_s}{4N_0} \sum_{i=1}^{N_t} \lambda_i |\beta_{ji}|^2\right) \qquad (7.48)$$

For Rayleigh fading, the upper bound of PEP is written as follows:

$$P(\mathbf{S}, \hat{\mathbf{S}}) \le \left(\frac{1}{\prod_{i=0}^{N_t}\left(1 + \frac{E_s}{4N_0}\lambda_i\right)}\right)^{N_r} \qquad (7.49)$$

At a high SNR, we express the term $1 + \frac{E_s}{4N_0}\lambda_i$ as follows:

$$1 + \frac{E_s}{4N_0}\lambda_i \approx \frac{E_s}{4N_0}\lambda_i \qquad (7.50)$$

and Equation (7.49) is simplified as follows:

$$P(\mathbf{S}, \hat{\mathbf{S}}) \le \left(\prod_{i=0}^{N_t} \frac{E_s}{4N_0}\lambda_i\right)^{-N_r} = \left(\prod_{i=1}^{r} \lambda_i\right)^{-N_r} \left(\frac{E_s}{4N_0}\right)^{-rN_r}$$

$$= \left(\prod_{i=1}^{r} \lambda_i^{1/r}\right)^{-rN_r} \left(\frac{E_s}{4N_0}\right)^{-rN_r} \qquad (7.51)$$

where r is the rank of $\mathbf{A}(\mathbf{S}, \hat{\mathbf{S}})$. Now, we define three design criteria for the space–time coding in slow Rayleigh fading. The first design criterion is the rank criterion. The maximum diversity $N_t N_r$ can be achieved if a codeword difference matrix $\mathbf{B}(\mathbf{S}, \hat{\mathbf{S}})$ has full rank for any two codeword vector sequences $\mathbf{S}$ and $\hat{\mathbf{S}}$. If it has the minimum rank r over two tuples of distinct codeword vector sequences, the diversity is rN_r. The second design criterion is about coding gain. Since the determinant of $\mathbf{A}(\mathbf{S}, \hat{\mathbf{S}})$ is the product of the eigenvalues, we calculate the determinant and call it the determinant criterion. Assume rN_r is the target diversity gain. We should maximize the minimum determinant $\prod_{i=1}^{r} \lambda_i$ of $\mathbf{A}(\mathbf{S}, \hat{\mathbf{S}})$ along the pairs of distinct codewords with the minimum rank. Therefore, we can minimize the PEP. This determinant criterion is related to coding gain but does not calculate an accurate coding gain. Thus, this criterion should be considered as one design rule of the space–time coding. In [15], one more design criterion was discussed. The third design criterion is the trace criterion. In order to maximize the minimum Euclidean distance among all possible codewords, the minimum trace $\prod_{i=1}^{r} \lambda_i$ of $\mathbf{A}(\mathbf{S}, \hat{\mathbf{S}})$ should be maximized.

Example 7.3 *Orthogonal Space–Time Block Code*
Design orthogonal space–time block code with 2, 4, and 8 transmit antennas for real symbols.

Solution
From [9], orthogonal designs are suggested. When the symbol s_i is real and N_t is 2, 4, and 8, $\mathbf{S}_2$, $\mathbf{S}_4$, and $\mathbf{S}_8$ are defined as follows:

$$\mathbf{S}_2 = \begin{bmatrix} s_1 & s_2 \\ -s_2 & s_1 \end{bmatrix}$$

$$S_4 = \begin{bmatrix} s_1 & s_2 & s_3 & s_4 \\ -s_2 & s_1 & -s_4 & s_3 \\ -s_3 & s_4 & s_1 & -s_2 \\ -s_4 & -s_3 & s_2 & s_1 \end{bmatrix}$$

$$S_8 = \begin{bmatrix} s_1 & s_2 & s_3 & s_4 & s_5 & s_6 & s_7 & s_8 \\ -s_2 & s_1 & s_4 & -s_3 & s_6 & -s_5 & -s_8 & s_7 \\ -s_3 & -s_4 & s_1 & s_2 & s_7 & s_8 & -s_5 & -s_6 \\ -s_4 & s_3 & -s_2 & s_1 & s_8 & -s_7 & s_6 & -s_5 \\ -s_5 & -s_6 & -s_7 & -s_8 & s_1 & s_2 & s_3 & s_4 \\ -s_6 & s_5 & -s_8 & s_7 & -s_2 & s_1 & -s_4 & s_3 \\ -s_7 & s_8 & s_5 & -s_6 & -s_3 & s_4 & s_1 & -s_2 \\ -s_8 & -s_7 & s_6 & s_5 & -s_4 & -s_3 & s_2 & s_1 \end{bmatrix}$$

Example 7.4 *Performance of Space–Time Block Codes*

Consider the following MIMO systems:

MIMO system #1: 2 transmit antennas, 2 and 1 receiver antenna, s_i is real, and

$$S_2 = \begin{bmatrix} s_1 & s_2 \\ -s_2 & s_1 \end{bmatrix}$$

and

MIMO system #2: 4 transmit antennas, 1 receiver antenna, s_i is complex, and

$$S_4^c = \begin{bmatrix} s_1 & s_2 & s_3 & s_4 \\ -s_2 & s_1 & -s_4 & s_3 \\ -s_3 & s_4 & s_1 & -s_2 \\ -s_4 & -s_3 & s_2 & s_1 \\ s_1^* & s_2^* & s_3^* & s_4^* \\ -s_2^* & s_1^* & -s_4^* & s_3^* \\ -s_3^* & s_4^* & s_1^* & -s_2^* \\ -s_4^* & -s_3^* & s_2^* & s_1^* \end{bmatrix}$$

Compare their performances with a single antenna system.

Solution

From computer simulation, we can compare 2×2 and 2×1 Alamouti scheme and single antenna systems. The simulation configuration of MIMO system #1 is as follows: AWGN channel, perfect channel estimation, BPSK, and ML receiver. Figure p7.2 illustrates the bit error rate (BER) performance comparison of 2×2 and 2×1 Alamouti scheme and single antenna systems.

The simulation configuration of MIMO system #2 is as follows: AWGN channel, perfect channel estimation, QPSK, and ML receiver (Figure p7.3).

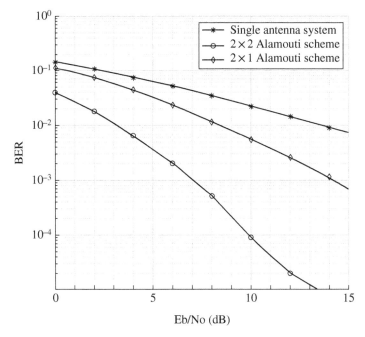

Figure p7.2 Performance comparison of 2×2 and 2×1 Alamouti scheme and single antenna system for Example 7.4.

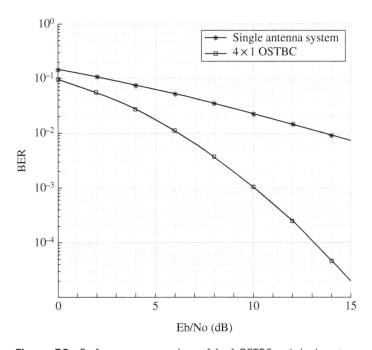

Figure p7.3 Performance comparison of 4×1 OSTBC and single antenna system.

As we can observe from the figures, increasing the number of antennas provides us with a better performance.

Space–time trellis codes (STTCs) have been proposed by Tarokh [16] in order to increase capacity in MIMO systems. STTCs are based on a joint design of channel coding, modulation and diversity scheme and provide us with a trade-off between throughput, diversity, and complexity. STTCs are able to mitigate the effects of fading and provide us with a significant performance improvement. Now, we discuss the STTC design. The STTC encoder is similar to the trellis-coded modulation (TCM) encoder. Figure 7.7 illustrates a STTC encoder. The input sequence c_t is a block of information (or coded bits) at time t and is denoted by $(c_t^1, c_t^2, \ldots, c_t^m)$. The kth input sequence c_t^k goes through the kth shift register and is multiplied by the STTC encoder coefficient set $\mathbf{g}^k$. It is defined as follows:

$$\mathbf{g}^k = [(g_{0,1}^k, g_{0,2}^k, \ldots, g_{0,N_t}^k), (g_{1,1}^k, g_{1,2}^k, \ldots, g_{1,N_t}^k), \ldots, (g_{v_m,1}^k, g_{v_m,2}^k, \ldots, g_{v_m,N_t}^k)] \qquad (7.52)$$

Each $g_{l,i}^k$ represents an element of M-ary signal constellation set and v_m represents the memory order of the kth shift register. If QPSK modulation is considered, it has one of

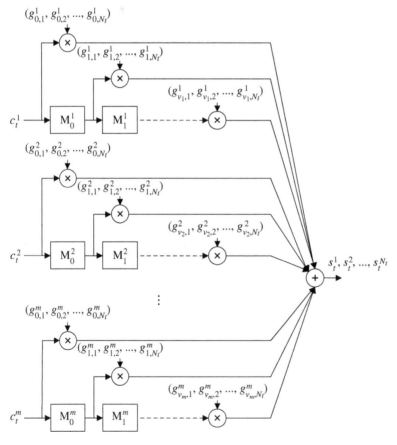

Figure 7.7 Space–time trellis encoder.

signal constellation set $\{0, 1, 2, 3\}$. The STTC encoder maps them into an M-ary modulated symbol and is denoted by $(s_t^1, s_t^2, \ldots, s_t^{N_t})$. The output of the STTC encoder is calculated as follows:

$$s_t^i = \sum_{k=1}^{m} \sum_{l=0}^{v_k} g_{l,i}^k c_{t-j}^k \bmod 2^m \tag{7.53}$$

where $i = 1, 2, \ldots, N_t$. The outputs of the multipliers are summed modulo 2^m. The modulated symbols s_t^i are transmitted in parallel through N_t transmit antennas. The total memory order of the STTC encoder is

$$v = \sum_{k=1}^{m} v_k \tag{7.54}$$

and v_k is defined as follows:

$$v_k = \left\lfloor \frac{v + k - 1}{m} \right\rfloor \tag{7.55}$$

The trellis state of the STTC encoder is 2^v. We assume that r_t^j is the received signal at the received antenna j at time t, the receiver obtains perfect CSI, and the branch metric is calculated as the squared Euclidean distance between the actual received signal and the hypothesized received signals as follows:

$$\sum_{j=1}^{N_r} \left| r_t^j - \sum_{i=1}^{N_t} h_{ji}^t s_t^i \right|^2 \tag{7.56}$$

The STTC decoder uses the Viterbi algorithm to select the path with the lowest path metric. In order to achieve full diversity, the STTC encoder requires a long memory and a large number of antennas. Thus, many states and branches of the trellis diagram are needed. The complexity of the STTC decoder increases in proportion to them. This is one disadvantage of the STTC.

Example 7.5 *STTC Diversity Gain*
Consider a 2×1 space–time trellis coded QPSK scheme with two transmit antennas with the following coefficient set of the generator matrix:

$$\mathbf{g}^1 = [(0, 2), (2, 0)] \text{ and } \mathbf{g}^2 = [(0, 1), (1, 0)].$$

Find the diversity gain.

Solution
The STTC encoder can be implemented by a shift register, multiplier, and adder. Figure p7.4 illustrates an example of the STTC encoder with a constraint length of 2 and an input block length of 2. As we can observe from Figure p7.4, each output of the STTC encoder depends on both the current input block and the previous input block. This process is pretty similar to conventional convolutional encoding. The STTC can be represented by the trellis diagram as shown in Figure p7.5. Figure p7.6 illustrates QPSK signal constellation and mapping for the trellis diagram. Similar to convolutional codes, each state and branch in the trellis diagram represents the memory state and output block, respectively.

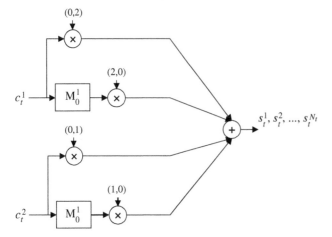

Figure p7.4 Example of STTC encoder.

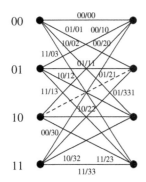

States

Branch labels $(c_t^1 c_t^2 / s_t^1 s_t^2)$

Figure p7.5 Trellis diagram for STTC with four states, QPSK and two transmit antennas.

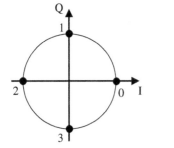

Figure p7.6 QPSK signal constellation and mapping.

$$0 \leftrightarrow +1$$
$$1 \leftrightarrow j$$
$$2 \leftrightarrow -1$$
$$3 \leftrightarrow -j$$

The error event probability of trellis codes is equivalent to the PEP. Thus, we consider two paths in the trellis diagram as shown in Figure p7.7. The dashed lines in Figure p7.7 diverge at time t_1 and remerge at time t_2. The first dashed line represents all zero input sequences $(00, 00)$ and their output sequences are calculated using the following equation:

$$(s_t^1, s_t^2) = c_t^1(0, 2) + c_{t-1}^1(2, 0) + c_t^2(0, 1) + c_{t-1}^2(1, 0) \bmod 4.$$

Figure p7.7 Paths diverging at time t_1 and remerging at time t_2.

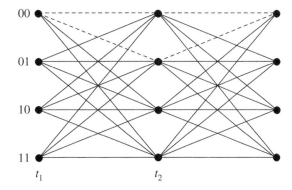

The output at time t_1 is

$$(s_1^1, s_1^2) = c_1^1(0,2) + c_0^1(2,0) + c_1^2(0,1) + c_0^2(1,0) \bmod 4$$
$$= 0 \cdot (0,2) + 0 \cdot (2,0) + 0 \cdot (0,1) + 0 \cdot (1,0) \bmod 4$$
$$= (0,0) \leftrightarrow (+1,+1)$$

and the output at time t_2 is

$$(s_2^1, s_2^2) = c_2^1(0,2) + c_1^1(2,0) + c_2^2(0,1) + c_1^2(1,0) \bmod 4$$
$$= 0 \cdot (0,2) + 0 \cdot (2,0) + 0 \cdot (0,1) + 0 \cdot (1,0) \bmod 4$$
$$= (0,0) \leftrightarrow (+1,+1)$$

Thus, the output sequences are $(+1, +1, +1, +1)$. The other diverging dashed line represents the nonzero input sequence $(01, 00)$. Their output sequences are calculated as follows:
The output at time t_1 is

$$(s_1^1, s_1^2) = c_1^1(0,2) + c_0^1(2,0) + c_1^2(0,1) + c_0^2(1,0) \bmod 4$$
$$= 0 \cdot (0,2) + 0 \cdot (2,0) + 1 \cdot (0,1) + 0 \cdot (1,0) \bmod 4$$
$$= (0,1) \leftrightarrow (+1,j)$$

and the output at time t_2 is

$$(s_2^1, s_2^2) = c_2^1(0,2) + c_1^1(2,0) + c_2^2(0,1) + c_1^2(1,0) \bmod 4$$
$$= 0 \cdot (0,2) + 0 \cdot (2,0) + 0 \cdot (0,1) + 1 \cdot (1,0) \bmod 4$$
$$= (1,0) \leftrightarrow (j,+1)$$

Thus, the codeword difference matrix $\mathbf{B}$ is

$$\mathbf{B} = \begin{bmatrix} 0 & 1-j \\ 1-j & 0 \end{bmatrix}$$

and the codeword distance matrix $\mathbf{A}$ is

$$\mathbf{A} = \mathbf{B}\mathbf{B}^H = \begin{bmatrix} 0 & 1-j \\ 1-j & 0 \end{bmatrix} \begin{bmatrix} 0 & 1+j \\ 1+j & 0 \end{bmatrix} = \begin{bmatrix} 2 & 0 \\ 0 & 2 \end{bmatrix}$$

Thus, the STTC has rank 2 and the diversity gain is $2 (=rN_r = 2 \cdot 1)$. This is full diversity. The determinant of the STTC is $4 (=2 \cdot 2 - 0 \cdot 0)$. A good design for the STTC is to achieve full diversity and then increase coding gain for full diversity through maximizing the minimum determinant of the codeword distance matrix $\mathbf{A}$.

Summary 7.3 Space–Time Coding Design

1) Space–time coding is a joint design of channel coding, modulation and diversity scheme. There are two types of space–time coding: space–time block codes (STBCs) and space–time trellis codes (STTCs).
2) The upper bound of PEP is

$$P(\mathbf{S}, \hat{\mathbf{S}}) \leq \left(\prod_{i=1}^{r} \lambda_i^{\frac{1}{r}} \right)^{-rN_r} \left(\frac{E_s}{4N_0} \right)^{-rN_r}$$

3) The rank criterion: The maximum diversity $N_t N_r$ can be achieved if a codeword difference matrix $B(\mathbf{S}, \hat{\mathbf{S}})$ has full rank for any two codeword vector sequences $\mathbf{S}$ and $\hat{\mathbf{S}}$. If it has a minimum rank r over two tuples of distinct codeword vector sequences, the diversity is rN_r.
4) The determinant criterion: The second design criterion is about coding gain. Since the determinant of $A(\mathbf{S}, \hat{\mathbf{S}})$ is the product of the eigenvalues, we can calculate the determinant. Assume rN_r is the target diversity gain. We should maximize the minimum determinant $\prod_{i=1}^{r} \lambda_i$ of $A(\mathbf{S}, \hat{\mathbf{S}})$ along the pairs of distinct codewords with minimum rank. Therefore, we minimize the PEP. This determinant criterion is related to coding gain but does not calculate an accurate coding gain.
5) The trace criterion: In order to maximize the minimum Euclidean distance among all possible codewords, the minimum trace $\prod_{i=1}^{r} \lambda_i$ of $A(\mathbf{S}, \hat{\mathbf{S}})$ should be maximized.

7.3.3 Spatial Multiplexing Design

In order to increase the transmission rate of $N_t \times N_r$ MIMO system, the best way is to transmit N_t independent symbols via one of each transmit antenna simultaneously and receive N_r observations via one of each receive antenna. Thus, the receiver has N_r observations of N_t unknown symbols. A spatial multiplexing technique transmits multiple data streams via different transmit antennas in the same time and frequency. The received signal includes the multiple data streams, and each transmitted data stream is extracted from the received signal. Thus, the spatial multiplexing technique can achieve a high multiplexing gain and increase a high channel capacity. This idea is based on BLAST architecture [7]. There are two types of BLAST technique. Diagonal BLAST (D-BLAST) can achieve the Shannon limit but it has significant complexity. V-BLAST has a lower capacity than the Shannon limit but the complexity is low. Figure 7.8 illustrates the transmitter architecture with four antennas and data sequence mapping of D-BLAST and V-BLAST.

In the MIMO system, N_t data sequences are transmitted simultaneously in the same frequency band with different antennas, and these various data sequences can be separated

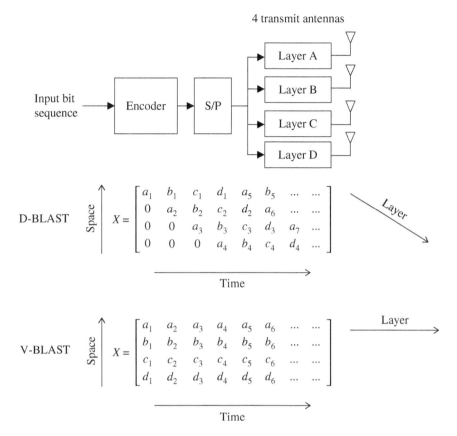

Figure 7.8 D-BLAST and V-BLAST transmitter and data sequences.

at the receiver. The transmitter does not need CSI and the total transmit power is maintained regardless of the number of transmit antennas. The receiver is based on interference mitigation techniques such as zero forcing (ZF), minimum mean-squared error (MMSE), successive interference cancellation (SIC), matched filter (MF), maximum likelihood (ML), and so on. These techniques were discussed in Chapter 3. In the MIMO system as spatial multiplexing, the complexity is a critical issue. The higher number of antennas brings better system performance but significantly increases system complexity. ZF detection uses the estimated channel response matrix **H**. Its complexity is low but system performance is also low. MMSE detection considers both **H** and the noise variance. Thus, its complexity is higher than ZF detection. Its performance is better than ZF detection at low or middle SNR, but their performance becomes similar at high SNR. ML detection is the optimal solution. However, the complexity is very high because it checks all possible hypotheses. Figure 7.9 illustrates the classification of MIMO detection algorithms.

V-BLAST provides a good trade-off between system performance and complexity. V-BLAST requires multiple and successive calculations and is based on SIC using QR decomposition. Assume a MIMO system with N_t transmit antennas and N_r receive antennas ($N_t = N_r = N$). As we discussed in Chapter 3, matrix factorization is useful for

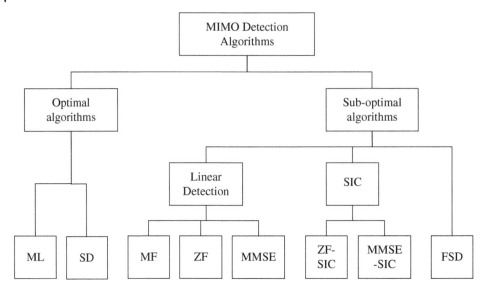

Figure 7.9 MIMO detection algorithms.

analysis. The QR decomposition of the channel response matrix **H** is defined as follows:

$$\mathbf{H} = \mathbf{QR} \tag{7.57}$$

where the matrix **Q** is an orthogonal matrix as follows:

$$\mathbf{Q}^H \mathbf{Q} = \mathbf{I}_N \tag{7.58}$$

The matrix **R** is an upper triangular matrix as follows:

$$\mathbf{R} = \begin{bmatrix} r_{11} & \cdots & r_{1N} \\ \vdots & \ddots & \vdots \\ 0 & \cdots & r_{NN} \end{bmatrix} \tag{7.59}$$

When we transmit $s_i[t]$ at receive antenna i and receive $y_i[t]$ at receive antenna i, the received symbol $y_i[t]$ is expressed as follows:

$$\begin{bmatrix} y_1[t] \\ \vdots \\ y_N[t] \end{bmatrix} = \begin{bmatrix} h_{11} & \cdots & h_{1N} \\ \vdots & \ddots & \vdots \\ h_{N1} & \cdots & h_{NN} \end{bmatrix} \begin{bmatrix} s_1[t] \\ \vdots \\ s_N[t] \end{bmatrix} + \begin{bmatrix} n_1[t] \\ \vdots \\ n_N[t] \end{bmatrix} \tag{7.60}$$

$$\mathbf{y} = \mathbf{Hs} + \mathbf{n} \tag{7.61}$$

At the receiver, we calculate the following equation:

$$\widetilde{\mathbf{s}} = \mathbf{Q}^H \mathbf{y} = \mathbf{Q}^H (\mathbf{Hs} + \mathbf{n}) = \mathbf{Rs} + \widetilde{\mathbf{n}} \tag{7.62}$$

$$\begin{bmatrix} \widetilde{s}_1[t] \\ \vdots \\ \widetilde{s}_N[t] \end{bmatrix} = \begin{bmatrix} r_{11} & \cdots & r_{1N} \\ \vdots & \ddots & \vdots \\ 0 & \cdots & r_{NN} \end{bmatrix} \begin{bmatrix} s_1[t] \\ \vdots \\ s_N[t] \end{bmatrix} + \begin{bmatrix} n_1[t] \\ \vdots \\ n_N[t] \end{bmatrix} \tag{7.63}$$

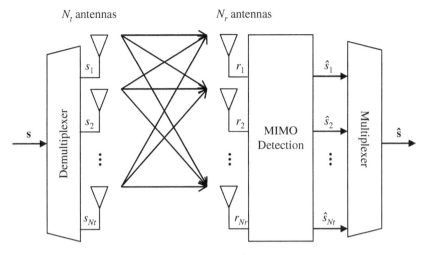

Figure 7.10 MIMO system for spatial multiplexing.

Due to the upper triangular structure, the last element $\tilde{s}_N[t]$ of the matrix **s** in Equation (7.63) is not affected by interferences and can be directly separated. The element $\tilde{s}_{N-1}[t]$ can be obtained by subtracting the N row from the $N-1$ row. Likewise, we can find the other elements.

Consider a spatial multiplexing system with N_t transmit antennas and N_r receive antennas and assume $N_r \geq N_t$. The received signal **r** ($N_r \times 1$ column vector) can be expressed as follows:

$$\mathbf{r} = \mathbf{Hs} + \mathbf{n} \tag{7.64}$$

where **H**, **s**, and **n** represent $N_r \times N_t$ MIMO channel matrix, $N_t \times 1$ transmit signal and $N_r \times 1$ white Gaussian noise vector, respectively. The element of **r**, r_j, is expressed as a superposition of all elements of **s**. Figure 7.10 illustrates the MIMO system for spatial multiplexing.

Maximum likelihood detection to find the most likely $\hat{\mathbf{s}}$ is as follows:

$$\hat{\mathbf{s}}_{ML} = arg \min_{s \in S} \|\mathbf{r} - \mathbf{Hs}\|^2 \tag{7.65}$$

where $\| \; \|$ denotes the norm of the matrix. The most likely $\hat{\mathbf{s}}$ is an element of set **S**. Thus, it is a simple solution to search all possible elements of set **S** and select one to satisfy Equation (7.65). This is known as a nondeterministic polynomial (NP) hard problem. The complexity increases exponentially according to the number of transmit antennas and the modulation order. Linear detection techniques such as MF, ZF, and MMSE use a MIMO channel inversion. The transmitted symbol estimation is calculated by the MIMO channel version, multiplication and quantization. The MF detection technique is one of the simplest detection techniques as follows:

$$\hat{\mathbf{s}}_{MF} = \text{Qtz}(\mathbf{H}^H \mathbf{r}) \tag{7.66}$$

where Qtz( ) represents quantization. The estimated symbols are obtained by multiplying the received symbols by Hermitian operation of the MIMO channel matrix. The ZF detection technique uses the pseudo-inverse of the MIMO channel matrix. When the MIMO channel matrix is square ($N_t = N_r$) and invertible, the estimated symbols by ZF detection are expressed as follows:

$$\hat{\mathbf{s}}_{ZF} = \text{Qtz}(\mathbf{H}^{-1}\mathbf{r}) \tag{7.67}$$

When the MIMO channel matrix is not square ($N_t \neq N_r$), it is expressed as follows:

$$\hat{\mathbf{s}}_{ZF} = \text{Qtz}((\mathbf{H}^H\mathbf{H})^{-1}\mathbf{H}^H\mathbf{r}) \tag{7.68}$$

As we can observe from Equations (7.67, 7.68), the ZF detection technique forces the amplitude of interferers to be zero by ignoring a noise effect. Thus, the MMSE detection technique considering a noise effect provides a better performance than the ZF detection technique. The MMSE detection technique minimizes the mean-squared error. It is expressed as follows:

$$\hat{\mathbf{s}}_{MMSE} = \text{Qtz}((\mathbf{H}^H\mathbf{H} + N_0\mathbf{I})^{-1}\mathbf{H}^H\mathbf{r}) \tag{7.69}$$

where I and N_0 represent an identity matrix and a noise. As we can observe from Equation (7.69), an accurate estimation of the noise is required. If the noise term N_0 is equal to zero, the MMSE detection technique is the same as the ZF detection technique. In linear detections, an accurate estimation of the MIMO channel matrix is an essential part and these detections are useful at a high SNR. The SIC detection technique is located between ML detection and linear detection. It provides a better performance than linear detections. SIC detection uses nulling and cancellation to extract the transmitted symbols from the received symbols. When one layer (a partial symbol sequence from one transmit antenna) is detected, an estimation of the transmitted layer is performed by subtracting from the already detected layers. The nulling and cancellation are carried out until all layers are detected. The SIC detection shows good performance at a low SNR. One disadvantage is that the SIC suffers from error propagation. When a wrong decision is made in any layer, the wrong decision affects the other layers. Thus, the ordering technique is used to minimize the effect of error propagation. In the nulling and cancellation of the ordering technique, the first symbol with a high SNR is transmitted as the most reliable symbol. Then, the symbols with a lower SNR are transmitted. Both linear detection and SIC detection cannot achieve the same performance as ML detection, although they have a lower complexity than ML detection.

Example 7.6 *Performance of Spatial Multiplexing Technique*
Consider a 2×2 MIMO system for spatial multiplexing as shown in Figure p7.8.
Compare the performances of optimal and sub-optimal MIMO detection algorithms.

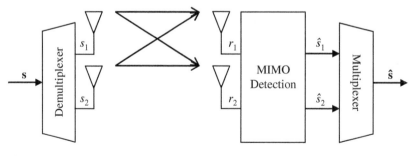

Figure p7.8 2×2 MIMO system for spatial multiplexing.

Solution

From computer simulation, we can compare MIMO detection algorithms: ML and SIC. The simulation configuration is as follows: 2×2 MIMO, QPSK, flat Rayleigh fading, AWGN, and perfect channel estimation. Figure p7.9 illustrates BER performance comparison of MIMO detection algorithms: ML, MMSE-SIC, and ZF-SIC. As we can observe, the optimal MIMO detection algorithm (ML) and sub-optimal detection algorithms (MMSE-SIC and ZF-SIC) are compared. The ML receiver has better performance than MMSE-SIC and ZF-SIC receivers, but the complexity of the ML receiver grows exponentially when increasing the number of transmit antennas.

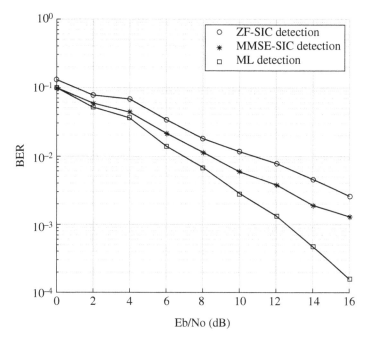

Figure p7.9 Performance comparison of MIMO detection algorithms (ML, MMSE-SIC, ZF-SIC).

Summary 7.4 Spatial Multiplexing Design

1) Spatial multiplexing techniques can achieve a high multiplexing gain and increase a high channel capacity.

2) ML detection finds the most likely $\hat{s}$ as follows:

$$\hat{\mathbf{s}}_{ML} = arg \min_{s \in S} \|\mathbf{r} - \mathbf{Hs}\|^2$$

where $\| \ \|$ denotes the norm of the matrix.

3) The MF detection technique is one of the simplest detection techniques as follows:

$$\hat{\mathbf{s}}_{MF} = \text{Qtz}(\mathbf{H}^H \mathbf{r})$$

where Qtz( ) represents quantization.

(Continued)

4) ZF detection is expressed as follows:

$$\hat{\mathbf{s}}_{ZF} = \text{Qtz}((\mathbf{H}^H\mathbf{H})^{-1}\mathbf{H}^H\mathbf{r})$$

5) The MMSE detection technique is expressed as follows:

$$\hat{\mathbf{s}}_{MMSE} = \text{Qtz}((\mathbf{H}^H\mathbf{H} + N_0\mathbf{I})^{-1}\mathbf{H}^H\mathbf{r})$$

where I and N_0 represent an identity matrix and a noise.

7.3.4 Massive MIMO

Massive MIMO (also known as large-scale antenna system, full dimension MIMO, or very large MIMO) was introduced in 2010 [14]. This became an essential technique of 5G systems, especially in the sub-6 GHz bands. The network configuration of massive MIMO systems is considered to be a base station equipped with large antenna arrays simultaneously serving many mobile devices. Compared with 4G MIMO techniques, massive MIMO provides us with higher spectral efficiency by spatial multiplexing of many mobile devices, and energy efficiency by a reduction of radiated power. The technical characteristics of massive MIMO can be summarized as follows:

 (i) TDD operation is required due to the reciprocity.
 (ii) Channel hardening removes the fast fading effect. The link quality varies slowly, which is helpful for resource allocation problems.
(iii) Closed loop link budget in proportional to the number of antennas in a base station. The link budget improvement is helpful for overall QoS improvement in a cell.
(iv) Relatively low complexity of precoding and decoding algorithms.
 (v) Full digital processing is helpful for both spectral efficiency and energy efficiency. In addition, it reduces accuracy and resolution of RF design.

According to [4, 14], if we can have unlimited antennas, unlimited capacity can be achieved under some conditions: (i) spatially correlated channels; (ii) MMSE channel estimation; and (iii) optimal linear combining.

Despite these advantages, there are practical limitations of massive MIMO. For example, more antennas brings a better performance. However, the performance limit depends on coherence time and bandwidth. In particular, high mobility requires smaller coherence time and more pilot signal. In addition, it has limited orthogonal pilots due to pilot contamination. The narrow beam generated by massive MIMO is very sensitive to mobile device mobility or antenna array sway.

We consider the uplink massive MIMO system in a single cell [17]:

$$\mathbf{y} = \sqrt{\rho}\sum_{k=1}^{K}\mathbf{h}_k x_k + \mathbf{n} = \sqrt{\rho}\mathbf{H}\mathbf{x} + \mathbf{n} \tag{7.70}$$

where K mobile devices with a single antenna simultaneously transmit K symbols $\mathbf{x} = [x_1, ..., x_K]^T$, and the base station with M antennas receives the symbol $\mathbf{y}$, $\mathbf{H} = [h_1, ..., h_K]^T$ is the channel matrix between the mobile device and the base station, $\mathbf{n}$ is Gaussian noise, and ρ is the average SNR. The channel matrix of massive MIMO (K single antenna terminals $\ll M$ antennas of a base station) can be decomposed into small-scale fading $\mathbf{g}_k^m$ and large-scale fading β_k as follows:

$$\mathbf{h}_k^m = \sqrt{\beta_k}\mathbf{g}_k^m, k = 1, \ldots, K, m = 1, \ldots, M \tag{7.71}$$

If the channel matrix is independent and identically distributed and the channel vector $\mathbf{h}_k \in \mathbb{C}^{M \times 1}$ is pairwisely orthogonal, the channel offers favorable propagation. The channel condition for favorable propagation is

$$\mathbf{h}_i^H\mathbf{h}_j = \begin{cases} 0, i \neq j, i, j = 1, \ldots, K, \\ \|\mathbf{h}_k\|^2 \neq 0, k = 1, \ldots, K \end{cases} \tag{7.72}$$

The condition Equation (7.72) will never be satisfied in practice. Thus, asymptotically favorable propagation conditions can be defined as follows:

$$\frac{\mathbf{h}_i^H\mathbf{h}_j}{M} \to 0, \ M \to \infty \tag{7.73}$$

Assuming the base station knows the channel matrix $\mathbf{H}$ and $\|\mathbf{h}_k\|^2$ is given, the sum-capacity is defined as follows [17]:

$$C = \log|\mathbf{I} + \rho\mathbf{H}^H\mathbf{H}| \tag{7.74}$$

Using the Hadamard inequality ($|\det(\mathbf{X})| \leq \prod_{k=1}^{n} \|x_k\|$ if the matrix $\mathbf{X}$ has columns x_k), we have

$$C = \log|\mathbf{I} + \rho\mathbf{H}^H\mathbf{H}| \leq \log\left(\prod_{k=1}^{K}[\mathbf{I} + \rho\mathbf{H}^H\mathbf{H}]_{k,k}\right) = \sum_{k=1}^{K}\log(1 + \rho\|\mathbf{h}_k\|^2) \tag{7.75}$$

We can interpret Equation (7.75) as the favorable propagation condition as Equation (7.73) provides us with the maximum sum-capacity because the equality of Equation (7.75) holds if and only if $\mathbf{H}^H\mathbf{H}$ is diagonal. The capacity can be achieved by one of MIMO detection algorithms (ML, SIC, MMSE, etc.) in the previous section. For example, ML detection Equation (7.65) can be used as follows:

$$\hat{\mathbf{s}}_{ML} = arg \min_{s \in S} \|\mathbf{y} - \sqrt{\rho}\mathbf{H}\mathbf{x}\|^2 \tag{7.76}$$

where S is the finite alphabet of s_k and Equation (7.76) is a least-square problem with a finite constraint.

In a downlink massive MIMO system in a single cell, the received signal at the kth user can be defined as follows:

$$y_k = \sqrt{\rho}\mathbf{h}_k^T\mathbf{x} + n_k = \sqrt{\rho}\mathbf{H}^T\mathbf{x} + \mathbf{n} \tag{7.77}$$

where the base station with M antennas transmits $\mathbf{x} \in \mathbb{C}^{M \times 1}$ to all K users with a single antenna, ρ is the average SNR, $\mathbf{n}$ is Gaussian noise, and $\mathbf{H}$ is the channel matrix. The sum-capacity of the broadcast channel can be expressed as follows [3]:

$$C = \max_{\{q_k\}} \log \det(\mathbf{I} + \rho\mathbf{H}^*\mathbf{D}_q\mathbf{H}^T) \tag{7.78}$$

where $\mathbf{D}_q$ is the diagonal matrix with the kth diagonal element $q_k(q_k \geq 0, \sum_{k=1}^{K} q_k \leq 1)$. It can be achieved by precoding techniques such as dirty paper coding or others. For example, assuming a linear precoding technique, the linear precoded signal vector can be expressed as follows:

$$\mathbf{x} = \sqrt{\alpha}\mathbf{W}\mathbf{s} \tag{7.79}$$

where $\mathbf{s} = [s_1, \ldots, s_K]^T$, $\mathbf{W} \in \mathbb{C}^{M \times K}$ is the precoding matrix, and α is constant satisfying $\alpha = 1/E(tr(\mathbf{W}\mathbf{W}^H))$. Using Equation (7.79), Equation (7.77) is rewritten as follows:

$$y_k = \sqrt{\alpha \rho}\, \mathbf{h}_k^T \mathbf{W} \mathbf{s} + n_k \tag{7.80}$$

and the precoding matrix can be defined in term of the precoder algorithms (maximum ratio transmission [MRT], ZF, and MMSE) as follows:

$$\mathbf{W} = \begin{cases} \mathbf{H}^*, & \text{MRT algorithm} \\ \mathbf{H}^*(\mathbf{H}^T\mathbf{H}^*)^{-1}, & \text{ZF algorithm} \\ \mathbf{H}^*\left(\mathbf{H}^T\mathbf{H}^* + \frac{K}{\rho}\mathbf{I}\right)^{-1}, & \text{MMSE algorithm} \end{cases} \tag{7.81}$$

Example 7.7 *Performance of Massive MIMO*

Consider massive MIMO systems with different numbers of transmit antennas for spatial multiplexing. Compare the performances of massive MIMO systems according to the number of transmit antennas.

Solution

From computer simulation, we can compare massive MIMO systems with 32, 64, 128, 256, and 512 transmit antennas. The simulation configuration is as follows: 32 mobile devices with single antenna, MMSE receiver, 64QAM, TDD, channel hardening, AWGN, and perfect channel estimation. Figure p7.10 illustrates the BER performance comparison of massive MIMO systems. As we can observe from the figure, more transmit antennas provides us with a better performance.

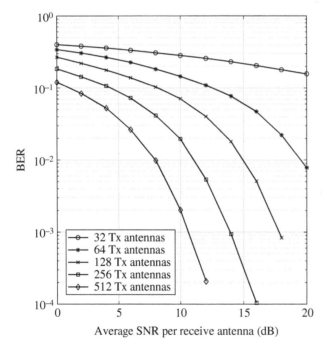

Figure p7.10 Performance comparison of massive MIMO (transmit antennas = 32, 64, 128, 256, and 512).

Summary 7.5 Massive MIMO

1) Massive MIMO has become an essential technique of 5G systems, especially in sub-6 GHz bands.
2) The technical characteristics of massive MIMO can be summarized as follows:
   a. TDD operation is required due to the reciprocity.
   b. Channel hardening removes the fast fading effect. The link quality varies slowly. It is helpful for resource allocation problems.
   c. The closed loop link budget is proportional to the number of antennas in a base station. The link budget improvement is helpful for overall quality-of-service improvement in a cell.
   d. There is a relatively low complexity of precoding and decoding algorithms.
   e. Full digital processing is helpful for both spectral efficiency and energy efficiency.

7.4 5G Multiple Access Techniques

As we briefly reviewed in Chapter 6, 5G multiple access schemes are based on multicarrier techniques. The candidates can be categorized as orthogonal multiple access (OMA) and nonorthogonal multiple access (NOMA). The structure of the 5G OMA scheme is based on conventional orthogonal frequency division multiple access (OFDMA) structure. It is possible to include additional functions such as precoding, windowing, and filtering. Depending on the additional functions, they are divided into CP-OFDM, filter bank multicarrier (FBMC), universal filtered multicarrier (UFMC), generalized frequency division multiplexing (GFDM), guard interval DFT-s-OFDM, and so on. OFDMA has been widely used in 4G systems but further improvements such as lower out-of-band emission (OOBE) are required. Those additional functions will be helpful for meeting 5G requirements. Figure 7.11 illustrates an example of the OFDM spectrum and the FBMC spectrum with eight subcarriers and the prototype filter (K = 4) [18]. As we can observe from Figure 7.11, the FBMC spectrum provides us with lower OOB emissions.

NOMA schemes allow us to multiplex each signal by different power allocation coefficients or signatures such as codeword, sequence, interleaver, and preamble. NOMA techniques can be categorized as power domain multiple access, code domain multiple access, and multiple domain multiple access. Figure 7.12 illustrates 5G multiple access techniques.

7.4.1 OFDM System Design

The OFDM technique is based on frequency division multiplexing (FDM), which transmits multiple signals in multiple frequencies simultaneously. Figure 7.13 illustrates FDM symbols with three carriers with different carrier frequencies, and each subcarrier separated by a guard band.

At the receiver, individual subcarriers are detected and demodulated. One disadvantage of FDM is a long guard band between the carriers. This long guard band makes the spectral efficiency of the FDM system worse. On the other hand, OFDM uses a similar concept but

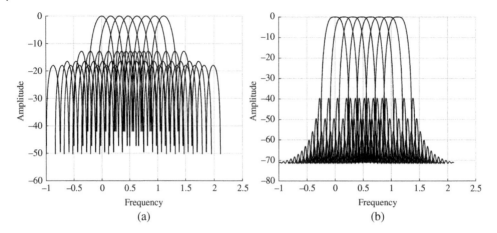

Figure 7.11 Spectrum comparison of (a) OFDM and (b) FBMC with eight subcarriers and a prototype filter (K = 4).

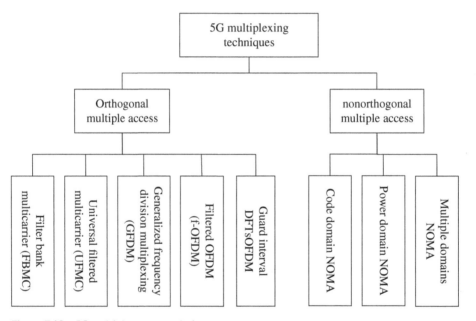

Figure 7.12 5G multiple access techniques.

increases the spectral efficiency by reducing the guard band between the subcarriers. This can be achieved by orthogonality characteristic of the OFDM system.

Figure 7.14 illustrates OFDM symbols with three subcarriers. These subcarriers are overlapping. A part of the subcarrier C passes through the frequencies of the subcarrier $C-1$ and the subcarrier $C+1$. The side lobes radiated by the adjacent subcarriers ($C-1$ and $C+1$) cause interference to the subcarrier C. However, this overlapping is acceptable due to the orthogonality. The OFDM system uses multiple subcarriers. Thus, it needs multiple local oscillators to generate them and multiple modulators to transmit them. However,

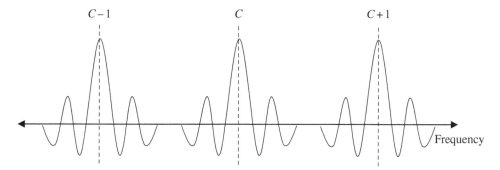

Figure 7.13 FDM with three carriers.

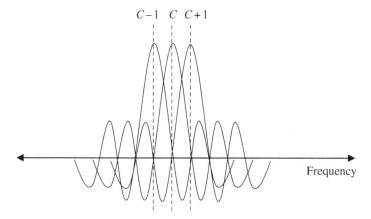

Figure 7.14 OFDM with three subcarriers.

a practical OFDM system uses fast Fourier transform (FFT) to generate this parallel data sequence. This is a big benefit because a local oscillator is expensive and not easy to implement. In the transmitter of the OFDM system, the data sequences are passed to inverse fast Fourier transform (IFFT) and these data sequences are converted into parallel data sequences which are combined by multiple subcarriers while maintaining the orthogonality between subcarriers. In the receiver, the parallel data sequences are converted into the serial data sequences by FFT. Although the OFDM system overcomes interferences in the frequency domain by orthogonality, the interference problem still exists in the time domain. One of the major problems in wireless communication systems is ISI. This is caused by multipaths, as discussed in Chapter 3, and one important reason is a distorted original signal. In the OFDM system, a cyclic prefix (CP) or zero padding (ZP) is used to mitigate the effects of multipath propagation. This can be represented as a guard period located just in front of the data, and able to mitigate delay spreads. We consider an OFDM system with N parallel data sequences as shown in Figure 7.15.

The baseband modulated symbol of the OFDM system can be represented as follows:

$$x(t) = \frac{1}{\sqrt{T_s}} \sum_{k=0}^{N-1} X_k e^{j2\pi f_k \frac{t}{T_s}}, \quad nT_s \le t \le (n+1)T_s \tag{7.82}$$

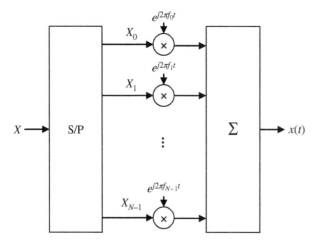

Figure 7.15 OFDM transmitter with N parallel data sequences.

where X_k is the baseband modulated symbol such as BPSK, QPSK, or QAM, and N is the total number of subcarriers. In this OFDM symbol, we can observe one subcarrier $(c_{k_1}(t))$ is orthogonal to another subcarrier $(c_{k_2}(t))$ as follows:

$$\frac{1}{T_s} \int_0^{T_s} c_{k_1}(t) c_{k_2}{}^*(t)\, dt = \frac{1}{T_s} \int_0^{T_s} e^{j2\pi f_{k_1} \frac{t}{T_s}} e^{-j2\pi f_{k_2} \frac{t}{T_s}}\, dt \tag{7.83}$$

$$= \frac{1}{T_s} \int_0^{T_s} e^{j2\pi(f_{k_1} - f_{k_2})\frac{t}{T_s}}\, dt = \begin{cases} 1, k_1 = k_2 \\ 0, k_1 \neq k_2 \end{cases} \tag{7.84}$$

The subcarrier spacing is expressed as follows:

$$\Delta f = f_k - f_{k-1} = \frac{1}{T_s} \tag{7.85}$$

Thus, Equation (7.82) is expressed as follows:

$$x(t) = \frac{1}{\sqrt{T_s}} \sum_{k=0}^{N-1} X_k e^{j2\pi k \frac{t}{T_s}}, \quad nT_s \leq t \leq (n+1)T_s \tag{7.86}$$

In addition, we can regard this signal as a discrete OFDM symbol when sampling the signal in every T_s/N. Thus, the OFDM symbol is expressed as follows:

$$x(n) = x\left(\frac{nT_s}{N}\right) = \frac{1}{\sqrt{T_s}} \sum_{k=0}^{N-1} X_k e^{j2\pi k \frac{1}{T_s} \frac{nT_s}{N}} = \frac{1}{\sqrt{T_s}} \sum_{k=0}^{N-1} X_k e^{j\frac{2\pi kn}{N}} \tag{7.87}$$

We represent the OFDM transmitter using IFFT (IDFT) as shown in Figure 7.16.

When we insert a cyclic prefix as a guard interval, we have the following OFDM symbol:

$$x(t) = \frac{1}{\sqrt{T_s}} \sum_{k=0}^{N-1} X_k e^{j2\pi k \frac{t}{T_s}}, \quad nT_s - T_g \leq t \leq (n+1)T_s \tag{7.88}$$

where T_g is a cyclic prefix length. This baseband signal is up-converted to a carrier frequency f_c and we obtain the following for the transmitted OFDM signal:

$$s(t) = Re\{\sqrt{2}x(t)e^{j2\pi f_c t}\} \tag{7.89}$$

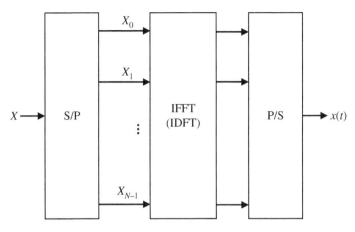

Figure 7.16 OFDM transmitter using IFFT/IDFT.

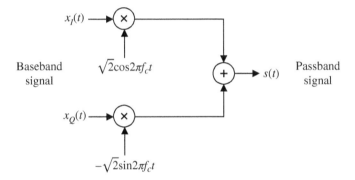

Figure 7.17 Up-conversion from the baseband signal to the passband signal.

The complex baseband signal $x(t)$ is represented in terms of real and imaginary parts as follows:

$$x(t) = x_I(t) + jx_Q(t) \tag{7.90}$$

Equation (7.89) is rewritten as follows:

$$s(t) = \sqrt{2}(x_I(t) \cos 2\pi f_c t - x_Q(t) \sin 2\pi f_c t) \tag{7.91}$$

The up-conversion from the baseband signal $x(t)$ to the passband signal $s(t)$ is illustrated in Figure 7.17.

In the receiver, we detect the following received signal $r(t)$:

$$r(t) = s(t) + n(t) \tag{7.92}$$

and then perform down-conversion from the passband signal to the baseband signal as shown in Figure 7.18.

We perform the synchronization process using the baseband signal $y(t)$. The OFDM signal is very sensitive to synchronization errors such as ISI and inter-carrier interference

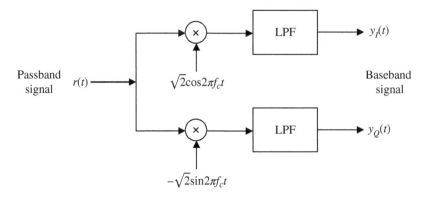

Figure 7.18 Down-conversion from the passband signal to the baseband signal.

(ICI). Thus, this process is very important and should be implemented very carefully. Generally, the synchronization of the OFDM system is composed of three stages: symbol timing synchronization, carrier frequency/phase offset synchronization, and sampling clock/sampling frequency synchronization. After removing the CP, the baseband signal is extracted by a FFT process as follows:

$$y_k(n) = \frac{1}{\sqrt{T_s}} \int_{nT_s}^{(n-1)T_s} y(t) e^{-j2\pi k \frac{t}{T_s}} \, dt = \widetilde{X_k} + I_k + N_k \tag{7.93}$$

where $\widetilde{X_k}, I_k,$ and N_k are the estimated signal, interference, and AWGN, respectively. Equation (7.93) includes interferences. Therefore, we need to remove the undesired part and equalization should be carried out. The blocks of the conventional OFDM system are illustrated in Figure 7.19. The OFDMA is a multiple access scheme based on the OFDM technique. The subcarriers in the OFDM system are allocated to users. However, the subcarriers are shared by multiple users in the OFDMA system. The OFDMA system uses not only time domain resource but also frequency domain resource. Thus, we can achieve a higher spectral efficiency than the other multiple access schemes. In addition, its structure is well matched with MIMO systems. Therefore, many broadband wireless communication systems have adopted MIMO-OFDM/OFDMA systems.

Example 7.8   OFDM System Design
Consider the following design requirements, and design the OFDM system.

Requirements	Values
Speed	80 kmph
Carrier frequency	2 GHz
Tolerable delay spread	10 μs
Bandwidth	500 kHz
Target data rate	1 Mbps

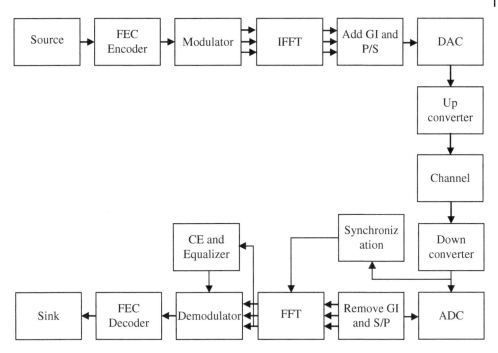

Figure 7.19 Conventional OFDM-based communication system.

Solution

From the required maximum speed (80 kmph [=22 m s^{-1}]) and the carrier frequency (2 GHz [wavelength = 0.15 m = 3 × 10^8 m s^{-1}/2 × 10^9 s^{-1}]), we calculate the maximum Doppler shift (f_m) as follows:

$$f_m = \frac{v}{\lambda} = \frac{22 \text{ m/s}}{0.15 \text{ m}} = 146 \text{ Hz}$$

From this result and the tolerable delay spread (10 μs), the coherence time is

$$T_c = \frac{0.423}{146 \text{ Hz}} = 2.9 \text{ ms}$$

and the coherence bandwidth is

$$B_c \approx \frac{1}{5\tau_{rms}} = \frac{1}{5 \cdot 10\mu s} = 20 \text{ kHz}$$

From the tolerable delay spread, the guard interval is 40 μs (10 μs × 4) and the OFDM symbol duration is 0.24 ms (40 μs × 6). The DFT period is 0.2 ms (0.24 ms − 40 μs). The OFDM symbol duration is the inverse of the subcarrier spacing. Thus, the subcarrier spacing is calculated by the DFT period as follows:

$$\text{Subcarrier spacing} = \frac{1}{0.2 \text{ ms}} = 5 \text{ kHz}$$

This value satisfies the condition that subcarrier spacing should be less than 20 kHz. The ICI power corresponding to the Doppler shift is calculated as follows:

$$P_{ici} \le \frac{1}{12}\left(2\pi(146)\left(\frac{1}{5 \times 10^3}\right)\right)^2 = 0.0028 = -25.5 \text{ dB}$$

This ICI power is less than noise and co-channel interference. The required total number of data subcarriers is calculated as follows:

$$\frac{500\,\text{kHz}}{5\,\text{kHz}} = 100$$

This result means the total number of data subcarriers should be smaller than 100. The sampling rate for pilot spacing is

$$f_p \le \frac{1}{2 \cdot 10\,\mu s \cdot 5\,\text{kHz}} = 10$$

and the normal CP is $18\,\mu s$ ($=0.24\,\text{ms} \times 0.075$). Thus, we can configure the parameters of the OFDM system as follows: since the target data rate is 1 Mbps, we need to contain 200 bits per one OFDM symbol ($=1\,\text{Mbps} \times 0.2\,\text{ms}$). We can choose 100 data subcarriers. The modulation scheme is QPSK modulation without coding or 16 QAM with code rate $\frac{1}{2}$. Thus, the DFT size can be chosen as 128. The number of pilot subcarriers can be selected as 12. When we choose 10 guard subcarriers and 6 null subcarriers, subcarriers of the OFDM system can be composed of data, pilots, guard subcarriers, and null subcarriers as follows:

128 DFT size = 100 data subcarriers + 12 pilots subcarriers

+ 10 guard subcarriers + 6 null carriers

In [19], the optimal pilot subcarrier allocation for AWGN channel is described. The pilot subcarrier set is expressed as follows:

$$\left\{ i, i + \frac{N}{N_p}, i + \frac{2N}{N_p}, \dots, i + \frac{(N_p - 1)N}{N_p} \right\}$$

where $i = 0, 1, 2, \dots, N/N_p - 1$ and N_p is the number of pilot subcarriers. One possible pilot allocation set is [0 10 21 32 42 53 64 74 85 96 106 117]. The interval of pilot subcarriers is 10 or 11. We should insert pilot subcarriers around both edges of the OFDM symbol and also consider guard carriers and null carriers. Thus, one possible subcarrier allocation of the OFDM symbol is illustrated in Figure p7.11. The parameters of the OFDM system are summarized in Table p7.1.

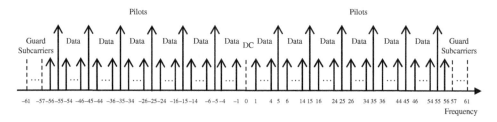

Figure p7.11 Subcarrier allocation in the OFDM symbol for Example 7.8.

Table p7.1 OFDM system parameters.

Parameters	Description	Value
N	DFT size	128
N_d	Number of data subcarriers	100
N_p	Number of pilot subcarriers	12
N_g	Number of guard subcarriers	10
Δf	Subcarrier spacing	5 kHz
T_{OFDM}	OFDM symbol duration	0.24 ms
T_g	Guard interval	40 µs
T_{cp}	Normal CP	18 µs
M-ary/R	Modulation and code rate	QPSK/no coding or 16QAM/1/2

Summary 7.6 OFDM System Design

1) The OFDM symbol duration is the inverse of the subcarrier spacing.
2) The ICI degrades the OFDM system performance. A simple upper bound on the ICI power is defined as follows:

$$P_{ici} \leq \frac{1}{12}(2\pi f_m T_s)^2$$

3) The guard interval is chosen as at least fourfold the rms delay spread.
4) The OFDM symbol duration is practically defined as at least fivefold or sixfold the guard interval.
5) The pilot spacing in the frequency domain should be smaller than the variation of channel in the frequency domain ($f_p \leq 1/2\tau_{max}\Delta f$).
6) The maximum pilot spacing in the time domain is described as $T_p \leq 1/2f_m T_{OFDM}$.
7) The raised cosine function as windowing is defined as follows:

$$w_T(t) = \begin{cases} \dfrac{1 + \cos\left(\pi + \frac{\pi}{\beta T_t}t\right)}{2} & 0 \leq t \leq \beta T_t \\ 1 & \beta T_t \leq t \leq T_t \\ \dfrac{1 + \cos\left(\frac{\pi}{\beta T_t}(t - T_t)\right)}{2} & T_t \leq t \leq (1 + \beta)T_t \end{cases}$$

where β and T_t are the roll-off factor and $T_s + T_g$, respectively.

7.4.2 FBMC, GFDM, and UFMC

The FBMC with offset quadrature amplitude modulation (OQAM) is one candidate for 5G waveforms. Basically, the FBMC-OQAM system adopts pulse-shaping filters and does not require a CP. Thus, it can provide us with improved spectral efficiency, better spectral shaping, lower ISI, and low OOB emissions. We consider an FBMC-OQAM system with N subcarriers and M complex input symbols [20]. The complex input symbols can be written as follows:

$$C_m^n = R_m^n + jI_m^n, \ 0 \le n \le N-1, \ 0 \le m \le M-1 \tag{7.94}$$

where N and M are a positive integer. R_m^n and I_m^n are the real and imaginary parts of the mth symbol on the nth subcarriers, respectively. The mth symbols on all subcarriers form a data block as follows:

$$\boldsymbol{C_m} = [C_m^0, C_m^1, \dots, C_m^{N-1}]^T, \ 0 \le n \le N-1 \tag{7.95}$$

The real and imaginary parts of the symbol are staggered in the time domain by $T/2$ where T is the symbol period. The symbols are passed through a bank of synthesis filters and modulated with N subcarriers where the subcarrier spacing is $1/T$. This means the real and imaginary parts of the complex symbol are transmitted with a time offset of half symbol duration ($T/2$). The modulated signal in the time domain with M symbols and N subcarriers can be expressed as follows [21]:

$$s(t) = \sum_{m=0}^{2M-1} \sum_{n=0}^{N-1} x_m^n h(t - mT/2) e^{j\frac{2\pi}{T}nt} e^{j\phi_m^n} \tag{7.96}$$

where x_m^n is the mapping signal from the complex input symbols with the following property:

$$x_m^n = \begin{cases} (1-\gamma)R_m^n + \gamma I_m^n, \text{if m is even} \\ \gamma R_m^n + (1-\gamma)I_m^n, \text{if m is odd} \end{cases}, \ \gamma \in \{0,1\} \tag{7.97}$$

$h(t)$ is the impulse response of the prototype filter, and $e^{j\phi_m^n}$ is a phase term to be $\frac{\pi}{2}(m + n) - \pi mn$ [21]. Basically, the overlapping ratio of consecutive symbols is highly related to the length of the prototype filter. We consider the prototype filter designed by [19]. Basically, the prototype filter response is designed as K (overlapping factor) times longer than N subcarriers. Thus, the length of the prototype filter response is $L = KN$. The FBMC-OQAM signal is composed of N subcarriers and spreads beyond one FBMC-OQAM symbol period. Thus, the combined signal causes a high peak-to-average power ratio (PAPR). In order to implement Equation (7.94), we need N up-samplers and N filters and the filtering process should be applied to each subcarrier. This is a big burden to a transmitter. Thus, the polyphase network (PPN) implementation as the equivalent time domain version is used to reduce the complexity. Figure 7.20 illustrates a FBMC transmitter and receiver.

GFDM uses circular shifted filters for pulse shaping and reduces out-of-block leakage. Due to the flexible structure of GFDM, OFDM and single carrier frequency division multiplexing (SC-FDM) can be regarded as special cases [22]. GFDM is based on an independent modulation block consisting of a number of subcarriers and subsymbols. The subcarriers

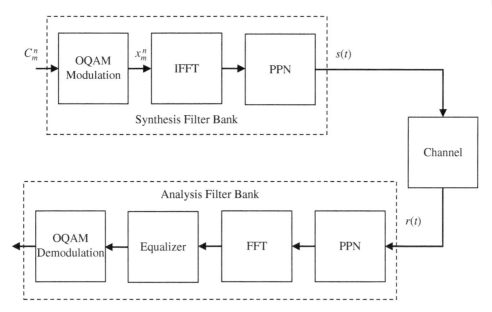

Figure 7.20 FBMC transmitter and receiver.

are filtered with a prototype filter circularly shifted in time and frequency. It allows us to reduce the OOB emissions. However, the subcarrier filtering causes nonorthogonal subcarriers and increases ISI and ICI. On the receiver side, an efficient technique such as matched file with iterative interference cancellation [23] is used and it achieves the same performance as OFDM systems. We consider a GFDM system with N time samples and M frequency samples. The transmit signal of the GFDM system is represented as follows:

$$s(t) = \sum_{m=0}^{M-1} \sum_{n=0}^{N-1} x_m^n g((t - mN)_{NM}) e^{j\frac{2\pi}{N}nt}, 0 \le t \le NM - 1 \tag{7.98}$$

where x_m^n is the transmit symbol with n subcarrier and m subsymbol, $g((t - mN)_{NM})e^{j\frac{2\pi}{N}nt}$ is the circular time and frequency shifted version of the prototype pulse-shaping filter. In the prototype pulse-shaping filter term, $(\ )_{NM}$ represents the NM modulo operation. Figure 7.21 illustrates a GFDM transmitter and receiver.

Unlike filtering each subcarrier of FBMC, the total bandwidth of UFMC is divided into sub-bands of equal size and the sub-bands are filtered [24]. The bandwidth of the filter is wider than the one of pulse-shaping modulation and the length in the time domain is shorter. Thus, a ZP prefix is adopted and the interference by the tail of the filter is eliminated. We consider N subcarriers are divided into K sub-bands and each sub-band has $L = N/K$ consecutive subcarriers. The transmit signal of the UFMC system is represented as follows [25]:

$$s(t) = \sum_{k=0}^{K-1} s_k(t) * f_k(t) \tag{7.99}$$

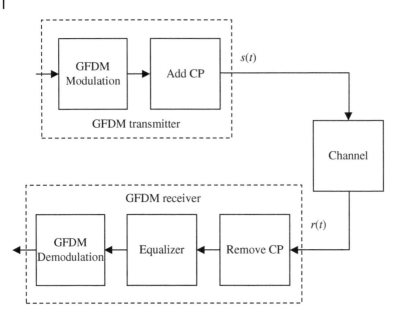

Figure 7.21 GFDM transmitter and receiver.

where the operation * is the convolution, $f_k(t)$ is the filter coefficient of sub-band k, and $s_k(t)$ is the OFDM signal over sub-band k as follows:

$$
\begin{aligned}
s_k(t) &= \sum_{m=0}^{M-1} s_{k,m}(t - m(N + N_g)) \\
&= \begin{cases} s_{k,m}(t - m(N + N_g)), m(N + N_g) \leq t \leq m(N + N_g) + N - 1 \\ 0, m(N + N_g) \geq t, m(N + N_g) + N - 1 \leq t \end{cases}
\end{aligned}
\tag{7.100}
$$

where N_g is the length of the ZP prefix, M is the number of symbol blocks, and $s_{k,m}(t)$ is the signal at the subcarrier k and symbol m as follows:

$$
s_{k,m}(t) = \sum_{l=(k-1)L}^{kL-1} x_{l,m} e^{j\frac{2\pi}{N} tl}, \quad 0 \leq t \leq N - 1
\tag{7.101}
$$

where $x_{l,m}$ is the lth transmit symbol at the symbol m. In the receiver, the signal length is $N + N_g$ and it is zero-padded to have $2N$ length. Thus, $2N$ point FFT is performed. After the $2N$ point FFT is carried out, only even numbers of subcarriers are detected. Figure 7.22 illustrates the transmitter and receiver of UFMC.

Example 7.9 *Comparison of OFDM and UFMC*

Consider the following parameters, and compare the spectrums of OFDM and UFMC:

FFT size = 512, UFMC sub – band size = 40 subcarriers,

number of sub – bands in UFMC = 5, filter length = 43,

modulation = 4QAM, and SNR = 10 dB.

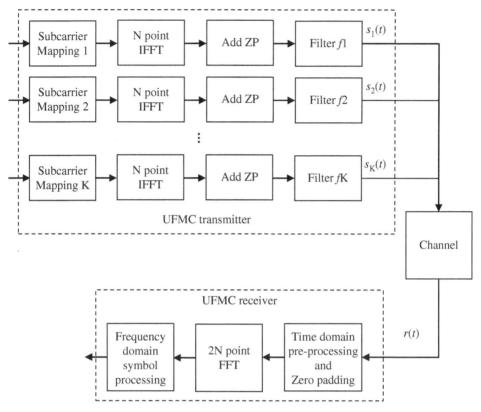

Figure 7.22 UFMC transmitter and receiver.

Solution

From the computer simulation, we can obtain Figure p7.12. As we can observe from the figure, UFMC provides us with lower OOB emissions.

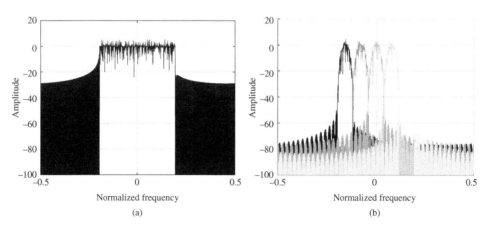

Figure p7.12 Comparison of (a) OFDM with 200 subcarriers and (b) UFMC with 5 sub-bands and 40 subcarriers at each sub-band.

Summary 7.7 FBMC, GFDM, and UFMC

1) FBMC adopts pulse-shaping filters and does not require a CP. Thus, it can provide us with improved spectral efficiency, better spectral shaping, lower inter-symbol interference, and low OOB radiation.
2) GFDM uses circular shifted filters for pulse shaping and reduces out-of-block leakage. Due to the flexible structure of GFDM, OFDM, and SC-FDM can be regards as special cases.
3) The total bandwidth of UFMC is divided into sub-bands of equal size, and the sub-bands are filtered. The bandwidth of the filter is wider than the one of pulse-shaping modulation, and the length in the time domain is shorter. Thus, a zero padding (ZP) prefix is adopted and the interference by the tail of the filter is eliminated.

7.5 5G Channel Coding and Modulation

In order to achieve high spectral efficiency, channel coding and modulation are key components of the physical layer in 5G communication systems. Cellular communication systems have evolved from 1G to 5G and provided us with different services. In terms of error correction coding techniques, there was a big jump from 2G to 3G because turbo codes [26] and LDPC codes [27, 28] were included. It was a paradigm shift. However, error correction coding schemes in 3G and 4G are almost the same. Another big jump from 4G to 5G is required because 5G faces new challenges such as much higher spectral efficiency and severe interferences in heterogeneous networks. In 5G systems, LDPC codes and polar codes are used. Spectral efficiency η represents the information rate over a given bandwidth and can be defined as follows:

$$\eta = \frac{R}{W} \text{ [bits/s/Hz]} \tag{7.102}$$

when one coding scheme transmits R [bits s^{-1}] over an AWGN of bandwidth W [Hz]. Shannon described the relationship between the spectral efficiency and SNR for reliable transmission as follows:

$$\eta < \log_2(1 + \text{SNR}) \tag{7.103}$$

As we can observe from Equation (7.103), the spectral efficiency is increased depending on SNR. Basically, high spectral efficiency can be achieved when adopting a high-order modulation and low code rate at a high SNR. However, the transmit power is limited in practical wireless communication systems as follows:

$$\text{SNR} > 2^\eta - 1 \tag{7.104}$$

and a high-order modulation scheme is vulnerable to the wireless channel impairments of a practical wireless communication system and degraded bit error performance. A low code rate provides us with a low BER but redundancy is increased. Thus, the high-order modulation and low code rate is restrictively used.

7.5.1 LDPC Codes

In 1962, R. Gallager [27] originally invented LDPC codes in his PhD thesis. However, the LDPC codes did not get much attention until D.J.C. Mackay and R.M. Neal [28] rediscovered them, because the era of transistors had just started and the hardware technology did not cover the complexity of LDPC encoding and decoding at that time. After turbo codes emerged in 1993, many researchers made an effort to understand how the turbo codes achieve near the Shannon limit and tried to find another new error correction code. In 1996, Mackay and Neal designed a new linear block code including many similar features of turbo codes such as randomness, large block length, and iterative decoding. They soon realized that the new codes are almost the same as Gallager's LDPC codes. After that, irregular LDPC codes as a generalization of Gallager's LDPC codes were introduced by Luby et al. [29] in 1998. The irregular LDPC codes have became the most powerful current error control codes. When comparing with the turbo codes, LDPC codes have several advantages. Firstly, a random interleaver is not required. Secondly, it has a better block error rate and a lower error floor. Thirdly, iterative decoding of LDPC codes is a simpler operation even if it requires more iterations. The most highlighted advantage is that it is patent-free.

As the name implies, LDPC codes are linear block codes with a sparse parity check matrix $\mathbf{H}$. The sparseness of the parity check matrix $\mathbf{H}$ means that it contains relatively few 1s among many 0s. The sparseness enables LDPC codes to increase the minimum distance. Typically, the minimum distance of LDPC codes linearly increases according to the codeword length. Basically, LDPC codes are the same as conventional linear block codes except for the sparseness. The difference between LDPC codes and conventional linear block codes is the decoding method. The decoder of the conventional linear block codes is generally based on ML decoding, which receives n bits codeword and decides the most likely k bits message among the 2^k possible messages. Thus, the codeword length is short and the decoding complexity is low. On the other hand, LDPC codes are iteratively decoded using a graphical representation (Tanner graph) of $\mathbf{H}$. The Tanner graph consists of bit (or variable, symbol) nodes and check (or parity check) nodes. The bit nodes and the check nodes represent codeword bits and parity equations, respectively. The edge represents a connection between bit nodes and check nodes, if and only if the bit is involved in the corresponding parity check equation. Thus, the number of edges in a Tanner graph equals the number of 1s in the parity check matrix $\mathbf{H}$. Figure 7.23 illustrates an example of a Tanner graph. The squares represent check nodes (or parity check equations) and the circles represent bit nodes in the figure.

The regular LDPC code by Gallager is denoted as (n, b_c, b_r) where n is a codeword length, b_c is the number of parity check equations (or 1s per column), and b_r is the number of coded bits (or 1s per row). The regular LDPC code has the following properties: (i) each coded bit is contained in the same number of parity check equations; and (ii) each parity check equation contains the same number of coded bits. The regular LDPC code by Gallager is constructed by randomly choosing the locations of 1s with the fixed numbers in each row and column. The rows of the parity check matrix are divided into b_c sets. Each set has n/b_r rows. The first set contains r consecutive 1s descending from left to right. The other sets are obtained by column permutations of the first set.

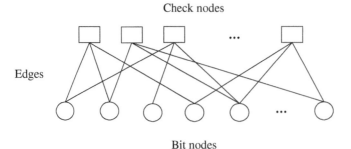

Figure 7.23 Example of a Tanner graph.

Example 7.10 *Regular LDPC Code Construction by Gallager*
Construct the parity check matrix of a (12, 3, 4) regular Gallager LDPC code.

Solution
Firstly, the rows of the parity check matrix are divided into three sets. The first set contains four consecutive 1s in each row as follows:

$$H = \begin{bmatrix} \text{The first set} \\ \text{The second set} \\ \text{The third set} \end{bmatrix} = \begin{bmatrix} 111100000000 \\ 000011110000 \\ 000000001111 \\ \hline 000000000000 \\ 000000000000 \\ 000000000000 \\ \hline 000000000000 \\ 000000000000 \\ 000000000000 \end{bmatrix}$$

Secondly, the second and third set is obtained by column permutation of the first set as follows:

$$H = \begin{bmatrix} 111100000000 \\ 000011110000 \\ 000000001111 \\ \hline 010010001001 \\ 100101000100 \\ 001000110010 \\ \hline 010001000011 \\ 001000101100 \\ 100110010000 \end{bmatrix}$$

As we can observe from the above parity check matrix, each coded bit is contained in three parity check equations (3 bits per column) and each parity check equation contains four coded bits (4 bits per row).

Another LDPC code construction by Mackay and Neal fills 1s in the parity check matrix H from left column to right column. The locations of 1s are randomly chosen in each column until each row with the fixed numbers is assigned. If some row is already filled, the row is not assigned and the remaining rows are filled. One important constraint is that the 1s in each column and row should not be square-shaped. It is important to avoid a cycle of length 4. However, it is not easy to satisfy this constraint. The numbers of b_r and b_c should be small compared with the code length.

Example 7.11 *Regular LDPC Code Construction by Mackay and Neal*
Construct the parity check matrix of a (12, 3, 4) regular Mackay and Neal LDPC code.

Solution
Firstly, the location of 3 bits in each column is randomly chosen from left column to right column by avoiding overlapping until some row with 4 bits appears as follows:

$$H = \begin{bmatrix} 1\,0\,0\,1\,0\,0\,1\,0\,0\,0\,0\,0 \\ 0\,0\,1\,1\,0\,0\,0\,1\,0\,0\,0\,0 \\ 0\,1\,0\,1\,0\,0\,0\,0\,1\,0\,0\,0 \\ 0\,0\,1\,0\,1\,0\,1\,0\,1\,0\,0\,0 \\ 0\,1\,0\,0\,1\,0\,0\,1\,0\,0\,0\,0 \\ 1\,0\,0\,0\,0\,1\,0\,1\,1\,0\,0\,0 \\ 0\,0\,1\,0\,0\,1\,0\,0\,0\,0\,0\,0 \\ 0\,1\,0\,0\,0\,1\,1\,0\,0\,0\,0\,0 \\ 1\,0\,0\,0\,1\,0\,0\,0\,0\,0\,0\,0 \end{bmatrix}$$

When filling in the 9th column, the 4th row and the 6th row of the above matrix contain 4 bits. Thus, we should not assign 1s in the 4th row and the 6th row. We keep filling in the columns, avoiding overlapping. The fully filled rows are as follows:

$$H = \begin{bmatrix} 1\,0\,0\,1\,0\,0\,1\,0\,0\,0\,0\,0 \\ 0\,0\,1\,1\,0\,0\,0\,1\,0\,0\,0\,0 \\ 0\,1\,0\,1\,0\,0\,0\,0\,1\,1\,0\,0 \\ 0\,0\,1\,0\,1\,0\,1\,0\,1\,0\,0\,0 \\ 0\,1\,0\,0\,1\,0\,0\,1\,0\,0\,0\,0 \\ 1\,0\,0\,0\,0\,1\,0\,1\,1\,0\,0\,0 \\ 0\,0\,1\,0\,0\,1\,0\,0\,0\,1\,0\,0 \\ 0\,1\,0\,0\,0\,1\,1\,0\,0\,0\,0\,0 \\ 1\,0\,0\,0\,1\,0\,0\,0\,0\,1\,0\,0 \end{bmatrix}$$

When filling in the 10th column, the 3rd row of the above matrix contains 4 bits. In the same way, we construct the parity check matrix of a (12, 3, 4) regular LDPC code as follows:

$$H = \begin{bmatrix} 1\,0\,0\,1\,0\,0\,1\,0\,0\,0\,1\,0 \\ 0\,0\,1\,1\,0\,0\,0\,1\,0\,0\,0\,1 \\ 0\,1\,0\,1\,0\,0\,0\,0\,1\,1\,0\,0 \\ 0\,0\,1\,0\,1\,0\,1\,0\,1\,0\,0\,0 \\ 0\,1\,0\,0\,1\,0\,0\,1\,0\,0\,1\,0 \\ 1\,0\,0\,0\,0\,1\,0\,1\,1\,0\,0\,0 \\ 0\,0\,1\,0\,0\,1\,0\,0\,0\,1\,1\,0 \\ 0\,1\,0\,0\,0\,1\,1\,0\,0\,0\,0\,1 \\ 1\,0\,0\,0\,1\,0\,0\,0\,0\,1\,0\,1 \end{bmatrix}$$

Similar to Gallager's LDPC code construction, the above parity check matrix contains 3 bits per column and 4 bits per row.

The decoding process of LDPC codes is based on the iteration scheme between bit nodes and check nodes in a Tanner graph. A decoding scheme of LDPC codes is known as a message passing algorithm, which passes messages forward and backward between the bit nodes and check nodes. There are two types of message passing algorithms: the bit flipping algorithm based on a hard decision decoding algorithm, and the belief propagation (BP) algorithm based on a soft decision decoding algorithm. The belief propagation algorithm calculates the maximum a posteriori probability. That is to say, it calculates the probability $P(c_i \mid E)$, which means we find a codeword c_i on the event E (all parity check equations are satisfied). In the belief propagation algorithm, the message represents the belief level (probability) of the received codewords. Each bit node passes a message to each check node connected to the bit node. Each check node passes a message to each bit node connected to the check node. In the final stage, a posteriori probability of each codeword bit is calculated. We should calculate many multiplication and division operations for the belief propagation algorithm. Thus, the implementation complexity is high. In order to reduce the complexity, it is possible to implement it using log likelihood ratios. Multiplication and division are replaced by addition and subtraction, respectively. We call this a sum-product decoding algorithm. In order to explain the belief propagation algorithm, the Tanner graph is modified.

Figure 7.24 illustrates an example of the Tanner graph for LDPC decoding. v_j, x_i, and y_i represent check nodes, bit nodes and received codeword bits, respectively. We express the received codeword as follows:

$$y_i = x_i + n_i \tag{7.105}$$

where n_i is Gaussian noise with zero mean and standard deviation σ. We define two messages (estimations): $q_{ij}(x)$ and $r_{ji}(x)$. The message $q_{ij}(x)$ and the message $r_{ji}(x)$ represent the message from the bit node x_i to the check node v_j and the message from the check node v_j to the bit node x_i, respectively. They can be expressed in the Tanner graph as shown in Figure 7.25.

The message $q_{ij}(x)$ means the probability $P(x_i = x \mid y_i)$ or the probability $x_i = x$ satisfying all check node equations except v_j. The message $r_{ji}(x)$ means the probability that the parity check node (parity check equation) v_j is satisfied when all bit nodes have x except x_i. Thus, message passing can be described as shown in Figure 7.26.

In the AWGN channel, we have the following initial value of $q_{ij}^{\text{initial}}(x)$:

$$q_{ij}^{\text{initial}}(x) = P(x_i = x \mid y_i) = \frac{1}{1 + e^{-\frac{2xy_i}{\sigma^2}}} \tag{7.106}$$

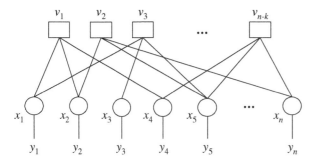

Figure 7.24 Tanner graph example for LDPC decoding.

Figure 7.25 Two messages in the Tanner graph.

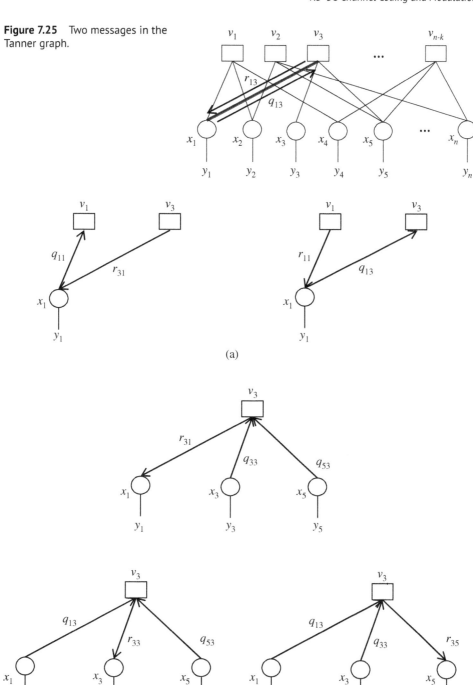

Figure 7.26 Examples of (a) bit node and (b) check node message passing in the Tanner graph.

where $x = +1$ or -1 (assume BPSK modulation). When the received vector y with L sequence is given, Gallager described the probability that the parity check nodes contain an even or odd number of 1s is expressed as follows:

$$P^e = \frac{1}{2} + a\frac{1}{2} \prod_{i=1}^{L}(1 - 2p_i) \tag{7.107}$$

where

$$a = \begin{cases} +1 \text{ for even parity} \\ -1 \text{ for odd parity} \end{cases} \tag{7.108}$$

and p_i is $P(x_i = -1|y_i)$, which is the probability that the codeword bit at i is equal to -1. Thus, the message $r_{ji}(+1)$ is expressed as follows:

$$r_{ji}(+1) = \frac{1}{2} + \frac{1}{2} \prod_{i' \in V_{j/i}} (1 - 2q_{i'j}(-1)) \tag{7.109}$$

where $V_{j/i}$ denotes a bit node set connected to the check node v_j except x_i. We express $r_{ji}(-1)$ as follows:

$$r_{ji}(-1) = 1 - r_{ji}(+1) \tag{7.110}$$

The message $q_{ij}(+1)$ is expressed as follows:

$$q_{ij}(+1) = \alpha_{ij}(1 - p_i) \prod_{j' \in C_{i/j}} r_{j'i}(+1) \tag{7.111}$$

and the message $q_{ij}(-1)$ is expressed as follows:

$$q_{ij}(-1) = \alpha_{ij}p_i \prod_{j' \in C_{i/j}} r_{j'i}(-1) \tag{7.112}$$

where $C_{i/j}$ denotes a check node set connected to the bit node x_i except v_j and the constants α_{ij} are selected to ensure that $q_{ij}(+1) + q_{ij}(-1) = 1$. In this way, we start calculating $r_{ji}(x)$ using the initial values of $q_{ij}(x)$. The message $q_{ij}(x)$ is calculated by $r_{ji}(x)$. Then, we calculate the a posteriori probability (APP) ratio for each codeword bit as follows:

$$Q_i(+1) = \alpha_i(1 - p_i) \prod_{j \in C_i} r_{ji}(+1) \tag{7.113}$$

$$Q_i(-1) = \alpha_i p_i \prod_{j \in C_i} r_{ji}(-1) \tag{7.114}$$

where the constants α_{ij} are selected to ensure that $Q_i(+1) + Q_i(-1) = 1$. Lastly, the hard decision outputs are calculated as follows:

$$\hat{x}_i = \begin{cases} +1, \text{if } Q_i(+1) \geq 0.5 \\ -1, \text{if } Q_i(+1) < 0.5 \end{cases} \tag{7.115}$$

The iteration process is continued until the estimated codeword bits satisfy the syndrome condition or the maximum number of iterations is finished.

Summary 7.8 Belief Propagation Algorithm for LDPC Codes

1) Initialization of $q_{ij}^{initial}(x)$ is

$$q_{ij}^{initial}(x) = P(x_i = x \mid y_i) = \frac{1}{1 + e^{-\frac{2xy_i}{\sigma^2}}}$$

2) The message $r_{ji}(x)$ from check nodes to bit nodes is

$$r_{ji}(+1) = \frac{1}{2} + \frac{1}{2} \prod_{i' \in V_{j/i}} (1 - 2q_{i'j}(-1))$$

$$r_{ji}(-1) = 1 - r_{ji}(+1)$$

where $V_{j/i}$ denotes a bit node set connected to the check node v_j except x_i.

3) The message $q_{ij}(x)$ from bit nodes to check nodes is

$$q_{ij}(+1) = \alpha_{ij}(1 - p_i) \prod_{j' \in C_{i/j}} r_{j'i}(+1)$$

$$q_{ij}(-1) = \alpha_{ij} p_i \prod_{j' \in C_{i/j}} r_{j'i}(-1)$$

where $C_{i/j}$ denotes a check node set connected to the bit node x_i except v_j.

4) The APP ratio for each codeword bit is

$$Q_i(+1) = \alpha_i(1 - p_i) \prod_{j \in C_i} r_{ji}(+1)$$

$$Q_i(-1) = \alpha_i p_i \prod_{j \in C_i} r_{ji}(-1)$$

5) The hard decision output is

$$\hat{x}_i = \begin{cases} +1, \text{if } Q_i(+1) \geq 0.5 \\ -1, \text{if } Q_i(+1) < 0.5 \end{cases}$$

7.5.2 Coding and Modulation for High Spectral Efficiency

In this section, channel coding schemes for high spectral efficiency are discussed. The turbo codes achieve very low error probability, close to the Shannon limit. The important design criteria for the turbo codes are to find suitable component codes that maximize the effective free distance [30], and to optimize the weight distribution of the codewords at a low E_bN_0 [31]. One disadvantage of the original turbo codes is that the error floor occurs at BER 10^{-5} due to poor minimum Hamming distance. Possible solutions are to: (i) design

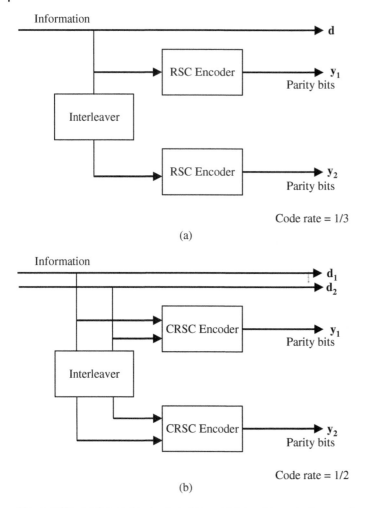

Figure 7.27 (a) Original turbo encoder and (b) duo-binary turbo encoder.

a good interleaver; (ii) increase the number of memories; and (iii) use the non-binary turbo codes such as duo binary turbo codes or 3D turbo codes. Duo-binary turbo codes [32] are composed of two circular recursive systematic constituent (CRSC) codes with two inputs. Its information bits are encoded pairwise. CRSC encoders do not need any tail bits. In [33], many advantages of duo-binary turbo codes are described as follows: (i) better convergence; (ii) larger minimum distances; (iii) less sensitivity to puncturing patterns; (iv) reduced latency; and (v) robustness of the decoder. In particular, the decoder of duo-binary turbo codes can be implemented much more simply because the gap between the MAP algorithm and its simplified version as component decoders is very small. It is very well matched with a high order modulation [34]. Figure 7.27 illustrates the original turbo encoder and duo-binary turbo encoder.

Example 7.12 *Performance of Turbo Codes*
Compare the BER performance of turbo codes.

Solution
We consider turbo codes as defined in CCSDS [35]. Computer simulations are carried out in order to evaluate the performance of turbo codes. The simulation configuration is summarized in Table p7.2. Figure p7.13 illustrates the BER performances of the turbo codes. As we can observe from the figure, the number of iterations is critical to turbo code performance. More than six iterations are required to saturate performance. In addition, the frame size is critical to turbo code performance.

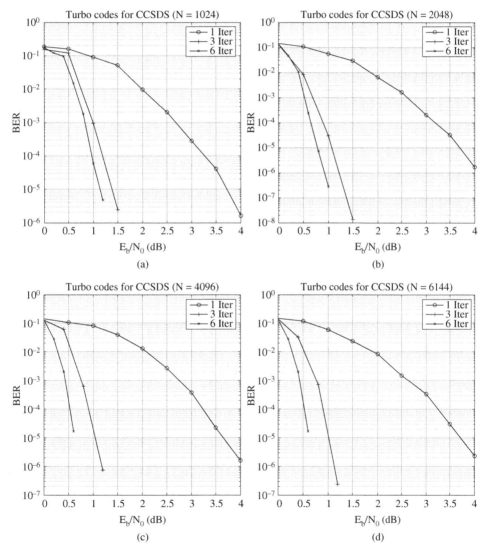

Figure p7.13 Turbo code BER performances with frame size (a) 1024, (b) 2048, (c) 4096, and (d) 6144.

Table p7.2 Simulation configuration for turbo codes.

Parameters	Values
Code rate	1/3
Frame size	1024, 2048, 4096, 6144
Generator polynomial	Poly2trellis(5, [23 33],23)
Modulation	BPSK
Decoder	MAP with 3 bits soft input
Channel	AWGN
Iteration	1, 3, 6
Simulation stop condition	Target error = 50 or max. transmission = 5e8

Example 7.13 *Performance of Duo-Binary Turbo Codes*
Compare the performance of duo- binary turbo codes.

Solution
In computer simulation, the frame error rate (FER) performance of duo-binary turbo code is investigated. Simulation configuration is as follows: 8-state duo-binary convolutional turbo codes, Max-log-MAP decoding, frame size 8000, 10 iterations and AWGN.

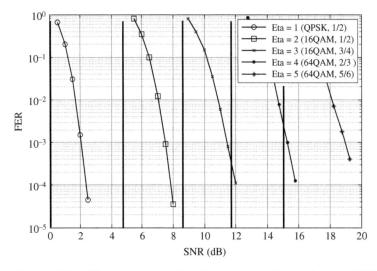

Figure p7.14 FER performance of duo-binary turbo codes, for Example 7.13.

As we can observe from Figure p7.14, spectral efficiencies (η = 1, 2, 3, 4, and 5) are achieved by different modulation schemes and code rates ([QPSK, 1/2], [16QAM, 1/2], [16QAM, 3/4], [64QAM, 2/3], and [64QAM, 5/6]), respectively. Each vertical line represents the minimum required SNR to achieve each spectral efficiency. As we can see, the minimum required SNR is very low. In addition, practical wireless communication systems include many other factors (synchronization overhead, frequency, and phase offset, etc.) that degrade the performance. Thus, it is very challenging to meet high spectral efficiency (beyond 5 bps/Hz) in practice.

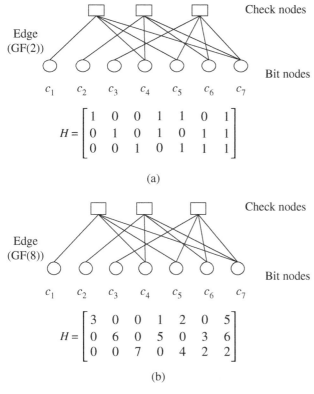

$$H = \begin{bmatrix} 1 & 0 & 0 & 1 & 1 & 0 & 1 \\ 0 & 1 & 0 & 1 & 0 & 1 & 1 \\ 0 & 0 & 1 & 0 & 1 & 1 & 1 \end{bmatrix}$$

(a)

$$H = \begin{bmatrix} 3 & 0 & 0 & 1 & 2 & 0 & 5 \\ 0 & 6 & 0 & 5 & 0 & 3 & 6 \\ 0 & 0 & 7 & 0 & 4 & 2 & 2 \end{bmatrix}$$

(b)

Figure 7.28 Tanner graph and parity check matrix of (a) binary LDPC code and (b) non-binary LDPC code over GF(8).

Non-binary LDPC codes [36] can include non-zero elements of the **H** matrix like Reed-Solomon (RS) codes. Non-binary LDPC codes using iterative belief propagation (BP) show us good performance at medium code lengths ($500 \leq N \leq 3000$) and high-order modulation communications (greater than 16QAM). However, the decoding complexity remains a major obstacle for their commercial application. Figure 7.28 illustrates a comparison of a binary LDPC code and a non-binary LDPC code as an example.

Example 7.14   *Performance of LDPC Codes*
Consider (8176, 7156) LDPC code [35]. The parity check matrix for the (8176, 7156) LDPC code is formed by using a 2×16 array of 511×511 square circulants. The base parity check matrix is 1022×8176 and rank 1020. The structure of the parity check matrix is shown below:

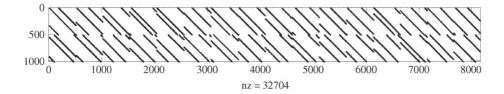

Evaluate the BER performance of the LDPC code.

Table p7.3 Simulation parameters for (8176, 7156) LDPC code.

Parameters	Values
Code rate	7156/8176
Frame size	7156
Modulation	BPSK
Decoder	Iterative message passing algorithm
Channel	AWGN
Iteration	50
Simulation stop condition	Target error = 50 or max. transmission = 1e8

Solution

Computer simulation is carried out in order to evaluate the performance of the (8176, 7156) LDPC code. The simulation configuration is summarized in Table p7.3.

Figure p7.15 shows the BER performance of the (8176, 7156) LDPC code. As we can see, the (8176, 7156) LDPC code with a high code rate shows us good performance, achieving BER 10^{-6} at 3.8 dB.

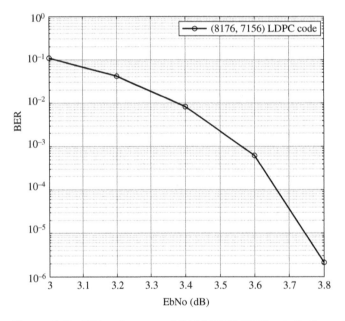

Figure p7.15 BER performance of (8176, 7156) LDPC code for Example 7.14.

The LDPC codes have been verified and widely used in cellular systems. However, several concerns remain:

(i) Long frame size: In order to maintain a good performance, a long frame size is required.

(ii) Long latency: The belief propagation (BP) algorithm of LDPC decoding is based on an iteration scheme. Typically, LDPC codes need about 25 iterations to converge.

(iii) Waterfall region (a sudden drop region in performance): The BER curve of LDPC codes produces a waterfall region. It may cause a BER performance fluctuation.

(iv) Difficult to support multiple code rates.

(v) Encoding design complexity.

Thus, polar codes are used for short frame length in 5G systems.

Example 7.15 *Performance of Non-binary LDPC Codes*

Compare the performance of non-binary LDPC codes.

Solution

Computer simulation is carried out in order to evaluate spectral efficiency of non-binary LDPC codes. Simulation configuration is set as follows: regular (2,4) LDPC over GF (Galois Field) (2^8), target BER 10^{-5}, gray labeling, belief propagation decoding, frame size N = 2000 and 40 000, and AWGN.

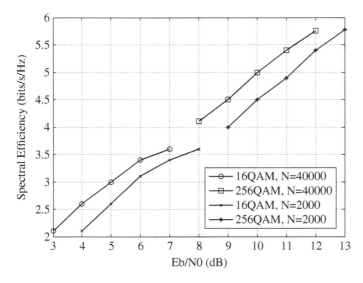

Figure p7.16 Spectral efficiency comparison of non-binary (2,4) LDPC codes over GF (2^8).

As we can observe from Figure p7.16, spectral efficiency increases according to modulation order and frame size. Non-binary LDPC code with large codeword lengths achieved high spectral efficiency (beyond 5 bps/Hz) at relatively low power. The spectral efficiency of the regular (2,4) GF (2^q) LDPC code increases with the field order q, code length, and modulation order.

Adaptive coding and modulation (ACM) techniques can be classified into regular ACM and band ACM. The regular ACM changes modulation order and coding rate according to channel conditions. In order to change the mode, it is important to know the CSI accurately in a timely manner. In a TDD system, we assume the downlink CSI is the same as in the uplink. In a FDD system, the CSI is measured in a receiver and fed back to a transmitter.

Depending on the modulation type and the code rates, the data rate of the system is then decided. On the other hand, the band ACM is part of the hybrid automatic repeat request (HARQ) techniques, which are used, for example, in terrestrial cellular systems. It selects a good subchannel and a bad subchannel and then allocates radio resources into subchannels with different modulations and coding rates.

Example 7.16 *Performance of ACM*
Compare the throughput of ACM modes.

Solution
In order to evaluate throughput with ACM, computer simulations were carried out, as an example, in cellular system environments (SISO, OFDMA, ITU-PB 3 km channel, convolutional code, 10 MHz bandwidth). Figure p7.17 illustrates ACM throughput in terms of modulation order and code rate. As we can observe from the figure, a high order modulation and high coding rate scheme gives us a very good throughput, but it requires a high carrier-to-interference plus noise ratio (CINR). In order to achieve the benefits of the technique, it is important to switch the modes when the pre-defined thresholds are crossed. This is turn requires that the received signal can be measured reliably to tell when the threshold values have been reached.

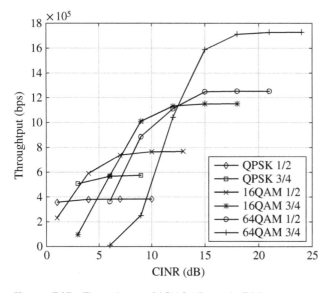

Figure p7.17 Throughputs of ACM for Example 7.16.

Summary 7.9 Coding and Modulation for High Spectral Efficiency

1) The turbo codes achieved very low error probability, close to the Shannon limit. The important design criteria of the turbo codes are to find suitable component codes that maximize the effective free distance, and to optimize the weight distribution of the codewords at a low $E_b N_0$.
2) Duo-binary turbo codes are composed of two circular recursive systematic constituent (CRSC) codes with two inputs. The advantages are (i) better convergence, (ii) larger minimum distances, (iii) less sensitivity to puncturing patterns, (iv) reduced latency, and (v) robustness of the decoder.
3) Non-binary LDPC codes can include non-zero elements of the **H** matrix like Reed-Solomon (RS) codes. Non-binary LDPC codes using iterative belief propagation (BP) show us good performance at medium code lengths ($500 \leq N \leq 3000$) and high order modulation communications (greater than 16QAM).
4) ACM provides us with good BER performance. In order to achieve the benefits of the technique, it is important to switch the modes when the pre-defined thresholds are crossed.

Problems

7.1 Define the throughput at each protocol layer: PHY, MAC, network layer.

7.2 Describe the pros and cons of approaches for increasing network throughput.

7.3 Compare approaches for increasing network throughput in terms of CapEx and OpEx.

7.4 Describe the design considerations for MIMO systems when increasing the number of antennas.

7.5 Compare SVD and QR decomposition of MIMO channels.

7.6 Describe the encoding and decoding process of 4×4 OSBTC.

7.7 Compare throughputs of 2×2 and 4×4 OSBTC and spatial multiplexing.

7.8 Describe the pros and cons of multi-user MIMO and massive MIMO.

7.9 Compare MIMO detection algorithms in terms of performance and complexity.

7.10 Describe the MIMO channel characteristics: channel parameterization, channel hardening, pilot contamination, and favorable propagation.

7.11 Describes the pros and cons of OMA and NOMA.

7.12 Consider the following design requirements and design the OFDM system:

Requirements	Values
Speed	150 kmph
Carrier frequency	3.5 GHz
Tolerable delay spread	10 μs
Bandwidth	10 MHz
Target data rate	20 Mbps

7.13 Compare CP-OFDM, FBMC, UFMC, and GFDM in terms of complexity and OOBE.

7.14 Compare regular and irregular LDPC codes.

7.15 Compare turbo codes, duo-binary turbo code, LDPC codes, and non-binary LDPC codes in terms of complexity, throughput, and BER performance.

References

1 Garey, M.R. and Johnson, D.S. (1979). *Computers and Intractability: A Guide to the Theory of NP-Completeness*. San Francisco, USA: W.H. Freeman and Co.

2 Kim, H. (2015). *Wireless Communications Systems Design*. Wiley, ISBN-10: 1118610156.

3 Tse, D. and Viswanath, P. (2005). *Fundamentals of Wireless Communication*. Cambridge University Press.

4 Björnson, E., Hoydis, J., and Sanguinetti, L. (2018). *Massive MIMO Networks: Spectral Energy, and Hardware Efficiency*. Now Publishers https://doi.org/10.1561/2000000093.

5 Hoydis, J., Hoek, C., Wild, T., and ten Brink, S. (2012). Channel measurements for large antenna arrays. In: *Proceedings of the IEEE ISWCS*, 811–815.

6 Foschini, G.J. (1996). Layered space-time architecture for wireless communication in a fading environment when using multi-element antennas. *Bell Labs Technical Journal* 1 (2): 41–59.

7 Wolniansky, P.W., Foschini, G.J., Golden, G.D., and Valenzuela, R.A. (1998). V-BLAST: an architecture for realizing very high data rates over the rich-scattering wireless channel. In: *Proceedings of the URSI International Symposium on Signals, Systems, and Electronics*, Oct. 1998, 295–300.

8 Alamouti, S. (1998). A simple transmit diversity technique for wireless communications. *IEEE Journal on Selected Areas in Communications* 16 (8): 1451–1458.

9 Tarokh, V., Jafarkhani, H., and Calderbank, A.R. (1999). Space-time block codes from orthogonal designs. *IEEE Transactions on Information Theory* 45 (5): 1456–1467.

10 Hassibi, B. and Hochwald, B.M. (2002). High-rate codes that are linear in space and time. *IEEE Transactions on Information Theory* 48 (7): 1804–1824.

11 Heath, R.W. and Paulraj, A.J. (2002). Linear dispersion codes for MIMO systems based on frame theory. *IEEE Transactions on Signal Processing* 50 (10): 2429–2441.

12 Song, S., Yang, Y., Xionq, Q. et al. (2004). A channel hopping technique I: theoretical studies on band efficiency and capacity. In: *Proceedings of the International Conference on Communications, Circuits and Systems (ICCCAS)*, vol. 1 June 2004, 229–233.

13 Sugiura, S., Chen, S., and Hanzo, L. (2010). Coherent and differential space time shift keying: a dispersion matrix approach. *IEEE Transactions on Communications* 58 (11): 3219–3230.

14 Marzetta, T.L. (2010). Noncooperative cellular wireless with unlimited numbers of base station antennas. *IEEE Transactions on Wireless Communications* 9 (11): 3590–3600.

15 Ionescu, D.M. (1999). New results on space-time code design criteria. In: *IEEE WCNC*, 684–687.

16 Tarokh, V., Seshadri, N., and Calderbank, A.R. (1998). Space-time codes for high data rate wireless communication: performance criterion and code construction. *IEEE Transactions on Information Theory* 44 (2): 744–765.

17 Ngo, H.Q., Larsson, E., and Marzetta, T. (2014). Aspects of favorable propagation in massive MIMO. In: *Proceedings of the 22nd EUSIPCO*, 76–80. Sep. 2014.

18 Bellanger, M. (2001). Specification and design of prototype filter for filter band based multi-carrier transmission. In: *IEEE International Conference on Acoustic, Speech, and Signal Processing*, 2417–2420. May 2001.

19 Negi, R. and Cioffi, J. (1998). Pilot tone selection for channel estimation in a mobile OFDM system. *IEEE Transactions on Consumer Electronics* 44: 1122–1128.

20 Siohan, P., Siclet, C., and lacaille, N. (2002). Analysis and design of OFDM/OQAM systems based on filter band theory. *IEEE Transactions on Signal Processing* 50: 1170–1183.

21 Chang, R.W. (1966). Synthesis of band-limited orthogonal signals for multi-channel data transmission. *Bell System Technical Journal* 45: 1775–1796.

22 Michailow, N., Matthé, M., Gaspar, I.S. et al. (2014). Generalized frequency division multiplexing for 5th generation cellular networks. *IEEE Transactions on Communications* 62 (9): 3045–3061.

23 Datta, R., Michailow, N., Lentmaier, M., and Fettweis, G. (2012). GFDM interference cancellation for flexible cognitive radio PHY design. *In: Proceedings of the 76th IEEE VTC Fall*, Québec City, QC, Canada, Sep. 2012, 1–5.

24 Vakilian, V., Wild, T., Schaich, F. et al. (2013). Universal-filtered multi-carrier technique for wireless systems beyond LTE. In: *Proceedings of the IEEE GLOBECOM Workshops*, Atlanta, GA, USA, Dec. 2013, 223–228.

25 Cai, Y., Qin, Z., Cui, F., and Li, G.Y. (2018). Modulation and multiple access for 5G networks. *IEEE Communications Surveys & Tutorials* 20 (1): 629–646 First Quarter.

26 Berrou, C., Glavieux, A., and Thitimajshima, P. (1993). Near Shannon limit error-correcting coding and decoding: turbo-codes. In: *Proceedings of ICC '93*, Geneva, 1064–1070. 23–26 May 1993.

27 Gallager, R.G. (1963). *Low-Density Parity-Check Codes*. Cambridge, MA: MIT Press.

28 MacKay, D.J.C. and Neal, R.M. (1996). Near Shannon limit performance of low density parity check codes. *Electronics Letters* 32: 1645–1646.

29 Luby, M.G., Mitzenmacher, M., Shokrollahi, M.A., and Speilman, D.A. (1998). Improved low-density parity check codes using irregular graphs and belief propagation. In: *IEEE International Symposium on Information Theory (ISIT)*, 171. 16–21 Aug, 1998.

30 Divslar, D. and McEliece, R.J. (1996). Effective free distance of turbo codes. *Electronics Letters* 32 (5): 445–446.

31 D. Divsalar and F. Pollara. (1995). On the Design of Turbo Codes. *TDA Progress Report 42-123*. Jet Propulsion Lab, Pasadena, California. https://ntrs.nasa.gov/archive/nasa/casi.ntrs.nasa.gov/19960009524.pdf.

32 Douillard, C. and Berrou, C. (2005). Turbo codes with rate-m/(m+1) constituent convolutional codes. *IEEE Transactions on Communications* 53: 1630–1638.

33 Berrou, C., Jézéquel, M., Douillard, C. et al. (2001). Duo-binary turbo codes associated with high-order modulations. In: *2nd ESA Workshop on Tracking Telemetry and Command Systems for Space Applications, TTC'2001*. Noordwijk, the Netherlands, Oct. 2001.

34 Goff, S.L., Glavieux, A., and Berrou, C. (1994). Turbo-codes and high spectral efficiency modulation. In: *Proceedings of IEEE International Conference on Communications (ICC) 1994*, 645–649. May 1994.

35 CCSDS (2011). *TM Synchronization and Channel Coding*. Blue Book Recommended Standard 131.0-B-2. Washington, DC: CCSDS https://public.ccsds.org/Pubs/131x0b2ec1s.pdf.

36 Davey, M.C. and Mackay, D. (1998). Low-density parity check codes over GF(q). *IEEE Communications Letters* 2: 165–167.

8

Ultra-Reliable and Low Latency Communication Systems

Enhanced mobile broadband communication (eMBB) is an extension of 4G broadband services, but ultra-reliable and low latency communication (URLLC) requires a different angle of cellular communications and networks. The research and development challenges of URLLC go beyond the upgrade to the 4G systems. Two key metrics for URLLC systems are low latency and high reliability. The URLLC systems should satisfy a certain level (e.g. 99.999% successful reception rate) of reliability while maintaining user plane latency below a set value (e.g. 1 ms). In 5G systems, multiple latency definitions are used: end-to-end (E2E) latency, user plane latency, and control plane latency. E2E latency is the time that a packet travels from source to destination. It takes time to receive a service across the whole network, and this includes transmitter and receiver processing time, over-the-air transmission time, network queuing, retransmission, routing delay, and so on. In the 3GPP standard [1], user plane latency is defined as the one-way transmission time to successfully deliver a packet from the layer 2 and 3 service data unit (SDU) ingress point to the layer 2 and 3 SDU ingress point of the radio interface, assuming the user equipment is in active state. Control plane latency is defined as the transition time from a most battery-efficient state (e.g. idle state) to the start of continuous data transfer (e.g. active state). In URLLC of 5G systems, the minimum requirements of user plane latency and control plane latency are 1 and 20 ms, respectively [1]. The reliability is defined as the ability of a network to successfully transfer data within a time period. There are several reliability and availability definitions. In the 3GPP standard [1], reliability is defined as the capability to transmit a given amount of traffic within a predetermined time with high success probability. Node reliability is defined as the probability communicating between nodes. The probability can be calculated by packet error probability, packet dropping probability, and queuing delay violation probability. Control plane reliability represents the probability of successful metadata decoding. Availability represents how often the service provides to an end user. It is defined as the probability of an available service in a given coverage and time. It is related to channel impairments and network deployments. For example, 99.9% availability means 1 among 1000 end users do not receive the service. In this chapter, we mainly deal with user plane latency and reliability, and discuss their key techniques.

Design and Optimization for 5G Wireless Communications, First Edition. Haesik Kim.
© 2020 John Wiley & Sons Ltd. Published 2020 by John Wiley & Sons Ltd.

8.1 Design Approaches of URLLC Systems

Simply speaking, latency is a measure of network delay. The network delay is caused by many issues such as router status, distance between network components, network traffics, network architecture and operation, and so on. More specifically, user plane latency for URLLC communications is composed of transmission processing time, transmission time, and reception processing time. In addition, the latency has deterministic components or stochastic components. For example, the deterministic components are transmission time interval (TTI), frame size, decoding and encoding processing time, and so on. These are what we determine and anticipate accurately. On the other hand, the stochastic components are retransmission time, queuing delay, synchronization, and so on. These are what we determine stochastically. In 5G systems, many new features including frame structure (mini-slot, scalable TTI, etc.), multi-access edge computing (MEC), network slicing, hybrid automatic repeat request (HARQ), and uplink (UL) grant-free transmission are adopted to reduce the latency. The frame structure is key for processing time and transmission time, because a longer frame length means longer signal processing time and transmission time. New features (mini-slot, scalable TTI, and so on) of the 5G frame structure allow for the reduction of the processing and transmission times. A scalable frame structure allows us to transmit the same amount of data in a shorter time. Mini-slot enables us to switch transmission rapidly between uplink and downlink. Another important aspect is to reduce the probability of retransmission. In the protocol stack of cellular communications, a cyclic redundancy check (CRC) is included to check the integrity of the received packet. By applying HARQ, data transmission is acknowledged by the recipient. Based on certain decision rules using CRC, the integrity of the received data is checked. If it does not pass the criterion, negative acknowledge (NACK) is sent to request a retransmission. If it passes, successful reception acknowledge (ACK) is sent. The HARQ is a key tool to maintain a certain level of reliability. However, the retransmission has a big cost due to increasing delay and computing power. In 4G, the minimum processing time of ACK/NACK feedback is 3 ms. In 5G, the processing time is significantly reduced as 0.2–1 ms for downlink and 0.3–0.8 ms for uplink [2]. It is important to reduce the retransmission to achieve lower latency and high reliability. MEC reduces the E2E latency significantly by allocating computing resources in the network edge such as radio access networks. Network slicing also allows us to reduce the latency by dedicated computing resources. UL grant-free transmission enables us to have fast uplink access. In this mechanism, a mobile user can transmit data without sending scheduling requests or receiving resource allocation from a network. This approach can reduce the latency significantly but may cause random collisions and suffer from low reliability.

The reliability is a fundamental topic of communications and network systems. In order to communicate with a certain error probability, many physical layer techniques such as channel coding and multiple input multiple output (MIMO) techniques have been developed and combat against many different types of impairments such as multipath fading, shadowing, Doppler effect, inter-cell and intra-cell interferences, phase noise, frequency offset, IQ imbalance, jitter, delayed packet reception, collisions, and so on. In the MAC layer, retransmission techniques are adopted. In higher layers, multiconnectivity and multipath TCP are studied to achieve higher reliability and availability. Various techniques are used to increase the reliability. Key techniques such as MIMO and low-density parity-check (LDPC) codes are already discussed in the previous chapter. Multiconnectivity and highly reliable network topologies are new features of 5G systems. In 3GPP Release 12, dual connectivity was introduced. User equipment (UEs) can be configured to use radio resources from two evolved Node Bs (eNBs): one for control plane and the other for user plane. This scenario is developed for non-standalone mode or small cell. After that, multiconnectivity can be used to improve reliability or throughput, depending on the configuration. A mobile user with multiconnectivity can have data duplication from different radio access networks. Thus, we can achieve ultra-reliability. Multiconnectivity is powerful for ultra-reliability but it is not efficient in terms of radio resource use. On the other hand, if we regard the multiple connections as aggregating radio resources from different radio access networks to a single user, throughput will be improved. Thus, more research works are focused on throughput boosting configuration. The multiconnectivity concept looks similar to a carrier aggregation technique. Carrier aggregation allows a single UE to use multiple frequency blocks (component carriers) simultaneously from a single eNB, but multiconnectivity uses radio resources from multiple eNBs. 5G networks can extend the level of reliability and availability by redundant network access paths. Basically, 5G networks are designed in order to guarantee no network outage. A highly reliable network can be provided by using redundant network access paths. Thus, when network links or components do not work properly, the access paths are rerouted by backup or redundant network components. Table 8.1 summarizes three approaches for reducing the latency.

Table 8.1 Approaches for reducing the latency.

5G techniques	Reducing transmission processing time	Reducing transmission time	Reducing reception processing time	Remarks
Short packet transmission (mini-slot, scalable TTI, etc.)	v	v	v	Deterministic components
MEC	v		v	
High-speed device design	v		v	Deterministic components
Network topology	v		v	
Network traffic management	v		v	Stochastic components
Network slicing	v		v	
HARQ		v		Stochastic components
UL grant-free transmission		v		Stochastic components
Scheduling policy	v	v	v	Stochastic components
Resource allocation	v	v	v	Stochastic components
Synchronization			v	Stochastic components

Wireless communications system design is a complex process. Many design parameters and metrics are trade-off relationships. In order to improve the latency and reliability of wireless communications systems, some metrics might be sacrificed. The URLLC system itself has a trade-off relationship because high reliability requires long latency. When using HARQ, a high enough number of retransmissions is required to guarantee the ultra-reliability, but a higher number of retransmissions requires a longer latency. In addition, reliability and data rate are a trade-off relationship. In coding theory, a higher code rate provides us with a higher data rate. However, the error probability is higher and reliability is lower. Energy efficiency and latency are a trade-off relationship as well. Lean carriers of 5G systems avoid always-on transmission and minimize transmission that is not related to user data delivery. This is helpful for improving energy efficiency and reducing interference. However, the always-on transmission mode will be helpful for quick response. In order to improve latency, mobile devices need to wake up more frequently and check for incoming packets. Thus, wireless communications system designers should find good trade-off points or optimize the systems under reasonable design requirements. In this chapter, we introduce a theoretical background for short packet transmission, analysis latency of 4G and 5G systems, and discuss one 5G key techniques to improve latency.

Summary 8.1 URLLC Design Approaches

1) The research and development challenges of URLLC go beyond the upgrade of the 4G systems. Two key metrics of URLLC systems are low latency and high reliability.
2) The latency has deterministic components (what we determine and anticipate accurately, e.g. TTI, frame size, decoding processing time, etc.) or stochastic components (what we determine stochastically, e.g. retransmission time, queuing delays, etc.).
3) In 5G systems, many new features including frame structure (mini-slot, scalable TTI, etc.), MEC, network slicing, HARQ, and UL grant-free transmission, are adopted to reduce the latency.
4) Reliability is a fundamental topic of communications and network systems. In order to communicate with a certain error probability, many physical layer techniques such as channel coding and MIMO techniques have been developed to combat many different types of impairments. In the MAC layer, retransmission techniques are adopted. In higher layers, multiconnectivity and multipath TCP are studied to achieve higher reliability and availability.
5) Many design parameters and metrics are trade-off relationships, such as reliability vs latency, reliability vs data rate, energy efficiency vs latency, etc.

8.2 Short Packet Transmission

In 5G systems, frame structure has been changed. The new frame structure includes many new features, such as scalability, short packet length, and others. In particular, supporting short packet transmission is a new challenge for 5G systems. For example, when short packets are transmitted via wireless channels, how much metadata (preamble) should we take into account? How much performance degradation is caused in terms of other performance metrics (e.g. throughput, energy efficiency)? What channel impairments are accentuated? Does traditional communication theory fit well? What is the theoretical background? Short packet transmission is a typical mode of URLLC and massive machine type communication (mMTC) applications because sensing data are generated as short length information. It requires a different design approach. From 1G to 4G and 5G eMBB mode, the main design goal is to improve the throughput and increase the number of mobile users in a cell. However, the URLLC mode should be designed in terms of the level of reliability, throughput and latency an application requires. The packet transmission delay can be defined as how long it takes to get all the packets into the physical medium in the first place. The packet transmission delay D_t can be simply calculated by packet size p and data rate r as follows:

$$D_t = p/r \tag{8.1}$$

For example, we have 1024 bytes packet size and 1 Mbps data rate. The packet transmission delay is 8.2 ms ($= 1024 \times 8/10^6$). Thus, if packet size increases, the transmission delay increases. The propagation delay can be defined as how long it takes one bit to travel from a transmitter of the physical medium to a receiver. The propagation delay D_p can be simply calculated by distance d and propagation speed s as follows:

$$D_p = d/s \tag{8.2}$$

where propagation speed depends on physical medium. For example, copper and wireless link have speeds of 2×10^8 and 3×10^8 m s^{-1}, respectively. If the distance between a transmitter and a receiver is 1 km and the data is transmitted via wireless link, the propagation delay is 3.4 µs ($= 1000/3 \times 10^8$). Thus, the propagation delay increases as the distance increases. Packet delay is defined as the time from when the first bit leaves a transmitter until the last bit is received at a receiver. Thus, packet delay is composed of packet transmission delay and propagation delay. In the above example, the packet delay is 8.2034 ms. The propagation delay is much smaller than the transmission delay in cellular systems. The packet size is the dominant factor in the transmission delay. As we reviewed in the previous chapter, the channel capacity is the maximal achievable rate for a given error probability. The fundamental limit was derived in discrete memoryless channel (DMC) and additive white Gaussian noise (AWGN) channel by Shannon [3]. In this limit, large packets are assumed and the Shannon capacity equation does not include the packet size. Namely, the channel capacity is accurate for an infinite codeword length. However, if we deal with short packet transmission, it is not accurate. Thus, asymptotic channel capacity for finite block length was studied in the 1960s by Feinstein and Gallager [4, 5]. In 2010, the finite block length problem was reformulated and non-asymptotic achievability for the finite block length was derived in [6]. The finite block length theory is highly related to short packet transmission and URLLC applications. In particular, the finite block length codeword could represent one realization of the block fading channel. It is useful when we deal with outage capacity in the block fading channel. In error correction coding theory, a transmitter sends an n bits codeword via a noisy channel. The codeword is composed of k bits message and $n - k$ bits redundancy. A receiver decodes the n bits received codeword and

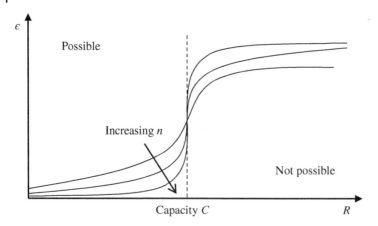

Figure 8.1 Trade-off of error probability and code rate.

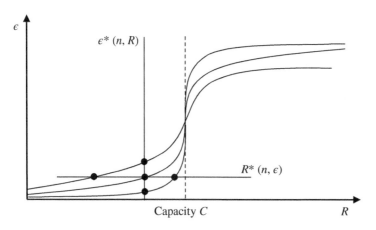

Figure 8.2 Vertical and horizontal asymptotic view.

estimates the k bits message. Figure 8.1 illustrates the relationship between error probability and code rate. When fixing the codeword length n, we observe the relationship between error probability ε (or reliability) and code rate R (or transmission rate). If code rate $(R = k/n)$ is lower (namely, more redundancy), we can expect lower error probability ε. We can regard this problem as high transmission rate systems with low reliability (e.g. 1 Gbps transmission rate system with 90% reliability) or low transmission rate systems with high reliability (e.g. 1 Mbps transmission rate system with 99.999% reliability). When increasing the codeword length n, the error probability is lower.

Figure 8.2 illustrates vertical asymptotic and horizontal asymptotic views. In information theory, vertical asymptotic analysis deals with the error exponent while fixing the rate. Horizontal asymptotic analysis deals with maximum achievable rate for codeword length n while fixing the error probability.

In short packet transmission, we are more interested in horizontal asymptotic analysis. We consider a mathematical communication model in AWGN channel as shown in Figure 8.3.

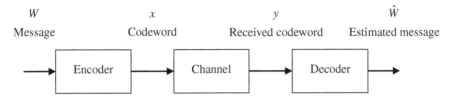

Figure 8.3 Communication model.

A message $W \in \{1, 2, \ldots, M\}$ is encoded into a codeword $\boldsymbol{x}$. The codeword of length n is transmitted through an AWGN channel. The code rate is $R = \frac{1}{n}\log_2 M$. The codeword is in the set

$$\{\boldsymbol{x} \mid \boldsymbol{x}^2 = n\sigma_x^2\} \subset \mathbb{R}^n \tag{8.3}$$

where σ_x^2 is the average transmitted power. This means an equal power constraint. The channel distorts each of the codewords independently. The channel can be described by a probability density function as follows:

$$p_{y|x}(\boldsymbol{y} \mid \boldsymbol{x}) = \prod_{i=1}^{n} \frac{1}{\sqrt{2\pi\sigma_w^2}} e^{-\frac{(y_i - x_i)^2}{2\sigma_w^2}} \tag{8.4}$$

where σ_w is a noise variance. The received codeword $\boldsymbol{y}$ is the output of the channel. A decoding algorithm finds the estimated message $\hat{W}$ from the received codeword $\boldsymbol{y}$. The probability of error is defined as follows:

$$\varepsilon = P[\hat{W} \neq W] \tag{8.5}$$

and the maximum coding rate $R^*(n, \varepsilon)$ is defined as the largest code rate among all codes with n and ε. The capacity C can be expressed as follows:

$$C = \frac{1}{2}\log_2(1 + \rho) \tag{8.6}$$

where $\rho = \sigma_x^2/\sigma_w^2$ is the reference signal-to-noise ratio (SNR) at the receiver and $\sigma_x^2 + \sigma_w^2 = \sigma_y^2$ where σ_y^2 is the received signal variance. The channel dispersion V measures the stochastic variability of the channel relative to a deterministic channel with the same capacity [6]. It is defined as follows:

$$V = \frac{\rho(2 + \rho)}{2(1 + \rho)^2} \tag{8.7}$$

The normal approximation of the maximum coding rate is

$$R^*(n, \varepsilon) = C - \sqrt{\frac{V}{n}}Q^{-1}(\varepsilon) + \frac{\log_2 n}{2n} \tag{8.8}$$

The normal approximation in Equation (8.8) was proved to be a valid $O(1/n)$ asymptotic approximation for achievability bound and converse bound in [6]. The achievability bound means a performance that can be achieved by some encoding and decoding algorithm. The converse bound means a performance outperforming any choice of encoding and decoding algorithms. Figure 8.4 illustrates the normal approximation of the maximum coding rate as a function of the block length at 1 dB and $\varepsilon = 10^{-3}$.

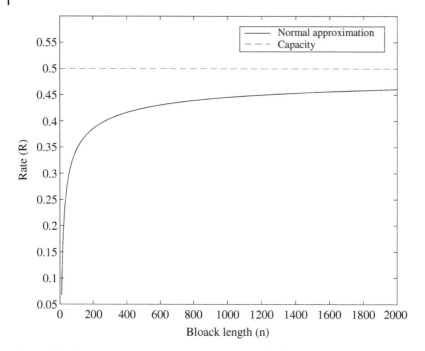

Figure 8.4 Normal approximation as a function of the block length.

In URLLC applications, one of our interests is to find answers about how small a block length is needed to achieve a certain transmission rate and reliability. As we can observe from Figure 8.4, choosing a small block length is efficient as the block length increases. This approach can be theoretical background when dealing with a low latency system with a certain reliability guarantee. The capacity or outage capacity can be obtained from the approximation of coding rate by limiting block length and reliability as follows:

$$C = \lim_{\varepsilon \to 0} \lim_{n \to \infty} R^*(n, \varepsilon) \tag{8.9}$$

As we can observe from Equation (8.9), the capacity represents the maximum transmission rate of reliable connectivity with no restrictions of block length and no errors. Now, we drive an upper bound of code rate and a lower bound of error probability by the Neyman-Pearson test. We consider the following hypotheses:

$$\mathcal{H}_1 : \quad \boldsymbol{y} \sim p_{y|x}$$
$$\mathcal{H}_0 : \quad \boldsymbol{y} \sim p_y \tag{8.10}$$

for a given $\boldsymbol{x}$. When choosing an output pdf p_y, the log-likelihood function is defined as follows:

$$\Lambda(\boldsymbol{x}, \boldsymbol{y}) = \frac{1}{n} \ln \frac{p_{y|x}(\boldsymbol{y} \mid \boldsymbol{x})}{p_y(\boldsymbol{y})} \geq \gamma \tag{8.11}$$

where γ is a threshold. If $\Lambda(\boldsymbol{x}, \boldsymbol{y}) \geq \gamma$, the hypothesis $\mathcal{H}_1$ is selected. Otherwise, the hypothesis $\mathcal{H}_0$ is selected. The probability of Neyman-Pearson missed detection (MD) and false alarm (FA) are expressed as follows:

$$P_{MD}(\boldsymbol{x}, \gamma) = P(\Lambda(\boldsymbol{x}, \boldsymbol{y}) < \gamma \mid \mathcal{H}_1, \boldsymbol{x})$$
$$P_{FA}(\boldsymbol{x}, \gamma) = P(\Lambda(\boldsymbol{x}, \boldsymbol{y}) \geq \gamma \mid \mathcal{H}_0, \boldsymbol{x}) \tag{8.12}$$

and Equation (8.12) depends on both $\boldsymbol{x}$ and γ. The probability of detection P_D can be expressed as $P_D = 1 - P_{MD}$. The hypotheses in Equation (8.10) are modified by the Neyman-Pearson test as follows:

$$\mathcal{H}_1 : \quad (\boldsymbol{x}, \boldsymbol{y}) \sim p_{y|x}p_x$$
$$\mathcal{H}_0 : \quad (\boldsymbol{x}, \boldsymbol{y}) \sim p_y p_x \tag{8.13}$$

and the probability of Neyman-Pearson missed detection (MD) and false alarm (FA) are also modified as follows:

$$P_{MD}(\gamma) = \sum_{x \in C} P_{MD}(\boldsymbol{x}, \gamma) p_x(\boldsymbol{x})$$
$$P_{FA}(\gamma) = \sum_{x \in C} P_{FA}(\boldsymbol{x}, \gamma) p_x(\boldsymbol{x}) \tag{8.14}$$

where C is the selected code. Equation (8.14) is independent of $\boldsymbol{x}$. For a fixed error probability P_e, finite blocklength n, $p_x(\boldsymbol{x}) = \frac{1}{M}, \boldsymbol{x} \in C$, and the chosen p_y, the code rate R is upper-bounded by

$$R \leq \overline{R} \tag{8.15}$$

where

$$\overline{R} = -\frac{1}{n} \log_2 P_{FA}(\gamma) \tag{8.16}$$

and where γ is set by $P_{MD}(\gamma) = P_e$. For a fixed code rate R and finite block length n, the error probability P_e is lower-bounded by

$$P_e \geq \underline{P}_e \tag{8.17}$$

where

$$\underline{P}_e = P_{MD}(\gamma) \tag{8.18}$$

and where γ is set by $\overline{R}$. As we can observe from Equations (8.15–8.18), missed detection (MD) and false alarm (FA) probabilities are directly related to the bounds. Those bounds allow us to evaluate the performance of encoding and decoding algorithms for short packet transmission. The capacity can be calculated by Equation (8.9). Non-asymptotic upper and lower bounds on $R^*(n, \varepsilon)$ are derived in [7]. Figure 8.5 illustrates upper and lower bounds of the maximum coding rate in terms of the block length at 1 dB and $\varepsilon = 10^{-3}$. As we can observe from Figure 8.5, in order to operate at 80% of capacity (code rate = 0.4), we need block length between 177 and 271. The capacity is not so much a practical metric when dealing with short packet transmission.

Example 8.1 *Short Packet Transmission*
Consider non-asymptotic upper and lower bounds on $R^*(n, \varepsilon)$ in terms of the block length n at 1 dB and error probability $\varepsilon = 10^{-5}$. How long a block length do we need to operate at 80% of capacity?

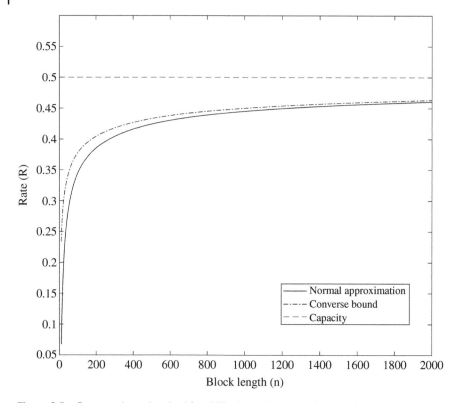

Figure 8.5 Converse bound and achievability bound ($\approx$ normal approximation).

Solution

From Equation (8.8) and reference [7], we have Figure p8.1. As we can observe from the figure, the code rate 0.4 is 80% of capacity. We can read upper and lower bounds and the required block length is $487 \leq n \leq 587$. Comparing with Figure 8.5, Example 8.1 requires a lower error probability. The required block length is longer than the case of a higher error probability.

In addition, this approach is useful for evaluating the performance of error correction codes. The traditional way to evaluate error correction codes is a waterfall curve describing the relationship between error probability and $E_b N_0$. In this curve, a lower code rate basically results in a better performance. When comparing different code rates, the curve does not provide us with a fair comparison. Thus, a normalized rate is defined in [6] as follows:

$$R_{\text{norm}} = \frac{R}{R^*(n, \varepsilon, SNR_{\text{min}})} \tag{8.19}$$

where SNR_{min} denotes the minimum SNR at which the error correction code admits decoding with error probability below ε. The denominator of the right term in Equation (8.19) can be replaced by Equation (8.8) approximately for block length as low as 100 [6]. Another approach is to optimize ARQ systems. Assuming that we have a (n, k) block code and decoding errors are independent for different retransmissions, a long-term ARQ throughput can be defined as (code rate) $(1 - \text{error probability})$. The objective of the ARQ optimization

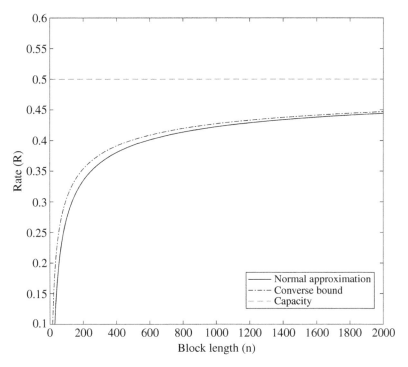

Figure p8.1 Converse bound and achievability bound ($\approx$ normal approximation).

problem is to maximize the throughput as follows:

$$T(k) = \max_n \frac{k}{n}(1 - \varepsilon(k, n)) \tag{8.20}$$

For many channels, the normal approximation in Equation (8.8) is tight [6], and we can equivalently maximize

$$\check{T}(k) = \max_n \frac{k}{n}\left(1 - Q\left(\frac{nC - k}{\sqrt{nV}}\right)\right) \tag{8.21}$$

where C and V are the channel capacity and channel dispersion, respectively [6]. Equation (8.21) can be expressed in terms of code rate R as follows:

$$T^*(k) \approx \max_R R\left(1 - Q\left(\sqrt{\frac{kR}{V}}\left(\frac{C}{R} - 1\right)\right)\right) \tag{8.22}$$

The tight approximation to the optimal error probability as a function of k is as follows [6]:

$$\check{\varepsilon}(k) = \left(\frac{kC}{V}\ln\frac{kC}{2\pi V}\right)^{-1/2}\left(1 - \frac{1}{\ln\frac{kC}{2\pi V}}\right) \tag{8.23}$$

As $k \to \infty$, the dominant terms can be retained as follows:

$$\check{\varepsilon}(k) \sim \frac{1}{\sqrt{\left(\frac{kC}{V}\right)\ln\left(\frac{kC}{V}\right)}} \tag{8.24}$$

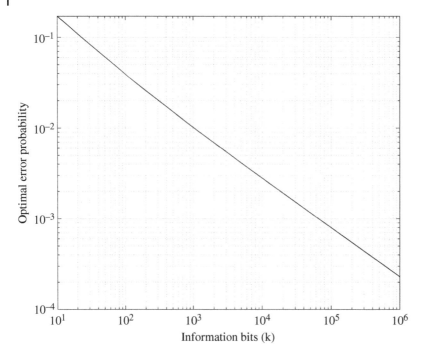

Figure 8.6 Optimal error probability in terms of the information bits.

Figure 8.6 illustrates optimal error probability, maximizing the long-term throughput under ARQ feedback for AWGN channel with SNR 1 dB.

Example 8.2   *Optimization of ARQ System*
Consider that we have a (n, k) block code and AWGN channel and decoding errors are independent for different retransmissions. When transmitting 10 000 information bit at SNR 1 dB, what error probability maximizes the long-term throughput?

Solution
From Figure 8.6, the optimal error probability maximizing the long-term throughput under ARQ feedback for a AWGN channel with SNR 1 dB is as high as 2.8×10^{-3}.

Based on memoryless block fading model, short packet application over MIMO fading channels is described in [8, 9]. Figure 8.7 illustrates an example of memoryless block fading model. In the figure, n_c is the number of time-frequency slots in which the channel is not changed. Namely, it is a coherence interval and the fading channel matrix does

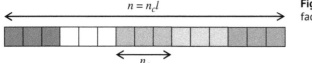

Figure 8.7 Memoryless block fading model.

not change over the coherence interval. l is the number of the coherence interval. As we reviewed the MIMO fading channels in Chapter 7, the ergodic capacity of MIMO fading channels is an ensemble average of instantaneous capacity over all possible MIMO channel matrices. The outage capacity of MIMO fading channels is more useful than ergodic capacity because there is delay limitation. The outage capacity represents the maximum data rate without errors. It is a useful metric for a delay-constrained communication link over slow fading channels. In particular, it is suitable for short packet transmission. When n_c is fixed and l is large enough, a MIMO fading channel varies rapidly over the packet duration. Error correction coding is required over many coherence intervals. On the other hand, when n_c is large enough and l is fixed (e.g. $l = 1$), MIMO fading is constant over the packet duration. We regard this MIMO fading channel as a quasi-static channel. The realization of the MIMO fading channel matrix may be small. In the MIMO channel, signal outages occur during the channel fading, and it may be difficult for the receiver to collect the transmitted information correctly. However, the probability of channel outage is typically small for low rates. A reliable communication link can be made by choosing a sufficient large packet size. For single antenna systems, the outage capacity can be defined as the supremum of the rate R satisfying $P_{\text{outage}}(R) \leq \varepsilon$ [9]:

$$C_{\text{outage}} = \sup\{R \mid P_{\text{outage}}(R) \leq \varepsilon\} \tag{8.25}$$

where the outage probability is given as follows [10]:

$$P_{\text{outage}}(R) = P\left[\log(1 + |H|^2\rho) < R\right] \tag{8.26}$$

where ρ and H are the power constraint and channel matrix, respectively. We can interpret that a reliable communication with short packet error probability in the quasi-static channel is feasible if and only if $\log(1 + |H|^2\rho) > R$. If we consider fast convergence to outage capacity, channel dispersion is zero for the quasi-static channel: namely, $V = 0$. In this case, asymptotic expression of the maximum coding rate $R^*(n, \varepsilon)$ is described in [11] as follows:

$$R^*(n, \varepsilon) = C_{\text{outage}} + \mathcal{O}\left(\frac{\log n}{n}\right) \tag{8.27}$$

where the big $\mathcal{O}$ notation describes the limit of a function and $\mathcal{O}\left(\frac{\log n}{n}\right)$ comprises remainder terms of the order $\frac{\log n}{n}$. Equations (8.25) and (8.26) are fitted in a single antenna channel model. However, Equation (8.27) is available for MIMO channels as well as with/without channel state information. As we can observe from Equation (8.27), $R^*(n, \varepsilon)$ converges to the outage capacity as n goes to infinity, which means that the main component of channel impairments is deep fading, and also the outage capacity is a useful metric for delay-constrained communication link over slow fading channels. Thus, error correction coding is not so effective in this channel and other wireless channel impairment mitigation techniques should be used. The outage capacity and probability of Equations (8.25) and (8.26) for MIMO channels can be expressed [8] as follows:

$$\lim_{n_c \to \infty} R^*(l, n_c, \varepsilon) = C_{\text{outage}} = \sup\left\{R \mid \underset{Q^l}{\text{Inf}}\, P_{\text{outage}}(R, \mathbf{Q}^l) \leq \varepsilon\right\} \tag{8.28}$$

where Inf is the infimum over all positive definite matrices $\mathbf{Q}^l$ and the outage probability is

$$P_{\text{outage}}(R, Q^l) = P\left[\frac{1}{l}\sum_{k=1}^{l}\log\det(\mathbf{I} + \mathbf{H}_k^H\mathbf{Q}_k\mathbf{H}_k) \leq R\right] \tag{8.29}$$

where $\mathbf{I}$ is the identity matrix, $\mathbf{H}_k$ is the $m_t \times m_r$ channel matrix, and $m_t \times m_t$ matrices $\mathbf{Q}^l$ are $\{\mathbf{Q}_1, \mathbf{Q}_2, ..., \mathbf{Q}_l\}$ and satisfy

$$\frac{1}{l}\sum_{k=1}^{l}\text{tr}(\mathbf{Q}_k) \leq \rho \tag{8.30}$$

When $l = 1$, Equation (8.29) is identical to Equation (8.26).

Summary 8.2 Short Packet Transmission

1) The packet transmission delay can be defined as how long it takes to get all the packet into the physical medium in the first place. The propagation delay can be defined as how long it takes one bit to travel from a transmitter of the physical medium to a receiver. Packet delay is defined as the time from when the first bit leaves a transmitter until the last bit is received at a receiver.

2) The finite block length theory is highly related to short packet transmission and URLLC applications. In particular, the finite block length codeword could represent one realization of the block fading channel.

3) The channel dispersion V measures the stochastic variability of the channel relative to a deterministic channel with the same capacity [6]. It is defined as follows:

$$V = \frac{\rho(2+\rho)}{2(1+\rho)^2}$$

where $\rho = \sigma_x^2/\sigma_w^2$ is the reference SNR at the receiver and $\sigma_x^2 + \sigma_w^2 = \sigma_y^2$ where σ_y^2 is the received signal variance.

4) The normal approximation of the maximum coding rate is

$$R^*(n, \varepsilon) = C - \sqrt{\frac{V}{n}}Q^{-1}(\varepsilon) + \frac{\log_2 n}{2n}$$

5) The normal approximation was proved to be a valid $O(1/n)$ asymptotic approximation for achievability bound and converse bound.

6) The traditional way to evaluate error correction codes is a waterfall curve describing the relationship between error probability and $E_b N_0$. In this curve, a lower code rate basically results in a better performance. When comparing different code rates, the curve does not provide us with a fair comparison. Thus, normalized rate is defined as follows:

$$R_{\text{norm}} = \frac{R}{R^*(n, \varepsilon, SNR_{\text{min}})}$$

where SNR_{min} denotes the minimum SNR at which the error correction code admits decoding with error probability below ε.

8.3   Latency Analysis

In a cellular network, there are many network components affecting the E2E latency and each component causes a delay. The cellular network is composed of a radio access network and core networks. The wireless transmission and signal processing are the main elements of the latency calculation. In core networks, the packet exchanges happen via a wired medium such as fiber or copper. The signaling, routing, and packet processing is the main element. In addition, depending on scenarios (e.g. handover, HARQ, etc.), the latency calculation will be different. In [12], the delay models of 4G cellular systems are studied. Figure 8.8 illustrates the delay models for uplink and downlink [12]. In uplink transmission, the first step is to send a scheduling request to a base station (eNB). After receiving a scheduling grant from a base station, a mobile station (UE) is ready to transmit the data packet. If the timing is not aligned, the initial time alignment is performed by the random access procedure from a base station to a mobile station. The timing alignment is about waiting time requirement after the packet is ready for the transmission until the beginning of the next TTI. In addition, the random access procedure serves as an uplink grant acquisition mechanism. The signal establishing procedure including a request, grant and data is performed in subframe with a fixed duration. The data processing time is proportional to the transmission frame size. The control signal processing time is typically shorter than the data processing time. However, it typically has a more complex procedure and protection mechanism. Although the HARQ mechanism is not included in the Figure 8.8, HARQ is a key component of the 5G system and results in significant delay. When considering uplink transmission in frequency division duplexing (FDD), a base station receives a packet in subframe n, and the acknowledgement of HARQ is reported in subframe $n + 4$. If a retransmission is needed, it will be done in subframe $n + 8$. Thus, the HARQ round trip time (RTT) is 8 ms for an uplink in FDD. In time division duplexing (TDD) mode, the RTT relies on TDD configuration. In core networks, the main delay component is the traffic congestion of packets. Typically, latency by 4G core network components is 1–20 ms. As an example, a simple latency calculation for an uplink user plane of 4G systems is as follows [12]:

(i)   Average waiting time for a physical uplink control channel (PUCCH) at a periodicity of 10 ms: 5 ms.
(ii)   Time UE sends scheduling request on PUCCH: 1 ms.
(iii)   Time eNB decodes scheduling request and creates the scheduling grant: 3 ms.
(iv)   Transmission time of scheduling grant: 1 ms.
(v)   UE processing time including decoding of scheduling grant and encoding of uplink data: 3 ms.
(vi)   Transmission time of uplink data: 1 ms.
(vii)   Data decoding time at eNB: 3 ms.
(viii) Thus, the total delay is 17 ms. Another simple latency calculation for a downlink user plane of 4G systems is as follows [12]:
(ix)   Processing time of data: 3 ms.
(x)   TTI alignment time: 0.5 ms.
(xi)   Transmission time of downlink data: 1 ms.
(xii)   Data decoding time at UE: 3 ms.

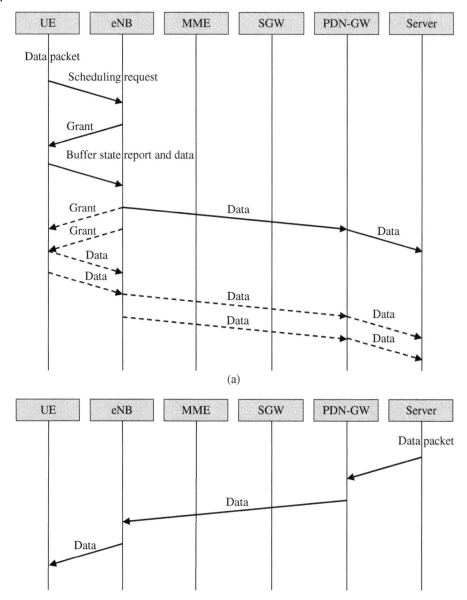

*UE: User equipments, eNB: evolved Node B (base station), MME: mobility management entity, SGW: Serving gateway, PDN-GW: Packet data network gateway

(b)

Figure 8.8 Delay model for (a) uplink and (b) downlink.

Thus, the total delay is 7.5 ms. However, in these calculations, grant acquisition delay, HARQ retransmission, synchronization delay, and others are not included.

Based on a HARQ latency model as shown in Figure 8.9 [12], we can formulate the user plane downlink transmission delay including HARQ delay. As we can observe from Figure 8.9, it takes t_{UE} and t_{eNB} to process the packet and prepare for the transmission in a

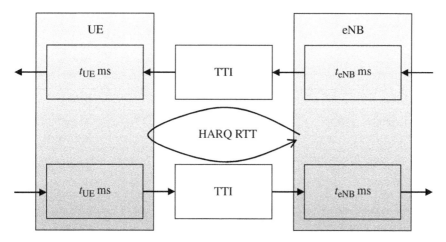

Figure 8.9 HARQ latency model for FDD.

mobile station (UE) and a base station (eNB), respectively. The HARQ RTT is simply calculated as $t_{UE} + t_{eNB} + 2TTI$. The fractions of processing times are represented by w, x, y, and z where $w + x = 1$ and $y + z = 1$. The one-way latency can be computed as follows:

$$d_{one\ way} = yt_{eNB} + TTI + wt_{UE} + n_{HARQ}(t_{eNB} + t_{UE} + 2TTI) \qquad (8.31)$$

where n_{HARQ} is the number of HARQ retransmissions. When we have 0 or 1 retransmission, the error probability of the first transmission is p, and $w = x = y = z = 1/2$, Equation (8.31) can be rewritten as follows:

$$d_{one\ way} = \left(\frac{1}{2} + p\right)(t_{eNB} + t_{UE} + 2TTI) \qquad (8.32)$$

From Equation (8.32), $d_{one\ way} = 0.5(t_{eNB} + t_{UE} + 2TTI)$ for 0% block error ratio (BLER) and $d_{one\ way} = 0.7(t_{eNB} + t_{UE} + 2TTI)$ for 20% BLER. If we have $t_{UE} = t_{eNB} = 2$ ms and TTI = 1 ms, $d_{one\ way} = 0.5(2 + 2 + 2 \cdot 1) = 3$ ms for 0% BLER and $d_{one\ way} = 0.7(2 + 2 + 2 \cdot 1) = 4.2$ ms for 20% BLER. Using the same HARQ latency model, we can roughly calculate the 5G one-way latency. For example, 4G needs 14-symbol TTI for 15 kHz subcarrier spacing and the frame size is 1 ms. However, 5G has two-symbol TTI for 15 kHz subcarrier spacing and the frame size is 0.14 ms. If we consider 60 kHz subcarrier spacing, the frame size is 0.035 ms. The shorter frame size reduces the latency significantly. Assuming that a 5G transmitter and receiver have same processing power as 4G, and the 4G processing delay is given, the one-way latency comparison is summarized in Table 8.2.

The latency calculation in the TDD model is different from the FDD model. Figure 8.10 illustrates the HARQ latency mode when we have a TDD frame structure. As we can observe from Figure 8.10, the user plane one-way latency is composed of node processing delays (t_{eNB}, t_{UE}), radio frame alignment (t_{FA} is the time for frame alignment and depends on the frame structure), and TTI duration. When we have 2.5 ms processing time (1.5 ms at a receiver and 1 ms at a transmitter) and 1 ms TTI duration, the user plane latency in TDD mode can be represented as follows:

$$d_{UP,TDD} = 3.5 + t_{FA} + pt_{RTT} \qquad (8.33)$$

Table 8.2 User plane latency calculations for 5G and 4G FDD.

	4G (3GPP R.10)	5G NR configuration #1 (FDD)	5G NR configuration #2 (FDD)
Subcarrier spacing	15 kHz	15 kHz	60 kHz
Number of OFDM symbols per TTI	14-symbol TTI (1 ms)	2-symbol TTI (0.14 ms)	2-symbol TTI (0.035 ms)
Processing delay			
a. Transmission processing delay	1 ms	0.14 ms	0.035 ms
b. Frame alignment time	0.5 ms	0.07 ms	0.017 ms
c. TTI	1 ms	0.14 ms	0.035 ms
d. Receiver processing delay	1.5 ms	0.21 ms	0.052 ms
One way latency ($= a + b + c + d$)	4 ms	0.57 ms	0.142 ms

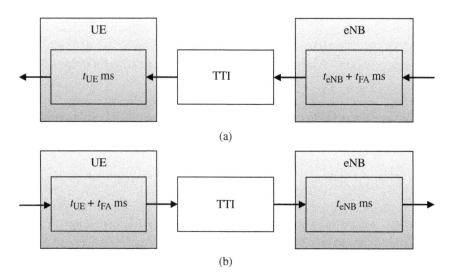

Figure 8.10 HARQ latency model for (a) TDD downlink and (b) uplink.

where t_{RTT} is the average HARQ RTT and p is the error probability of the first HARQ transmission. Tables 8.3–8.6 shows the user plane latency calculations in downlink and uplink for different TDD configurations when BLER is 0% and 10% [13].

In [13], the control plane latency of 4G systems is analyzed. The control plan latency is defined as the required time for a UE to transit from idle state (a battery efficient state) to active state (a continuous data transfer state). In the idle state, there is a radio resource control (RRC) connection in the UE. Thus, the UE monitors the paging channel to detect a call and acquire cell information. Once the RRC is established, the UE enters a connected

Table 8.3 User plane downlink latency analysis with 0% HARQ BLER [13].

Step	Description	UL/DL configuration						
		0	1	2	3	4	5	6
1	eNB processing delay	1 ms	1 ms	1 ms	1 ms	1 ms	1 ms	1 ms
2	Frame alignment	1.7 ms	1.1 ms	0.7 ms	1.1 ms	0.8 ms	0.6 ms	1.4 ms
3	TTI duration	1 ms	1 ms	1 ms	1 ms	1 ms	1 ms	1 ms
4	UE processing delay	1.5 ms	1.5 ms	1.5 ms	1.5 ms	1.5 ms	1.5 ms	1.5 ms
	Total one-way delay	**5.2 ms**	**4.6 ms**	**4.2 ms**	**4.6 ms**	**4.3 ms**	**4.1 ms**	**4.9 ms**

Table 8.4 User plane uplink latency analysis with 0% HARQ BLER [13].

Step	Description	UL/DL configuration						
		0	1	2	3	4	5	6
1	UE processing delay	1 ms	1 ms	1 ms	1 ms	1 ms	1 ms	1 ms
2	Frame alignment	1.1 ms	1.7 ms	2.5 ms	3.3 ms	4.1 ms	5 ms	1.4 ms
3	TTI duration	1 ms	1 ms	1 ms	1 ms	1 ms	1 ms	1 ms
4	eNB processing delay	1.5 ms	1.5 ms	1.5 ms	1.5 ms	1.5 ms	1.5 ms	1.5 ms
	Total one-way delay	**4.6 ms**	**5.2 ms**	**6 ms**	**6.8 ms**	**7.6 ms**	**8.5 ms**	**4.9 ms**

Table 8.5 User plane downlink latency analysis with 10% HARQ BLER [13].

Step	Description	UL/DL configuration						
		0	1	2	3	4	5	6
1	eNB processing delay	1 ms	1 ms	1 ms	1 ms	1 ms	1 ms	1 ms
2	Frame alignment	1.7 ms	1.1 ms	0.7 ms	1.1 ms	0.8 ms	0.6 ms	1.4 ms
3	TTI duration	1 ms	1 ms	1 ms	1 ms	1 ms	1 ms	1 ms
4	UE processing delay	1.5 ms	1.5 ms	1.5 ms	1.5 ms	1.5 ms	1.5 ms	1.5 ms
5	HARQ retransmission	0.1*10 ms	0.1*10.2 ms	0.1*9.8 ms	0.1*10.5 ms	0.1*11.6 ms	0.1*12.4 ms	0.1*11.2 ms
	Total one-way delay	**6.2 ms**	**5.62 ms**	**5.18 ms**	**5.65 ms**	**5.46 ms**	**5.34 ms**	**6.02 ms**

Table 8.6 User plane uplink latency analysis with 0% HARQ BLER [13].

		UL/DL configuration						
Step	**Description**	**0**	**1**	**2**	**3**	**4**	**5**	**6**
1	UE processing delay	1 ms	1 ms	1 ms	1 ms	1 ms	1 ms	1 ms
2	Frame alignment	1.1 ms	1.7 ms	2.5 ms	3.3 ms	4.1 ms	5 ms	1.4 ms
3	TTI duration	1 ms	1 ms	1 ms	1 ms	1 ms	1 ms	1 ms
4	eNB processing delay	1.5 ms	1.5 ms	1.5 ms	1.5 ms	1.5 ms	1.5 ms	1.5 ms
5	HARQ retransmission	0.1*11.6 ms	0.1*10 ms	0.1*10 ms	0.1*10 ms	0.1*10 ms	0.1*10 ms	0.1*11.5 ms
	Total one-way delay	**5.76 ms**	**6.2 ms**	**7 ms**	**7.8 ms**	**8.6 ms**	**9.5 ms**	**6.05 ms**

state and then an active state. Figure 8.11 illustrates an example of control plane flow from the idle state to the connected state [13]. As we can observe from Figure 8.11, control plane flow from the idle state to connected state is as follows. Firstly the UE waits for random access channel (RACH) scheduling and sends RACH preamble to the eNB. The eNB detects the preamble and transmits a random access response. The UE decodes the scheduling grant, timing alignment, and cell radio network temporary identifier (C-RNTI) assignment, and then requests a RRC connection to the eNB. The eNB handles the L2 (data link layer) and RRC connection and sends the RRC connection setup to the UE. The UE handles the RRC and transmits a RRC connection setup complete and non-access stratum (NAS) service request to the eNB. The eNB handles Uu (radio interface allowing information transfer between UE and eNB) and S1-C (or S1-MME [mobility management entity], interface delivering signaling protocols between eNB and MME) interface and requests NAS connection to the MME. The MME handles the NAS connection setup and sends it to the eNB. The eNB handles the interface and transmits RRC security mode command and connection reconfiguration, including TTI alignment, to the UE. The UE handles the RRC connection and transmits the RRC connection setup complete to the eNB. Each step requires a specific delay. Based on Figure 8.11, Table 8.7 summarizes an example of control plane delay calculation comparison (4G, 5G with 1/7 ms TTI, and 5G with 1/7 ms TTI and 1/3 processing delay) in terms of UE. Table 8.8 calculates an example of a control plane delay calculation for steps 11–17 [13]. In Table 8.8, t_1 and t_2 depend on traffic congestion, routing delay and processing power, and others. Excepting these delays, the estimated delay from the idle state to the connected state is from 76 ms (with 3 ms msg2 window and 1 ms RACH cycle) to 80 ms (with 5 ms msg2 window and 5 ms RACH cycle). In order to improve the latency, several solutions were proposed in 4G LTE [13]. The first approach is to combine the RRC connection request and NAS service request. If two request messages are processed in parallel, overall latency can be reduced by approximately 20 ms. The second approach is to reduce processing delay in both UE and eNB by improving processing power. The processing delay is actually the major part of the delay, accounting for approximately 75% of the

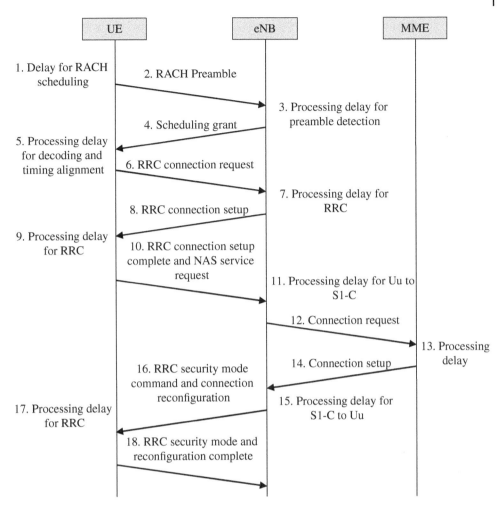

Figure 8.11 Delay model for the control plane from idle state to connected state.

transition [13]. The third approach is to reduce RACH scheduling period, in which case the average waiting time at the UE will be reduced. The fourth approach is to put dormant state in connected mode. Thus, the transition from a dormant state to active state is less than 10 ms.

The cellular systems allow a user to be moved from one cell to another or to be changed to a cell with better signal quality. A handover is defined as a procedure in which a connected call or data session is transferred from a source call to a target cell without disconnecting the session. The handover procedure is generally composed of three steps: preparation, execution, and completion. In preparation steps, the UE evaluates the signal quality and send a measurement report to an eNB. The eNB decides a handover based on the information from the UE. In execution steps, the UE detaches from the source cell and synchronizes to the target cell. New radio resources including RRC connection reconfiguration, sequence number (SN) status transfer and UL allocation are prepared. In completion steps, the radio

Table 8.7 Control plane latency calculation (Steps 1–10) of 4G FDD, based on Figure 8.11.

Steps	Description	4G	5G NR (TTI 1/7 ms)	5G NR (TTI 1/7 ms and 1/3 processing delay)
1	Average delay due to RACH scheduling period	0.5	1/14	1/14
2	RACH preamble	1	1/7	1/7
3–4	Preamble detection and transmission of RA response (time between the end of RACH transmission and UE's reception of scheduling grant and timing adjustment)	2 + 1	2 + 1/7	2/3 + 1/7
5	UE processing delay (decoding of scheduling grant, timing alignment and C-RNTI assignment + L1 encoding of RRC connection request)	5	5	5/3
6	Transmission of RRC connection request	1	1/7	1/7
7	Processing delay in eNB (L2 and RRC)	4	4	4/3
8	Transmission of RRC connection setup (and UL grant)	1	1/7	1/7
9	Processing delay in the UE (L2 and RRC)	15	15	5
10	Transmission of RRC connection setup complete (including NAS service request)	1	1/7	1/7
	Total delay	**31.5 ms**	**26.8 ms**	**9.5 ms**

Table 8.8 Control plane latency calculation (Steps 11–17) of 4G FDD [13].

Steps	Description	Min. delay (ms)	Average delay (ms)
11	Processing delay in eNB (Uu → S1-C)	4	
12	S1-C transfer delay	t_1	t_1
13	MME processing delay (including UE context retrieval of 10 ms)	15	15
14	S1-C transfer delay	t_2	t_2
15	Processing delay in eNB (S1-C → Uu)	4	4
16	Transmission of RRC security mode command and connection reconfiguration (+ TTI alignment)	1.5	1.5
17	Processing delay in UE (L2 and RRC)	20	20

resources of the source cell are released. Figure 8.12 illustrates an example of the handover scenario, where the MME and serving gateway are not changed. Depending on different scenarios, the procedures are changed and the handover latency is calculated including different delay components such as multiple-attempt handover, RRC procedure delay, UE processing time, RACH procedure, and so on. As one example, the handover latency can be calculated by the time that the UE receives the RRC connection reconfiguration from the source eNB and sends RRC connection reconfiguration complete to the target eNB. Basically, this latency is covered by execution steps. Table 8.9 shows us the rough handover latency calculation [13].

In the 5G non-standalone handover mechanism, we should consider two configurations: NR-to-NR handovers with or without LTE mobility anchor. In case of NR-to-NR handover without LTE mobility anchor, the handover time for NR to NR signaling change will be similar to 4G macro cell handover time and it requires approximately 45 ms as we calculated. However, when we consider LTE mobility anchor change, it requires a longer handover time (approximately 75 ms [14]) because of more handover procedures (radio resource release, LTE-to-LTE handover, new resource allocations, etc.). The 3GPP Study Group works on handover improvement by multiconnectivity techniques and others. When a UE establishes multiconnectivity links via NR and LTE and the UE traffics are aggregated, the eNB can change the traffic path depending on the quality of NR and LTE links. The NR-to-LTE path switching time will be about 20 ms [14]. If 5G NR split bearer is involved, an additional signaling is required to switch, and the path switching time will be about 140 ms [15]. [In multiconnectivity, there is a split bearer for which traffics are routed via the master and secondary base stations. The split bearer is either a master cell group [MCG] bearer or a secondary cell group [SCG] bearer.] When the UE switches the data path from NR to LTE in 5G CN level interworking, it takes about 125 ms [15].

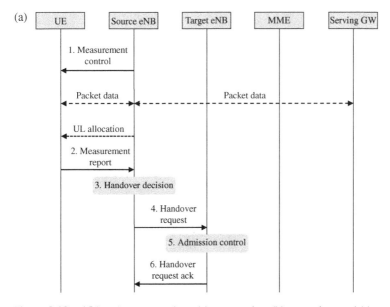

Figure 8.12 4G handover procedure: (a) preparation, (b) execution, and (c) completion.

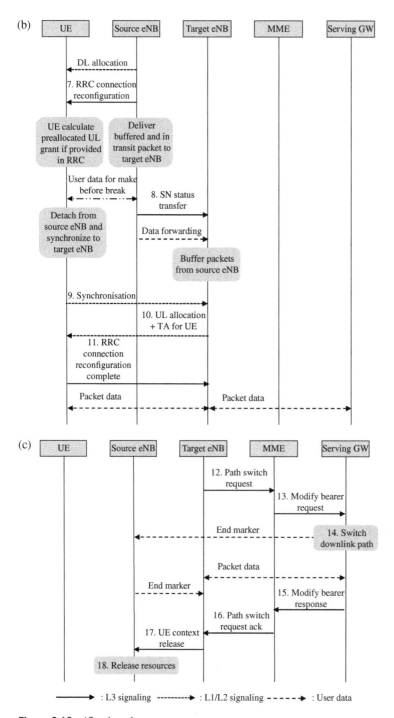

Figure 8.12 (*Continued*)

Table 8.9 Handover latency calculation based on Figure 8.12b [13].

Step	Description	Delay (ms)
7	RRC connection reconfiguration including mobility control info	15
8	SN status transfer	0
9.a	Target cell search	0
9.b	UE processing time for RF/baseband retuning, security update	20
9.c	Delay to acquire first available PRACH in target eNB	0.5/2.5
9.d	PRACH preamble transmission	1
10	UL allocation + TA for UE	3/5
11	UE sends RRC connection reconfiguration complete	6
	Minimum/typical total delay	**45.5/49.5**

Summary 8.3 Latency Analysis

1) Wireless transmission and signal processing are the main elements of the latency calculation. In core networks, the packet exchanges happen via a wired medium such as fiber or copper. The signaling, routing, and packet processing are the main elements. In addition, depending on scenarios (e.g. handover, HARQ, etc.), the latency calculation will be different.

2) Using the same HARQ latency model, we can roughly calculate the 5G one-way latency. For example, 4G needs 14-symbol TTI for 15 kHz subcarrier spacing and the frame size is 1 ms. However, 5G has two-symbol TTI for a 15 kHz subcarrier spacing and the frame size is 0.14 ms. The shorter frame size reduces the latency significantly.

3) The control plane latency is defined as the required time for a UE to transit from idle state (a battery efficient state) to active state (a continuous data transfer state). In the idle state, there is a radio resource control (RRC) connection in the UE. Thus, the UE monitors the paging channel to detect a call and acquire cell information. Once the RRC is established, the UE enters into the connected state and then active state.

4) In order to improve the latency, several solutions were proposed in 4G LTE. The first approach is to combine the RRC connection request and the NAS service request. The second approach is to reduce processing delays in both UE and eNB by improving processing power. The third approach is to reduce the RACH scheduling period. The fourth approach is to put dormant state in connected mode. Thus, the transition from a dormant state to active state is less than 10 ms.

8.4 Multi-Access Edge Computing

As we briefly reviewed in Chapter 6, MEC is typically located at the edge of a network and a user is within one hop of a network. We can obtain many benefits from MEC, such as low latency, high throughput, better security, traffic reduction, and context and location awareness. It allows us to enable new applications including automated vehicles and virtual and augmented reality. The MEC features are summarized as follows [15]:

(i) On-premises: MEC can be operated in standalone and provide a mobile user with proper services.
(ii) Proximity: MEC servers are located in close vicinity to a mobile user.
(iii) Low latency: The computing power of MEC is enough to process applications in real time. It allows us to support latency-critical 5G applications and also alleviate the burden of traffics of backhauls.
(iv) Location awareness: Since a MEC server is close to a mobile user, it allows us to provide location-based services.
(v) Network contextual information: MEC is able to use the information about radio network conditions and local contextual information in order to optimize network and applications operation.

There are multiple design and optimization problems. For example, how many tasks and which tasks should be offloaded to the MEC server? How do we maximize resource utilization and achieve optimal resource allocation and scheduling? What is the main objective (low latency, traffic reduction, low energy, or others) of MEC usage? These questions are about resource management problems. The MEC servers have a limited computing power. The offloading and resource allocation are the key research challenges for supporting 5G applications. In order to meet various requirements such as different demands of users, different network environments, different applications, and so on, then efficient resource allocation schemes including multiple objectives should be designed and optimized. In addition, there are reliability and mobility problems, such as how to handover among MEC servers. How do we maintain the reliability under time-varying environments of wireless connection and user mobility? In an automated vehicle scenario, a moving vehicle may cause frequent handovers among MEC servers. It may affect the overall network performance. When the coverage of MEC networks is limited and a MEC server no longer provides the vehicle with a latency-critical service, the vehicle may not receive the computation results from a MEC server. Thus, there are some research activities to investigate computation migration, mobility-aware resource allocation and offloading, mobility-aware fault tolerant MEC systems, and so on.

Another design issue is network integration and configuration of MECs and cloud networks – for example, how to configure and coordinate different MEC servers and applications in 5G infrastructures. The MECs are deployed at the edge of networks such as small or macro base stations, and computing resources are distributed in the network. However, this approach causes more complex and heterogeneous networks. The time-varying environments and various computing tasks will be another design and optimization challenge, as well as security and privacy. When there is a task offloading to some MEC server, the tasks are computed locally and the data transfer may not be secured. In order to protect mobile

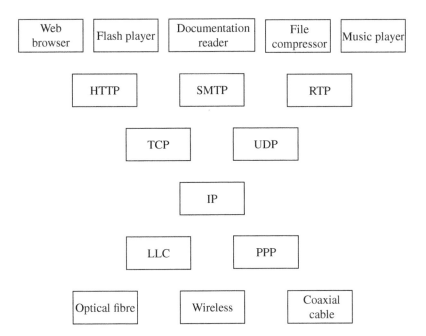

Figure 8.13 The hourglass model of layered system architecture.

user data, encryption schemes and physical layer security techniques are investigated for tasks and resource sharing on MEC networks. Lastly, we should consider deployment and operation of MEC networks. What is the optimal number of MEC servers deployed in terms of CapEx and OpEx?

Besides design and optimization problems, a more fundamental problem of network design is known as the hourglass model of layered system architecture, as shown in Figure 8.13. As we can observe from the figure, the layers on the top and bottom contain many protocols, but the center of the protocol stack contains only the IP layer. It looks like an hourglass. In this model, a single IP protocol allows us to maximize interoperability and minimize the number of interfaces. Thus, millions of applications can run over any network, and it was one reason for the internet success. However, the traditional architecture is about to change. Depending on applications, network conditions are considered during the application development phase. For example, when a video stream service is designed, the network throughput is a key metric of the services, and the video compress rate can be adjusted according to the traffic change. In addition, the internet environment has changed. Numbers of mobile internet users have grown rapidly. The traffic may be stuck with a backbone network. The MEC network architecture allows us to converge the network and the applications and improve network performance while maintaining the benefits of the hourglass model.

The key part of the MEC software is split into three components: terminal components, edge components, and remote components [15]. Terminal components perform some preliminary processing to determine the need for further computing capability supports. The edge components perform some operations, including offloading computation for leveraging low latency and high network performance. The remote components include some operations to be performed in data centers, including large storage and databases. This approach is different from software modularization. The software modularization is designed for improving software development and maintenance, but MEC software design focuses on distributed computing to meet specific network performance at the network edge.

In multi-access edge computing, mobile applications are offloaded to edge servers to reduce the latency and computing power. There are many offloading methods and radio resource managements. According to the objective function, the resource managements can be categorized as minimizing the overall latency, maximizing resource utilization, or minimizing energy consumption. The first approach is to formulate the optimization problem to minimize the overall latency by managing the transmit power, beamforming, task and resource allocation. The second approach is to find offloading tasks based on task characteristics and channel conditions, and then allocate radio resources for each user. The third approach of minimizing energy consumption is similar to the others. Resource management adopts conventional optimization methods to solve convex optimization problems. In [16–18], the optimization problems are formulated to achieve a low latency communication. They use a latency model composed of wireless transmission latency, network latency, and computation latency. The user experienced latency, T_k, can be defined as follows:

$$T_k = T_k^t + T_k^n + T_k^c + T_k^r \approx T_k^t + T_k^n + T_k^c \tag{8.34}$$

where T_k^t is the transmission latency when sending the task from the kth user to a base station, T_k^n is the network latency when sending the kth user data from a base station to an edge server, T_k^c is the computation latency for computing the task at the edge server, and T_k^r is the latency when sending the computation results from a base station to the kth user. However, the data size of the computation results is typically small and T_k^r can be ignored. As we reviewed in the previous section, T_k^t is highly related to the packet size and can be expressed as follows:

$$T_k^t = \frac{d_k}{r_k} \tag{8.35}$$

where d_k and r_k are the data size of the kth user computation task and the kth user data rate, respectively. The network latency is related to task assignment and the data transportation latency between a base station and an edge server. Thus, T_k^n can be represented as follows:

$$T_k^n = \sum_{m \in M} \alpha_{k,m} \tau_{k,m} \tag{8.36}$$

where $\alpha_{k,m} \in \{0, 1\}$ is the task assign indicator. $\alpha_{k,m} = 1$ indicates that the kth user is served by the mth edge server. The set of user task assignment can be defined as $A = \{\alpha_{k,m} \mid k \in K, m \in M\}$. $\tau_{k,m}$ is the network latency between the kth user associated base station and the mth edge server. The computation latency is related to each task's computational complexity and computation resource at edge servers. Thus, T_k^c can be expressed as follows:

$$T_k^c = \sum_{m \in M} \alpha_{k,m} \frac{c_k}{g_{k,m}} \tag{8.37}$$

where c_k is the required computation resource for the kth user task and $g_{k,m}$ is the allocated computation resource to the kth user at the mth edge server. The set of computation resource allocation can be defined as $G = \{g_{k,m} \mid k \in K, m \in M\}$. From Equations (8.35–8.37), the user-experienced latency is represented as follows:

$$T_k = \frac{d_k}{r_k} + \sum_{m \in M} \alpha_{k,m} \left(\tau_{k,m} + \frac{c_k}{g_{k,m}} \right) \tag{8.38}$$

Now, the optimization problem can be formulated to minimize the user-experienced latency as follows [16]:

$$\min_{A,P,V,G} \left(\sum_{k \in K} T_k \right)$$

subject to

$$C_1 : T_k \leq T_k^{\max}, \quad \forall k \in K,$$

$$C_2 : p_k \leq P_k^{\max}, \quad \forall k \in K,$$

$$C_3 : \sum_{k \in K} \alpha_{k,m} g_{k,m} \leq g_m^{\max}, \quad \forall m \in M,$$

$$C_4 : \sum_{m \in M} \alpha_{k,m} = 1, \quad \forall k \in K,$$

$$C_5 : \alpha_{k,m} \in \{0,1\}, \quad \forall k \in K, \forall m \in M \tag{8.39}$$

where $T_k^{\max}$ is the maximum tolerable latency of the kth user, $P_k^{\max}$ is the maximum uplink transmit power of the kth user, and $g_m^{\max}$ is the total computation resources at the mth server. In addition, P and V represent uplink transmit power and receive beamforming, respectively. In the problem expressed in Equation (8.39), the constraint C_1 means that the user-experienced latency does not exceed the maximum tolerable latency. The constraint C_2 represents the limitation of each user transmit power. The constraint C_3 represents that the computation resource allocation at edge servers do not exceed their maximum. The constraints C_4 and C_5 mean that a user can be served by one edge server at a time. The optimization problem in Equation (8.39) includes the integer variable in the task assignment and non-convex objective function and is known as a mixed integer nonlinear programming problem [19]. Thus, the optimization problem is transformed to an equivalent problem and then the integer variables in task assignments are relaxed into continuous variables [16]. From uplink and downlink duality in TDD MIMO systems [20], the problem in Equation (8.39) can be transformed as follows:

$$\min_{A,W,G} \left(\sum_{k \in K} T_k \right)$$

subject to

$$C_1, C_3, C_4, C_5,$$

$$\tilde{C}_2 : \sum_{l \in L} \mathbf{w}_{k2}^{l2} \leq P_k^{\max}, \quad \forall k \in K \tag{8.40}$$

where $\mathbf{w}_k^l$ is the downlink beamforming vector of the lth base station for the kth user. The set of downlink beamforming vectors can be defined as $W = \{\mathbf{w}_k \mid k \in K\}$. The uplink receive beamforming and transmit power are expressed as follows:

$$v_k = \frac{\mathbf{w}_k^T}{\mathbf{w}_{k2}^2}, \quad \forall k \in K \tag{8.41}$$

and

$$p_k = \mathbf{w}_{k2}^2, \quad \forall k \in K \tag{8.42}$$

respectively. In order to solve the problem in Equation (8.40), binary variables $\alpha_{k,m}$ are relaxed to continuous variables $\widetilde{\alpha}_{k,m}$, and the set of user task assignments is redefined as $\widetilde{A} = \{\widetilde{\alpha}_{k,m} \mid k \in K, m \in M\}$. Thus, we have the following optimization problem:

$$\min_{A,W,G} \left(\sum_{k \in K} T_k \right)$$

subject to

$$C_1, \widetilde{C}_2, C_3, C_4,$$
$$\widetilde{C}_5 : \widetilde{\alpha}_{k,m} \in [0,1], \quad \forall k \in K, \forall m \in M \tag{8.43}$$

Now, the problem in Equation (8.43) can be solved by the block coordinate descent method [16].

It is possible to design the computation task process using a Markov decision process (MDP). If we model it as a MDP, we can use a machine learning technique to solve the optimization problem without a priori knowledge of the environment [21]. In [22], a task offloading problem is described to minimize the weighted sum of power consumption and latency and optimize the task offloading decisions using machine learning. Computational tasks can be offloaded from an end user device to the gateway according to channel conditions, task queue and end user computing resources. The network state, s^k, of an end user device in each time k is denoted as follows [22]:

$$s^k = (g^k, T^k, r_d^k) \in S \tag{8.44}$$

and the end user device chooses an action

$$a^k = \left(O^k, P_t^k \right) \in A \tag{8.45}$$

Each end user device (an agent) decides to offload the computation task and choose the transmit power. The cost function is expressed as follows:

$$C^k = C_l^k + C_o^k + \delta^k \tag{8.46}$$

where δ^k is a penalty function when the task transmission fails, C_l^k is the cost function of a local computing mode, and C_o^k is the cost function of the offloading computing mode. The cost function can be regarded as latency and power consumption. Computation tasks can be performed at the end user device or offloaded to the gateway and performed at the edge server. Local computing mode ($O^k = 0$) means that the end user device does not offload the computation task and also the cost function includes the local computation power consumption, the local task execution latency, and zero transmission power. Offloading computing mode ($O^k = 1$) means that the end user device decides to offload the computation task and transmit it to the gateway with the transmit power $P_t^k \in P_t$. If the transmission between the end user device and the gateway fails and the outage occurs, the computation task ($\mathcal{O}^k = -1$) fails. In local computing mode, the total power consumption of one computation task is expressed as follows:

$$P_c^k = f_d P_d m^k \tag{8.47}$$

where f_d is the fixed CPU frequency of an end user device, P_d is the power consumption per CPU cycle, and m is the task size. $f_d P_d$ represents computing power consumption per bit at the end user device. The local computing latency, L_d^k, is defined as follows:

$$L_d^k = f_d m^k / D_d \tag{8.48}$$

where D_d is the computation capacity of the end user device. Thus, the cost function in the local computing mode is represented as follows:

$$C_l^k = P_c^k + \beta L_d^k \tag{8.49}$$

where β is the weight factor to adjust between power consumption and task execution latency. In offloading computing mode, the cost function is expressed as follows:

$$C_o^k = P_s^k + P_t^k + \beta(L_s^k + L_t^k) \tag{8.50}$$

where $P_s^k = f_s P_s m^k$ is the computation power at the edge server, P_t^k is the transmission power at the end user device, $L_s^k = f_s m^k / D_s$ is the computation latency at the edge server, and L_t^k is the transmission latency. Thus, the cost function in Equation (8.46) is rewritten as follows:

$$C^k = P_c^k + P_s^k + P_t^k + \beta(L_s^k + L_t^k + L_d^k) + \delta^k \tag{8.51}$$

In order to minimize the cost function in Equation (8.51), a task offloading scheme should be found. The optimization problem is now formulated as follows:

$$\min_{\beta, \mathbf{P_t}, \mathcal{O}} \left(\sum_{k \in K} C^k \right)$$

subject to

$$C_1 : 0 \leq \beta \leq 1,$$
$$C_2 : 0 \leq P_t^k \leq P_{\max},$$
$$C_3 : \mathcal{O}^k = \{0, 1, -1\} \tag{8.52}$$

where the constraint C_1 represents the weight factor range, the constraint C_2 represents the transmit t power limit, P_{max}, of the end user device when offloading the computation power to the gateway, and the constraint C_3 means the task mode (local computing, offloading computing, and computation fail). The optimization problem in Equation (8.52) is a mixed integer nonlinear programming problem and the integer variable $\mathcal{O}^k$, continuous variable $\mathbf{P_t}$, and the discrete variable δ^k should be optimized. It is difficult to find an optimal solution. One approach is to decompose the problem into multiple sub-optimization problems and then solve them separately. Another approach is to use a machine learning technique because it is possible to model it as a MDP. The transition probability is defined as the transition from state s^k to s^{k+1} with the cost function C^k when the action a^k is taken as follows:

$$P = (s^{k+1}, C^k \mid s^k, a^k) \tag{8.53}$$

The long-term expected cost is given as follows [22]:

$$V(s, \pi) = E_{\pi} \left[\sum_{k=1}^{K} \gamma^k C^k \right] \tag{8.54}$$

where $s^k = (g^k, T^k, r_d^k)$, $\gamma \in [0, 1]$ is the discount factor, and E is the statistical conditional expectation with transition probability P. As we reviewed the reinforcement learning in Chapter 5, we need to find the optimal policy π^* to minimize the cost $V(s, \pi)$. For any given network state s, the optimal policy π^* can be found as follows:

$$\pi^* = \arg\min_{\pi} V(s, \pi), \quad \forall s \in S \tag{8.55}$$

Now, we define the action value function Q and explore the optimal task offloading policy. The Q value, $Q(s, a)$, is defined as follows:

$$Q(s, a) = E_{\pi}[C^{k+1} + \gamma Q_{\pi}(s^{k+1}, a^{k+1}) \mid s^k = s, a^k = a] \tag{8.56}$$

and the Q value, $Q(s, a)$, is updated based on the current cost function C^k and the discounted Q value, $Q(s^{k+1}, a), \forall a \in A$ as follows:

$$Q\left(s^k, a^k\right) \leftarrow (1 - \alpha) Q\left(s^k, a^k\right) + \alpha \left(C^k + \gamma \min_{a} Q(s^{k+1}, a) \right) \tag{8.57}$$

where C^k and α are the costs observed for the current state and the learning rate, respectively. As we can observe from Equation (8.57), the Q value is calculated with all possible actions and chosen as the minimum Q value. Thus, the computation task offloading optimization problem in Equation (8.52) can be solved by the Q learning algorithm.

Computational task scheduling of a MEC system is one of the key design issues to reduce latency. A mobile device should decide whether to perform a task locally or to offload a task to a MEC server and execute the task remotely. In [23, 24], the task scheduling policies for MEC systems are described. They adopt a MDP based on the queueing state, execution state,

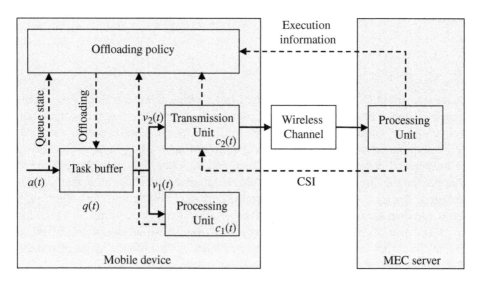

Figure 8.14 MEC system model for task scheduling.

and transmission state. We consider the MEC system model as shown in Figure 8.14 [23]. A mobile device needs to execute a computation-intensive and delay-sensitive task, and a MEC server acts as a small data center installed at a base station. Depending on the offloading policy, a mobile device can execute the task locally or send it to the MEC server via a transmission unit, and then execute the task remotely at the MEC server. Since the battery life of the mobile device is limited, the average power consumption at the mobile device is constrained by $\overline{P}_{max}$. The MEC model assumes equal-length time slots and task generation with the probability α. In each time slot, the decision about local or remote computation is made by the offloading policy of the mobile device. The number of tasks in the task buffer at the beginning of the t time slot, $q[t]$, is described as follows:

$$q[t+1] = \min((q[t] - v_l[t] - v_c[t])^+ + a[t], Q) \tag{8.58}$$

where $(x)^+ = \max(x, 0)$ and $a[t] \in \{0, 1\}$ is the task arrival indicator. $a[t] = 1$ means that a task arrives at the t time slot. Q is the capacity of the task buffer. We assume it is large enough. $v_l[t]$ and $v_c[t]$ represent computational task scheduling decision indicators at the t time slot. There are four possible computational task scheduling decisions as follows:

$$V = \left\{ (v_l[t], v_c[t]) \mid (0,0), (0,1), (1,0), (1,1) \right\} \tag{8.59}$$

For example, $(v_l[t], v_c[t]) = (1, 0)$ means that a task is sent to the local processing unit ($v_l[t] = 1$) and the MEC server does not execute ($v_c[t] = 0$). As we can observe from Equation (8.59), the tasks are computed in the local processing unit or remote MEC server. The computation model is defined. Firstly, the processing state of the local processing unit, $c_l[t]$, can be expressed as follows:

$$c_l[t] \in \{0, 1, \ldots, N-1\} \tag{8.60}$$

where $N = C/(f_l \Delta)$ is the time slot for task computation, where C is the local CPU cycles, f_l is the CPU operating frequency, and Δ is the time slot length. Power consumption, P_l, is required to compute. For example, $c_l[t] = 0$ means that the local CPU is idle and there is no power consumption at the local processing unit. When offloading the task to the MEC server, the transmission state is represented as follows:

$$c_t[t] \in \{0, 1, \ldots, M\} \tag{8.61}$$

where M is the data packet size. The achievable throughput at the t time slot, $r(\gamma[t], P_t)$, is expressed as follows [23]:

$$r(\gamma[t], P_t) = B\log_2 \left(1 + \frac{\gamma[t]P_t}{N_0 B}\right) \geq R \tag{8.62}$$

where $\gamma[t]$ is the channel gain at the t time slot, P_t is the transmit power, B is the bandwidth, N_0 is the spectral density of a noise and each pack includes R bits. Similar to the local processing unit, the time slot for task computation at the MEC server is $N_m = C/(f_m \Delta)$ where f_m is the CPU operating frequency at the MEC server. For example, $c_t[t] = m$ means that the mth packet of a task is scheduled to offload in the t time slot. Now, the system state can be modeled under MDP as follows [23]:

$$\tau[t] = (q[t], c_t[t], c_l[t]) = (i, m, n) \tag{8.63}$$

where the state space S is represented as follows: $S = \{0, 1, ..., Q\} \times \{0, 1, ..., M\} \times \{0, 1, ..., N-1\}$, where $\times$ is the Cartesian product. In order to characterize the computational task scheduling policy, a set of probabilistic parameters mapping the system state to the probability space is defined as follows [24]:

$$g_\tau^k \in [0, 1], \quad \forall \tau \in S, \quad k = 1, 2, 3, 4 \tag{8.64}$$

where k represents four possible cases as follows: the first case is $c_t[t] = 0$, $c_l[t] = 0$. Both local processing unit and transmission unit are idle. The second case is $c_t[t] \neq 0$, $c_l[t] = 0$. The processing unit is idle but the transmission unit is occupied. The third case is $c_t[t] = 0$, $c_l[t] \neq 0$. The transmission unit is idle and the mobile device can offload a task to the MEC server. The fourth case is $c_t[t] \neq 0$, $c_l[t] \neq 0$. Both the processing unit and the transmission unit are occupied. In order to analyze the average delay and power consumption, one-step state transition probability from τ to τ' is defined as follows:

$$\chi_{\tau, \tau'} = P(\tau \rightarrow \tau') \tag{8.65}$$

and the steady-state distribution, π_τ, can be obtained by solving the following equation set [25]:

$$\sum_{\tau' \in S} \chi_{\tau, \tau'} \chi_{\tau'} = \pi_\tau, \quad \forall \tau \in S$$

$$\sum_{\tau \in S} \pi_\tau = 1 \tag{8.66}$$

According to Little's theorem [25], the average queueing delay can be represented as follows [23]:

$$t_q = \frac{1}{\alpha} \sum_{i=0}^{Q} i P(q[t] = i) = \frac{1}{\alpha} \sum_{i=0}^{Q} i \sum_{m=0}^{M} \sum_{n=0}^{N-1} \pi_{(i, m, n)} \tag{8.67}$$

where α is the task arrival rate. The local execution time for each task is

$$t_c = t_{tx} + N_c + t_{rx} \tag{8.68}$$

where the average transmission time for each task, t_{tx}, is

$$t_{tx} = M \sum_{j=1}^{\infty} j (1 - \beta)^{j-1} \beta$$

$$\beta = P(r(\gamma[t], P_t) \geq R) \tag{8.69}$$

N_c is the execution time at the MEC server, and t_{rx} is the feedback loop time to receive computation results. β is the probability of the channel not in outage. Thus, the average processing time of a task, t_p, is represented as follows [23]:

$$t_p = \eta N + (1 - \eta) t_c \tag{8.70}$$

where η is the proportion of computation tasks and can be expressed as follows [23]:

$$\eta = \frac{\sum_{\tau \in S_1} \pi_\tau g_\tau^1 + \sum_{\tau \in S_3} \pi_\tau g_\tau^3}{\sum_{\tau \in S_1} \pi_\tau g_\tau^1 + \sum_{\tau \in S_2} \pi_\tau g_\tau^2 + 2\sum_{\tau \in S_3} \pi_\tau g_\tau^3} \tag{8.71}$$

where the state set S_k is defined as follows:

$$S_1 = \{(i, m, 0) \mid i \geq 1, m \in \{0, 1, \ldots, M\}\}$$
$$S_2 = \{(i, 0, n) \mid i \geq 1, n \in \{0, 1, \ldots, N-1\}\}$$
$$S_3 = \{(i, 0, 0) \mid i \geq 2\} \tag{8.72}$$

Thus, the average delay to the computation task is the sum of the average queueing delay and the average processing time as follows:

$$\overline{T} = t_q + t_p \tag{8.73}$$

The average power consumption at the mobile device can be expressed as follows:

$$\overline{P} = \sum_{\tau \in S} \pi_\tau (\mu_\tau^l P_l + \mu_\tau^{tx} P_{tx}) \tag{8.74}$$

where μ_τ^l and μ_τ^{tx} are the probabilities of local processing and successful packet transmission as follows:

$$\mu_\tau^l = \begin{cases} g_\tau^1 + g_\tau^3, & \tau = (i, 0, 0), \forall i \geq 2 \\ g_\tau^1, & \tau = (i, 0, 0) \cup (i, m, 0), \forall i \geq 1, m > 0 \\ 1, & \tau = (i, m, n), \quad \forall i \geq 0, m \geq 0, n > 0 \\ 0, & \text{otherwise} \end{cases} \tag{8.75}$$

and

$$\mu_\tau^{tx} = \begin{cases} \beta(g_\tau^2 + g_\tau^3), & \tau = (i, 0, 0), \forall i \geq 2 \\ \beta g_\tau^2, & \tau = (i, 0, 0) \cup (i, 0, n), \forall i \geq 1, m > 0 \\ \beta, & \tau = (i, m, n), \quad \forall i \geq 0, m > 0, n \geq 0 \\ 0, & \text{otherwise} \end{cases} \tag{8.76}$$

respectively. P_l and P_{tx} are the required power consumptions. Now, the power constrained delay minimization problem for MEC systems is defined as follows [23]:

$$\min_{g_\tau^k} \left(\overline{T} = t_q + t_p = \frac{1}{\alpha} \sum_{i=0}^{Q} i \sum_{m=0}^{M} \sum_{n=0}^{N-1} \pi_{(i,m,n)} + \eta N + (1 - \eta) t_c \right)$$

subject to

$$C_1 : \overline{P} \leq \overline{P}_{max}$$

$$C_2 : \sum_{\tau' \in S} \chi_{\tau, \tau'} \chi_{\tau'} = \pi_\tau, \quad \forall \tau \in S$$

$$C_3 : \sum_{i=0}^{Q} \sum_{m=0}^{M} \sum_{n=0}^{N-1} \pi_{(i,m,n)} = 1$$

$$C_4 : \sum_{k=1}^{4} g_{(i,m,n)}^k = 1, \quad \forall i, m, n$$

$$C_5 : g_{(i,m,n)}^k \geq 0, \quad \forall i, m, n, k \tag{8.77}$$

where the constraint C_1 means that the average power is constrained, the constraints C_2 and C_3 denote the balance equations, and the constraints C_4 and C_5 represent the conditions of probabilistic parameters. These mean that π_τ can be obtained by the equation set Equation (8.66) if $g^k_{(i,m,n)}$ is determined. The problem in Equation (8.77) is non-convex and the solution can be obtained easily; thus, it is reformulated to a series of linear programming problems as follows [23]:

$$\min_{x,\eta} \left(\frac{1}{\alpha} \sum_{\tau \in S} \sum_{k=1}^{4} i x^k_\tau + \eta N + (1-\eta)t_c \right)$$

subject to

$$C_1 : v_l(\boldsymbol{x})P_l + \beta v_{tx}(\boldsymbol{x})P_{tx} \leq \overline{P}_{max}$$

$$C_2 : \Gamma(\boldsymbol{x},\eta) = 0$$

$$C_3 : F_\tau(\boldsymbol{x}) = 0, \quad \forall \tau = (i,m,n) \in S$$

$$C_4 : \sum_{i=0}^{Q} \sum_{m=0}^{M} \sum_{n=0}^{N-1} \sum_{k=1}^{4} x^k_{(i,m,n)} = 1$$

$$C_5 : x^k_{(i,m,n)} \geq 0, \quad \forall i,m,n,k, \quad \eta \in [0,1] \tag{8.78}$$

where $x^k_\tau = \pi_\tau g^k_\tau$ is the occupation measure, and $\sum_{k=1}^{4} g^k_\tau = 1$ and $\pi_\tau = \sum_{k=1}^{4} x^k_\tau$. This represents the probability in the state $\tau = (i,m,n)$ while the decision k is made [26]. The problem in Equation (8.78) is obtained by replacing π_τ with x^k_τ of the problem in Equation (8.77). The term $\Gamma(\boldsymbol{x},\eta)$ of constraint C_2 is expressed as follows:

$$\Gamma(\boldsymbol{x},\eta) = (1-\eta) \sum_{\tau \in S_1} x^1_\tau - \eta \sum_{\tau \in S_2} x^2_\tau + (1-2\eta) \sum_{\tau \in S_3} x^3_\tau \tag{8.79}$$

and the term $F_\tau(\boldsymbol{x})$ of the constraint C_2 is expressed as follows:

$$F_\tau(\boldsymbol{x}) = \eta \sum_{\tau' \in S} \sum_{k=1}^{4} \widetilde{\chi}_{\tau',\tau,k} x^k_{\tau'} - \sum_{k=1}^{4} x^k_\tau = 0 \tag{8.80}$$

where $\widetilde{\chi}_{\tau',\tau,k}$ is the probability that the current state τ' and the decision k is made while the next state τ is independent with $g^k_\tau : \sum_{k=1}^{4} \widetilde{\chi}_{\tau',\tau,k} g^k_{\tau'} = \chi_{\tau',\tau}, \quad \forall \tau', \tau v_l(\boldsymbol{x})$ and $v_{tx}(\boldsymbol{x})$ are linear functions of the variable $\mathbf{x}$ as follows:

$$v_l(\boldsymbol{x}) = \sum_{i=1}^{Q} x^1_{(i,0,0)} + \sum_{i=2}^{Q} x^3_{(i,0,0)} + \sum_{i \geq 1} \sum_{m=1}^{M} x^1_{(i,m,0)} + \sum_{i \geq 1} \sum_{m=0}^{M} \sum_{n=1}^{N-1} \sum_{k=1}^{4} x^k_{(i,m,n)} \tag{8.81}$$

and

$$v_{tx}(\boldsymbol{x}) = \sum_{i=1}^{Q} x^1_{(i,0,0)} + \sum_{i=2}^{Q} x^3_{(i,0,0)} + \sum_{i \geq 1} \sum_{n=1}^{N-1} x^1_{(i,0,n)} + \sum_{i \geq 1} \sum_{m=1}^{M} \sum_{n=0}^{N-1} \sum_{k=1}^{4} x^k_{(i,m,n)} \tag{8.82}$$

respectively. The optimal solution and value of the problem in Equation (8.78) are expressed as (x^*,η^*) and $\overline{T}'(\eta^*)$, respectively. If we find x^*, the optimal task scheduling policy, $g^{k^*}_\tau$, can be found as follows:

$$g^{k^*}_\tau = \frac{x^{k^*}_\tau}{\sum_{k=1}^{4} x^{k^*}_\tau}, \quad \forall \tau \in S, k \in \{1,2,3,4\} \tag{8.83}$$

The problem in Equation (8.78) is still non-convex, but we can regard it as a linear programming problem in terms of variable x_τ^k.

Summary 8.4 MEC

1) The MEC features are summarized as follows: on-premises, proximity, low latency, location awareness, and network contextual information.
2) The MEC network architecture allows us to converge the network and the application and improve network performance while maintaining the benefits of the hourglass model.
3) There are many MEC design problems: design and optimization problems, resource management problems, reliability and mobility problems, security and privacy, and deployment and operation of MEC networks.
4) There are many offloading methods and radio resource managements. According to the objective function, the resource managements can be categorized as minimizing the overall latency, maximizing resource utilization, or minimizing energy consumption. The first approach is to formulate the optimization problem to minimize the overall latency by managing the transmit power, beamforming, task and resource allocation. The second approach is to find offloading tasks based on task characteristics and channel conditions and then allocate radio resources for each user. The third approach of minimizing energy consumption is similar to the others. They adopt conventional optimization methods to solve convex optimization problems.

Problems

1 Describe the requirements of the URLLC system after defining specific use cases.

2 Compare the latency definitions.

3 Describe the trade-off relations among communication and network metrics, including throughput, latency, energy efficiency, connection density, and others.

4 Describe deterministic components of the 5G physical layer and find one component causing the longest latency.

5 Stochastic components of 5G systems should be analyzed in terms of probability. Select one component and model it using a probability model.

6 In order to combat many different channel impairments, describe the physical layer and MAC layer techniques. Compare their pros and cons.

7 Survey 5G techniques and network policies to reduce latency in 3GPP standard documents.

8 In short packet transmission theory, describe trade-off of error probability and code rate in terms of both vertical asymptotic view and horizontal asymptotic view.

9 Consider non-asymptotic upper and lower bounds on R*(n,ε) in terms of the block length n at 2 dB and error probability $\varepsilon = 10^{-6}$. What block length do we need to operate at 90% capacity?

10 Consider that we have a (n, k) block code and AWGN channel and decoding errors are independent for different retransmissions. When transmitting 10^5 information bits at SNR 2 dB, what error probability maximizes the long-term throughput?

11 Describe the downlink signaling process of 5G systems and then perform a latency analysis.

12 Compare the HARQ latency models of FDD and TDD according to packet size decrease.

13 Taking into account different scenarios (e.g. small/macro cell, TDD/FDD, single/multi antenna, etc.), formulate the resource allocation problems of MEC in order to minimize the E2E latency.

References

1 3GPP (2017). 3GPP TS 22.261, v16.0.0, Service requirements for next generation new services and markets. https://portal.3gpp.org/desktopmodules/Specifications/SpecificationDetails.aspx?specificationId=3107.

2 Bertenyi, B., Nagata, S., Kooropaty, H. et al. (2018). 5G NR radio interface. *Journal of ICT Standardization* 6 (Combined Special Issue 1 and 2).

3 Shannon, C. (1948). A mathematical theory of communication. *Bell System Technical Journal* 27: 379–423, 623–656.

4 Feinstein, A. (1954). A new basic theorem of information theory. *Transactions of the IRE Professional Group on Information Theory* 4 (4): 2–22.

5 Gallager, R. (1965). A simple derivation of the coding theorem and some applications. *IEEE Transactions on Information Theory* 11 (1): 3–18.

6 Polyanskiy, Y., Poor, H., and Verdu, S. (2010). Channel coding rate in the finite block-length regime. *IEEE Transactions on Information Theory* 56 (5): 2307–2359.

7 Y. Polyanskiy, (2010). Channel coding: non-asymptotic fundamental limits. PhD dissertation. Princeton University.

8 Durisi, G., Koch, T., and Popovski, P. (2016). Towards massive, ultra-reliable, and low-latency wireless communication with short packets. *Proceedings of the IEEE* 104 (9): 1711–1726.

9 Durisi, G., Koch, T., Östman, J. et al. (2016). Short-packet communications over multiple-antenna Rayleigh-fading channels. *IEEE Transactions on Communications* 64 (2): 618–629.

10 Effros, M., Goldsmith, A., and Liang, Y. (2010). Generalizing capacity: new definitions and capacity theorems for composite channels. *IEEE Transactions on Information Theory* 56 (7): 3069–3087.

11 Yang, W., Durisi, G., Koch, T., and Polyanskiy, Y. (2014). Quasi-static multiple antenna fading channels at finite blocklength. *IEEE Transactions on Information Theory* 60 (7): 4232–4265.

12 3GPP (2016). 3GPP TR 36.881, v1.0.0, Study on latency reduction techniques for LTE. https://portal.3gpp.org/desktopmodules/Specifications/SpecificationDetails.aspx?specificationId=2901.

13 3GPP (2018). 3GPP TR 36.912, v15.00, Feasibility study for further advancements for E-UTRA (LTE-Advanced). https://www.etsi.org/deliver/etsi_tr/136900_136999/136912/15.00.00_60/tr_136912v150000p.pdf.

14 Samsung. (2017). 4G–5G Interworking: RAN level and CN level interworking. *Samsung White Paper*. https://www.samsung.com/global/business/networks/insights/white-paper/4g-5g-interworking.

15 A. Reznik (editor), R. Arora, M. Cannon, et al. (2017). Developing Software for Multi-Access Edge Computing. *ETSI White Paper No. 20*. https://www.etsi.org/images/files/ETSIWhitePapers/etsi_wp20_MEC_SoftwareDevelopment_FINAL.pdf.

16 Q. Liu, T. Han, and Nirwan Ansari. (2018). Joint radio and computation resource management for low latency multi-access edge computing. *2018 IEEE Global Communications Conference (GLOBECOM)*. https://ieeexplore.ieee.org/document/8647792.

17 Pang, A.-C., Chung, W.-H., Chiu, T.-C., and Zhang, J. (2017). Latency-driven cooperative task computing in multi-user fog-radio access networks. In: *IEEE 37th International Conference on Distributed Computing Systems (ICDCS)*, 615–624.

18 Sardellitti, S., Scutari, G., and Barbarossa, S. (2015). Joint optimization of radio and computational resources for multicell multi-access edge computing. *IEEE Transactions on Signal and Information Processing over Networks* 1 (2): 89–103.

19 Boyd, S. and Vandenberghe, L. (2004). *Convex Optimization*. Cambridge University Press.

20 Schubert, M. and Boche, H. (2005). Iterative multiuser uplink and downlink beamforming under SINR constraints. *IEEE Transactions on Signal Processing* 53 (7): 2324–2334.

21 Xu, J. and Ren, S. (2016). Online learning for offloading and autoscaling in renewable-powered multi-access edge computing. In: *2016 IEEE Global Communications Conference (GLOBECOM)*, 1–6.

22 X. Liu, Z. Qin, and Y. Gao. (2019). Resource allocation for edge computing in IoT networks via reinforcement learning. *2019 IEEE International Conference on Communications (ICC)*, Shanghai, China, May 2019.

23 J. Liu, Y. Mao, J. Zhang, and K.B. Letaief. (2016). Delay-optimal computation task scheduling for multi-access edge computing systems. *2016 IEEE International Symposium on Information Theory (ISIT)*, Barcelona, Spain, 10–15 July 2016.

24 Zhang, W., Wen, Y., Guan, K. et al. (2013). Energy optimal mobile cloud computing under stochastic wireless channel. *IEEE Transactions on Wireless Communications* 12 (9): 4569–4581.

25 Ross, S.M. (2014). *Introduction to Probability Models*. Academic Press.

26 Altman, E. (1999). *Constrained Markov Decision Processes*. Chapman and Hall/CRC.

9

Massive Machine Type Communication Systems

9.1 Introduction

Massive machine type communication (mMTC) is a communication link supporting a number of devices attached to the internet or communicating with each other, with or without human intervention. It is also called massive machine-to-machine (M2M) communication. This communication link is designed for Internet of Things (IoT) services. The International Telecommunications Unions (ITU) documentation ITU-T Y.2060 [1] defines the concept and scope of the IoT. The ITU definition of IoT is as follows [1]: "The IoT can be viewed as a global infrastructure for the information society, enabling advanced services by interconnecting (physical and virtual) things based on existing and evolving interoperable information and communication technologies." In this definition, things are objects of the physical world (e.g. electrical equipment, etc.) or the virtual world (e.g. application software, etc.). The IoT device is defined as "a piece of equipment with the mandatory capabilities of communication and optional capabilities of sensing, actuation, data capture, data storage and data processing." The devices collect information and send it to network for further analysis. The fundamental characteristics of IoT systems include interconnectivity, heterogeneity, dynamic changes and enormous scale. The mMTC systems should be designed to cover them. In order to develop mMTC systems, we should design them from a different perspective. The key challenges are to develop massive communication links for low-cost devices that are distributed over a wide area and consume ultra-low power. The key requirements of the mMTC can be summarized as massive connectivity, low-cost devices, ubiquitous coverage, low data rate, and ultra-low power consumption. More than ten standards have already been developed to facilitate mMTC applications and services. As unlicensed spectrum technologies, long range (LoRa) is suitable for mMTC services. The unlicensed spectrum technology is composed of two parts: LoRa (physical layer) and LoRaWAN (upper layers). The LoRa as physical layer technology includes a spread spectrum modulation technique using chirp spread spectrum (CSS). Due to the linearity characteristic of chirp pulses, the frequency differences between the transmitter and the receiver are in line with the time differences. We do not need accurate RF correction and complexity algorithms. They can be easily compensated. It allows us to reduce the RF device cost. In addition, the coverage is usually a few kilometers. The CSS signals with low power are difficult to intercept. The use of a two-layer security mechanism (network level and application level) makes the network more robust. On the

Design and Optimization for 5G Wireless Communications, First Edition. Haesik Kim.
© 2020 John Wiley & Sons Ltd. Published 2020 by John Wiley & Sons Ltd.

other hand, the disadvantages of the LoRa are as follows: first, a patent fee is required to use the LoRa. Secondly, it has centralized architecture. The customers of the mMTC services access the network but may not manage their own gateway. It is difficult to build private networks. Lastly, the LoRa alliance supports device certifications but there is no open standard. As licensed spectrum technologies, narrowband Internet of Things (NB-IoT) is developed by 3GPP and the specification was fixed in 3GPPP Release 13 in June 2016. The NB-IoT, as a subset of the LTE standards, uses limited bandwidth and relaxes the high throughput configuration. The key features are summarized as follows: data rate 250 kbps, bandwidth 180 kHz, 50 K connections per cell, battery life up to 10 years, module cost under $5, transmit power 20 or 23 dBm, and uplink latency less than 10 seconds. The NB-IoT includes many benefits such as long battery life, wide coverage, better scalability, quality of service (QoS), and security compared to unlicensed technologies, and coexistence with legacy cellular systems. However, the disadvantages of NB-IoT are as follows: no support for roaming and voice transmission, and relatively low data rate.

In this chapter, we consider general mMTC architectures to meet requirements such as massive connectivity, low-cost devices, ubiquitous coverage, low data rate, and ultra-low power consumption. In particular, energy efficiency and connection density are key metrics of mMTC applications. We discuss one practical optimization tool, power optimization and wireless sensor networks (WSNs), and focus on design and optimization to improve energy efficiency.

9.2 Design Approaches of mMTC Systems

IoT technologies will bring a big impact to a broad range of market sectors including automotive, agriculture/aquaculture, factory automation, healthcare, smart homes and cities, retail, public safety, and the military. Depending on the target applications, the key design considerations of IoT systems will be different. In general, we should consider the following aspects of IoT systems: connectivity solutions, device requirements (e.g. battery life, processing power, memory, bandwidth, throughputs, sensing, actuation, etc.), network topology, security mechanisms, power management mechanisms, data processing mechanisms, and management by IoT device or server, and so on. The focus in this book is on connectivity solutions. We look into design challenges and approaches of mMTC systems in this section.

Traditional cellular systems are designed in accordance with large packet size, high data rates, and downlink-dominated communication links. However, in mMTC systems, the design approach needs to be fundamentally changed to small packet size, low data rate, and uplink-dominated communication links. In addition to that, we assume that the requirements of mMTC systems include massive numbers of devices (up to 300 K devices) in a single cell, sporadic user activity, and low complexity and energy-constrained devices. In order to meet these requirements, we need to find answers to the following questions: how do we achieve ultra-low power consumption of mMTC devices? How do we manage the radio resources for sporadic activity and mixed traffic? How do we establish connections to a massive number of devices in a single cell? What network topologies and deployments are suitable for the applications? As we discussed in Chapter 8, short packet transmissions associated with mMTC also present other design challenges. In 3GPP, there are three parallel tracks for connectivity solutions for IoT systems. Firstly, enhanced machine-type communication (eMTC, also called CAT-M1 or LTE-M) is one type of lower power wide area network (LPWAN) radio technology by 3GPP Release 13. It modifies LTE radio access network for mMTC applications by reducing air interface capabilities. It can deliver up to 1 Mbps throughput and allows us to use essential features (e.g. voice transmission, full mobility, etc.) of LTE. In addition, it can support IoT services on existing LTE base stations. The technical features can be summarized as follows: frequency hopping with narrowband retuning for frequency diversity; transmission time interval (TTI) bundling and repetition for large coverage; reduced hybrid automatic repeat request (HARQ), positioning and multicast support, and so on. Secondly, NB-IoT (also called CAT-M2) scales down to simplicity for low-cost, low-throughput and delay-tolerant applications with reduced functionalities. NB-IoT can be deployed in an existing LTE band. When comparing NB-IoT with eMTC, NB-IoT has advantages in terms of coverage, cost, power consumption, and connection density. Thus, the customers of IoT services would select NB-IoT solutions when requiring lower cost, wider coverage and longer battery life. On the other hand, eMTC has advantages in terms of throughput, portability and voice transmission. eMTC would be selected in the scenarios involving voice call, high throughput and portability. Thus, both NB-IoT and eMTC are suitable for different scenarios and applications. They may be cooperative in a complementary manner. The technical features of NB-IoT can be summarized as follows: two uplink mode support, single HARQ process, reduced broadcast system information, and so on. Thirdly, extended coverage global system for mobile communications Internet of Things (EC-GSM-IoT) is based on eGPRS. It supports high throughput, wide coverage, low complexity, and low energy. One interesting feature is that EC-GSM-IoT can be deployed by a simple software update on existing 2G infrastructures (GSM networks). However, it does not receive as much attention as NB-IoT or eMTC. The technical features of EC-GSM-IoT can be summarized as follows: new logical channels for extended coverage, relaxed idle mode, and positioning support. Table 9.1 summarizes the features of eMTC, NB-IoT, and EC-GSM-IoT.

Among these IoT standards, we review the NB-IoT standard [2]. This standard is designed for synergies with LTE. As we can observe from Table 9.1, downlink and uplink techniques are based on the LTE transmission scheme. The frame, subframe and slot length of NB-IoT are the same as for LTE. The orthogonality between the NB-IoT physical resource block (PRB) and the LTE PRB are preserved and their coexistence is allowed because NB-IoT complies with the OFDM numerology of LTE. The NB-IoT subcarriers can be deployed within the LTE spectrum as inside an LTE carrier or a LTE guard band. In addition, a standalone carrier can be deployed using any spectrum with more than 180 kHz bandwidth. Likewise, the NB-IoT physical signals and channels are based on LTE. However, they are redesigned to meet the requirements of IoT services and multiplexed in the time domain. Table 9.2 summarizes the physical signals and channels of NB-IoT.

In the time domain, each NB-IoT frame consists of 10 subframes of 1 ms length and each subframe consists of two slots with seven OFDM symbols. As we can observe from Table 9.2, the NB-IoT downlink has three physical signals and three physical channels.

Table 9.1 Features of 3GPP IoT standards.

	eMTC	NB-IoT	EC-GSM-IoT
Deployment	In-band LTE	Standalone, in-band, and guard-band LTE	In-band GSM
Bandwidth	1.4 MHz	180 kHz	2.4 MHz (200 kHz per channel)
Peak rate	1 Mbps for uplink and downlink	250 kbps for downlink, 250 kbps (multi tone) or 20 kbps (single tone) for uplink	474 kbps (EDGE) for downlink and uplink, 2 Mbps (EGPRS2B) for downlink and uplink
Number of antennas	1	1	1–2
Duplex	Full or half	Half	Half
Device transmit power	20/23 dBm	20/23 dBm	23/33 dBm
Power saving	Power saving mode (PSM), discontinuous reception (DRX) as Extended I-DRX, C-DRX	PSM, Extended I-DRX, C-DRX	PSM, Extended I-DRX
Latency	10–15 ms	1.6–10 s	700 ms – 2 s
Downlink techniques	OFDMA, 16 QAM, 15 kHz tone spacing	OFDMA, 15 kHz tone spacing,	TDMA/FDMA, GMSK, and 8PSK
Uplink techniques	SC-FDMA, 16 QAM, 15 kHz tone spacing	SC-FDMA, 15 kHz and 3.75 kHz tone spacing	TDMA/FDMA, GMSK, and 8PSK

Both narrowband primary synchronization signal (NPSS) and narrowband secondary synchronization signal (NSSS) are used for cell search, cell identity detection, and time and frequency synchronization. NPSS is transmitted in subframe #5 in every 10 ms frame and NSSS is transmitted in subframe #9 with a 20 ms period. NRS is transmitted in all subframes and the main purpose is phase reference for the modulation of the downlink channels. Narrowband Physical Broadcast Channel (NPBCH) is transmitted in subframe #0 in every frame and includes the master information block (MIB). The MIB is not changed over the 640 ms TTI. Narrowband physical downlink control channel (NPDCCH) carries control information such as paging, resource allocation and scheduling information, random access channel (RACH) response, HARQ acknowledgement, power control, and so on. The size of the control information is 23 bits. NPDSCH is the data-bearing channel. It is composed of user unicast data, paging message and system information. Uplink of NB-IoT supports both single- and multiple-tone transmission. The multiple-tone transmission is based on SC-FDMA with 15 kHz tone spacing. The single-tone transmission support both 15 and 3.75 kHz tone spacing. The NB-IoT uplink has one physical signal and two physical channels. DMRS is transmitted in one or three SC-FDMA symbols and multiplexed with the data. Narrowband physical random access channel (NPRACH) is newly designed because LTE PRACH uses a wider bandwidth of 1.08 MHz. NPRACH resources can be allocated in set of

Table 9.2 NB-IoT signals and channels.

	NB-IoT physical signals and channels	Remark
Downlink physical signal	Narrowband primary synchronization signal (NPSS)	LTE uses three PSSs but all NB-IoT cells share one NPSS
	Narrowband secondary synchronization signal (NSSS)	
	Narrowband reference signal (NRS)	
Downlink channels	Narrowband physical broadcast channel (NPBCH)	LTE uses 40 ms TTI but NB-IoT uses 649 ms TTI
	Narrowband physical downlink control channel (NPDCCH)	
	Narrowband physical downlink shared channel (NPDSCH)	• LTE uses turbo codes but NB-IoT uses convolutional codes • LTE uses higher order modulation but NB-IoT uses QPSK • LTE uses multiple spatial multiplexing layers but NB-IoT uses single layer
Uplink channels	Demodulation reference signal (DMRS)	
	Narrowband physical random access channel (NPRACH)	LTE uses multi-tone transmission with 1.25 kHz subcarrier spacing but NB-IoT uses single tone transmission with 3.75 kHz tone spacing
	Narrowband physical uplink shared channel (NPUSCH)	• LTE uses minimum bandwidth of one PRB but NB-IoT bandwidth allocation is smaller than one PRB • LTE use higher order modulation but NB-IoT uses $\pi/2$ BPSK or $\pi/4$ QPSK • LTE uses multiple spatial multiplexing layers but NB-IoT uses single layer

12, 24, 36, and 48 subcarriers. In order to extend coverage, the preamble can be repeated up to 128 times. The role of NPRACH is to make a connection between mobile devices and a base station. Narrowband physical uplink shared channel (NPUSCH) carries both data and control information. Formats 1 and 2 of NPUSCH are used for carrying uplink data and signaling HARQ acknowledgement for downlink, respectively. Figure 9.1 illustrates NB-IoT frame and subframe structure, and allocation of different physical signals and channels.

When implementing NB-IoT devices, a low-cost design is essential. The low-cost NB-IoT devices may be equipped with a low-cost local oscillator and it may cause large carrier frequency offset. In addition, NB-IoT devices are operated at a low signal-to-noise ratio (SNR) due to the limited power capability. Those conditions make synchronization difficult. Namely, large frequency offset and symbol timing should be estimated at a low SNR. When a NB-IoT device switches on, the first thing that happens is cell search and initial acquisition. It should find a suitable cell and obtain control information by a synchronization process. The synchronization is composed of timing alignment, time and frequency offset

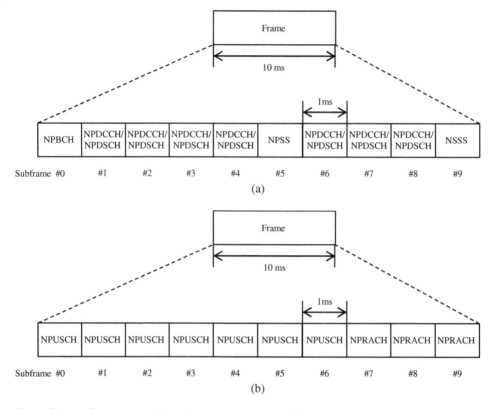

Figure 9.1 (a) Downlink and (b) uplink frame structure of NB-IoT.

correction, and control information (e.g. cell ID) acquisition. NPSS allows us to obtain the symbol timing and the carrier frequency offset and NSSS is used for obtaining the narrowband physical cell identity (NB-PCID) and frame timing within an ambiguity of 80 ms. The frame timing is a key step to align the start of a possible broadcast channel detection. After obtaining symbol timing, carrier frequency offset, cell identity and framing timing in the synchronization procedure, a NB-IoT device finds a master information block (MIB) in the NPBCH subframe #0 of every frame. The MIB includes key control information such as operation mode (standalone, in-band, or guard band), frequency raster offset, and so on. After synchronization is complete, the NB-IoT devices send a random access preamble using NPRACH. The base station transmits a random access response including timing advance command and scheduling of uplink resource using NPDSCH. The NB-IoT device sends its identity to the base station using NPUSCH. The base station transmits a contention resolution message to resolve any contention. Figure 9.2 summarizes the NB-IoT access procedure.

In order to support different scenarios, the network sets up three different NPRACH resource configurations. Each configuration has different repetition values of random access preamble. NB-IoT devices determine their coverage class by estimating the downlink received signal power, and transmits random access preamble in the NPRACH resources. The remaining steps such as connection release are similar to LTE.

NB-IoT device   Base station

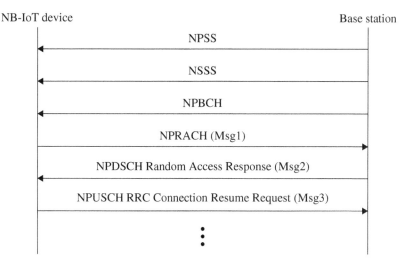

Figure 9.2 NB-IoT connection establishment.

In 5G, there is 5G mMTC development. The 5G standard in the first phase focuses on enhanced mobile broadband (eMBB) services. In the second phase, URLLC and mMTC are discussed. The 5G mMTC technologies are not yet defined. However, 3GPP considers both NB-IoT and eMTC as candidates to meet the 5G LPWAN requirements. In 3GPP 5G NR, there is no separate study for LPWAN. In 3GPP Release 15, there are two ongoing works for further enhancement of eMTC and NB-IoT. Therefore, both NB-IoT and eMTC will be the 5G mMTC technologies. The mMTC design of 5G faces many research challenges to meet the requirements. Key research challenges and design approaches of 5G mMTC can be summarized as follows:

(i) The signaling challenge for unpredictable and sporadic mMTC device activities: A grant-based access control mechanism is suitable when the traffic is somehow predictable. Traditional cellular systems adopt this mechanism and it has worked well so far. However, in mMTC scenarios, grant-based signaling may be inefficient because the signal transmissions are sporadic and uncoordinated. As we briefly discussed in Chapter 8, a grant-free access mechanism does not require a large overhead and is efficient in mMTC scenarios even if it suffers from collision problems. In 3GPP, a conventional radio resource control (RRC) connection is established by the steps: random access, initial attach, and authorization. However, cellular IoT signaling reduces the procedure for short packet transmission and data can be delivered during the signaling procedure [3].

(ii) Resource management for massive connections: If a LTE access reservation mechanism is used in massive connection scenarios, the throughput performance would be significantly degraded because there is no collision resolution procedure in the protocol. Thus, resource management to support massive connections should be developed.

Table 9.3 mMTC design approaches.

Approaches 5G techniques	Improving energy efficiency	Improving connection density	Improving radio resource utilization	Remarks
Power control schemes	v		v	MAC
Low power RF and BB design	v			PHY
Resource allocation and scheduling	v	v	v	MAC
Grant-free access mechanism		v	v	MAC
Radio access schemes		v	v	PHY and MAC

(iii) Power control and management mechanism: One requirement of IoT devices is a long battery life. In order to meet this requirement, power control and management mechanism should be improved in terms of sleep/idle mode procedures, transmission power control, and low power RF and baseband design.

(iv) Massive access schemes: In the massive connection scenario of mMTC, the collision rate will be high for a conventional access procedure. The high collision rate results in longer latency, lower energy efficiency, QoS degradation and lower spectrum utilization. Thus, radio access schemes should be improved for massive connectivity.

Table 9.3 summarizes approaches for improving energy efficiency.

Summary 9.1 Design Approaches of mMTC

1) Massive machine type communication (mMTC) is a communication link supporting a number of devices attached to the internet or communicating with each other, with or without human intervention.
2) In mMTC systems, the design approaches needs to be fundamentally changed to a small packet size, low data rate, and uplink-dominated communication links.
3) In 3GPP, there are three connectivity solutions for IoT systems: eMTC, NB-IoT, and EC-GSM-IoT.
4) Key research challenges and design approaches for 5G mMTC can be summarized as follows: (i) signaling challenge for unpredictable and sporadic mMTC device activities; (ii) resource management for massive connections; (iii) power control and management mechanism; (iv) massive access schemes.

9.3 Robust Optimization

As we discussed in Chapter 4, a standard form of an optimization problem is as follows:

$$\min_{\mathbf{x}} f(\mathbf{x})$$

subject to

$$C_1 : g_j(\mathbf{x}) \leq a_j, \ j = 1, 2, \ldots, m$$
$$C_2 : h_k(\mathbf{x}) = b_k, \ k = 1, 2, \ldots, p \tag{9.1}$$

where the functions $f(\mathbf{x})$, $g_j(\mathbf{x})$, and $h_k(\mathbf{x})$ are exactly known. In convex optimization problems, they are convex. However, in wireless communications and network system design, the objective functions and constraint functions may not be precisely known or may be corrupted by some noise. In fact, most real-world optimization problems involve uncertainty. In this case, an optimal solution of the problem shown in Equation (9.1) may provide us with poor performance. Thus, we need a new approach to deal with unknown perturbations or some degree of uncertainty in optimization problems. The uncertainty is caused by noise, random nature, measurement errors, or unknown knowledge of data. This scenario is common in wireless communication and network problems.How do we treat the uncertainty in optimization problems? There are two classical methods: stochastic programming and sensitivity analysis. Stochastic programming assumes the probability distribution of the parameters. The functions are a collection of random variables. It chooses the best solution in the collections. However, stochastic programming causes high complexity of the optimization problems, with heavy data requirements. Sensitivity analysis finds a solution with fixed values for parameters and then observes how the associated solution is affected by small perturbations. This method is easy to apply for linear programming. However, this is a post process of optimizations. Namely, in order to determine the impact of parameters, the outcomes are recalculated under different assumptions. It is not practically helpful for finding solutions that are robust for data with uncertainty. As a complementary approach to stochastic programming and sensitivity analysis, robust optimization (RO) finds an acceptable solution under all possible realizations of the uncertain inputs. The solution of robust optimization is protected against data deviations. Robust optimization is a subfield of optimization to find solutions that offer robustness against uncertainty. Thus, it is a sort of worst-case oriented methodology. This approach is useful when (i) some parameters of the problems include estimation errors or data may be contaminated; (ii) the objective or constraint functions are sensitive to perturbations; and (iii) we cannot afford to ignore low probability. In robust optimization, an optimal feasible solution is robust if it remains a deterministic dataset under any realization of the data. Simply speaking, robust optimization is composed of two steps. The first step is to define a deterministic dataset within an uncertainty set. The second step is to find the best solution that is feasible for all possible realizations of the uncertain inputs. Thus, the data uncertainty is modeled as hard constraints. Figure 9.3 illustrates the approach of robust optimization.

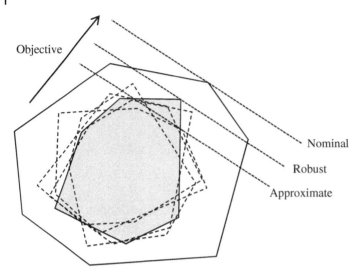

Objective

Nominal

Robust

Approximate

Figure 9.3 Robust feasible set vs nominal feasible set.

We consider uncertain parameter δ belonging to an uncertainty set Δ, an objective function $f_0(\mathbf{x})$ to optimize, and constraint function $f_i(\mathbf{x}, \delta_i)$. A standard form of robust optimization using a bounded uncertainty set is as follows:

$$\min_{\mathbf{x}} f_0(\mathbf{x})$$

subject to

$$C_1 : f_i(\mathbf{x}, \delta_i) \leq 0, \quad \forall \delta_i \in \Delta_i, i = 1, 2, \ldots, m \tag{9.2}$$

where $\mathbf{x} \in \mathbb{R}^n$ is the optimization variable, and the uncertainty parameters $\delta_i \in \mathbb{R}^k$ take arbitrary values in the uncertainty set Δ_i. The goal of the problem in Equation (9.2) is to find the $\mathbf{x}^*$ minimizing $f_0(\mathbf{x})$ among all possible solutions which are feasible for all possible realizations of δ_i within Δ_i. As we can observe from Equation (9.2), the objective function is irrelevant to the uncertainty parameters. We can introduce an auxiliary variable t and minimize t subject to the additional constraint $\max_{\delta_0} f_0(\mathbf{x}, \delta_0) \leq t$. The uncertainty set has a Cartesian product structure $\Delta = \Delta_1 \times \Delta_2 \times \cdots \times \Delta_m$ with $\delta_i \in \Delta_i$. The problem in Equation (9.2) is known as a semi-infinite optimization problem [4] and is also known to be computationally intractable [5]. Thus, we focus on some geometries of Δ_i and this allows us to find computationally tractable solutions. There are two types of uncertainty geometry model: ellipsoidal models and polytopic models. We consider the following robust linear programming problem:

$$\min_{\mathbf{x}} \mathbf{c}^T \mathbf{x}$$

subject to

$$\mathbf{a}_i^T \mathbf{x} \leq b_i, \quad \forall \mathbf{a}_i \in \Delta_{\mathbf{a}_i}, \forall b_i \in \Delta_{b_i}, i = 1, 2, \ldots, m \tag{9.3}$$

where $\mathbf{a}_i$ and b_i are uncertain parameters belonging to the uncertainty sets $\Delta_{\mathbf{a}_i}$ and Δ_{b_i}. $\mathbf{c}$ is the uncertain coefficient. Without loss of generality, we assume that the objective function is irrelevant to the uncertainty parameters because of the dual nature of the problem:

$$\min_{\mathbf{x}} \max_{\mathbf{c} \in \Delta_{\mathbf{c}}} \mathbf{c}^T \mathbf{x} \qquad\qquad \min_{\mathbf{x},t} t$$

subject to   subject to

$$\mathbf{a}_i^T \mathbf{x} \le b_i, \qquad\qquad \mathbf{c}^T \mathbf{x} \le t, \forall \mathbf{c} \in \Delta_{\mathbf{c}} \qquad (9.4)$$

$$\forall \mathbf{a}_i \in \Delta_{\mathbf{a}_i}, \forall b_i \in \Delta_{b_i}, \quad \leftrightarrow \qquad \mathbf{a}_i^T \mathbf{x} \le b_i,$$

$$i = 1, 2, \ldots, m \qquad\qquad \forall \mathbf{a}_i \in \Delta_{\mathbf{a}_i}, \forall b_i \in \Delta_{b_i},$$

$$i = 1, 2, \ldots, m.$$

Robust linear programming is tractable for most practical uncertainty sets of interest [4]. Ellipsoidal uncertainty sets were considered in order to trade off performance and robustness by controlling the size of the ellipsoidal sets [4, 6]. The key features of the ellipsoidal uncertainty model are as follows: (i) en ellipsoid uncertainty geometry can be expressed in a simple mathematical representation using the mean and covariance matrix of the uncertain dataset; (ii) it is possible to express complicated uncertainty sets; and (iii) in the case of uncertain data with a stochastic model, the stochastic uncertainty model can be replaced by a deterministic ellipsoidal uncertainty model. In Equation (9.3), the uncertainty of b_i and $\mathbf{c}$ can be ignored if the worst-case scenario is assumed at the lower bound of the interval in the problem. The problem Equation (9.3) can be reformulated and is referred to as the robust counterpart problem as follows:

$$\min_{\mathbf{x}} \mathbf{c}^T \mathbf{x}$$

subject to   (9.5)

$$\mathbf{a}_i^T \mathbf{x} \le b_i, \quad \forall \mathbf{a}_i \in \Delta_{\mathbf{a}_i}, \quad i = 1, 2, \ldots, m$$

where the uncertainty set $\Delta_{\mathbf{a}_i}$ is the user-specified primitive uncertainty set. A solution is called robust feasible if it satisfies the uncertainty constraints for all realizations of the uncertainty parameters. It can be ellipsoidal geometry and expressed as follows:

$$\Delta_{\mathbf{a}_i} = \{\mathbf{a}_i = \bar{\mathbf{a}}_i + \mathbf{P}_i \mathbf{u}_i | \mathbf{u}_{i2} \le 1\}, \quad i = 1, \ldots, m \qquad (9.6)$$

where $\bar{\mathbf{a}}_i$ is the nominal value of $\mathbf{a}_i$ representing the center of the ith ellipsoid and $\mathbf{P}_i \in \mathbb{R}^{n \times n}$ is a symmetric positive semi-definite matrix for all i. Figure 9.4 illustrates the concept of the uncertainty set.

Figure 9.4 The concept of the uncertainty set.

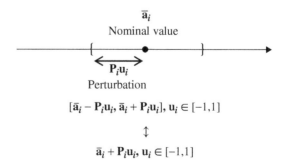

$\bar{\mathbf{a}}_i$
Nominal value

$\mathbf{P}_i \mathbf{u}_i$
Perturbation

$[\bar{\mathbf{a}}_i - \mathbf{P}_i \mathbf{u}_i, \bar{\mathbf{a}}_i + \mathbf{P}_i \mathbf{u}_i], \mathbf{u}_i \in [-1,1]$

$\updownarrow$

$\bar{\mathbf{a}}_i + \mathbf{P}_i \mathbf{u}_i, \mathbf{u}_i \in [-1,1]$

If $P_i = I$, the uncertainty sets are spheres. If $P_i = 0$, $\mathbf{a}_i$ is fixed and the problem becomes a linear programming problem without uncertainty. Now, we reformulate the problem as follows:

$$\min_{\mathbf{x}} \mathbf{c}^T \mathbf{x}$$

subject to

$$\begin{bmatrix} \max_{\mathbf{a}_i} \mathbf{a}_i^T \mathbf{x} \\ \mathbf{a}_i \in \boldsymbol{\Delta}_{\mathbf{a}_i} \end{bmatrix} \leq b_i, \quad i = 1, 2, \dots, m \tag{9.7}$$

In Equation (9.7), the maximization problem of the constraint term can be rewritten using Cauchy-Schwarz as follows:

$$\max_{\mathbf{a}_i} \{ \mathbf{a}_i^T \mathbf{x} \mid \mathbf{a}_i \in \boldsymbol{\Delta}_{\mathbf{a}_i} \} = \bar{\mathbf{a}}_i^T \mathbf{x} + \max \{ \mathbf{u}_i^T \mathbf{P}_i \mathbf{x} \mid \mathbf{u}_{i2} \leq 1 \} = \bar{\mathbf{a}}_i^T \mathbf{x} + \mathbf{P}_i^T \mathbf{x}_2 \tag{9.8}$$

Thus, the problem in Equation (9.7) is rewritten as follows:

$$\min_{\mathbf{x}} \mathbf{c}^T \mathbf{x}$$

subject to

$$\bar{\mathbf{a}}_i^T \mathbf{x} + \mathbf{P}_i^T \mathbf{x}_2 \leq b_i, \quad i = 1, 2, \dots, m \tag{9.9}$$

which is recognized as second-order cone programming (SOCP). Thus, a robust linear programming problem with ellipsoidal uncertainty can be solved efficiently by the interior point methods described in Chapter 4. The ellipsoidal uncertainty model allows us to transform a computationally intractable semi-infinite problem into a convex optimization problem. Polyhedral uncertainty set is a special case of ellipsoidal uncertainty sets. In the optimization problem in Equation (9.3), the uncertainty sets $\boldsymbol{\Delta}_{\mathbf{a}_i}$ have polytopic geometry as follows:

$$\boldsymbol{\Delta}_{\mathbf{a}_i} = \{ \mathbf{a}_i \mid \mathbf{D}_i \mathbf{a}_i \leq \mathbf{d}_i \} \tag{9.10}$$

where $\mathbf{D}_i \in \mathbb{R}^{k_i \times n}$ and $\mathbf{d}_i \in \mathbb{R}^{k_i}$ are given as an input. The uncertainty sets $\boldsymbol{\Delta}_{b_i}$ are given as an interval in $\mathbb{R}$. Thus, Equation (9.3) is rewritten as follows:

$$\min_{\mathbf{x}} \mathbf{c}^T \mathbf{x}$$

subject to

$$\mathbf{a}_i^T \mathbf{x} \leq b_i, \quad \forall \mathbf{a}_i \in \boldsymbol{\Delta}_{\mathbf{a}_i}, \quad i = 1, 2, \dots, m \tag{9.11}$$

where $\boldsymbol{\Delta}_{\mathbf{a}_i} = \{ \mathbf{a}_i \mid \mathbf{D}_i \mathbf{a}_i \leq \mathbf{d}_i \}$ and b_i represents the lower end of the interval. The problem in Equation (9.11) can be rewritten as follows:

$$\min_{\mathbf{x}} \mathbf{c}^T \mathbf{x}$$

subject to

$$\begin{bmatrix} \max_{\mathbf{a}_i} \mathbf{a}_i^T \mathbf{x} \\ \mathbf{D}_i \mathbf{a}_i \leq \mathbf{d}_i \end{bmatrix} \leq b_i, \quad i = 1, 2, \dots, m \tag{9.12}$$

Duality allows us to solve the problem with a polytopic uncertainty set. Since the dual of the constraint term becomes

$$
\begin{array}{ll}
\max_{\mathbf{a}_i} \mathbf{a}_i^T \mathbf{x} & \min_{\mathbf{p}_i \in \mathbb{R}^{k_i}} \mathbf{p}_i^T \mathbf{d}_i \\[2mm]
\text{subject to} & \text{subject to} \\[2mm]
\mathbf{D}_i \mathbf{a}_i \leq \mathbf{d}_i \quad \leftrightarrow & \mathbf{p}_i^T \mathbf{D}_i = \mathbf{x} \\[2mm]
& \mathbf{p}_i \geq 0
\end{array}
\tag{9.13}
$$

the robust linear optimization problem becomes

$$
\min_{\mathbf{x}} \mathbf{c}^T \mathbf{x}
$$

subject to

$$
\begin{aligned}
\mathbf{p}_i^T \mathbf{d}_i &\leq b_i \\
\mathbf{p}_i^T \mathbf{D}_i &= \mathbf{x}, \quad i = 1, 2, \ldots, m \\
\mathbf{p}_i &\geq 0
\end{aligned}
\tag{9.14}
$$

As we can observe from Equation (9.14), the complexity of the problem has polynomial growth with the size of the nominal problem and the uncertainty set. There are various uncertainty constraint sets. Table 9.4 summarizes tractable reformulation for different types of uncertainty sets.

The robust optimization assumes that all variables make decisions that must be made before the actual realization of the uncertain data is known. However, in real-world problems, the variables do not correspond to actual decisions, and can tweak themselves according to varying data. Thus, some decision variables need to be adjusted to corresponding parts of varying data. When a multi-period optimization problem with uncertain data is considered, and the uncertain data is revealed progressively, a subset of the decision variables can be selected after observing realizations of some uncertain data. This approach allows us to adjust the earlier decision under a small dataset. In stochastic programming, this approach is called recourse. In robust optimization, it is called adjustable robust optimization (ARO). In ARO, the here-and-now decision of robust optimization is relaxed, and a wait-and-see decision is taken into account. ARO formulates this decision environment

Table 9.4 Tractable robust counterparts of uncertain linear optimization problems.

Uncertainty	Uncertainty set	Tractability	Illustration
Box	$\delta_\infty \leq 1$	LP	
Ellipsoidal	$\delta_2 \leq 1$	SOCP or CQP	
Polyhedral	$\mathbf{D}_i \mathbf{a}_i \leq \mathbf{d}_i$	LP	

and has a recourse action. We consider the two-stage adjustable robust linear programming problem as follows:

$$\min_{\mathbf{x}} \mathbf{c}^T \mathbf{x}$$

subject to

$$\mathbf{A}(\delta)\mathbf{x} + \mathbf{B}\mathbf{y}(\delta) \leq \mathbf{d}, \quad \forall \delta \in \Delta \tag{9.15}$$

where $\mathbf{x} \in \mathbb{R}^n$ is the first stage here-and-now decision variable (which needs to be determined now) before $\delta \in \mathbb{R}^L$ is realized, while the second stage wait-and-see decision variable $\mathbf{y} \in \mathbb{R}^k$ can be chosen after the uncertain parameters are realized. $\mathbf{c} \in \mathbb{R}^n$, $\mathbf{A} \in \mathbb{R}^{m \times n}$ and $\mathbf{d} \in \mathbb{R}^m$ are uncertain coefficients. Δ is the user-specified uncertainty set. $\mathbf{B} \in \mathbb{R}^{m \times k}$ is a fixed recourse (or a certain coefficient matrix). The problem in Equation (9.15) includes many certain parameters and the complexity is high. Computationally tractable reformulation is helpful for solving the problem. Thus, the second-stage decision variable function $\mathbf{y}(\delta)$ can be approximated by affine decision rules as follows [7]:

$$\mathbf{y}(\delta) = \mathbf{y}^0 + \mathbf{Q}\delta \tag{9.16}$$

where $\mathbf{y}^0 \in \mathbb{R}^k$ and $\mathbf{Q} \in \mathbb{R}^{k \times L}$ are the coefficients of the decision rule to be optimized. The problem in Equation (9.15) is rewritten as follows:

$$\min_{\mathbf{x}} \mathbf{c}^T \mathbf{x}$$

subject to

$$\mathbf{A}(\delta)\mathbf{x} + \mathbf{B}\mathbf{y}^0 + \mathbf{B}\mathbf{Q}\delta \leq \mathbf{d}, \quad \forall \delta \in \Delta \tag{9.17}$$

As we can observe from Equation (9.17), the problem is affine in the uncertain variable δ and the decision variables $\mathbf{x}$, $\mathbf{y}^0$ and $\mathbf{Q}$, and becomes a three-stage problem. The ARO is less conservative than the robust optimization because the feasible set of the ARO is larger than that of the robust optimization. However, it is difficult to formulate the ARO problem explicitly because the dependency of parameters is not known in many cases. The single-stage approach has one step: find the static solution and reveal its uncertainty. Its complexity is low for linear programming problems. In a multistage approach, we have the following process: decision → uncertainty revealed → decision adjustment → uncertainty revealed → decision adjustment .... Decomposition algorithms are needed to solve the problem and the complexity is known as NP hard for linear programming problems. ARO is efficient to solve multistage optimization problems. Due to its complexity, robust optimization is implemented in software packages. We can summarize the steps of the ARO as follows:

Initial conditions: Define the system model and formulate the problem.
- ***Step 1***: Solve the nominal problem

Repeat
- ***Step 2***: Determine the uncertain parameters and the uncertainty set
- ***Step 3***: Check quality of the nominal solution and stop if the nominal solution is robust enough
- ***Step 4***: Determine the adjustable variables and the decision rules
- ***Step 5***: Formulate the robust counterpart

- **Step 6**: Try to approximate and reformulate the problem and then solve the adjustable robust counterpart
- **Step 7**: Check the solution and go to step 2 or 4 if not enough

Until Quality of the robust solution is enough.

Example 9.1 *Robust Linear Programming with Box Model*

Consider the following simple robust linear programming problem:

$$\max_{x,y} x + y$$

subject to

$$ax \le 10, x \ge 0$$

$$by \le 10, y \ge 0$$

where $x, y \in \mathbb{R}$ are the optimization variables and the uncertainty parameters $a, b \in \mathbb{R}$ take arbitrary values in the uncertainty set $[0, 2]$. Find the optimal solution of the robust linear programming problem.

Solution

The linear constraints

$$ax \le 10, x \ge 0 \quad \text{for all } 0 \le a \le 2$$

$$by \le 10, y \ge 0 \quad \text{for all } 0 \le b \le 2$$

can be rewritten as follows:

$$\max_{0 \le a \le 2,\, x \ge 0} ax \le 10, x \ge 0$$

$$\max_{0 \le b \le 2,\, y \ge 0} by \le 10, y \ge 0$$

We can have the following simple constraints:

$$x \le 5, x \ge 0$$

$$y \le 5, y \ge 0$$

The constraints can be represented in a box shape as shown in Figure p9.1. From the figure, $(x, y) = (5,5)$ maximizes the objective function. The optimal solution of the robust linear programming problem is $(5,5)$.

Example 9.2 *Robust Linear Programming with Ellipsoidal Model*

Consider the following simple robust linear programming problem

$$\max_{x,y} x + y$$

subject to

$$ax + by \le 1, x \ge 0, y \ge 0$$

where $x, y \in \mathbb{R}$ are the optimization variables and the uncertainty parameters $a, b \in \mathbb{R}$ take arbitrary values in the ellipsoidal uncertainty sets $\Delta_a = \{a = \bar{a} + P_a u \mid \|u\|_2 \le 1\}$ and $\Delta_b = \{b = \bar{b} + P_b u \mid \|u\|_2 \le 1\}$. Transform the original problem to a second-order conic programming problem.

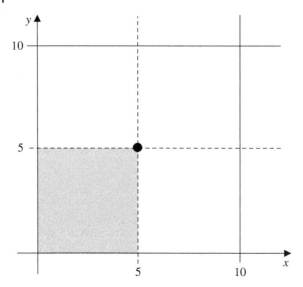

Figure p9.1 The constraints of the problem in Example 9.1.

Solution

The ellipsoidal uncertainty sets can be illustrated in Figure p9.2. The optimization variables x, y should be satisfied with the following constraints:

$$ax + by \leq 1, \quad x \geq 0, \quad y \geq 0 \quad \text{for all } (a, b) \in \Delta_{a,b}$$

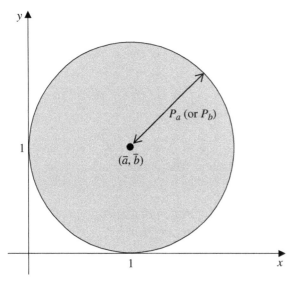

Figure p9.2 The ellipsoidal uncertainty set for Example 9.2.

The above constraints can be rewritten as follows:

$$\max_{(a,b)\in\Delta_{a,b}} ax + by \leq 1, \quad x \geq 0, \quad y \geq 0$$

where the constraint function $ax + by$ can be rewritten as follows:

$$ax + by = (\bar{a} + P_a)x + (\bar{b} + P_b)y = (\bar{a}x + \bar{b}y) + (P_a x + P_b y)$$

The above constraints can be rewritten as follows:

$$(\bar{a}x + \bar{b}y) + \max_{P_a^2+P_b^2\leq1} (P_a x + P_b y) \leq 1, \quad x \geq 0, \quad y \geq 0$$

$$\max_{P_a^2+P_b^2\leq1} (P_a x + P_b y) \leq 1 - (\bar{a}x + \bar{b}y), \quad x \geq 0, \quad y \geq 0$$

$$(x, y) \leq 1 - (x + y), \quad x \geq 0, \quad y \geq 0$$

where $\|(x, y)\|$ is the length of (x, y). Thus, the problem transforms as follows:

$$\max_{x,y} x + y$$

subject to

$$(x, y) \leq 1 - (x + y), \quad x \geq 0, y \geq 0$$

This problem is of the same form as the second-order conic programming problem and now relatively easier than the original problem.

It is possible to have many different outcomes for robust counterparts of other optimization problems. A robust counterpart of a SOCP with uncertainty sets can be formulated by semidefinite programming (SDP) [8]. However, the robust optimization problems as the counterparts of convex optimization problems are not always tractable problems. In [9], the tractability of robust counterparts of convex optimization problems is summarized. For example, the robust counterparts of a SOCP with uncertainty and a SDP with uncertainty are NP-hard. There are many robust optimization applications in wireless communication systems. For example, robust geometric programming is applied to power control problems in wireless communications. The problem is formulated to minimize the total power consumption subject to constraints on the outage probability between receiver and transmitters in log-normal fading channel [10]. When array antenna response is not known precisely, the problem is formulated as robust optimization with an ellipsoidal uncertainty set and is equivalent to a SOCP [11]. In a beamforming design, weights allocation to the array lie within a box constraint and the antenna design problem is transformed to a regularized version of the nominal beamforming problem [12].

Robust stochastic optimization is useful when we deal with stochastic models with uncertain data [13]. In robust stochastic optimization, the objective function and constraints of the problem can be described by probabilities of the events. The robust stochastic optimization problem can be defined as follows:

$$\min_{\mathbf{x}} P(f_0(\mathbf{x}, \boldsymbol{\delta}_0))$$

subject to

$$P(f_i(\mathbf{x}, \boldsymbol{\delta}_i)) \leq \alpha_i, \quad i = 1, 2, \ldots, m \tag{9.18}$$

where $\mathbf{x} \in \mathbb{R}^n$ is the optimization variable, α_i is the limit of the probabilities, and the uncertainty parameters $\boldsymbol{\delta}_i \in \mathbb{R}^k$ takes arbitrary values in the uncertainty set $\boldsymbol{\Delta}_i$. We assume that the probability distribution function of $\mathbf{\Delta}_i$ is known. The problem in Equation (9.18) can be transformed to the robust stochastic linear programming problem as follows:

$$\min_{\mathbf{x}} \mathbf{c}^T \mathbf{x}$$

subject to

$$P(\mathbf{a}^T \mathbf{x} \le b) \ge \gamma \tag{9.19}$$

where the uncertainty parameter $\mathbf{a}$ is expressed as a Gaussian random vector with mean $\bar{\mathbf{a}}$ and covariance $\mathbf{\Sigma}$ and the constraint term holds with the probability of the Gaussian random variable $\mathbf{a}^T \mathbf{x}$ greater than the limit γ. The mean μ and the variance σ^2 of the constraint function $\mathbf{a}^T \mathbf{x}$ can be expressed by $\bar{\mathbf{a}}^T \mathbf{x}$ and $\mathbf{x}^T \mathbf{\Sigma} \mathbf{x}$, respectively. This problem is also called a chance-constrained linear programming problem. The cumulative distribution function of the constraint function $\mathbf{a}^T \mathbf{x}$ is described as follows:

$$F(\delta) = \frac{1}{2} \left(1 + \text{erf} \left(\frac{\delta - \mu}{\sqrt{2\sigma^2}} \right) \right) \tag{9.20}$$

where the error function is

$$\text{erf}(x) = \frac{2}{\sqrt{\pi}} \int_0^x \exp(-t^2) \ dt \tag{9.21}$$

The probability function of the constraint term can be expressed as follows:

$$P(\mathbf{a}^T \mathbf{x} \le b) = \frac{1}{2} \left(1 + \text{erf} \left(\frac{b - \bar{\mathbf{a}}^T \mathbf{x}}{\sqrt{2\mathbf{x}^T \mathbf{\Sigma} \mathbf{x}}} \right) \right) \tag{9.22}$$

and the constraint term is rewritten as follows:

$$\sqrt{2} \text{erf}^{-1}(2\gamma - 1) \mathbf{\Sigma}^{1/2} \mathbf{x}_2 + \bar{\mathbf{a}}^T \mathbf{x} \le b \tag{9.23}$$

When $2\gamma - 1 \ge 0$, the constraint term in Equation (9.23) is the same as that of a SOCP problem. Thus, the problem in Equation (9.19) is rewritten as follows:

$$\min_{\mathbf{x}} \mathbf{c}^T \mathbf{x}$$

subject to

$$\sqrt{2} \text{erf}^{-1}(2\gamma - 1) \mathbf{\Sigma}^{1/2} \mathbf{x}_2 + \bar{\mathbf{a}}^T \mathbf{x} \le b \tag{9.24}$$

This means that the constraint described by the probability can promote a linear programming problem to a SOCP problem.

Example 9.3 *Robust Stochastic Linear Programming*

Consider the following robust stochastic linear programming problem:

$$\min_{x,y} x + y$$

subject to

$$P(ax + by \ge 2) \ge \gamma, \quad x, y \ge 0$$

where a and b have Gaussian distribution with mean μ_a and μ_b and variance σ_a^2 and σ_b^2, respectively. They are independent. Transform the original problem into an equivalent deterministic problem.

Solution

Since the two parameters a and b are independent, the constraint term $ax + by$ also has a Gaussian distribution with mean $\mu_a x + \mu_b y$ and variance $\sigma_a^2 x^2 + \sigma_b^2 y^2$. Thus, the constraint probability is the probability that uncertain variable $ax + by$ is greater than or equal to 2. We assume that β is the value of the standard Gaussian distribution with mean of 0 and variance of 1. The value can be easily obtained from a simple Gaussian function. The constraint term is equivalent to the following equation:

$$\frac{2 - \mu_a x + \mu_b y}{\sqrt{\sigma_a^2 x^2 + \sigma_b^2 y^2}} \geq \beta$$

$$2 - \mu_a x + \mu_b y \geq \beta \sqrt{\sigma_a^2 x^2 + \sigma_b^2 y^2}$$

and the problem with the constraint term described by the probability can be transformed with an equivalent nonlinear deterministic constraint as follows:

$$\min_{x,y} x + y$$

subject to

$$2 - \mu_a x + \mu_b y \geq \beta \sqrt{\sigma_a^2 x^2 + \sigma_b^2 y^2}, \quad x, y \geq 0.$$

Summary 9.2 Robust Optimization

1) A standard form of robust optimization using a bounded uncertainty set is as follows:

$$\min_{\mathbf{x}} f_0(\mathbf{x})$$

subject to

$$C_1 : f_i(\mathbf{x}, \boldsymbol{\delta}_i) \leq 0, \quad \forall \boldsymbol{\delta}_i \in \Delta_i, \quad i = 1, 2, \dots, m$$

where $\mathbf{x} \in \mathbb{R}^n$ is the optimization variable, and the uncertainty parameters $\boldsymbol{\delta}_i \in \mathbb{R}^k$ take arbitrary values in the uncertainty set Δ_i. The goal of the problem is to find the $\mathbf{x}^*$ minimizing $f_0(\mathbf{x})$ among all possible solutions which are feasible for all possible realizations of $\boldsymbol{\delta}_i$ within Δ_i.

2) Robust optimization (RO) finds an acceptable solution under all possible realizations of the uncertain inputs. The solution of robust optimization is protected against data deviations. Robust optimization is a subfield of optimization, in order to find a solution offering robustness against uncertainty.

3) We can summarize the steps of the adjustable robust optimization as follows:

   Initial conditions: Define the system model and formulate the problem

   - ***Step 1***: Solve the nominal problem

   Repeat

   - ***Step 2***: Determine the uncertain parameters and the uncertainty set
   - ***Step 3***: Check quality of the nominal solution and stop if the nominal solution is robust enough
   - ***Step 4***: Determine the adjustable variables and the decision rules
   - ***Step 5***: Formulate the robust counterpart
   - ***Step 6***: Try to approximate and reformulate the problem and then solve the adjustable robust counterpart
   - ***Step 7***: Check the solution and go to step 2 or 4 if not enough

   Until Quality of the robust solution is enough.

9.4 Power Control and Management

Energy efficiency is a key metric of machine-type communication systems. IoT devices and connectivity solutions must be designed for low power so that their battery life is extended. Capabilities of IoT devices and mobile handheld devices are improving due to new features but require more power consumption. However, the battery capacity is improving slowly. In this circumstance, the power management of devices is essential for mMTC services. In the 3GPP standard, two power-saving schemes for mMTC services are adopted: power-saving mode (PSM) and extended discontinuous reception (DRX) [14]. The PSM uses a deep sleep mode by switching off the device while staying in the network. In this mode, the IoT device is not reachable from the network but it allows the device to wake up and transmit data to the network. This scenario is acceptable for IoT networks because the downlink latency is not significant and infrequent paging monitoring is allowed. The extended DRX is similar to the DRX of LTE systems, except for a longer timer value. The extended DRX allows IoT devices to enter in an idle mode so they do not listen for a certain period, then are periodically active to listen for a paging message from the network in order to receive incoming data. For both schemes, power control is an important part of an energy-efficient network. The role of the power control mechanism is to adjust the transmit power, save its own power, and not interfere with neighboring cells or users. In addition, it is helpful for increasing the utilization of the spectrum in wireless communications. The power control methods are classified into centralized or distributed, iterative or non-iterative, and synchronous or asynchronous [15]. Cellular systems basically use centralized and synchronous power control mechanisms. Ad-hoc network systems use distributed and asynchronous power control mechanisms. Since there is no central coordinator or information about other devices, it depends upon local link gain and estimated signal-to-interference-plus-noise ratio (SINR). In mMTC applications, distributed networks are often considered. The basic mechanism of 5G power control is similar to the previous 3G and 4G power control methods. There are two types of 5G power control: open loop control and closed loop control. Open loop power control adjusts the PRACH transmission power. Closed loop power control receives an input from mobile stations and determines PUCCH or PUSCH channel powers. The open loop and closed loop power control mechanisms are described in [16]. A mobile station (or UE) determines a transmission power for PRACH $P_{PRACH,b,f,c}(i)$ on active uplink bandwidth part (BWP) b of carrier f for serving cell c based on downlink reference signal for serving cell c in transmission occasion i as follows [16]:

$$P_{PRACH,b,f,c}(i) = \min(P_{CMAX,f,c}(i), P_{PRACH,target,f,c} + PL_{b,f,c}) \text{ [dBm]} \tag{9.25}$$

where $P_{CMAX,f,c}(i)$ is the configured maximum UE output power for carrier f of serving cell c within transmission occasion i, $P_{PRACH,target,f,c}$ is the target reception power provided by higher layers for the active uplink BWP b of carrier f of serving cell c, and $PL_{b,f,c}$ is a path loss for the active uplink BWP b of carrier f based on the downlink reference signal associated with the PRACH transmission on the active downlink BWP of serving cell c. We can interpret Equation (9.25) as the following steps: (i) calculate the target reception power and path loss (P_1); (ii) compare P_1 with the configured maximum output power (P_2); and (iii) select either P_1 or P_2. It looks like a simple procedure but it is actually not simple to calculate accurate $P_{PRACH,target,f,c}$ and $PL_{b,f,c}$. If a mobile station transmits a PUSCH on active uplink BWP b of carrier f of serving cell c using a parameter set configuration with index j, reference signal index q_d, and PUSCH power control adjustment state with index l, the mobile station determines the PUSCH transmission power $P_{PUSCH,b,f,c}(i,j,q_d,l)$ in the transmission occasion i as follows [16]:

$$P_{PUSCH,b,f,c}(i,j,q_d,l) = \min \begin{pmatrix} P_{CMAXf,c}(i), P_{O\_PUSCH,b,f,c}(j)+ \\ 10\log_{10}(2^\mu M_{RB,b,f,c}^{PUSCH}(i))+ \\ \alpha_{b,f,c}(j)PL_{b,f,c}(q_d)+ \\ \Delta_{TF,b,f,c}(i) + f_{b,f,c}(i,l) \end{pmatrix} \text{[dBm]} \qquad (9.26)$$

where $P_{O\_PUSCH,b,f,c}(j)$ is $P_{O\_Nominal\_PUSCH,f,c}(j)+P_{O\_UE\_PUSCH,b,f,c}(j)$, $M_{RB,b,f,c}^{PUSCH}(i)$ is the bandwidth of the PUSCH resource assignment expressed in number of resource blocks, $\alpha_{b,f,c}(j)$ is a value of higher layer parameter, $PL_{b,f,c}(q_d)$ is a downlink path loss estimate calculated by the mobile station using reference signal index q_d for active downlink BWP of serving cell c, $\Delta_{TF,b,f,c}(i) = 10\log_{10}((2^{BPSK,K_s} - 1)\beta_{offset}^{PUSCH})$ for $K_s = 1.25$, and $\Delta_{TF,b,f,c}(i) = 0$ for $K_s = 0$ where K_s is provided by higher layer, and $f_{b,f,c}(i,l)$ is the PUSCH power control adjustment state l for active uplink BWP b of carrier f of serving cell c. As we can observe from Equation (9.26), closed loop power control is more elaborate than open loop power control. Both open loop and closed loop power control are centralized and synchronous power control mechanisms. In the realization of mMTC applications, power management is a major research challenge. We design power control schemes and optimize the mMTC network in terms of energy efficiency.

9.4.1 Linear Programming for Power Control in Distributed Networks

Distributed power control is useful in ad-hoc networks. We can design a power control scheme based on local link gain, estimated SINR and target threshold [17]. Distributed power control satisfies certain SINR thresholds in the network as follows:

$$p_i(k+1) = \frac{\gamma_i}{SINR_i(k)}p_i(k) \qquad (9.27)$$

where $p_i(k)$ is a transmit power of the ith link in the kth time slot, γ_i is the threshold of a lower SINR for each link i, and:

$$SINR_i(k) = \frac{g_{ii}p_i(k)}{\sum_{i \neq j}g_{ij}p_j(k) + n_i} \qquad (9.28)$$

where g_{ij} and n_i are the channel response from a transmitter of the ith link to a receiver of jth link and additive white Gaussian noise (AWGN), respectively. In a distributed manner, each user measures autonomously its current SINR and makes its power level decision for the next step in order to achieve its target threshold. This scheme is the standard distributed power control and it converges to the Pareto optimal that is the minimal power operational point for the network of links. There are several extensions such as asynchronous implementation [18], joint power control [19], and integer programming [20]. As one example, we consider integer programming for power control. Integer programming is a subset of linear programming. Most of the characteristics of integer programming are similar to linear programming except one thing: some or all of the variables are restricted to be integers.

We assume one simple scenario including one small cell with one mobile device and one neighboring small cell with one mobile device. The power level is constrained as integers less than or equal to some positive integer C and the boundary of the power level is from 0 (minimum power level) to 20 (maximum power level). The objective is to assign an optimal power to each mobile device and minimize the total power. The problem can be formulated as follows:

$$\min_{p_1,p_2}(p_1 + p_2)$$

subject to

$$C_1 : \max\left(\frac{g_{11}}{n_1}p_1 - \frac{\gamma_1 g_{21}}{n_1}p_2, \frac{g_{12}}{n_2}p_1 - \frac{\gamma_1 g_{22}}{n_2}p_2\right) \geq \gamma_1$$

$$C_2 : \max\left(-\frac{\gamma_2 g_{11}}{n_1}p_1 + \frac{g_{21}}{n_1}p_2, -\frac{\gamma_2 g_{12}}{n_2}p_1 + \frac{g_{22}}{n_2}p_2\right) \geq \gamma_2$$

$$C_3 : p_1, p_2 \in [0, 1, 2, \ldots, 20] \tag{9.29}$$

where g, γ and n are the channel responses, thresholds and noises of each link, respectively. We assume that they have the following values:

$$g_{11} = \frac{4}{5}, \ g_{21} = \frac{4}{5}, \ g_{12} = \frac{1}{5}, \ g_{22} = \frac{2}{3},$$

$$\gamma_1 = \gamma_2 = \frac{3}{4}, \ n_1 = n_2 = 1 \tag{9.30}$$

Now, we can drive the following equations from the first constraint of Equation (9.29):

$$\frac{g_{11}}{n_1}p_1 - \frac{\gamma_1 g_{21}}{n_1}p_2 \geq \gamma_1 \tag{9.31}$$

$$\frac{4}{5}p_1 - \frac{3}{5}p_2 \geq \frac{3}{4} \tag{9.32}$$

$$\frac{4}{3}p_1 - \frac{5}{4} \geq p_2 \tag{9.33}$$

and

$$\frac{g_{12}}{n_2}p_1 - \frac{\gamma_1 g_{22}}{n_2}p_2 \geq \gamma_1 \tag{9.34}$$

$$\frac{1}{5}p_1 - \frac{1}{2}p_2 \geq \frac{3}{4} \tag{9.35}$$

$$\frac{2}{5}p_1 - \frac{3}{2} \geq p_2 \tag{9.36}$$

The feasible area of the above two Equations (9.33) and (9.36) can be represented as shown in Figure 9.5.

Likewise, we drive the following equations from the second constraint of Equation (9.29):

$$-\frac{\gamma_2 g_{11}}{n_1}p_1 + \frac{g_{21}}{n_1}p_2 \geq \gamma_2 \tag{9.37}$$

$$-\frac{3}{5}p_1 + \frac{4}{5}p_2 \geq \frac{3}{4} \tag{9.38}$$

$$\frac{3}{4}p_1 + \frac{15}{16} \leq p_2 \tag{9.39}$$

Figure 9.5 The shaded area satisfying the first constraint.

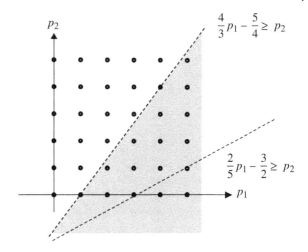

and

$$-\frac{\gamma_2 g_{12}}{n_2} p_1 + \frac{g_{22}}{n_2} p_2 \geq \gamma_2 \tag{9.40}$$

$$-\frac{3}{20} p_1 + \frac{2}{3} p_2 \geq \frac{3}{4} \tag{9.41}$$

$$\frac{9}{40} p_1 + \frac{9}{8} \leq p_2 \tag{9.42}$$

The feasible area of the above two Equations (9.39) and (9.42) can be represented as shown in Figure 9.6.

Now, we can have the intersection of Figures 9.5 and 9.6 that satisfies both sets of constraints and find the optimal solution of the power control problem as shown in Figure 9.7.

Therefore, the optimal solution of the power control problem can be found $p_1 = 3$ and $p_2 = 2$ which satisfies the objective function from the shaded area of Figure 9.7. Now, we assume that the channel responses, thresholds and noises of each link have different values

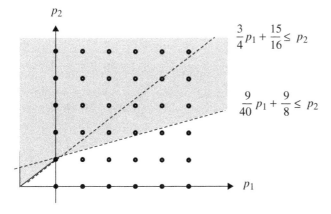

Figure 9.6 The shaded area satisfying the second constraint.

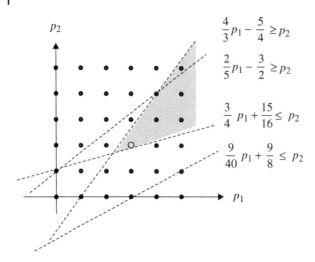

$$\frac{4}{3}p_1 - \frac{5}{4} \geq p_2$$

$$\frac{2}{5}p_1 - \frac{3}{2} \geq p_2$$

$$\frac{3}{4}p_1 + \frac{15}{16} \leq p_2$$

$$\frac{9}{40}p_1 + \frac{9}{8} \leq p_2$$

Figure 9.7 The shaded area satisfying both constraints.

as follows:

$$g_{11} = 1, \ g_{21} = 10, \ g_{12} = \frac{1}{2}, \ g_{22} = 1,$$

$$\gamma_1 = \gamma_2 = \frac{3}{4}, \ n_1 = n_2 = 1 \tag{9.43}$$

We can drive the following equations from the first constraint of Equation (9.29):

$$\frac{2}{15}p_1 - \frac{1}{10} \geq p_2 \tag{9.44}$$

and

$$\frac{2}{3}p_1 - 1 \geq p_2 \tag{9.45}$$

The feasible area of the above two Equations (9.44) and (9.45) can be represented as shown in Figure 9.6a. Likewise, we drive the following equations from the second constraint of Equation (9.29).

$$\frac{3}{40}p_1 + \frac{3}{40} \leq p_2 \tag{9.46}$$

and

$$\frac{3}{8}p_1 + \frac{3}{4} \leq p_2 \tag{9.47}$$

The feasible area of the above two Equations (9.46) and (9.47) can be represented as shown in Figure 9.8b. Now, we can observe from Figure 9.8a,b that, contrary to the previous example, there is no optimal solution that satisfies both constraints. In this case, we can keep the previous power values.

9.4.2 Power Control Problem Formulations

We consider one network consisting of N point-to-point links with independent and flat fading channels. The ith receiver receives the signal with the power level $(p_1, \ldots, p_N)$ from the ith transmitter. The channel response between the ith receiver and jth transmitter

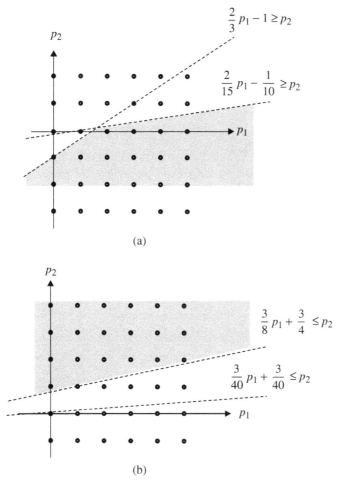

Figure 9.8 The shaded areas satisfying (a) the first constraint and (b) the second constraint.

is represented as g_{ij}. In [21], the power control mechanism is designed by maximizing the minimum expected value of the receiver signal-to-interference ratio (SIR) subject to non-negative transmit power constraints. Thus, the optimization problem is defined as follows:

$$\max_{\{p_i\}_{i=1}^{N}} \left(\min_i \mathrm{E}(SIR_i)\right)$$

subject to

$$p_i > 0, \quad i = 1, 2, \dots, N \tag{9.48}$$

where $\mathrm{E}(SIR_i)$ is the expected value of the ith SIR as follows:

$$\mathrm{E}(SIR_i) = \mathrm{E}\left(\frac{g_{ii}p_i}{\sum_{j=1, i \neq j}^{N} g_{ij}p_j}\right) = \frac{G_{ii}p_i}{\sum_{j=1, i \neq j}^{N} G_{ij}p_j} \tag{9.49}$$

where $G_{ij} = E(g_{ij})$. The SIRs at all receivers are identical at the optimum [21]. Thus, Equation (9.48) can be rewritten as follows:

$$\max_{t,\{p_i\}_{i=1}^N} t$$

subject to

$$\frac{G_{ii}p_i}{\sum_{j=1,i\neq j}^N G_{ij}p_j} = t, \quad i = 1, 2, \ldots, N$$

$$p_i > 0, \quad i = 1, 2, \ldots, N. \tag{9.50}$$

The problem in Equation (9.50) can be solved by the Perron-Frobenius theorem. By substituting α for $1/t$, it can be rewritten as follows:

$$\min_{\alpha,\{p_i\}_{i=1}^N} \alpha$$

subject to

$$\mathbf{Ap} = \alpha\mathbf{p},$$

$$p_i > 0, \quad i = 1, 2, \ldots, N \tag{9.51}$$

where $\mathbf{p} = [p_1, \ldots, p_N]$ and the matrix $\mathbf{A}$ is

$$A_{ij} = \begin{cases} G_{ij}/G_{ii}, & i \neq j \\ 0, & i = j \end{cases} \tag{9.52}$$

In order to solve Equation (9.51), we should find the largest eigenvalue of the matrix $\mathbf{A}$. When we have $\mathbf{A} \in \mathbb{R}^{n \times n}$ and $\mathbf{A} \geq 0$, there is the Perron-Frobenius eigenvalue λ_{PF} of the matrix $\mathbf{A}$ that is real and non-negative, with associated non-negative left and right Perron-Frobenius eigenvectors. We have $|\lambda| \leq \lambda_{PF}$ for any other eigenvalue λ. The Perron-Frobenius eigenvalue λ_{PF} is the largest. The associated Perron-Frobenius eigenvector allows us to find the optimal power allocation for the problem in Equation (9.51).

Based on the outage probability of the receivers, the power control problem can be formulated [21]. The outage probability P_i of the ith receiver can be defined as the probability that the SINR of the ith receiver is lower than threshold γ as follows:

$$P_i = P\left(g_{ii}p_i \leq \gamma\left(\sum_{j=1,i\neq j}^N g_{ij}p_j + n_i\right)\right) \tag{9.53}$$

We assume that AWGN is not significant compared with the interference and we try to simplify the problem. Thus, the outage probability in Equation (9.53) is rewritten as follows:

$$P_i = P\left(g_{ii}p_i - \gamma\sum_{j=1,i\neq j}^N g_{ij}p_j \leq 0\right) \tag{9.54}$$

When the channel responses are independent, exponentially distributed random variables, the outage probability density function can be expressed as follows [22]:

$$P_i = 1 - \prod_{i\neq j}^N \left(\frac{1}{1 + \frac{\gamma G_{ij}p_i}{G_{ii}p_i}}\right) \tag{9.55}$$

Now, the robust power control mechanism is designed by minimizing the maximum outage probability subject to box transmit power constraints (the minimum transmit power p_{min} and the maximum transmit power p_{max}). Thus, the optimization problem is defined as follows:

$$\min_{\{p_i\}_{i=1}^N} \left(\max_i P_i \right)$$

subject to   (9.56)

$$p_{min} \leq p_i \leq p_{max}, \quad i = 1, 2, \dots, Na$$

The problem in Equation (9.56) can be equivalently rewritten as follows:

$$\min_{\{p_i\}_{i=1}^N} \left(\max_i \prod_{\substack{i \neq j}}^N \left(1 + \frac{\gamma G_{ij} p_i}{G_{ii} p_i} \right) \right)$$

subject to   (9.57)

$$p_{min} \leq p_i \leq p_{max}, \quad i = 1, 2, \dots, N$$

By introducing t, the problem in Equation (9.57) can be rewritten as follows:

$$\min_{t, \{p_i\}_{i=1}^N} t$$

subject to

$$\prod_{\substack{i \neq j}}^N \left(1 + \frac{\gamma G_{ij} p_i}{G_{ii} p_i} \right) \leq t, \quad i = 1, 2, \dots, N$$ (9.58)

$$p_{min} \leq p_i \leq p_{max}, \quad i = 1, 2, \dots, N$$

The problem in Equation (9.58) is regarded as geometric programming. Geometric programming is not convex but can be transformed to convex optimization through changing variables, objective and constraint functions [23]. The standard form of geometric programming is as follows:

$$\min_{\mathbf{x}} f_0(\mathbf{x})$$

subject to

$$C_1 : f_i(\mathbf{x}) \leq 1, \quad i = 1, 2, \dots, m$$ (9.59)

$$C_2 : h_i(\mathbf{x}) = 1, \quad i = 1, 2, \dots, p$$

where $f_0, \dots, f_m$ are posynomials and $h_1, \dots, h_p$ are monomials. A monomial is a function $h : \mathbb{R}_{++}^n \to \mathbb{R}$ defined as follows:

$$h_i(\mathbf{x}) = c_i x_1^{a_1^i} x_2^{a_2^i} \dots x_n^{a_n^i}$$ (9.60)

where $c_i > 0$ and $a_j^i, j = 1, \dots, n$ are exponents. A sum of monomial functions is called a posynomial as follows:

$$f_i(\mathbf{x}) = \sum_{k=1}^{K_i} c_{ik} x_1^{a_1^{ik}} x_2^{a_2^{ik}} \dots x_n^{a_n^{ik}}$$ (9.61)

where $c_{ik} > 0$ and $a_j^{ik}, j = 1, \dots, n$ are exponents. In the problem in Equation (9.58), the objective is a monomial, the first constraint is a posynomial, and the second constraint is a monomial. Thus, it is possible to transform to convex optimization. We can solve the transformed problem efficiently.

9.4.3 Beamforming for Transmit Power Minimization

As we discussed in Chapter 7, there are various forms of MIMO techniques. Among them, beamforming is generally known as the forming of antenna beams in the desired direction with a certain power. Beamforming can be used at the front-ends of both transmitter and receiver in order to achieve spatial selectivity. Receive beamforming is widely used in wireless communication systems. However, it requires multiple antenna in a receiver. It is not suitable for mMTC environments. On the other hand, transmit beamforming is suitable for multi-user environments including mMTC systems. In multi-user systems, it can deliver independent streams to each user and reduce interference due to the dedicated beams, where the dedicated beams are generated by adding signal components coherently or destructively at the intended user or unintended users, respectively. Thus, transmit beamforming delivers signal power to a certain user and less energy to others. It is helpful for energy efficiency improvement in mMTC systems. Basically, transmit beamforming is more complex than receive beamforming because receive beamforming affects one user, but transmit beamforming should be designed while taking into account all users in cellular networks. In addition, channel station information at transmitter (CSIT) is essential for transmit beamforming. It is difficult to obtain accurate CSIT in a practical wireless communication system, and the performance of beamforming is very sensitive to channel state information. Figure 9.9 illustrates the receive and transmit beamforming structure.

We consider transmit beamforming with N transmit antennas and M users with single antenna. The transmit signal at time t, $\mathbf{x}(t)$, can be represented as follows:

$$\mathbf{x}(t) = \sum_{m=1}^{M} s_m(t)\mathbf{w}_m \tag{9.62}$$

where $s_m(t)$ and $\mathbf{w}_m$ are the mth user symbol and beamforming vector, respectively. The received signal at the mth user, $r_m(t)$, can be expressed as follows:

$$r_m(t) = \mathbf{h}_m^H \mathbf{x}(t) + n_m(t) \tag{9.63}$$

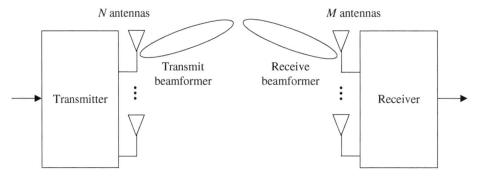

Figure 9.9 Transmit and receive beamforming.

where $\mathbf{h}_m$ and $n_m(t)$ are the channel response of the mth user and AWGN at the receiver, respectively. We assume that the symbols and the noise are statistically independent. The SINR at the mth user, $SINR_m$, can be represented as follows:

$$SINR_m = \frac{|\mathbf{w}_m^H \mathbf{h}_m|^2}{\sum_{l=1,l\neq m}^{M} |\mathbf{w}_l^H \mathbf{h}_m|^2 + \sigma_m^2} \tag{9.64}$$

where σ_m^2 is the noise power. We can design the transmit beamformer in order to minimize the total transmit power of a base station subject to the constraint on SINR balancing. We assume that CSIT, $\mathbf{h}_m$, is known at the transmitter. The transmit beamformer design can be formulated as follows [24]:

$$\min_{\{\mathbf{w}_m\}_{m=1}^{M}} \sum_{m=1}^{M} \mathbf{w}_m^2$$

subject to

$$\frac{|\mathbf{w}_m^H \mathbf{h}_m|^2}{\sum_{l=1,l\neq m}^{M} |\mathbf{w}_l^H \mathbf{h}_m|^2 + \sigma_m^2} \geq \gamma_m^T, \quad m = 1, 2, \ldots, M \tag{9.65}$$

where γ_m^T is a predefined threshold SINR. The problem in Equation (9.65) is not convex optimization. However, we consider from the characteristics of beamforming that the beamforming vector goes through an arbitrary phase shift. The problem in Equation (9.65) can be transformed as follows [24]:

$$\min_{\{\mathbf{w}_m\}_{m=1}^{M}} \sum_{m=1}^{M} \mathbf{w}_m^2$$

subject to

$$(\mathbf{w}_m^H \mathbf{h}_m)^2 \geq \gamma_m^T \sum_{l=1,l\neq m}^{M} \mathbf{w}_l^H \mathbf{h}_m \mathbf{h}_m^H \mathbf{w}_l + \gamma_m^T \sigma_m^2, \quad m = 1, 2, \ldots, M \tag{9.66}$$

$$\Re(\mathbf{w}_m^H \mathbf{h}_m) \geq 0, \quad m = 1, 2, \ldots, M$$

$$\Im(\mathbf{w}_m^H \mathbf{h}_m) = 0, \quad m = 1, 2, \ldots, M$$

where $\Re()$ and $\Im()$ denote the real part and imaginary part, respectively. This problem contains a quadratic objective function and linear equality and inequality constraints. We can regard it as a convex quadratic optimization problem. As we discussed in Chapter 4, we can solve the problem using two classes of algorithms: active-set method and interior point method. If $\mathbf{h}_m$ is not known and the channel correlation matrix is known at the transmitter, the problem in Equation (9.65) is rewritten as follows [24]:

$$\min_{\{\mathbf{w}_m\}_{m=1}^{M}} \sum_{m=1}^{M} \mathbf{w}_m^2$$

subject to

$$\frac{|\mathbf{w}_m^H \mathbf{R}_m \mathbf{w}_m|^2}{\sum_{l=1,l\neq m}^{M} |\mathbf{w}_l^H \mathbf{R}_m \mathbf{w}_l|^2 + \sigma_m^2} \geq \gamma_m^T, \quad m = 1, 2, \ldots, M \tag{9.67}$$

where $\mathbf{R}_m = E(\mathbf{h}_m \mathbf{h}_m^H)$ is the channel correlation matrix. It can be approximated as a Kronecker product of the correlation matrices at transmitter and receiver. This problem is not a convex optimization problem. We can transform the problem using semidefinite relaxation (SDR). SDR is a computationally efficient approximation technique. It can be applied to nonconvex, quadratically constrained quadratic programs (QCQPs). In many practical applications including beamforming, IoT network localization, waveform design and so on, SDR allows us to have empirical approximations. We consider the following QCQP problem [25]:

$$\min_{\mathbf{x}} \mathbf{x}^T \mathbf{C} \mathbf{x}$$

subject to

$$\mathbf{x}^T \mathbf{A}_i \mathbf{x} \geq b_i, \quad i = 1, 2, \ldots, m \tag{9.68}$$

where the inequality notation $\geq$ can be replaced by either $\leq$ or $=$. $\mathbf{C}$ and $\mathbf{A}_i \in \mathbb{S}^n$ are all positive semidefinite, where $\mathbb{S}^n$ is the set of all real symmetric $n \times n$ matrices. $\mathbf{x} \in \mathbb{R}^n$ and $b_i \in \mathbb{R}$. The SDR uses the definition $\mathbf{X} = \mathbf{x}\mathbf{x}^T$ to make the problem linear. In addition, the condition $\mathbf{X} = \mathbf{x}\mathbf{x}^T$ implies that rank $(\mathbf{X}) = 1$. A function $f(\mathbf{x}) = \mathbf{x}^T \mathbf{C} \mathbf{x}$ is convex if and only if $\mathbf{C}$ is positive semidefinite. The objective function and the constraint function satisfy the following:

$$\mathbf{x}^T \mathbf{C} \mathbf{x} = \mathrm{Tr}(\mathbf{x}^T \mathbf{C} \mathbf{x}) = \mathrm{Tr}(\mathbf{C} \mathbf{x}^T \mathbf{x}) \tag{9.69}$$

and

$$\mathbf{x}^T \mathbf{A}_i \mathbf{x} = \mathrm{Tr}(\mathbf{x}^T \mathbf{A}_i \mathbf{x}) = \mathrm{Tr}(\mathbf{A}_i \mathbf{x}^T \mathbf{x}) \tag{9.70}$$

where $\mathrm{Tr}()$ is a trace. Thus, the problem in Equation (9.68) can be transformed as follows:

$$\min_{\mathbf{X}} \mathrm{Tr}(\mathbf{C}\mathbf{X})^2$$

subject to

$$\mathrm{Tr}(\mathbf{A}_i \mathbf{X}) \geq b_i, \quad i = 1, 2, \ldots, m \tag{9.71}$$

$$\mathbf{X} \geq 0$$

$$\mathrm{rank}(\mathbf{X}) = 1$$

where $\mathbf{X} \in \mathbb{S}^n$ and $\mathbf{X} \geq 0$ indicates that $\mathbf{X}$ is positive semidefinite. As we can observe from Equation (9.71), the objective and constraint functions become convex in $\mathbf{X}$. Comparing Equations (9.71) and (9.68), the rank constraint is included. It is nonconvex. Thus, we drop the rank constraint and obtain the following relaxed problem:

$$\min_{\mathbf{X}} \mathrm{Tr}(\mathbf{C}\mathbf{X})$$

subject to

$$\mathrm{Tr}(\mathbf{A}_i \mathbf{X}) \geq b_i, \quad i = 1, 2, \ldots, m \tag{9.72}$$

$$\mathbf{X} \geq 0$$

The problem in Equation (9.72) is known as the SDR of the problem in Equation (9.68). The optimal solution may be found by the interior point method or other numerical algorithms. Now, we define $\mathbf{W}_m = \mathbf{w}_m \mathbf{w}_m^H$ and reformulate the problem in Equation (9.67) using SDR as follows:

$$\min_{\{\mathbf{w}_m\}_{m=1}^M} \sum_{m=1}^M \operatorname{Tr}(\mathbf{W}_m)$$

subject to

$$\operatorname{Tr}(\mathbf{W}_m \mathbf{R}_m) \geq \gamma_m^T \sum_{l=1, l \neq m}^M \operatorname{Tr}(\mathbf{W}_l \mathbf{R}_m) + \gamma_m^T \sigma_m^2, \quad m = 1, 2, \ldots, M \quad (9.73)$$

$$\mathbf{W}_m \geq 0, \quad m = 1, 2, \ldots, M$$

The reformulation allows us to solve the problem by numerical algorithms. Robust stochastic optimization can be used for the transmit beamforming design. The robust downlink beamforming design problem can be formulated using outage probability [26]. The non-outage probability of the mth user is expressed as follows:

$$P_m = P\left(\frac{\mathbf{w}_m^H (\widetilde{\mathbf{R}}_m + \Delta_m) \mathbf{w}_m}{\sum_{l=1, l \neq m}^M \mathbf{w}_l^H (\widetilde{\mathbf{R}}_m + \Delta_m) \mathbf{w}_l + \sigma_m^2} \geq \gamma_m^T \right) \quad (9.74)$$

where the actual channel correlation matrices, $\mathbf{R}_m$, are expressed as follows:

$$\mathbf{R}_m = \widetilde{\mathbf{R}}_m + \Delta_m \quad (9.75)$$

where $\widetilde{\mathbf{R}}_m$ and Δ_m are the estimated channel correlation matrices and the errors of the mth user, respectively. Δ_m are random matrices. We assume that real-valued diagonal and complex-valued upper or lower triangle elements of Δ_m are zero mean and independent Gaussian values with a variance of $\sigma_{\Delta_m}^2$ [26]. We assume that the non-outage probability in Equation (9.74) can be rewritten as follows [26]:

$$P_m = P\left(\operatorname{Tr}((\widetilde{\mathbf{R}}_m + \Delta_m) \mathbf{W}_m) \geq \gamma_m^T \sum_{l=1, l \neq m}^M \operatorname{Tr}((\widetilde{\mathbf{R}}_m + \Delta_m) \mathbf{W}_l) + \gamma_m^T \sigma_m^2 \right) \quad (9.76)$$

$$P_m = P(\operatorname{Tr}((\widetilde{\mathbf{R}}_m + \Delta_m) \mathbf{Z}_m) \geq \gamma_m^T \sigma_m^2) \quad (9.77)$$

where $\mathbf{Z}_m = \mathbf{W}_m - \gamma_m^T \sum_{l=1, l \neq m}^M \mathbf{W}_l$. The actual channel correlation matrices are Hermitian, and $\operatorname{Tr}((\widetilde{\mathbf{R}}_m + \Delta_m) \mathbf{Z}_m)$ is regarded as a real-valued Gaussian random variable [26]. Using the Gaussian error function, non-outage probability is given as follows:

$$P_m = \frac{1}{2} + \frac{1}{2} \operatorname{erf}\left(\frac{\operatorname{Tr}(\widetilde{\mathbf{R}}_m \mathbf{Z}_m) - \gamma_m^T \sigma_m^2}{\sqrt{2} \sigma_{\Delta_m}^2 \mathbf{Z}_m} \right) \quad (9.78)$$

From Equation (9.78), the non-outage probability constraint is defined as follows:

$$\operatorname{Tr}(\widetilde{\mathbf{R}}_m \mathbf{Z}_m) - \gamma_m^T \sigma_m^2 \geq \sqrt{2} \sigma_{\Delta_m}^2 \operatorname{erf}^{-1}(2p_m - 1) \mathbf{Z}_m \quad (9.79)$$

because the non-outage probability of the mth user is greater than the predefined probability p_m $(P_m \geq p_m)$. Thus, we can formulate the robust non-outage probability constrained transmit beamforming problem as follows:

$$\min_{\{\mathbf{w}_m\}_{m=1}^{M}} \sum_{m=1}^{M} \mathrm{Tr}(\mathbf{W}_m)$$

subject to

$$\mathrm{Tr}(\widetilde{\mathbf{R}}_m \mathbf{Z}_m) - \gamma_m^T \sigma_m^2 \geq \sqrt{2}\sigma_{\Delta_m}^2 \, \mathrm{erf}^{-1}(2p_m - 1)\mathbf{Z}_m, \quad m = 1, 2, \ldots, M \quad (9.80)$$

$$\mathbf{W}_m \geq 0, \quad m = 1, 2, \ldots, M$$

The problem in Equation (9.80) includes a linear convex objective function and convex second-order cone and SDP constraint functions. This problem is convex and can be solved by numerical algorithms.

Example 9.4 *Transmit Beamforming for Power Minimization with SINR Constraints*

Consider a single cell mMTC network composed of a base station with N antennas and M users with single antennas. The downlink channel response is known at the transmitter. The transmit signals are separated spatially by the transmit beamforming vectors $\mathbf{w}_m$. The squared norm $\|\mathbf{w}_m\|^2$ represents the power allocation to m users and the normalization $\mathbf{w}_m/\|\mathbf{w}_m\|$ represents the beamforming direction. Find the optimal transmit beamforming vectors in order to minimize the total transmit power in the cell.

Solution

Firstly, we formulate the optimization problem as follows:

$$\min_{\{\mathbf{w}_m\}_{m=1}^{M}} \sum_{m=1}^{M} \left\| \mathbf{w}_m \right\|^2$$

subject to

$$SINR_m \geq \gamma_m^T, \quad m = 1, 2, \ldots, M$$

where γ_m^T is a predefined threshold SINR and $SINR_m$ is SINR at the mth user as follows:

$$SINR_m = \frac{|\mathbf{h}_m^H \mathbf{w}_m|^2}{\sum_{l=1, l\neq m}^{M} |\mathbf{h}_l^H \mathbf{w}_m|^2 + \sigma_m^2}$$

where σ_m^2 is the noise power. As we can observe from the optimization, the objective function is convex but the constraint function is not convex. The absolute values in the SINR make $\mathbf{w}_m$ and $e^{j\theta_m}\mathbf{w}_m$ equivalent for any phase rotation θ_m. Thus, the constraint function can be transformed as follows:

$$\frac{1}{\gamma_m^T \sigma_m^2} |\mathbf{h}_m^H \mathbf{w}_m|^2 \geq \sum_{l=1, l\neq m}^{M} \frac{1}{\sigma_m^2} |\mathbf{h}_m^H \mathbf{w}_l|^2 + 1$$

The transformed constraint functions can be rewritten as follows:

$$\frac{1}{\sqrt{\gamma_m^T \sigma_m^2}} \Re(\mathbf{h}_m^H \mathbf{w}_m) \geq \sqrt{\sum_{l=1, l\neq m}^{M} \frac{1}{\sigma_m^2} |\mathbf{h}_m^H \mathbf{w}_l|^2 + 1}$$

where $\Re()$ denotes the real part and this constraint is a second-order cone constraint. We can regard the problem as a convex quadratic optimization problem. The strong duality and Karush–Kuhn–Tucker (KKT) conditions hold for the optimization problem. The Lagrangian function of the optimization problem can be defined as follows [24]:

$$L(\mathbf{w}_1, \ldots, \mathbf{w}_M, \lambda_1, \ldots, \lambda_M)$$

$$= \sum_{m=1}^{M} \mathbf{w}_m^2 + \sum_{m=1}^{M} \lambda_m \left(\sum_{l=1, l\neq m}^{M} \frac{1}{\sigma_m^2} |\mathbf{h}_m^H \mathbf{w}_l|^2 + 1 - \frac{1}{\gamma_m^T \sigma_m^2} |\mathbf{h}_m^H \mathbf{w}_m|^2 \right)$$

where $\lambda_m \geq 0$ is the Lagrange multiplier and it is associated with the mth user. We could have KKT conditions that $\partial L / \partial \mathbf{w}_m = 0$, $m = 1, \ldots, M$ at the optimal solution as follows:

$$\mathbf{w}_m + \sum_{l=1, l\neq m}^{M} \frac{\lambda_l}{\sigma_m^2} \mathbf{h}_l \mathbf{h}_l^H \mathbf{w}_m - \frac{\lambda_m}{\gamma_m^T \sigma_m^2} \mathbf{h}_m \mathbf{h}_m^H \mathbf{w}_m = 0$$

$$\left(\mathbf{I}_N + \sum_{l=1}^{M} \frac{\lambda_l}{\sigma_m^2} \mathbf{h}_l \mathbf{h}_l^H \right) \mathbf{w}_m = \frac{\lambda_m}{\sigma_m^2} \left(1 + \frac{1}{\gamma_m^T} \right) \mathbf{h}_m \mathbf{h}_m^H \mathbf{w}_m$$

$$\mathbf{w}_m = \left(\mathbf{I}_N + \sum_{l=1}^{M} \frac{\lambda_l}{\sigma_m^2} \mathbf{h}_l \mathbf{h}_l^H \right)^{-1} \mathbf{h}_m \frac{\lambda_m}{\sigma_m^2} \left(1 + \frac{1}{\gamma_m^T} \right) \mathbf{h}_m^H \mathbf{w}_m$$

$$\mathbf{w}_m = \widetilde{\mathbf{w}}_m^* \alpha$$

where $\mathbf{I}_N$ is the identity matrix. The term $\alpha = \frac{\lambda_m}{\sigma_m^2} \left(1 + \frac{1}{\gamma_m^T} \right) \mathbf{h}_m^H \mathbf{w}_m$ is scalar and the term $\widetilde{\mathbf{w}}_m^* = \left(\mathbf{I}_N + \sum_{l=1}^{M} \frac{\lambda_l}{\sigma_m^2} \mathbf{h}_l \mathbf{h}_l^H \right)^{-1} \mathbf{h}_m$ includes the beamforming direction. Thus, the optimal beamforming vectors $\mathbf{w}_m^*$ are represented as follows:

$$\mathbf{w}_m^* = \sqrt{p_m} \frac{\left(\mathbf{I}_N + \sum_{l=1}^{M} \frac{\lambda_l}{\sigma_m^2} \mathbf{h}_l \mathbf{h}_l^H \right)^{-1} \mathbf{h}_m}{\left(\mathbf{I}_N + \sum_{l=1}^{M} \frac{\lambda_l}{\sigma_m^2} \mathbf{h}_l \mathbf{h}_l^H \right)^{-1} \mathbf{h}_m}, \quad m = 1, \ldots, M$$

where p_m is the beamforming power for the mth user and the Lagrange multiplier can be obtained from the following equation [24]:

$$\lambda_l = \frac{\sigma_m^2}{\left(1 + \frac{1}{\gamma_m^T} \right) \mathbf{h}_l^H \left(\mathbf{I}_N + \sum_{l=1}^{M} \frac{\lambda_l}{\sigma_m^2} \mathbf{h}_l \mathbf{h}_l^H \right)^{-1} \mathbf{h}_m}, \quad \text{for all } l$$

Summary 9.3 Power Control and Management

1) Energy efficiency is a key metric of machine-type communication systems. IoT devices and connectivity solutions must be designed for low power so that their battery life is extended.
2) The basic mechanism of 5G power control is similar to the previous 3G and 4G power control methods.
3) In a 3GPP standard, two power-saving schemes for mMTC services are adopted: power-saving mode (PSM) and extended discontinuous reception (DRX)

(Continued)

4) A power control mechanism can be designed by maximizing the minimum expected value of the receiver signal-to-interference ratio subject to non-negative transmit power constraints. After transforming to a convex optimization problem, it can be solved by interior point methods.
5) Transmit beamforming delivers a signal power to the certain user and less energy to others. It is helpful for energy efficiency improvements in mMTC systems.

9.5 Wireless Sensor Networks

In IoT networks, all node-equipped sensors collect data periodically and send their information to the internet directly. A server connected to the internet analyzes and interprets the data. On the other hand, wireless sensor networks (WSNs) are regarded as a subset of IoT networks. WSNs are defined as a group of sensors for monitoring the physical conditions of the environment, collecting the related information, and sending the data to central nodes. In WSNs, the collected data can be analyzed and utilized locally or can be sent to the internet.

Original study of WSNs began in the military in order to detect Soviet submarines in 1950s. There was some academic research in the 1960s and 1970s. In the 1980s, a distributed sensor network (DSN) programme was run in the Defense Advanced Research Projects Agency (DARPA) in the US. The research on DSNs affected WSNs. After a market demand for WSNs appeared in the 1990s and 2000s, academia and industry recognized the potential for high volume of deployment in industrial and consumer applications.

WSNs provide us with many advantages such as (i) many observations of environments, (ii) diverse characteristics, (iii) large area coverage, and (iv) robustness to failures. As mentioned in previous sections, mMTC systems are resource-constrained networks. In particular, power consumption, channel bandwidth and data traffic are limited in the networks, and they should be efficiently managed. IoT networks deal with many different types of sensing data such as accelerometers, gyroscopes, barometers, humidity, chemical data, proximity data, and so on. Huge amounts of data will be produced in IoT networks. One key question is how to collect and manage the large volume of data accurately and efficiently. In order to collect the data efficiently, improve battery life, and better use the channel bandwidths and traffics, data fusion will be useful in mMTC systems. Data fusion techniques integrate the data from multiple sensors or sources and produce more consistent and accurate information than any individual sensing data. It can be helpful for managing the big data of IoT systems. An IoT network includes sensing nodes with low power and low accuracy. Data fusion techniques allow us to create accurate data from them.

The key idea of data fusion is to combine data from different sensors and achieve better performance. It also known as data merging, entity resolution, or consolidation. In the real world, there are data conflicts such as representation, attributes, and so on. For example, representation conflict is caused by different applications, architectures, theories and methods (e.g. km/s vs mph, Celsius vs Fahrenheit, kilograms vs pounds, etc.). Conflict resolution is needed. In addition, data fusion allows us to transform many noisy data to few accurate data and reduce transmit power by transmitting only necessary data. In particular, it is an efficient technique for managing huge amounts of data in IoT environments. In [26, 27], research challenges of data fusion techniques in IoT environments are summarized as follows:

(i) Data imperfection: sensor data may not be precise, accurate and certain in WSNs.
(ii) Ambiguities and inconsistencies: IoT environments may result in data ambiguities and inconsistencies.
(iii) Conflicting nature: the data conflicts in different architectures and applications should be taken into account and managed by the data fusion algorithms.
(iv) Data correlation and alignment: these problems (especially sensor registration problems) are common in WSNs.
(v) Trivial data: IoT networks are composed of a huge numbers of sensors and sensing parameters. Processing of trivial data may affect the data fusion accuracy.
(vi) Dynamically iterative process: data fusion is not a static but a dynamic process.
(vii) Operational timing: when IoT devices are spread over a wide area and real-time processing is required, the transmission timing will be different and synchronization among them will be a research challenge.
(viii) Data dimensionality: measurement data may be preprocessed locally or globally.

Level of preprocessing would be one research challenge. As we discussed for optimization theories in previous chapters, there is no perfect algorithm solving all problems in all IoT environments. It is important to select or develop the algorithm satisfying the specific application and environment. Data fusion techniques as multidisciplinary techniques are widely used in many different fields. It is not easy to establish classification in terms of one aspect. Thus, they can be classified in multiple ways: types of data source [28], Dasarathy's classification [29], abstraction level [30], JDL data fusion classification [31], and types of architecture [32]. Sensor data may be complementary, competitive or cooperative. Dasarathy's classification, as one well-known data fusion classification, focuses on the input and output relationship of data fusion techniques, composed of (i) data in–data out, (ii) data in–feature out, (iii) feature in–feature out, (iv) feature in–decision out, and (v) decision in–decision out. In [30], four abstraction levels are defined: signal level, pixel level, characteristic, and symbol. JDL data fusion classification, as the most popular model, is based on five processing levels, an associated database, and information bus as shown in Figure 9.10.

The JDL data fusion model is a functional model, and it was the first to describe the data fusion model using a common terminology. As we can observe from Figure 9.10, the data fusion process is related to the refinement of objects, situations, threats, and processes. The last classification [32] is based on architecture types: centralized, distributed, and hierarchical architectures. In centralized architecture, source/sensor nodes are cheap and do not have computational capability. Central nodes receive the information from all source nodes and the fusion process is performed in the central node. In this architecture, it is relatively easy to find an optimal data fusion rule. However, it requires a large communication resource and includes a single point of failure at the central node. On the other hand, each source node in a distributed architecture is able to process the measurement data before

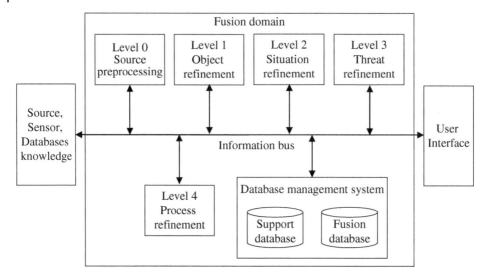

Figure 9.10 JDL data fusion model.

transmission to central nodes. Depending on connectivity conditions, each source node can communicate and cooperate with other source nodes. It allows us to have less traffic congestion and higher survivability due to multiple points of failure at source nodes. However, each source node has its own processing power and fuses the data, so the source nodes are expensive. In addition, there are some technical problems such as how to manage fusion responsibility, communication resources, and operation of networks. The hierarchical architecture combines two architectures. The central and cluster nodes are in a hierarchy. The cluster nodes are able to process source data and send the processed data to a higher-level node to be fused. A higher-level node may give feedback to a lower-level node. Depending on system requirements, a suitable architecture is designed. Figure 9.11 illustrates architecture types.

There are many data fusion problems in terms of system requirements, architectures, data attributes, and others. The problems can be categorized by data imperfection, correlation, inconsistency, and disparateness [26]. Multiple data fusion techniques have been developed to solve different types of problems. Table 9.5 summarizes the data fusion techniques. As we can observe from the table, one data fusion algorithm cannot cover all data fusion problems, and proper algorithms should be selected according to the properties of the problem. For example, as we reviewed with machine learning techniques in Chapter 5, we can solve classification problems using a support vector machine (SVM). In order to detect faults in sensor networks, SVM can be used with the following steps: (i) signal separation based on frequency and amplitude; (ii) modeling of system faults using an adaptive time-based observer; (iii) combining sensor data; and (iv) training of SVM for fault prediction [33]. In addition, when combined with other algorithms, we can achieve a better performance. Light Detection and Ranging (LIDAR) is an essential sensor for automated vehicles. LIDAR is composed of a laser, a scanner, and a GPS receiver. It measures the distance between a

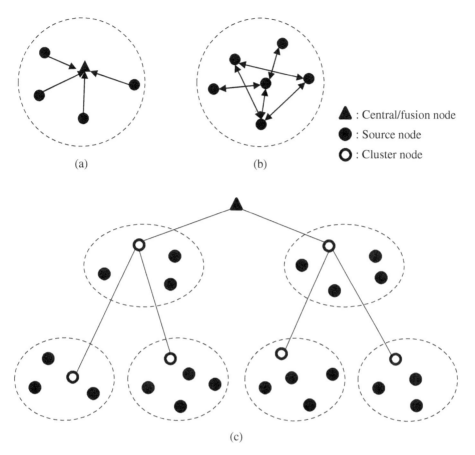

: Central/fusion node
: Source node
: Cluster node

Figure 9.11 Architectures of data fusion: (a) centralized architecture, (b) distributed architecture, and (c) hierarchical architecture.

vehicle and objects by illuminating the target with a laser and measuring the reflected light with a sensor. Both SVM and Naive Bayes classifiers can be used to perform data fusion for hyperspectral and LIDAR data processing [34]. Each algorithm produces 88% and 58% classification accuracy, but data fusion using both algorithms results in 91% accuracy [34]. IoT networks consist of resource-limited IoT devices and operate in stochastic environments under uncertainty. IoT systems can be modeled using Markov decision processes with states, actions, a transition model, reward function and policy. If we can model IoT systems as a Markov decision process, machine learning such as reinforcement learning can be used to solve the problems of IoT systems.

Example 9.5 *Bayesian Theorem for Multisensor Data Fusion*

Consider a centralized sensor network modeled by Bayesian theorem. In the model, the sensor nodes are described by a likelihood matrix. There are two sensors with three observations whose likelihood matrices are described as follows:

Table 9.5   Data fusion techniques.

	Data fusion techniques
Inference and decision methods	Bayesian theory, fuzzy logic, Dempster–Shafer evidence theory, abductive reasoning, semantic method
Classification methods	Machine learning, artificial neural network
State estimation methods	Kalman filter, extended Kalman filter, unscented Kalman filter, particle filter, covariance consistency method, ML
Inconsistent data fusion methods	Sensor validation techniques, stochastic adaptive sensor modeling

Table p9.1   Likelihood matrices of two sensors.

$P_1(z\,|\,x)$	z_1	z_2	z_3	$P_2(z\,|\,x)$	z_1	z_2	z_3
x_1	0.4	0.4	0.2	x_1	0.4	0.2	0.4
x_2	0.4	0.4	0.2	x_2	0.2	0.4	0.4
x_3	0.2	0.2	0.6	x_3	0.4	0.4	0.2

where $\mathbf{x}$ and $\mathbf{z}$ are the state value and observation, respectively. They have different detection probabilities. The prior probability is $P(\mathbf{x}) = (1/3, 1/3, 1/3)$. Compare individual detection and combined detection.

Solution
By Bayesian theorem, the posterior probabilities of the state $\mathbf{x}$ after observing $\mathbf{z}$ are represented as follows:

$$P(\mathbf{x}\,|\,z_i) = \beta P(z_i\,|\,\mathbf{x})P(\mathbf{x})$$

where β is a constant for normalizing. When we observe z_1 of the sensor 1, the posterior probability is calculated as follows:

$$P_1(\mathbf{x}\,|\,z_1) = \beta P(z_1\,|\,\mathbf{x})P(\mathbf{x}) = \beta(0.4, 0.4, 0.2) \odot (1/3, 1/3, 1/3)$$
$$= (0.1333, 0.1333, 0.0666)/0.3332 = (0.4, 0.4, 0.2)$$

where $\odot$ is an elementwise multiplication. Likewise, we can calculate the others and have the following table:

Table p9.2 Posterior probabilities of two sensors.

$P_1(x\,|\,z)$	x_1	x_2	x_3	$P_2(x\,|\,z)$	x_1	x_2	x_3
z_1	0.4	0.4	0.2	z_1	0.4	0.2	0.4
z_2	0.4	0.4	0.2	z_2	0.2	0.4	0.4
z3	0.2	0.2	0.6	z_3	0.4	0.4	0.2

In order to combine the information from both sensors, we should integrate the observations. We consider the observation set $\mathbf{Z}_n = \{\mathbf{z}_1, \mathbf{z}_2, \ldots, \mathbf{z}_n\}$ and construct a posterior probability $P(\mathbf{x}\,|\,\mathbf{Z}_n)$ as follows:

$$P(\mathbf{x}\,|\,\mathbf{Z}_n) = \frac{P(\mathbf{Z}_n\,|\,\mathbf{x})P(\mathbf{x})}{P(\mathbf{Z}_n)} = \frac{P(\mathbf{z}_1, \mathbf{z}_2, \ldots, \mathbf{z}_n\,|\,\mathbf{x})P(\mathbf{x})}{P(\mathbf{z}_1, \mathbf{z}_2, \ldots, \mathbf{z}_n)}$$

Given the state $\mathbf{x}$, the information from the ith source is independent of the information from other sources. Thus, we have

$$P(\mathbf{z}_i\,|\,\mathbf{x}, \mathbf{z}_1, \mathbf{z}_2, \ldots, \mathbf{z}_{i-1}, \mathbf{z}_{i+1}, \ldots, \mathbf{z}_n) = P(\mathbf{z}_i\,|\,\mathbf{x})$$

From $P(\mathbf{x}, \mathbf{y}\,|\,\mathbf{z}) = P(\mathbf{x}\,|\,\mathbf{z})P(\mathbf{y}\,|\,\mathbf{z})$,

$$P(\mathbf{z}_1, \mathbf{z}_2, \ldots, \mathbf{z}_n\,|\,\mathbf{x}) = \prod_{i=1}^{n} P(\mathbf{z}_i\,|\,\mathbf{x})$$

Thus, the posterior probability is expressed as follows:

$$P(\mathbf{x}\,|\,\mathbf{Z}_n) = (P(\mathbf{Z}_n))^{-1}P(\mathbf{x})\prod_{i=1}^{n} P(\mathbf{z}_i\,|\,\mathbf{x})$$

Now, the combined likelihood function is represented as follows:

$$P_{1,2}(\mathbf{z}_1, \mathbf{z}_2\,|\,\mathbf{x}) = P_1(\mathbf{z}_1\,|\,\mathbf{x})P_2(\mathbf{z}_2\,|\,\mathbf{x})$$

When we observe $\mathbf{z}_1 = z_1$ of the sensor 1 and $\mathbf{z}_2 = z_1$ of the sensor 2, the posterior probability is calculated as follows:

$$\begin{aligned} P(\mathbf{x}\,|\,z_1, z_1) &= \beta P_{1,2}(z_1, z_1\,|\,\mathbf{x}) = \beta P_1(z_1\,|\,\mathbf{x})P_2(z_2\,|\,\mathbf{x}) \\ &= \beta(0.4, 0.4, 0.2) \odot (0.4, 0.2, 0.4) \\ &= (0.16, 0.08, 0.08)/0.32 \\ &= (0.5, 0.25, 0.25) \end{aligned}$$

When comparing this result and the observation from single sensor 1, sensor 2 brings a slight loss of detection performance. However, if we expand the number of samples and sources, the results may be stable with accuracy.

Centralized data processing may cause heavy data traffic congestion and require many relay nodes. However, distributed data processing allows us to reduce energy consumption due to fewer packet transmissions and improved network scalability. In the DSNs, the algorithms are designed to maximize the efficiency of communication links. Conventional operation is as follows. Each sensor node collects the information. The extracted information is compressed without loss and transmitted to other nodes. Depending on the network architecture and system requirements, the packet transmission may be limited. For example, communication between neighboring nodes is frequently performed, and transmission to long distant nodes or sink/central nodes is infrequently performed. The data collected from sensor nodes are used for estimation or decision on a hypothesis. The nodes receiving the compressed information update local estimates using data fusion techniques. The processed data are transmitted to sink/central nodes. In order to solve the estimation problem, there are two approaches to distributed estimation:

(i) Sensor nodes collect all data and local estimation is performed. Then, based on the estimation, sensor nodes interact with neighboring nodes iteratively [35, 36].

(ii) Sensor nodes continuously interact with neighboring nodes while measuring new sensor information [37].

In distributed systems, we need to combine the information for multiple sensing nodes, calculate a common estimate of sensing data, and agree with a common view in the network. This problem can be formulated in an agreement problem. The consensus algorithm is an iterative procedure that allows a network to agree on a certain value (e.g. average, maximum, or minimum) for a set of initial values. The average consensus problem can be formulated when an agent with computation capability and communication tracks the average of time-varying signals together with neighboring agents. The term "consensus" means that the system reaches values of consensus states such as average, maximum, minimum, and so on. The key idea of consensus algorithms is to have a set of agents to agree on a global value using local information exchange. The objective of consensus algorithms is to minimize the disagreement among the sensing nodes. The consensus problem is sometimes called an agreement problem, gossip algorithms, synchronization, and rendezvous. Its applications cover distributed agreement and synchronization problems, load balancing, coordination of autonomous agents, distributed data fusion in sensor networks, and so on. This algorithm is suitable for DSNs.

In order to describe the interactions and information flows in DSNs, graph models are widely used. The graph model is a mathematical abstraction representing the relations among the elements. In the model, vertices and edges represent elements and relations, respectively. In the DSNs, the vertices are the sensors and the edges are communication links between nodes to exchange information with each other. The connectivity described by Laplacian matrix in the graph model determines the capacity of the network to reach a consensus and characterizes the convergence rate of the consensus algorithms [38]. A graph is defined as $G = (V, E)$ where V is the set of vertices v_i, $i = \{1, \ldots, N\}$ and $E \subseteq V \times V$ is the set of edges $e_{ij}(v_i, v_j)$ representing connections between two vertices. If an edge has a direction, the graph is called a directed graph. The direct edge e_{ij} has j head and i tail. If the edge does not have a direction, it is called an undirected graph and $e_{ij} = e_{ji}$ for all pairs $\{i, j\}$. Figure 9.12 illustrates examples of directed and undirected graphs.

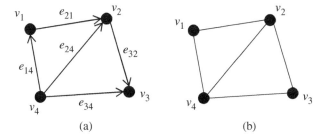

Figure 9.12 Examples of (a) directed and (b) undirected graphs.

If a weight is associated with edges, a graph is called a weighted graph. When we have a weight $W : E \to \mathbb{R}$, $W(e_{ij}) \neq 0$ if $e_{ij} \in E$, and $W(e_{ij}) = 0$ otherwise. If two vertices are joined by an edge, they are called endpoints of the edge. If two vertices are endpoints of the same edge, they are adjacent to each other. The adjacency matrix $\mathbf{A}$ of the graph G is the matrix with the element a_{ij} given by $a_{ij} > 0$ if $e_{ij} \in E$, and $a_{ij} = 0$ otherwise. If the graph G is weighted, $a_{ij} = W(e_{ij})$ for all $e_{ij} \in E$. If the graph G has no self-loops, the diagonal elements of the adjacency matrix are equal to 0 ($a_{ii} = 0$). If the graph G is undirected, the adjacency matrix $\mathbf{A}$ is symmetric ($a_{ij} = a_{ji}$). In undirected graphs, vertices adjacent to a vertex i are called neighbors of a vertex i. In directed graphs, neighbors of a vertex i are the vertices with an outgoing edge to the vertex i. The set of neighbors of a vertex i is defined as follows:

$$\mathcal{N}_i = \{j \in V \,|\, e_{ij} \in E\} \tag{9.81}$$

The in-degree and out-degree of a vertex i are determined by the sums of the weights of the outgoing and incoming edges as follows:

$$d_i^{in} = \sum_{j=1}^{N} a_{ji}, \quad d_i^{out} = \sum_{j=1}^{N} a_{ij} \tag{9.82}$$

If $d_i^{in} = d_i^{out}$, a vertex i is called balanced. If all vertices are balanced, a graph is called balanced. The degree matrix $\mathbf{D}$ of a graph G is defined as the diagonal matrix whose element is given by $D_{ij} = d_i^{out}$ if $i = j$, and $D_{ij} = 0$ otherwise. When we have graphs with unit weight, $D_{ii} = \mathcal{N}_i$ for all $i \in V$. The Laplacian matrix or connectivity matrix $\mathbf{L}$ of the graph G is defined as $\mathbf{L} = \mathbf{D} - \mathbf{A}$. The properties of the Laplacian matrix are important in the convergence analysis of the consensus algorithms.

Property 9.1 Laplacian Matrix

In the graph G, properties of the Laplacian matrix $\mathbf{L} \in \mathbb{R}^{N \times N}$ are as follows:

(a) The eigenvalues of the Laplacian $\mathbf{L}$ are located inside a circle in the complex plane with centers in $\mathbf{L}_{ii}$ and radii by $\sum_{j=1, j \neq i}^{N} |\mathbf{L}_{ij}|$.
(b) The eigenvalues of the Laplacian $\mathbf{L}$ have non-negative real parts and they are all inside a circle with radius $2d_m^{out}$ ($d_m^{out} = \max_{i \in V} d_i^{out}$).
(c) $\mathbf{L} \cdot \mathbf{1} = \mathbf{0}$ where $\mathbf{0}$ is the vector of all zeros, $\mathbf{1}$ is the vector of all ones, and the Laplacian $\mathbf{L}$ has at least one null eigenvalue with associated eigenvector.

(d) In undirected graphs, the eigenvalues of the Laplacian **L** are arranged in non-increasing order as follows: $2d_m^{out} \geq \lambda_1 \geq \ldots \geq \lambda_N = 0$.
(e) The second smallest eigenvalue λ_{N-1} is algebraic connectivity representing the degree of connectivity of the graph G.
(f) The algebraic multiplicity of the null eigenvalue of the Laplacian **L** is equal to the number of connected components. This is a condition to reach a consensus.
(g) If the graph G has l connected components, rank $(\mathbf{L}) = N - l$.

Now, we use the graph model and discuss consensus algorithms in DSNs. When a sensor node measures data and the measurement data include an error, a consensus algorithm reduces the effect of an error and finds an accurate estimate by interaction among sensor nodes. The global optimality is achieved. Consider a DSN composed of N nodes with an associated value $x_i, i = \{1, 2, \ldots, N\}$ defined as the state of node i. The state is initialized by the measurement data and iteratively updated by the received information from neighboring nodes. If node i and node j reach a consensus, we have $x_i = x_j$. Let $\mathbf{x}(t)$ be a vector formed with all sensor measurements at time index t, and $\mathbf{x}(0) = [x_1(0), x_2(0), \ldots, x_N(0)]^T$ be the vector of initial states in the network. The common consensus $\overline{\mathbf{x}}$ of the initial measurements can be expressed as follows:

$$\text{Average consensus} : \overline{\mathbf{x}} = \frac{1}{N} \sum_{i=1}^{N} x_i(0) \tag{9.83}$$

$$\text{Weighted average consensus} : \overline{\mathbf{x}} = \frac{\sum_i^N d_i^{out} x_i(0)}{\sum_i^N d_i^{out}} \tag{9.84}$$

$$\text{Maximum consensus} : \overline{\mathbf{x}} = \max_i x_i(0) \tag{9.85}$$

$$\text{Minimum consensus} : \overline{\mathbf{x}} = \min_i x_i(0) \tag{9.86}$$

The network connectivity is expressed by the coefficients a_{ij} where $a_{ij} = 1$ and $a_{ij} = 0$ represent direct connection and disconnection, respectively, between nodes i and j. They are the elements of the adjacency matrix in the graph. When consensus algorithms converge on the state, they have a bounded state value and are tolerant of changes in the network topology. However, they are sensitive to noise and delay. When consensus algorithms converge on the state derivative, they are robust to noise and delay. However, they do not have a bound state value and are sensitive to changes in the network topology. In a continuous time system, the minimization of the disagreement can be obtained by a simple algorithm to reach a consensus. The state evolution of each sensor node can be expressed as a first-order differential equation as follows [39]:

$$x_i'(t) = \sum_{j \in \mathcal{N}_i} a_{ij}(x_j(t) - x_i(t)) \tag{9.87}$$

where $\mathcal{N}_i$ represents the set of neighbors of node i. The sensor nodes are updated by interaction with their neighboring nodes. We can rewrite the state evolution by the following linear system:

$$\mathbf{x}'(t) = -\mathbf{L}\mathbf{x}(t) \tag{9.88}$$

If we have undirected graphs, we can regard Equation (9.88) as a gradient descent algorithm. In the sensor network, each sensor node has a dynamic system evolving in time. In [40], based on self-synchronization of a population of mutually coupled oscillators, the generalized form of Equation (9.87) can be expressed as follows [40]:

$$x_i'(t) = g_i(y_i) + \frac{K}{z_i} \sum_{j \in \mathcal{N}_i} a_{ij} f(x_j(t) - x_i(t)), \quad i = 1, \dots, N \tag{9.89}$$

where $g_i(y_i), f(), K$ and z_i are, respectively, a function of local measurement y_i taken by node i, a nonlinear odd function increasing monotonically and describing the mutual coupling among the sensor nodes, a global control loop gain representing the coupling strength, and a local coefficient depending on the SNR at sensor node i. In Equation (9.89), the summation means the coupling with all other sensor nodes. The solution of the differential Equation (9.88) is given as follows:

$$\mathbf{x}(t) = \exp(-\mathbf{L}t)\mathbf{x}(0) \tag{9.90}$$

and the state of the sensor nodes reach a consensus as follows:

$$\lim_{t \to \infty} \mathbf{x}(t) = \frac{1}{N} \mathbf{1} \mathbf{1}^T \mathbf{x}(0) \tag{9.91}$$

In a discrete system, Equation (9.87) can be rewritten as the difference equation as follows [41]:

$$x_i[k+1] = \sum_{j \in \mathcal{N}_i \cup \{i\}} w_{ij} x_j[k], \quad k \geq 0 \tag{9.92}$$

where w_{ij} is a weighting factor and the degree of confidence satisfying $\sum_{j \in \mathcal{N}_i \cup \{i\}} w_{ij} = 1$. We represent the iterative algorithm in the matrix form as follows:

$$\mathbf{x}[k+1] = \mathbf{W}\mathbf{x}[k] \tag{9.93}$$

where $\mathbf{W}$ is the weight matrix for a network characterized by the graph model and can be expressed as follows:

$$\mathbf{W} = \mathbf{I} - \epsilon \mathbf{L} \tag{9.94}$$

where ϵ is the coefficient to converge. The weight matrix is also called the transition matrix. When iterating Equation (9.93) k times, we have

$$\mathbf{x}[k] = \mathbf{W}^k \mathbf{x}[0] \tag{9.95}$$

When we have the eigenvectors $\mathbf{v}_l$ of $\mathbf{W}$ associated with the eigenvalues λ_l and the eigenvalues are real, Equation (9.95) is rewritten as follows:

$$\mathbf{x}[k] = \sum_{l=1}^{N} \lambda_l^k \mathbf{v}_l \mathbf{v}_l^T \mathbf{x}[0] \tag{9.96}$$

The state of sensor nodes reach a consensus asymptotically if satisfying

$$\lim_{k \to \infty} \mathbf{x}[k] = \frac{1}{N} \mathbf{1} \mathbf{1}^T \mathbf{x}[0] = c\mathbf{1} \tag{9.97}$$

where $c \in \mathbb{R}$ is the consensus value ($c = \frac{1}{N} \mathbf{1}^T \mathbf{x}[0]$) and $c\mathbf{1}$ is the consensus vector belonging to the agreement space.

Example 9.6   *Consensus Algorithm*

Consider a simple sensor network with three sensor nodes with the initial state [0.1, 0.4, 0.8] modeled in Figure p9.3.

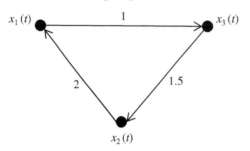

Figure p9.3   Graph model for the sensor network in Example 9.6.

Evaluate the evolution of the states.

Solution

From Equation (9.95), we have the consensus algorithm as follows:

$$\mathbf{x}'(t) = -\mathbf{L}\mathbf{x}(t)$$

The initial state is given as follows:

$$\mathbf{x}(0) = \begin{bmatrix} 0.1 \\ 0.4 \\ 0.8 \end{bmatrix}$$

and the weight matrix $\mathbf{L} \in \mathbb{R}^{3 \times 3}$ can be obtained from Figure p9.3 as follows:

$$\mathbf{L} = \begin{bmatrix} 2 & -2 & 0 \\ 0 & 1.5 & -1.5 \\ -1 & 0 & 1 \end{bmatrix}$$

Now, we can iterate the consensus algorithm with initial values and find the evolution of the states. Figure p9.4 illustrates the evolution of the state $\mathbf{x}(t)$ and convergence to 0.5.

Signal detection is an important component of communication systems. The detection task is performed by measuring signal strength. However, during the process there are many problems to solve, such as channel impairments, definition of detection threshold, data interpretation, and so on. The detection theory is based on statistical methods. As we reviewed Bayesian theory, maximum likelihood (ML) and maximum a posteriori (MAP) in Chapter 3, they are important tools for minimizing probability errors in the decision process. In order to find an optimal detection system, we assume that a WSN has a parallel topology with N sensor nodes and one fusion node as shown in Figure 9.13, and each sensor node has a computing power and transmits its decision to the fusion node. We obtain an observation y_i from a sensor node and perform the binary hypothesis test defined as H_0: signal is absent, and H_1: signal is present. The measurement data at each sensor are statistically independent. Each sensor employs the detection rule to make a decision for H_1 if the threshold is exceeded or for H_0 otherwise as follows:

$$u_i = \begin{cases} 0, & \text{if } H_0 \text{ happens} \\ 1, & \text{if } H_1 \text{ happens} \end{cases}, \quad i = 1, \dots, N \tag{9.98}$$

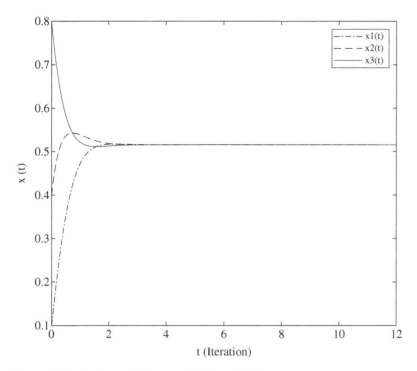

Figure p9.4 Evolution of the states in Example 9.6.

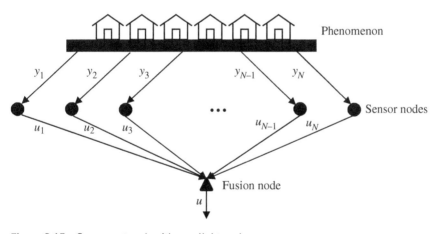

Figure 9.13 Sensor network with parallel topology.

where u_i is a local decision variable. In the sensor network, each sensor collects the measurement, make a local decision, and send its decision to the fusion node. The fusion node makes a global decision $u = f(u_1, \ldots, u_N)$.

In order to make a global decision, the data fusion algorithms are used. If each sensor node sends the measurement to the fusion node, the optimal decision rule can be found by collecting measurements, forming a likelihood ratio and comparing it with a threshold as follows:

$$\Lambda(\mathbf{y}) = \frac{P(y_1, y_2, \ldots, y_N \mid H_1)}{P(y_1, y_2, \ldots, y_N \mid H_0)} \overset{H_1}{\underset{H_0}{\gtrless}} \gamma \tag{9.99}$$

where γ is a threshold. In this case, each sensor node will send raw data to the fusion node and a high throughput is required. In the system model as shown in Figure 9.13, each sensor node sends the local decision u_i to the fusion node. In [42], based on Bayesian theory and the Neyman-Pearson formulation, the optimal decision rule is given by the likelihood ratio test as follows:

$$\Lambda(\mathbf{u}) = \frac{P(u_1, u_2, \ldots, u_N \mid H_1)}{P(u_1, u_2, \ldots, u_N \mid H_0)} \overset{H_1}{\underset{H_0}{\gtrless}} \gamma \tag{9.100}$$

Since we assumed independent local decisions, Equation (9.100) can be rewritten as follows:

$$\frac{\prod_{i=1}^{N} P(u_i \mid H_1)}{\prod_{i=1}^{N} P(u_i \mid H_0)} = \prod_{i=1}^{N} \Lambda(u_i) \overset{H_1}{\underset{H_0}{\gtrless}} \gamma \tag{9.101}$$

In addition, the local decision variable will be 0 or 1. If we define the subset S_1 containing all local decision variables $u_i = 1$ and the subset S_0 containing all local decision variables $u_i = 0$, Equation (9.101) can be rewritten as follows:

$$\prod_{i \in S_0} \frac{P(u_i \mid H_1)}{P(u_i \mid H_0)} \prod_{i \in S_1} \frac{P(u_i \mid H_1)}{P(u_i \mid H_0)} \overset{H_1}{\underset{H_0}{\gtrless}} \gamma \tag{9.102}$$

We define the probabilities of miss-detection and false alarms for each sensor node as follows:

$$P_{Mi} = P(u_i = 0 \mid H_1), \quad P_{Fi} = P(u_i = 1 \mid H_0) \tag{9.103}$$

and Equation (9.102) can be rewritten as follows:

$$\prod_{i \in S_0} \frac{P_{Mi}}{1 - P_{Fi}} \prod_{i \in S_1} \frac{1 - P_{Mi}}{P_{Fi}} \overset{H_1}{\underset{H_0}{\gtrless}} \gamma \tag{9.104}$$

From Equation (9.104), the log-likelihood ratio test can be found as follows:

$$\sum_{i=1}^{N} \left(\log\left(\frac{1 - P_{Mi}}{P_{Fi}} \right) u_i + \log\left(\frac{P_{Mi}}{1 - P_{Fi}} \right) (1 - u_i) \right) \overset{H_1}{\underset{H_0}{\gtrless}} \log \gamma \tag{9.105}$$

$$\sum_{i=1}^{N} \log\left(\frac{(1 - P_{Mi})(1 - P_{Fi})}{P_{Mi} P_{Fi}} \right) u_i \overset{H_1}{\underset{H_0}{\gtrless}} \log\left(\gamma \prod_{i=1}^{N} \frac{1 - P_{Fi}}{P_{Mi}} \right) \tag{9.106}$$

$$\sum_{i=1}^{N} \alpha u_i \overset{H_1}{\underset{H_0}{\gtrless}} \eta \tag{9.107}$$

where α is a weighting factor and η is an adjusted threshold. As we can observe from Equation (9.107), the optimal decision rule at the fusion node becomes a weighted sum of the local decisions. The weight depends on the reliabilities of sensor nodes.

Distributed estimation has been investigated since the 1970s. Early-stage research topics included finding an optimal fusion from local estimates and reconstructing a global estimate. In the 1980s, the graph model was widely used. Track fusion using cross-covariance and decentralized structures for parallel Kalman filtering were developed. In 1990s, ML and MAP linear estimation fusion were developed. In the 2000s, due to advanced VLSI and communication technologies, distributed estimation for ad-hoc sensor networks was actively investigated, and consensus-based distributed Kalman filters and diffusion-based distributed filters were developed. In IoT networks, distributed estimation also plays an important role. Depending on the target applications and requirements, estimation algorithms should be selected and suitable algorithms will improve the performance significantly. As we reviewed least squares (LS), minimum mean-squared error (MMSE), ML, and MAP in Chapter 3, they all have their own pros and cons. For example, when we have a huge amount of sensor nodes and data, ML and MAP provide us with accurate estimates. However, when we deal with a small amount of data, they are inefficient and we need a simpler algorithm to converge quickly. In addition, it is not easy to formulate all distributions. In the static sensor fusion problem, a linear MMSE estimate will be a good choice. In order to estimate a time-invariant variable, we assume that a WSN has a parallel topology with N sensor nodes and one fusion node, as shown in Figure 9.14.

We consider a random variable $\mathbf{x}$ to be estimated and N sensor nodes generating the measurement as follows:

$$y_i = H_i x_i + n_i, \quad i = 1, \ldots, N \tag{9.108}$$

where x_i, H_i, and n_i are the state, measurement matrix, and Gaussian noise, respectively. The Gaussian noise is uncorrelated with the state x_i as well as other measurements of Gaussian noise. The global MMSE estimate $\hat{\mathbf{x}}$ of $\mathbf{x}$, given $\mathbf{y}$, is represented as follows:

$$\mathbf{P}^{-1}\hat{\mathbf{x}} = \mathbf{H}^T \mathbf{R}_{\mathbf{n}}^{-1} \mathbf{y} \tag{9.109}$$

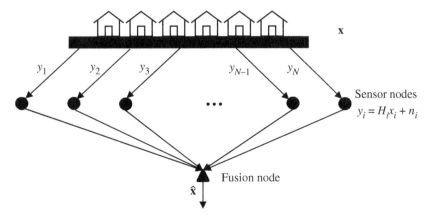

Figure 9.14 System model for distributed estimation.

where $\mathbf{R}_n$ is the covariance matrix of Gaussian noise, and $\mathbf{P}$ is the estimate error covariance corresponding to $\hat{\mathbf{x}}$. The corresponding error covariance is expressed as follows:

$$\mathbf{P}^{-1} = \mathbf{R}_\mathbf{x}^{-1} + \mathbf{H}^T \mathbf{R}_\mathbf{n}^{-1} \mathbf{H} \tag{9.110}$$

and acts as a normalizing factor. The right side of Equation (9.109) can be rewritten as follows:

$$\mathbf{H}^T \mathbf{R}_\mathbf{n}^{-1} \mathbf{y} = \sum_{i=1}^{N} H_i^T R_{n_i}^{-1} y_i \tag{9.111}$$

and the term $H_i^T R_{n_i}^{-1} y_i$ of Equation (9.111) can be rewritten as follows:

$$H_i^T R_{n_i}^{-1} y_i = P_i^{-1} \hat{x}_i \tag{9.112}$$

Thus, we have

$$\mathbf{P}^{-1} \hat{\mathbf{x}} = \sum_{i=1}^{N} P_i^{-1} \hat{x}_i \tag{9.113}$$

where the estimate error covariance corresponding to $\hat{\mathbf{x}}$ is

$$\mathbf{P}^{-1} = \sum_{i=1}^{N} P_i^{-1} - (N-1) \mathbf{R}_\mathbf{x}^{-1} \tag{9.114}$$

As we can observe from Equations (9.113) and (9.114), the complexity of the fusion node decreased. Each estimate of a sensor node is weighted by the inverse of the estimate error covariance and we can allocate sensor nodes with higher confidence to more trustable places. In dynamic sensor fusion problems, we should estimate the states at every time step because the state involves time-variant variables such as position, temperature, velocity, and so on. We consider a linear model with N sensor nodes and a centralized architecture like Figure 9.14. Each sensor node can transmit information to the fusion node at every time step. The state to be estimated is modeled as follows:

$$\mathbf{x}_{k+1} = \mathbf{F}\mathbf{x}_k + \mathbf{w}_k \tag{9.115}$$

where $\mathbf{x}_k$, $\mathbf{F}$, and $\mathbf{w}_k$ are the state at time t_k, system dynamic matrix, and Gaussian noise with zero mean and covariance matrix $\mathbf{R}_\mathbf{w}$, respectively. The measurements observed by N sensor nodes are as follows:

$$\mathbf{y}_k^i = \mathbf{H}_k^i \mathbf{x}_k + \mathbf{n}_k^i, \quad i = 1, \dots, N \tag{9.116}$$

where $\mathbf{y}_k^i$, $\mathbf{H}_k^i$, and $\mathbf{n}_k^i$ are the measurement of the sensor i at time t_k, the measurement matrix, and Gaussian noise with zero mean and covariance matrix $\mathbf{R}_n^i$, respectively. The Kalman filter provides us with an optimal solution for the distributed estimation problem. In terms of fusion nodes, the global observation can be represented as follows:

$$\mathbf{y}_k = \mathbf{H}\mathbf{x}_k + \mathbf{n}_k \tag{9.117}$$

and the global estimate is given by the Kalman filter as follows:

$$\hat{\mathbf{x}}_{k|k} = \hat{\mathbf{x}}_{k|k-1} + \mathbf{P}_{k|k} \mathbf{H}' \mathbf{R}_n^{-1} (\mathbf{y}_k - \mathbf{H} \hat{\mathbf{x}}_{k|k-1}) \tag{9.118}$$

$$\mathbf{P}_{k|k}^{-1} = \mathbf{P}_{k|k-1}^{-1} + \mathbf{H}' \mathbf{R}_n^{-1} \mathbf{H} \tag{9.119}$$

$$\widehat{\mathbf{x}}_{k+1|k} = \mathbf{F}\widehat{\mathbf{x}}_{k|k} \tag{9.120}$$

$$\mathbf{P}_{k+1|k}^{-1} = \mathbf{F}\widehat{\mathbf{P}}_{k|k}\mathbf{F}' + \mathbf{R}_w \tag{9.121}$$

where $\widehat{\mathbf{x}}_{k|k} = E(\mathbf{x}_k \mid \mathbf{y}_0, \dots, \mathbf{y}_k)$ and $\mathbf{P}_{k|k} = E((\mathbf{x}_k - \widehat{\mathbf{x}}_{k|k})(\mathbf{x}_k - \widehat{\mathbf{x}}_{k|k})' \mid \mathbf{y}_0, \dots, \mathbf{y}_k)$. Equations (9.118) and (9.119) comprise the update step and Equations (9.120) and (9.121) comprise the prediction step. The term $\mathbf{H}'\mathbf{R}_n^{-1}\mathbf{H}$ is rewritten as follows:

$$\mathbf{H}'\mathbf{R}_n^{-1}\mathbf{H} = \sum_{i=1}^{N} \mathbf{H}^{i'}\mathbf{R}_n^{i-1}\mathbf{H}^i = \sum_{i=1}^{N}(\mathbf{P}_{k|k}^{i-1} - \mathbf{P}_{k|k-1}^{i-1}) \tag{9.122}$$

Thus, the global error covariance matrix and the estimate are represented in terms of the local covariance and estimates as follows:

$$\mathbf{P}_{k|k}^{-1} = \mathbf{P}_{k|k-1}^{-1} + \sum_{i=1}^{N}(\mathbf{P}_{k|k}^{i-1} - \mathbf{P}_{k|k-1}^{i-1}) \tag{9.123}$$

$$\mathbf{P}_{k|k}^{-1}\widehat{\mathbf{x}}_{k|k} = \mathbf{P}_{k|k-1}^{-1}\widehat{\mathbf{x}}_{k|k-1} + \sum_{i=1}^{N}(\mathbf{P}_{k|k}^{i-1}\widehat{\mathbf{x}}_{k|k}^{i} - \mathbf{P}_{k|k-1}^{i-1}\widehat{\mathbf{x}}_{k|k-1}^{i}) \tag{9.124}$$

From Equations (9.123) and (9.124), two architectures for distributed Kalman filtering are suggested. Firstly, each sensor node calculates the local estimates ($\widehat{\mathbf{x}}_{k|k}^{i}$ and $\mathbf{P}_{k|k}^{i}$) and transmits them to the fusion node at every time step. Based on Equations (9.123) and (9.124), the fusion node calculates the global estimate. This approach is simple in terms of sensor nodes, but the fusion node needs a high computational power. In addition, communications between nodes are required at every time step. Secondly, the global error covariance matrices can be calculated by each sensor node if there is any information about what sensor nodes have communicated. It allows the fusion node computation to be reduced.

Summary 9.4 Wireless Sensor Networks

1) In IoT networks, all nodes equipped with sensors collect data periodically and send their information to the internet directly. A server connected to the internet analyzes and interprets the data. On the other hand, wireless sensor networks (WSNs) are regarded as a subset of IoT networks. WSNs are defined as a group of sensors for monitoring the physical conditions of the environment, collecting the related information, and sending the data to central nodes.
2) The key idea of data fusion techniques is to combine data from different sensors and achieve better performance.
3) Centralized data processing may cause heavy data traffic congestion and many relay nodes, but distributed data processing allows us to reduce energy consumption due to fewer packet transmissions and improved network scalability. In distributed sensor networks, the algorithms are designed to maximize efficiency of communication links.
4) The key idea of consensus algorithms is to have a set of agents to agree on a global value using local information exchange.

(Continued)

> 5) The detection theory is based on statistical methods. Bayesian theory, ML and MAP are important tools to minimize the probability errors in the decision process.
> 6) In IoT networks, distributed estimation plays an important role. Depending on the target applications and requirements, the estimation algorithms should be selected carefully, and suitable algorithms will improve the performance significantly.

Problems

9.1 Describe the requirements of IoT systems.

9.2 Describe the design considerations for mMTC systems for a factory.

9.3 Compare IoT connectivity solutions: LoRa, NB-IoT, eMTC, and EC-GSM-IoT.

9.4 Describe the pros and cons of mMTC design approaches in Table 9.3.

9.5 Describe the pros and cons of uncertainty geometry models: ellipsoidal model, polytopic model and box model.

9.6 Consider the following simple robust linear programming problem

$$\max_{x,y} 2x - y$$

subject to

$$ax \leq 8, \quad x \geq 0$$
$$by \leq 2, \quad y \geq 0$$

where $x, y \in \mathbb{R}$ are the optimization variables and the uncertainty parameters a, $b \in \mathbb{R}$ take arbitrary values in the uncertainty set $[0, 2]$. Find the optimal solution of the robust linear programming problem.

9.7 Consider the following simple robust linear programming problem:

$$\max_{x,y} x + 2y$$

subject to

$$ax - by \leq 3, \quad x \geq 0, \quad y \geq 0$$

where $x, y \in \mathbb{R}$ are the optimization variables and the uncertainty parameters a, $b \in \mathbb{R}$ take arbitrary values in the ellipsoidal uncertainty sets $\Delta_a = \{a = \bar{a} + P_a u \mid u_2 \leq 1\}$ and $\Delta_b = \{b = \bar{b} + P_b u \mid u_2 \leq 1\}$. Transform the original problem to the second-order conic programming problem and find the optimal solution.

9.8 Consider the following robust stochastic linear programming problem:

$$\min_{x,y} 2x - y$$

subject to

$$P(ax + by \geq 5) \geq \gamma, \quad x, y \geq 0$$

where a and b have Gaussian distributions with mean μ_a and μ_b and variance σ_a^2 and σ_b^2, respectively. They are independent. Transform the original problem into an equivalent deterministic problem and find the optimal solution.

9.9 Compare open-loop and closed-loop power control methods of 3G, 4G, and 5G.

9.10 Taking into account different scenarios (e.g. small/macro cell, TDD/FDD, single/multi-antenna, etc.), formulate the problems of small cells in order to minimize the total transmit power of a base station.

9.11 Consider signal power x which can be zero (hypothesis H_0) or k (hypothesis H_1), each hypothesis with a probability $1/2$. The measurement of the signal is perturbed by AWGN of variance σ^2. Find the decision threshold for ML and MAP criterion.

References

1 International Telecommunication Union. (2012). *Y.2060 – Overview of the Internet of Things*. https://www.itu.int/rec/T-REC-Y.2060-201206-I.

2 3GPP. (2016). *TR 45.820 V13.0.0, Cellular System Support for Ultra-low Complexity and Low Throughput Internet of Things*. https://portal.3gpp.org/desktopmodules/Specifications/SpecificationDetails.aspx?specificationId=2719.

3 3GPP. (2017). *TS 24.301 V14.4.0, Non-Access-Stratum (NAS) Protocol for Evolved Packet System (EPS); Stage 3*. https://portal.3gpp.org/desktopmodules/Specifications/SpecificationDetails.aspx?specificationId=1072.

4 Ben-Tal, A. and Nemirovski, A. (1998). Robust convex optimization. *Mathematics of Operations Research* 23 (4).

5 Ben-Tal, A. and Nemirovski, A. (1999). Robust solutions of uncertain linear programs. *Operations Research Letter* 25 (1).

6 El Ghaoui, L. and Lebret, H. (Oct 1997). Robust solutions to least-squares problems with uncertain data. *SIAM Journal on Matrix Analysis and Applications* 18 (4): 1035–1064.

7 Ben-Tal, A., El Ghaoui, L., and Nemirovski, A. (2009). *Robust Optimization*, Princeton Series in Applied Mathematics. Princeton University Press.

8 Ben-Tal, A. and Nemirovski, A. (2002). Robust optimization methodology and applications. *Mathematical Programming* 92 (3): 453–480.

9 Bertsimas, D., Brown, D.B., and Caramanis, C. (2011). Theory and applications of robust optimization. *SIAM Review* 53 (3): 464–501.

10 Hsiung, K.L., Kim, S.J., and Boyd, S. (2005). Power control in lognormal fading wireless channels with uptime probability specifications via robust geometric programming. In: *Proceedings American Control Conference*, 3955–3959.

11 Lorenz, R. and Boyd, S. (2005). Robust minimum variance beamforming. *IEEE Transactions on Signal Processing* 53: 1684–1696.

12 Mutapcic, A., Kim, S.J., and Boyd, S. (2007). Beamforming with uncertain weights. *IEEE Signal Processing Letters* 14: 348–351.

13 Birge, J.R. and Louveaux, F. (1997). *Introduction to Stochastic Programming*. New York, NY: Springer.

14 Wang, Y.E., Lin, X., Adhikary, A. et al. (2017). A primer on 3GPP narrowband internet of things. *IEEE Communications Magazine* 55 (3): 117–123.

15 Ulukus, S. and Yates, R.D. (1998). Stochastic power control for cellular radio systems. *IEEE Transactions on Communications* 46 (6): 784–798.

16 3GPP. (2018).*TS 38.213 V15.3.0, NR; Physical Layer Procedures for Control*. https://portal .3gpp.org/desktopmodules/Specifications/SpecificationDetails.aspx?specificationId=3215.

17 Foschini, G.J. and Miljanic, Z. (1993). A simple distributed autonomous power control algorithm and its convergence. *IEEE Transactions on Vehicular Technology* 42 (4): 641–646.

18 D. Mitra, (1993). An asynchronous distributed algorithm for power control in cellular radio systems. *Proceedings of the 4th Winlab Workshop, Third Generation Wireless Information Networks*, Rutgers University.

19 Yates, R. and Huang, C.Y. (1995). Integrated power control and base station assignment. *IEEE Transactions on Vehicular Technology* 44 (3): 638–644.

20 Wu, C. and Bertsekas, D.P. (2001). Distributed power control algorithms for wireless networks. *IEEE Transactions on Vehicular Technology* 50 (2).

21 Kandukuri, S. and Boyd, S. (2002). Optimal power control in interference limited fading wireless channels with outage probability specifications. *IEEE Transactions on Wireless Communications* 1 (1): 46–55.

22 Stuuber, G.L. (2011). *Principles of Mobile Communication*. Springer.

23 Beightler, C.S. and Philips, D.T. (1976). *Applied Geometric Programming*. Wiley.

24 Bengtsson, M. and Ottersten, B. (2002). Optimal and suboptimal transmit beamforming. In: *Handbook on Antennas in Wireless Communications*. CRC.

25 Luo, Z., Ma, W., So, A.M. et al. (2010). Semidefinite relaxation of quadratic optimization problems. *IEEE Signal Processing Magazine* 27 (3): 22–34.

26 Chalise, B.K., Shahbazpanahi, S., Czylwik, A., and Gershman, A.B. (2007). Robust downlink beamforming based on outage probability specifications. *IEEE Transactions on Wireless Communications* 6 (10): 3498–3503.

27 Khaleghi, B., Khamis, A., Karray, F.O., and Razavi, S.N. (2011). Multisensor data fusion: a review of the state-of-the-art. *Information Fusion* 14: 28–44.

28 Durrant-Whyte, H.F. (1988). Sensor models and multisensor integration. *International Journal of Robotics Research* 7 (6): 97–113.

29 Dasarathy, B.V. (1997). Sensor fusion potential exploitation-innovative architectures and illustrative applications. *Proceedings of the IEEE* 85 (1): 24–38.

30 Luo, R.C., Yih, C.-C., and Su, K.L. (2002). Multi-sensor fusion and integration: approaches, applications, and future research directions. *IEEE Sensors Journal* 2 (2): 107–119.

31 Joint Directors of Laboratories (JDL). (1991). *Data Fusion Lexicon*. Technical Panel for C3, Code 420. https://apps.dtic.mil/dtic/tr/fulltext/u2/a529661.pdf.

32 H. Xinhan and W. Min, Multi-sensor data fusion structures in autonomous systems: a review. *IEEE International Symposium on Intelligent Control*, 817–821, 2003.

33 Banerjee, T.P. and Das, S. (2012). Multi-sensor data fusion using support vector machine for motor fault detection. *Information Sciences* 217: 96–107.

34 Bigdeli, B., Samadzadegan, F., and Reinartz, P. (2014). A decision fusion method based on multiple support vector machine system for fusion of hyperspectral and LIDAR data. *International Journal of Image and Data Fusion* 5 (3): 196–209.

35 Schizas, I.D., Ribeiro, A., and Giannakis, G.B. (2008). Consensus in Ad Hoc WSNs with noisy links: part I—distributed estimation of deterministic signals. *IEEE Transactions on Signal Processing* 56: 350–364.

36 Schizas, I.D., Giannakis, G.B., Roumeliotis, S.I., and Ribeiro, A. (2008). Consensus in Ad Hoc WSNs with noisy links: part II—distributed estimation and smoothing of random signals. *IEEE Transactions on Signal Processing* 56 (2): 1650–1666.

37 Kar, S., Moura, J.M.F., and Ramanan, K. (2012). Distributed parameter estimation in sensor networks: nonlinear observation models and imperfect communication. *IEEE Transactions on Information Theory* 58: 3575–3605.

38 Fax, J.A. and Murray, R.M. (2004). Information flow and cooperative control of vehicle formations. *IEEE Transactions on Automatic Control* 49 (9): 1465–1476.

39 Olfati-Saber, R. and Murray, R.M. (2004). Consensus problems in networks of agents with switching topology and time-delays. *IEEE Transactions on Automatic Contro* 49 (9): 1520–1533.

40 Barbarossa, S. and Scutari, G. (2007). Decentralized maximum-likelihood estimation for sensor networks composed of nonlinearly coupled dynamical systems. *IEEE Transactions on Signal Processing* 55 (7): 3456–3470.

41 Ren, W., Beard, R.W., and Atkins, E.M. (2005). A survey of consensus problems in multi-agent coordination. In: *Proc. of the American Control Conference*, vol. 3, 1859–1864.

42 Varshney, P.K. (1997). *Distributed Detection and Data Fusion*. New York, NY: Springer-Verlag.

Index

Design and Optimization for 5G Wireless Communications, First Edition. Haesik Kim.
© 2020 John Wiley & Sons Ltd. Published 2020 by John Wiley & Sons Ltd.